DO-IT-YOURSELF HOME IMPROVEMENT MANUAL

DO-IT-YOURSELF HOME IMPROVEMENT MANUAL

Octopus

First Published 1986 by
Octopus Books Limited
59 Grosvenor Street
London W1
Reprinted 1987

ISBN 0 7064 2318 6
Printed in Hong Kong

CONTENTS

INTRODUCTION

Your home is quite a complex assortment of materials and constructional techniques. This book covers both interior and exterior repairs. In general terms a wider range of skills is needed to repair and maintain the house interior than is necessary for work on the exterior. However, there are two big advantages with indoor repairs: they are easy to get at, by and large, and you are at least working under cover. In this book we start by looking at some of the commoner jobs and problems and how to tackle them.

The major features

Most homes are built in a fairly traditional way. The shell of the house is divided up into rooms by interior walls and floors. The walls may be solid and load-bearing – meaning that they carry the weight of floor and ceiling joists and other walls – or may be simple partitions carrying no load other than their own weight. This distinction is important if you intend to modify the layout of your home by removing interior walls or creating new door openings.

Solid walls have their surfaces covered with a layer of plaster, which provides a smooth basis for interior decorating. Non-load-bearing partition walls may be of lightweight blockwork, also plastered, or may consist of a framework of timber covered with sheets of plasterboard.

Plasterboard partition walls can be easily damaged, and fixings to them must be made into the timber frame behind the plaster-board if they are to support any weight.

Floors are formed by timber joists that span each room. Floorboards of natural timber or man-made board are nailed to their upper surfaces, and at first-floor and second-floor levels ceilings are fixed to the joist's undersides. In old houses the ceiling will be formed of laths and plaster – narrow strips of wood are nailed across the gaps between the joists, and plaster is forced up against them to form the ceiling surface. In modern homes, sheets of plasterboard are used instead. Older homes usually have timber ground floors, with a gap between the joists and the ground beneath them; in most modern homes the ground floor is solid concrete.

So much for the basic structure. Window and door frames are set into openings in the walls; inner sills complete the window frame, while architrave mouldings conceal the edges of door frames and cover the join between them and the plaster. At floor level, the plaster is protected by another wooden moulding, the skirting board. At ceiling level the angle between wall and ceiling may be concealed by a decorative cornice or coving. Storeys are linked by a timber staircase – one of the most complex bits of joinery found in most homes.

Within this framework run the various services to the house. Plumbing and heating pipework is largely concealed under floors, and is surface-mounted only where it runs to appliances and equipment. Electric wiring is usually completely concealed – under floors, above ceilings and buried in the plaster – emerging only at light-switches and socket outlets, but may be surface-mounted in channelling or conduit in buildings, such as flats, with concrete floors and ceilings.

By taking a careful look around your own home, you will be able to identify many, if not all, of these features. You will also become aware of the scale of the repair work needed – from minor patching of damaged plaster to the refixing of loose floorboards.

The outside shell of a house is also a complex assortment of features, built with a variety of materials and techniques, with but one practical purpose: to protect its occupants from the weather. However picturesque the building may appear, it has to keep wind and rain at bay, and if it is not given its fair share of maintenance and repair it will soon deteriorate. This book aims to help you keep your house in sound condition by telling you about the sort of problems that can arise, and what to do to put them right.

Problem areas in the home

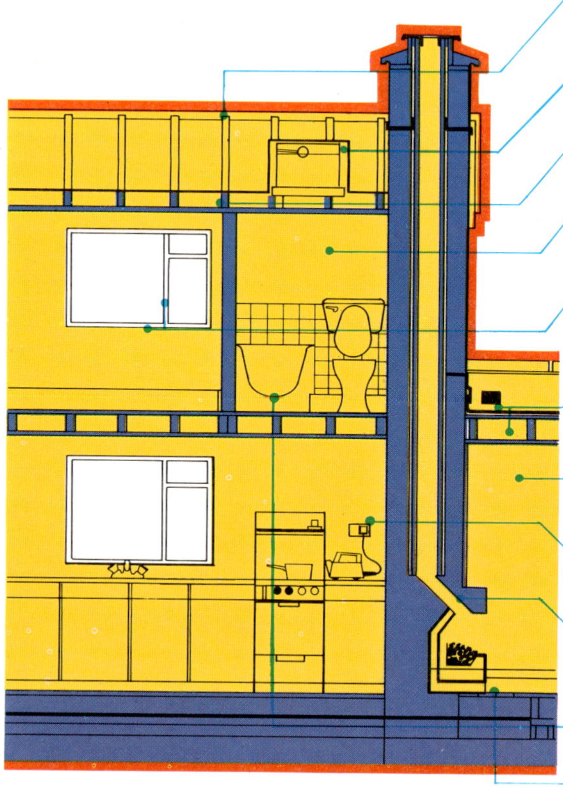

Looking after a tool kit properly is just as important as doing a job well. Not only should the right tool be readily to hand but it should be kept in its proper place. This purpose-designed toolbox, made largely from Finnish birch plywood, contains a selection of tools appropriate for home repairs. Compartments allow heavy and delicate tools to be stored safely apart.

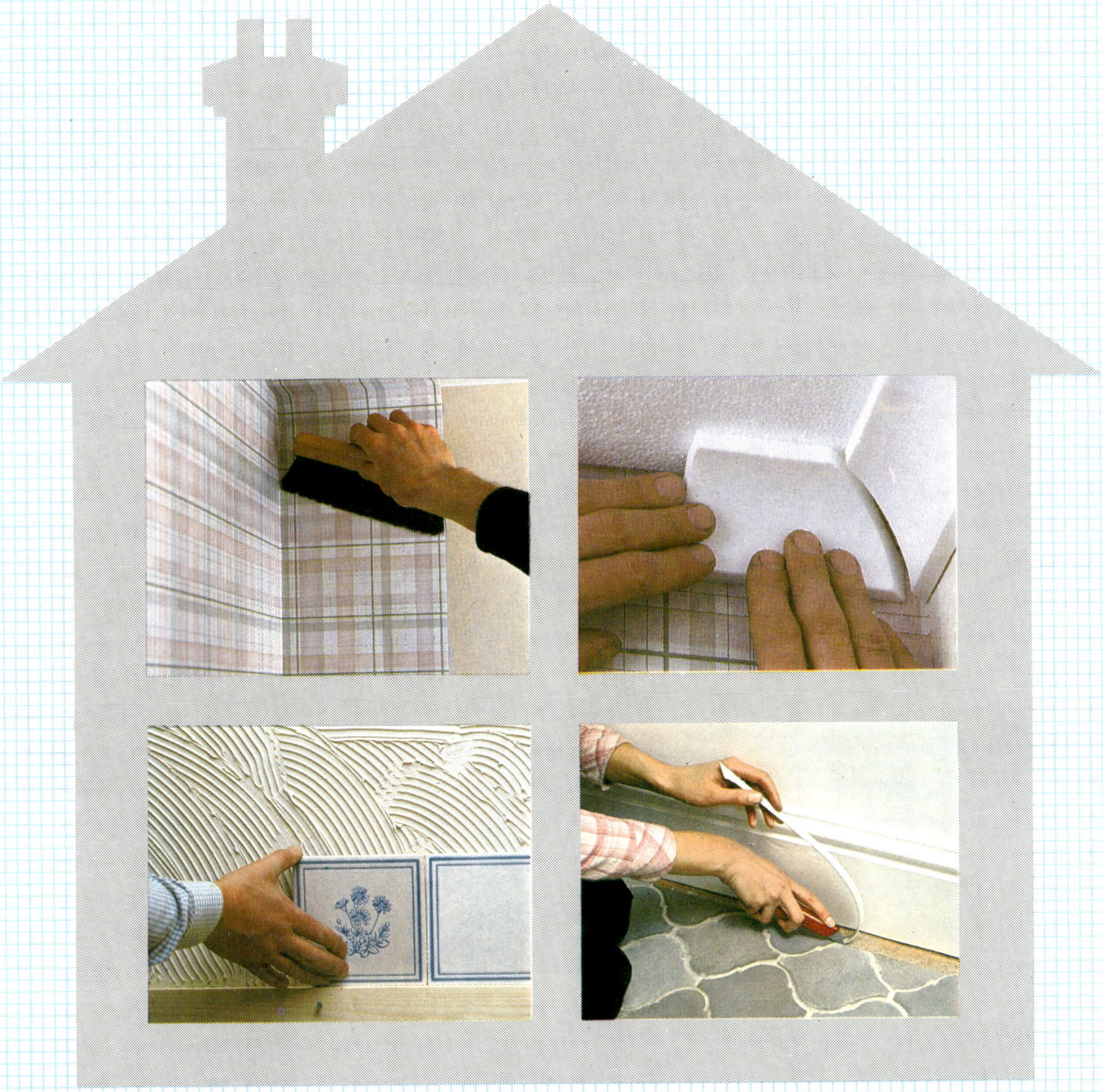

HOME DECORATING

Hanging a length of wallpaper or painting a door may be your idea of the ultimate in practical skills, but millions of people take such activities in their stride. Many do these jobs very well indeed, but for some there is room for improvement. There is a right way to hang wallcoverings, there is a correct sequence to follow when painting a panelled door. Do you know all the answers?

If you think you do, just dip into the following pages at random and find out what gaps there are in your knowledge. In this chapter many years of practical experience have been distilled to help you with a wide range of decorating tasks around the home.

Before you begin

Interior decorating is not difficult and most people will soon become a dab hand with a brush or get the hang of wallpapering quite quickly and be able to produce first-class results. It will help enormously if you assemble a good kit of decorating equipment, choose the right paint and paper, and settle on an appropriate and attractive colour scheme.

Not everyone has a flair for interior design so choosing a colour scheme can be difficult and the results sometimes disappointing. However, there are a few ground rules which, if borne in mind, will help you avoid many of the most common pitfalls.

Unless a room is being refurnished from scratch, including carpets and curtains, it is best to use the colours in existing furnishings as the basis for a colour scheme.

Then the size and shape of the room, its aspect and use, should be considered.

Light colours will make a room seem more spacious, whereas darker colours will make it seem smaller. You can also change the shape of a room by combining light and dark colours. A long, narrow room, for example, looks more square if dark colours are used on the end walls and light colours on the side walls.

Features in a room, such as a chimney breast, can be brought forward by painting them a dark colour with the recess walls painted in a light colour. The opposite effect will be achieved by reversing the colours.

Cold rooms which get very little sun need rich, warm colours to bring them to life. Bright rooms, on the other hand, can be decorated with cool, pale colours.

Patterns should also be matched to a room. A wallpaper with a large motif is best in a big room – in a small room it can be overbearing.

Jazzy, multi-coloured patterns are hardly conducive to relaxation so they are not a good choice for a lounge or bedroom.

These basic guidelines might have to be compromised somewhere along the way but, by and large, they will help greatly in achieving satisfying results.

The right choice of pattern and quality of paper and paint will help on the practical side. The easiest wallpaper designs to use are simple, random designs. These present far fewer problems when pattern matching, papering uneven corners and so on.

Anyone tackling their first wallpapering job would be well advised to cut their teeth on a vinyl or medium thick paper. These will withstand a reasonable amount of pulling around without damage. Thin papers can tear easily after pasting and when being positioned on the wall – more especially if there is some intricate cutting involved.

Above A selection of painting equipment. Left to right: paint pads, roller and tray; a range of brushes; and stripping equipment – blowtorch, hot-air stripper, sandpaper, scrapers and shavehook.
Right and far right Colour schemes must be chosen bearing in mind the shape and size of the room. Light colours make a room look more spacious.

Paint, both gloss and emulsion, can be bought in non-drip and liquid forms. Non-drip paints have a jelly-like consistency and they will not run or splash about so they are especially useful when developing a good painting technique. Solid emulsion is ideal when decorating the ceiling of a furnished room, for example, as it makes no mess at all.

Lastly, remember that good decorating equipment will last a lifetime of use and help you to achieve good results every time.

Equipment

The amount of equipment and materials needed will depend on the types of surface to be decorated and the condition of existing surfaces.

Brushes The size of a brush is denoted by the widths of the bristles. A range of sizes is needed to enable narrow and wide surfaces to be painted more easily and to a higher standard.

For most interior work a useful kit will comprise 25, 50 and 75mm brushes. The smaller sizes are used on narrow items such as window frames; the 75mm brush is needed for covering wide areas.

For walls and ceilings a 125mm brush is best (or a paint roller or paint pad).

A useful addition is a small, 12mm cutting-in brush. This has angled bristles which enable window frames to be painted without smudging paint on the glass. For painting behind a radiator and other awkward places, a crevice brush is needed. This has a long wire handle which can be bent to get the bristles into tight corners.

Pure bristle brushes are a good investment – the bristles are well bulked and have a strong, stiff, springy feel. They hold paint well and produce a good finish.

Roller A paint roller enables ceilings and walls to be covered quickly. Rollers are made in various materials – a good one made from lamb's-wool or mohair will cover a surface well and will not spatter paint around. A roller tray is also needed.

Paint pads Available in a range of sizes and shapes for use with both emulsion and gloss paint. The larger pads come into their own for speedy and effortless coverage of walls and ceilings which are smooth.

A pad consists of a piece of foam covered with mohair pile. It is held in a metal or plastic holder. Though it can be loaded straight from a paint tin or roller tray, special applicators are available.

Filling knife For filling surface cracks. The blade is flexible: wide and narrow types are available.

Paint scraper Has a stiff blade for stripping paint from flat surfaces.

Shavehooks For stripping paint from mouldings, tight corners and other intricate places. There are two types – one has a triangular head, the other has curves and straight portions and is more versatile.

Blowtorch For fast stripping of old paint. A canister of gas is fitted to a burner taking care to ensure a good seal. When the canister is empty, a new one is fitted.

Electric paint stripper A blast of hot air softens old paint ready for stripping.

Chemical stripper A liquid or paste stripper which is dabbed or spread on to old paint to soften and shrivel it for stripping.

Glasspaper Sheets of glasspaper or an abrasive block are used to rub down surfaces to smooth them and provide a key for the new paint. A power operated sander makes this work much easier.

Sponge For washing down surfaces.

White spirit or brush cleaner For cleaning equipment used with gloss paint.

Painting technique

Always prepare ceilings first, then the walls and finally any woodwork or metal (window frames). See section dealing with metalwork.

Preparing ceilings and walls

In new houses or extensions, plastered walls and ceilings can be painted within a few weeks. Old ceilings should be washed with sugar soap or household detergent, then rinsed with plenty of clean water and allowed to dry.

Always wash walls from the skirting upwards to prevent dirty streaks running down and drying out. These could show through the new paint.

Fill any holes or cracks with cellulose filler and leave them flush with the surface. Any dried water stains should be coated first with oil-based primer sealer to make sure the following paint conceals them. An aluminium sealer is needed on a ceiling that has become discoloured with nicotine stains. Any flaking paint should be scraped off before using oil-based primer sealer. Powdery surfaces need the same oil-based sealer applied over them.

Flaking paint often indicates dampness, so cure the cause of this before decorating.

Preparing woodwork

Never remove paintwork which is in a sound condition. The only exception is where a thick film is preventing windows and doors from closing properly.

Wash down sound paintwork with sugar soap or household detergent then rub down with fine grade glasspaper and rinse off. Any small chips can be filled with fine surface filler.

Where paint is peeling, pitted or badly chipped, strip it off back to bare wood before repainting.

When stripping with a blowtorch, place a metal tray below to catch burning paint peelings. Always keep the blowtorch moving to avoid a concentration of heat scorching the wood. Be careful around windows where heat can crack the glass.

An electric heat stripper is equally quick and has the advantage of not scorching the wood in mouldings where paint stripping takes longer. It's also safer to use since there are no burning paint peelings to worry about.

Chemical stripper is only economically justified for small areas or for mouldings or around glass. After stripping, the bare wood should be cleaned thoroughly with white spirit or the solvent recommended by the manufacturers. If traces of chemical are left they can affect the new paint.

Preparing metal

Treat sound paintwork as for wood. Flaking or rusted surfaces should be stripped back to bare metal. Rust can be removed with a

1. *Stripping paintwork using a blowtorch and shavehook.*
2. *A chemical paint stripper is dabbed on using an old brush. Paste types are applied with a spatula.*
3. *Small chips in paintwork are filled with fine surface filler.*
4. *An electric hot air stripper.*
5. *An electric sander takes the elbow work out of rubbing down paintwork.*
6. *Remove door fittings before painting.*

wire brush. Apply a coat of rust inhibiting metal primer before repainting.

Painting walls and ceilings

Apply the paint in bands about 500mm wide working away from the window. Working away from the light makes it easier to see which areas have been covered. Close the windows to slow down the drying rate of the paint so that wet edges can be joined up before they start to dry. Open the windows to accelerate drying when the job is finished.

Always plan to paint a complete ceiling or wall in one continuous work session. If a break is taken halfway through, allowing the paint to dry, then the dried paint line will show when the ceiling is completed. Breaks can be taken in corners when painting walls.

If using a roller it will first be necessary to use a small brush to apply a narrow band of paint around window frames and in corners and other areas where the roller will not reach. A roller is used in a criss-cross, random fashion.

To load the roller correctly, push it backwards and forwards in the paint to cover it then run it up and down the sloping part of the tray to spread the paint evenly around it. Never let the roller spin freely or leave the surface sharply when painting or paint splashes will result.

A paint pad can be used more quickly without fear of splashing. Load it by immersing the pile in the paint before wiping away the excess on the can. If using a special applicator trough, this incorporates a roller which transfers paint to the pad.

Emulsion

Usually two coats of emulsion paint are sufficient to cover a ceiling or wall and leave a smooth, even finish. However, sometimes a third coat will be needed to get a good finish. The first coat of emulsion paint can be diluted with water following the instructions on the can. Do not dilute non-drip emulsion.

1. *Start painting a ceiling adjacent to the window and work away from the light.*
2. *A roller is loaded by rolling it back and forth in the tray.*
3. *Special applicator troughs are available for loading paint pads.*
4. *Before using a roller, paint corners with a small brush.*
5. *Paint in random directions when using a roller.*
6. *A paint pad is also used working in random directions.*

Emulsion paint is sold in various finishes such as matt or silk. If there are bumps and hollows in a wall it is best to use a matt finish to disguise the faults – a shiny emulsion will highlight them.

If a wall has been patched with filler in lots of places then it is best to first hang lining paper, or a textured paper which is especially formulated to be painted. Lining paper should be hung in vertical lengths when it is to be painted over.

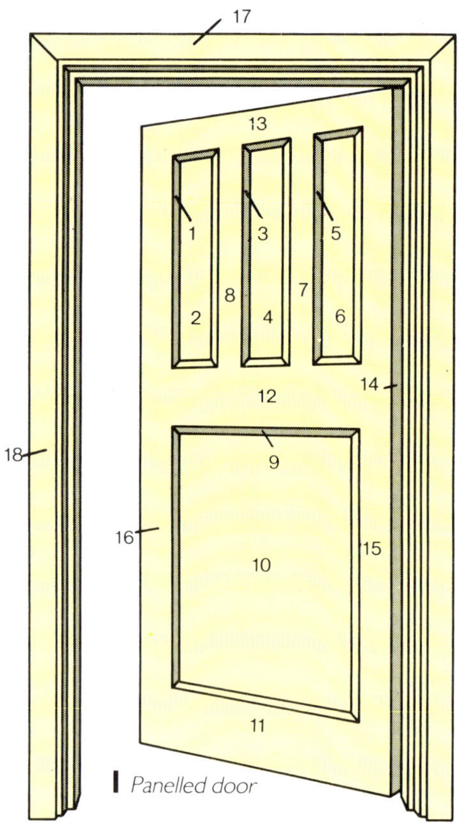

1 *Panelled door*

2 *Flush door*

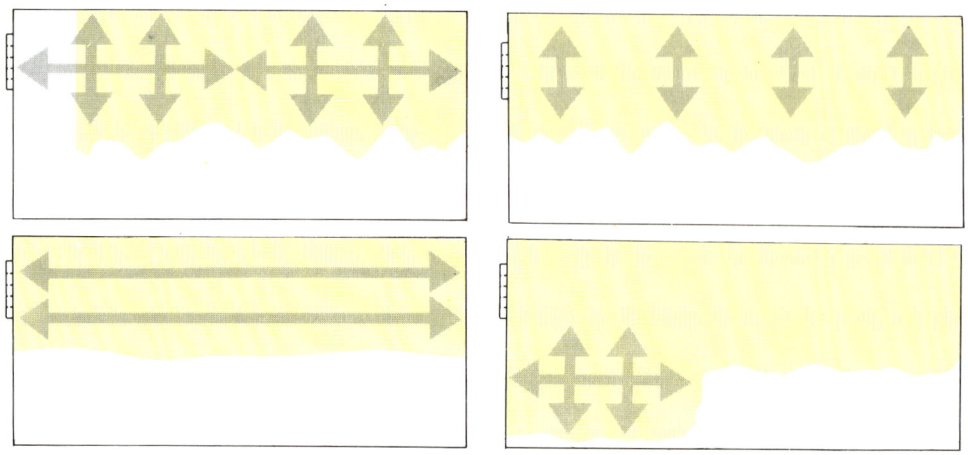

3 *Sash window*

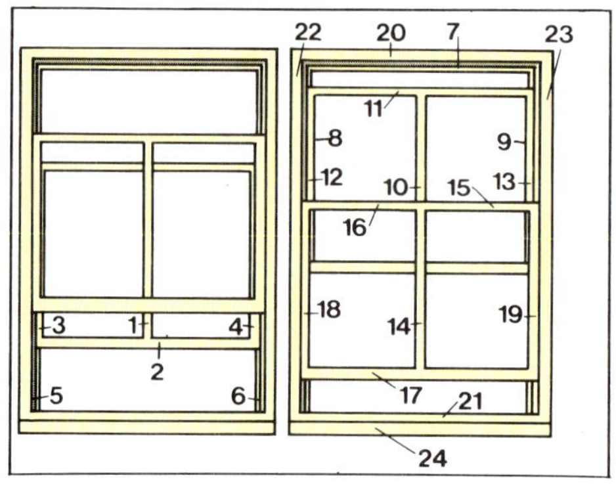

4 *Casement window*

1. *The order for painting a panelled door.*
2. *A flush door is painted by laying on then brushing out in the order shown.*
3. *A sash window is opened as on the left for painting sections 1 to 6; it is then repositioned as on the right to coat sections 7 to 24.*
4. *The order for painting a casement window. Always paint the sill last, so that it does not get smudged.*
5. *Applying primer to bare wood.*
6. *Using an angled cutting-in brush to paint a window frame neatly. Alternative methods of keeping paint off the glass are to stick masking tape on the pane or to use a purpose-made paint shield.*

Doors

Remove all door fittings such as handles and keyhole plates – trying to work around them causes paint runs. Clean out the keyhole and the top edge of the door to prevent dirt being picked up on the bristles and being transferred to the paint. Finally, open the door and put a wedge below it.

With a panelled door, paint the mouldings first with a small brush then switch to a 50mm brush to complete (in the following order) the panels, vertical centre sections, horizontal sections at the top, middle and bottom, vertical outside sections, edges and door frame.

Paint a flush door in square sections working from the top on the hinge side, downwards to finish at the bottom corner on the handle side. Use a 75mm brush to cover the surface more quickly and to join up the squares before the paint starts to dry.

For a smooth finish, always paint flat surfaces as follows. Dip the tops of the bristles in the paint and wipe away any excess on the side of the tin. To lay on the paint make two or three down strokes, then cross-brush the area. Lay off the paint with vertical strokes and finish with light upward strokes using the tips of the bristles. Then reload the brush and paint the adjoining section.

Windows

Paint openable windows as early in the day as possible so they will be dry for closing at night. Use a small brush and paint (in the following order) the rebates, any cross bars, top and bottom horizontal rails, side vertical rails and edges, the window frame. It is important that the correct order of painting is followed so that you do not miss parts or smudge the work.

Metalwork

Use a coat of metal primer on bare surfaces, followed by undercoat and gloss. Previously painted metal is treated as for wood. Always make absolutely sure that any rust is removed before priming.

Paint types

When the old paintwork is to remain, apply one or two coats of undercoat, as needed to hide completely the old colour. Finish off with a coat of gloss.

When painting bare wood, first use a brush or lint-free rag to dab shellac knotting over knots and resinous patches; this seals in any resin which might otherwise bleed through the following paint coats. Next apply a coat of wood primer to seal the wood and fill any cracks. Follow up with undercoat and gloss. Always allow full drying time between each coat.

Planning

If you are planning a painting job, you will want to work out how much paint to buy. You should also try to calculate roughly how long the job will take. This will allow you to plan both your total time and when you will finish each coat, so that you can work out the times of breaks.

How much paint will you need?
Work out how much paint to buy before going to the shop. First measure the length and width of the room. It is best to use metric measurements for this since paint is sold in litres. Round up the dimensions of the room to the nearest half metre and add them together. Then multiply the result by the height of the room and multiply the result by two. This will give you the total area of your walls. It is difficult to estimate the sizes of windows without calculating them exactly, but as a rough guide, subtract 2 square metres for a small window, 4 square metres for a medium sized window, and 5 square metres for a large one. You should allow 2 square metres for each door. You should also add on extra for any protruding chimney breasts or similar features.

Stairways often have triangular walls. Work out the area of these by multiplying the length by the height of the wall and dividing by two.

Covering power
The actual quantity of paint that you will need will depend on the covering power of the type you are going to use. It will also depend on the surface you are painting. For example, liquid gloss and emulsion paints cover a larger area per litre than non-drip gloss. Also, bare plaster will be more absorbent, and therefore take more paint, than a surface that has been prepared. To find the exact covering power of a particular brand of paint, look at the details on the can. As a rule of thumb, expect non-drip gloss and silk-finish paints to cover about 12 sq m per litre; solid emulsion to cover about 14 sq m per litre; undercoat, eggshell and vinyl silk to cover about 15 sq m; and liquid gloss to cover about 17 sq m.

How many coats?
Of course, the number of coats you need will also influence how much paint you require. Several factors determine how many coats you should apply. In ideal conditions, follow the instructions on the can. But sometimes you will need more coats than the manufacturer recommends. For example, if you are covering a dark colour with a lighter one, you should allow extra coats to cover up the old colour. The surface itself is also important. When you are painting over bare wood, use a coat of primer and an undercoat before you start applying the gloss. When covering old gloss paint you may also need one or two undercoats to provide a surface that will take the new gloss paint.

How long will it take?
When you are planning a decorating job, remember that you should allow enough time for preparation and cleaning up afterwards. When working out how long the whole job will take, bear in mind the time each coat of paint will take to dry.

Preparation nearly always takes longer than you think it will. The time you allow for filling holes and rubbing down will obviously vary according to the condition of the surfaces, but allow 2 to 3 hours for priming the walls of a room 3m × 4m.

Troubleshooting

Even with the most careful planning, problems can sometimes occur. Below you will find descriptions of some of the most common painting problems you are likely to encounter.

Blisters Mostly found when painting in wet conditions outside the house. Inside, they can be caused by painting over old, soft paint. If there are a lot of blisters, strip back to bare wood and repaint. An isolated blister can be cut out; should sound paint be found underneath then fill the depression with fine surface filler and apply new undercoat and gloss. If bare wood is found then use shellac knotting (if necessary) followed by primer; then proceed as above.
Brush marks Caused by not rubbing down old paintwork properly, or by applying too thick a coat of paint or by using poor quality brushes. Using old, thick paint is another cause; thick paint should be thinned, but never overthinned, following the instructions on the can.
Specks Pimples on the surface show more prominently in a shiny finish. The cause is specks of dust getting on the brush or into the paint.
Runs, sags and wrinkles All these are caused by poor painting techniques. The paint has been applied too thickly, or not spread evenly. If noticed immediately when the paint is fresh and wet then they can be brushed out lightly. If attempted when the paint has started to dry the surface will be smeared.
Dull gloss Due to poor preparation, not allowing sufficient drying time between coats, incorrect use of thinners, or overbrushing the paint.
No hiding power When the previous colour shows through the top coat the problem is usually due to using the wrong undercoat below the gloss or not applying a sufficient number of undercoats. Other causes are not stirring the paint properly, overthinning the paint or overbrushing the gloss.

Cures
Should any of the problems above occur, then let the paint harden and dry for about four days. The surface should then be rubbed down lightly using fine grade glasspaper; wipe away and dust then apply another finishing coat.

Problems in kitchens and bathrooms
You may experience problems with paintwork breaking up because of condensation in these rooms. If this happens you will obviously want to redecorate, but you should try to eliminate the condensation.

The best way to prevent condensation is to provide good ventilation by fitting an extractor fan and ensuring that all vents are unobstructed. Another solution is to apply anti-condensation paint to the walls. This contains an insulating substance. It can be painted over in any colour.

When repainting, check the manufacturer's instructions on the paint can to make sure that the paint is suitable for kitchens and bathrooms. In addition, avoid using gloss paint on kitchen and bathroom walls, as it exaggerates the effect of condensation.

Outdoor woodwork
When tackling outdoor woodwork, the essential point is to prepare carefully. Exterior woodwork takes a battering from the weather and if it is to remain in good condition its surface must be prepared well before you apply any paint. If the existing paintwork is in quite good condition this is simply a matter of sanding down the surface to provide a good base for the new paint. Use wet and dry paper and rinse the surface with clean water when you have rubbed it down. Next apply the undercoat and when this is dry, sand the surface once more, this time using dry paper. You can then put on the finishing coat.

More often, however, the paint on exterior woodwork has started to deteriorate before you repaint it. If this is the case, start by scraping the surface thoroughly. Remove all the old paint. If it has started to flake, you will probably be able to do this with an ordinary hand paint scraper. If it is more stubborn use either an orbital sander or a purpose-made hot-air paint stripper. When you have got all the old paint off the woodwork, brush away the dust and apply a coat of primer. When this has dried, fill any holes or cracks with a proprietory wood filler. Put on the undercoat when this has set. For best results you should then apply two top coats. If you follow this procedure carefully, your outdoor paintwork will last well and it will provide an excellent protection against the weather.

Wallpapering technique

Before you start papering, make sure you have all the equipment you need and that you have plenty of space in which to work.

Wallpapering equipment

Pasting table A fold-away pasting table is a good investment. It saves having to provide a makeshift surface or borrowing the kitchen table for pasting wallpaper. Measuring about 2m long by about 600mm wide, it can also be used as a general worktable for matching patterns and marking and cutting lengths of paper. Inexpensive and easy to store, it will last a lifetime of wallpapering jobs.

Paste bucket Any clean bucket will do.

Paste brush A 100 or 125mm wide paint brush is suitable. An old brush is often best since it will not shed loose bristles when pasting.

Hanging brush Use for smoothing wallpaper on to the wall.

Shears A proper pair of wallpaper shears, about 250mm long, are needed to cut accurate, long straight lines when trimming paper to a neat fit. A pair of normal household scissors are not a good substitute though a sharp pair is useful when cutting the paper to fit around light switches,

1

2
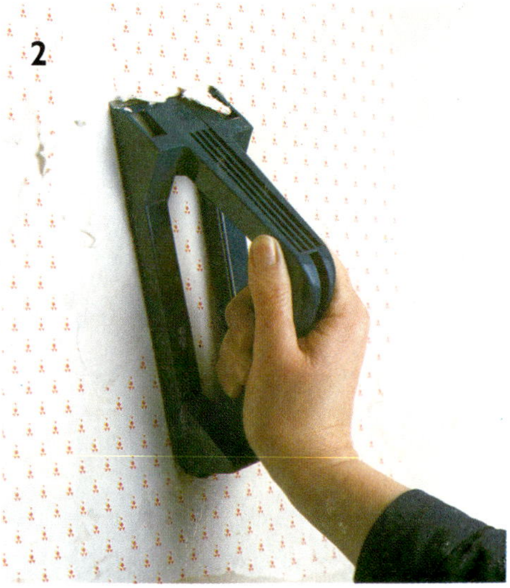

Above Hang lining paper horizontally.
Below and right Equipment for hanging wallcoverings. Although a short stepladder is illustrated it is important that the one you use is long enough to allow the top part of the paper to be hung while working within comfortable reach.

1. *Easy-strip wallcoverings are formulated so that the top layer peels away to leave a paper backing on the wall.*
2. *Standard wallcoverings have to be scraped off. Soak the surface with hot water if the paper is difficult to remove and then use a proprietary scraper.*
3. *Washable wallcoverings are the most difficult to strip off. First the surface has to be broken down to allow the soaking water to get through and loosen the old paste. A wire brush or, as here, a Skarsten scraper can be used to score the surface covering.*
4. *Fill cracks slightly proud of the surface using cellulose filler.*
5. *Rub the filler smooth when dry.*

3

4
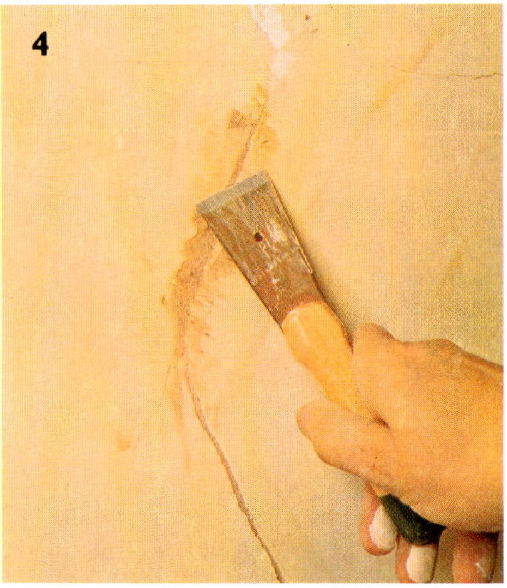

5

fireplaces and other intricate features.
Knife A sharp handyman's knife is useful, especially for trimming vinyls.
Plumb bob Wallpaper must be hung vertically. This means having to mark a guide line on the wall. This is done by suspending a chalked plumb bob down the wall then snapping a chalk line impression on to the wall. A long, 1m spirit level which gives a vertical reading is a good alternative.
Pencil For marking out cutting lines.

Folding boxwood rule A 600mm or 1m folding rule is ideal for measuring and marking the paper. A steel tape is a useful alternative.
Wooden seam roller Not essential but useful for smoothing the edges of the paper firmly to the wall. Never use it on papers which have a raised texture which would be flattened by the pressure.
Paste Buy the correct paste for the wallpaper being used. Standard paste is used for normal wallpaper; heavy-duty type is used for thick paper; for vinyls a paste containing a fungicide is needed. Universal pastes which can be mixed with differing amounts of water are available. These cover a variety of wallpaper types.
Size Before ordinary wallpaper is hung on bare plaster the wall should be sized. This helps ensure that the paper will stick to the wall properly. Size also makes the wall more slippery so the paper slides into position more easily. Size can be made from many normal wallpaper pastes – check the instructions.
Scraper For removing old paper.
Lining paper Thin, white paper sold in rolls. It is used to cover cracked walls or below heavy and expensive wallcoverings; without it any imperfections in the wall would show through the wallcovering.

As a good general rule always take the utmost care to keep your equipment in the very best condition. After using, wash, clean and rub dry the tools; carefully pack away unused paste and store in a dry, clean cupboard. Sometimes it may be worthwhile to repackage powdered adhesives into a well sealed jar.

Left to right, top to bottom: Pasting brush, paste bucket, steps; hanging brush, edge roller, sponge, filling knife, serrated scraper, proprietary scraper; various grades of glasspaper, pastes, wallpaper shears, folding rule, knife, pencil, plumb bob and line; pasting table (folded).

Paper stripping

Always strip off any existing paper. This can be simple or tough work. Some modern wallcoverings can be removed simply by loosening the bottom edge from the wall and pulling upwards to leave a thin, white backing paper on the wall. If this is soundly fixed over the complete wall and none of its edges are overlapping then it can be left in place and papered over. If not it should be stripped off. Some clean-strip wallcoverings can be similarly removed.

Occasionally an ordinary paper is found which can be pulled away in large sheets leaving only isolated patches still sticking in place. In cases like these a weak paste or perhaps a damp wall will have made the paper so easily removable.

Normal papers which are firmly adhering are removed by soaking with hot water and then by scraping. A little household detergent added to the water can help.

Washable papers are usually difficult to remove. The surface must first be broken down to allow the water to soak through. Score the surface with a wire brush or even an old piece of hacksaw blade, then soak thoroughly and scrape the paper off. If the going is really tough and a large area is involved then, as a last resort, a steam stripping machine could be obtained from a local hire shop. This machine will enable you to remove several layers of old paper.

Faced with a bare wall, go over the surface with coarse glasspaper wrapped around a wood block to remove any remaining nibs of paper. Then wash the wall with hot water to clear all traces of the old paste.

1

2

3

4

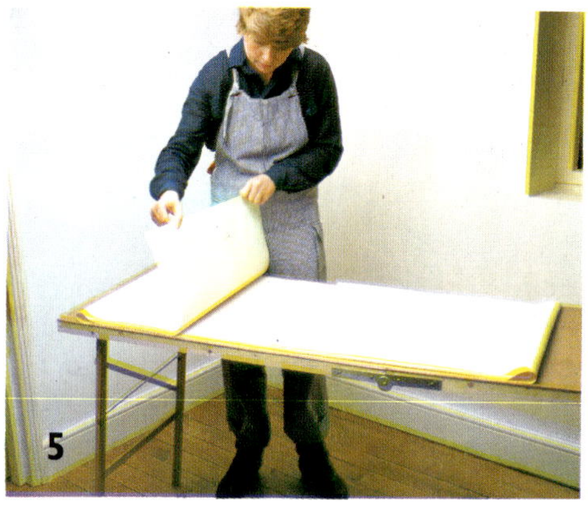
5

6

Cutting and pasting

1. Match the pattern before cutting out each length of paper. With some patterns it is economical to work from two rolls and minimise wasted paper. The smaller the size of the pattern repeat, the smaller the likely amount of wastage.

2. Use wallpaper shears to make long, accurate cuts. Make sure your shears are sharp.

3. Every bit of the paper has to be well pasted. First a wide band is pasted right down the middle of the piece.

4. The paper is then pulled towards you to slightly overlap the edge of the table; the paste is then brushed outwards to the edge.

5. When half the paper has been pasted, its edge is folded to the centre. The other half is then pasted and folded similarly.

6. Snapping a 'chalked' stringline on the wall as a guide to the first length of paper.

Preparing to hang paper

Normally wallpaper is hung starting near a window or on the wall which is adjacent to the window wall. Successive lengths are then hung working away from the window light. This is done so that, should the edges of two lengths be overlapped slightly, a shadow will not be cast which would make the error more noticeable.

The first length of paper must be hung vertically – this ensures that the following lengths will also be vertical. Hold the roll of paper in place and make a mark at the top of the wall 12mm in from the edge of the roll. This ensures that 12mm of the paper will be turned on to the window wall.

Suspend the plumb bob from the top of the wall and smear the string with chalk. Allow the string to stop swinging then press it against the skirting board; with the other hand, snap the string against the wall to leave a chalk mark. Use a pencil and a straight-edge to mark a more definite line through the chalk. If the wall is flat, a long spirit level can be used to mark verticals.

Should a fairly large pattern motif be used then it is important to centralise it on the chimney breast. In this case draw the vertical guide line on the breast and start papering at that point, working backwards to the window.

Fill any cracks or holes with a cellulose filler and a filling knife. If a smooth finish can't be obtained then leave the filler proud of the surface, let it harden and rub it smooth with glasspaper.

Next brush size all over the wall. Mix up the powder with water following the instructions on the packet closely.

Finally, where the walls are crazed or in a generally poor state, though structurally sound, hang lining paper. This is used in the same way as normal wallpaper except that it must be hung horizontally on the wall. The edges of each piece must be butted up closely (never overlapped) and the ends cut tightly into the corners of the walls. In extreme cases cross-lining is needed to get a smooth surface. This means having to hang two layers of lining paper – the first vertically and the second horizontally.

Hang lining paper with the same paste as that used for the final wallcovering.

When buying wallcoverings you must always ensure that the batch number on each roll is the same but it is still a good idea to unravel a metre or two of paper from several rolls and take them into a good light so that a check can be made to ensure there is no colour variation in the pattern from roll to roll. If there is a slight difference in one roll then keep this for hanging on a separate wall so that the variation will not be apparent.

Cut the first length of paper 100mm longer than needed to allow for a 50mm excess at the top and bottom of the wall. Place the paper on the paste table positioning it so that the top edge and one side overlaps the table by about 3mm. Having pasted the overlapping edges the paper can be repositioned so that the unpasted edge overlaps the table.

First paste a wide band down the middle of the paper and then brush outwards to the edges in herring-bone fashion. When half the length has been pasted, fold over the top edge to the centre line. The other half of the length can then be pasted and its top edge folded to meet the other one in the middle.

Thin papers and vinyls can be hung immediately after pasting. Medium weight papers should be left for a few minutes for the paste to soak in well. Heavy papers must be left to soak for up to ten minutes before you hang them.

Hanging

Hold the paper to the wall and unpeel the top half. Position its edge against the marked pencil line. Make sure that 50mm of paper is extended on to the ceiling. It's a good idea to turn under the top edge (paste side to paste side) to prevent paste smearing on to the ceiling. Ensure that this first half is aligned exactly with the pencil line.

Using the wallpaper brush, smooth down the middle of the paper and then brush outwards to the edges. This prevents air being trapped under the paper. When the top half is smoothed in place unpeel the lower half and brush this out as before. If the top half was aligned perfectly with the pencil line the lower half will automatically follow it. The 12mm margin should then be brushed tightly into the corner and smoothed on to the window wall.

Now return to the top edge. Run the back of the scissors into the angle of the ceiling and wall to leave a crease line across the paper. Pull the edge away from the wall, cut along the crease line, then brush the paper back into place. Repeat this at the skirting.

The first length of paper is critical; if it is not vertical then problems will start to accumulate with successive lengths. The pattern will be misaligned and edges of lengths will start to overlap. So if the top half of the paper wanders away from the vertical, peel it off and reposition it.

Check that paste has not got on to the face of the paper. If it has then wipe it off with a clean sponge and water. Also remove any paste which gets on to the ceiling or skirting before it dries.

Before cutting out the next length, offer up the roll and check with the first length where the pattern matches – and make sure to allow a 50mm excess at the top for final trimming. With more experience, pattern matching of lengths can be tackled on the paste table.

With some patterns, the amount of wasted paper can be alarming. It is often more economical to work from two rolls at once to minimise wastage.

The second and subsequent lengths are hung in exactly the same way. Position the top edge closely against the edge of the first length and align the pattern. Make sure, on brushing out, that the edges butt up closely all the way down.

When two lengths are hung and the paste is nearly dry, run the seam roller down the joint to press down the edges. Continue hanging lengths on the wall until the last full-width piece has been brushed in place.

Hanging

1. *The edge of the first length of paper is aligned with the chalk mark on the wall.*
2. *The paper is smoothed working from the middle outwards to expel air and prevent bubbles forming.*
3. *The back of the shears is pressed along the ceiling line to leave a crease line through the paper.*
4. *Carefully trimming along the crease line with the shears.*
5. *When the top of the paper is smoothed back into place it should fit neatly. This process is then repeated at the skirting.*
6. *The next length being positioned carefully to ensure alignment of the pattern. Provided that the first piece of paper was exactly vertical, the second and subsequent sheets should also be in exactly the right position.*

1

2

3

4

5
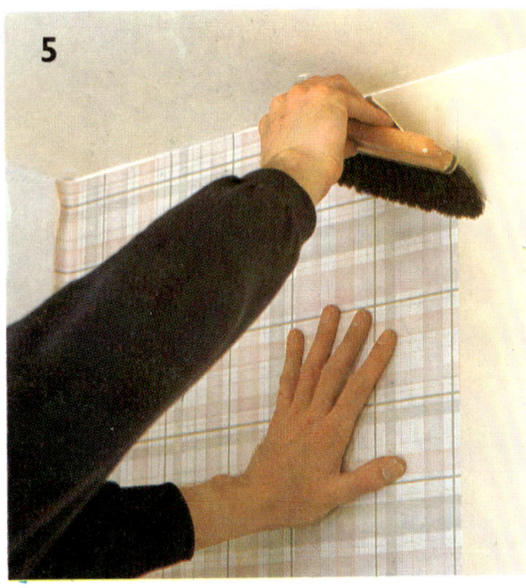

6
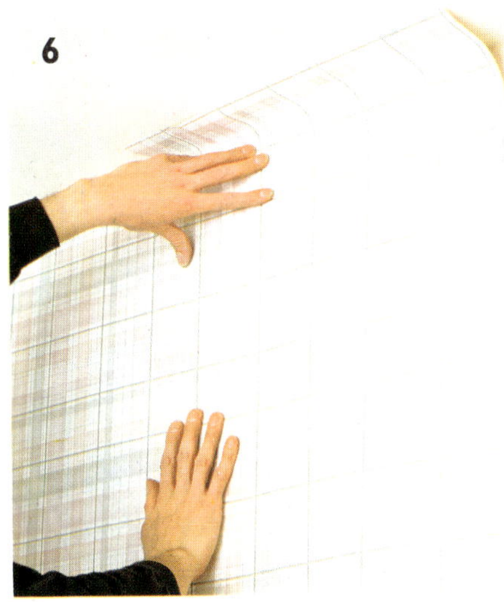

1

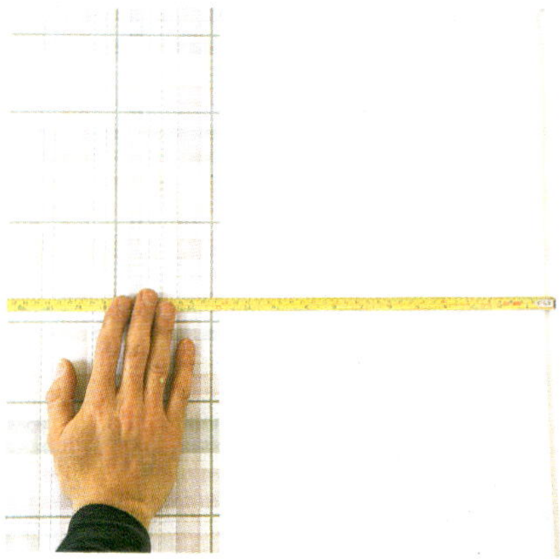

2

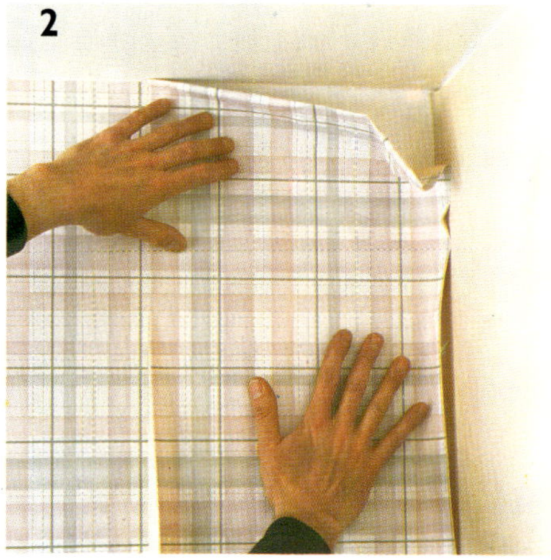

3

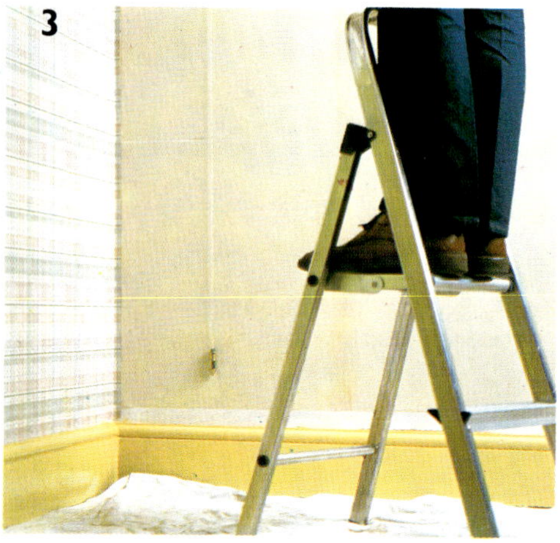

4

Internal corners

1. *Hang complete lengths of paper until only a part length is needed to reach to the corner. Use a rule to measure the distance to the corner. This amount of paper is cut from the next length allowing about 10mm to turn the corner.*

2. *Carefully hang this piece of paper, brushing it tight into the corner and smoothing the margin onto the return wall.*

3. *A plumb bob is suspended on the next wall as a guide to hanging the offcut piece of paper.*

4. *The offcut is then hung with its edge tight into the corner to overlap the edge of the previous piece. The pattern must be matched as closely as possible.*

1

2

External corners

1. *On an external corner, such as a chimney breast, hang the first piece on the facing wall, allowing for about 20mm of paper to turn onto the side wall. Do not smooth down the 20mm edge until you have papered the side wall.*

2. *Hang the offcut on the side wall with its edge tight to the external corner, then smooth down over it the loose edge of the piece hung on the facing wall. Joins made on a side wall in this way will always be less noticeable than those made on a facing wall.*

Corners and obstructions

Internal corners

Measure the distance from the edge of the last length into the corner. Do this at the top, middle and bottom of the wall. Since many corners are out of true, these measurements could differ, so do take care when recording distances.

Select the largest measurement and add 10mm to it. So, if the three measurements are 190, 195 and 200mm the final figure will be 210mm – this amount should then be cut from the next length. Make sure the cut is made from the correct side of the length. Keep the offcut piece of paper safely – this will be hung on the return wall.

Paste then hang the first piece, using the tips of the brush bristles to smooth the edge tightly into the corner. Smooth down the 10mm overlap on to the return wall, and continue.

Whenever a corner is turned, the first piece of paper on the new wall must be hung following a plumb line as was the starting length. Measure the width of the offcut and mark a vertical line on the wall at this distance from the corner. Paste then hang the offcut, brushing its edge into the corner to overlap the edge of the previous length. Obviously there will be a slight break in the pattern but this will not be readily noticeable. Do, however, ensure that the pattern is matched as closely as possible.

External corners

Work up to the last full width before the corner. As before, take three measurements from the edge of the last length to the corner and add 25mm to the largest measurement. Cut this amount from the length then paste and hang it, turning the edge around the corner. Do not brush down the edge – leave it loose.

Hang a plumb line for the offcut on the new wall which should be marked at the same distance from the corner as is the width of the offcut. Smooth the offcut on to the wall then brush the loose edge of the first piece down over it. Again match the pattern as closely as possible.

For appearance it is always best to overlap the paper at external corners on whichever wall it will be least noticed. In some circumstances it might be better to brush down the edge of the first piece on to the new wall and then hang the offcut to overlap it.

Window reveals

Paper the reveal first, turning 10mm of paper on to the facing wall. The cut and hang the paper on the facing wall cutting it to the outline of the reveal.

Other problem areas

If dealing with a modern, flush light switch or socket then brush on the top part of the paper down to the fitting. Turn off the electricity supply at the mains before loosening the screws holding the switch cover to the wall. Next, cut a hole in the paper slightly less in area than the size of the cover. Pull the cover through the hole and then hang the remainder of the length. Trim around the hole made in the paper to leave a 5mm margin inside the cover. Screw back the cover and restore the electricity supply.

An older-style switch is often mounted on a block which cannot be removed. Smooth down the top part of the paper until the switch is reached then press the paper against the switch to ascertain its position. Using small scissors make star-shaped cuts in the paper, working outwards from the centre of the switch to a point about 10mm beyond the mounting block. Brush the paper around the block, use the back of the scissors to make a crease around it, then trim along the crease line and brush the paper back into place.

Doorways

Working from the last full length of paper before the door frame, carefully measure out and cut a length of paper which will overlap the doorway by about 50mm all round. Paste the paper and brush the top part on to the wall above the door. Mark a crease line along the top of the door frame. Trim along the crease and finish by making a short diagonal cut working outwards from the top corner of the frame.

The lower half of the paper can now be brushed on to the wall and creased, then trimmed to fit neatly at the side of door frame. The diagonal cut made in the paper will not be noticeable when the length has been hung.

Fireplace surround

Where the mantelshelf reaches to within 20mm or so of the corners of the chimney breast wall, it is best to hang the top half of the length then make a neat horizontal cut in the paper level with the mantelshelf.

The lower half then can be fitted separately working downwards to the skirting. Crease the paper into each shape, withdraw it, snip along the line, brush it back into place and so on. A small pair of sharp scissors will help you to make the short, intricate cuts that are needed.

By the time the paper is trimmed completely, the paste might have dried; if so, you will have to repaste the edges and brush on the paper.

Where there is a long distance between the edge of the mantelshelf and the corner, a cut line would be noticeable. Here the paper must be hung in one piece.

1. *Papering neatly around a doorway. Cut away most of the waste, leaving about 50mm all round for final trimming. By making a diagonal cut outwards in the paper working from the top corner of the frame, you will be able to smooth the paper neatly into the side and along the top of the frame.*

2. *Tackling a reveal. After papering the inside walls, turning a small margin onto the outside wall, the paper on the facing wall is cut to the exact outline of the reveal and is smoothed over the edge of the first piece.*

3. *Modern, flush fitting light switches are simple to paper around. Having turned off the electricity at the mains, the cover plate can be pulled forward allowing the paper to be trimmed as needed to leave a small margin inside the area occupied by the cover plate.*

4. *Star-shaped cuts made around an old-style light switch enable the paper to be trimmed accurately and neatly.*

5. *To trim paper around a fireplace means gradually creasing and trimming working from the top downwards.*

6. *When the paper has been cut to shape all the way down it can be smoothed into place.*

Other papering techniques

On the previous pages you will find information about the basics of wallpapering. But you may want to use one of the modern ready-pasted wallpapers, for which a different technique is required. Another technique which requires special skills is papering a ceiling. Finally in this section you will find hints and tips to help you with papering problems.

Ready-pasted paper

Using a ready-pasted wallcovering means not having to bother with a paste table or paste. The paste is already on the back of the wallcovering but in a dried form. To activate it the paper is immersed in water for the time recommended on the instructions – usually about a minute.

A plastic water trough can be obtained with the wallcovering, though any container which is long enough and deep enough to accept a loosely rolled length of paper will suffice. It's a good idea to place some newspapers below and around the trough to catch any water splashes.

Each length of paper is cut as normal and is then rolled up loosely with the pattern facing inwards. The roll is then immersed in water. It is important to roll the paper loosely otherwise the water might not reach and wet the paste. Long rolls should first be immersed with the pattern facing outwards and then be rerolled in the trough so that the free end is for the top of the wall.

Take hold of the top of the paper and gradually pull it upwards. Try to keep the tail of the paper in the trough so that water drains back into it. Smooth the length on to the wall using a clean sponge – always working from the middle of the length to the edges.

Sometimes excess paste will squelch out at the edges – this can be wiped away with a separate sponge kept solely for this job.

Sometimes when complicated lengths have to be trimmed around light switches or other obstacles, the paste might dry out before the length has been smoothed on to the wall. So keep a jar of paste handy to repaste any dried edges.

At corners, a latex adhesive is needed to stick down overlapping edges.

In kitchens and bathrooms where walls have been lined with sheet expanded polystyrene to combat condensation, cover it with lining paper before using ready-pasted paper.

Novamura

This is unusual in that the wall, not the paper, is covered with paste. The paper is then hung as normal and smoothed with a sponge.

Ready-pasted

1. *A trough filled with water replaces a pasting table and paste brush when hanging ready-pasteds.*
2. *After immersing in the water the paper is gradually raised from the trough leaving the tail in it.*
3. *A sponge is used to smooth the paper on to the wall, working from middle to the edges. It's a good idea to have a small amount of ordinary wallpaper paste on hand to enliven any 'dried' edges of ready pasted material.*

Novamura

1. *Novamura is a simple wallcovering to hang. The special paste is brushed on to the wall over the area to be covered by one length of the material.*
2. *Then, working straight from the roll, the wallcovering is smoothed out carefully, with the aid of a sponge.*
3. *At picture rails, skirtings and so on the material is trimmed to fit in the same way as standard wallpaper.*

1

2

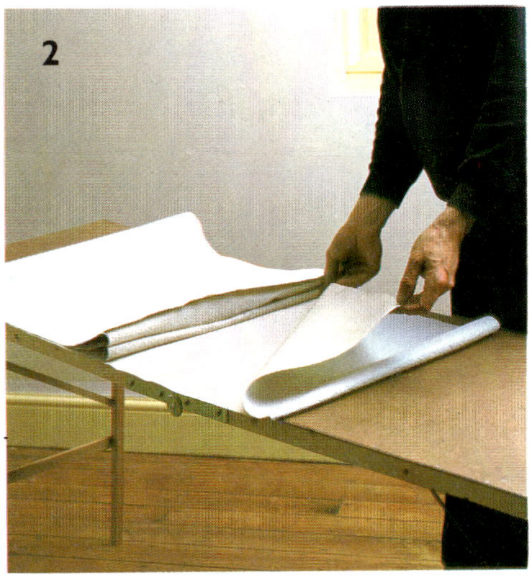

3

4

5

6

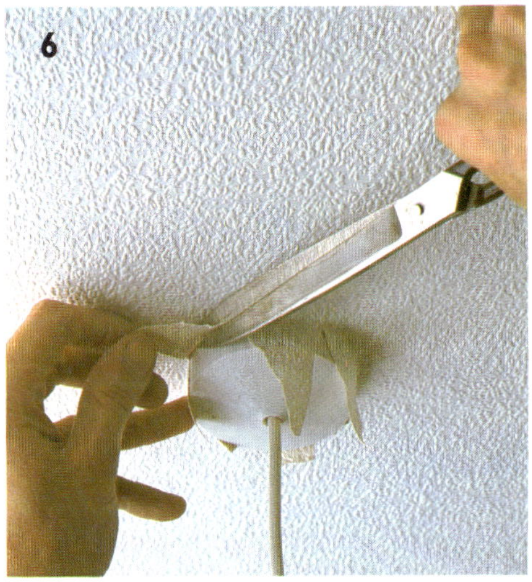

Ceilings

Preparing a ceiling for papering is precisely the same as preparing a wall. Hanging the paper is basically the same as for wallpaper except that there is the law of gravity to overcome! The first time you try papering a ceiling it may be a good idea to have some help handy.

In general, the starting point for papering is parallel with the main window. Successive lengths are then hung, working away from the light so that should any edge be slightly overlapped a shadow will not be cast.

However, if by working at right angles to the window much shorter lengths of paper will be needed then this can be done. The dimensions of the ceiling might also govern which way the paper is hung – bearing economy in mind. A roll of paper is about 10m long, so in a room 4m wide only two lengths would be obtained from a roll with 2m of paper wasted. In a case like this it could be far more economical to paper in the other direction.

Assuming a start is to be made by the window, mark a line across the ceiling which allows for 50mm of paper to be turned on to the window wall for final trimming. If the walls are to be papered then allow for 5mm to be turned on to the window wall. Each length should be cut to allow for 50mm excess at each end – again for final trimming.

Arrange a strong working platform across the room which enables the ceiling to be reached comfortably. Use scaffold boards supported on trestles, strong boxes or step-ladders.

Paste the paper and fold it concertina fashion – paste side to paste side. Make each fold about ½m long. Unfold the first portion of paper and align it with the pencil mark on the ceiling. Use a spare roll to support the paper while the first fold is being brushed on to the ceiling, working from the middle outwards. Subsequent folds are then released and brushed out in turn, making sure the guide line is followed.

At the ceiling-to-wall angle trim the paper as in wallpapering. Leave a 5mm margin on the walls only if wallpaper is to be used. Hang subsequent lengths similarly, closely butting up the edges.

To paper around a ceiling rose, paper up to the fitting, make a hole in the paper and then make a series of short diagonal cuts outwards from the centre of the rose. Hang the rest of the length then return to the rose. Turn off the electricity at the mains and remove the casing of the rose. Then finally trim the paper so that a small margin is left that will be hidden beneath the casing. Smooth down the paper and replace the fitting.

Papering ceilings

1. *Snapping a chalked string line on the ceiling as a guide to the first length.*
2. *Pasting and folding the paper in concertina fashion – each fold should be about ½m long.*
3. *Use a spare roll to support the paper while it is being unfolded and brushed into place on the ceiling following the marked guide line.*
4. *When the wall is reached the paper is creased into the wall-to-ceiling angle and then trimmed carefully with the shears.*
5. *When the ceiling rose is reached, make a hole in the paper and pull the rose through. Continue to hang the paper.*
6. *Return to the rose, make star-shaped cuts, then gradually trim it neatly around the rose plate.*

Papering tips

1. *If a bubble is noticed soon after a length of paper has been hung, then the edge of the paper should be pulled away from the wall to release the trapped air, then brushed back into place. If the bubble is not noticed until later then cut a cross through the bubble with a sharp knife, peel back the flaps and brush on some paste.*
2. *Use a brush or a small roller to smooth the flaps back into place. If done carefully the cuts will not be noticeable.*

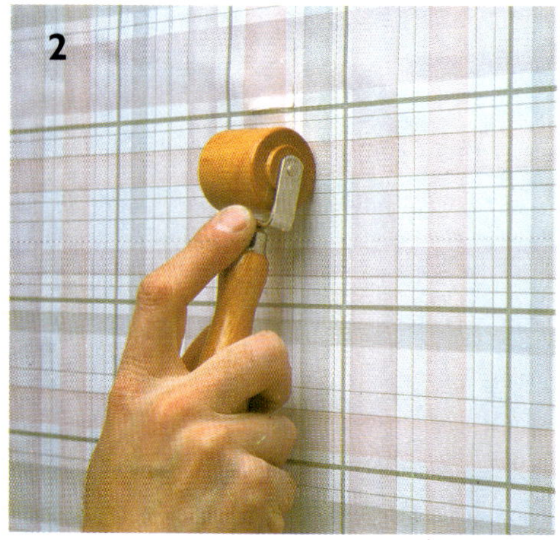

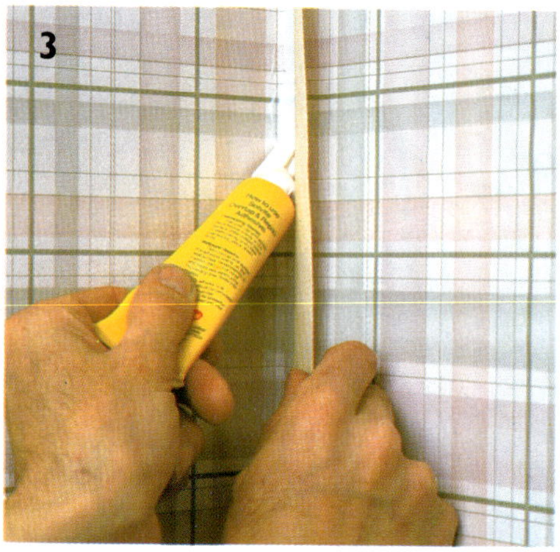

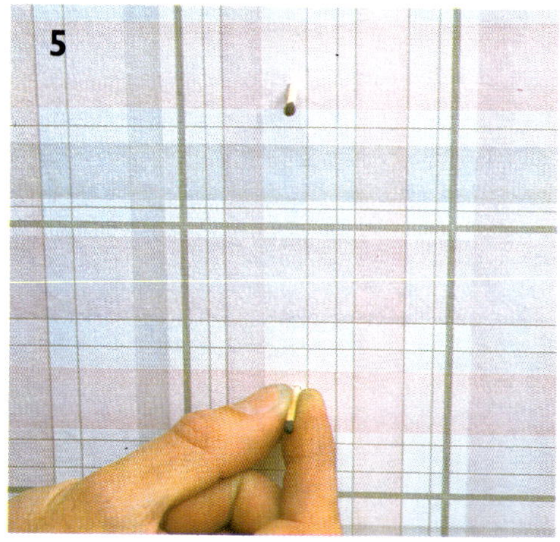

Wallpapering and problems

Blisters in paper are usually caused by not brushing out correctly and leaving trapped air underneath. Check each length as it is hung by looking at it side-on. If a bubble is spotted early, the edge of the paper can be peeled back past the bubble and the paper brushed back into place. Should the bubble be spotted too late, then use a sharp knife to cut a cross through the centre of the bubble. Brush some paste on to the back of the paper then smooth it back into place. If done carefully the cuts will not be noticeable.

Failure to stick over large areas can be caused by not sizing a porous wall or by using a paste which is too thin. Always mix up paste according to the instructions and don't continue to use paste for more than a couple of days after mixing it. Before mixing another batch of paste, clean out the bucket. Lining the bucket with a pedal bin liner which can be thrown away saves having to clean out the bucket.

A common problem is failure of the pattern to match all the way down with the previous length. This is caused by the paper stretching irregularly. One cause of this is not allowing each length to soak for approximately the same amount of time.

Stretching is also caused by allowing the paper to drop down suddenly after brushing the top on to the wall. This is a particular problem when hanging long lengths on stairwell walls. Always support the lower half of the paper then lower it gently for brushing on to the wall.

If confronted with a pattern-matching problem then aim to match the pattern at eye level where it will be most noticed.

Finding somewhere to rest a messy paste brush is solved by tying a piece of string tautly across the bucket. Rest the brush bristles on the string.

The free end of a roll of paper is not always the top of the pattern. Unroll a metre or so to check which way up it should go. With some patterns it is easy to hang a length upside down so, before pasting, get into the habit of writing *Top* on the back edge of the paper – and check this before hanging.

After taking a fixture off the wall, put a matchstick in each screw hole, leaving about 5mm protruding. Press the wallpaper over the matchsticks so that they pop through to indicate the exact positions of the screw holes when putting back the fixture.

If wallpaper shears become clogged with paste, clean, straight lines are difficult to cut. Wipe the shears regularly and if the paste has hardened stand the shears in hot water for a couple of minutes and then clean. Taking care of your shears will keep them sharp and efficient.

3. *Unlike ordinary wallpaper, vinyl wallcoverings will not stick down on overlaps made in corners and so on. A special latex adhesive is needed.*
4. *To avoid the possibility of hanging a length upside down, which is possible with some patterns, write TOP on the relevant edge before pasting a length.*
5. *A simple method of locating screw holes in the wall when refixing wall lights and other fixtures. Push matchsticks in the screw holes and, when papering, brush the paper over them so that they pop through to show positions of screw holes when refitting the fixture.*

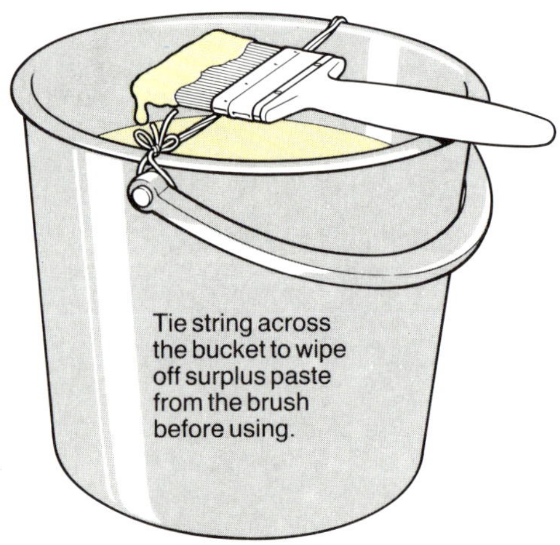

Plastering

Plaster provides an inexpensive surface covering for interior walls, but is easily damaged, especially on corners and angles, and cracks easily if there is any movement in the house structure. It is also affected by damp, which can cause the plaster to crumble away from the masonry behind.

Patching cracks

Small cracks in plaster can be filled with patching plaster or a proprietary filler, mixed up to a firm consistency. First, use the edge of your filling knife to rake out any loose material from the crack, and if possible undercut the edges of the crack so that the filler can key in better. Brush out any dust from the crack with an old paintbrush, and then dampen it with water so that the existing plaster does not suck all the moisture out of the filler and cause cracks.

Press the filler into the crack, working at right angles to the crack direction; then draw your filling knife blade along the crack to remove excess filler and leave to harden. Ideally, the filler should be left slightly proud of the surrounding surface, so that it can be sanded off to a flush finish when it has set.

Repairing corners

Chipped corners are less easy to repair. For small chips, use a fairly stiff filler mix and match the shape of the corner, smoothing it off with glasspaper once it has hardened. Where the damage is more extensive, you will get better results by cutting away the plaster about 50mm (2in) from the corner and then replastering it in one operation. One way of doing this is to pin a batten to one face of the corner so that its edge is level with the surface of the plaster on the other face. The gap between the batten edge and the existing plaster is then filled with new plaster, applied to the dampened brickwork and finished off flush with the existing plaster by running a batten up over the surface. Score the surface of the new plaster lightly, ready for the finishing skim coat to be applied. Repeat the process on the other face of the corner, holding the batten in place against the already plastered face to prevent damage to the corner.

Once the first coat has dried, the surface is moistened again and a thin skim coat of plaster is applied over both surfaces. This

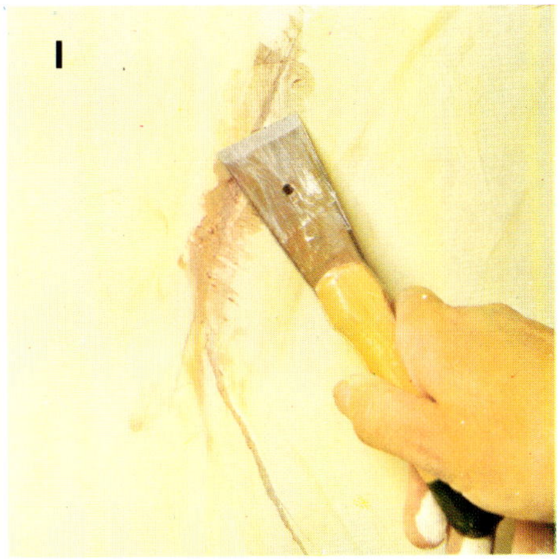

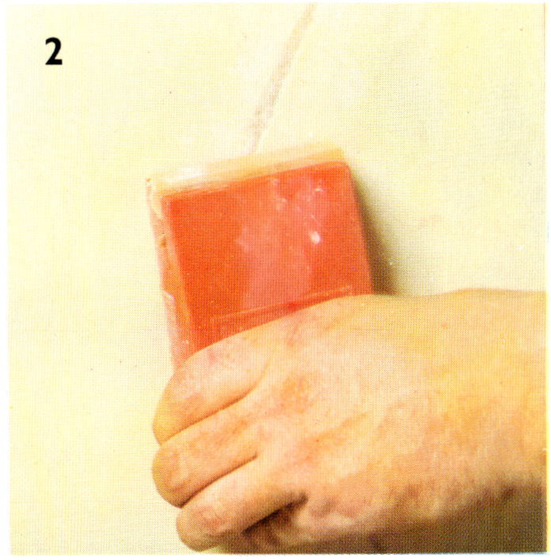

Filling cracks

1. Apply fillers with a broad filling knife, finishing some proud and others flush.
2. When the filler is dry, carefully rub it down level with the wall using fine grade glasspaper.
3. Pin a batten to a damaged corner to provide a square working edge and remove it when the repair is completed.

Tools and materials needed for plastering. From top to bottom and left to right: Plastic bucket for mixing plaster, metal hawk for holding plaster mix, two-knot damping brush for wetting existing plaster, wood float for applying undercoats, gauging trowel for measuring small quantities of materials, angled trowel for finishing corners, steel float for applying finishing coat, scrim tape, plaster.

coat is polished with a dampened steel float. You can then smooth over the sharp corner angle with a moistened finger.

If the corner being repaired is particularly prone to damage, it can be reinforced with expanded metal angle beading which is pinned to the masonry, or held in place with dabs of plaster, and then plastered over. In this case you will not need corner battens, since the nosing of the angle beading forms an edge for you to plaster to.

Repairing lath-and-plaster ceilings

Lath-and-plaster ceilings fail because the plaster that was forced up between the laths no longer provides a strong enough key to support the plaster's weight. You can repair small sagging areas by wedging them back up against the laths and pouring quick-setting plaster over the laths from above – by lifting floorboards above ground-floor ceilings, or from the loft for first-floor ones. Larger areas will have to be pulled down and replaced with plasterboard.

Damage to lath-and-plaster ceilings – from a misplaced foot in the loft, for example – can be repaired by bridging the hole with expanded metal mesh which is then covered with a layer of plaster.

Patching plasterboard

Small holes in plasterboard can be patched with scrim (coarse cloth) and plaster. Begin by cutting away the surface of the board for about 25mm (1in) round the hole, to a depth of 3mm (⅛in) or so. Cut a piece of scrim big enough to cover this area, put blobs of plaster around the perimeter of the hole and stretch the scrim over it, bedding it in the plaster blobs. When these have set, skim over the repair with two or three coats of plaster to bring its surface level with that of the surrounding plaster. Polish with a dampened steel float when almost set. A self-adhesive wall repair tape is also available. The glass mesh is stuck smoothly over the prepared area and plastered as previously described.

Larger holes must be repaired with a patch of plasterboard. Cut away the damaged board until you reach the centres of the joists or uprights at each side of it, and complete a rectangular opening in the board. Wedge and nail lengths of timber between the joists or uprights to form a rectangular frame, so that these pieces will support the other two edges of the patch. Cut a piece of plasterboard to fit the hole, and pin it in place in the opening. Use plaster or filler to fill the gaps between the patch and the surrounding plaster, and bed fine scrim or paper tape in the wet plaster around the edges of the patch, applying more plaster over it and feathering out the edges for a neat finish. Finally, sponge a thin slurry of plaster all over the repair, ready for redecorating.

Replastering

To replaster a large damaged area, cut back to a sound edge and dampen the brickwork. Then float on the first coat of plaster proud of the surrounding surface, and draw a long batten up over the patch to remove the excess, resting it on the surrounding plaster at either side. Score the surface and leave to dry, ready for the final skim coat.

Where the area to be patched is too large to be bridged by a levelling batten, place patches of plaster, as thick as the final plaster should be, at intervals across the area, and use these as reference levels for the batten technique. Again score the first coat, and dampen it before applying the final skim coat.

1

2

3

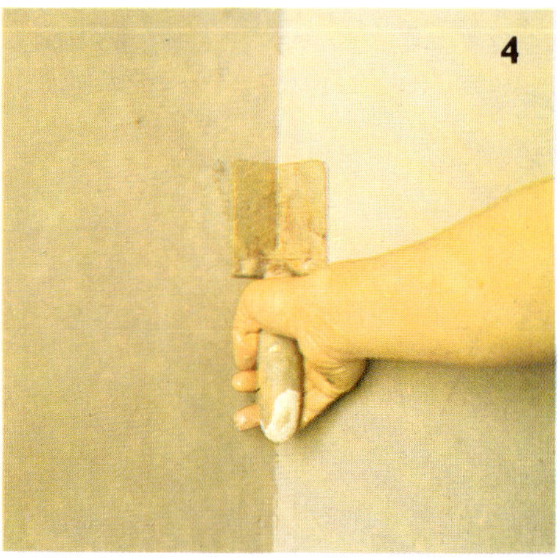

4

1. *Fix a timber rule to the wall above a reveal and work flush to its surface.*

2. *Scratch a coat of wall rendering to provide a key for the finish. This is known as devilling.*

3. *Plaster to a batten fixed slightly proud of the surface at a corner. Wait until the plaster has set before turning the batten round to repair the other side of the corner. When both patches are dry, sand the corner to a smooth finish.*

4. *Use an angled trowel to provide a smooth finish at internal corners.*

1

2

3

4

5

6

Ceramic tiles

Careful planning is the secret of successful tiling. Whether a room is being half tiled or fully tiled to the ceiling, the aim is to leave a neat, balanced effect. Plan to have a full size tile at the top of the wall or in the top course of a half-tiled wall. Narrow pieces of cut tiles are untidy and should also be avoided where they will be readily noticed – in corners, above washbasins, around windows and so on. A balanced wall will have equal-size cut tiles at both ends.

To avoid pitfalls in advance and to establish exactly where the tiles are going to fall, use a measuring staff. Make this with a long piece of wood marked out in tile increments according to the size of tiles being used. With the help of the measuring staff, the best start point can be found.

Corners, floors, skirtings and work-surfaces are rarely true, so never use these or similar features as a base for tiling. The only way to ensure that the tiles are hung vertically and horizontally is to fix battens to the wall and work from these.

Materials Tile adhesive is supplied in ready-mixed or powder form. For large jobs the ready-mixed type is best. If the tiles are likely to be splashed by excessive water (such as in a shower area) then a water resistant adhesive is needed.

Grout is supplied in powder form for mixing with water. It is used to fill the joints between the tiles.

Tools In addition to basic measuring and marking equipment, the following are needed. For spreading the adhesive on to the wall and drawing it out to leave a series of ridges, a spatula or small trowel plus a plastic comb are needed. The special plastic comb can be obtained with the adhesive.

Various gadgets are made for cutting tiles. One of these will be needed to trim tiles to fit in corners and so on.

For cutting out L-shaped tiles and other shapes, a special pair of tile nippers can be used; a suitable alternative is an ordinary pair of pincers.

Surface preparation

A sound, level and dry surface is essential. Old tiles, provided that they are flat and firmly fixed, can remain. The odd loose one can be refixed with tile adhesive. A plastered wall might look flat but check it first with a long, wooden straight-edge. Place the wood in all directions on the surface to see if any noticeable see-saw action is detectable. Small undulations can be filled with cellulose filler or else a special thick-bed adhesive can be used to overcome the unevenness when tiles are being hung. In bad cases there is no alternative but to completely replaster the wall or to line it with plasterboard to provide a suitable surface.

Remove any wallpaper or loose paint from the wall. Sound gloss paint should be rubbed down to leave a surface to which the adhesive will bond.

Tiling

1. *A measuring staff is essential for establishing the best arrangement for the tiles in the room. Hold the staff on the wall vertically and horizontally in various places and you will be able to see at a glance where the best starting point is to avoid leaving narrow pieces of tile around windows, above washbasins and so on. To make a staff just mark off a long piece of wood in tile increments, allowing about 2mm for each joint.*

2. *Using the measuring staff to ascertain in advance likely problems.*

3. *A horizontal batten is fixed to the wall to support the bottom row of tiles. This is removed when the wall has been tiled, the space remaining is then tiled.*

4. *After spreading adhesive over an area of about 1 sq. metre tiling can begin. The first tile is placed in the angle formed by the horizontal batten and vertical guide line (or batten if used). Tiling then continues in horizontal rows.*

5. *Scoring a tile with a tile cutter after marking out the exact cutting line carefully.*

6. *With this type of cutter the glaze is scored, the tile is placed in its jaws and, by simply squeezing the handles, the tile will break cleanly.*

Finishing off

1. *To fill an awkward space first make a cardboard pattern.*
2. *Transfer the outline of the pattern to the tile.*
3. *Score deeply through the marked guide line on the tile using the tile cutter. Then, using tile clippers or pincers, carefully nibble away the waste portion of the tile. Clean up the cut edge with a tile file and fit the tile into the space on the wall.*
4. *To prevent hold-ups when tiling, fix a horizontal batten to the wall above obstacles such as a sink and continue to tile with whole tiles. Remove the batten the following day and fill in the gap with cut tiles.*
5. *When tiling over a previously half-tiled wall, the top can be finished neatly by fixing quadrant shaped ceramic trim.*
6. *The final job is to work grout cement into the joints between the tiles using a slightly damp sponge or a rubber squeegee blade. Work the grout well into the gaps.*

Laying

Fix a horizontal batten to the wall at a point which will eventually leave a full tile in the top course. A vertical batten is needed also near a corner as a guide to the first vertical row of tiles.

Using a spatula or trowel, spread adhesive over about 1 sq. m of wall, then comb through it to leave ridges. Place the first tile snugly into the angle formed by the two battens. Subsequent tiles are laid in horizontal courses until the area covered with adhesive is completed.

Position each tile with a slight twisting movement, butting its edges tightly to the neighbouring tiles. Many tiles have little nibs (called spacer lugs) on the edges to ensure uniform joint lines are left between tiles. If there are no spacer lugs then use pieces of card or special spacers to keep the joints uniform.

Although the two guide battens should ensure that the tiles are going up horizontally and vertically, it is wise to check each completed sq. m of tiles with a spirit level and make any necessary adjustments quickly.

A wipe over with a dryish sponge will remove any adhesive from the surface of the tiles before it dries. This can be done later when the adhesive has dried but it means a lot of dust and elbow work.

Hang as many full-size tiles as possible before cutting tiles to fit odd spaces. The two battens fixed to the wall can be removed after 24 hours and the spaces left filled with cut tiles.

To cut a tile, first score through the glazed surface with a tile cutter. There are various types of cutter, one of the most useful being that which works in a pincer-like action. With other cutters, having

scored the tile it is then placed on two matchsticks (placed in line with the score mark) and pressed down on either side to snap it cleanly.

Awkwardly shaped tiles are cut by making a template of the required shape and transferring this to the tile. Score deeply into the glaze along the guide line then nibble away the waste with pincers.

When an obstacle such as a washbasin is reached, a horizontal batten can be fixed to the wall to allow tiling to continue with full tiles. Later on the batten can be removed and the spaces filled in with cut tiles.

A space for an accessory such as a soap tray can be filled temporarily by a tile or two tiles, as needed. Fix these tiles with a small blob of adhesive. When the wall has been completed for 24 hours, remove the temporary tiles, spread adhesive on the back of the accessory and fix it in place. Secure it with adhesive tape until the adhesive has set.

Where tiles are hung over a previously half-tiled wall the top edge can be finished neatly either with a smooth layer of filler or wood beading. An even neater method is to cut slivers of tile and bed them down in adhesive.

After all the tiles have been in place for 24 hours, use a slightly damp sponge to work grout mix into the joints. Remove surplus grout with a damp cloth.

Brick tiles

As an alternative to traditional materials, there is a wide range of products available for decorating complete walls or feature areas in a room.

Brick tiles are made in a lightweight material and have the look and feel of genuine bricks. Usually they are fireproof and so can be used also around fireplaces. Various colours are available and the bricks are fixed to the wall using a special adhesive which shows between the tiles to act as mortar joints.

An authentic brick tile is also available. This can be fixed to an emulsion-painted wall allowing the paint colour to show through and serve as recessed mortar joints. Alternatively, a special pointing compound can be used to fill in the joints; several colours can be obtained. Special corner pieces are used so that a chimney breast, for example, can be tiled yet still retain the appearance of a genuine wall.

Brick panels made from expanded polystyrene measure about 600 × 300mm and are fixed with adhesive. Each panel comes complete with pointed mortar joints and can be cut with a sharp knife. Corner bricks are available.

Whichever type of 'brick' is used it is essential to spend time in planning for the appearance of a genuine wall. An authentic look will be lost if, for example, thin slivers of a brick appear at corners. It is best to mark on to the wall the required brickwork bonding pattern before work begins.

Other types

Stone wall tiles are similar to brick tiles. They have a texture which simulates hand-picked quarry stones. For authenticity, sizes, shapes and colour shades are random. The tiles are fixed with a special mastic adhesive which also serves as the pointing between tiles.

For best results it is worthwhile laying out the tiles on the floor to establish the best arrangement before tiling the wall.

The appearance of genuine, ceramic tiles can be achieved using panels of plastic or enamelled fibreboard. Each panel comprises a number of tiles and is fixed to the wall with a panel adhesive.

The plastic type is bendable and so will cope with uneven walls – it can even be turned around a corner. Where cutting is needed, this is done with scissors. Plastic panels are not suitable for areas subject to excessive heat.

Enamelled fibreboard panels are fixed direct to even walls or, where an undulating surface is encountered, to wall battens. Cutting panels is done with a saw.

Mirrors

Strategically placed mirrors or mirror tiles can be used to create an illusion of space in a room, to make a room brighter by reflecting window light, or just as an eye-catching feature – perhaps in an alcove or behind display shelving.

Smaller mirrors can be fixed with mirror screws, clips or corner plates. A large mirror needs additional support provided by screwing to the wall a batten on which it can rest. Any wall which is reasonably flat makes a good surface for a mirror; if the wall is badly undulating then it will be necessary to first fix a base board of plywood or chipboard to provide a smooth surface. However it is fixed, a mirror should first be held in place and its positioning checked with a spirit level. It must be truly vertical.

Dome-head mirror screws are best for screw fixing. If the holes are not already drilled then these can be made with an electric drill and a special spear-point bit. The holes should be drilled at least 25mm away from the edge.

To drill a hole, lay the mirror on a flat

A selection of the many different types of material available for introducing unusual effects on walls.

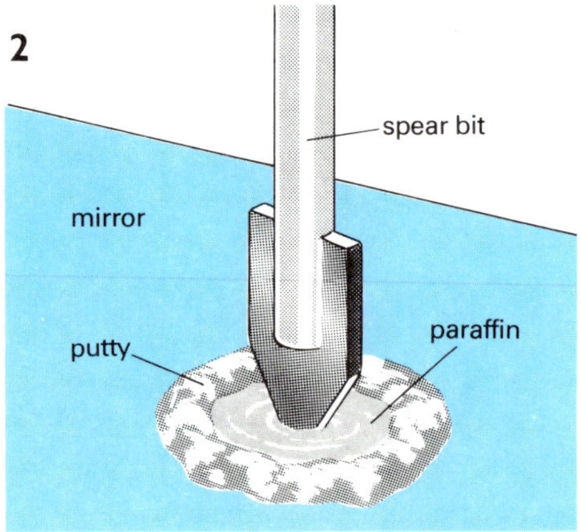

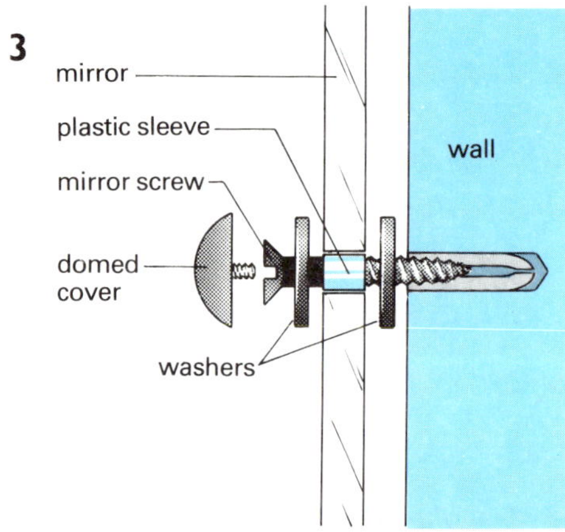

1. *Mirror clips provide a firm yet neat method for fixing a mirror.*
2. *For fixing with screws, holes first have to be drilled with a special spear-point bit.*
3. *Dome-head mirror screws come complete with spacer washers – one being used on each side of the mirror.*
4. *Peel protective paper from the fixing tabs on the back of a mirror tile and press it firmly into place on the wall, applying pressure only over the tabs.*

surface, stick a small ring of Plasticine around the drilling position and pour into it a few drops of water. Drill the holes first from the back of the mirror then, as the point of the bit breaks through on the mirror side, turn the mirror over and complete the hole from the front.

Mirror screws are often provided with spacer washers which fit between the mirror and the wall, plastic sleeves which fit in the hole in the mirror, and extra washers which go between the screw heads and the mirror surface. Never over-tighten the screws or the mirror might crack. The screw head is concealed beneath a screw-on dome cover.

When using mirror clips, two fixed clips are screwed to the wall to support the mirror. Two more sliding clips are added at the top (and possibly one on either side) to retain the mirror. The screws for these are tightened sufficiently to allow the clips to slide in and out. The mirror is positioned on the fixed clips and then the sliding clips are pushed into position.

Mirror tiles are available in many types and styles – colours, patterns and even murals comprising about six tiles. If the tiles are to be used in a kitchen or bathroom then first check their suitability for steamy conditions. The wall must be clean and dry, and free from loose material. Tiles must not be fixed over vinyl wallpaper because they will soon come adrift.

On the back of each tile there are four adhesive tabs; remove the paper covering from each and press the tile to the wall. The tabs might be provided in a separate packet.

If a wall is slightly undulating then some distortion in the reflection will result. This can be overcome by using an additional tab over the existing one. In extreme cases, the wall must be lined first with chipboard or plywood.

Mirror tiles can be bought in different sizes and can be used in many ways to produce interesting and imaginative results. They can be put in virtually any room in your house or apartment.

In the bathroom they can cover a wall, although they will of course suffer from condensation when the bath is in full use. Mirror tiles can also be used to reflect other decorations by, for instance, running a line of tiles behind a selection of indoor plants, or by fixing them within the recess of an old, disused fireplace.

Carpets

Laying carpets is a job within the capability of many do-it-yourselfers equipped with the right tools and a certain amount of patience. The most difficult part is tensioning the carpet correctly across the room, and for this reason it is probably best to lay your first carpet in a small room free of too many awkward corners. Unless you are skilled at the job, leave carpeting through rooms with expensive carpet to the professionals.

Preparation

Begin by clearing the room completely of furniture, and inspect the floor thoroughly, punching down raised nail heads and fixing loose boards. Then lay stout brown paper over the floor, and, for a traditional carpet, fix gripper strips all round the perimeter of the room about 12mm (½in) in from the skirting board with the spikes facing the skirting. Use masonry nails for the job on concrete floors. Next, cut your underlay to reach from gripper strip to gripper strip, and tape the joins neatly.

Ready to lay

Unroll the carpet across the room, and position it so that it reaches from wall to wall. You will probably be faced with alcoves, bays and other awkward obstacles, and it may be necessary to join offcuts of carpet to the main piece to reach into these.

Begin by fixing the carpet to the gripper strips along the longest uninterrupted wall. Hook the carpet over the strip, pressing it down firmly so that the spikes grip the carpet backing and the edge of the carpet tucks down neatly into the gap between the strips and the skirting board.

Now pull the carpet across the room to the opposite wall. Make any cuts that are necessary to fit around obstacles, and hook the carpet over the strips at that side, using the knee kicker to stretch the carpet taut across the room. Repeat the trimming and fitting process along the other two walls.

Foam-backed carpets can be laid with special gripper strips with modified spikes, or can be stuck down at the edges of the floor with double-sided tape.

At doorways, the carpet should be finished off with a special threshold strip, nailed to the floor.

If you have to join pieces of carpet, use special self-adhesive seaming tape, or hessian tape and latex adhesive. Cut the meeting edges absolutely parallel, lay one edge on the tape and press the other down alongside it, hammering the join to ensure good adhesion.

With cheap carpets, particularly those with long pile, you can avoid using gripper strips by simply tacking the carpet to the floorboards at about 150mm (6in) intervals round the edge.

Laying stair carpet

Stair carpet should always be put down over an underlay, although this can be fitted in the form of pads tacked to each tread with one edge overhanging the nosing by about 50mm (2in). The carpet itself can be tacked in place down the staircase, but a neater result will be achieved by using special staircase grippers which are pinned into the angles between treads and risers.

Lay the carpet with the pile facing down the stairs. Start laying at the foot of the flight, tacking the carpet to the face of the first riser. Take it over the first tread, and press the fold of carpet into the first gripper strip. Continue working up the staircase, keeping the carpet as taut as possible until you reach the last riser before the landing. Here, the carpet should be tacked under the last nosing, so that the landing carpet just overlaps it.

Where the flight contains angled treads (called winders), a series of folds are needed to take up the slack as the carpet turns the angles. You may find it easier to cut the carpet just below the nosing and tack it in place, since the bulky folds can be difficult to accommodate neatly.

Other floorcoverings

Vinyl floorcoverings in sheet and tile form are perfect for use in kitchens, bathrooms, utility rooms and WCs where a durable, smooth and easy-to-clean floor surface is required. Sheet floorcoverings are now made in widths of up to 4m (13ft) – wide enough to cover all but the widest rooms in a single piece. Tiles are usually 300mm (about 12in) square, although other sizes, and occasionally interlocking shapes, are also available.

Laying floor tiles

Like other floorcoverings, floor tiles will give their best only if the floor is smooth.

Minor cracks in timber and chipboard floors can be filled with an all-purpose filler, and at the same time the floor should be checked for protruding nails which should be hammered into the surface or extracted.

If there are many cracks, or the boards are uneven, the floor should be resurfaced by nailing down sheets of hardboard over it.

Solid floors should also be checked over. Again, minor cracks can be smoothed with filler, but if the floor is uneven it should be resurfaced using a self-smoothing screed. This is a watery cement mortar-like ma-

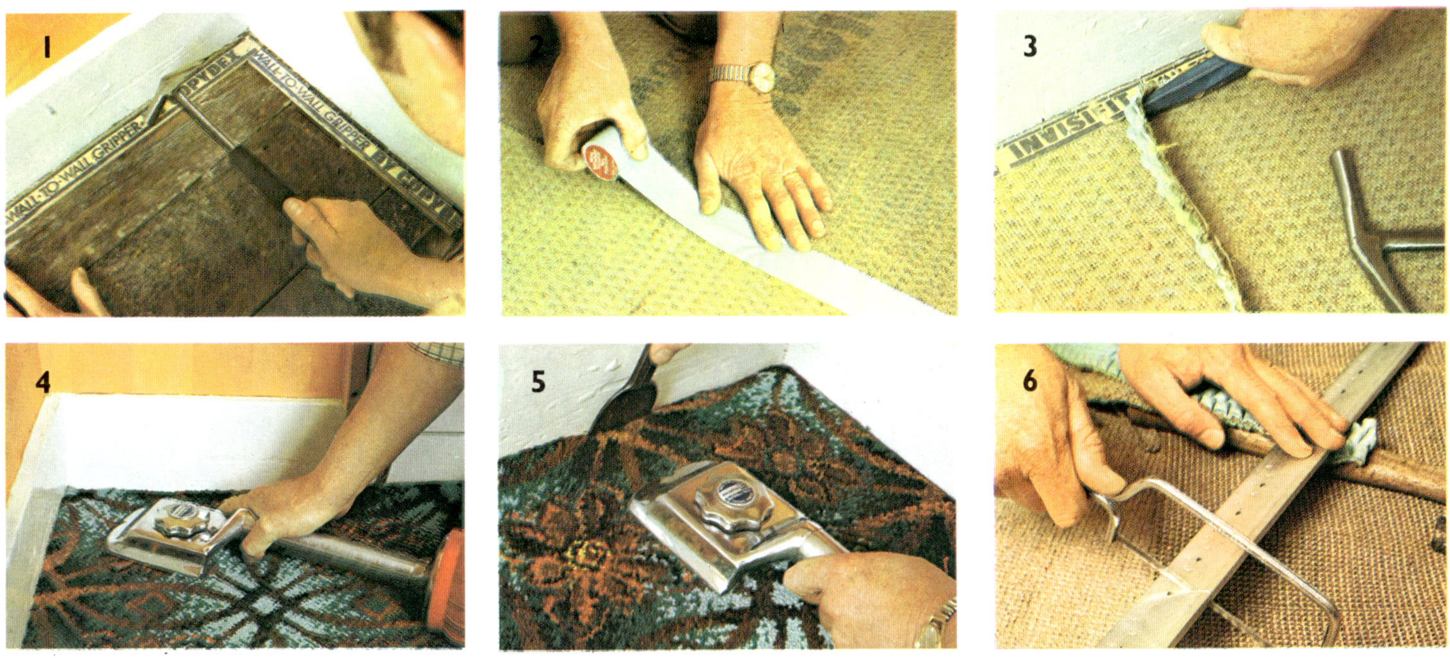

Carpeting

1. *Fit a traditional carpet by fixing gripper strips round the room 12mm from the walls, except at doorways where a special threshold strip is used.*
2. *Make butt seams in rubber underlay and join them with single-sided adhesive tape.*
3. *Butt underlay against gripper strips and trim with sharp knife.*
4. *Stretch carpet on to gripper pins with knee kicker. Put the knee kicker on the carpet and adjust it so that the pins grip the backing but do not damage the pile. Kick the pad with your knee while smoothing the carpet with your free hand.*
5. *Cut carpet about 6mm oversize. Tuck surplus between gripper and skirting using bolster chisel or a paint scraper.*
6. *Protect carpet in doorways with threshold strip cut to length. These are of various sections for use with different adjoining floorcoverings.*

Note *If you are laying foam-backed carpet, do not attempt to stretch it. Lay it on the floor, align two edges with two of the walls, and cut the remaining two edges to fit the other walls. Attach it to the floor with tacks or double-sided tape. Cut the carpet with a sharp trimming knife.*

terial which is poured on to the floor, roughly spread out, and then left to smooth over and harden. At the same time as these repairs are being carried out, the floor should be checked for dampness and steps taken to eradicate this problem.

Ceramic tiles need a particularly stable sub-floor. A solid floor is ideal, but in the case of a timber floor the surface should be covered with sheets of 9.5mm thick plywood, or tongued and grooved flooring grade chipboard fixed down to the floor with countersunk screws at 300mm intervals. In this case, a floor bonding agent should be brushed over the surface before the tile adhesive is spread.

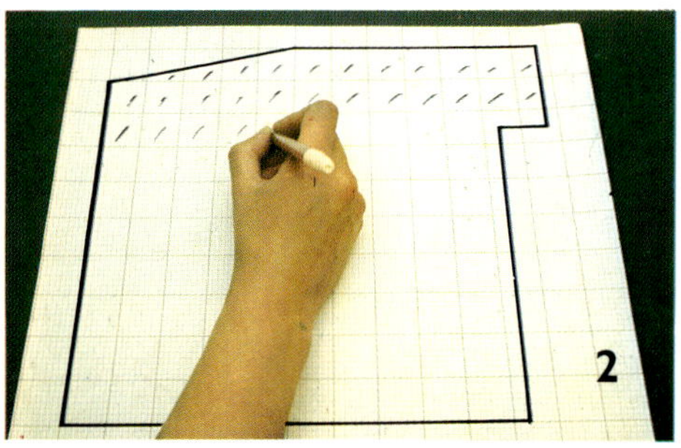

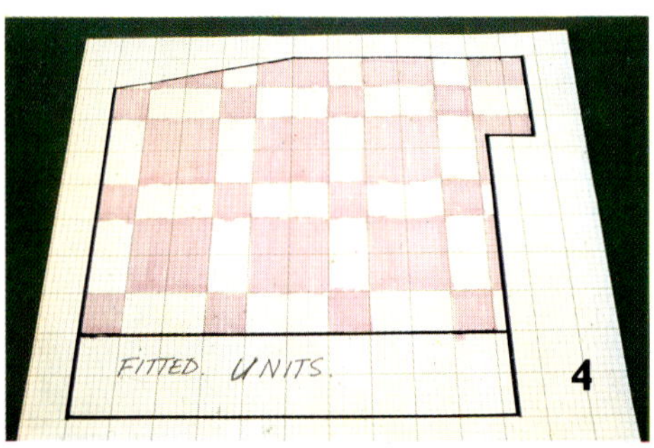

1–3. *Draw scale plan of floor, one square per tile, to find quantity.*
4. *Shade in design for patterns.*

Laying floor tiles

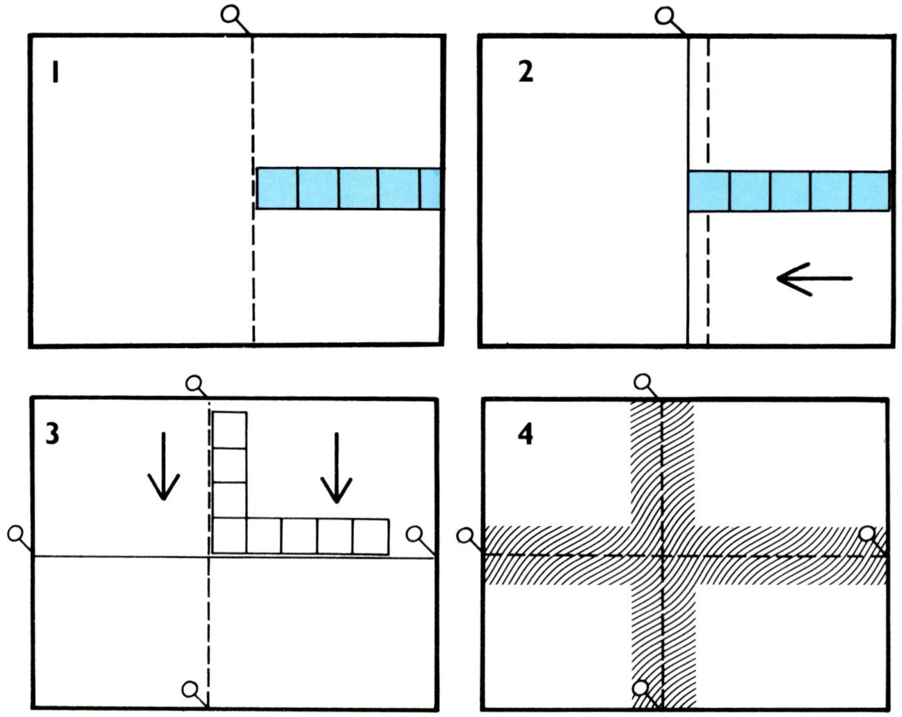

1. *Mark centre line and check that edge tiles are at least a half-tile wide.*
2. *If not move line a half-tile width to one side.*
3. *Mark centre line in other direction, check as before and move line if necessary.*
4. *Spread adhesive along the floor, on either side of the chalk marks.*
5. *Lay central tiles 1 and 2 first and then work outwards until centre is filled.*
6. *Lay border tiles last. Place tile to be cut (A) on adjacent last complete tile. Place a full tile against skirting and mark cutting line on (A). This will give you the correct tile size for the edge. Mark each tile separately for accurate cutting.*

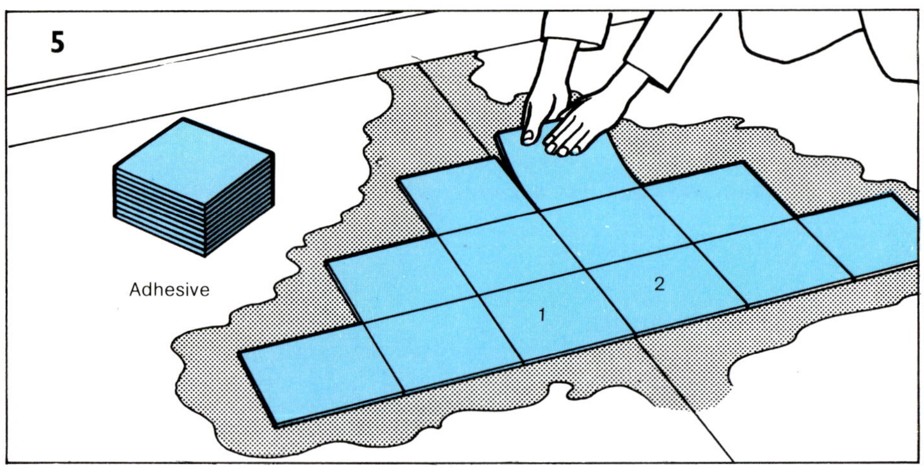

Marking out

All types of tiles are laid from the mid-point of the room to give border tiles of equal width around the perimeter. Use two chalked string lines to mark the centre point, then loose lay a row of tiles from the centre to check that the border tiles are at least half a tile wide. If they are not, move the string line half a tile width off centre and remark the line.

Then, again, loose lay the tiles to check to see that they fit properly and give the desired effect.

Laying tiles

Work from the centre point, spreading adhesive to cover about 1 sq. m at a time. Lay the main area of the whole tiles first, then cut and fit the border tiles.

Some vinyl tiles are self-adhesive. Simply peel off the backing and press them into place.

Carpet tiles are usually loose-laid, and in this case temporarily tack down the first few tiles in the centre of the room (stick them down if the floor is solid) to stop them moving when the other tiles are butted closely against them. When all the tiles are laid, pull out the tacks.

After four days, ceramic floor tiles must be grouted with floor grout.

Laying 2m and 4m wide sheet vinyl

Sheet vinyl is a soft material and it tends to show any unevenness in the floor surface, so the first step is to ensure that this is perfectly smooth and dry.

All types of vinyl should be allowed to relax before laying and this involves leaving it loosely rolled, pattern side inwards, for at least 24 hours in the room where it will be fitted. If the room is heated, this will make the vinyl more supple and easier to handle.

If laying the vinyl coincides with room redecoration it is possible to make the task of fitting a lot easier and neater if the skirtings are removed temporarily and replaced on top of the vinyl which then needs only to be roughly trimmed around the perimeter of the room. Modern skirtings are usually surprisingly easy to prise away from the wall and nail back again.

If the room is a complicated shape and 4m wide vinyl is chosen, which can be rather awkward to handle in a confined place, it is a good idea to make a template using paper-felt underlay or brown paper cut to the room shape. The template is placed on the vinyl which is cut roughly to shape, about 50mm oversize, and then lifted into position for final laying.

Whether or not a template is used, the next step is to get the vinyl into the room with the surface smooth and surplus material lapping against the walls. Make sure that the pattern lines up with the longest wall that will be seen as you enter the room.

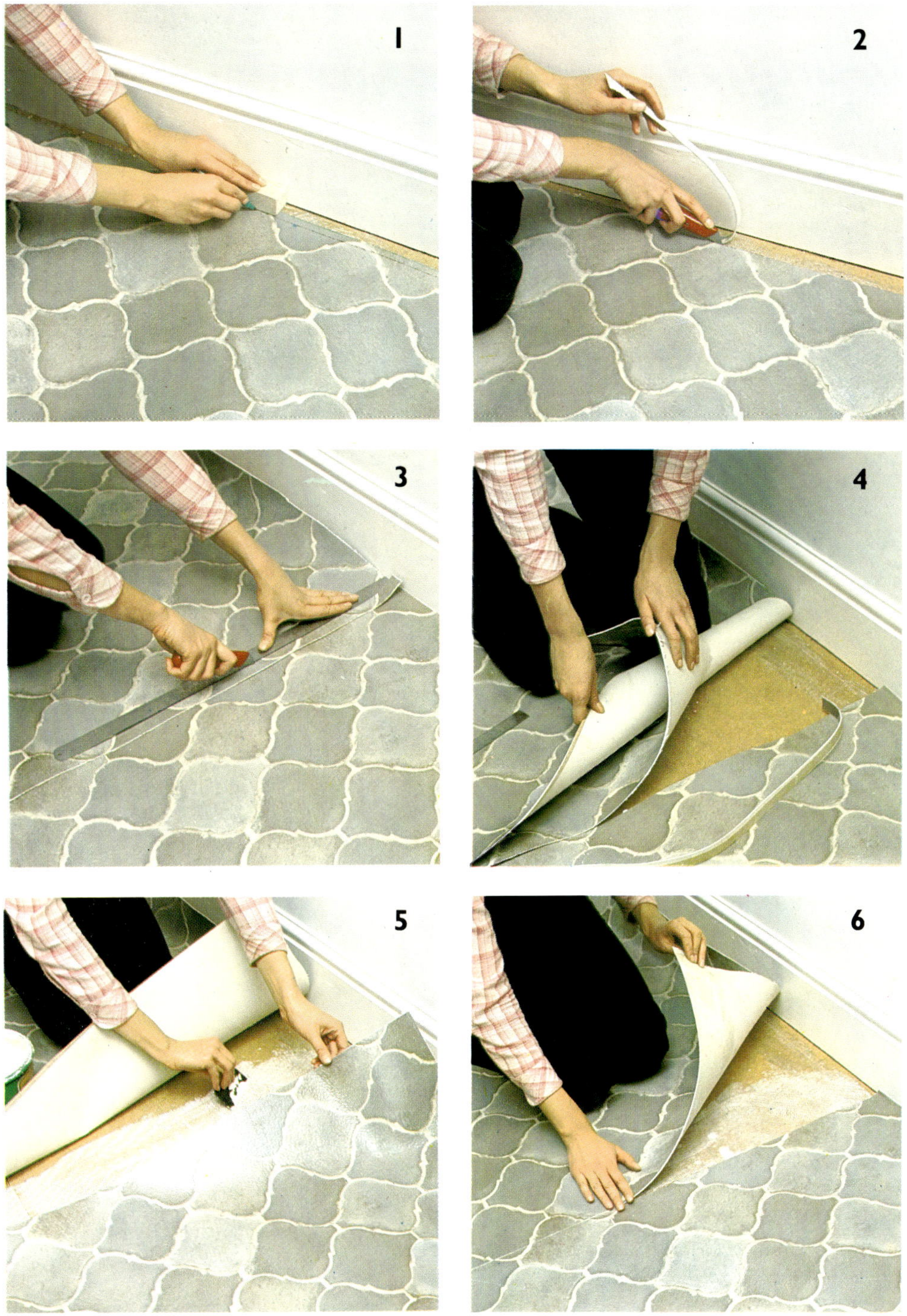

Laying sheet vinyl

1. *Trimming 2m wide vinyl sheet against a skirting. Modern lay-flat types are very flexible and are best trimmed as described in the text. Conventional types are not supple enough to allow marking on the back, so use the method shown. Take a small wood block and pull vinyl the width of this block away from the skirting. Hold block against the skirting and, with a ball pen against the block, mark a trimming line on the vinyl.*

2. *Use a sharp trimming knife to cut the vinyl to this line. Wherever possible guide the blade with a steel rule when making straight cuts. When the vinyl is pushed back against the skirting it will resume its original position and fit neatly to the wall.*

3. *The patterns of adjoining sheets should be carefully matched. Lay a steel rule on the overlap and cut through both sheets.*

4. *Pull back the vinyl and remove the offcuts. Check that the sheets butt together neatly.*

5. *Spread vinyl adhesive on the floor under the join.*

6. *Press the vinyl back into place.*

Remove doors to make fitting easier.

Fit internal corners by marking the approximate corner position on the back of the vinyl, then trim the corner little by little until the vinyl fits perfectly. At external corners and around door frames, make slanting release cuts from the edge of the vinyl to where it touches the floor.

Finally, trim all around against the skirting. The neatest method is to mark a cutting line as accurately as possible with a series of dots on the back of the vinyl, rule a line to link the dots, and then trim to the line with scissors.

With 2m wide vinyls, there will probably be a seam between adjacent sheets, and this can be trimmed by overlapping the sheets, and then, by using a steel rule as a guide, cutting through both sheets together using a sharp trimming knife. This method cannot be used with bold patterns.

Lay-flat vinyl needs only to be stuck down at doorways using double-sided adhesive tape. Conventional vinyls must be stuck down along all edges and seams using a 75mm wide band of vinyl flooring adhesive.

Wooden flooring

Real wood floorcoverings come in a variety of types. Wood mosaic panels – fingers of wood made up into squares – are one of the most attractive, and are easy to lay in a variety of patterns. Woodstrip floorcoverings are either small, solid planks, usually with tongue-and-groove edges, or panels consisting of hardwood veneer bonded to a plywood backing cut to provide lugs that make fixing the strips to the sub-floor easier. These are usually laid at right angles to existing floorboards on timber sub-floors.

Laying mosaic panels

These panels, which are either loose-laid if they are tongue-and-groove, or stuck down with adhesive, are best laid over hardboard on timber floors. In either case, a narrow expansion gap must be left all around the edge of the floor to prevent the panels buckling and lifting in damp weather. The first row of panels is laid to a string line positioned 12mm (½in) from the skirting board, and should be dry-laid to begin with so that you can adjust the position of the row to get cut pieces of equal length at each end. When you are ready to start laying panels, spread the adhesive and bed the panels down firmly, butting each panel firmly against its neighbours. If you are laying tongue-and-groove panels, tap them firmly together with a hammer and a wood block to close the join.

With all the whole panels laid, pieces can be cut to fit the gaps at the ends of the rows. Remember to allow for the expansion gap at the skirting board.

The next job is to cover the expansion gap by pinning lengths of quadrant beading to the skirting board. At doorways, fit a tapered threshold strip. Finish off by dusting the floor carefully and applying the floor sealer as directed by the panel manufacturer – usually two or three coats of varnish. This will not be necessary with factory-finished panels.

Laying woodstrip flooring

Once again, you must allow an expansion gap at the skirting board. Start laying strips to a string line next to the skirting board; on timber sub-floors pin tongue-and-groove

Woodblock flooring

Laying self-adhesive woodblock flooring:

1. *Remove protective membrane after laying self-adhesive hardboard underlay.*
2. *Lay out wood block in desired pattern.*
3. *Gently bond with mallet.*
4. *Square off herringbone edges by marking along edge strip, leaving gap for expansion along skirting.*
5. *Cut off protruding portions with sharp knife held against straight-edge.*
6. *Fit edge strip into place.*

types down through the tongue of each plank; on solid floors use the recommended adhesive. You will probably need several strips, butted end to end, to fill each row. Stagger the joints between strips in successive rows, and at the far side of the room saw or plane the last strip to fit the gap. Finish off as for mosaic panels by fitting quadrant beading around the skirting boards and a threshold strip in doorways, and seal the surface if you are laying unfinished strips.

Laying woodstrip panels

Provided that the sub-floor has been well prepared (level, firm, stable and dry) it is a simple job to lay a woodstrip panel floor.

The panels are laid on a special, ready-mixed adhesive and each panel is tongued and grooved at the edges so that the familiar basket weave pattern is formed automatically as the panels are locked tightly together.

Since the walls in a room are not usually square to each other it is best to start laying the panels in the middle of the room, working outwards to the skirtings where they can be trimmed to fit.

First, lay string lines from the midpoints of opposite walls. The starting point is where the strings cross. To establish how the panels will fall at the perimeter, lay a row of panels dry outwards to the skirtings. To avoid leaving thin pieces at the skirtings, alter the starting point by half a panel width one way.

Before work starts have a bowl of water and a sponge ready so that adhesive can be wiped off the panels and hands immediately, otherwise things can become messy. Some white spirit and a cloth are needed to remove adhesive which has nearly dried on the panels.

Spread sufficient adhesive over an area to be occupied by four panels. Align a groove of the first panel with the string line and press it on to the adhesive. Further panels are added by sliding them into place so that the tongues and grooves engage tightly. Lay the panels immediately while the adhesive is tacky.

Continue to lay panels out to the skirtings. At the perimeter of the room it is important to leave a 10mm gap to allow for any future movement of the wood. This gap is best filled with a special cork strip, though a quadrant or scotia moulding pinned to the skirting board makes a suitable alternative.

To cut a panel to fit, lay the panel to be cut immediately over the last full panel in the row. On top lay another panel with one edge positioned 10mm from the skirting (don't include the tongue). On the panel to be cut, mark the rear edge of the topmost panel. This is then the line of cut.

Cut the panel with a fine-tooth saw or a power saw. Trim off the tongue nearest the skirting and lay the panel. Awkward shapes are best cut using a coping saw, pad saw or power jig saw, having first made a template of the required shape.

If an exact half-panel is needed, split it down the middle by easing it backwards and forwards until the two halves separate. Don't saw it or the teeth will quickly become clogged with glue. Each quarter of a panel can be further separated by easing off individual fingers. This is useful when fitting a tricky piece around a radiator pipe or door frame.

Some panels are supplied with a finishing coat which eliminates the need for waxing and polishing. Unfinished panels must be well sanded before applying a floor seal.

Mosaic panels

1. *Setting out the panels before starting the job. A panel is laid against one wall with edging strip placed between it and the skirting. A string line is stretched across the room following the edge of this panel.*
2. *The line that the string follows is marked on the floor and the panel then can be pushed right into the corner. It can then be seen that the walls are not at right angles.*
3. *A second panel is then positioned to project beyond the edge of the first panel by a distance equal to the depth of the marking batten.*
4. *Press the batten against the wall and draw the outer edge of the batten on to the panels as a cutting guide line.*
5. *Cut along the marked guide line, lay edging strip against the second skirting, and check the fit.*
6. *Spread adhesive over the area of four panels.*

Flooring repairs

Timber floors do not often give much trouble, and such problems as do arise are frequently caused by the boards being lifted, for repairs to plumbing or electrical services under them, and improperly replaced. Many of these can be cured quite easily, with a few woodworking tools and a certain amount of upheaval, as carpets and furniture have to be moved to give access.

Repairing holes and gaps

Unless your floorboards will be on show, repairs to holes and gaps are carried out mainly to stop draughts and dust rising through them. Small holes can be stopped up with wooden plugs or wood filler; gaps between boards can be filled with thin strips of wood glued, tapped in and planed flush.

Large holes, usually the result of damage, should be cut out completely and replaced with new wood. If the boards are tongue-and-groove, your first job is to use a padsaw to cut along the join between the damaged board and its neighbour, to sever the tongue. Next, the end of the board should be prised up with a claw hammer or floorboard bolster, once the nail heads holding it have been punched in. Wedge the end of the board up so that you can saw off the damaged section at the centre of the next joist along. Cut a piece of new board to fit the gap, remove the lower lip along its grooved edge and slot it into place, nailing it down to the exposed halves of the joists at each end.

An alternative method is to cut out the damaged section using a padsaw, cutting at an angle of 45° between two holes drilled in the board. The new piece of board is cut to fit, and is supported on fillets of wood screwed to the sides of the joists.

If the gaps between boards are sizeable right across the floor, it is better to fit and re-lay all the boards, nailing each one in turn tightly against its neighbour as you work. This process will leave a large gap along the skirting board at one side of the room, which should be filled with a new board cut down to the required width.

Boards that are improperly fixed squeak and bang when trodden on, and may warp, causing ridges to show through your floorcoverings. Nail down all loose boards securely; to force a warped edge back into place use screws, rather than nails which will be pulled up by the spring in the board.

Sanding floorboards

If you want to clean up old floorboards and leave them exposed, you should hire a floor sanding machine. This is rather like a cylinder lawn mower, and rotates belts of abrasive paper against the floor surface, picking up the dust like a vacuum cleaner as it goes along.

Before using the machine, punch down all nail heads carefully, to prevent them tearing the abrasive belts. Then begin to sand the floor at an angle of 45° to the board direction, using coarse abrasive. Change to medium and finally to fine, running this time parallel with the boards. To reach right into the skirting boards, you will need a small rotary or orbital sander, again used with a selection of abrasive papers. Once the surface is completely stripped, sweep up carefully, and if you intend to paint or varnish the floor, wipe it over with a rag dipped in white spirit. Then you can apply the finish of your choice.

Re-screeding concrete floors

You can patch small areas of damage in concrete floors with a cement-based filler or ordinary mortar. But if the surface is crumbling and dusty, the best solution is to cover it with a new screed, using a self-levelling floor screeding compound. Sweep the floor to remove all loose material, mix up the compound with water as recommended, and pour it out on to the floor surface. Trowel it out to cover the entire surface; the mix is runny enough to level itself out, and dries to leave a hard, smooth surface layer a few millimetres thick, and the perfect base for new floorcoverings.

Sanding floors

1. *Floor sander used first diagonally and then,* **2**, *parallel to boards. The diagonal movement will take more off the surface of the wood than when you are sanding with the grain. In both cases, tilt the sander before starting the machine and lowering the drum on to the floor. As the sander starts to move, you will have to restrain it so that it does not move too fast, but do not hold it back too much or it will make a hole in the floor.*
3. *Edge finisher with sanding disc.*
4. *Orbital sander for light sanding. Pour self-levelling screed on floor and trowel over surface.*

Flooring repairs

1. *To take up a small section of a floorboard, first drill two holes at one end of the section. Then cut across the board with a pad saw so that one end of the damaged section is free.*
2. *Lift up the damaged section and wedge it up with a piece of timber. Then cut the other end of the board with a panel saw.*
3. *Fill small gaps between boards with strips of wood, glued and tapped into place with a hammer.*

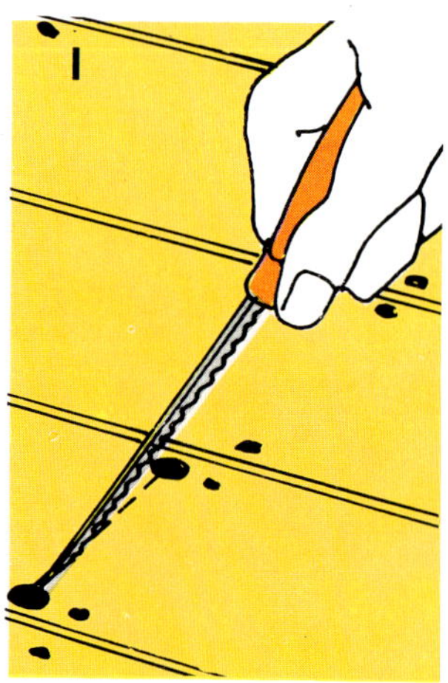

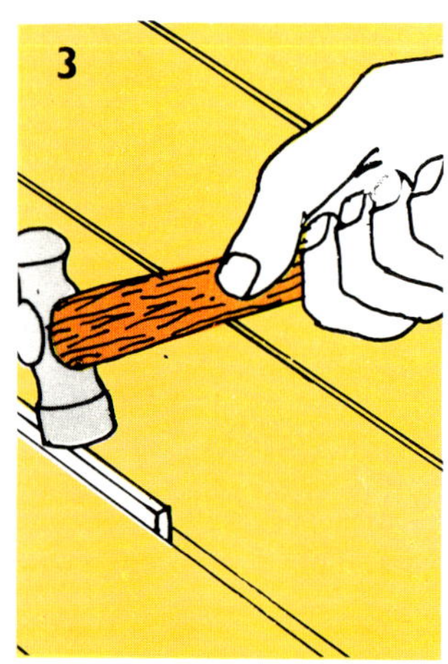

Doors

Hanging a new door is a relatively straightforward exercise, and is illustrated here step by step. Most doors are hung on ordinary butt hinges, although rising butts are used where the door has to clear a thick floorcovering as it opens. Two hinges, set 150mm (6in) down from the top of the door and 230mm (9in) up from the bottom, are fitted on most doors, while on heavy doors a third hinge may be added midway between the other two.

Hanging the door

With all the preparatory work completed, the door should be held in the open position so that the hinge positions can be marked on the door frame and the recesses cut. Of course, if you are hanging a door in an existing frame, you will have fitted the hinges to the door to match the existing hinge positions. The door is then fixed with first one screw per hinge, and a check is made that it swings and closes correctly. If adjustments are needed, the recesses can be chiselled out or packed as necessary. Where rising butts are being used, you may have to bevel off the inside of the door's top edge so it clears the frame as it opens.

The last stage is to mark the latch position on the door frame, and chop out the wood to receive the latch plate.

Door repairs

You can stop a door rattling by fitting self-adhesive foam draught strip around the edges of the stop bead against which the door closes. For a permanent cure, however, you should reposition the latch plate in which the door catch engages. This will involve chiselling out the recess on the door frame by a few millimetres on the side furthest from the door face, and replacing the plate.

Sticking doors can be caused by a build-up of paint on the door edges, by loose hinge screws or by opening joints on a framed door. To cure the first, plane off about 3mm (1/8in) of wood along the door edge, prime, undercoat and repaint. To cure the second, tighten the screws in the top hinge after wedging the door up slightly in the open position. If they will not grip use longer screws, or plug the old screw holes with thin dowel.

If the joints in a framed door have opened up, open the door and wedge it up slightly at the outer edge. Then tap glued hardwood wedges into the mortises (cutting a starter slot with a chisel first if necessary) to tighten up the joints. Leave the door wedged up overnight, and trim off the wedges flush with the door edges when the glue has set.

Doors may squeak either because the hinges need oiling or because the door is catching on the frame. The first of these problems can be cured simply with a small quantity of oil. The second problem should be tackled in the same way as for sticking doors. But check where the door is catching and sand any slight protrusions.

Rising butts

Hinge position

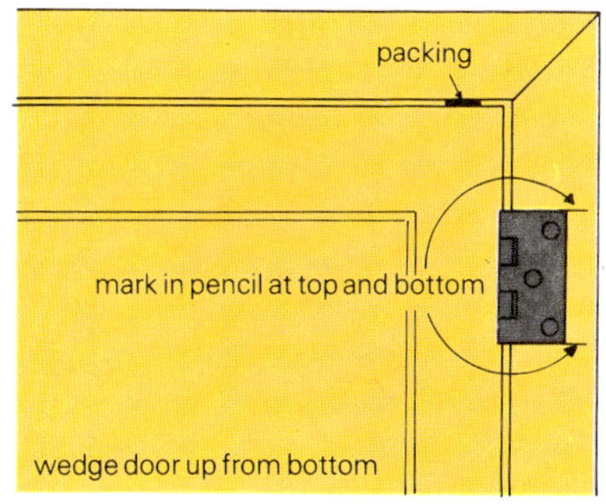

Swing direction

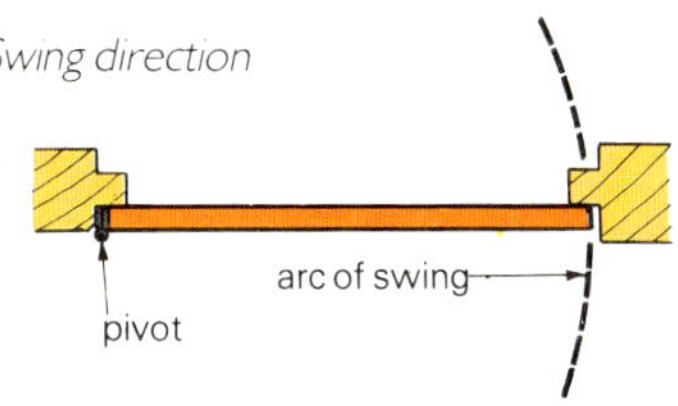

Points to remember when hanging doors: Bevel the top edge with riding butt hinges. Pack the door in place when marking hinge positions on door posts. Check the arc of swing carefully.

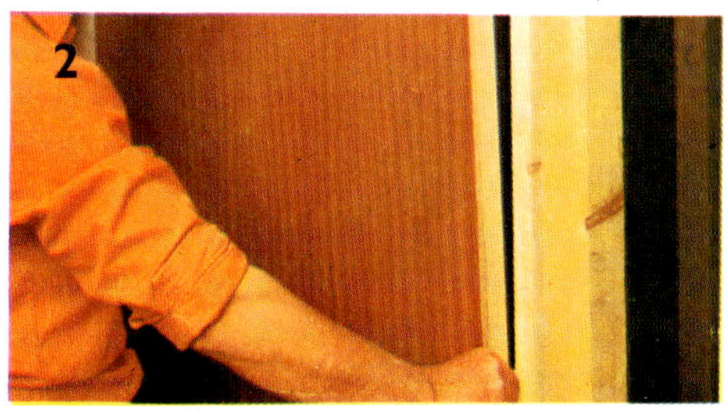

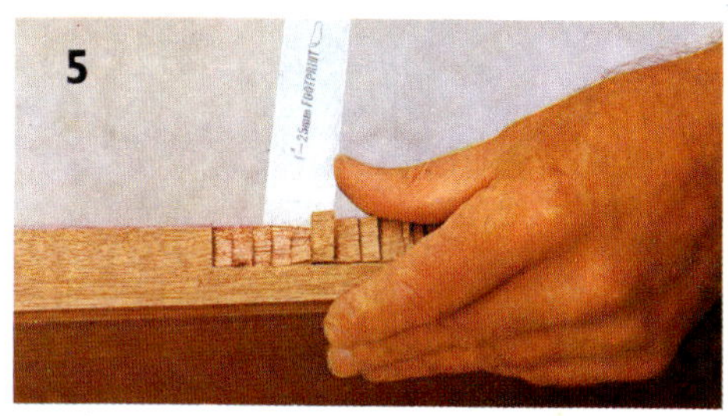

Hanging doors

1. *New doors have protruding ends to the stiles to protect them in transit. Saw these off.*
2. *Check the fit of the door in its frame. There should be about 2mm clearance at top and sides.*
3. *Using the hinge as a template, mark its position on the door edge. Cut round it with a chisel.*
4. *Make a series of angled cuts with the chisel to the depth of the hinge. Keep within the outline.*
5. *Slice crossways with the chisel along the bottom of the recess.*
6. *Pare away the waste timber and clean up.*
7. *Try the hinge for fit in the recess – the leaf should lie flush. Drill pilot holes for the screws.*

Ceiling decor

Polystyrene tiles both decorate and insulate. Although they can be used in any room they are especially suited to kitchens and bathrooms where they combat condensation. They are an ideal covering for a poor, though stable ceiling. Sizes are normally 300mm and 600mm square.

A clean, dry, sound surface is needed so any paper or flaking paint must be removed. A special adhesive paste is used and this must be spread evenly over the complete back of each tile before it is pressed into place.

Find the centre of the ceiling by stretching a string line from the mid-points of opposite walls. Tiling can begin where the lines cross but check first to see if an unsightly narrow strip of tiles will be left at the perimeter. If so, the starting point should be moved half a tile's width to one side. Fluorescent strip lighting can also be a deciding factor when establishing the starting point.

As each tile is laid in place use a square of hardboard to press it to the ceiling for a few seconds until the adhesive grips it. If a tile is pressed with the fingers the surface will be indented.

Continue hanging the tiles until only part tiles are needed to fill the gaps at the edges. Measure out and mark each tile carefully before cutting it with a sharp knife. Place the tile on a flat surface, with the decorative face uppermost, hold a straight-edge on the tile and then cut through it with firm pressure. Make a cardboard template as a guide before cutting tiles to fit awkward shapes.

The tiles can be painted with emulsion paint if preferred. This job is easier if the tiles are painted before they are hung. Never paint expanded polystyrene with gloss paint – it breaks down the material and makes it highly inflammable.

The edge of the ceiling can be finished with polystyrene coving.

A textured ceiling is achieved with a thick, paint-like compound sold under various brand names. These compounds can be used on any sound, dry, clean surface and are especially useful for covering a cracked ceiling. The cracks should be filled first with cellulose filler.

There are two types of compound. One is self-texturing – it is applied using either a brush or roller and leaves a stippled surface automatically. A roller gives a deeper texture. Patterned rollers are also available.

The other type is applied with a brush over a small area. It is then given a texture in one of a number of ways. A basic stipple effect is created by wrapping a sponge in polythene and bouncing it up and down on the compound. Other effects can be created by, for example, twisting a comb on the compound to leave a series of swirls. It's best to practise first on a piece of hardboard before tackling the real thing.

Ceiling centrepieces and other mouldings made of polystyrene can be used to enhance a plain ceiling. These are easy to fix using a special adhesive.

Ceiling coving

Cracks which continually reopen at the angle of the ceiling to wall are caused by normal, seasonal movement of the house. There is little chance of any filling material keeping the crack sealed permanently. The only real solution is to hide it behind coving.

Gypsum plaster coving is available in two girths, 100 and 127mm. The 100mm size comes in 3m lengths; 127mm size is in 3, 3.6 and 4.2m lengths. The special coving adhesive is sold in 5kg bags. This is mixed with water to a creamy consistency; mix up enough for only one length of coving at a time as it sets quickly.

The first stage is to draw guide lines on the ceiling and wall. The lines enclose the

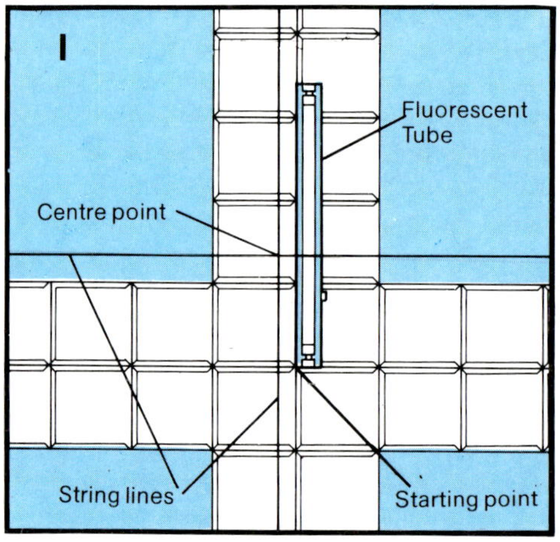

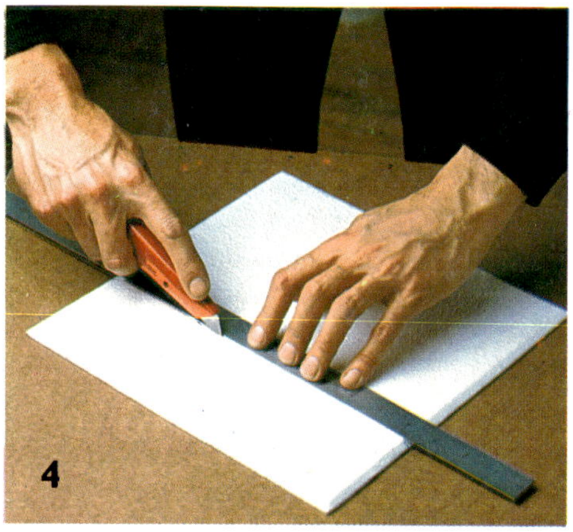

Tiling a ceiling

1. *Adjust first line of tiles to run along one edge and end of fluorescent light fitting. This will minimize cutting and make the job look neater.*
2. *Spreading adhesive all over the back of a polystyrene tile.*
3. *Use a piece of hardboard to press the tile into place. Tiles are delicate and indent easily under finger pressure.*
4. *A sharp knife and a straight-edge are needed to cut a tile cleanly.*

area to be occupied by the coving. For 100mm coving the guide lines should be drawn 67mm from the angle; for 127mm coving each line should be 83mm from the angle. The area between the lines should be cleaned and any wallpaper or loose paint removed. Finally, score the area with a filling knife to provide a good key for the adhesive. 1

Supplied with the coving is a template which is used for marking out mitres at the coving ends to suit internal or external corners. Cut the coving with a fine-tooth saw then lightly sandpaper any rough edges.

Butter adhesives on to the back of the coving along the two surfaces which will be 2 in contact with the wall and the ceiling. Fix the coving in place immediately. Though light in weight, longer lengths should preferably be handled by two people to eliminate the risk of breakages. Dampen the fixing area then immediately press the coving between the guide lines. The adhesive should grip the coving after a few seconds. If it doesn't, then knock a couple of nails into the wall tight to the bottom edge, with another midway between these two but tight to the top edge. Pull the nails out later and fill the holes.

Scrape off any adhesive which squelches out from behind the coving and use it to fill gaps at the edges or between lengths of coving. Use a wet paint brush to remove any last traces of adhesive.

For Victorian style houses, decorative plaster coving, mouldings and ceiling centrepieces would fit better into the style. Fitting is as for plain types.

3

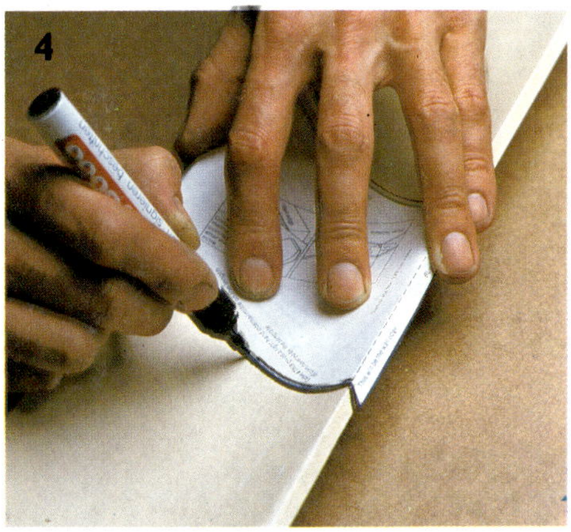

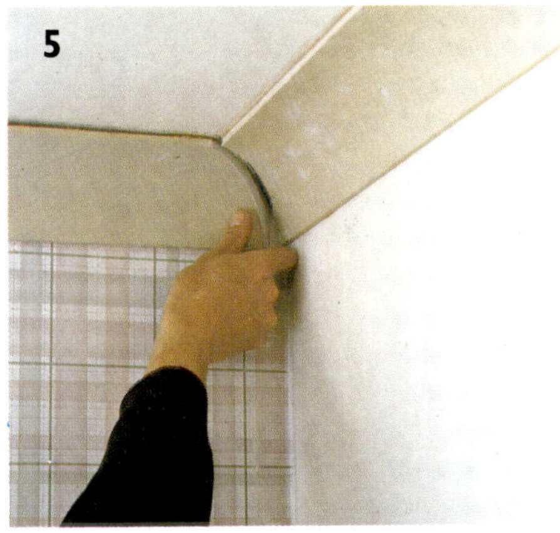

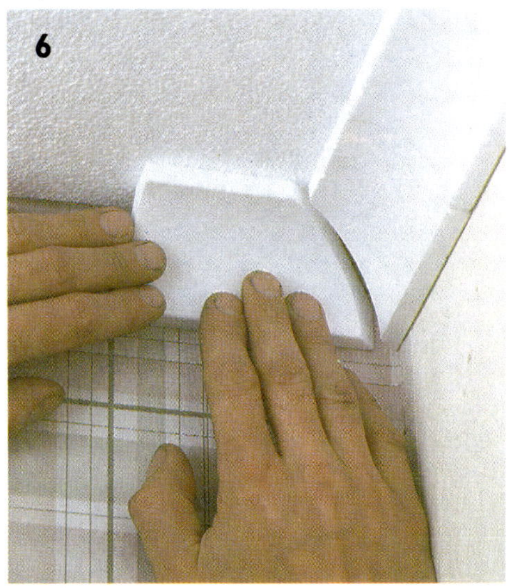

Putting up coving

1. *Adhesive is buttered on to the back edges of the coving.*
2. *Pressing a length of coving firmly into place between guide lines marked on the wall.*
3. *Filling gaps with excess adhesive.*
4. *A template is supplied to enable mitre joints to be marked out.*
5. *A neat joint made in a corner.*
6. *Expanded polystyrene coving is supplied with special corner pieces.*

Self-texturing paint compounds are an interesting alternative for ceilings. They are applied more thickly using a roller.

Window repairs

The commonest problems with windows are the sticking of moving parts, damage caused by rot and cracked or broken glass. Where hinged casements or sliding sashes stick, the trouble may be caused by the accumulation of paint on the meeting surfaces, and it can often be cured by stripping back to bare wood and repainting. If more clearance is needed, the sticking edge can be planed to remove a little more wood. Another cause of sticking with both types of window is sagging – where the joints in the casement or sash open up and allow it to sag out of square. You may be able to correct the sagging *in situ* by recessing L-shaped metal repair brackets into the surface at each corner of the sash or casement, covering them with wood filler and painting them; alternatively, you will have to remove it from the frame, square it up on your workbench and drive small glued hardwood wedges into the mortises at each joint to tighten it up. Take care not to overdo this, or you may crack the glass. Before replacing the sash or casement, check that the top and bottom edges are well painted; they are often left bare, and water can then penetrate, leading to rot.

Repairing rot damage

If rot damage is not extensive, you may be able to patch the damaged areas with wood filler after cutting away rotten wood. Where the casements or sashes show signs of extensive rot damage, you can replace rails or glazing beads with new mouldings, which are available from most timber merchants. This will involve careful cutting away of the old wood, and you may have to strip down the sash or casement completely. The alternative is to buy a complete replacement casement or sash if your window is a standard size, or otherwise to have one made for you. Rotten sills can be patched with new wood, jointed to the old with glue and wooden dowels to reinforce the repair. The window frames themselves can be patched on a small scale, and gaps between the wood and the masonry should be filled with non-setting mastic.

Replacing sash cords

One of the trickiest repairs is replacing the sash cords on sliding sash windows. When one breaks, you should always replace both cords at the same time; if you do not, the one you did not replace is sure to break in the near future.

Start by removing the staff beads with a chisel, and open up the pocket piece at each side of the window. Retrieve the weight from the side where the cord is broken, and wedge the inner sash up so you can pull the weight from the other side out through its pocket and cut it off its cord. Now you can lower the inner sash and lift it out of the frame. The sash cord will be tacked into a groove in the side of the sash; prise out the tacks to release it.

The procedure is repeated to remove the outer sash. Wedge it up, remove the weights and prise off the parting bead. Then you can lift the sash out and remove the cords.

Rehang the outer sash first. Holding the sash cord in a hank, tie a length of string to one end and attach a bent nail or a small lead weight to the other end of the string. Pass this over the outer pulley and let it drop inside the weight compartment. You

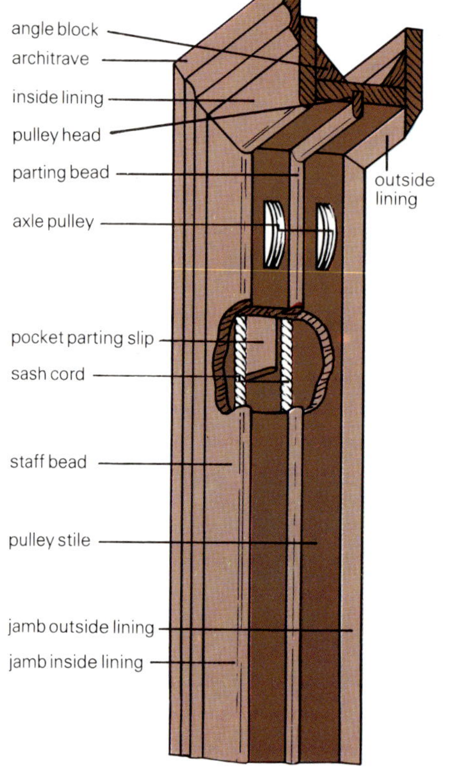

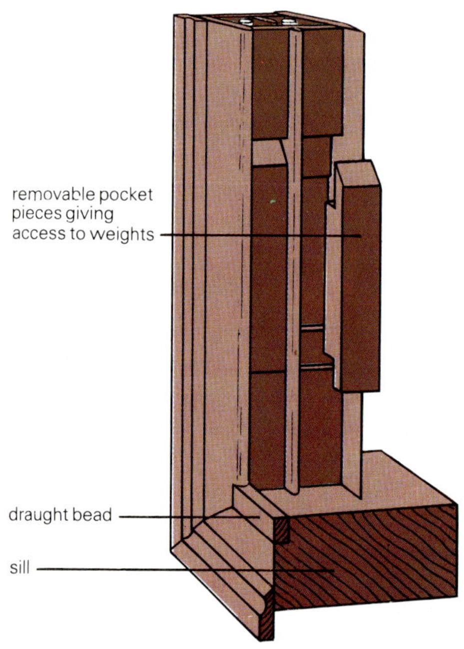

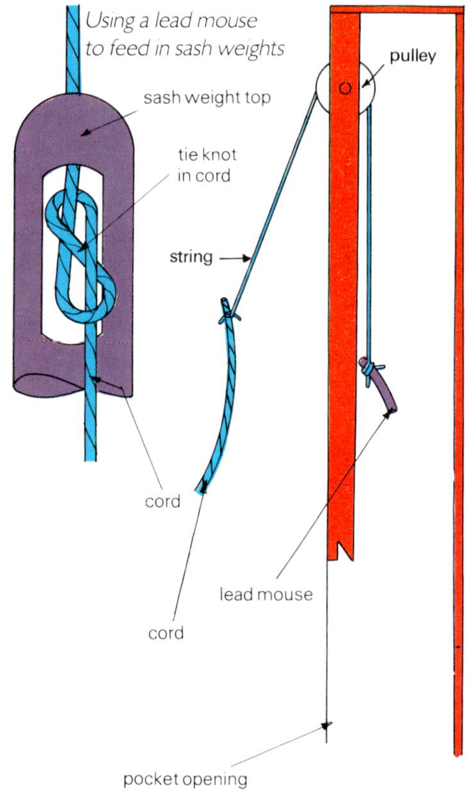
Using a lead mouse to feed in sash weights

can then retrieve it and use it to pull the sash cord through, ready to be tied to the weight. Now haul up the weight until it hangs just below its pulley, and pin the cord temporarily in place alongside the parting bead groove. Let it hang down towards the pocket, and cut the cord about 50mm (2in) above the top of the pocket piece. Repeat the process at the other side. Hold the outer sash in the frame, resting on the sill, and attach the cords to the sides of the sash with tacks. You should then be able to push the sash up to its closed position, checking that the weights drop almost to the bottom of the weight compartment as you do so.

Now replace the parting bead, and repeat the recording procedure for the inner sash; here, of course, the weights will be in the up position when the sash is closed, and drop as it is opened. Finally, replace the pocket pieces and the staff beads, and make good any damage to the beads with filler.

When carrying out this job, it is a good opportunity to repaint the sashes, since their sides cannot normally be reached for redecoration. If several coats of paint have already been applied, check that the sash is not sticking before adding another coat; it may be necessary to strip the old paint first if there is a severe build-up of paint.

Glazing

Replacing a cracked or broken pane of glass is a relatively straightforward job, requiring more care and patience than skill. The most important point is to measure the rebate accurately before ordering the glass, and to make sure that you have enough putty for the job – linseed oil putty for wooden-framed windows, metal casement putty for metal ones. You will also need small nails called glazing sprigs to hold the glass in place in a wooden window, and special clips for metal windows.

Wear stout gloves to remove the pieces of broken glass from the frame, hack out the old putty with a chisel or a glazier's hacking knife, pull out glazing sprigs or clips with pliers and clean the rebate. Prime any bare wood or metal.

Measure the rebate both vertically and horizontally; if the frame is not a perfect rectangle, take the measurements of the shorter sides in each case, and subtract 3mm (⅛in) from each measurement to give you the ordering size. If you are using patterned glass, be sure to tell your glass merchant which way the pattern should run.

Apply bedding putty evenly round the rebate, locate the pane of glass along the bottom of the rebate and press it into position with gentle but firm hand pressure applied to the edge, NOT the centre, of the pane. Fix the glazing sprigs or clips to the rebate to hold the pane in place, and trim away the excess putty on the inside of the pane.

Next, apply the facing putty all round the rebate, and use your putty knife to finish it off at an angle of about 45° to the glass. Mitre the corners neatly, cut away any surplus putty and seal the putty to glass and frame by brushing over it gently with an old paintbrush or using a moistened finger. Leave the putty to harden for about 14 days, and then undercoat and topcoat it to protect it from the weather, taking the paint line on to the face of the glass by about 2mm to form a watertight seal.

If you decide to cut the glass yourself, lay the sheet on a flat table covered with an old blanket. Mark the cutting line 3mm outside the measured dimension of the rebate to allow for the thickness of the cutter. Lay a straight-edge between the marks and make a single firm but smooth stroke of the cutter across the glass against the straight-edge. Lay the score line over one edge of the straight-edge and press evenly for a clean break.

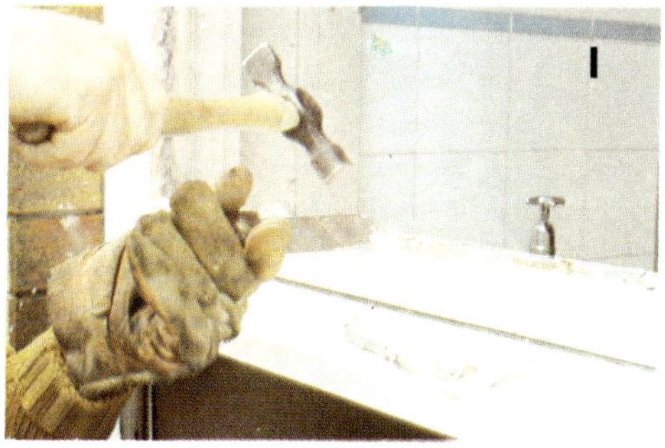

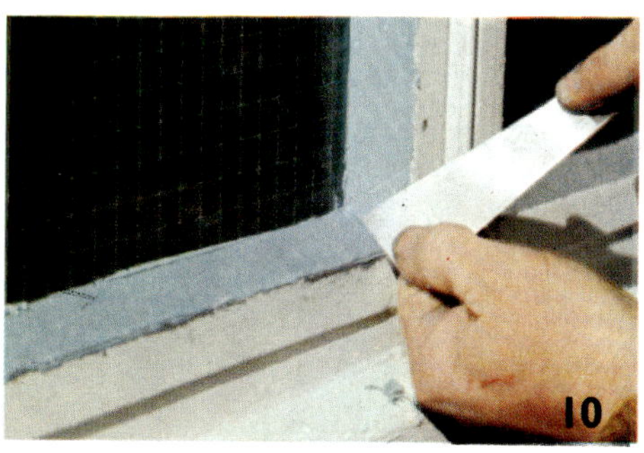

Glazing

1. *Remove all the old or broken glass carefully, wearing stout gloves.*
2. *Brush out the rebate.*
3. *Prime any bare wood or metal.*
4. *Measure the rebate accurately.*
5. *With patterned glass, make sure the pattern runs the correct way.*
6. *Press bedding putty all round the rebate.*
7. *Insert spacer blocks to support large panes.*
8. *Offer up the glass and press it gently into place.*
9. *Press in facing putty all round.*
10. *Finish off with a neat mitre, using a putty knife.*

1

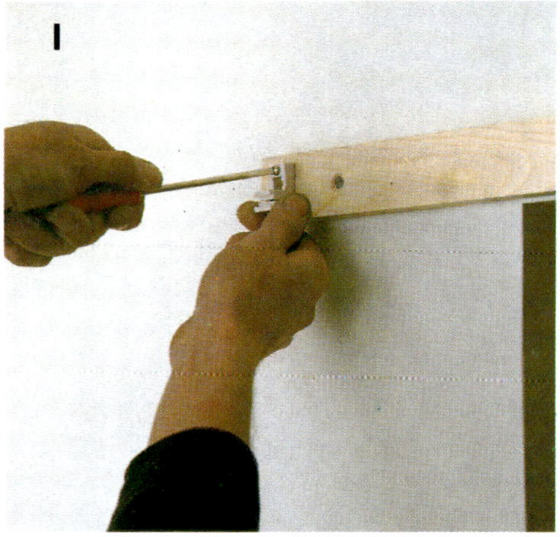

2

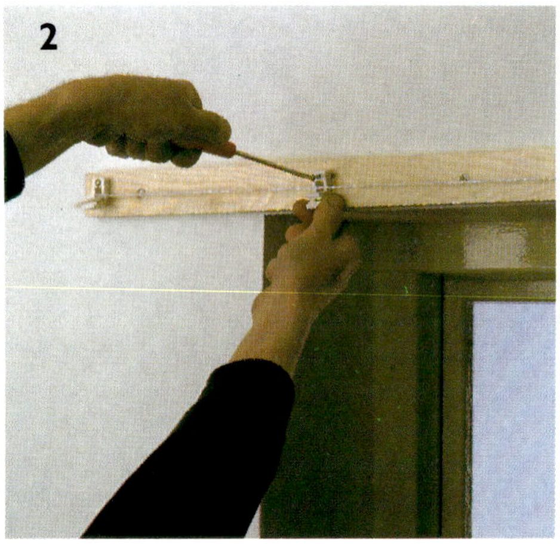

3

Curtain tracks

1. *Minimise hard drilling into a concrete lintel by fixing a horizontal timber batten along the top of the window opening. For an average window, three or four strong fixings will hold the batten securely. Using the wood screws supplied with the track, fix the end brackets in place equidistant from the sides of the window opening and equal heights above the sill or floor (neither may be horizontal).*

2. *Stretch a string line between the end brackets and fix the intermediate brackets equally spaced and in line with the string. This will give an accurate horizontal fitting.*

3. *Clip track in place on brackets.*

Finishing touches

This section includes a number of other interior jobs around the home. These include putting up tracks for curtains and fixings for blinds, working with decorative laminates, and putting up panelling around baths and pipes.

Curtain tracks

When choosing a curtain track make sure it will be strong enough to support the type of curtains to be hung – lined floor-to-ceiling curtains, for example, are very heavy. In most cases the track will be fixed to the face of the wall above the window, but special brackets or track may be required if the fixing is to be made in the top of the window recess, or to the ceiling. Also make sure that the track is long enough to allow an overhang of 250mm to 300mm on each side of the window opening depending on the fullness of the curtains.

The easiest way to put up curtain track is to screw it to the top of the frame, or to a batten fixed to the wall above the window frame. The problem with fixing directly to the wall is that it often hides a reinforced concrete lintel and fixing into this can be very difficult.

Always fix the number of brackets recommended by the manufacturer. Usually you need a bracket 25mm from each end, and intermediate brackets at about 300mm intervals. Fix the end brackets first – they should be equal heights above the sill for sill-length curtains, and equal heights above the floor for floor-length curtains. Be careful if you use a spirit level to level the brackets in case either the floor or the sill is out of true, which is quite common in old houses.

Once the end brackets are in position, string can be stretched between them so that the intermediate brackets can be fixed in a straight line. Fixing to the frame or to a batten is easy because the wood screws provided can be used, but fixing to the wall is more tricky. Use a masonry drill bit to make holes for plastic wallplugs into which the fixing screws can be inserted. But make sure the screws are long enough to go right through the plaster layer into the brickwork beneath.

If the masonry drill bit makes slow going this is due probably to a concrete lintel. In this case switch to a percussion masonry bit in an electric drill with hammer action. Even then the going can be hard, so reduce the number of fixings that have to be made by making just sufficient holes to fix a 12mm thick batten above the window, and then screw the brackets to this.

Once the brackets are fixed, normally the track just snaps into place.

Cornice poles

These are normally supported on brackets on either side of the window, and they must be securely fixed. After fixing one bracket at the desired height, and with a spirit level on the pole, mark the position of the other bracket. But check that the top of the window, the sill and the floor are also level.

1. *Cornice pole*

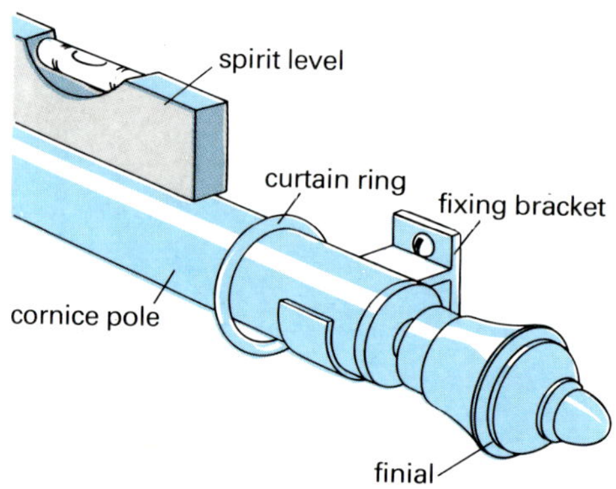

2. *Roller blind*

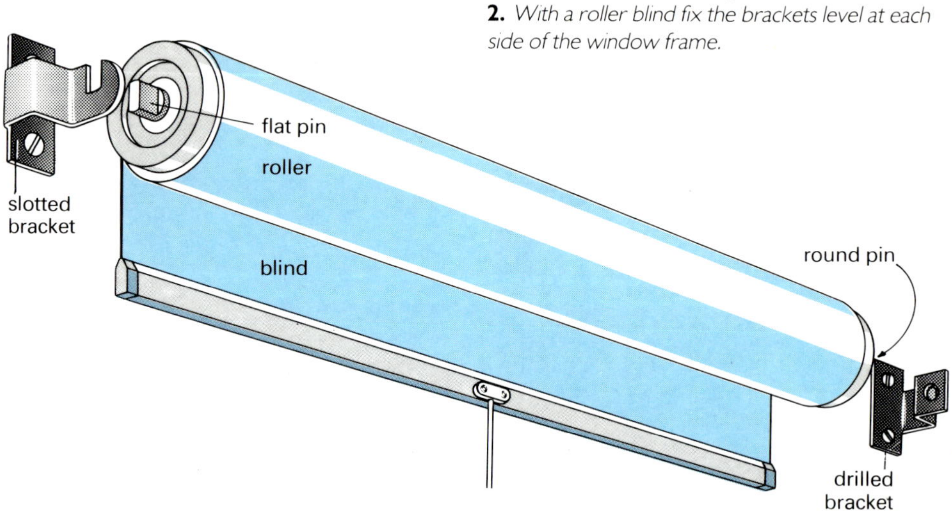

1. *Before fixing a cornice pole check that top of frame is level. Fix one end bracket and align pole with spirit level before fixing other bracket.*

2. *With a roller blind fix the brackets level at each side of the window frame.*

Roller blinds

These must be fixed level or the blind will not roll neatly. The slotted bracket must be fixed on the same side as the mechanism and flat pin of the roller.

Laminates

Plastic laminate can be used anywhere in the home to provide a hard-wearing and easy-to-clean surface. However, it is most widely used on worktops.

To work with laminates you will need a cutting knife, fitted with a special laminate-cutting blade, or a tungsten-tipped laminate cutter (rather like a tile cutter). With both of these, the surface is scored and then snapped along the marked line. You can also cut laminate with a power jig saw with a fine-tooth blade, while for curves special laminate scissors are the best bet. You will also need a notched adhesive spreader, and an edger or a block plane to bevel the edges of the sheet once it is stuck in place. When measuring laminate, allow 3mm (⅛in) overhang for trimming. Position it on thin battens over the worktop when the adhesive is touch dry. Slide out the first batten and press down one edge. Proceed in this way to prevent air being trapped. Some contact adhesives allow some slippage.

Working with laminates

1. *Score against straight-edge with laminate cutter or special blade in knife until dark line appears.*
2. *Snap laminate firmly upwards.*
3. *Fine-tooth panel saw can be used to cut laminate if well supported.*
4. *Apply contact adhesive to both surfaces with notched spreader and leave until touch dry.*
5. *Place timber battens on surface and lay laminate on top of them.*
6. *Position sheet with 3mm overhang, slide out battens one by one and roll down laminate.*
7. *Drawing pins at edges help to locate position.*
8. *Use block plane, file or metal scraper to trim flush with edge.*
9. *Remove trapped air by tapping smooth wood block over surface.*
10. *With resin adhesive, hold edge strip in place with adhesive tape. For iron-on edge strip, cover with brown paper and fix with a cool iron.*
11. *Or hammer with wood block if using contact adhesive.*
12. *Trim edge strips to a bevel.*

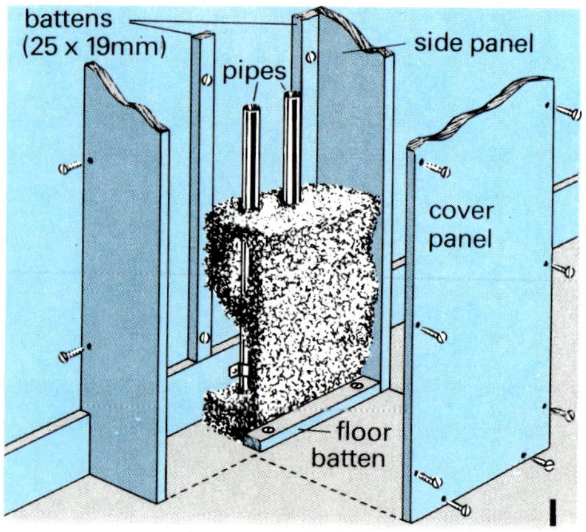

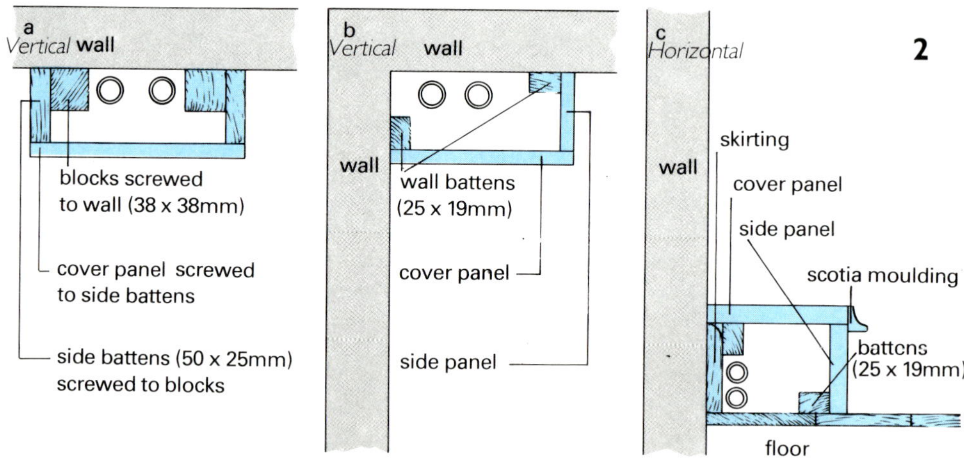

1. *The standard method of boxing-in pipes and insulating them against freezing. Vertical battens are screwed to the wall on each side of the pipe. Chipboard or plywood side panels are screwed to the battens, insulation is packed around the pipes and a cover is screwed in place.*
2. *Alternative methods of boxing-in vertical and (right) horizontal pipes.*
3. *Panelling a bath with moulded plastic panels.*
4. *A more elaborate framework of this nature is required for home-made panels.*

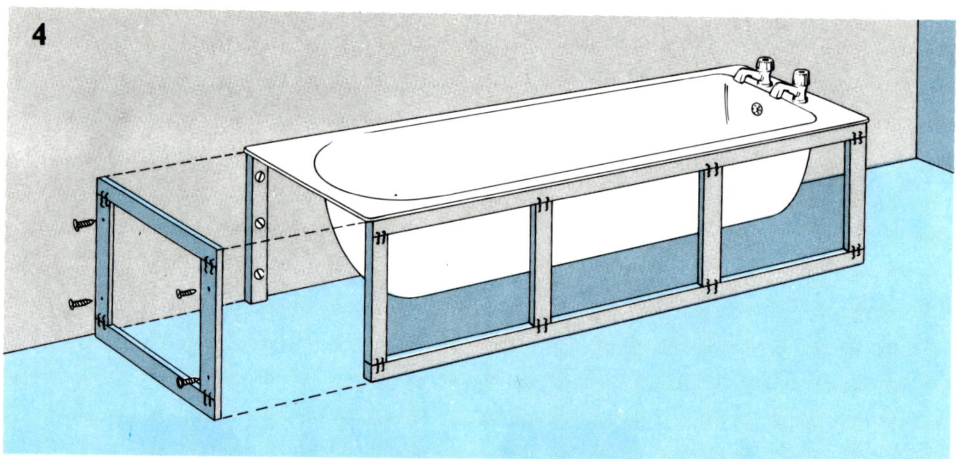

Boxing-in pipes

If the pipes protrude less than 50mm from the wall, the sides of the boxing can be made from 50 × 25mm timber fixed to timber blocks, which in turn are fixed to the wall using wallplugs and screws. Then screw a chipboard or plywood cover to the side pieces.

If the pipes protrude more than 50mm from the wall, or you want room to pack some insulation around them, screw 25 × 20mm vertical battens to the wall. Fix chipboard or plywood side pieces of the required depth to the battens, then pack the pipes with glass fibre insulation if desired, and fit a cover as before.

When the pipes are close to a corner, only one side piece will be required, the cover being fitted direct to the batten mounted on the side wall.

To box-in pipes running along a skirting, nail a 25 × 20mm batten to the floor, and another to the top of the skirting. Then fix plywood or timber cover panels to the battens to hide the pipes. For neatness, quadrant or scotia moulding can be fixed to the exposed corner.

Panelling a bath

Whether you are fixing a moulded plastic bath panel, or making your own, first build a framework under the bath sides to support the panels. The framework does not need to be elaborate.

A framework of 50 × 25mm battens is suitable. With a moulded plastic panel it may be sufficient to screw a batten to the floor running the length of the bath, another to the top of the panel on the inside edge where it tucks under the bath rim, and then fix two vertical battens to the walls at the ends of the bath. If the bath has an end panel, a batten is glued to the inside of the corner edge of this. Another is fixed to the top of this panel on the inside, and another to the floor under the end of the bath.

The panels are trimmed along the base to fit under the bath rim, holes are drilled into the battens, and then the panels are held with chromium plated screws fitted with chromium plated collars. Some moulded panels only require floor battens, the top edge being held in place by clips supplied with the panels.

For home-made panels made of lacquered hardboard or chipboard to be finished with ceramic tiles, use 50 × 25mm battens to make a side frame consisting of two horizontal rails and four uprights that will fit between the floor and under-bath rim. Hold the frame in place against wood blocks fixed to the floor and end walls.

If the bath needs an end frame, make this in a similar way, screwing the two frames together where they join. Next, screw the panels to the frame. In the case of lacquered hardboard, polished aluminium strips can be glued to one face of the corner joint for neatness.

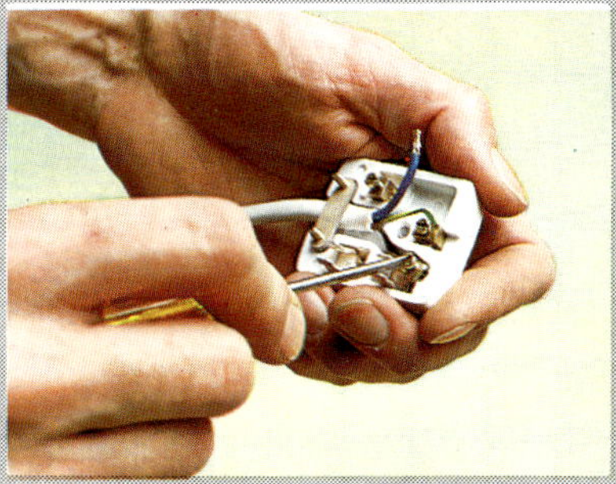

ELECTRICITY

Many people avoid doing electrical work on the grounds that it is too technical and potentially dangerous. But you need not concern yourself with technicalities. All you need is to be able to follow instructions and carry out simple manual tasks and to follow a few basic safety guidelines. Always switch off the supply before doing any electrical work and get any new installation checked by the electricity board. The components of a house installation are easily accessible and easy to work on. This section, written in non-technical language, shows you how to deal with everything from fitting a door bell to running an electrical supply to your workshop. You will find it an invaluable aid to any electrical work you decide to carry out.

The mains supply

The mains electricity supply in a house or flat is in two parts. First the electricity board's apparatus comprising the service fuse unit, the meter to register the electricity consumed, and, where night storage heating is installed, a time switch. This apparatus is sealed and must not be tampered with. You are responsible for any damage to the apparatus. Second, the consumer's installation which includes everything on the house side of the meter.

Your equipment at the mains consists of a double-pole main switch and one or more fuses.

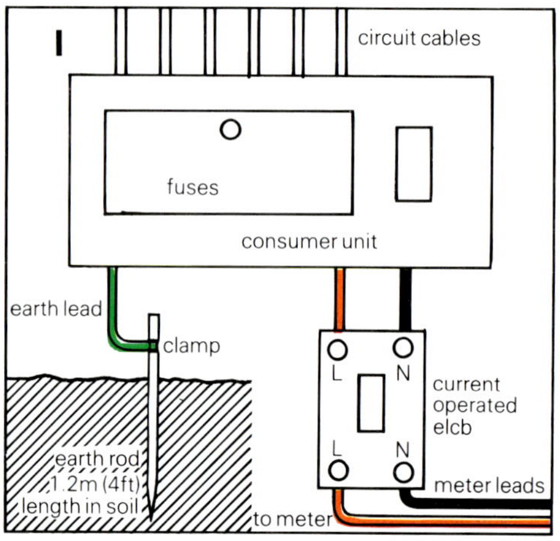

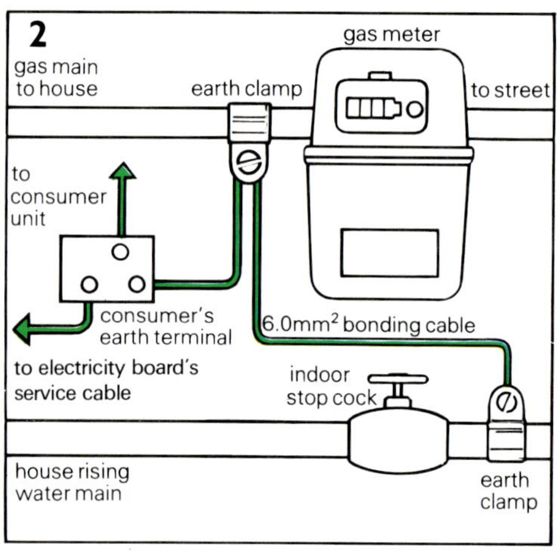

1. *Wiring layout of consumer unit with separate ELCB and earth rod.*
2. *Bonding to earth of mains water and gas pipes.*
3. *Typical mains installation.*

In the modern installation the main switch and the circuit fuses are contained in a single consumer unit. In some houses, especially in rural areas, there is also an earth leakage circuit breaker (ELCB) though in the latest models of consumer unit an ELCB is fitted in place of the conventional main switch even where the circuit is also protected by conventional earthing. In older installations, instead of a single consumer unit there are a number of main switch and fuse units – one for lighting, another for socket outlets, another for the cooker circuit and so forth.

Even in the modern installation a main switch and fuse unit is installed for a shower unit or a cooker circuit where these are added after the main installation has been completed and there are no spare fuses in the consumer unit. See page 57.

The electricity supply in Britain is standardised at 240 volts a.c., 50Hz single phase two-wire for dwellings. All appliances and lamps bought should be suitable for this supply. For certain heavy-load appliances such as electric boilers, a three phase supply may have to be used.

Extending an installation

As a consumer you are permitted to make any additions or alterations to your installation. You do not have to obtain permission from the electricity board or any other authority before work is started.

When a major extension or a major alteration to an installation is completed, such as a new ring circuit or a rewire you should notify the electricity board so that the board can test the wiring before it is connected with the mains. The wiring should conform to the current edition of the Institution of Electrical Engineers (IEE) Wiring Regulations although these are not mandatory. If the wiring conforms with the regulations the board must connect the new wiring upon receipt of the necessary completed application form.

The basic installation

An installation comprises a number of separate circuits each having a specific current rating according to the circuit function: for example, lighting, ring circuit, cooker, and shower unit. All circuits originate at the consumer unit.

The consumer unit contains several ways, one for each circuit, fitted with either a fuse unit or a miniature circuit breaker (MCB). The average size is six-way, but the tendency is to fit eight-way consumer units to allow for extensions.

Fuses or MCBs of different current ratings are colour coded: 5 amps (A) (white), 15A (blue), 20A (yellow), 30A (red) and 45A (green), but not all consumer units have facilities for a 45A fuse.

Lighting circuits

Lighting circuits are wired using two methods: (i) the loop-in, and (ii) the joint box, methods.

Loop-in method

With the loop-in method 1.0 or 1.5mm^2 twin and earth PVC sheathed feed cable is run from a 5A fuseway to each lighting point in turn and terminates at the last point. From each light a separate cable is run to the respective switch. The wires at the light are jointed at the ceiling rose, this serving as a joint box.

Joint box method

With the joint box method the feed cable from the 5A fuseway is run to a series of 15A four-terminal plastic joint boxes, one for each light and its switch. From each joint box two cables are run; one to the light, the other to the switch.

Ring circuits

A ring circuit is a multi-outlet 30A circuit supplying an unrestricted number of 13A socket outlets and fused connection units in a floor area not exceeding 100m^2.

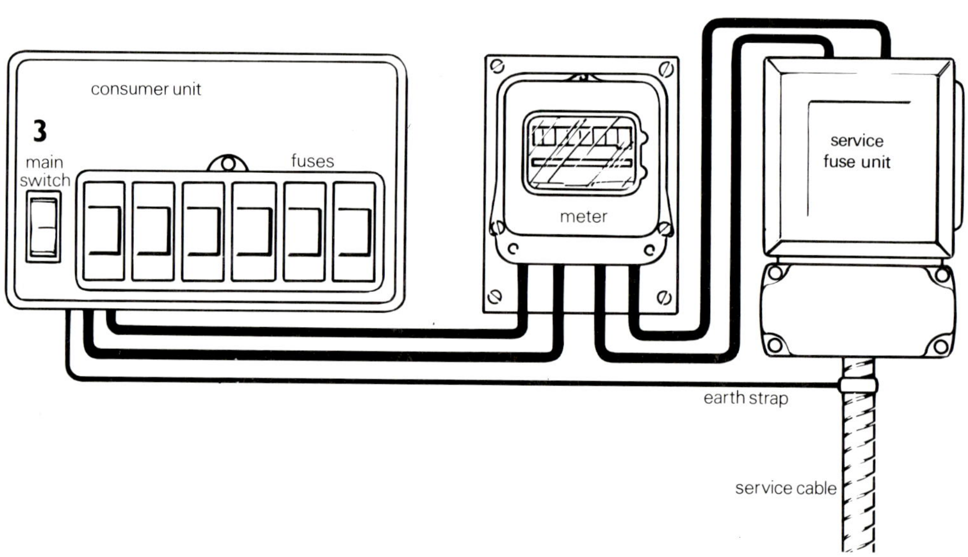

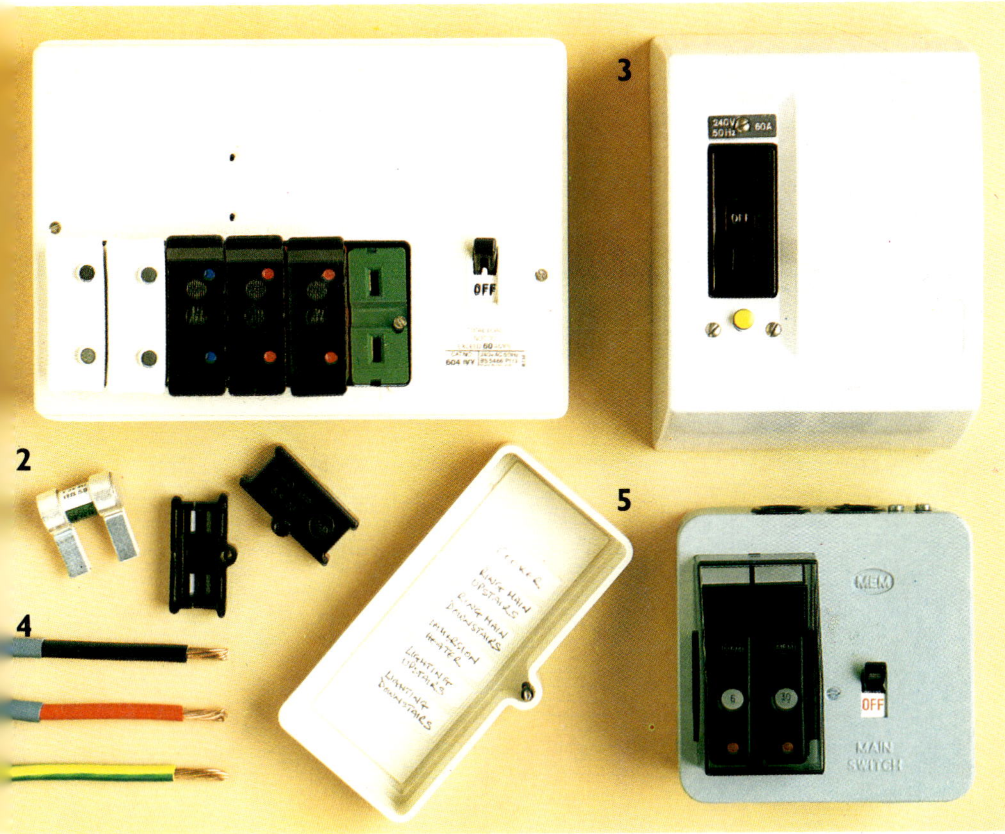

1. *Six-way consumer unit containing rewirable fuses.*
2. *Cartridge fuse unit.*
3. *Earth leakage circuit breaker.*
4. *Meter tails and earthing lead.*
5. *Two-way consumer unit containing miniature circuit breakers.*

A 2.5mm² twin and earth PVC sheathed cable starts at a 30A fuseway, is looped in and out of each 13A outlet and returns to the same fuseway, so forming a ring.

Spur cables of the same size may branch off the ring, each supplying one single or one double 13A socket outlet or one fused connection unit. A ring circuit can have as many spurs as there are original outlets (sockets and fused connection units) on the ring.

Radial circuits

A radial circuit is any circuit not wired in a ring such as circuits supplying a cooker, immersion heater or 13A outlets.

A multi-outlet radial circuit supplying 13A socket outlets and fused connection units can be of either 20A or 30A current rating; using 2.5mm² and 4mm² cable respectively, each may supply an unrestricted number of 13A sockets within a limited area – 20sq m and 50sq m respectively.

Cables and plugs

Cables used for home wiring are mainly twin and earth PVC flat sheathed cables containing one red and one black PVC insulated conductor and one uninsulated earth conductor.

The red conductor is used in the live pole of the circuit, the black in the neutral pole. (The black conductor is also used in the live pole for the switch wire of a lighting circuit linking the switch to the light. However, to identify it as the live, red PVC sleeving is placed over each end within the switch and lighting point.)

Also used in lighting circuits is three-core and earth PVC flat sheathed cable, for linking the two switches of a two-way switching circuit and for the cable running to a two-gang switch where two lights on the same fitting are switched independently from one position. The core colours of this cable are red, yellow, and blue. The colours have no significance in home wiring but identify the different wires at the switches.

At the ends of all cables where they terminate at switches, socket outlets, ceiling roses or other wiring accessories the bare earth conductors should be enclosed in green-yellow PVC sleeving. Sizes of the conductors of house wiring cables range from 1.0mm² to 16mm², the size chosen depending upon the current rating of the circuit.

Flexible cords

Flexible cords are made in numerous sizes and types. The most widely used is circular PVC sheathed – three-core for earthed electrical appliances, two-core for double-insulated appliances and for insulated lighting pendants.

Other types used are parallel-twin flex; unkinkable flex for electric irons and percolators; and braided circular flex for heaters as an alternative to circular PVC sheathed.

Lighting circuit

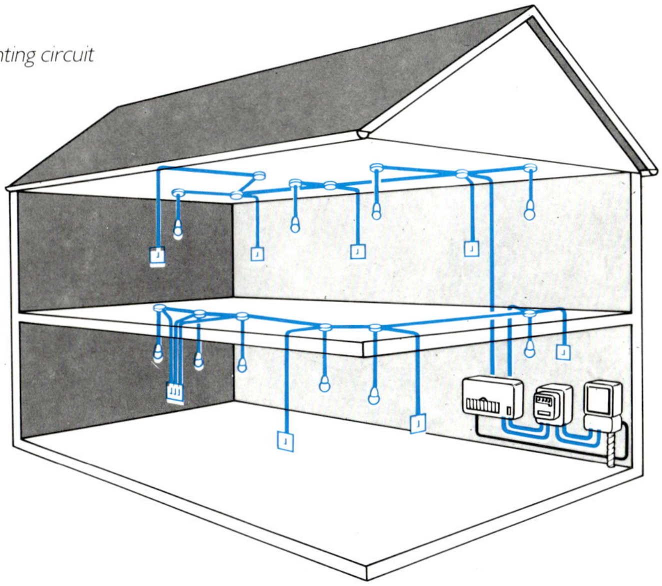

Ring circuit

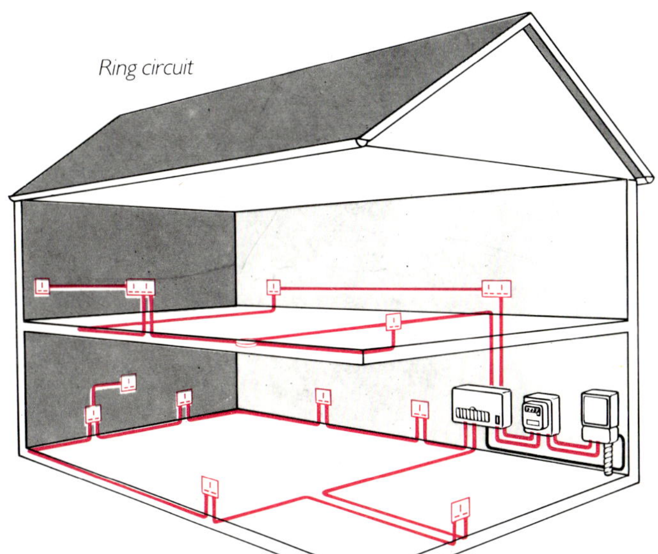

Plugs

Plugs used in the home are: (A) three-pin (flat) 13A fused plugs; (B) three-pin and two-pin (round) non-fused 2A, 5A and 15A plugs; and (C) moulded-on plugs such as those fitted to electric shavers.

The 13A fused plug is the standard plug. Round-pin plugs generally are obsolescent and the two-pin versions, except those fitted to shavers, are potentially dangerous as they provide no earthing for appliances required to be earthed.

Wiring a 13A fused plug

The three terminals of a fused plug are marked L for the live core of the flex, N for the neutral core, and E for earth.

When connecting a plug to old flex having the former colour coding red (live), black (neutral) and green (earth) take especial care that the wires are connected to the correct terminals of the plug. For safety always connect the green/yellow (or green) wire to the E terminal first followed by the brown (or red) to the L terminal and finally the blue (or black) to the N terminal.

Double check that the sheathing of the flex and not the unsheathed ends of the wires are clamped by the cord grip.

The flex connections to a three-pin round-pin plug are the same as for a fused plug. When connecting the two-core flex of a double-insulated appliance, the E (earth) terminal is left blank.

When a moulded-on plug needs replacing either replace the flex complete with a new moulded-on plug or cut off the old plug and fit a conventional plug.

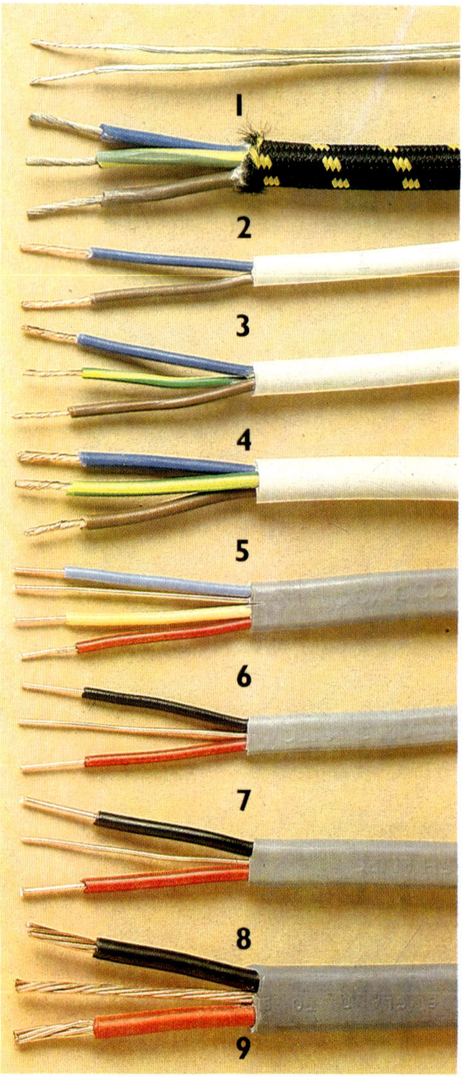

1. *Parallel twin unsheathed flex.*
2. *Circular braided three-core flex.*
3. *Two-core circular PVC-sheathed flex.*
4. *Three-core circular PVC-sheathed flex.*
5. *Heat-resistant circular three-core flex.*
6. *Three-core and earth PVC-sheathed cable.*
7. *Two-core and earth PVC-sheathed cable.*
8. *Two-core and earth PVC-sheathed cable.*
9. *Two-core and earth PVC-sheathed cable.*

Plug adaptors

The function of a multi-plug adaptor is to enable more than one portable appliance or portable lamp to be used from a socket outlet. To prevent overloading a socket outlet use only one adaptor and preferably one which has only two outlets and will not accept another adaptor which, with its numerous plugs and flexes, produces a potentially dangerous 'Christmas-tree'.

If you buy an adaptor which accepts plugs of lower rating than that of the socket, ensure it contains a protective 2A or 5A fuse.

Cable sizes

Circuit	Cable (mm²)
Lighting	1.0 or 1.5
Immersion heater	2.5
Ring circuit	2.5
Radial multi-13A-outlets (20A)	2.5
Radial multi-13A-outlets (30A)	4.0
Shower unit	4.0 or 6.0
Cooker	6.0 or 10.0
Meter leads	16.0

Running cables

PVC sheathed house wiring cables can be run under floors, in voids between ceilings and floors, in the loft, buried in the plaster of walls, fixed to wall and ceiling surfaces or in mini-trunking.

Cables under floors

Cables run in a ceiling void may rest on the ceiling but where they cross joists they are threaded through holes drilled in the joists at least 50mm below the tops of the joists. Under a suspended ground floor the cables may rest on the concrete screed, the earth or building structure without the need for any fixings except where cables are likely to be disturbed.

Cables in the loft

In a loft the cables can rest on the ceiling alongside joists. Where they cross joists they must be fixed to the tops of the joists but should be routed well away from access points and walkways. Where expanded polystyrene granules instead of glass fibre or vermiculite is used for loft insulation, the cables should be either run in PVC conduit or covered with PVC channel, since direct contact with the polystyrene may harm the PVC sheathing.

Cables down walls

PVC sheathed cables may be run down the cavities of hollow partition walls without the need for intermediate fixings for drops of up to 3m.

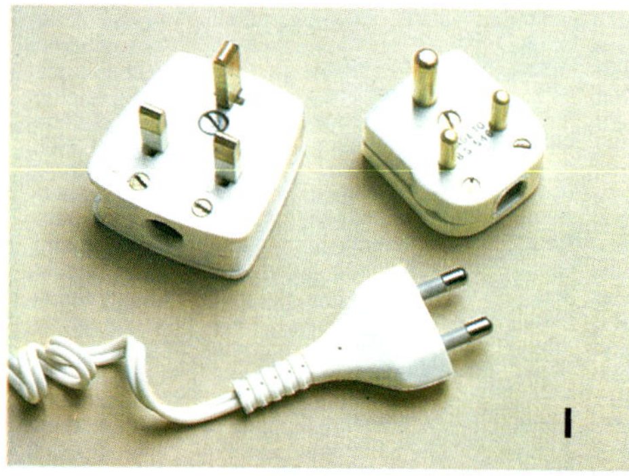

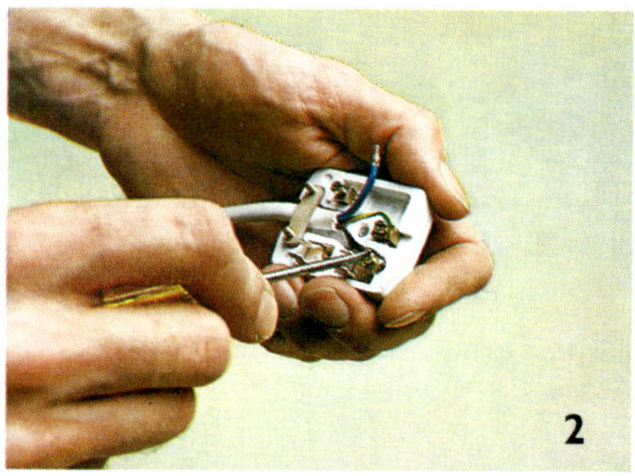

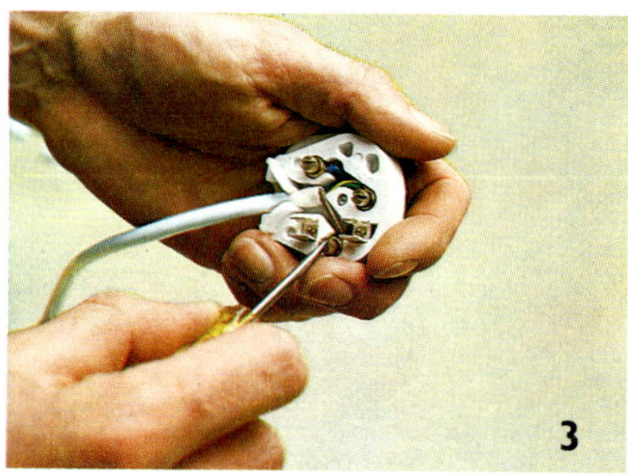

1. *Fused 13 amp plug, round-pin unfused plug and two-pin shaver plug.*
2. *Connecting flex to plug with post terminals and screw-down cord clamp.*
3. *This plug has clamp terminals and screwless cord grip.*

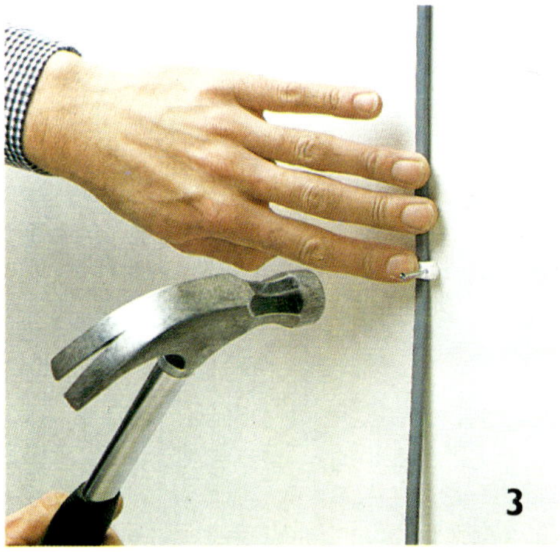

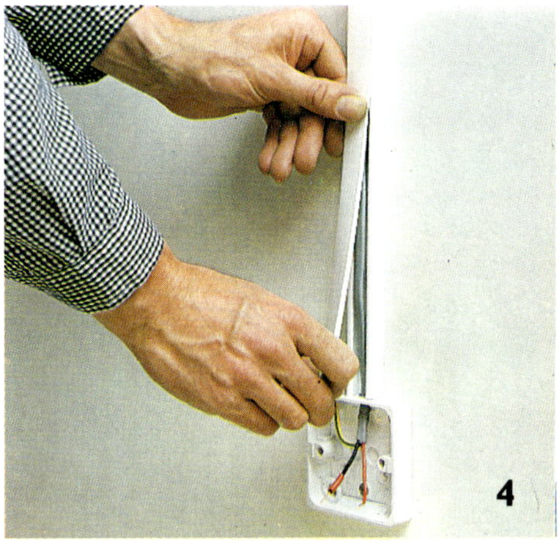

1. Threading cables through holes specially drilled in the joists.
2. Fixing cables to timber using single-pin plastic cable clips.
3. Fixing cable to the surface of a wall using single-pin plastic cable clips.
4. With mini-trunking, fix channel to the wall, lay in cable, and snap on cover.

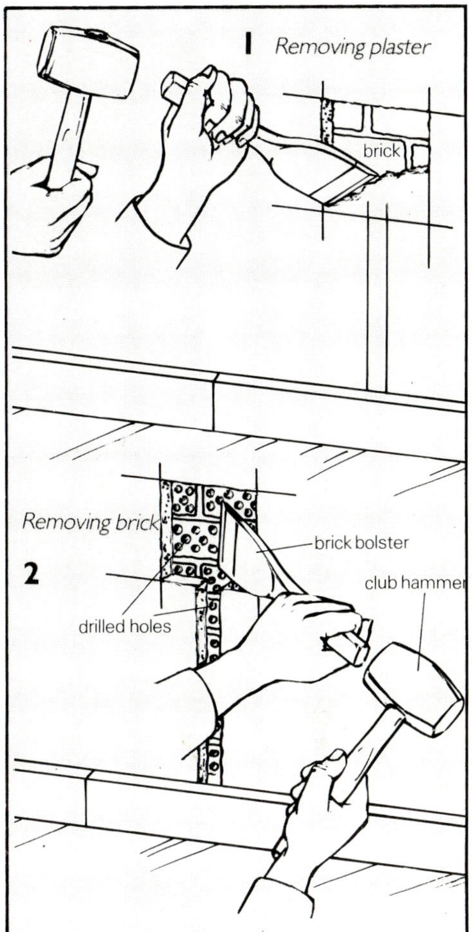

1. Mark the areas to be chased out on a wall and chip away the plaster.
2. Drill holes in the masonry before chipping it out with a bolster.

On solid walls the cables may be fixed to the wall surface or be buried in the plaster.

Surface fixings
The cables are fixed to the wall surface with plastic cable clips fitted with single steel pins. The maximum permitted distances between fixings are 400mm for vertically run cables and 250mm for horizontally run cables.

The clips are of different sizes to suit the various cables and are available in white for use with white sheathed cable.

Cables buried in plaster
PVC sheathed cables may be buried direct into the plaster of walls and plastered over without the need for any additional protection from mechanical damage in the form of conduit or channel. If conduit or channel is used the wider and deeper chases are likely to weaken the wall without protecting the cables from drilling, plugging or driving nails.

To minimise the risk of damage the cables must be run vertically above and/or below the respective switch or other wiring accessory where any person fixing shelves or other structures will expect the cable to be situated.

Solid floors
Where the floor is solid and it is not possible to run cables beneath to socket outlets in those rooms, in some instances the cables can be run behind the skirting boards and behind door frame architraves where they cross doorways. A more satisfactory method is to enclose the cable in mini-trunking which is fixed to the walls on the tops of skirting boards and around door frames. Special boxes and elbow fittings are used with the trunking. Moulded skirting is also available which can be used to conceal a number of cables.

Lighting

The modern ceiling rose has three terminal banks arranged in-line plus an earth terminal.

One outer bank has three terminal screws, two for the neutral feed wires, the other for the blue flex wire. The other outer bank has two terminal screws, one for the circuit switch wire, the other for the brown flex wire. The centre bank has three terminal screws all of which are for live feed wires where the circuit is wired on the loop-in system. The sleeved earth conductors of the circuit are connected to the earth terminal.

A circular sheathed flex is connected to the ceiling rose. A plastic pendant lampholder is connected to the other end.

Fixing a ceiling rose
The ceiling rose has an integral backplate for fixing direct to a ceiling, either to a joist or to a piece of 100 × 25mm timber having a hole drilled into it for the circuit cables and fixed between two joists, using gauge 8 woodscrews.

Fixing other pendants
Pendants other than those with conventional ceiling roses, have open-back ceiling plates. The pendant flex has a multi-way cable connector for joining the flex wires to the circuit wires. These wires and the connectors have to be housed in an enclosure of non-combustible material comprising a circular box and the ceiling plate.

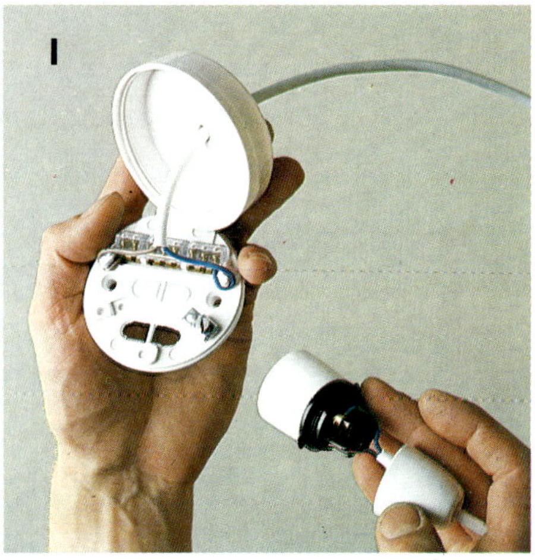

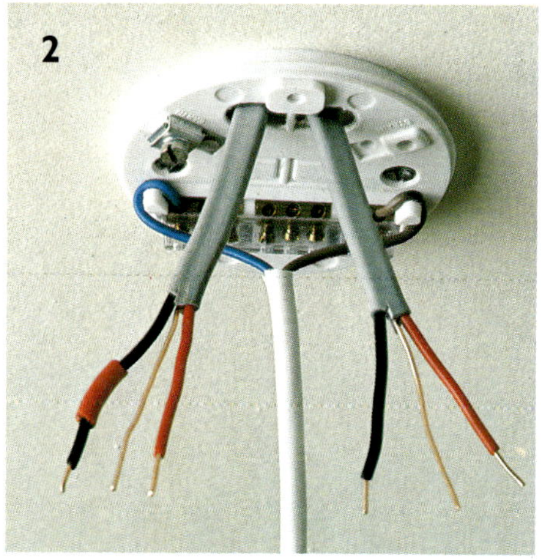

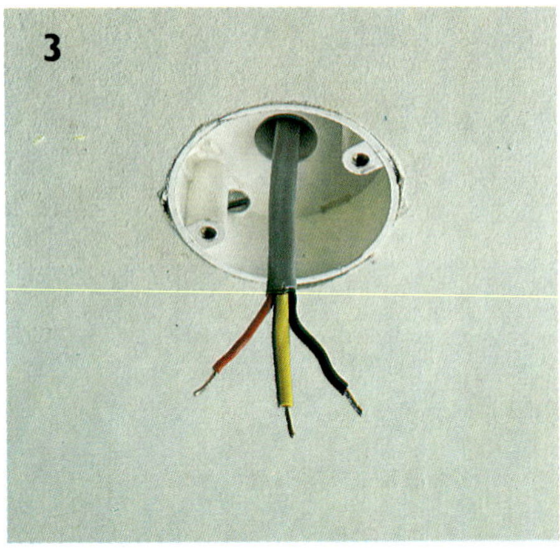

The box is of PVC, having a cable outlet and two screwed (M4 metric) lugs.

The box is sunk flush with the ceiling and fixed to timber fixed between two joists. The fitting ceiling plate is fixed to the box lugs using M4 metric screws.

Fixing close-mounted ceiling lights

This type of fitting, including fluorescent lighting fittings, usually contains a backplate for fixing direct to the ceiling either at one or more joists or to timber fixed between the joists.

The circuit cables are passed through a grommeted cable entry hole and connected to the wiring terminals. The live feed conductors of a loop-in system are connected to a cable connector housed in the fitting.

Fittings having no integral backplate and/or no live loop-in facilities require a BESA box fitted flush into the ceiling.

A batten lampholder is a close-mounted light fitting fixed to the ceiling or wall either on a pattress or over a BESA box. Loop-in types have an enclosed backplate.

Fixing wall lights

Wall lights, including single spotlights, have to be mounted on or over a metal or plastic box sunk flush into the wall. Wall lights having BESA backplates are fixed to BESA boxes. Those with other backplates are fitted over narrow boxes, termed architrave switch boxes.

Single spotlights can be fixed to surface mounted BESA boxes. Two or more spotlights are mounted on a lighting track. This track has a live end to which the circuit cable is fixed direct, no box being required. Lighting tracks also have the advantage that you can move the spots.

Batten lampholders in various versions may also be used as wall fittings.

Adding a light

Material required: A quantity of $1.0mm^2$ twin and earth PVC sheathed cable, a short piece of green/yellow PVC sleeving; one ceiling rose, flex and lampholder if a simple pendant. Otherwise, choose a suitable lighting fitting, e.g. pendant, close mounted ceiling fitting, wall light or spot light. Also required are: one rocker operated 1-gang 1-way plate switch and mounting box or alternatively a one-way 5A cord operated ceiling switch; cable clips, wood screws, wall plugs and where necessary a piece of fixing timber for the ceiling light and for a ceiling switch. A 15A four-terminal joint box will be required if the new light is wired using the joint box method, which it will be if it is a wall light.

Wiring the circuit

Locate the nearest loop-in ceiling rose containing live feed wires. Pierce a hole in the ceiling at the new light position or above the light if it is to be a wall light. From the loop-in ceiling rose run a length of the new cable to the new ceiling light. Pierce a hole in the ceiling above the switch position. From the new ceiling lighting point run a length of cable to the switch which means passing the cable through the hole in the ceiling and running it down the wall to the switch position. At the ceiling point knock out the thin section of plastic in the ceiling rose, thread in the cable and fix the rose. Connect the cables to the rose.

If the lighting fitting is of another type

Wiring ceiling-mounted light fittings

1. *Two-core circular sheathed flexible cord is connected to the ceiling rose and lampholder of a plain pendant.*
2. *Circuit cables protrude through the ceiling rose base which is fixed with woodscrews.*
3. *A BESA box is fixed flush with the ceiling for mounting the ceiling plate of heavy fittings.*
4. *A loop-in version of batten lampholder is fixed direct to the ceiling. This type is recommended for use in kitchens and bathrooms.*

1. *A BESA box being used for mounting a wall light. Circuit and flex wires are joined in a cable connector.*

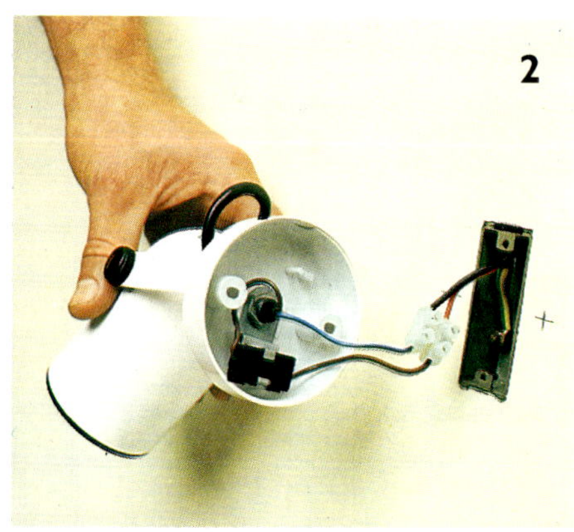

2. *Alternatively, screw the fitting to the wall over an architrave box.*

follow the instructions opposite.

At the switch position mark the fixing holes on the wall for a surface box or cut a chase for a flush box. Drill and plug the holes and fix the box. Thread in the cable and connect and fix the switch.

Turn off the main switch. Release the original ceiling rose from its fixings. Enlarge the knockout hole, thread in the new cable and refix the ceiling rose.

Prepare the end of the cable. Connect the red wire to the centre terminal bank. Connect the black wire to the terminal containing the black wires. Connect the sleeved earth wire to the earth terminal. Replace the ceiling rose cover and switch on the power. Where the new switch is a cord-operated ceiling switch fix this to a joist or a piece of timber fixed between the joists. Prepare the end of the cable and connect the wires to the respective terminals.

Where the new light is a wall light, run the new cable to a new joint box fixed between the joists. From the joint box run the cable down to the switch, and run a cable down to the wall light. Fix the wall light as described earlier.

Prepare the ends of the three cables at the joint box. Enclose the black wire of the cable running from the switch in red PVC sleeving and connect the wires to the joint box.

1

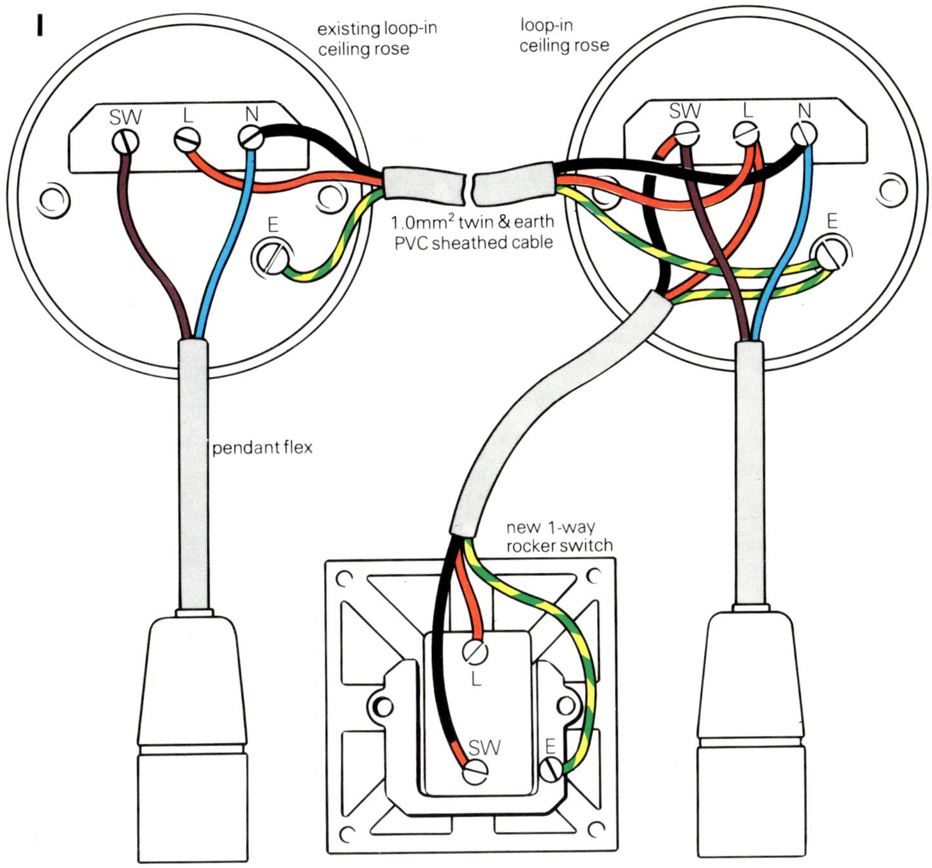

Switches

The modern rocker-operated 5A lighting switch is a square plateswitch containing 1, 2, or 3 switches on the one plate and has two screw holes for fixing to the lugs of a one-gang plastic shallow surface box or a metal plaster-depth flush box.

Each box contains an earth terminal to which is connected the sleeved earth conductor of the circuit cable. On the top edge and sometimes also on the bottom edge of a metal box is a PVC grommeted cable entry.

The traditional height for a lighting switch is 1.5m above floor level, but any other convenient height is satisfactory.

Installing a plateswitch

For surface mounting, hold the box in place against the wall and mark the positions of the fixing holes. Drill and plug the holes. Knock out a section of thin plastic on the top edge, thread in 100mm of cable and fix the box using gauge 8 wood screws. For flush mounting, cut a chase in the plaster so that when the box is inserted the front edge will be flush with the wall surface.

Prepare the end of the cable by stripping off the sheath, leaving about 12mm within the box. Slip green/yellow PVC sleeving over the bare earth wire and connect the wire to the box earth terminal.

Slip red PVC sleeving over the black

2

3

4

1. Wiring layout for feed and switch cables to new ceiling rose. Other cables – one or two feed cables, and switch cable – omitted for clarity.

2. New ceiling rose screwed to ceiling with feed and switch cables connected. Red sleeving identifies the switch return wire.

3. Existing loop-in ceiling rose with new feed wire pushed through from above prior to connecting.

4. 15-amp four-terminal joint box attached to batten between joists for ease of wiring.

5. Wiring connections at joint box.

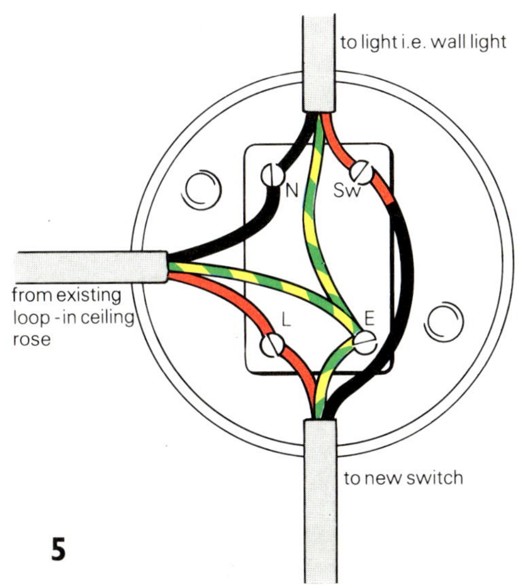

5

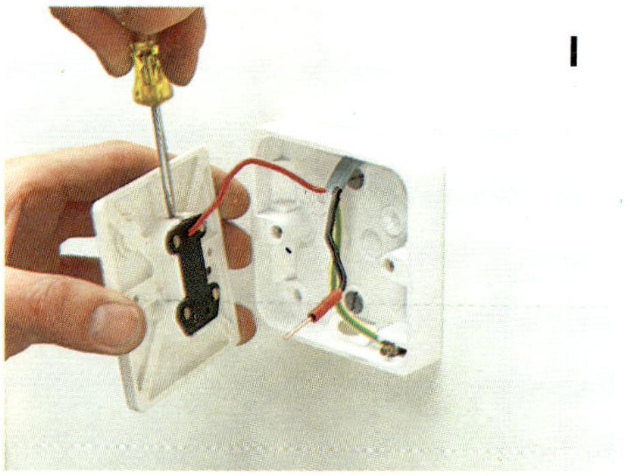

1. *Connecting the switch feed wire to one terminal of a 1-way switch.*
2. *Connecting the switch return wire to the other terminal. Red sleeving is slipped on to identify it as a live wire.*
3. *A 5-amp cord-operated ceiling switch with circuit wires connected to the switch terminals and green/yellow sleeved earth wire connected to the earth terminal on the pattress.*

switch wire. Connect the wires to the terminals and fix the switch using the two M3.5 metric screws supplied.

Cord-operated ceiling switch

A ceiling-mounted switch either has an integral backplate similar to that of a ceiling rose or it is mounted on a plastic pattress.

The ceiling switch or its pattress is fixed to a joist or to a piece of timber inserted between the joists. The ends of the cable are prepared as for a wall switch and the wires are connected to the respective terminals on the switch.

The connections for a two-way ceiling switch are the same as those for a plateswitch.

Installing a dimmer switch

A dimmer switch has the same number of terminals as the equivalent one-way or two-way rocker switch. It is a plateswitch and will usually fit the shallow switch mounting box. A few versions require a 25mm depth box. Fitting a dimmer switch therefore requires the same procedure as a rocker switch.

A dimmer switch can replace an existing rocker switch without modification to the wiring being necessary or a new box. A dimmer switch is unsuitable for controlling fluorescent lighting unless the fluorescent control gear is modified, a special dimmer is used and an extra wire run from the switch to the light.

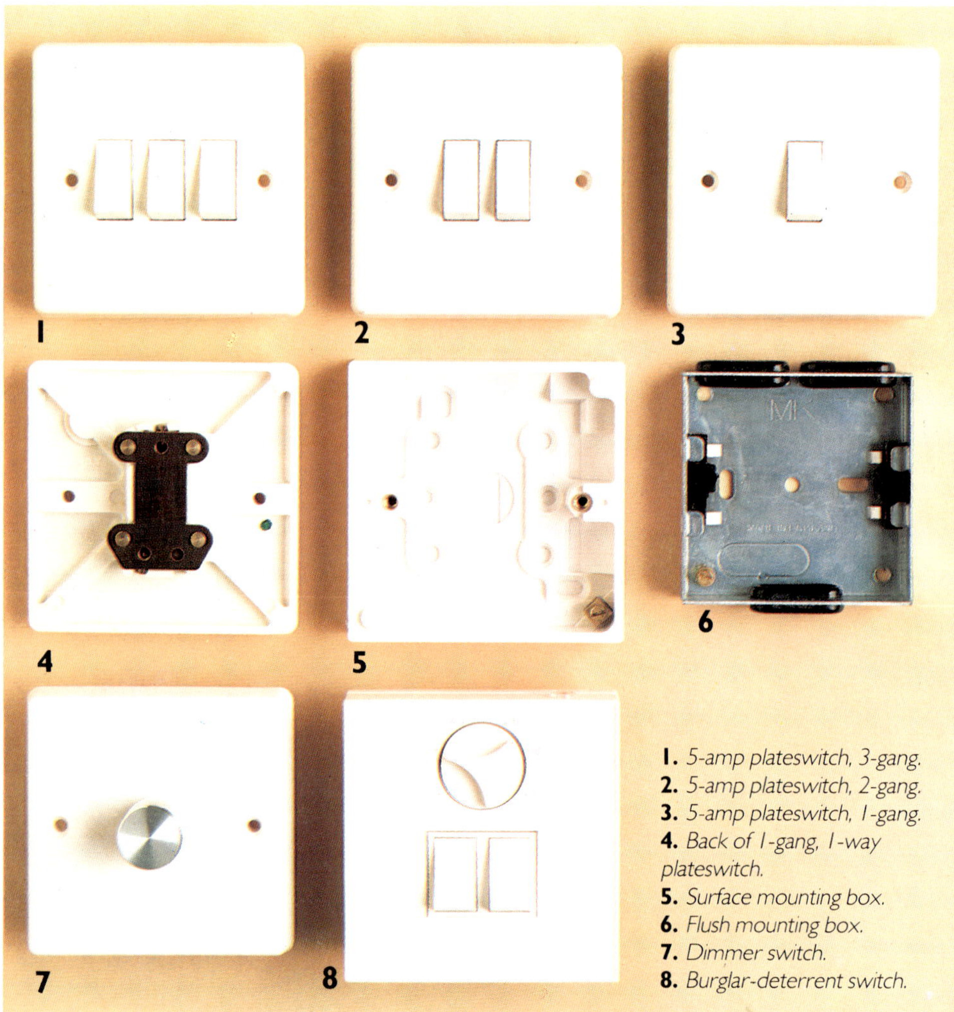

1. *5-amp plateswitch, 3-gang.*
2. *5-amp plateswitch, 2-gang.*
3. *5-amp plateswitch, 1-gang.*
4. *Back of 1-gang, 1-way plateswitch.*
5. *Surface mounting box.*
6. *Flush mounting box.*
7. *Dimmer switch.*
8. *Burglar-deterrent switch.*

Burglar deterrent switch

An electronic timing device in the form of a switch can be fitted in place of a rocker switch. The switch is solar operated and has an over-ride switch for use out of programmed hours.

Wiring a two-way switch

These materials are required: a quantity of $1.0mm^2$ three-core and earth PVC sheathed cable; earth wire sleeving; two two-way rocker switches plus a mounting box; or a one-way rocker switch plus a cord operated two-way switch; cable clips, wood screws and wall plugs.

Run the cable from the existing switch to the new switch position following the easiest route.

Turn off the main switch and remove the existing switch. Run the new cable into the existing box. Strip off the outer sheathing and about 9mm of insulation from the end of each of the three insulated wires. Slip PVC sleeving over the bare end of the earth conductor and connect it to the earth terminal in the box. Connect the yellow wire to the Common terminal of the two-way switch. Connect the red wire and the existing red wire to the L1 terminal; enclose the existing black wire in red PVC sleeving and connect this wire and the new blue wire to the L2 terminal. Fix the switch to the box using the original screws.

If the second switch is a wall switch fix the box to the wall, or if a flush box, fix it into a chase cut in the plaster. Insert the cable and prepare the end as at the first switch. Connect the red wire to the L1 terminal of the switch, connect the yellow wire to the Common terminal and connect the blue wire to the L2 terminal. Connect

1

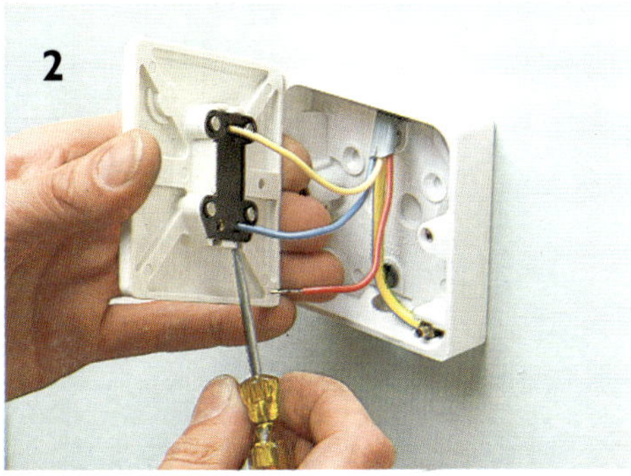

2

P 9

Fitting two-way switches

1. *Connecting first 2-way switch which replaces existing 1-way switch.*
2. *Connecting second 2-way switch to linking cable.*
3. *Connections at two-way switches with existing cable and linking cables.*

Note *A two-way switch has two live terminals (marked L1 and L2), a common terminal (marked c) and an earth terminal (marked E). Connect the three-core and earth cable as shown.*

3

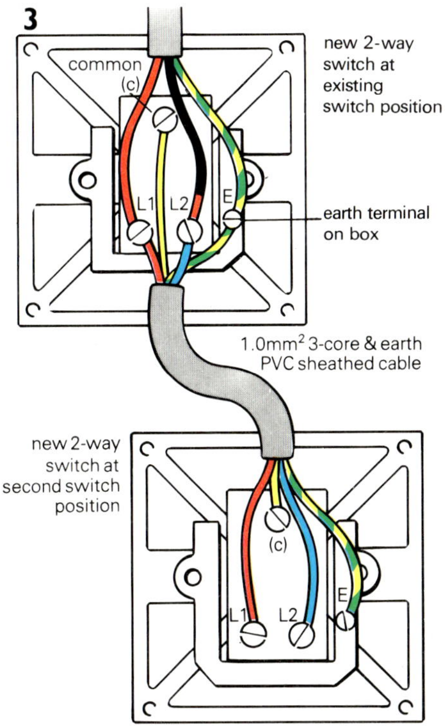

the earth wire to the box earth terminal.

If the second switch is of the cord operated type fix it to a joist or a piece of timber fixed between the joists. Connect the wires to the switch terminals as for a wall switch.

Fitting a door bell

Door chimes operate at a voltage of from 6 to 12 volts and bells require a voltage of 3 to 6 volts.

Many models of bells and chimes will accommodate batteries in the casing so making separate batteries unnecessary.

With the self-contained type it is necessary only to run a length of twin bell wire to the push fixed to the door post outside the front door or in any other position. The bell wire is fixed by enamelled tacks which are pushed through the wire between the conductors.

Bells and chime kits are available, the only necessary additions being the batteries or other power source. The alternative power source is a bell transformer which is connected to the mains and has an output of 3–5–8 volts from a three-terminal block. Some models of chimes require 12 volts for which a special transformer is available.

Another refinement is an illuminated bell push, some models of which contain a nameplate.

An illuminated push can be fitted only where the bell or chime is powered from a mains transformer for, if used with batteries, the batteries would last only a day or so.

An alternative to a bell is the buzzer which is especially useful for operation in conjunction with a bell from a second push as one can be distinguished from the other.

Mains transformer

The transformer must be one designed for the purpose, and it will then meet the requirements of the regulations. The transformer can be supplied from a 1.0mm² twin and earth PVC sheathed cable connected to the lighting circuit fuseway in the consumer unit and fixed next to the unit.

Fitting sockets

It is a fairly simple job to convert a single 13A socket outlet to a double.

Materials required: One 13A double socket outlet. One plastic two-gang surface mounting box. A short length of green/ yellow PVC sleeving.

Surface to surface conversion

Turn off the main switch. Release the existing single socket from its box and disconnect the six wires (two red, two black and two earth wires) from the socket terminals. Remove the box from the wall.

Knock out the section of thin plastic from the base of the new box. Thread in the cables and hold the box in position against the wall and mark the screw fixing holes. Drill and plug the holes for gauge 8 wood screws. Fix the box to the wall.

If the earth wires are not sleeved, slip a length of the green/yellow sleeving over the wires and connect them to the E terminal of the new socket outlet. Connect the red wires to the L terminal, and the black wires to the N terminal of the socket outlet. Fix the socket outlet to the box using the two screws supplied.

1

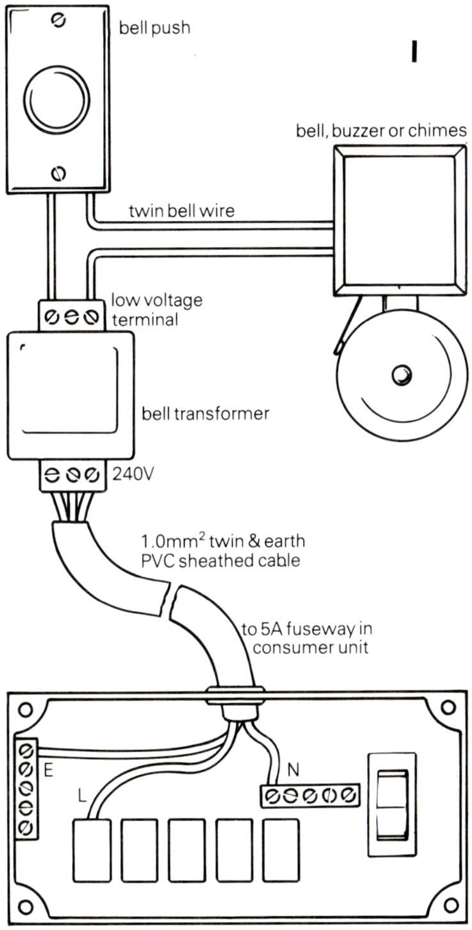

2

1. *Wiring layout for bell circuit and connection to consumer unit.*
2. *Mains transformer, bell and bell push.*

Wiring a socket on a spur

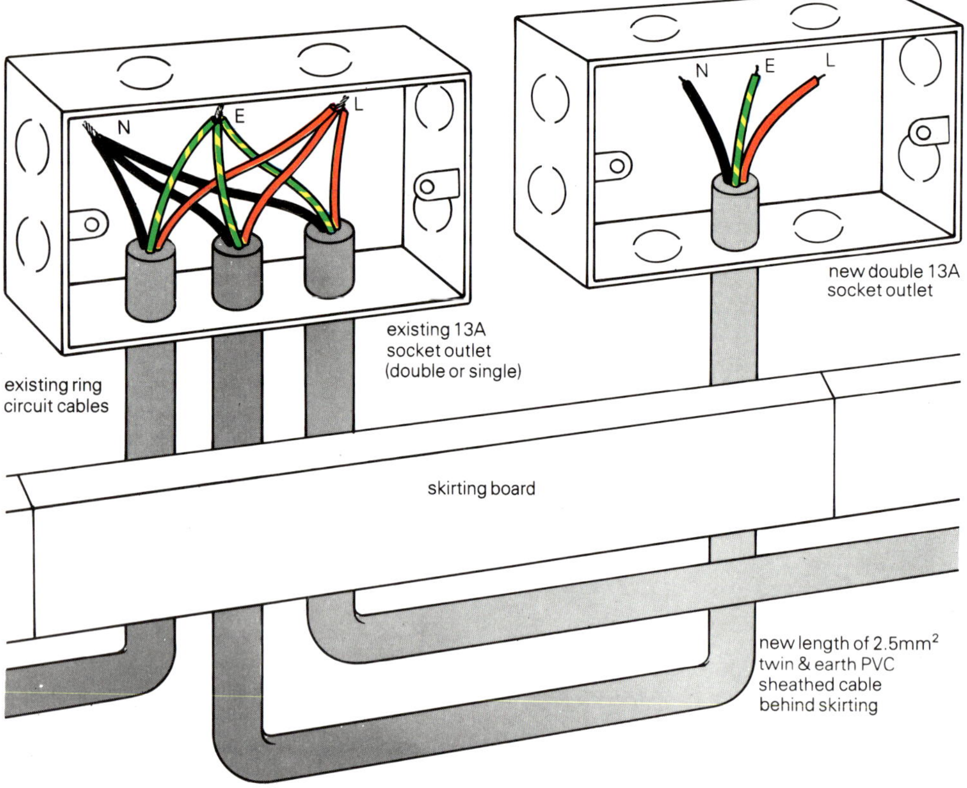

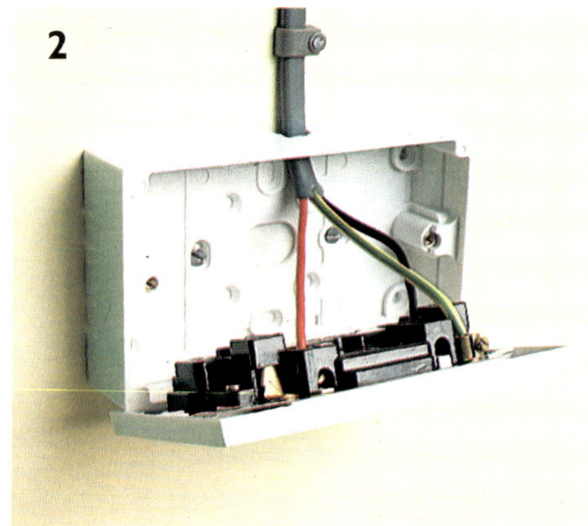

Flush to surface conversion
Remove the existing single-gang socket outlet from its flush box.

Knock out the section of thin plastic from the base of the new two-gang plastic box. Thread in the cables and fix the box to two of the screwed lugs of the metal flush box using the existing original screws removed with the single socket outlet. Connect the cables to the respective terminals of the new socket outlet after fitting sleeving to the earth wires if not already sleeved.

Fix the socket outlet to the box using the two screws supplied with the socket.

Identifying spur cables
A spur cable may only feed one double or one single socket outlet, so it is important to check that the single outlet you are converting is the only one on a spur. If it contains only one cable, examine the nearest socket outlet each side of it. One of these should have three cables and the other two or three (this may be feeding another spur). If

Surface-to-surface socket conversion

1. *Release the single socket from its surface box by removing the two fixing screws.*
2. *Knock out the appropriate areas of thin plastic for the cable and screws on the double box. Then thread the cable through the knockout, screw the box to the wall and attach the wires to their terminals on the double socket.*

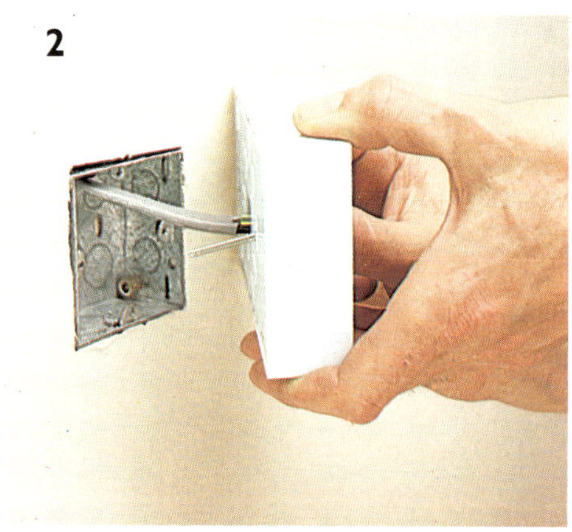

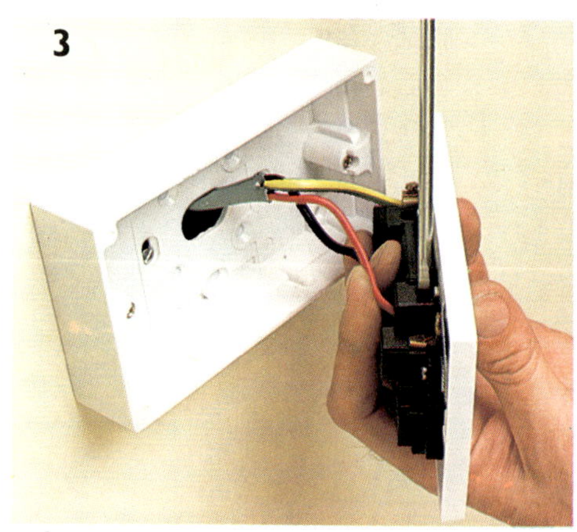

Flush-to-surface socket conversion

1. *Release the single socket from its flush position. Remove the wires from the terminals. Leave the metal flush box in position in the wall as shown.*

2. *Knock out the thin plastic in the back of the double moulded box and in the 51mm horizontally spaced screw holes. These holes should match exactly with the holes in the existing metal flush box. Attach the box to the lugs of the flush box with the original socket fixing screws.*

3. *Connect the double socket to the circuit wires and screw it onto the mounting box.*

neither has three cables, your chosen outlet is second on a spur and may not be converted. To check if a socket outlet having two cables is in a ring circuit, again examine the adjacent outlets. If one has three cables and the other has one, the outlet is the first of two on a spur, but if both adjacent outlets have two cables, it is part of a ring circuit and may be safely converted to a double.

Adding a socket

The simplest method of providing an additional 13A socket outlet is to supply it from a spur cable connected either to the terminals of an existing socket outlet on the ring circuit or to connect it to a 30A joint box in the ring cable. Both methods involve a minimum of disturbance to existing wiring.

Materials required: A quantity of 2.5mm² twin and earth PVC sheathed cable, green/yellow PVC sleeving, one double or single 13A socket outlet together with a surface or a flush mounting box; a PVC grommet for a flush box; a 30A three-terminal plastic joint box if the new cable is connected to the ring cable (not at a socket), cable clips, wood screws and wall plugs.

Turn off the main switch and release the nearest socket outlet from its box to check it has two cables. Raise a floorboard at this position and another near the new socket position and any other floorboards needed to be raised along the cable route. Ease out the plaster behind the skirting at the existing socket position and pass the cable up from the void and into the mounting box.

Prepare the end of the cable by stripping off the sheathing leaving about 12mm in the box. Connect the wires to the socket terminals: red alongside the existing red wires in the L terminal, the black wire alongside the existing black wires in the N terminal and the sleeved earth wire in the E terminal. Refix the socket to its box.

If the joint box method is used instead, insert the joint box, in the void, into one of the cables going up into the socket, having removed the section of sheathing. Connect these wires and the wires of the new cable to the three terminals in the 30A joint box.

Return to the new socket position and ease out the plaster behind the skirting board. Pass the end of the new cable up behind the skirting board. Knock out a section of thin plastic on the edge of the box if a surface type. If a flush box, knock out a blank on the bottom edge and fix a grommet in the hole.

Fix the box to the wall. If a flush box, first chop out a chase in the wall so that the front edge of the box is flush with the wall.

Thread in the end of the cable. Prepare the end of the cable by stripping off the sheathing in the box but leave about 12mm within the box. Strip about 9mm of insulation from the ends of the insulated wires and slip green/yellow PVC sleeving over the bare end of the earth wire.

Connect the red wire to the L terminal, the black wire to the N terminal and the sleeved earth wire to the E terminal. Fix the socket to the box using the two screws supplied with the socket.

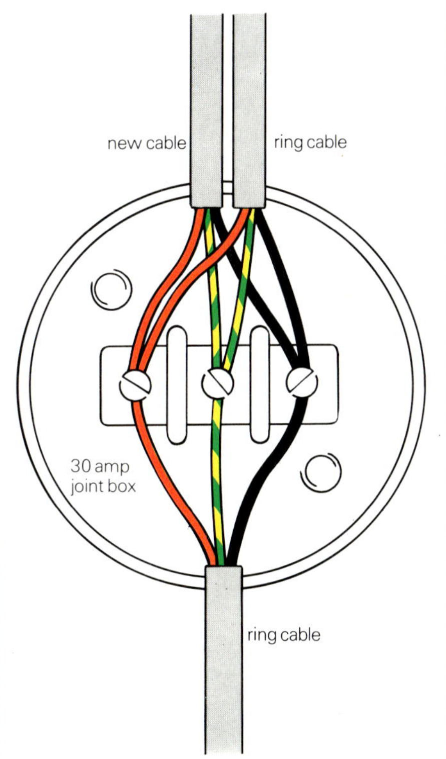

Wiring connections required at a three-terminal 30 amp joint box.

1

2

3

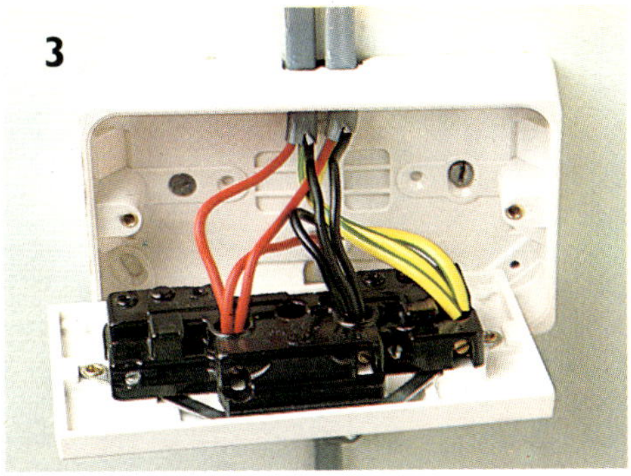

Adding a socket

1. *New socket mounting box on wall with cable fed through knockout.*
2. *Spur and ring cables at existing socket position.*
3. *Three wires connected side by side in existing socket terminals. Coil wires neatly in box before replacing socket plate.*

Installing appliances

Some appliances need to be wired direct into the domestic supply. These include items such as showers, immersion heaters and cookers.

Instant showers

A shower unit has an electrical loading of either 6kW or 7kW and therefore requires a circuit of 30A current rating, since the current demand is 25 or 29 amps respectively. The cable for this 30A circuit may be 4.0mm² provided it is supplied from either a cartridge circuit fuse or an MCB. Were the circuit fuse of the rewirable type, a 6.0mm² cable would be necessary since the current at which it would blow would be more than the current rating of 4.0mm² cable.

Materials required: A quantity of 4.0mm² (or 6.0mm²) twin and earth PVC sheathed cable; green/yellow PVC sleeving; one 30A double-pole cord-operated ceiling switch; one 30A main switch and fuse unit preferably fitted with an MCB or a cartridge fuse; two 1 metre-long 6.0mm² single core PVC insulated and sheathed cables, one red, the other black for connecting to the main switch and fuse unit; about 2m of 6.0mm² green/yellow PVC insulated cable.

Install the main switch and fuse unit next to the existing consumer unit and connect the mains leads and earth conductor to the mains and earth terminals respectively.

Run the twin and earth PVC sheathed cable to a point above the bathroom ceiling and pass the end through a hole pierced in the ceiling at the position of the switch. Run another length of the cable from the switch position to the shower unit. Connect and fix the ceiling switch in a position normally inaccessible to a person using the shower. Connect the cable to the shower unit.

At the mains end connect the circuit cable to the load or output terminals of the main switch and fuse unit. Fix all cables in position and get the electricity board to connect the mains leads to the meter.

Cookers

An electric cooker of 12kW or under can be supplied from a 30A circuit, for although this loading is equivalent to 50 amps the regulations take account of the diversity of use of the boiling rings and oven and a kettle plugged into the control unit when assessing the current demand on the circuit. A cooker in excess of 12kW requires a 45A circuit.

Materials required: A quantity of twin and earth PVC sheathed cable (6.0mm² for a 30A circuit; 10mm² for a 45A circuit); one cooker control unit with auxiliary 13A socket outlet, or a 50A double-pole cooker switch if an auxiliary socket outlet is not required; mounting box for the above; one cable outlet unit and box if a free-standing cooker; cable clips, wood screws and wall plugs. One main switch and fuse unit.

Decide the position for the cooker control unit which should be about 300mm to one side of the cooker and traditionally about 1.5m above floor level. Knock out two cable entry hole blanks from the mounting box and fit PVC grommets if a metal box. Fix the box to the wall or if a flush type fix it into a chase cut into the wall. Similarly, fix the box of the cable outlet unit about 500mm above floor level.

Install the main switch and fuse unit next to the consumer unit and connect the pair of tails and earth conductor to the unit. See page 59. From this, run the circuit cable to the cooker control unit following the most satisfactory route. From the cooker control unit, run a length of the same cable down to the cable outlet unit box. Prepare the ends of the cables. Connect the two cables in the control unit box to the respective terminals in the control unit and fix the unit to its box.

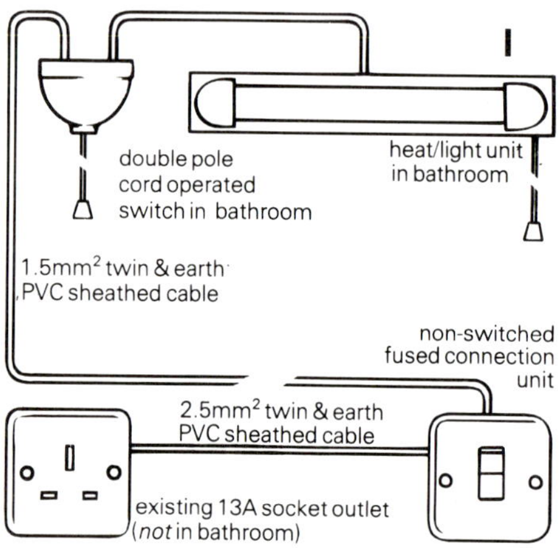

1. *Fused connection unit wired from ring main supplies heat/light unit via 30 amp DP ceiling switch.*
2. *Switched fused connection unit supplies oil-filled radiator.*

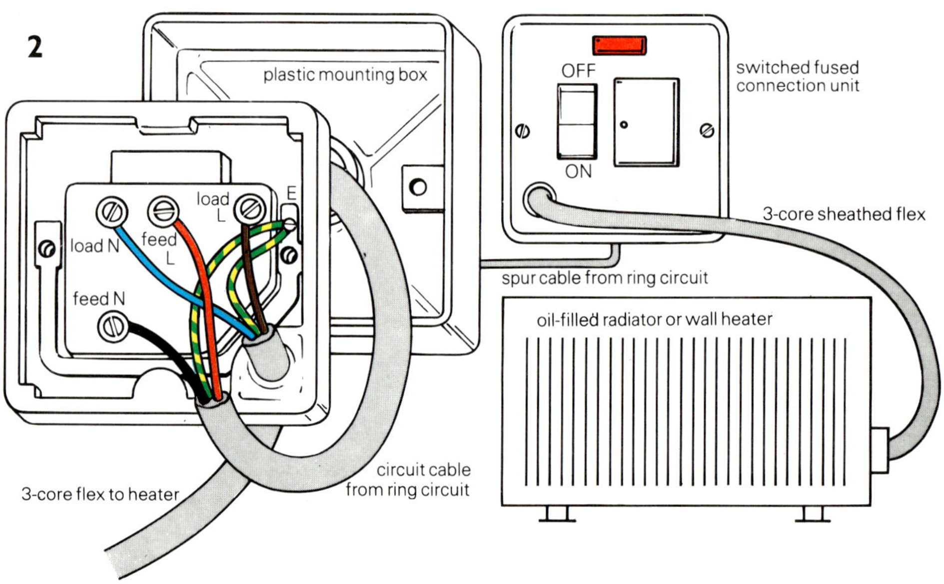

30 amp double pole cord-operated ceiling switch with cover removed, and wiring connections.

Wiring a shower unit

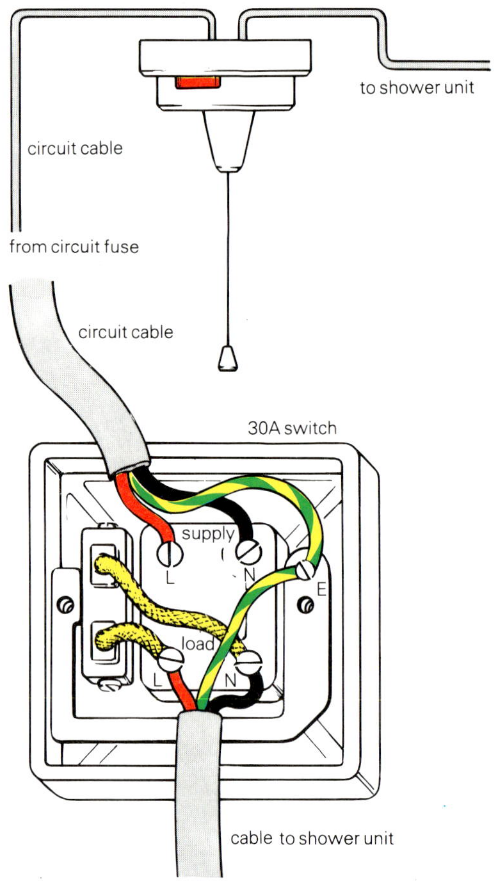

Connect the cable outlet unit to the cable running down from the control unit. If the cooker is in position, also connect the cooker trailing cable to the cable outlet unit. Fix the unit to its box. Connect the other end of the circuit cable to the main switch and fuse unit.

Wall heaters

A fixed appliance such as a wall heater, panel heater, towel rail, heat/light unit or shaver unit can be supplied from a ring circuit spur where the loading of the individual appliance does not exceed 3120 watts (13 amps). No socket outlets are permitted in bathrooms.

The basic materials required are: a quantity of 2.5mm² twin and earth PVC sheathed cable; green/yellow PVC sleeving; one 13A fused connection unit and a mounting box; as well as cable clips, wood screws and wall plugs.

The spur cable is connected to the ring circuit at a socket outlet or at a 30A joint box inserted into the ring cable. For wall heaters, towel rails and similar fixed appliances including a high level radiant heater in the bathroom, the spur cable terminates in a switched fused connection unit fixed near the appliance (as long as it cannot be reached from the bath) and connected to it by the appliance flex. In a small bathroom where a fused connection could be reached from the bath, the ap-

1. *Cooker cable outlet unit.*
2. *Flush cooker control unit.*
3. *Flush cooker control unit with extra socket.*
4. *Surface-mounted cooker control unit with extra socket.*
5. *Deep flush mounting box.*
6. *Wiring for free-standing cooker.*
7. *Wiring for separate oven and hob.*

pliance must be wired as for a heat/light unit.

A heat/light unit requires a separate isolating switch which, in a bathroom, must be a double pole cord-operated switch. For this circuit, fix a non-switched fused connection unit next to the socket outlet to which it is connected and from the unit run 1.5mm² twin and earth PVC sheathed cable to the ceiling switch. From the switch run a length of the cable to the heat/light unit.

A spur cable feeding a shaver supply unit in the bathroom is run direct into the unit, no fused connection unit being necessary. The cable must be 2.5mm².

Alternatively, the shaver unit can be supplied from the lighting circuit as should shaver sockets not of the bathroom type, and extractor fans.

Built-in split-level cooker

The one cooker control unit may serve both sections of a split-level cooker provided each is within 2m of the control unit. Otherwise, two units are required, these being linked together. The circuit cable and control unit is exactly as for a free-standing cooker but two cables are run from the control unit, one to each section of the cooker, and connected direct to the terminals of the section.

All cables connecting a cooker and cooker sections must be of the same size as the circuit cable, unlike other appliances which may be connected with flex.

Immersion heaters

An immersion heater installed in a hot-water storage cylinder has a loading of 3kW (maximum) and requires a 15 or 20A circuit. There are two principal types of top-entry immersion heater. One has a single element which extends to about 75mm from the base of the cylinder. The other type has two elements: a long one of the same length as a single-element heater, the other one about 300mm long.

Both types are supplied from a single circuit and both require a double-pole 20A isolating switch fixed in close proximity to the heater. The two-element immersion heater also requires a changeover switch. This switch, together with the isolating switch, forms a dual switch assembly on the one mounting box.

Other materials required are: a quantity of 2.5mm² twin and earth PVC sheathed cable; green/yellow PVC sleeving; a length

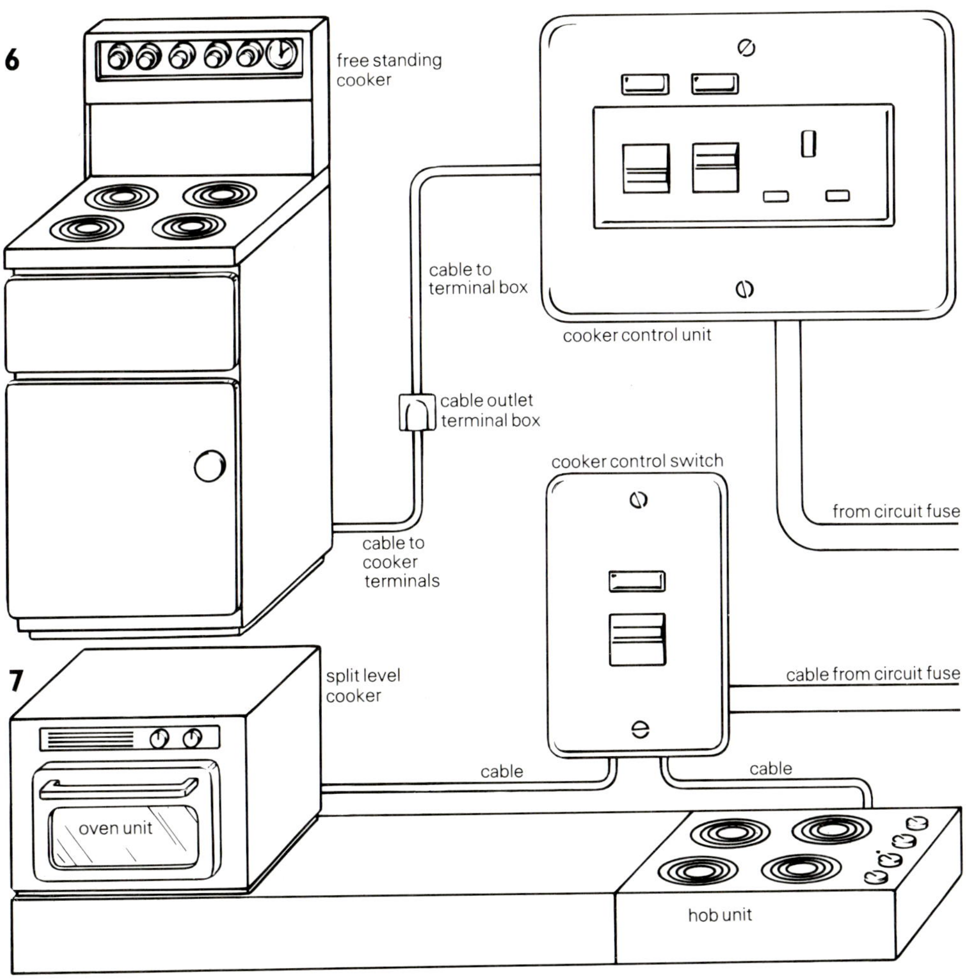

of 1.5mm^2 three-core heat resisting flexible cord for connecting the immersion heater to the isolating switch (two lengths for a two-element heater), cable clips, wood screws and wall plugs.

If there is no spare fuseway in the consumer unit it is necessary to install a main switch and fuse unit. This must be fitted with a fuse or MCB of 15A rating.

Before you start, check there is a boss provided in the cylinder to take an immersion element. Turn off the water supply to the cylinder and then drain it. If the boss is at the top you need only drain a few pints. Remove the blanking cap and screw in the immersion heater.

Run the circuit cable from the fuseway in the consumer unit, or from the switch and fuse unit if there is no spare fuseway, to the position of the isolating switch following the most convenient route for the cable and avoiding hot pipes.

Fix the mounting box of the isolating switch unit to the wall in the airing cupboard as close as possible to the immersion heater terminal head.

Connect the red and the black wires of the circuit cable to the mains L and N terminals respectively of the isolating switch, and the brown and blue wires of the heat-resisting flex to the corresponding load terminals of the switch. Connect the earth conductors to the earth terminal of the box. For a two-element immersion heater, the L load terminal of the isolating switch is connected to the common terminal of the changeover switch using a short length of 2.5mm^2 red PVC insulated cable. The brown wire of one flexible cord is connected to the L1 terminal of the changeover switch, the brown wire of the other flex is connected to the L2 terminal. The two blue flex wires are connected to the load N terminal of the isolating switch and all earth wires are connected to the E terminal in the box.

At the immersion heater, the brown wires are connected to the L terminals respectively, the two blue wires to the N terminal and the earth wires to the E terminal.

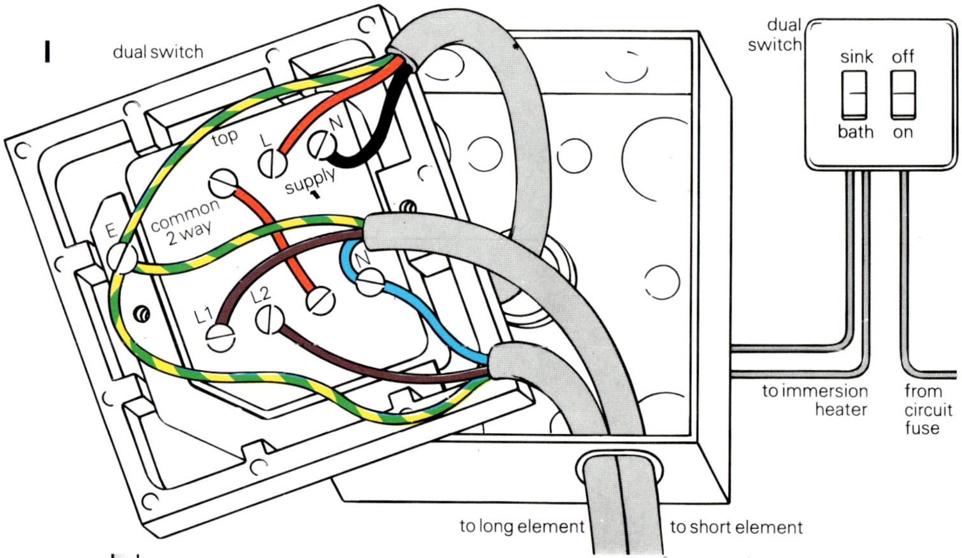

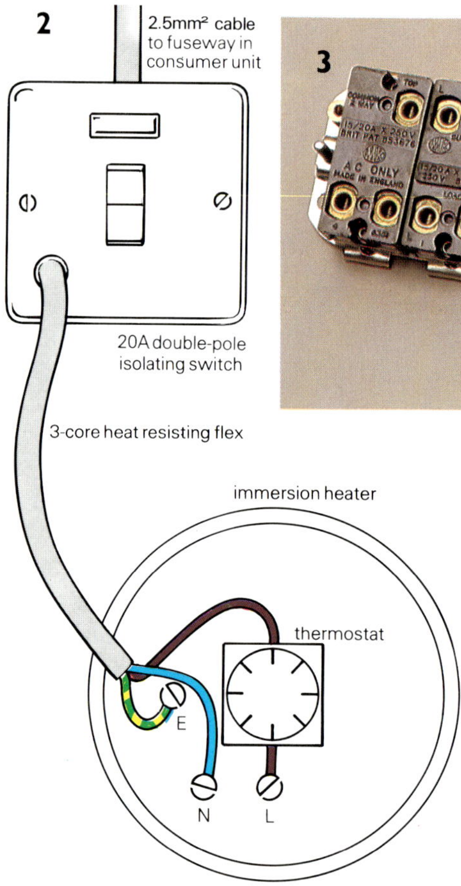

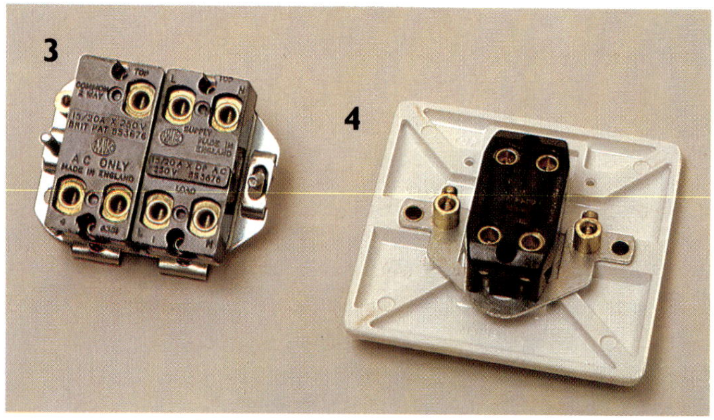

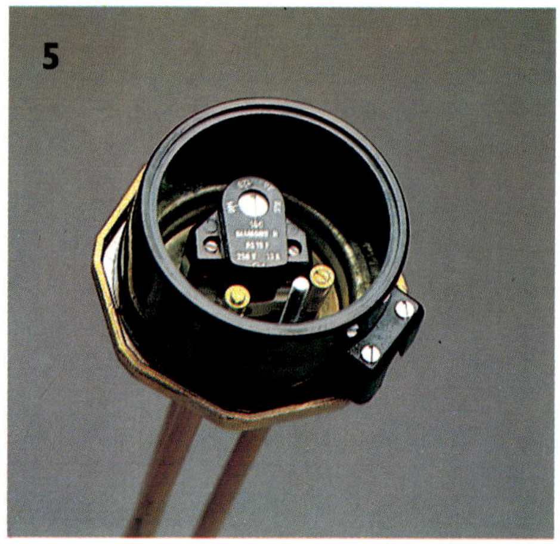

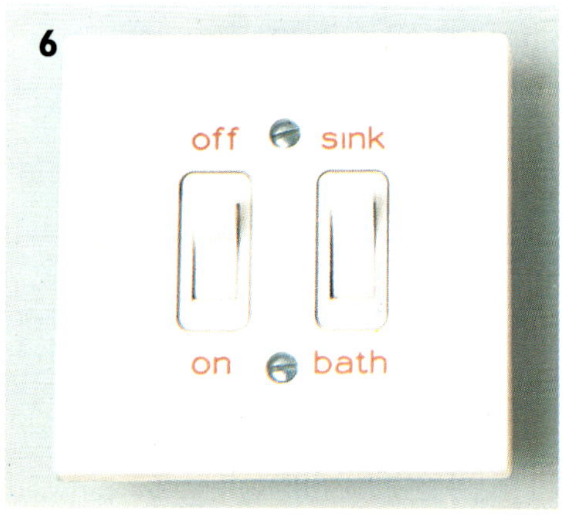

1. *Wiring connections at dual switch for two-element immersion heater.*
2. *Wiring connections to single-element immersion heater.*
3 & 4. *Rear view of dual and single immersion heater switches.*
5. *Head of immersion heater showing thermostat and terminals.*
6. *Dual switch for two-element immersion heater.*

Fuses

There are two types of circuit fuses, rewirable fuses containing ordinary fuse wire, and cartridge fuses.

The cartridge fuse is a small ceramic tube with a metal cap at each end. It contains a silver fuse element connected by a wire to each end cap. The cartridge is tightly packed with quartz granules (sand). These fuses are most commonly used in plugs.

Most consumer units are fitted with rewirable fuses, but the cartridge fuse is the superior of the two. Its advantages are that the fuses of various current rating have different physical dimensions (except the 15A and 20A which are of identical size) which prevents, say, a 5A cartridge being replaced by one of higher current rating,

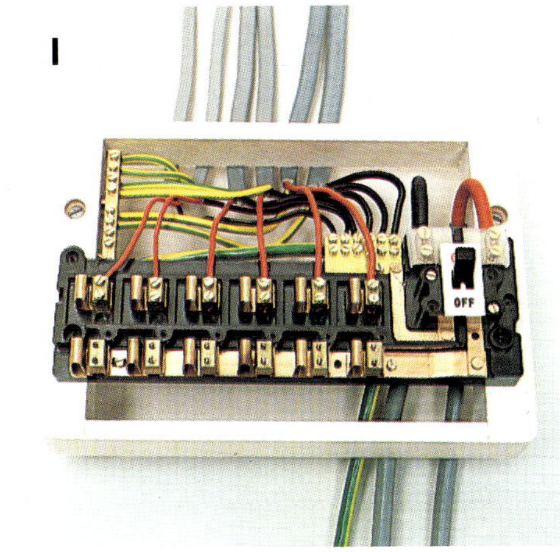

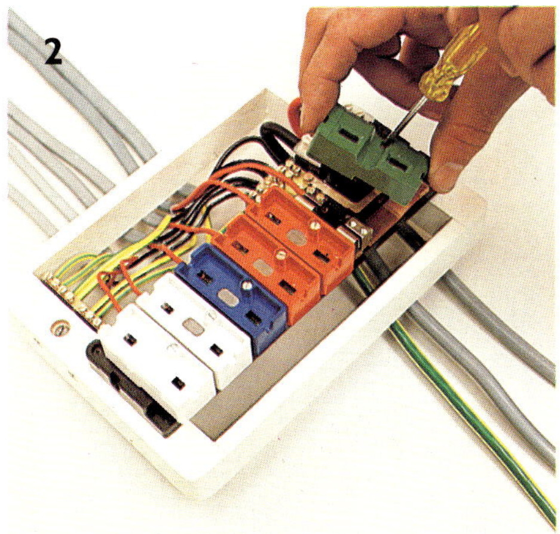

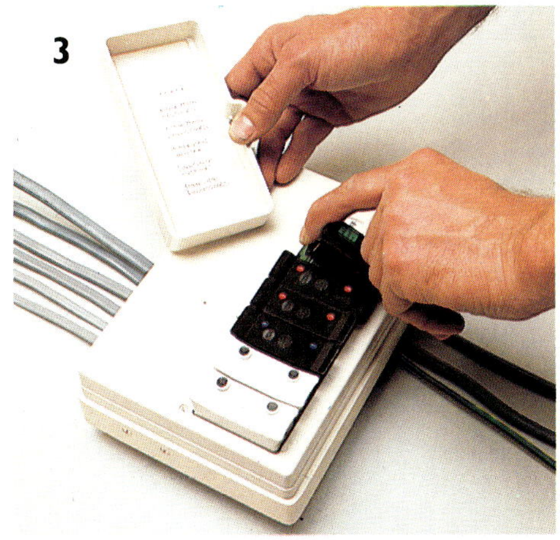

1. *Consumer unit fixed to wall by wood screws. Red live wires connected to respective fuseway terminals, black neutral and sleeved earth wires to their terminal blocks, and meter tails to switch terminals.*
2. *Fitting bases of fuse units over live contacts.*
3. *Fitting fuse carriers.*

and a cartridge fuse requires less current to melt the fuse element.

A rewirable fuse on the other hand can be fitted with a heavier fuse wire than its rated capacity and endanger the circuit cable and apparatus which may start a fire.

A rewirable fuse requires a current of twice its rating to blow whereas a cartridge fuse requires a current of only 1½ its rating to blow.

MCBs

A miniature circuit breaker is superior to circuit fuses and requires a current of only 1¼ its rating to operate. Also, when it trips the current the circuit is restored simply by switching on the MCB once any fault has been rectified.

Earth leakage circuit breaker (ELCB)

An ELCB is a safety device which trips if, through a fault in wiring or in an appliance, there is a slight leakage of electricity to earth, and isolates the circuit or circuits connected through it. It is required in modern houses that one socket is protected by an ELCB, to supply power tools used outdoors. An ELCB may also be present in other houses where earthing facilities are inadequate. There are various types and models of ELCB, and you should seek professional advice as to which suits your particular requirements. For individual appliances they can be incorporated in plugs, socket outlets or plug-in units; to protect whole circuits an ELCB may replace the main isolator switch in the consumer unit or be fitted as a separate unit next to the consumer unit.

Mending fuses

To mend a rewirable fuse, replace the blown fuse wire with a new piece of the correct current rating. When a cartridge fuse blows remove the blown cartridge and fit a new cartridge. Should a fuse blow again immediately after it is renewed or an MCB trips and the fault is not obvious, call in an electrician.

Fitting a switchfuse unit

A main switch and fuse unit (switchfuse unit) is really a one-way consumer unit comprising a double-pole isolating switch and a single-pole fuse which can be of a current rating of from 5A to 45A, of the rewirable or the cartridge type or it can have a miniature circuit breaker of the switch or push-button type.

The unit is installed to supply any circuit from a new lighting circuit to a cooker circuit or for an electricity supply to an outbuilding. Where more than one additional circuit is likely to be installed it is wise to fit a multi-way consumer unit instead of a switchfuse unit.

Where a number of night storage heaters are to be installed, each needs a separate circuit making a multi-way consumer unit necessary. Such a consumer unit is time controlled by a time switch usually fitted by the electricity board to limit the supply to the overnight off-peak hours when electricity is cheaper.

To install the switchfuse unit, fix the switchfuse unit (or multi-way consumer unit where there is to be more than one additional circuit) near the existing consumer unit and the electricity board's meter. To the mains terminal of the unit connect a pair of single-core PVC insulated and sheathed cables, one red, the other black. The red cable is connected to the L terminal, the black to the N terminal. A 6mm² green/yellow PVC insulated cable is connected to the E terminal of the unit.

The cables are left for the electricity board to connect to the mains. The size of cables depends on the load and on the board's requirements.

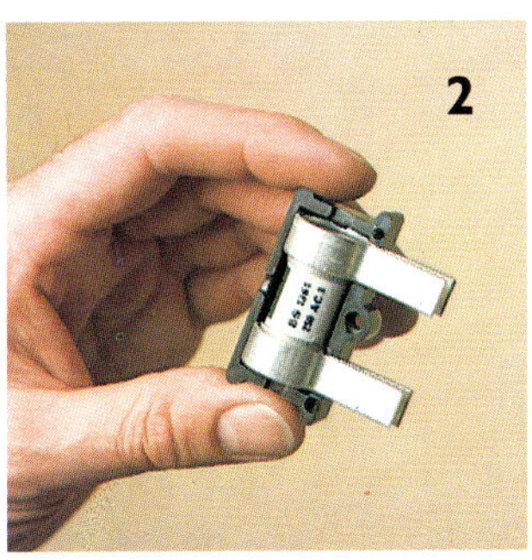

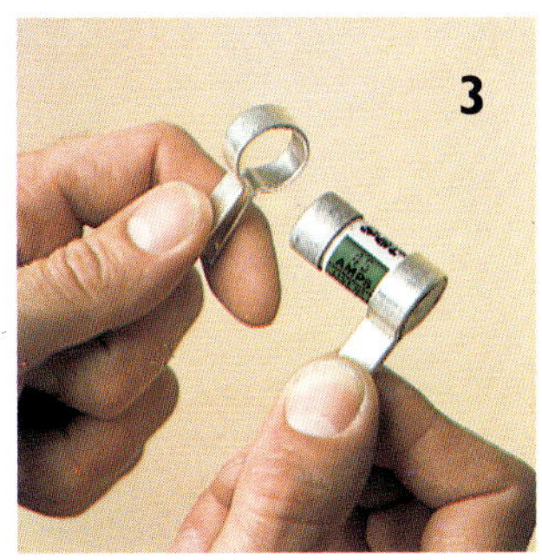

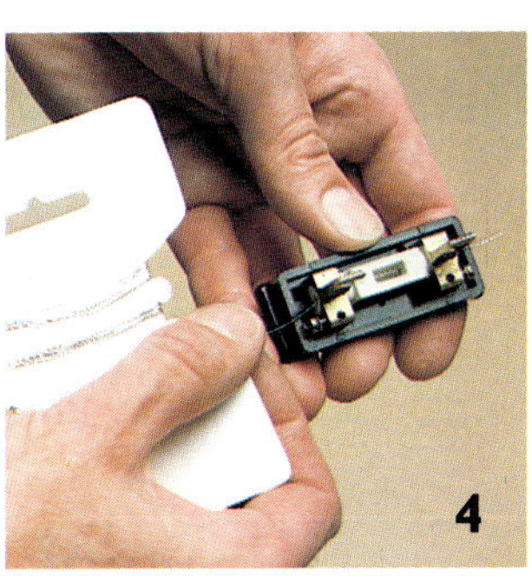

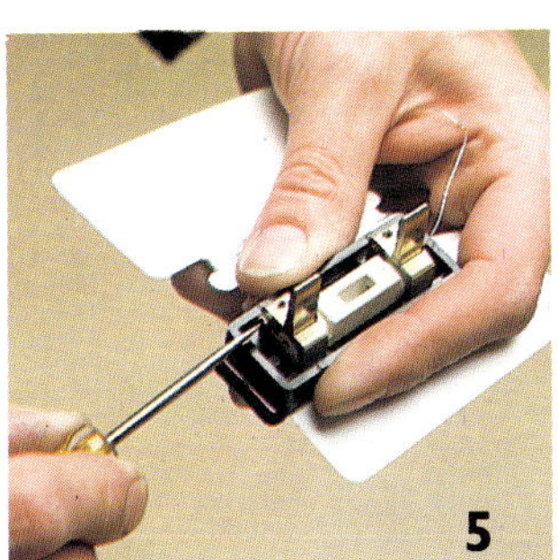

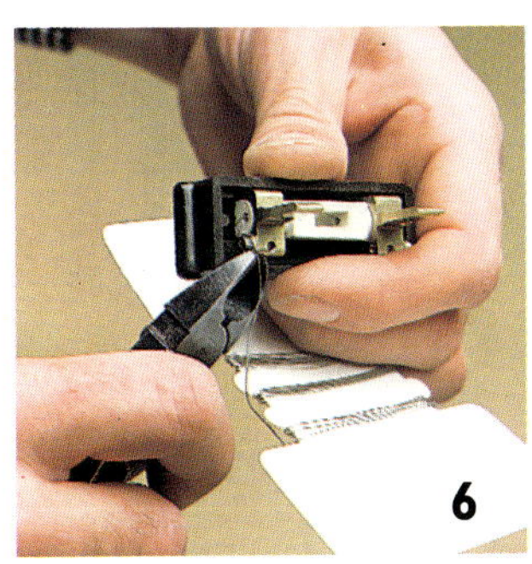

1. *Circuit fuses and miniature circuit breaker.*
2 & 3. *Fitting new circuit cartridge fuse.*
4, 5 & 6. *Mending rewirable circuit fuse.*

Outside supply

An electricity supply to a detached garage, outdoor workshop or greenhouse requires a separate circuit of 20A or 30A current rating. The circuit can be from a fuseway in the existing consumer unit with a double-pole 30A switch fixed near the consumer unit. If there is no spare fuseway it is necessary to install a main switch and fuse unit. This can be fitted with either a cartridge fuse or an MCB.

The cable running to the outbuilding can be twin and earth PVC sheathed (2.5mm^2 for a 20A supply, 4.0mm^2 for a 30A supply). The outdoor section of the cable can be run overhead fixed at a height of at least 3.5m above ground level, or it can be buried underground where it must be enclosed in high impact, rigid plastic conduit buried at least 500mm below ground level.

Overhead method

In addition to the cable, materials required are: a length of galvanised steel catenary wire (preferably stranded), a length of 2.5mm^2 green/yellow PVC insulated earth cable and a cable connector; a length of 100 × 50mm timber for fixing to the outbuilding to provide the fixing height for the overhead cable fixed to the catenary wire; two eye bolts or vine eyes and an adjuster; a main switch and fuse unit to be fixed in the outbuilding in addition to the one in the house.

Installing the cable

Run the cable out of the house through a hole drilled in the wall at the specified height. Fix one eye bolt and the adjuster to the house wall, the other to the timber at the outbuilding. Splice the catenary wire between the eye bolts and tension it, and attach the PVC sheathed cable to the catenary using cable ties. Join the earth wire to the catenary at the outbuilding end using the cable connector. Fix the PVC sheathed cable and the earth cable to the upright timber and pass the ends into the outbuilding through a hole drilled in the wall and connect the red and black wires to the L and N mains terminals of the switch and fuse unit fixed near the door.

Underground method

Dig the trench to the required depth and place a 50mm layer of builders' sand in the bottom of the trench. Install the 25mm conduit in the trench using wide bends at the corners and pass it through a hole drilled into the house wall above the damp proof course and at the other end into the outbuilding.

Dismantle the conduit and thread in the cable. Smear adhesive bought with the conduit over the ends before fitting the elbows and coat the joints with bituminous paint.

Fill in the trench, removing any sharp stones or flints. Connect up the cable as described above. In the outbuilding, socket outlets and a fused connection unit for the fixed lighting can be supplied from a radial circuit. See page 45.

1

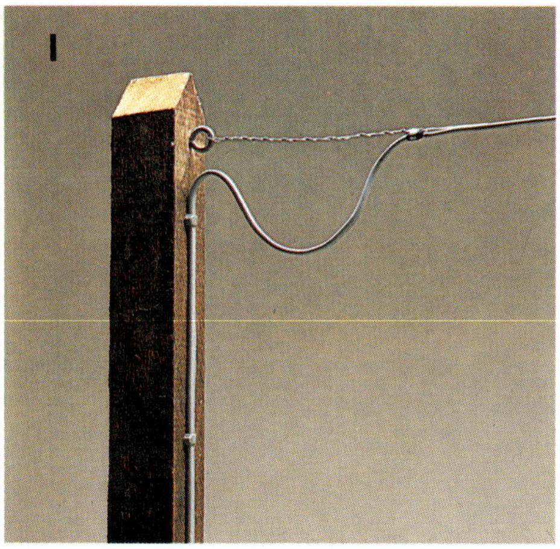

1. *Twin and earth PVC sheathed cable secured by cable ties to galvanised steel catenary wire. Loop keeps water drips away from walls.*

2. *Wiring layout for underground and overhead outside cables via 30 amp DP switch near consumer unit.*

2

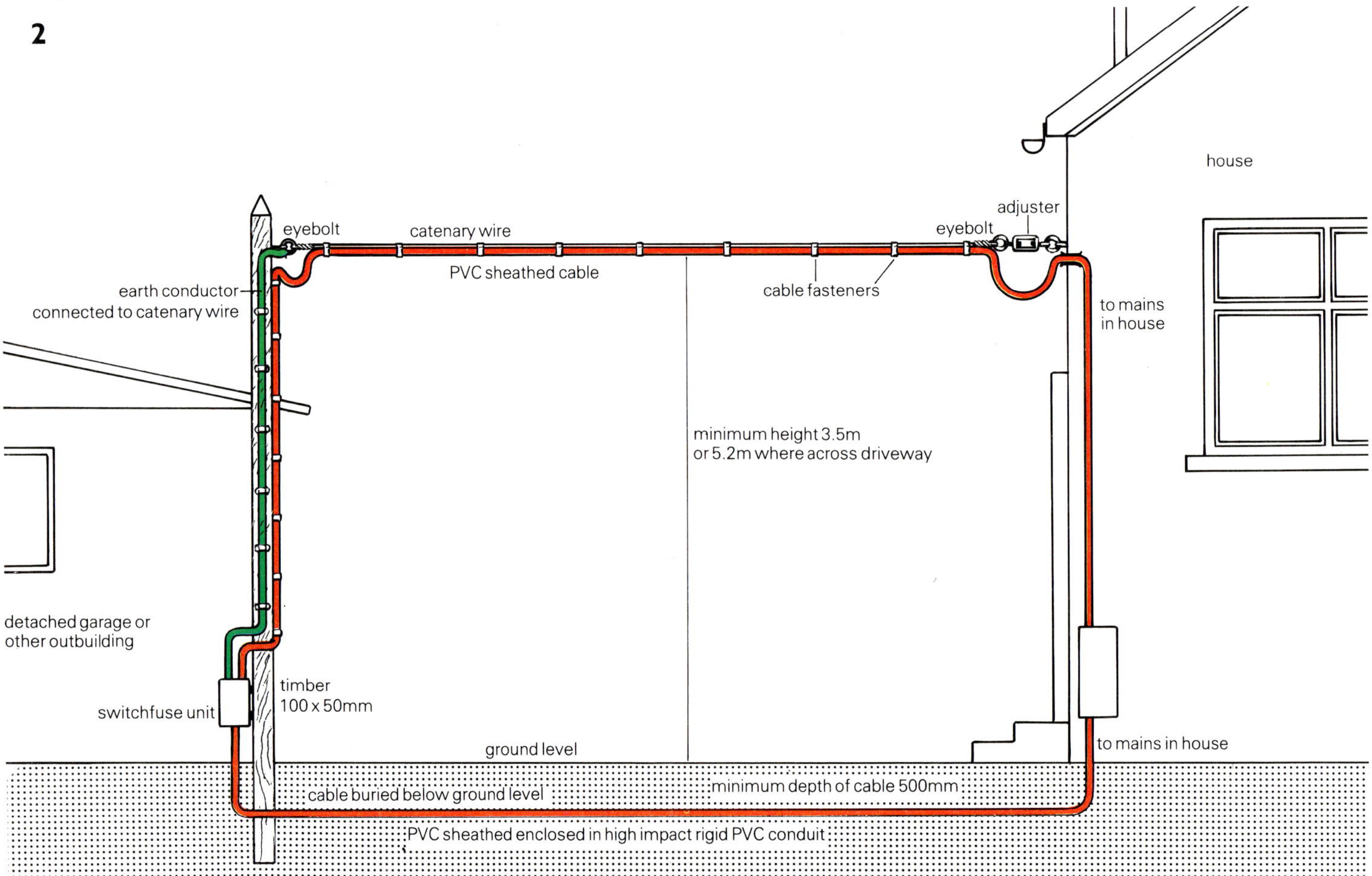

PLUMBING

Traditionally, plumbing has been one of those jobs which has always been left to the tradesman – a carry-over from the days of lead pipe. Nowadays, lead is obsolete and science has come to our aid in the shape of easy-to-make joints in copper and plastic pipe plus ready-packaged components complete with excellent instructions on their use.

With a little knowledge about how your supplies reach the taps and how other pipes dispose of waste water, you can plan and alter existing installations to suit yourself. This section will put you on the road to understanding how your house plumbing system works. It will also show you the basic techniques required to cut and join the various types of pipe and to put in fittings such as baths and basins.

The basic system

Be sure you understand the layout and operation of your household hot and cold water services and drainage system before attempting alterations or improvements to bathroom or kitchen plumbing.

Cold water services

Your responsibility for the water supply to your home begins at the water authority's stop-cock. This will be found at the bottom of a guard-pipe with a hinged metal cover, probably near to the front boundary of your property. From this point the service pipe travels underground to the house, usually rising into the home through the kitchen floor – often under the sink. Once above ground, this service pipe is usually referred to as the rising main.

Another stop-cock should be fitted into the rising main a few inches above the kitchen floor. Closing this stop-cock is the first step that must be taken if a pipe bursts, a cistern overflows or in virtually any plumbing emergency. It will usually be necessary to turn it off before carrying out plumbing improvements. Make sure that you know where it is and how to turn it off.

In some, usually older, houses every tap and the lavatory flushing cistern are supplied with water direct from the rising main. In most modern houses, though, only the cold tap over the kitchen sink – and perhaps a branch to an outside tap or a washing machine – is connected directly to the rising main. Other taps and the lavatory flushing cistern are supplied with water from a main cold water storage cistern, usually situated in the roof space. Water flows into this cistern from the rising main via a ball valve or float valve.

Hot water services

The main cold water storage cistern, which should have a capacity of 227 litres (50gal) also supplies the hot water storage cylinder with water under constant low pressure. Water in this cylinder may be heated solely by means of an electric immersion heater, solely by means of a boiler or – quite often – by means of a boiler during the winter and an immersion heater during the summer.

Note that a vent pipe rises from the dome of the cylinder and terminates open-ended over the cold water storage cistern. The distribution pipe taking hot water to the kitchen and bathroom is taken as a branch from this vent pipe *above the level of the hot water cylinder*. So the cylinder cannot be drained from the hot taps.

In normal use this is an important safety factor. To enable the cylinder to be drained when required, a drain-cock is provided near the boiler or, if the cylinder is heated by an immersion heater only, at the base of the cold pipe supplying the cylinder.

Never attempt to drain the cylinder from either of these drain-cocks without switching off the electric immersion heater and letting out the boiler fire.

This kind of system, in which water is heated solely by an immersion heater or in which water in the cylinder circulates directly through a boiler, is called a direct hot water system.

If your home has a central heating system heated by the same boiler that is used for hot water supply, you will have an indirect system. Even if you haven't a central heating system at present, an indirect system may have been installed if you live in a hard water area or if it was thought that central heating might be provided at some time in the future.

With an indirect hot water system, the water stored in the cylinder does not circulate through the boiler. It is heated indirectly by a closed coil or heat exchanger through which water heated in the boiler passes.

This closed coil or heat exchanger and the circulating pipes that connect it to the boiler are called the primary circuit. It is to the primary circuit that any central heating system must be connected.

The primary circuit of a conventional indirect hot water system is supplied with water from a small feed and expansion tank, usually sited near to the main cold water storage cistern in the roof space. A vent pipe from the primary circuit also terminates open-ended over this tank.

There are, it must be added, patent self-priming indirect cylinders that do not need a separate feed and expansion tank. They have a specially designed inner cylinder which serves as a heat exchanger. When the system is first filled with water from the main cold water storage cistern, water flows through this inner cylinder into the primary circuit. It is prevented from returning to the outer part of the cylinder by a giant air bubble or air lock that forms in the inner cylinder. A conventional indirect system gives a more positive separation of water in

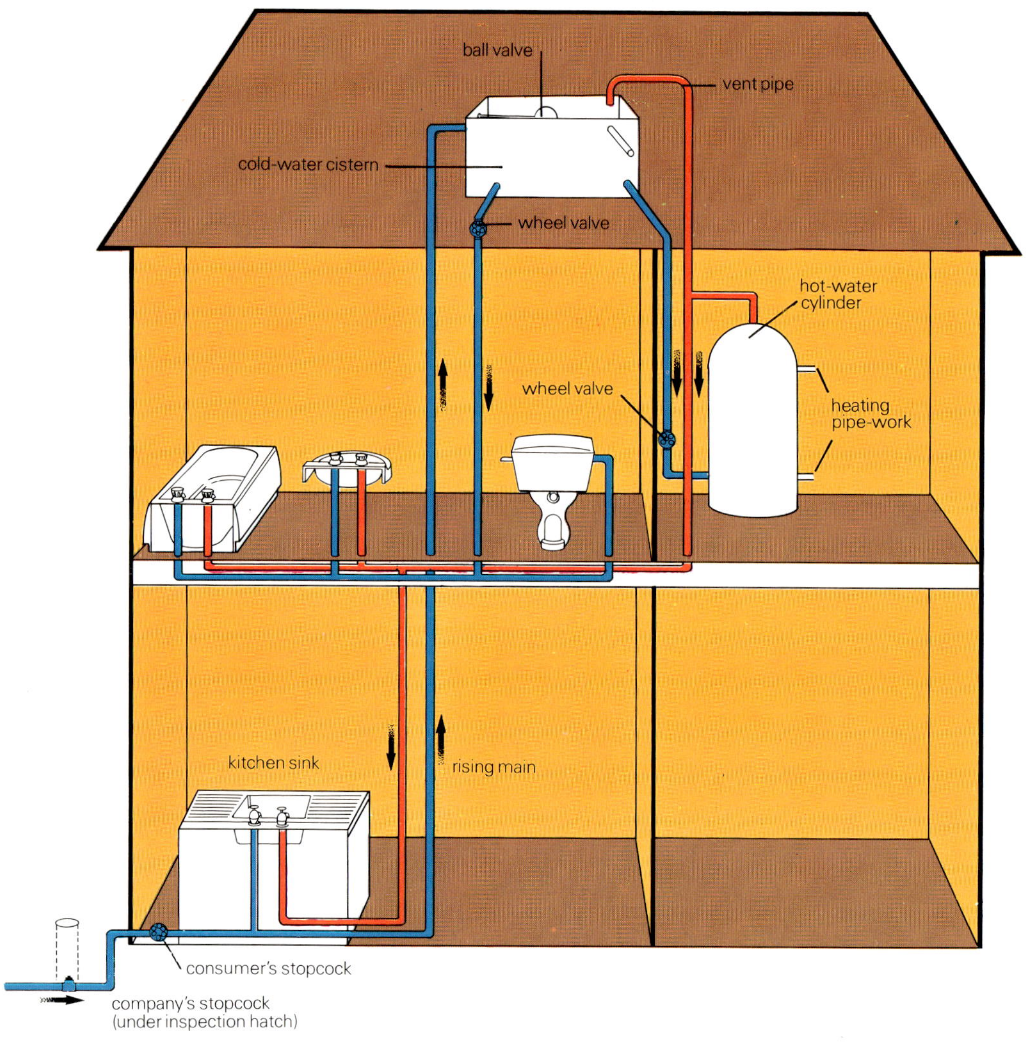

In a modern home only the cold water tap over the kitchen sink (the household's source of water for drinking and cooking) is connected directly to the rising main. All other cold taps, the lavatory flushing cistern and the hot water storage cylinder are supplied from a main cold water storage cistern in the roof space. Bathroom and kitchen hot water taps are supplied by a distribution pipe taken from the vent pipe above the hot water cylinder.

the primary circuit and the domestic hot water. It therefore affords a more certain protection from internal corrosion.

Some householders, investigating their hot and cold water systems, will find that they have a packaged plumbing system or a two-in-one unit. These are often used where a large house is converted into two or more flats or where an older home is modernised.

A packaged plumbing system is, quite simply, a cylinder hot water system in which the cold water storage cistern and the hot water cylinder are brought into close proximity to form one compact unit. Packaged plumbing systems may have direct, indirect or self-priming indirect cylinders.

Above-ground drainage

Houses where the plumbing was installed prior to the 1960s are likely to have a two-pipe above-ground drainage system. In such a system a rigid distinction is made between soil fittings such as lavatories and waste fittings such as baths, basins, bidets and sinks. The outlet pipes of soil fittings are connected direct to the main soil and vent pipe but the outlets of waste fittings discharge over a yard gully and are not allowed to connect directly to the drain. Where upper floor wastes are concerned this usually meant that the branch waste pipes discharged over a rainwater hopper-head and were then conveyed down to a yard gully through a length of rainwater down pipe.

In a single-stack drainage system all wastes discharge into one main soil and waste stack often made of UPVC or other plastic and usually contained within the fabric of the building.

The success of a single-stack drainage system depends upon very careful plumbing design. The Building Regulations require that you should always notify the district or borough council's building control officers before making any addition to a drainage system. This is particularly important – not only to comply with the law but also to safeguard your family's health – where an addition is to be made to a single-stack drainage system.

Working with pipes

The ability to join lengths of pipe to each other and to other plumbing fittings is a basic skill that must be acquired by every amateur plumber. Light gauge copper and stainless steel tubing is commonly used in hot and cold water supply. The easiest way to join pipes of these materials is with non-manipulative (type A) compression joints and fittings.

The basic compression coupling – for joining two lengths of pipe of the same diameter – consists of a joint body with, at each end, a brass or copper ring or olive and a screw-on cap-nut. When a tube end is thrust into the joint and the cap-nut tightened, the olive is compressed against the tube wall to make a watertight connection. As well as straightforward couplings there is a very wide range of other compression joints and fittings to meet virtually every plumbing need.

There are T junctions (usually referred to simply as tees) for use in taking a branch water supply pipe from an existing pipeline. There is a variety of bends, crosses and couplings with a compression joint at one end and a threaded joint (either male or female) at the other for connecting to screwed fittings, to cold water storage cisterns or to hot water cylinders. There are straight and bent tap and ball-valve connectors. These have a compression joint at one end and a 'cap and lining' joint at the other. Then there are plumbing fittings such as stop-cocks and gate valves that are manufactured with compression joint inlets and outlets.

All of these joints and fittings – and many others – can be seen at any good DIY centre and in the pages of the manufacturers' illustrated catalogues.

The only essential tools required to make compression joints are a hacksaw, a metal file and a couple of reliable wrenches but, where a project will necessitate making a number of joints, a wheel tube cutter can be a great time saver. You should also have a tin of jointing compound such as 'Boss White' and some vaseline or oil. A piece of chalk will be useful too in helping you make your first joints effectively.

How to make a simple coupling

First cut the tube ends squarely either with a hacksaw or a wheel tube cutter. A useful tip to ensure a square cut with a hacksaw is to join the edges of a piece of newspaper together around the pipe at the point where the cut is to be made and to use the paper as a template.

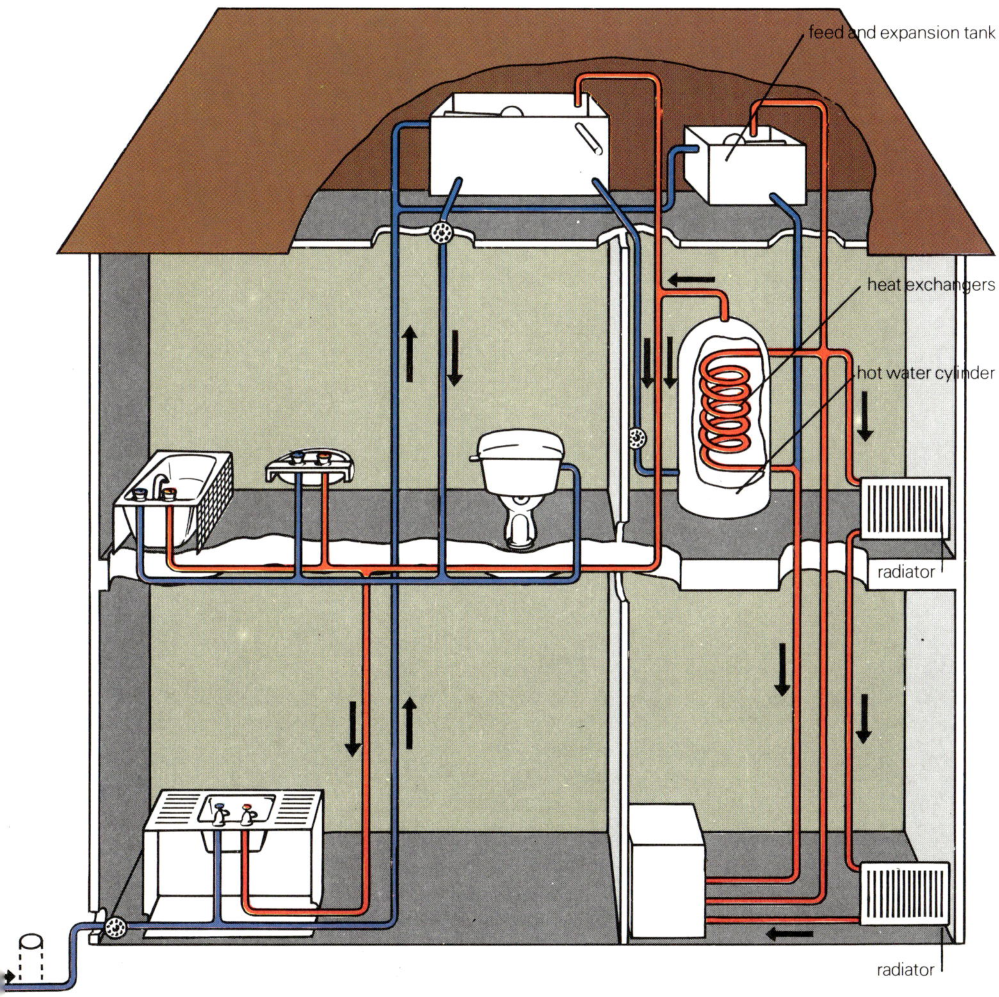

Where the same boiler provides central heating as well as hot water supply an indirect hot water system should be installed. With a system of this kind the domestic hot water is heated indirectly by a heat exchanger within the cylinder through which water, heated in the boiler, passes. In the primary and radiator circuits the same water is used over and over again, only the very small losses from evaporation being made up from the feed and expansion tank.

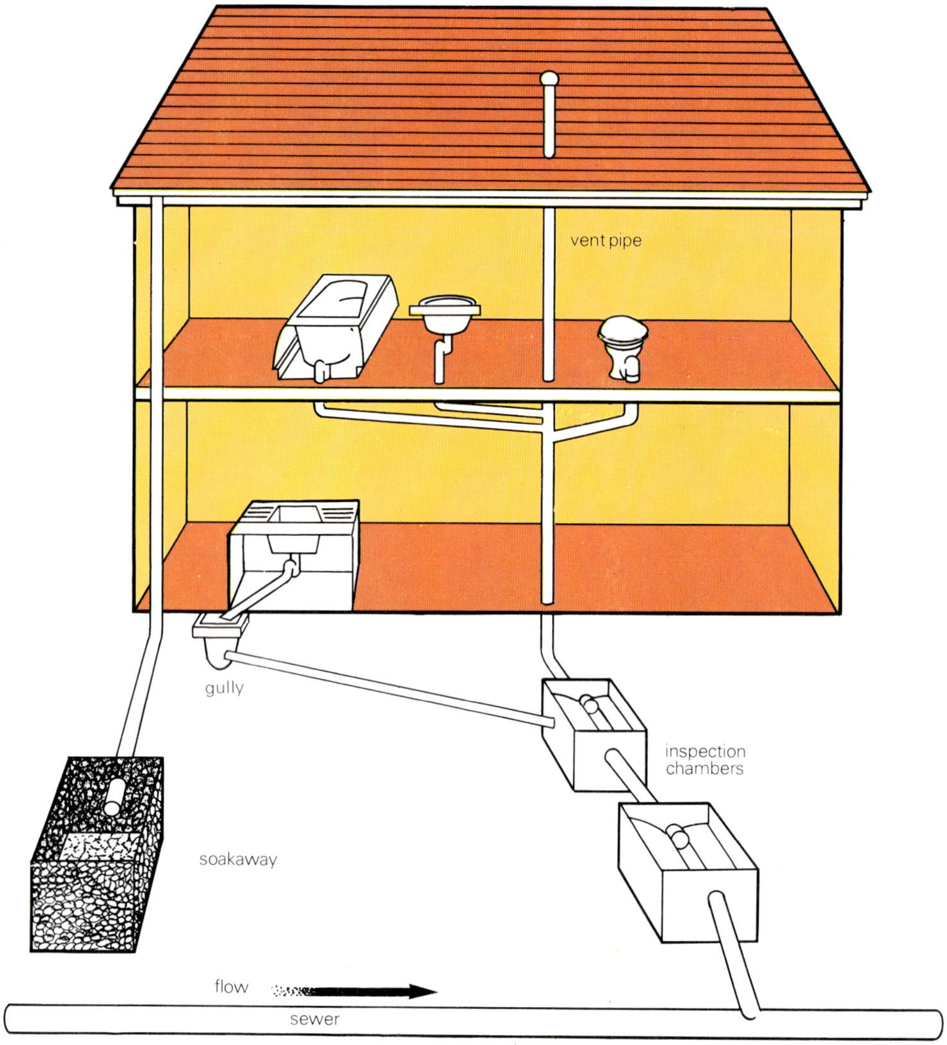

Modern homes usually have single-stack drainage systems. All wastes discharge into a single main soil and waste stack. This is usually made of plastic and is constructed within the fabric of the building, only a few inches of open vent pipe protruding from the roof. Even where this system is installed it is quite usual – as the illustration shows – for ground floor sinks, baths or basins to discharge over a yard gully.

Remove all burrs. Wheel cutters usually produce internal burr which can be removed with the reamer incorporated in the tool. A hacksaw produces external burr that must be removed with a file.

Dismantle the compression coupling and slip first the cap-nut and then the olive over the tube end. Make sure that you don't turn the olive round as you slip it on the pipe end. With some makes it doesn't matter but with others it is most important that the olive should be the right way round in the completed joint.

Push the tube end into the body of the fitting until the tube stop permits it to go no further. Smear some jointing compound on the olive and apply a little oil or vaseline to the screw threads of the joint body. It must be said that some manufacturers of compression fittings insist that no jointing compound is necessary when making their joints. However, it can do no harm and does ensure a watertight joint at first attempt.

Push the olive up to the joint body and screw on the cap-nut hand tight. Mark the tube end with a piece of chalk and make another mark on the cap-nut immediately adjacent to it. Hold the body of the coupling firmly with one wrench and – using the chalk marks as guide – grip the cap-nut firmly with the other wrench and tighten it by one and a quarter complete turns. Repeat the process with the other length of pipe in the other end of the coupling and the joint is made. Do not overtighten.

Once you have gained a little experience you'll find that you can take one or two short cuts when making compression joints. It won't be necessary to dismantle the couplings completely or to make the joint at each end of the coupling separately. Loosen the two cap-nuts. Thrust the two pipe ends through the olives into the body of the coupling. Then, after tightening up the cap-nuts hand tight, use one wrench on one and one on the other to tighten them both up at the same time. You'll find too that, after you have successfully made two or three joints, you'll be able to tighten by those one and a quarter turns without needing the chalk guide.

Inserting a tee junction into a vertical length of pipe – to take a branch to an outside tap or a washing machine for instance – can be difficult at times. Follow these instructions and you'll find that it is quite easy.

Cut off the water supply and drain the pipe. Cut a 19mm (3/4in) segment out of the pipe at the point at which the tee is to be inserted. Even though you have drained the pipe properly it is likely that a pint or so of water will flow out as you cut the pipe. Don't be alarmed but do be prepared to catch it!

Dismantle the cap-nuts and olives from the straight run of the tee. Slip a cap-nut and then an olive up the upper length of cut pipe. They'll promptly slide off again unless you secure them. Use a spring clothes

Copper or stainless steel tube can be cut with a hacksaw. A vice helps to ensure a square cut.

peg for this. Slip the other cap-nut and olive over the end of the lower length of cut pipe. Use another spring clothes peg to prevent them slipping down.

Spring the two cut ends of pipe into the body of the tee and screw up the cap-nuts as already described to make the joint. Make sure, before you finally tighten up, that the branch outlet of the tee is pointing in the right direction – towards the position of the garden tap or washing machine.

Stainless steel tubing

Stainless steel tubing is obtained in the same sizes as copper tubing and is joined by type A compression joints in exactly the same way. When cutting stainless steel tubing it is better to use a hacksaw than a tube cutter and, since stainless steel is harder than copper, you'll find that a little more force is needed to tighten up the cap-nuts effectively.

Most manufacturers make a range of chromium plated brass fittings for use with stainless steel tube and one manufacturer makes fittings of stainless steel for this.

Pipe sizes and metrication

Prior to metrication, the sizes of copper and stainless steel tube encountered in British domestic plumbing were ½in, ¾in and 1in. These were measurements of the internal diameter of the pipes. The ½in pipe was commonly used for the rising main and for branch hot or cold water supplies to sinks, basins and bidets, and for the branch supply to the lavatory flushing cistern. The main hot and cold supply pipes to the ¾in bath taps would be in ¾in pipe. This size was also used for the vent pipe from the hot water storage cylinder and – usually – for the cold supply pipe from the cold water cistern to the cylinder. A 1in diameter pipe was used for the flow and return pipes

1. *A wheel tube cutter provides an easy way of cutting copper tubing and ensures a square cut. The hand control – see right hand in illustration – is tightened and the cutter rotated around the pipe. It is best not to use a wheel tube cutter with stainless steel tubing as it work hardens the end and may make it liable to split.*

2. *Where copper tube is cut with a tube cutter there will be rough burr inside the tube end. This must be removed with a reamer before making a joint. Many tube cutters incorporate a reamer for this purpose.*

3. *Where copper or stainless steel tube is cut with a hacksaw the rough burr will be found on the outside of the pipe end. This can be removed with a metal file as illustrated. Should the pipe not have been cut absolutely square, the file can also be used to square off the end.*

between boiler and cylinder. Occasionally, too, the cold supply pipe from storage cistern to cylinder would be in the larger 1in diameter pipe.

The metric equivalents of ½in, ¾in and 1in tube are 15mm, 22mm and 28mm respectively and all compression joints are now sold in these metric sizes. They are not – as a glance at any rule with both metric and imperial measurements will confirm – exact translations of the imperial sizes. However, most of the difference is accounted for by the fact that the imperial dimensions were of the internal diameter while the metric measurements are of the external diameter of the pipes.

Fortunately for the amateur plumber the 15mm and 28mm metric sizes are sufficiently close to their imperial equivalents to permit compression fittings of these sizes to be used, without adaptation, with ½in and 1in copper or stainless steel tubing. When using a 22mm fitting to join modern 22mm tubing to existing ¾in tubing, some kind of an adaptor is necessary. The exact way in which the fitting is adapted will depend upon its make. Generally, it will involve using a larger olive and perhaps a larger cap-nut with the same joint body. Ask the supplier if you are in doubt.

Dezincification

In some parts of the country a corrosive water supply produces a phenomenon called dezincification in the brass of which compression fittings are usually made. Brass is an alloy of copper and zinc and, when dezincification takes place, the zinc dissolves away leaving a fitting unchanged in appearance but totally without strength.

The remedy used to be to use gunmetal fittings since gunmetal – an alloy of copper and tin – is not affected by dezincification. There is, however, nowadays a range of corrosion resistant brass fittings which are unaffected by dezincification. They are clearly marked CR on body and cap-nuts.

1. *To make a compression joint, unscrew the cap-nut and extract the ring or olive. Slip first the cap-nut and then the olive over the pipe end. Make sure that the olive is the same way round as it was in the joint. This is very important with some makes of compression joint. Where, as in the illustration, the pipe is in a vertical position, a spring clothes peg can be used to prevent the ring and cap-nut from slipping down.*

2. *Some makers of compression joints insist that no jointing compound is needed when making their joints. However, plumbers invariably add a smear of compound to the tube end and the olive. It does ensure a watertight joint at the first attempt.*

3. *Push the pipe into the body of the fitting as far as the tube stop. Push the olive down the pipe to the fitting and screw up the cap-nut hand tight. The application of a little oil to the thread will ease screwing on the cap-nut and subsequent tightening.*

4

5
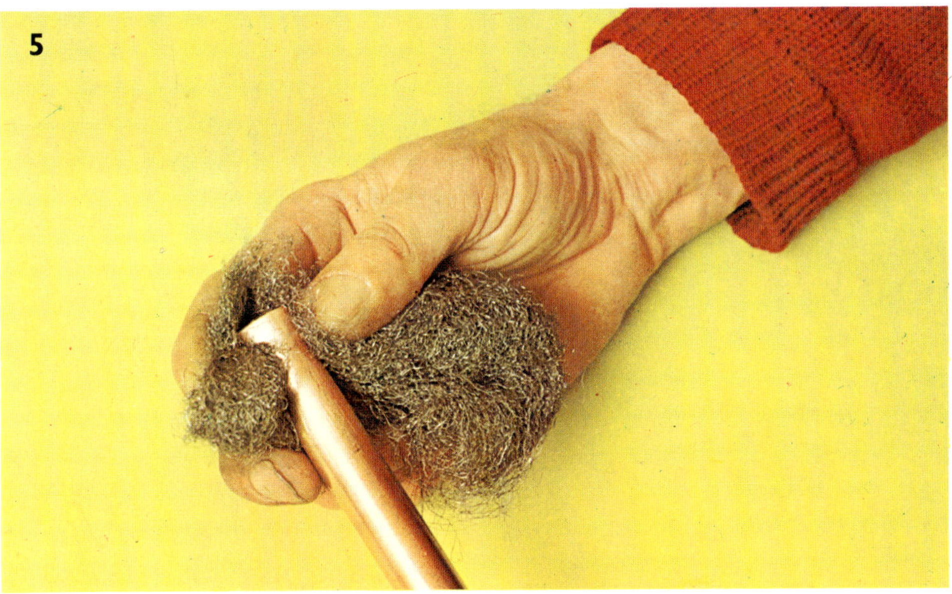

6

When purchasing compression fittings it is wise to ask the supplier for the kind of fittings that are used by *good quality plumbers in your particular area.*

Soldered capillaries

Soldered capillary joints and fittings provide an alternative to compression fittings for joining copper or stainless steel tubing. Soldered capillary fittings are smaller, neater and cheaper than compression types.

A capillary coupling – the basic capillary joint – is a metal sleeve that fits closely over the ends of the lengths of tube to be joined. The coupling is then heated, and molten solder encouraged to flow – by capillary attraction – into the narrow space between the outside of the tube end and the inside of the coupling.

There are two kinds of soldered capillary fittings on the market. Integral ring fittings incorporate within their body sufficient solder to complete the joint. The cheaper end-feed fittings are simply metal sleeves and molten solder has to be fed into the joint from a length of solder wire.

Tools required to make soldered capillary joints are a means of cutting the tubing to length – a hacksaw or tube cutter – and of cleaning the end of burr. You'll also need a blow torch, some wire wool or fine abrasive paper, some flux and – for end feed joints only – a roll of solder wire. Don't overlook the fire risk when using a blow torch. Have a sheet of heat-resistant material handy to interpose between the capillary fitting and any flammable surface – a skirting board or a rafter for instance – that may be behind the working area.

This is the way to make a capillary joint using copper tubing. The rather different technique used with stainless steel tubing will be described later.

Cut the tube ends absolutely square and

4. *Screw on the cap-nut hand tight then use a wrench or spanner of appropriate size to give it one full and one quarter turn. A chalk mark on the cap-nut and the body of the fitting can help in getting the tightening right. Do not overtighten. A little jointing compound on the olive will ensure a watertight joint, and if you smear oil on the thread of the nut it will tighten easily. After some experience you will be able to tighten correctly without the chalk marks.*

5. *Absolute cleanliness is the secret of success in making soldered capillary joints. After cutting the tube end squarely and removing all burrs, clean the tube end thoroughly either with wire wool, as illustrated, or with fine abrasive paper.*

6. *The interior of the soldered capillary fitting must also be thoroughly cleaned with wire wool or with abrasive paper. In the illustration a special wire brush is being used to clean the interior of an integral ring soldered capillary coupling. The solder is contained within the two rings that can be seen encircling the coupling.*

remove all burrs as described earlier for making compression joints. Clean the outside of the tube ends and the inside of the capillary sleeve with either fine wire wool or with fine abrasive paper. Thorough cleanliness is the secret of success when making joints of this kind. Smear flux on the surfaces that you have cleaned.

Insert the tube ends into the capillary sleeve as far as the tube stops. With an integral ring joint all that remains to be done is to heat the sleeve gently and evenly with the flame of the blow torch. The solder will melt and run to fill the space between the tube end and the sleeve. The joint is complete when a bright ring of solder can be seen all around the mouth of the coupling.

When this occurs, wipe off excess flux and leave undisturbed until cool enough to touch.

With an end-feed fitting, preparation is exactly the same but, when the fitting has been heated, solder wire is applied to the mouth of the joint. This will melt and flow between pipe and fitting to make the joint. Once again the joint is complete when a ring of solder appears all round the mouth of the fitting.

It can sometimes be helpful to know roughly how much solder will be needed to complete an end-feed capillary joint. A 15mm joint is likely to need about ½in of solder wire, a 22mm joint about ¾in and a 28mm joint about 1in. It is a good idea to bend over this amount of wire before you begin to make the joint. You will then have a good idea when it is almost complete.

Most soldered capillary fittings – couplings and tees for instance – have more than one joint. It is best to make all these joints at the same time. Where other joints of one fitting have to be made later then joints already made should be wrapped around with a damp cloth. This will prevent the solder from remelting.

Stainless steel tubing

Stainless steel tubing can be joined by the same capillary fittings that are used with copper tube but at least one manufacturer makes a range of stainless steel fittings for this purpose.

The tube ends are prepared in exactly the same way as the ends of copper tube but a special phosphoric acid flux – instead of the usual chloride based flux – *must be used*. This can burn the fingers so apply it with a brush or spatula.

When heating the joint apply the flame to the fitting only – not to the stainless steel tube. Remember that stainless steel does not conduct heat so readily as copper. Heat the fitting carefully, endeavouring to apply heat to the back as well as to the front. Your heat-resistant mat placed behind the fitting will help by reflecting the heat back.

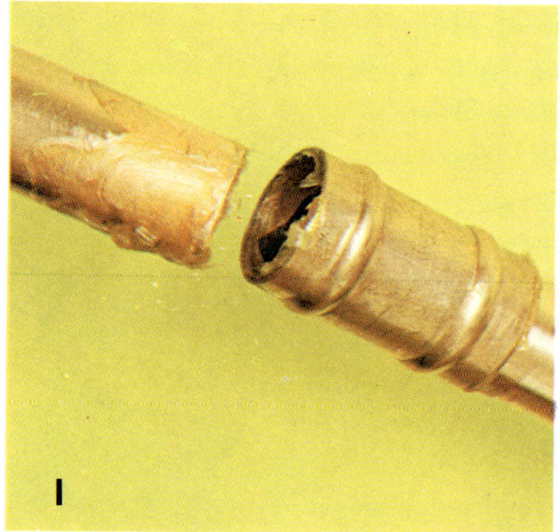

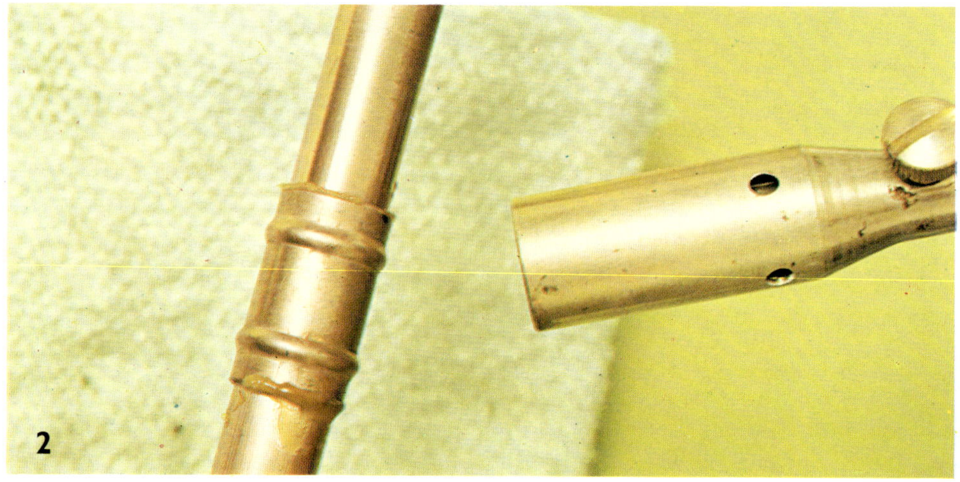

1. *Coat the exterior of the tube end and the interior of the fitting with flux and thrust the tube into the fitting as far as the tube stop. When making soldered capillary joints with stainless steel tubing, a phosphoric acid flux must be used. This should be applied with a brush or spatula.*

2. *Apply a steady heat to the soldered capillary fitting using a blow torch. The solder contained in the rings will melt and flow to fill the space between the tube end and the interior of the coupling. The joint is complete when a ring of bright solder appears all round the mouth of the fitting. Wipe off excess flux and leave undisturbed until cool enough to handle. Note the heat-resistant mat interposed between the joint and the wall or other surface behind it. This is an important fire precaution.*

3. *End-feed soldered capillary fittings are cheaper than integral ring ones. Preparation of the tube end and coupling is carried out in exactly the same way but, as the fitting is heated, solder wire is applied to its mouth. This solder melts and flows, by capillary action, to fill the space between the pipe end and the coupling. As with an integral ring fitting, the joint is complete when a bright ring of solder appears all around the mouth. Once again – note the protective heat-resistant mat.*

When applying end-feed solder wire apply it to the mouth of the fitting in two or three places to make sure that the molten solder flows throughout the space between tube and fitting.

Metrication

Exact fit is more important with capillary fittings than with compression ones. Metric size fittings cannot be used with existing

1

2

3

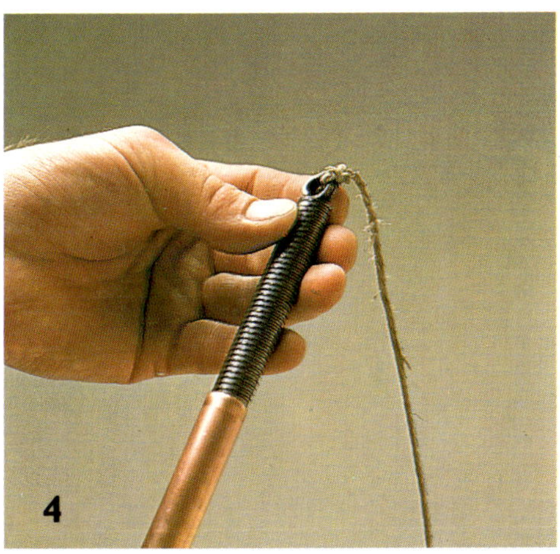
4

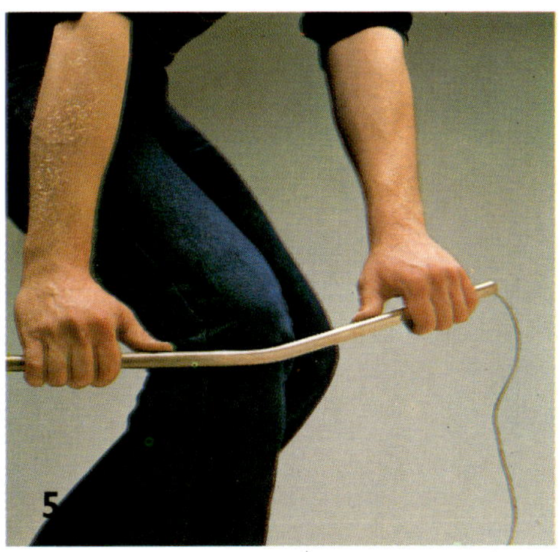
5

imperial size tube. However, conversion couplings – with the imperial size at one end and the metric size at the other – are freely available.

Bending copper tubing

When installing copper water supply and distribution pipes, changes of direction *can* be achieved by the use of the soldered capillary or compression bends that are included in every range of these fittings. However, a neater – and much cheaper – result can be obtained by bending the pipe itself.

You will find that the 15mm and 22mm copper tubes used in domestic plumbing can quite easily be bent by hand, over the knee. This, however, results in the pipe being deformed. The inside of the bend is wrinkled, the outside is flattened and the pipe becomes elliptical instead of circular in section.

By supporting the walls of the pipe as the bend is made this deformation can be avoided. This can be done with a bending machine or bending springs. Bending machines are expensive and it is best to hire one.

Bending springs support the walls of the tube internally. They can be used to achieve easy bends (a minimum radius of 40mm for 15mm tube and 60mm for 22mm tube). The spring – of the appropriate size for the tube that is to be bent – should be greased to facilitate withdrawal and inserted to the point at which the bend is to be made. Bend over the knee, overbending by a few degrees at first and then bringing the pipe back.

Insert a bar into the loop at the end of the spring, twist to reduce the spring's diameter and pull to withdraw. Slight wrinkling on the inside of the bend can be dressed out afterwards with a hammer. Never attempt this before withdrawing the spring. If you do you will find the spring quite impossible to remove.

Watertight screwed joints

At one time it was the practice to make screwed joints used in plumbing systems watertight by coating strands of hemp with jointing compound and binding them around the male thread of the screwed joint.

This was messy and uncertain in its effect but it is still found in many older houses

1. *Insert the pipe to be bent into the bending machine.*
2. *Put it the grooved section, so that the pipe is supported when it is bent.*
3. *With one foot on the lower arm of the machine, push the lever so that the pipe bends.*
4. *When using bending springs, tie string to one end, so that you can take the spring out.*
5. *Support the pipe on your knee as you bend it with a spring.*

and is a useful technique. Nowadays, PTFE plastic thread sealing tape provides a cleaner and more effective way of making screwed joints watertight. This tape can be purchased on reels from builders' merchants or DIY shops.

To ensure a watertight joint bind the tape anti-clockwise three times round the male thread before screwing it home. This prevents the tape being pulled off. A screwed joint sealed with PTFE tape can easily be undone again when required.

The swivel tap connectors used to connect water supply pipes to the screwed tails of pillar taps and ball-valves are normally provided with a fibre washer that makes the connection watertight without other treatment.

Plastic tubing

Plastic tubing may be used in domestic plumbing for cold water supply and distribution and for waste pipes and drains. Certain types (CPVC and polybutylene) may also be used for hot water distribution and central heating, special fittings being available to allow connections to boilers and hot-water cylinders.

One of the most versatile of plastics is UPVC. Where UPVC pipes are used for cold water supply they are joined by solvent welding. For waste pipes they may be either solvent welded or connected by push-fit ring sealed joints. Often both methods are used in one system.

Polypropylene is sometimes used for drainage work as it stands up to hot and chemical wastes better than UPVC. Polypropylene pipes cannot be solvent welded.

CPVC pipes are solvent-welded in the same way as UPVC. Polybutylene cannot be solvent welded and is joined with special push-fit fittings or, if required, using conventional brass compression fittings.

Fittings

Using the information on cutting and joining pipes on the previous pages, it is not difficult to put in fittings such as baths, basins and water-storage tanks. Plumbing in appliances like washing machines can also be tackled.

Sinks

To avoid an unnecessarily long interruption of the domestic hot and cold water services, a new sink should be fitted with its waste and overflow unit and with its taps before being moved into position.

If you choose a mixer rather than individual sink taps, be sure to choose a *sink* mixer. These have separate channels for the hot and cold water and the two streams mix in the air after leaving the nozzle. This is because it is illegal in any plumbing appliance to mix water from a storage cistern and water from the rising main. In a bathroom or shower where the cold water comes from the tank it can be mixed inside the mixer.

To drain the water supply pipes prior to connecting them to the new taps you must turn off the main stop-cock and open up all hot and cold taps.

Washing machines

Plumbing-in an automatic washing machine involves providing the machine with hot and cold water supplies and making arrangements for it to be drained.

The most usual way of dealing with the water supply is to cut off the supplies to the

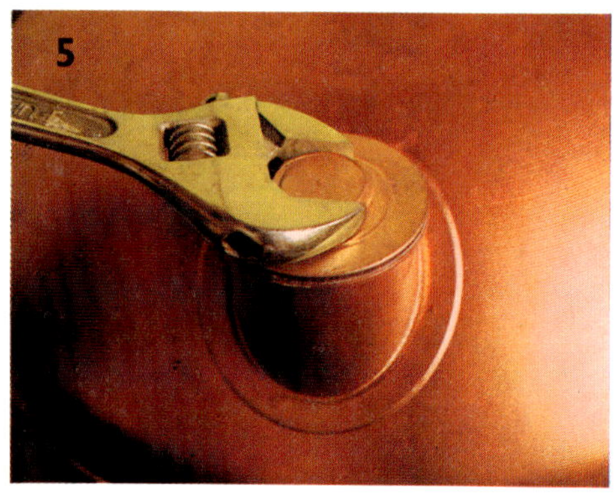

1. The modern method of making screwed joints watertight. Bind the PTFE thread sealing tape three times anti-clockwise round the male thread. *2. PTFE thread sealing tape is bound round the male thread of a connection to a hot water cylinder before screwing it home and, 3, around the projecting male thread of the flow connection of an indirect cylinder before connecting to it a compression fitting with a female screwed thread at one end and a compression joint – for connecting to the copper flow pipe from the boiler – at the other end.* *4. The sealing ring of an immersion heater boss cap is smeared with non-toxic compound before being screwed home.* *5. The boss cap is used to blank off the boss if an immersion or microbore element is not used.*

kitchen sink, drain the supply pipes and then to tee into these pipes as described earlier in this book (pages 61-3).

Make sure that the outlets of the tee junctions point towards the washing machine. Connect to the teepieces 15mm tubing sufficiently long to reach the washing machine's hose connectors. To the outer end of these lengths of 15mm copper tubing fit washing machine stop-cocks. These are attractively styled valves with a compression joint inlet and an outlet designed for connection to the washing machine hoses. They are provided with a plate which can be screwed to the wall.

Where the washing machine is to be fitted in close proximity to the existing hot and cold water supply pipes it may be possible to fit special valves into these pipes (perhaps without even having to cut off the water supply) and connect the hoses directly to these valves.

The waste hose of the washing machine may be simply hooked over the edge of the sink when required. Where this is not practicable the hose can be hooked permanently into an open-ended stand-pipe fixed to the kitchen wall and discharging via a waste trap either over a yard gully or into the main soil and waste stack of a single-stack drainage system.

The stand-pipe must have its inlet at least 60cm (24in) above floor level and must have an internal diameter of at least 35mm (1⅜in).

Fitting a kitchen sink unit

__1.__ Spread a layer of non-setting mastic under the flange of the slotted waste and bed this down into the outlet hole of the sink. Slip one of the washers provided over the tail of the waste projecting from below the sink and then the sleeve or banjo fitting to which is connected the flexible overflow pipe.
__2.__ Screw the overflow fitting on the other end of this flexible pipe to the overflow outlet of the sink. Two further washers – one soft and one hard – must be slipped over the tail of the waste before screwing on and tightening up the back-nut. The hard washer should be in direct contact with the back-nut. As the back-nut is tightened the waste flange will turn on the waste hole of the sink. Stop this by holding the outlet grid with a pair of pliers. Finally, screw on the trap. A bottle trap is shown but a simple U trap would be equally suitable.
__3.__ Slip a plastic washer over the tails of the taps or mixer before pushing them through the holes in the sink top. Underneath, before screwing up the back-nuts, use a top-hat or spacer washers to accommodate the shanks of the taps protruding through the thin material of the sink.
__4.__ The water supply pipes are connected to the tails of the taps with swivel tap connectors or cap and lining joints. A fibre washer ensures a watertight connection. The swivel tap connectors will have either compression or soldered capillary joint inlets for connection to the copper water supply pipes.

Baths

Baths are available in enamelled cast iron, pressed steel and either acrylic plastic or glass reinforced plastic. Plastic baths are recommended for DIY installation.

Plastic baths are very easily damaged by extreme heat. Never rest a lighted cigarette on the rim and be *very* careful when using a blow torch.

They are supplied with substantial padded metal or wooden frames or cradles. These must be assembled exactly as recommended by the manufacturer.

When replacing an old enamelled cast iron bath with a plastic one, the removal of the old bath is likely to be the most difficult part of the job. Remove the bath panel and, after cutting off the water supply and draining the pipes, disconnect the water supply pipes from the tap tails and disconnect the trap from the waste outlet. The overflow pipe may be taken through the bathroom wall to discharge in the open air. If this is the case saw through the overflow pipe flush with the wall and plug it.

If the old bath has adjustable feet, lower them before attempting to move it to reduce the risk of damaging the wall tiling or surround.

Cast iron baths are *very* heavy. It is best not to attempt to move it from the room intact. Drape a blanket over it and, wearing goggles, break it up with a club hammer.

Connect the hot and cold hoses of an automatic washing machine or dishwasher to the pipes supplying the kitchen taps. Use tee junctions to make the connections and fit wall-mounted stop-cocks so that the machine can be easily disconnected for servicing. The waste outlet can discharge into a stand-pipe over a yard gully as shown below and inset, or into the main soil and waste stack. Carefully consult the manufacturer's instructions before beginning – requirements can vary from one machine to another.

Basins

Wash basins are traditionally of ceramic material but basins of enamelled pressed steel or plastic, set into counter tops, are becoming increasingly popular.

Ceramic basins may be either wall-hung or pedestal. A pedestal basin should never be supported solely by the pedestal and the plumbing fittings. Modern pedestal basins are always supplied complete with concealed brackets or hangers.

Either individual ½in hot and cold taps or, provided that the bathroom cold water supply is from a storage cistern and not from the main, a basin mixer may be used. In a basin mixer the two streams of hot and cold water mix in the body of the fitting. Some modern mixer sets are supplied complete with pop-up wastes.

Ceramic basins have built-in overflows. The basins used in vanity units are provided with flexible overflow tubes that connect to the waste outlet in the same way as the waste and overflow unit of a modern sink or bath.

Cisterns

Cold water storage cisterns used always to be made of galvanised mild steel. Particularly when connected to copper pipes this material is very subject to corrosion. Neglected corrosion will ultimately result in a leaking cistern and hundreds – perhaps thousands – of pounds worth of damage to ceilings, decorations and furnishings.

A galvanised steel cistern showing early signs of corrosion can be saved and protected. Drain and dry the cistern. Remove every trace of rust by wire brushing (wear goggles to protect the eyes!) and with abrasives. Then apply two coats of a tasteless and odourless bituminous paint. This treatment will afford protection for several years and can be repeated when necessary.

Ultimately, though, a new cistern will be required and it is best to choose a plastic one. Plastic cisterns cannot corrode and are frost resistant. They are light, easily installed and – having rounded internal angles – are easy to keep clean.

Plastic cisterns may be of glass reinforced plastic (GRP), of polythene or of UPVC. Polythene cisterns are usually round or barrel shaped and flexible. They can there-

1

2

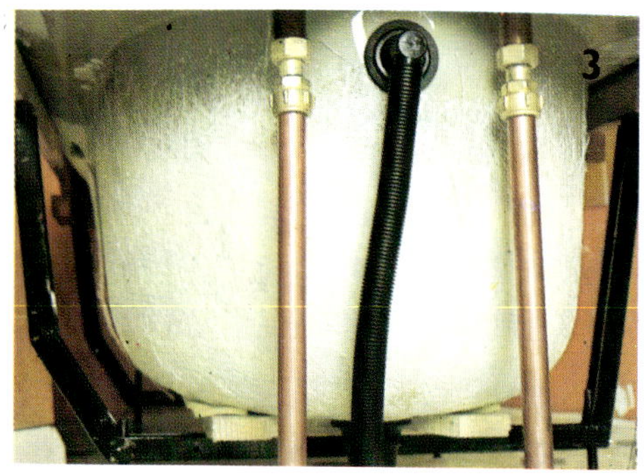

3

Plumbing-in a new bath

1. *Illustrated is a glass reinforced plastic (GRP) bath fitted into its frame. As much plumbing work as possible should be carried out before moving it into position. Modern bath waste assemblies include a flexible overflow pipe similar to the overflow of a modern sink, which connects to the waste outlet or to the trap. A plastic trap and waste pipe should always be used with a plastic bath as the bath flexes when in use. With copper pipework, the pipes will not flex with the bath, and the joint will be strained immediately. Plastic pipes will flex at the same rate as the bath, putting no strain on the joint.*

2. *Here the overflow outlet of the bath is being connected to the flexible overflow pipe. The waste outlet is bedded down in the outlet hole of the bath on a bed of non-setting mastic.*

3. *The plumbing in of the new bath is completed. The waste and trap are in position and the flexible overflow pipe connects to them. The two 22mm copper water supply pipes are connected to the tails of the taps with 22mm swivel tap connectors with a compression joint inlet.*

Plumbing-in a wash basin

1. *On sanitary ware it is important to prevent direct contact between metal and china. For this reason, and to provide a watertight seal, the waste is bedded into a ring of plumbing putty, taking care not to block the slot which connects to the overflow outlet. Push the waste firmly down into the basin outlet, slip on a plastic washer underneath the basin and tighten the back nut.*

2. *Screw the trap on to the waste outlet and connect the trap outlet to the waste pipe.*

3. *Attach the taps to the basin in a similar manner to the waste, bedding them down in the putty. Attach an angled swivel connector to the tail of each tap and bend the supply pipes so they cross over behind and within the pedestal to avoid sharp bends. Corrugated tap connectors are available which can easily be bent to the required shape without tools.*

4. *Alternatively, use straight swivel connectors and elbow joints to connect the supply pipes instead of bending.*

1

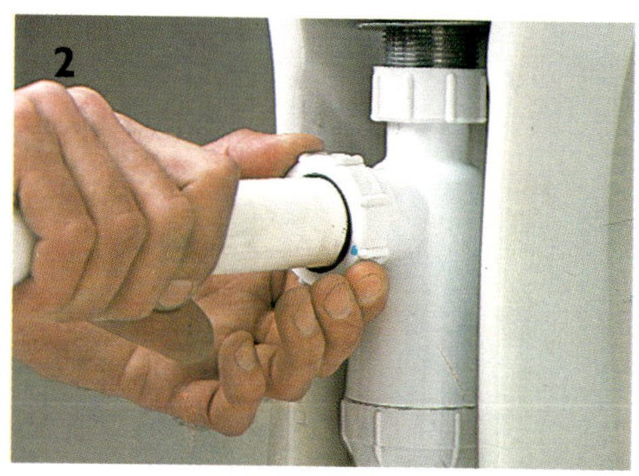

2

3

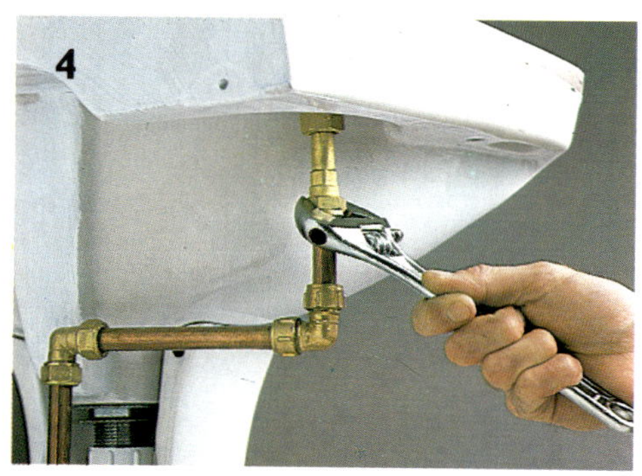

4

fore be flexed through small openings.

Where it is impossible to introduce a cistern of the required capacity of 227 litres (50gal) through a small trap door into the roof space, it is permissible to use two smaller cisterns, linking them together with a 28mm pipe about 2in above their bases. To avoid stagnation of the stored water the ball-valve inlet should be connected to one of the cisterns and the distribution pipes taken from the other.

Showers

No bathroom nowadays is complete without a shower. Showers save both time and money. It is possible to have four or five showers in the time – and with the same amount of hot water – as one sit-down bath.

A shower may be fitted over a bath or installed in its own separate shower cubicle. An independent shower in a cubicle can be provided wherever there is a floor space of 1m by 1m in plan – on a landing, in the corner of a bedroom or even in the cupboard under the stairs.

Where a shower is to be supplied with hot water from a cylinder storage hot water system there are certain design requirements that are essential to success. The hot and cold supplies to the shower must be under equal pressure. This means that they must both come from the cold water storage cistern. The cold supply must *not* come direct from the main.

The storage cistern must be sufficiently high above the shower sprinkler to give an adequate spray. Best results will be obtained if the base of the cold water storage cistern is about 1.5 metres above the shower sprinkler but the absolute minimum hydraulic head for a satisfactory

Installing a water-storage cistern

1. *Always measure carefully. The ball-valve inlet should be 75mm from the cistern rim and the overflow outlet 95mm from the rim. Outlets to distribution pipes should be 50mm from the cistern's base.*
2. *Having established the position of the tapping the fitting to be connected to it can be used as a template to mark the size of the hole.*
3. *A hole cutter provides the easiest way of making holes for connections.*
4. *Use a plastic washer on each side of the cistern wall to ensure a watertight seal. Do not use jointing compound.*
5. *Make connections squarely and do not overtighten.*
6. *A gate valve fitted into each outlet pipe permits the distribution pipes to be drained.*
7. *Use plastic washers on either side of the cistern to secure the ball valve. To prevent noise secure the rising main firmly to the roof timbers.*
8. *The completed installation.*

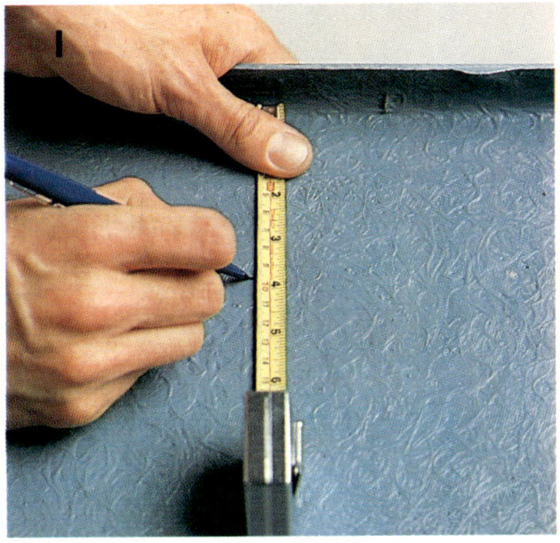

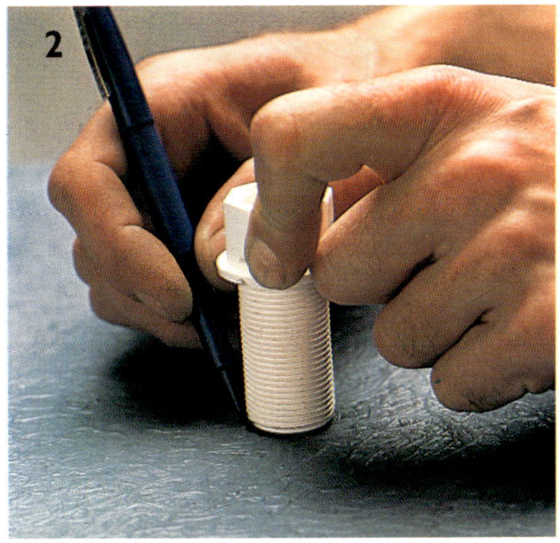

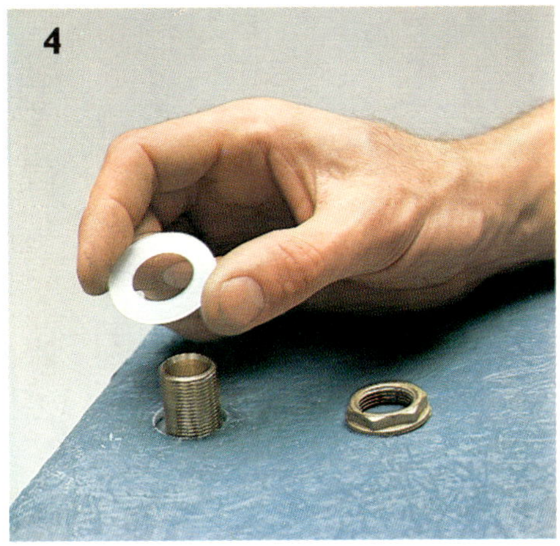

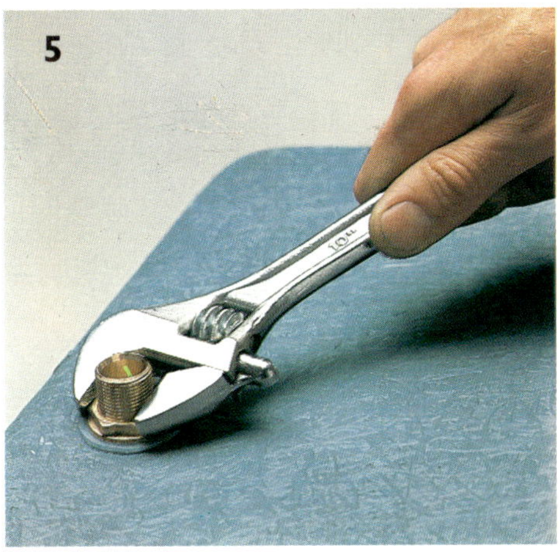

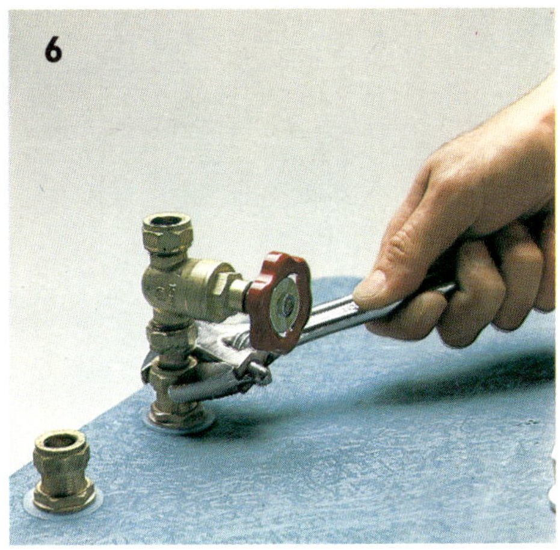

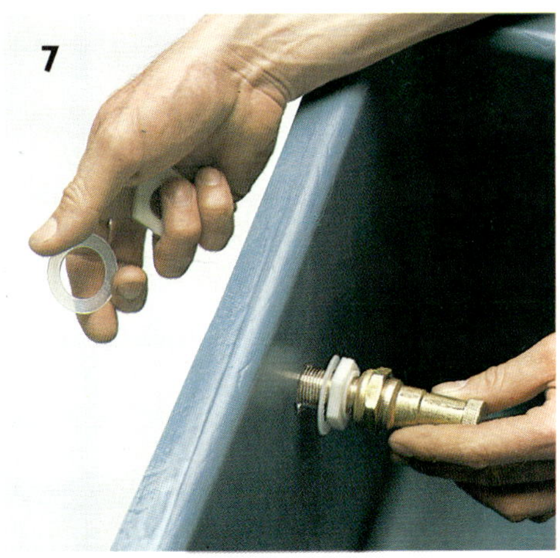

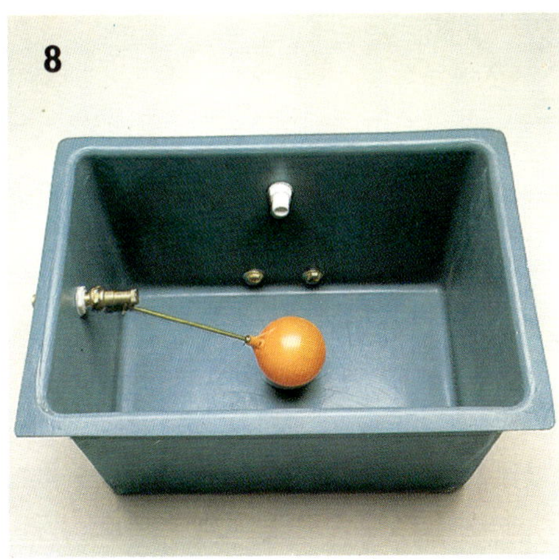

1
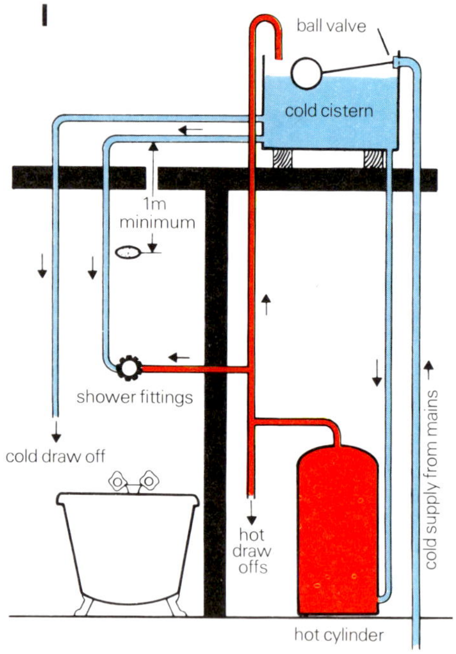

2

shower is 1 metre. As a safety precaution it is best if the cold supply to the shower is taken as a separate pipe from the cold water storage cistern and not as a branch from another cold water distribution pipe.

Where the cold water storage cistern is too low to give an adequate shower the best solution is usually to construct a substantial wooden platform in the roof space and to raise the cistern on to it, lengthening the connecting pipes by inserting new lengths of copper tube linked with compression joints. Where this isn't possible an electric booster pump may be installed to give adequate pressure.

Where these design requirements cannot be met, another alternative is to install an instantaneous electric shower. These need only to be connected to the rising main by means of a 15mm branch pipe and provided with a suitable supply of electricity. Water from the main is heated by powerful electric elements as it passes through the appliance. Increasing the flow of water lowers the temperature while reducing the flow raises the temperature. Modern instantaneous electric showers usually have an anti-scald cut-out device for safety.

All showers other than instantaneous electric ones require some kind of mixing valve to mix the streams of hot and cold water to the required temperature. The bath taps provide the simplest mixing valve. With both the basic push-on shower attachments and with the more sophisticated bath/shower mixers, the hot and cold taps are adjusted until the required temperature is achieved.

Manual mixing valves mix the hot and cold water in one fitting, control of temperature and – in some cases – flow, are obtained by turning a large knurled control knob.

1. *Cold supply to shower mixer should be taken direct from storage cistern.*
2. *Instantaneous electric shower can be connected to cold water main supply.*
3. *A mixer shower installed, replacing the taps.*

3

More sophisticated still are thermostatic mixing valves. These are able to accommodate minor differences in pressure between the hot and cold water supplies. They eliminate the risk of scalding if pressure on the cold side of the shower falls because, for instance, someone has flushed a lavatory or drawn off cold water from a basin tap. Where a thermostatic mixing valve is fitted there is no need to take a separate cold supply pipe to the shower from the cold water storage cistern. It can be taken as a branch from a pipe supplying other bathroom appliances but it must originate from the storage cistern, *not* from the main.

It is impossible to obtain a satisfactory shower using an instant electric type which features separate on/off and temperature controls. This type of shower heats the water as it passes through the heater and it is this feature which limits the amount of water available, as this will also vary with the season. In winter the mains water temperature is lower, so you will obtain even less hot water.

The best shower of all is the thermostatically controlled mixer type, which automatically compensates for normal pressure changes to the incoming water.

Waste disposal units

Sink waste disposal units are plumbed permanently into the outlet of the kitchen sink to dispose of soft kitchen wastes such as vegetable peelings, food scraps, dead flowers, apple cores and so on. A capacitor-start 420 watt (½hp) induction motor operates powerful steel blades to grind these wastes into a slurry that is then flushed into the drainage system by turning on the cold tap.

Where a standard waste disposal unit is to be fitted the sink must have an 89mm (3½in) outlet instead of the usual 38mm (1½in) outlet, although at least one unit is made with the option of a 38mm (1½in) outlet and a correspondingly lower handling capacity. Both enamelled steel and stainless steel sinks are available with outlets of this size. The outlets of existing stainless steel (but not enamelled steel) sinks can be enlarged to the size required with a special cutter usually available on hire from the manufacturer of the disposal unit.

The electrical power supply to the unit must be taken from a 13 amp outlet. A fused plug and socket connection is acceptable but a switched fused connection unit is preferable.

Plumbing problems and emergencies

For easy reference here are some tips for dealing with some common plumbing problems. Most of these cause great inconvenience and it is useful to be able to deal with them yourself as soon as they occur.

Dripping taps

The usual cause of a dripping tap is a washer that needs replacing. The method of taking the tap apart depends whether you have old-fashioned pillar taps or the newer shroud-headed type. With pillar taps, you must first turn off the water supply to the tap. Then unscrew the cover and you will see the headgear nut. Holding the spout of the tap, undo the headgear nut with a spanner. You will now be able to lift out the headgear, revealing the jumper, the brass component on which the washer is fitted. To remove the old washer you will either have to undo a small screw on the end of the jumper or prise the washer free. If you cannot take the washer off, you should replace the entire jumper unit. Otherwise replace the washer, reassemble the tap, and turn on the water supply. Leave the tap slightly open when turning on the water. This will help eliminate any air pockets in the pipes.

With a modern shrouded-head tap, the procedure is the same, except that the method of taking the tap apart is slightly different. You either remove the cap on the top of the shrouded-head and undo the screw beneath, or undo a screw at the side of the head.

Fitting taps

When replacing an old or broken tap with a new one, it is important to remember the correct sequence of fittings and washers that you attach to the tap when you connect it to the supply.

Above the surface of the sink or basin should be a ring of non-setting mastic (nearest the top of the tap) and a plastic washer. When these have been fitted, the tap can be inserted through the hole in the sink. Next a fibre washer is fitted to the tail of the tap, followed by the back nut. A tap connector can then be screwed on to the tail and connected to the supply pipe. For a good joint, wrap PTFE tape around the tail before fitting the connector.

Leaking pipes

Frost, corrosion, or a hole caused by an accident such as nailing through a pipe can all cause leaks. If you find a leak, turn off the water supply immediately and drain the pipe. Quickly check whether any electrical appliances or wiring have been affected by the leak. If this has happened, disconnect the relevant appliances or turn off the power supply and call in a qualified electrician.

As a temporary repair, use one of the commercially available kits. These consist either of a plastic putty that you mix with a hardener and force into the hole or of a waterproof adhesive tape that is wound round the affected length of pipe. Another alternative is a rubber-lined pipe clamp that is held together by a nut and bolt.

None of these solutions provides a lasting repair, however. For this, you need to cut out the length of pipe in which the leak has occurred and replace it with a new piece.

Blocked sinks

If water will not drain away, first check the outlet itself is not blocked. If it is clear, the most likely place for a blockage is in the trap directly under the sink. There are three main types of trap: the old S-bend type, and the modern P-trap and bottle trap. The S-bend type is usually made of lead and has a small screw at the bottom which you can undo to remove any debris. Take this off with a spanner and push a length of wire up both sides of the trap and pull out any debris. Keep a bucket under the trap.

With a modern P-trap or a bottle trap, you can unscrew and remove the whole trap. This allows you to clean it out under a tap.

If the trap is not blocked, use the length of wire to probe along the outlet pipe and pull out any debris that has collected there. If this fails, the blockage must be in the drainage system outside the house.

Frozen pipes

Thaw a frozen pipe as soon as possible after you discover it – the longer it is left frozen, the more likely it is to result in a burst. If it has already burst, turn off the water supply before attempting to thaw the pipe.

The best way to thaw a frozen pipe is to use a hot-air paint stripper. A hairdrier provides a reasonable alternative, although it does not generate as much heat and therefore will take longer. Do not use a blowtorch – the fire risk is much too great.

Blocked WC

Unblocking a WC is best done by a professional with specialist equipment, but if you prefer to tackle it yourself, the method depends on exactly where the blockage is sited. Look under the outside drain inspection cover. If it is full, the obstruction is in the exterior drains and you will have to clear them using rods. If it is empty, the problem is between the pan and the chamber.

You may be able to shift the obstruction by pushing wire down the pan. If this does not work, try plunging. The best way to do this is to use a mop with a plastic bag tied to the head. As you plunge the pan, get someone to stand at the inspection chamber and intercept anything lodged in the pan, so that it does not escape into the drainage system and cause another blockage farther away from the house.

If this method does not rectify the problem, call in a professional plumber.

Fitting a waste disposal unit

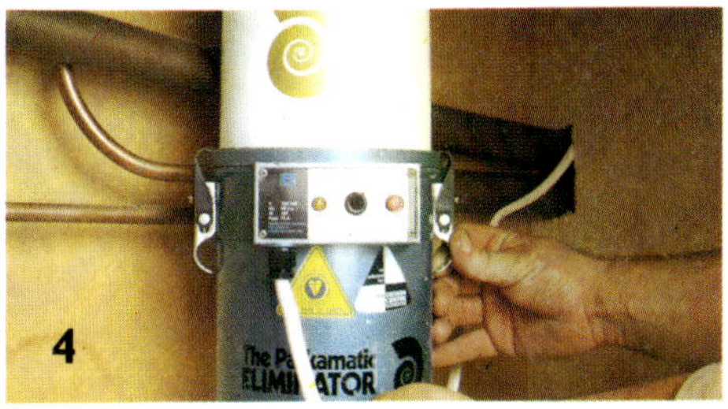

1. *A conventional waste and overflow unit fitted to the right-hand sink and, fitted to the left-hand sink, the key-hole plate assembly to which the disposal unit will be fitted.*

2. *Bottle traps should not be used with sink waste disposal units. An ordinary tubular trap (either of metal or plastic) should be fitted.*

3. *The main body of the waste disposal unit – containing the grinding blades – slots into the keyhole housing fitted to the sink outlet.*

4. *The motor unit clips on to the main body of the unit and the electrical connection is made.*

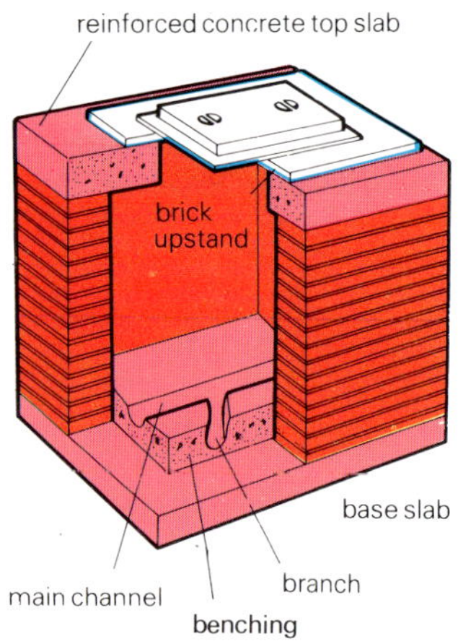

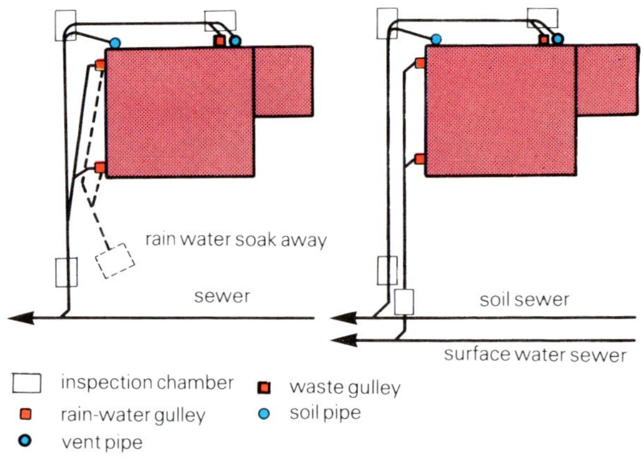

The left plan shows alternative ways for disposing of rainwater with a single-stack system. In a two-pipe system (right) it drains to a separate sewer.

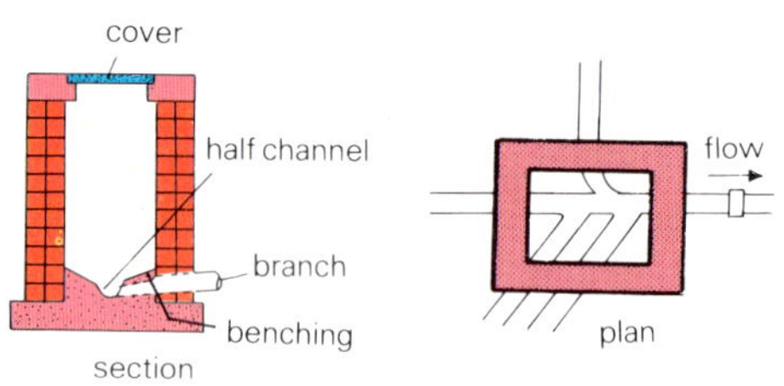

The diagrams above show a typical drainage inspection chamber as a cut-away, section, and plan view.

Drainage

The drains – the system of pipework, hoppers, gullies and underground pipes that carries waste water of all types away from the house – rarely get the regular checking and maintenance they deserve; too often, the only attention they get is when there is a blockage, yet a regular check-up would help to avoid these problems.

The importance of traps

Every water-using appliance – bath, basin, sink, wc, washing machine and so on – has a trap on the run of pipework that carries the waste water to the drains. The purpose of this is to provide a water seal in the pipe run that will prevent smells from the drains entering the house. On old lead pipework, the trap will be a U-shape bend with a small metal plug at the bottom; this can be unscrewed to allow a blockage to be cleared. You must take care when undoing it not to deform the soft pipework; you can then insert a length of wire to poke the blockage clear.

On modern plastic pipework, you will find a plastic trap – either a U-shape section joined to the appliance and the pipework with a screwed fitting, or else a one-piece bottle trap. In the former case, you can unscrew the fittings to remove the trap, which can then be unblocked, flushed through and replaced. In the case of the bottle trap, the base of the trap can be unscrewed to clear a blockage. Both types are sealed with rubber O-rings; make sure that these are replaced carefully when the trap is reassembled, or you will have leaks.

Before attempting to clear a blocked trap beneath a bath, basin or sink, put the plug in and have a bucket handy to catch the water in the trap itself.

Blockages in wcs can often be cleared by using a rubber or plastic cup plunger. If the blockage persists, you may have a blocked drain further down the system, and this will have to be tackled from one of the inspection chambers or manholes outside your house. To locate the blockage, lift the cover of the manhole nearest to the house; if it is empty, the blockage is between it and the house, whereas if it is full the blockage is further down still. Move on down the drain run until you find an empty chamber; the blockage will be between it and the last full chamber.

To clear a blocked drain you will need a set of drain rods – lengths of cane which can be screwed together like a chimney sweep's brush, and which can be fitted with an assortment of plungers and brushes to dislodge the blockage. At the full manhole, screw a couple of canes together, attach the plunger and feed it down the drain, adding more canes as you do so. Rotate the rods clockwise as you feed them in the drain, to prevent the screwed ferrules from undoing; if you do not do this you will lose the rods irretrievably in the drain. Place a board across the outlet from the next (empty) manhole, to catch the debris as you dislodge it and prevent it causing a blockage further down. When you have cleared the blockage, scrub through the drain run with the brush attachment, using plenty of clean water from a hose.

When outside gullies become blocked, lift the grating and scoop out the debris from the gully trap by hand (wearing rubber gloves) or by using an old tin as a scoop. Hose the gully through with clean water, scrub the grating and replace it. Fitting a gully cover made from exterior-quality plywood will prevent debris from blowing into the trap and causing another blockage.

Repairing manholes

If a manhole cover is cracked or broken, it should be replaced as a matter of urgency. You will probably have to buy a new rim as well as a new lid, since getting exactly the right size is likely to prove difficult. Chip away the concrete holding the old rim, using a club hammer and cold chisel. Clean up the surround, and bed the new rim in a 1:3 cement to sand mortar, checking with a spirit level that it is sitting level and is not twisted. Leave to harden for 24 hours before laying the new cover in place.

If the benching – the sloped mortar in the base of the manhole that supports the half-pipes crossing the chamber – is cracked, chip it away carefully taking care not to damage the pipes and replace it with a 1:4 cement to sharp sand mortar, finished with a steel trowel.

Joints in drainage pipes

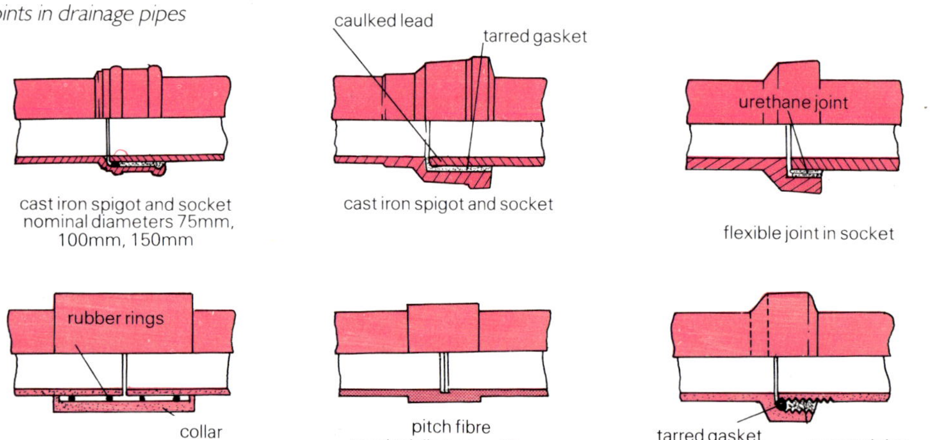

cast iron spigot and socket nominal diameters 75mm, 100mm, 150mm

cast iron spigot and socket

flexible joint in socket

nominal diameters 100mm, 125mm, 150mm up to 610mm

pitch fibre nominal diameters 75mm, 100mm, 125mm, 150mm, 200mm

glazed vitrified clay nominal diameters 75mm, 100mm, 150mm up to 760mm

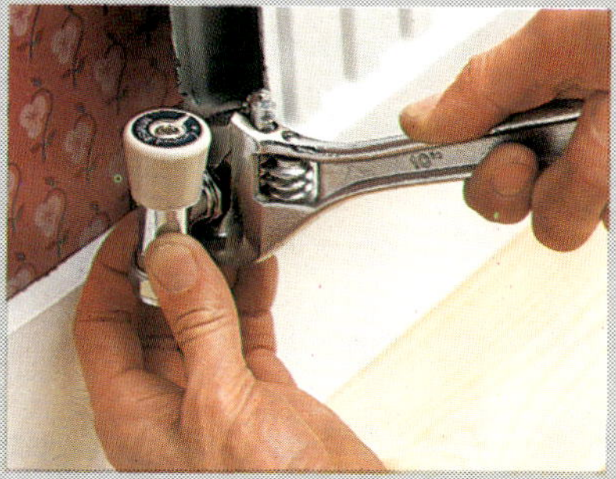

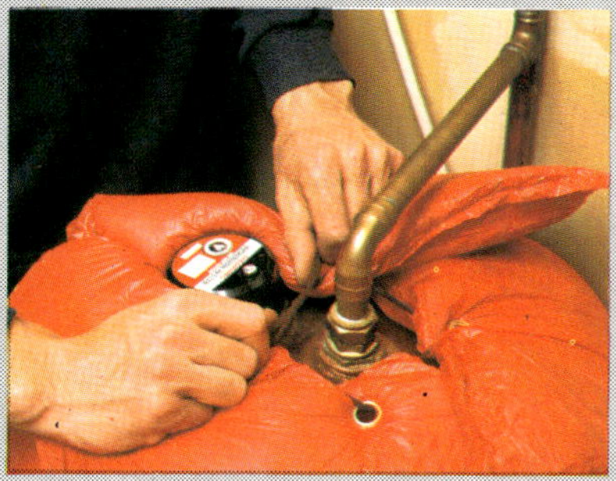

CENTRAL HEATING AND INSULATION

Mysterious pipes disappearing into walls and floors together with strange rumblings from a white box in the kitchen may well be the extent of your knowledge about central heating. But it is very useful to know how it all works so that if trouble should strike then at least you will know what emergency action should be taken. And when it comes to buying a new installation you will be able to talk intelligently to the supplier and choose the best system for your home. This section will give you all the basic information you need to have for this purpose.

Keeping warm is only a small part of the story. Economy of fuel, whether gas, electricity, oil or solid fuel, is just as important with ever-soaring costs these days. Insulation can help cut your costs, but make sure you don't get your sums wrong. It's not much good spending £4,000 on a fuel-saving device if it takes 40 years to recover the outlay.

Planning a system

To design and install central heating may seem a daunting task, but it can be made reasonably straightforward if kept to a basic system.

There are a number of different types of heating systems. This section deals mainly with gas fired systems which are the most popular.

Only a competent handyman should think of designing and installing his own system, but many other people would like to understand more about the system they are ordering, wish to order, or have to maintain. The hardest part is often making the calculations involved in the design and this subject is covered simply and without mystique in this section.

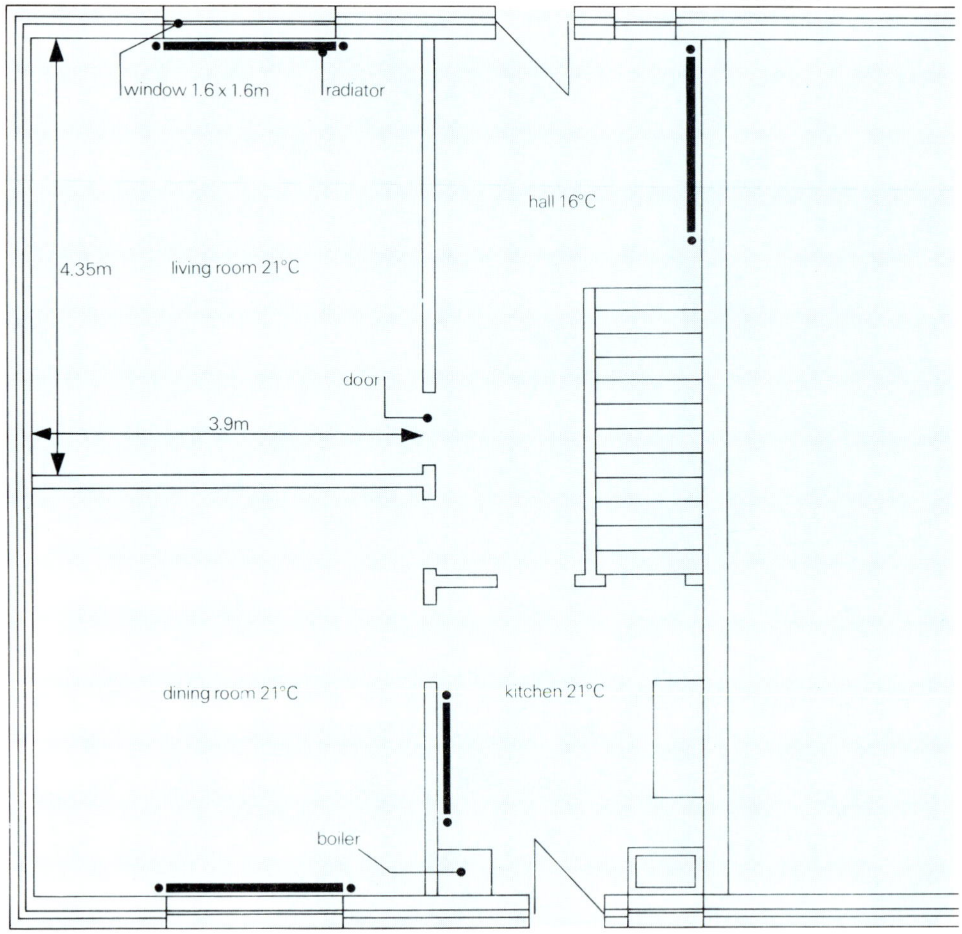

Planning your own heating system

Before you consider which system to install it is best to make a survey of your home. Draw up a sketch plan as accurately as you can and record these details.

1. Length, height and width of each room, the size of the windows and the height of the sill above the floor, which will help decide the size and position of radiators.
2. The construction, material and thickness of the floors.
3. The construction of the walls, their thickness and whether they are solid or cavity, plastered or masonry.
4. The type of windows, single or double glazed, metal or wooden frames.
5. The construction of ceilings and roof area, whether it is plasterboard or lath, whether it is insulated and to what thickness, and if it is ventilated.

You'll need to know all of these details accurately to calculate the *heat losses* which will determine the size of boiler you need, the amount of radiator area and the size of pipes and pump.

6. There is one other major consideration in calculating the heat losses. It is known as the *comfort conditions* necessary for each room. These are: (a) room temperatures, and (b) air changes or ventilation.

These are explained when we come to calculate heat losses, but they can be marked on your sketch plan.

7. Last, but not least, it is good practice to decide where each piece of equipment will be fixed. If you position these on your sketch it will simplify working out the pipework connections.

Choice of fuel

This is a choice to make before you decide on the boiler or heating appliances. The choice of fuel will affect where the boiler is sited, and will depend on whether there is storage space, on the economic cost of running and, of course, whether there is fuel service available. You have to weigh up the various advantages and disadvantages of one fuel against another, for your house.

Central heating fuels fall into four main categories.

Coal

The first problem with coal is storage. Secondly, the boiler will need cleaning thoroughly and regularly, probably every 24 to 48 hours. You also have to get rid of the ash. Deliveries can be irregular and the control of the heating is not quite so easy as with gas or electricity. It is normal in summer to use an immersion heater for domestic hot water; this is also usually the time when coal can be bought most cheaply.

The immersion heater is electric and is positioned in the boss provided in the hot water cylinder. Coal is not an entirely satisfactory material for providing both heating and hot water throughout the year, unlike the following fuels.

Electricity

This is not a fuel but an energy generated from a fuel. The supply to a British house is invariably 240 volts, 50 hertz.

Electric space heating can be classified as direct or indirect.

Indirect Known as the storage system, these are heavy radiators filled with refractory blocks which heat up at night on cheap, off-peak electricity and release the stored heat during the day.

Direct Here you use electricity at the standard rate, but it has the advantage of flexibility and immediate response. Electric fires are a direct system.

Direct and indirect systems can be used together and the advantages of electricity are that it is clean, silent, requires little maintenance and you use effectively all the energy you pay for.

However, electric heating can be very expensive indeed to run, and dangerous if not used correctly.

Oil

Until ten years ago oil was the most widely used fuel for domestic heating. Unfortunately, oil prices, as the whole world knows, have risen very sharply. You also have to weigh in the balance the uncertainty of delivery and the need to store large quantities of oil, with its inherent smell. Installation costs have proved more expensive than for other fuels. For these reasons oil has taken second place to gas in recent years.

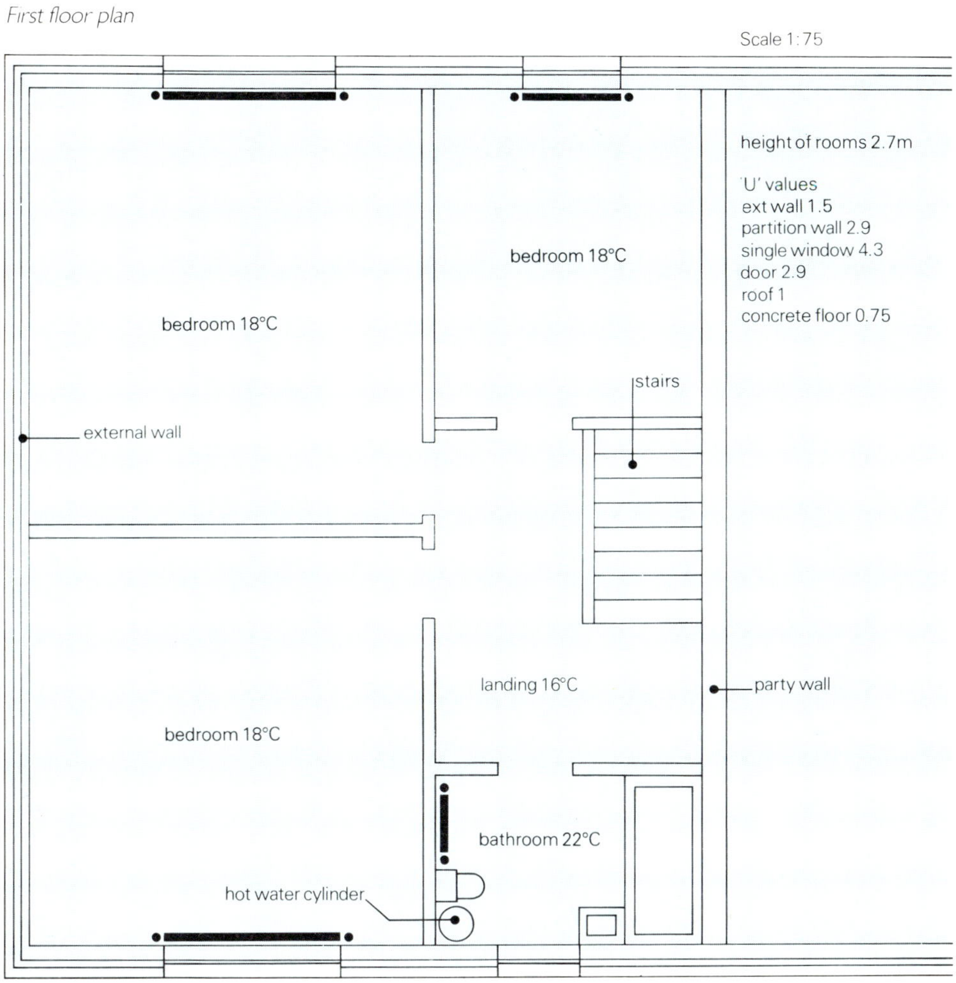

Thermostatic solid fuel room heater can supply hot water and feed a limited number of radiators.

Gas

Gas is clean, easily available and presents no storage problems where there is a main supply.

The installation of any gas main in a house should always comply with the local gas board regulations.

Gas is not always available in rural areas and it can be costly to have mains installed into a dwelling. However, if you are in this situation but want to use gas, you can buy containers of Calor Gas.

Wet systems

All fuels can be used with a wet or dry system. Wet systems are more common. They work in the following way.

1. The boiler heats water.
2. The water is circulated by a pump or gravity.
3. The hot water is carried through pipes into heat emitters: steel panel radiators, fan or natural convectors, or skirting-mounted convectors.
4. Pipework for single or two-pipe systems can be smallbore or microbore.

Smallbore means a minimum of 15mm diameter or upwards.

Microbore is 12mm diameter or below.

5. There are open and closed systems.

Open systems are those fed with water from a cold water tank known as the feed and expansion (F & E) tank by atmospheric pressure.

Closed or sealed systems are those that have a pressurised unit installed which isolates it from atmospheric pressure. This also enables the system to work at higher temperatures which can reduce the size of pipework needed.

Dry systems

These can work in one of two ways.

1. They can use a direct source of heat such as gas or electric fires.
2. They can consist of a ducted system, where warmed air is circulated by a fan through sheet metal ducting. Ducted systems can operate on any type of fuel.

Full, partial or background central heating

Full central heating means that every room has an emitter installed and that the temperature you require is reached and maintained when the outside temperature is as low as −1°C. A controlled system can be obtained by zoning. Here zone valves are used to shut off parts of the house while the rest is still being heated.

Partial central heating means that some rooms have no emitters. This is not ideal since heat will transfer from one room to another and may produce cold areas. Partial heating may be installed so that more heaters can be incorporated into the system later. If you want to do this be sure to allow for the heating load in the design stage.

Background heating can be full central heating with reduced temperatures in some or all rooms. This system can be topped up by using off-peak electric heaters, gas fires and in some cases oil heaters.

Central heating and hot water

It is economical to add the heating of domestic hot water into the central heating system. This can be done with all fuels except coal fired central heating in summer. The hot water and the central heating can be controlled independently and you should choose a control system that allows you to switch and time the water heating separately from the radiators.

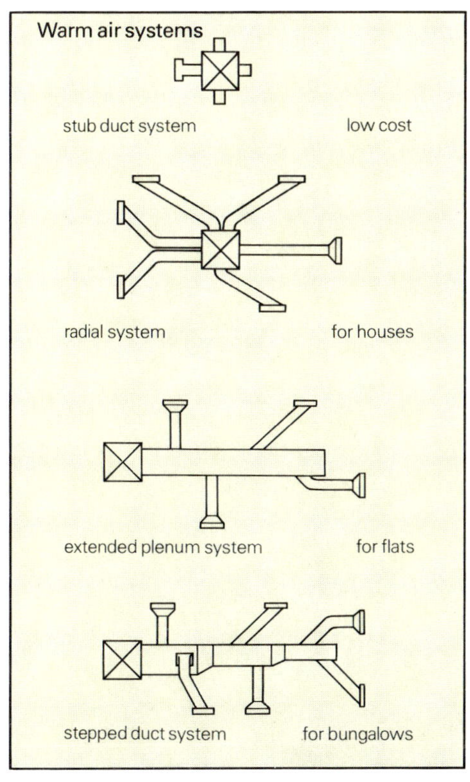

Basic calculations

Having decided on the fuel and coverage of the central heating that you require, the next thing is to calculate the size of the boiler, radiators, pipework and hot water cylinder.

This is where you will need your sketch plan, because to size the boiler heating load you have to calculate how much heat is being lost from each room through walls, windows and ceiling, and, of course, into the domestic hot water cylinder. To find the heating load you have to decide on or calculate:

1. Room temperatures and air changes
As a guide use these figures from the I.H.V.E. guide part B. The external air temperature is taken as −1°C:

Room	Temp.	Air changes
Living	21°C	0.33
Dining	21°C	0.33
Bathroom	22°C	0.67
Bedroom	18°C	0.17
Kitchen	21°C	0.67
Bed-sitting	21°C	0.33
Hall	16°C	0.50

Air changes occur through openings such as doors, windows and cracks. Ventilation allowances are essential to avoid stale air, but must be kept to a minimum or the air that is heated will be lost. These vary from room to room.

2. *U*-value
These are the heat losses through the fabric of the building, bricks, glass, metal and wood, and vary with the type of construction. Each construction material has a *U*-value which is its heat transference in watts per square metre from the internal to the external air.

The U-values for each fabric construction are given as a guide (above right).

The lower the *U*-value the lower the loss of heat, so that any construction that can be insulated gives a greater saving in heat and money.

Once you've got the *U*-values for the materials of your house these can be entered on the sketch plan.

3. Room heat loss
Technically this is known as $U \times A \times \Delta T$

U calculated *U*-value of construction

A Area of construction, that is, walls, floors and windows

ΔT Temperature difference between internal and external air. For example −1°C to +21°C=22°C.

Material	*U*-value
Single glazing with wood frames	4.3
Double glazing with wood frames	2.5
Single glazing with metal frames	5.6
Double glazing with metal frames	3.2
Cavity wall with plaster	1.5
Solid wall, 335mm thick, with plaster	1.6
Stud partition wall	2.9
Timber door	2.9
Floors, timber, suspended	0.99
Floors, concrete	0.75
Roofs, tiled and felted, no insulation	1.5
Roofs, tiled and felted, 100mm insulation	0.0

Example
For this we will take the living room shown on the ground floor plan. It is always advisable to write down each room as you do the calculations, setting out the figures in the form of a table as shown below.

To the fabric heat loss total must be added the volume of the room multiplied by its ventilation allowance multiplied by the temperature difference:

volume ventilation ΔT

$$3.9 \times 4.35 \times 2.7 \times 0.33 \times 22 = 332.5\text{W}$$

So the final total heat loss for the living room is:
1424.4W + 332.5W = 1756.9 watts.

This calculation is repeated for each room and the lobby area. When all the calculations are made add them together to obtain the total heat loss for the whole house. Say 10kW (10,000W).

The *U*-values given here are based on a house in a sheltered or normal outlook. If your house is exposed on a hill, or is a tall building then the factors used would be increased slightly.

To calculate the total boiler heating load you have to include the losses from the pipework and the hot water requirements.

4. Hot water cylinder load
The heat required for the water in the cylinder is calculated from the formula $V \times \Delta T \times s \div t$

V Volume of water in the cylinder (litres)

ΔT Temperature difference between cold and hot water (°C)

s specific heat of water (4.186)

t time to heat up the water in the cylinder (seconds)

Example
Assume that the capacity of the cylinder is 130 litres (V = 130 litres), that the cold water is heated from 10°C to 65°C (ΔT = 55°C) and that it takes 2 hours ($t = 2 \times 3600$ = 7200 seconds) to heat up the water.

Hot water cylinder load = $130 \times 55 \times 4.186 \div 7200$ = 4.15kW

5. Pipework losses
If the pipework is not lagged, the heat loss can be considerable: 15mm copper pipework freely exposed gives a loss of about 45 watts per metre run. For pipework insulated with 25mm thickness insulation the heat loss is reduced to about 1.25 watts per metre run.

The total pipework losses are estimated as 10% of the sum of room heat loss and cylinder load (from these examples, this equals 10% of 10 + 4.15 = 1.4kW).

Example: *Heating calculations for living room*

Construction	Width (m)	Length (m)	Height (m)	Area, A (m²)	U value	ΔT (°C)	Heat loss (W)
Cavity wall	0.0	4.35	2.7	11.75	1.5	21° to −1° = 22°	387.6
Cavity wall (less window)	3.9 (1.6)	0.0 (0.0)	2.7 (1.6)	7.97	1.5	21° to −1° = 22°	263.0
Window (single-glazed)	1.6	0.0	1.6	2.56	4.3	21° to −1° = 22°	242.2
Partition wall to hall including door (same *U*)	0.0	4.35	2.7	11.75	2.9	21° to 16° = 5°	170.3
Partition wall to dining room	3.9	0.0	2.7	10.53	2.9	21° to 21° = 0°	0.0
Concrete floor	3.9	4.35	0.0	16.97	0.75	21° to −1° = 22°	279.9
Ceiling	3.9	4.35	0.0	16.97	1.6	21° to 18° = 3°	81.4
Fabric heat loss total:							**1424.4W**

__1.__ Wall-hung gas-fired boiler with built-in programmer is compact and saves floor space. Some have matching range of wall cupboards.
__2.__ Floor-standing gas-fired boiler with built-in programmer fits neatly under kitchen worktop.
__3.__ Floor-standing oil-fired boiler with casing opened to show pipe connections.

Total boiler load

You can now obtain your total boiler load as follows.

Room heat loss (total)	=10.0kW
Hot water cylinder load	= 4.15kW
Pipework loss	= 1.4kW
Pre-heat (say 5% of the above)	= 0.75kW
Total boiler load	**=16.30kW**

(Pre-heat is not usually required on fully pumped circuits.)

Boiler types

Boilers are rated in kilowatts (kW) and have minimum and maximum outputs. From the example above a boiler can be chosen quite easily, but if you plan a future extension it would be prudent to rate the boiler higher.

The boiler is the most expensive item in a central heating system, so careful consideration is wise before choosing. There are many variations and one will be more suitable for your needs than others. How do you decide which?

For this exercise we will consider in detail the gas fired boiler only, but solid fuel and oil fired boilers can be used.

Solid fuel

There are three types of solid fuel boiler.
Sectional boilers made up of cast iron bolted together. These are fed by hand.
Gravity fed boilers are made of steel and are fed by a hopper. They are thermostatically controlled.
Pot type boilers are similar to the two above but the efficiency is lower.

There are also two types of solid fuel room heaters, open and closed, which can provide central heating and hot water. Their output is limited. Room heaters are kept alight throughout the winter and replenished up to three times every 24 hours.

Gas boilers

Gas fired boilers today use natural gas. There are four types:
1. Floor mounted, conventional flue.
2. Floor mounted, balanced flue.
3. Wall mounted, balanced flue.
4. Back boiler in chimney breast.

Without doubt gas fired boilers are the easiest to install. They are relatively easy to maintain and can be used in almost every situation except bedrooms. They can be positioned high or low on a wall so long as the feed and expansion tank are placed above.

Oil

Most oil fired domestic boilers used class D oil. This is gas oil which requires no preheating.

There are three types of oil fired boiler.
Pressure jet is the most common type of oil burner and will use kerosene when downrated.
Vaporisation uses kerosene and is rated class C oil burner. It is much quieter.
Wall flame is similar to a pressure jet.

Oil storage

You will normally need to store enough oil to last eight weeks: you can work this out using the kilowatt loading of your boiler, as follows:

> The volume of oil required per kilowatt is given by the formula
>
> $$\frac{t}{c \times E \times s}$$
>
> t time the boiler will be in operation during 8 weeks. Assuming 12 hours per day, this is 8 × 7 × 12 × 3600 = 672 × 3600 seconds.
> E Efficiency of the boiler (75% = 0.75)
> c calorific value of the oil; for class C heating oil this is 42.7kJ/kg = 42700J/kg
> s specific gravity of oil (0.835)
>
> So the volume of oil required to be stored *per kilowatt rating of the boiler* is
>
> $$\frac{672 \times 3600}{42700 \times 0.75 \times 0.835} \text{ litres}$$
> $$= 90.47 \text{ litres}$$

Storage tanks should be built above ground, in the open, and be constructed of steel. They are normally put on brick pipes and at a gradient to allow venting and draining,

One-pipe oil-supply system

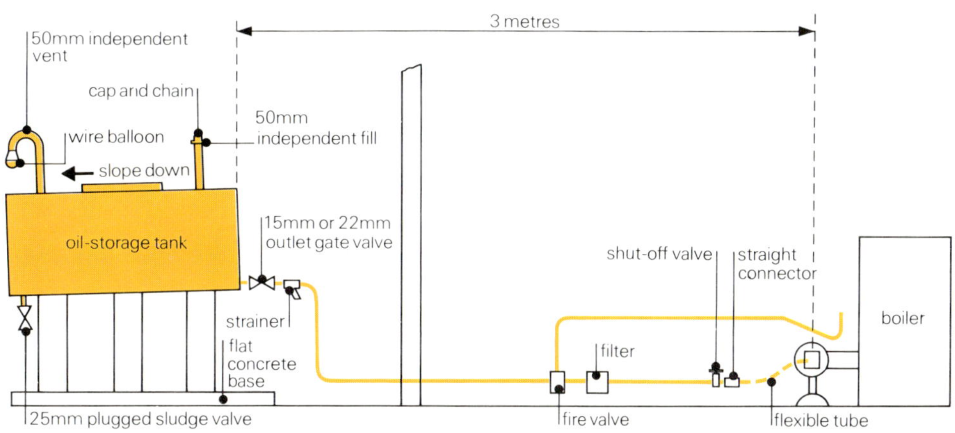

and placed within a brick compartment which is 'tanked' or made oil-tight to take the complete storage.

Tank rooms should comply with Fire Standards C.O.P. 3002 and British Standard 799.

Flues

Without a flue or chimney, normally brick built, your boiler would not function, but unless they are designed and installed correctly, chimneys lead to condensation.

All fuels produce gases and water vapour when burnt. A chimney provides a safe means of carrying away these gases. The hot flue gases and vapour rise because they are light than the colder outside air which displaces them from below. The height of the chimney influences the velocity at which these gases rise, together with the difference in temperature.

Designing a flue

Always install your flue to reduce the risk of condensation, bearing in mind the following:

1. If possible have a chimney or flue built inside the house.
2. Insulate it to reduce heat losses.
3. Line it with a non-absorbent and smooth impervious material.
4. It should be the correct size to comply with the boiler output.
5. Keep it as straight as possible. If bends are inevitable, then make them no less than 45° to the horizontal.

When installed inside the house the flue retains its own heat and reduces the risk of condensation. If the flue is outside the house then use a double skinned steel flue, with insulation between the skins. If an asbestos flue is used a drain tap has to be fitted at the lowest part of the flue, or at a suitable bend. Check with local health and building regulations before buying an asbestos flue.

A flexible stainless-steel flue liner provides a convenient method of lining an existing flue if installing a boiler in a fireplace opening. This type should not, however, be used with solid-fuel burning appliances as the waste gases will cause corrosion of the steel.

Sealed systems

This type of system uses a diaphragm or membrane tank together with a safety valve and pressure gauge, instead of the conventional open system using an F & E tank and open vent.

The sealed system can be used on both smallbore and microbore systems.

It is sometimes called a pressurised system, which means that it is not open to the atmosphere and can operate at higher temperatures which in turn can reduce the size of the piping.

Standard radiators cannot be used at these higher pressures as the surface of the radiator would be extremely uncomfortable to touch. Heat emitters that can be used are fan convectors, convector radiators and skirting heaters.

Control of the hot water cylinder water will be by the thermostatic valve which would keep the domestic hot water at 60°C to 71°C.

The position of the diaphragm within the system is important as it has to be in the right place to work with the pump.

Calculating the size of pressure vessel

This has to be calculated using four factors:

1. Static head on vessel
2. Cold fill pressure
3. Final temperature
4. Quantity of water in the system.

Manufacturers of sealed vessels provide information of the correct size to suit the system requirements. Set out right is an approximate guide to the size of expansion vessels required as produced by Wednesbury Tube Co., for a traditional boiler and radiator system.

The diaphragm is usually made of rubber and the expansion chamber is filled with air or nitrogen. Its function is to take up the expansion of water.

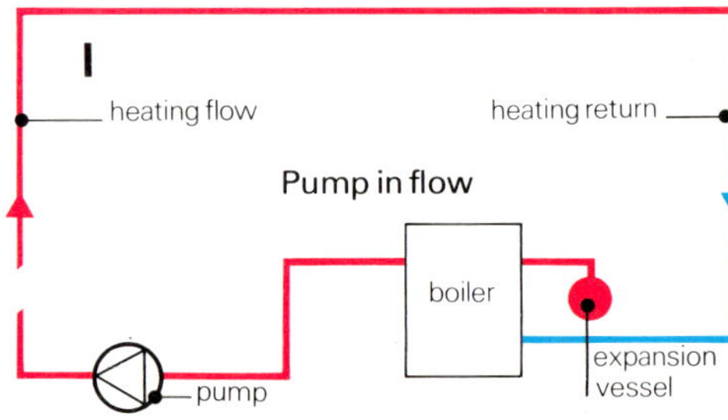

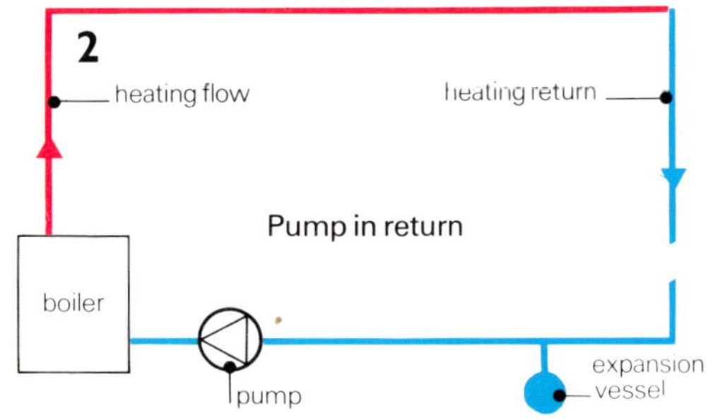

1. *Most common position of pump. Requires headroom over F & E tank.*
2. *Operates at lower pressure than* **1** *and requires no headroom.*

System output kW	Nominal vessel size in litres
6	4
12	8
18	12
24	18

1. *Liner connected direct to flue pipe of appliance when no condensation anticipated.*
2. *Fill space between liner and chimney with lightweight granular insulation.*
3. *Collecting condensate from a chimney.*

Where no condensation is anticipated, connect the lining directly to the flue pipe from the appliance.

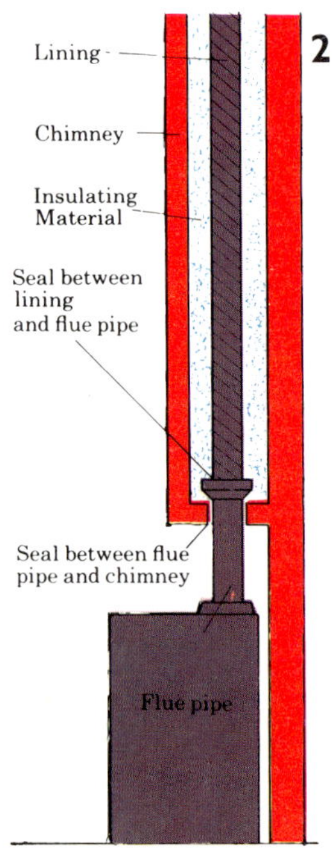

It is advisable to insulate the lining. An infill with lightweight granular material is suggested

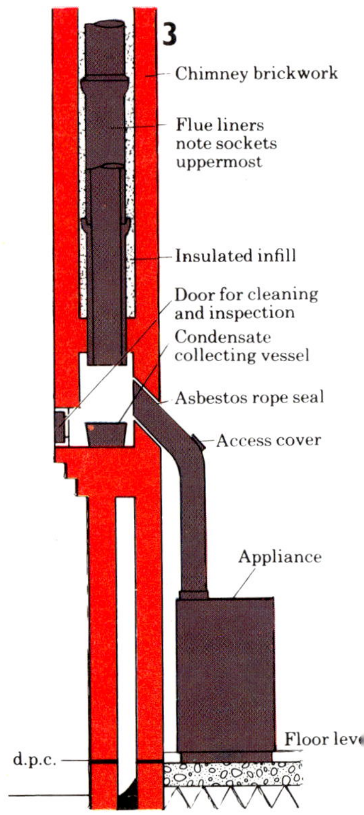

Collecting condensate from a chimney

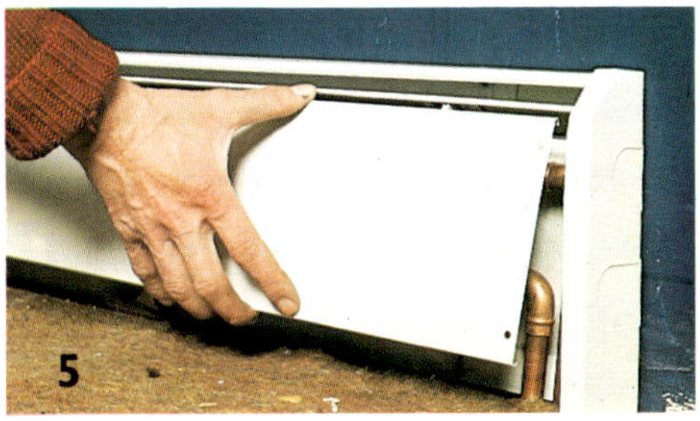

1. *Installing fan convector with outlets for two adjoining rooms.*
2. *Rear grille of* **1**.
3. *Completed installation.*
4. *Finned element of a skirting convector.*
5. *Fitting cover plate to* **4**. *Output is controlled by adjustable damper.*

You can fill the system directly from a domestic tap via a hose into the stop-cock with a non-return valve.

Another method which is used is that with a break between the mains supply and the system; this is to prevent backflow and contamination.

A leak in the system shows by a drop in pressure and refilling of water.

Safety valve
The safety valve is probably the most important fail-safe device. The correct valve must be used as the pressure in the system is different to that of an open system with an open vent.

Radiators

Before you start sizing any type of radiator it is essential to decide which type to use and where you are going to install them.

Positioning
The best place to put radiators is under windows where the downward currents of cold air will be heated, so giving the room an even temperature. This will also prevent wall stains above the emitters.

If you have to place the radiator against a wall, these stains can be prevented by fixing a shelf above it.

Types of domestic radiators
Panel radiators are made of light steel pressings welded together. They are reasonably attractive and cheap to buy. They present a large surface area. Single and double versions are commonly available in a variety of heights and lengths.

Although called radiators they radiate very little heat, working mainly by convection currents. They are easy to install and can be hung on light partitioning from brackets supplied with the radiators.

Their main disadvantage is that they are prone to attack by corrosion. To overcome this an inhibitor can be put into the system. This is usually a liquid (Fernox) which is put into the F & E tank.

There are many types of panel radiator on the market. When sizing always read the maker's instructions. Lockshield valves (lsv) and wheel head (wh) valves are fitted to either end.

Convector radiators are outwardly similar in appearance to panel radiators and are fitted with steel fins on the reverse face (or between the two panels of a double radiator) which greatly increase the surface area and thus the heat output. A double convector radiator may have a heat output up to 40% greater than the same size of panel radiator, and they are therefore more economical in terms of wall space. Fitting is as for panel radiators.

Fan convectors provide instant controlled heat. A fan capable of low, medium and boost output blows air over a finned heat exchanger. It can also be used in summer to give a cold air blow.

Fan convectors are small and efficient but the units themselves are expensive. Individual control is very easy because the heat output is governed by the fan which can be switched and thermostatically controlled. Installation is simple since there is only a flow and return water pipe. The only drawback is that you also need an electric socket outlet next to each unit. The fans can be noisy and need regular maintenance if they are to give good service.

Skirting heaters
These provide a neat and unobtrusive system. A skirting heater is a form of convector and special enclosures are available shaped to take the place of a skirting board. The drawback with this system is that it may be difficult to make connections around doorways: also it may not provide enough heat in large rooms.

1. *If wall space is limited, fit a double panel radiator or a convector radiator.*
2. *Ideal position for a radiator.*

1 *Radiator controls*

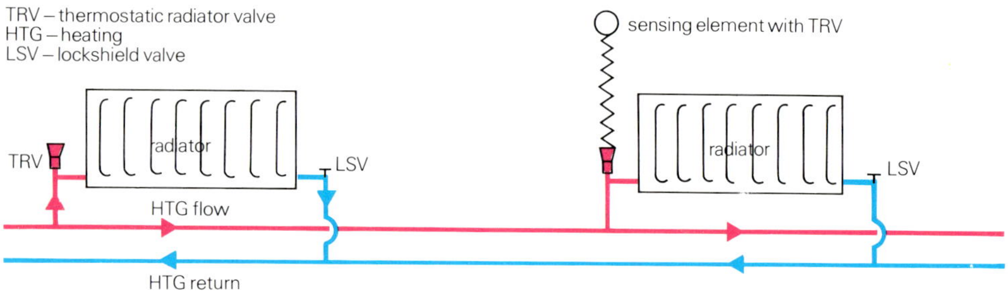

2 *Pumped heating with gravity hot water*

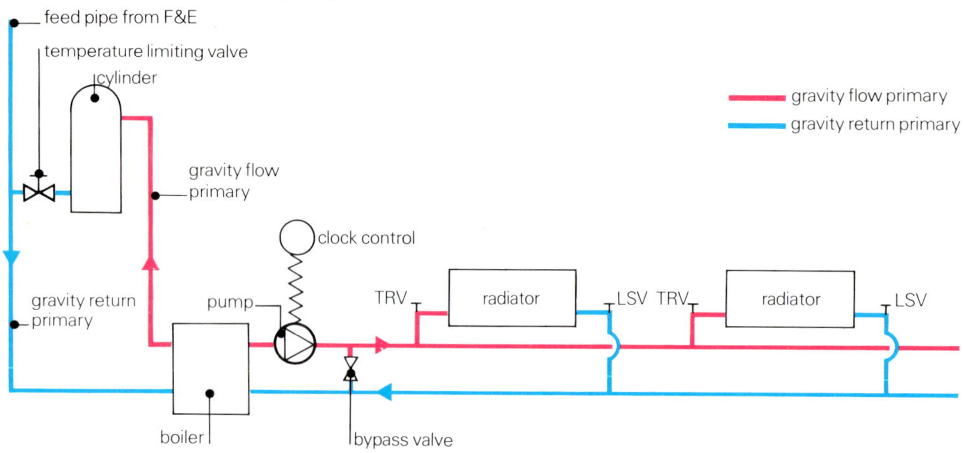

3 *Heating controlled with room thermostat Hot water cylinder controlled with thermostat*

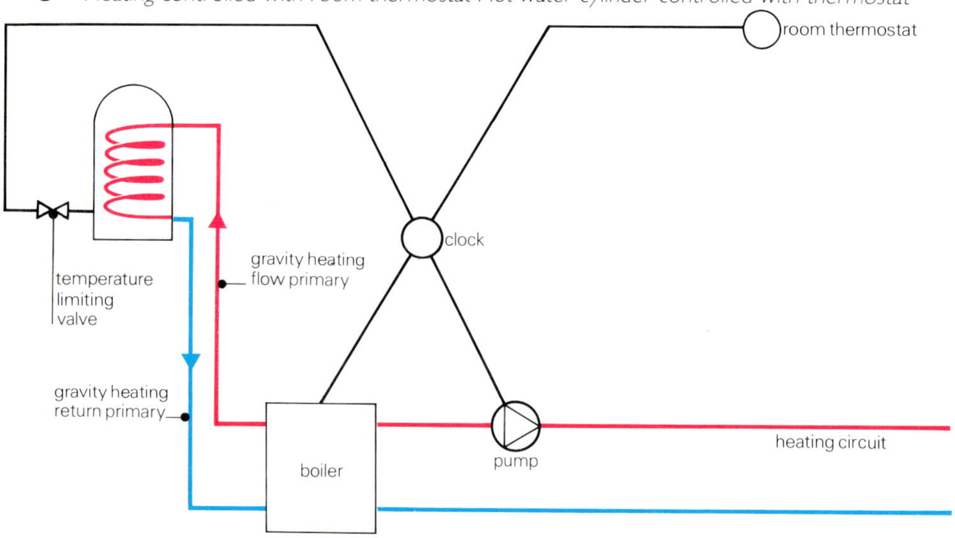

5 *Zoned valve heating with gravity hot water*

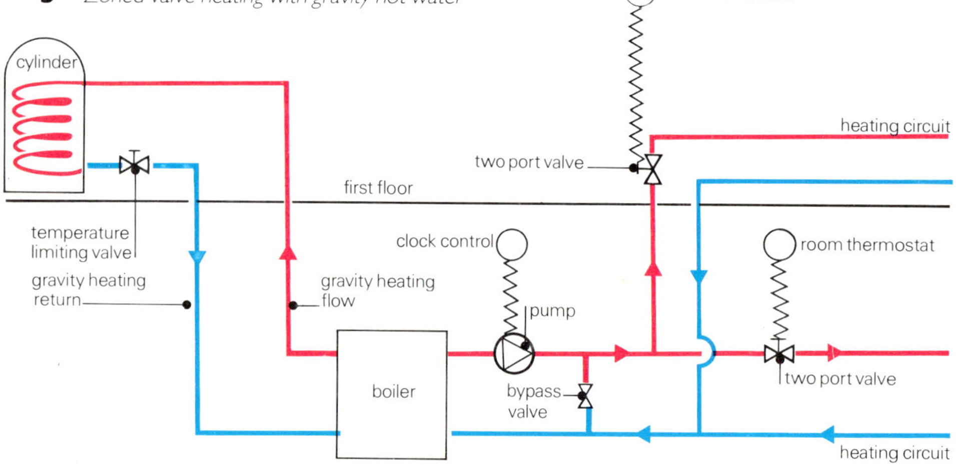

1

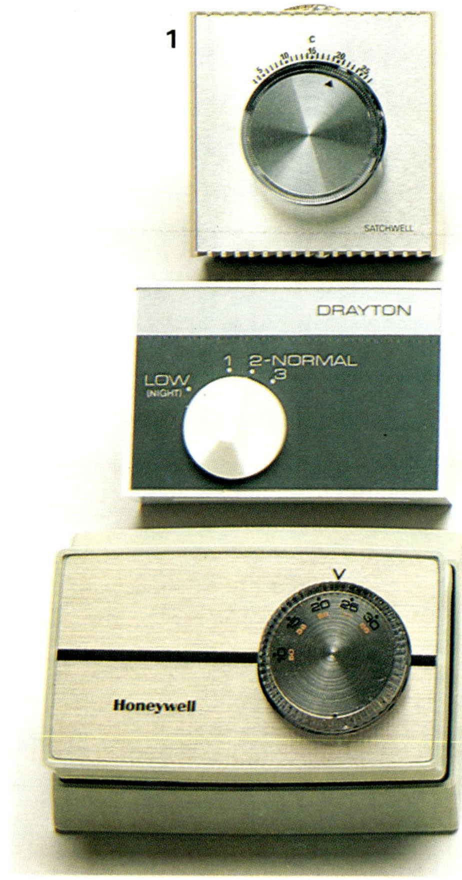

Use your sketch plan

The position of the radiators or fan convectors can now be drawn on the sketch plan, together with the boiler, hot water cylinder and the feed and expansion (F & E) tank. The sketch plan can be used equally well for both small and microbore systems.

At this stage you can decide on the type of controls you wish to install, whether to

4 *Heating controlled with room thermostat*

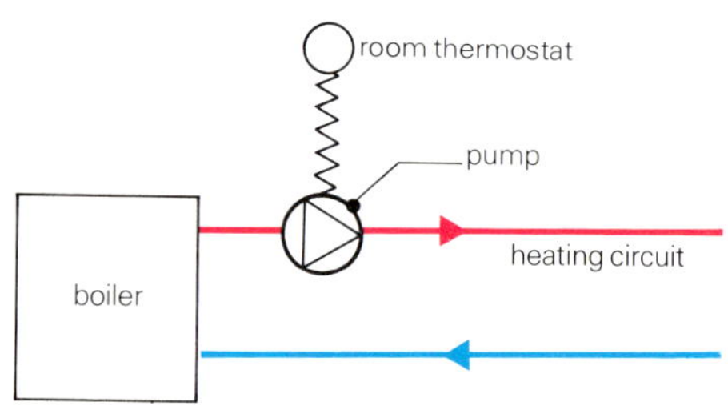

1. *Two-pipe heating system showing flow and return connections to radiators via TRVs (one with remote sensor) and LSVs.*
2. *Clock-controlled system with TRVs, and temperature limiting valve on cylinder. Bypass valve allows circulation in heating circuit when all TRVs are closed.*
3. *Simplest form of heating control – room thermostat switching pump.*
4. *As* **3**, *but with timer control and temperature limiting valve.*
5. *Individual control of ground and first floor heating circuits by means of zone valves.*

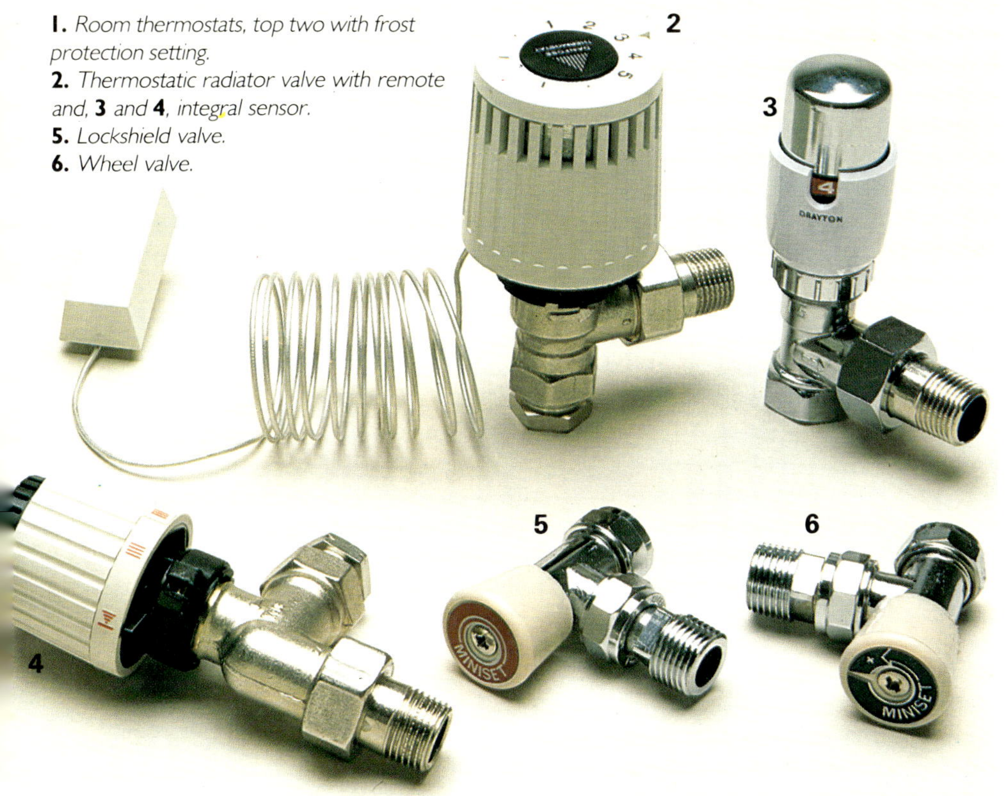

1. *Room thermostats, top two with frost protection setting.*
2. *Thermostatic radiator valve with remote and,* **3** *and* **4**, *integral sensor.*
5. *Lockshield valve.*
6. *Wheel valve.*

use small or microbore piping, and a pumped or gravity-driven system. All this will affect the positioning and design of your pipe runs to the individual units.

Controls

The spiralling cost of energy makes it more and more important to have effective control of your heating system.

Control systems allow you to conserve heat and energy without noticing any loss of comfort: a single degree of temperature more than you need adds up to 5% on the fuel bill. Most controls are accurate to plus or minus a degree centigrade.

There are two types of heating controls that you will come across:
1. Appliance controls on boilers or storage heaters.
2. Room and hot water controls for central heating systems.

Appliance controls
Most controls fitted to appliances are designed to provide a fail-safe, as well as controlling the temperature of the water within the appliance.

Gas-fired boilers require a thermostat to control the water temperature. If this is faulty there should be a safety valve installed in the boiler or flow pipework to release the pressure if it rises too high.

Boiler control alone is not ideal as this causes frequent firing. It is recommended to keep the control thermostat at 60°C or above to prevent condensation and the possibility of corrosion in the boiler.

Modern boilers, such as low water content types, use copper or steel heat exchangers. This causes even greater cycling and needs precise design.

Room and hot water controls
The simplest method is to use lockshield valves on the return pipework. These balance the system, and once they are set, they do not have to be touched unless an extension is added.

The wheel valves provide local control, so that a radiator or other heat emitter can be fully or partly shut down.

There are two other methods of controlling the radiators which in turn control room temperature.
1. By using air-sensing thermostatic radiator valves (TRVs). These have become very popular. They have to be installed on the flow side of the radiators, or they can cause a noise like machine gun fire when the valve partly opens.

With this method the pump is kept running continually, and is switched on and off by a clock control. The disadvantage is that temperature sensing is arbitrary. On the plus side each room can be controlled to the temperature that the system was designed for. Each or any room can be shut off without any detrimental effect to the overall system.

The hot water can be controlled on this system at a different temperature using a temperature limiting thermostat placed in the primary return, whether it is a gravity or pumped primary.
2. Room air thermostats control the whole house temperatures from one point.

The thermostat should be placed 1.5 metres (5ft) above floor level, away from radiators and other sources of heat and in a draught-free location.

Which is the best room is debatable. Many experts say that it should be placed in the hall, as this is usually the coldest area.

It is sometimes best to set the thermostat about 2°C higher than required so that anybody sitting in the living room will not feel cold.

The room thermostat can be used in many ways:
1. Switching a pump off and on.
2. Switching a boiler off and on.
3. Activating a zone valve.
4. Activating a diverter valve.

Heating system controls
In years gone by, systems had gravity primaries to the hot water cylinder, with a pumped heating circuit. Today it is more common and practical to have pumped primaries and heating. These are only some of the controls used. A fully pumped system can save boiler loads and provide a quick response to heating and hot water demands.

Diverter valve
This is the most common device. The diverter valve is a motorised valve under the control of two thermostats placed on the hot water cylinder and in the heating circuit. The valve has three ports – one inlet and two outlets. The inlet is the primary heating flow and the outlets are to the heating circuit and the hot water cylinder.

The function of the valve is to allow water pumped from the boiler to flow through the heating circuit or to the hot water cylinder, whichever has priority. This is usually the hot water cylinder – when the boiler is fired the water will heat up the hot water cylinder to the set temperature. Then the valve will open the port to the heating circuit and close the port to the domestic hot water cylinder. When both are satisfied the thermostats will shut off the pump.

Some diverter valves offer the facility of a mid-position where water can flow to both circuits.

The idea of diverter valves is to reduce boiler rating to a minimum, since the boiler output can be based only on the higher of the two circuits.

Frost thermostat

In conjunction with a room thermostat a frost thermostat can be used to prevent frost damage when the heating system is off for long periods. It is wired into the system to override the heating thermostat or clock when the ambient temperature around the frost thermostat approaches freezing point. It is usually placed on the outside of the house and set between 2°C and 5°C.

Zone valves using room thermostats

These work exactly as a room thermostat except that areas can be controlled independently. A typical application of this system would be to shut off upstairs bedroom radiators in daytime whilst heating downstairs living rooms.

Two-port valve system with full thermostatic control

Two-port valves serve only as on/off controls and are very basic.

Programmers and clock control

These have different functions to perform and are not the same. They can, however, be incorporated in the same control box. The usual purpose of the clock control is to turn the heating off when it is not specifically required in order to save fuel. The usual clock control has four tappets which can give two on and two off switchings to suit your heat needs.

For a working family it is usual to set one on for the early morning, say 5.30am to bring on the heating and give a warm house when getting ready for work. The off will be set for, say, half an hour before everybody leaves for work. In the evening the second on tapping can be set for one hour before arriving home, and the off setting for, say, 11pm before retiring.

A programmer is used in conjunction with a clock, but it allows you separate control of the heating and hot water. Modern programmers can be very complex with a range of perhaps six or 12 settings. The common settings are:

1. Heating and hot water continuously.
2. Heating and hot water, clock control.
3. Hot water clock control only.
4. Heating twice and hot water all day.
5. Heating and hot water off.

Many programmers are incorporated in the boiler panel and wired accordingly, being based on pumped heating and gravity fed hot water.

Fully pumped systems are normally controlled by a clock only.

Fully pumped heating and hot water with diverter control

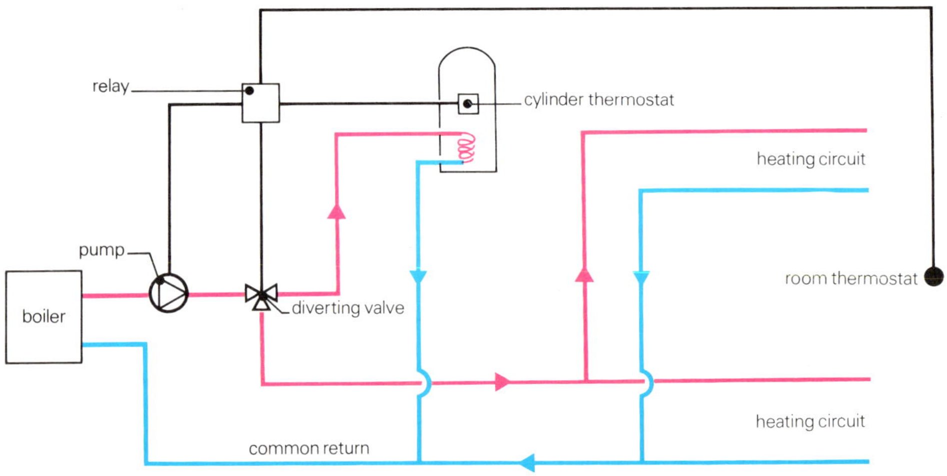

Above *Thermostats control motorised diverter valve via relay.*
1 & 2. *Thermostatic cylinder valves (temperature limiting valves) with remote sensor.*
3. *Thermostatic cylinder valve incorporating integral sensor.*
4. *Relay connected to room and cylinder thermostats controls.*
5. *Motorised diverter valve.*

1 & 2. *Six-position programmers.*
3. *Single function time switch.*
4. *Diverter-valve programmer.*
5. *Electronic programmer with 12 switching cycles per 24 hours.*
6. *Electronic optimising controller with built-in micro-computer can 'learn' timings.*

1
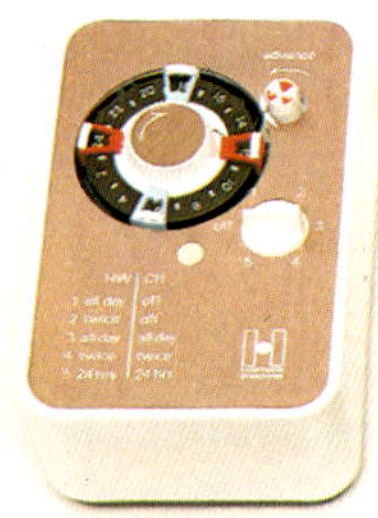
2
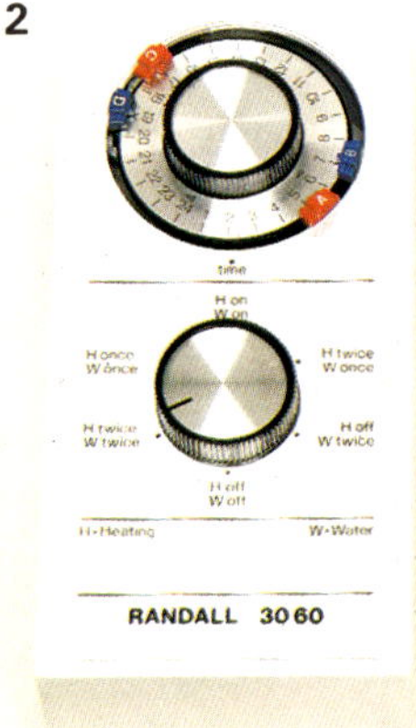

3

4
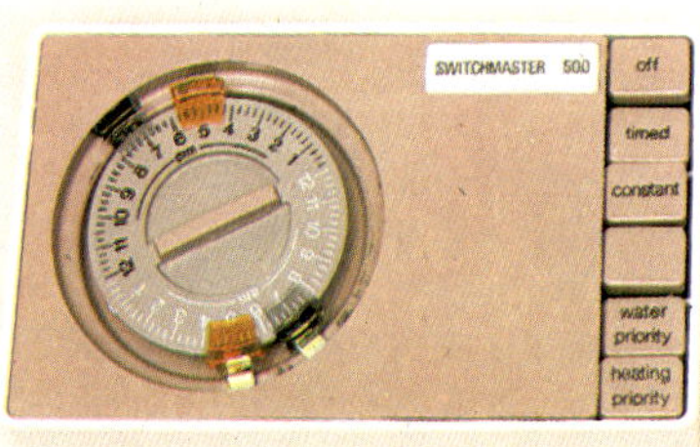

5
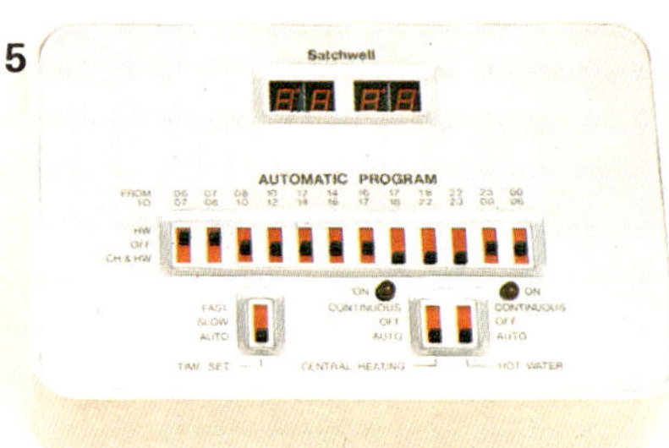

6
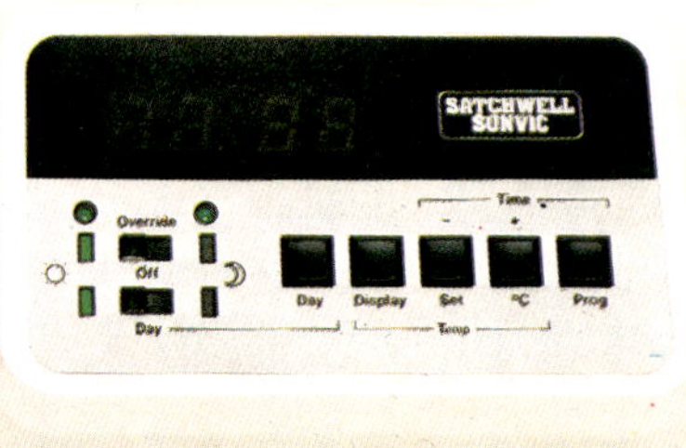

1 2 3
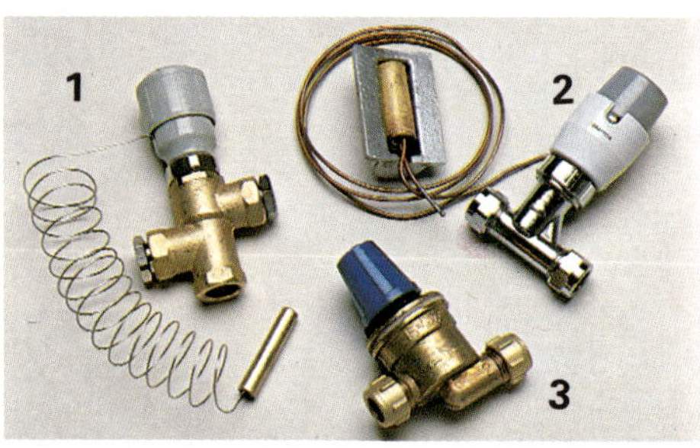

4 5
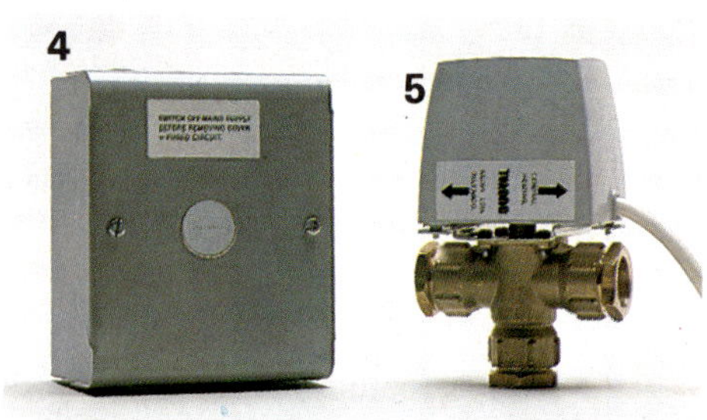

Tanks and pumps

Having positioned all the radiators and the boiler, with its controls, the hot water cylinder and the F & E tank have to be included along with the pipework and pump to complete the system.

Hot water cylinder
The majority of cylinders are copper with a 127-litre capacity. They are usually of the indirect type, which means that the water from the boiler flows through copper tubes known as a heat exchanger coil which prevents hot water from coming into contact with the water in the cylinder. This prevents furring-up of the system. A cylinder is usually put in the airing cupboard and if it is above the boiler can be gravity fed from it.

Gravity feed circulation
As the water in the pipes on the feed side of the boiler is heated it expands and becomes less dense. It therefore rises and is displaced by cooler water coming from the return side into the boiler, so beginning a circulation.

This system requires large pipes and is mainly found in older installations. To heat up a cylinder by gravity feed would take up to four hours.

Modern systems use pumped circulation which reduces the time taken to heat up the cylinder to 20–60 minutes depending on the size of pipe, usually 15 or 22mm, and the pressure produced by the pump.

Feed and expansion tank
This is always positioned above the highest point of the heating circuit, and if this happens to run into the roof space then the F & E tank must be above it. This is to ensure that the whole of the system is filled with water, which prevents air locking, which in turn would stop water circulation.

It is also sized to take the expansion of water from the open vent and is usually 45 litres nominal capacity. It can be galvanised steel or polyethylene.

Pipework, sizing and systems
From the sketch plan the pipework can now be shown connecting up the various pieces of equipment, and it can be sized.

Sizing involves intricate and lengthy calculation, but for most domestic heating the sizes of pipework can be based on the following loading for a given radiator layout and output:

Up to 3kW	15mm pipe
3kW to 10kW	22mm pipe
10kW to 18kW	25mm pipe

These sizes are based on a temperature difference on the flow and return pipework of 11°C. Smaller sizes should be avoided as they can give high water velocity which causes noise.

The best system of pipework uses two pipes. If sized correctly this gives complete control of the heating load.

The flow pipe is usually at 81°C and the return at 70°C, which means that each radiator connected will have the same temperature of flow and return water. The pipes can be installed in almost any position but take care to prevent air locking.

Pumps
Nearly every heating system has a pump to circulate water to each unit. It is important that you position it correctly in relation to the F & E tank and the heating open vent.

The pump produces a positive or negative pressure which can introduce air into the heating system or push water up the open vent to discharge over the F & E tank. These problems can be overcome as in the examples below.

Pumps should always be fitted with an isolating valve on each side so that the pump can be serviced without touching the rest of the heating system. Most pumps have an air cock on top to allow any air trapped inside to be discharged.

Pump sizing
Before any pump can be sized, the heating circuit with the highest radiator output or the longest run of piping has to be determined. This is known as the index circuit. From this the head of the system is calculated.

Head is the total pressure drop across the circuit. It is not necessary for this to be calculated in a modern domestic heating system since the domestic pumps usually have up to four selections of head ranging from zero to 45 kN.

The other factor you need to know is how much water the pump has to circulate around the system.

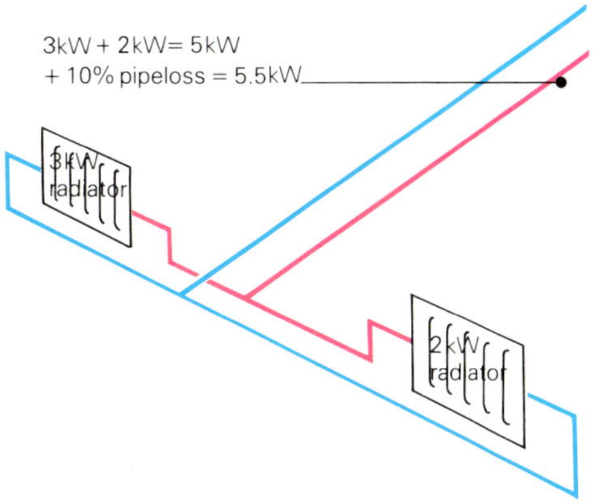

Pipe sizes are determined from output of radiators plus heat loss from pipes.

Air in the system
No matter how carefully you make your installation air is always present, and it is vital that it is dispersed as quickly as possible. It causes these problems which can seriously affect the system.

1. Air locking which can restrict the circulation of water, and result in some radiators not working.
2. Corrosion. A heating system has a mixture of copper and steel components and any air in the system will cause oxidation of the steel – rust.

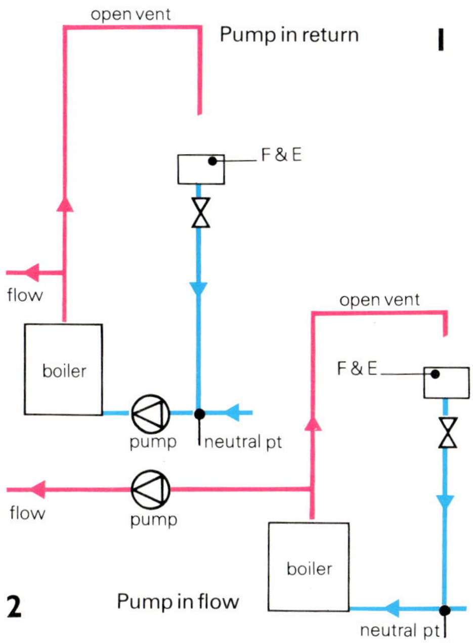

1. *Most common position of pump. Requires headroom over F & E tank.*
2. *Operates at lower pressure than* **1** *and requires no headroom.*
3. *With pump switched off, turn air vent valve anti-clockwise to release trapped air, then close. This process is known as 'bleeding' and should be carried out regularly to ensure the efficient operation of the system.*

3

Microbore heating

Microbore, as the word implies, is the use of narrow pipes with tube bores ranging from 6mm to 10mm diameter. Microbore is now readily accepted within the heating trade because of its many advantages. It can be used with open or pressurised systems using a two-pipe flow and return arrangement.

The design and calculations for microbore must be made more carefully than for smallbore; however, the majority of components used in a smallbore can be installed into a microbore system such as boiler, radiators and pump.

The advantages of microbore outweigh traditional systems because:

1. Installations are quicker; savings of up to 10% are common.
2. Disturbance of the household is reduced to a minimum.
3. It can be a flexible installation, permitting extensions at a later date.
4. The water content of the system is less which gives a faster heat-up and better response to controls.
5. Most important, a neater installation is possible, as the very small tubes can be easily concealed.
6. Assembly techniques are similar to a smallbore system but simpler. No specialist know-how is required.
7. The absence of many pipe fittings reduces the risk of leaks.
8. You can enjoy the economy of a low thermal capacity boiler.
9. Microbore can be installed in existing buildings and existing floorboards may not have to be lifted because the pipework can be surface mounted. It can also be buried in the concrete floor when new buildings are constructed.

Designing a microbore system

The design considerations are the same as for smallbore systems:

1. U-values and heat losses.
2. Temperatures in each room.
3. Boiler sizing.
4. Radiators, their position and sizing.
5. Feed and expansion tank.
6. Circuit temperature drop, 81 to 70°C.

The exceptions to smallbore design and calculations are the pipework layout, pump sizing, and pipework sizing. The use of manifold or manifolds and the pipework layout will be covered in the installation section.

The pump will have a slightly higher head due to the smaller bore which creates a higher velocity of water flow. The velocity has to be kept above 0.3 metres per second.

Microbore components and materials

Tube sizes have been reduced to 6, 8 and 10mm diameter, and are manufactured to BS2871 in soft tempered copper which allows easy manipulation by hand for all but very sharp bends. These can be formed with an external spring or hand bender. The following are the lengths available:

size mm	coil lengths
6mm	10 to 200m (33 to 660 ft)
8mm	10 to 150m (33 to 490 ft)
10mm	10 to 100m (33 to 330 ft)

The longer the length of coil, the less fittings you have and the fewer leaks.

Care must be taken when handling the coils as they are liable to kink and both ends should be covered to exclude dirt.

Radiator valves

Smallbore systems have a valve at each end of the radiator, but for microbore systems a valve has been designed which allows both inlet and outlet in one valve – known as a double entry valve.

When installing the valve the flow tapping is the one against the radiator.

In operation the valve controls the return from the radiator.

Manifold – the heart of the system

This is one of the major pieces of equipment that differs from the conventional smallbore system. It is simply a length of 22mm or 28mm copper tube with a central-

A selection of equipment and tools for a microbore heating and hot water system: boiler, high recovery hot water cylinder, panel radiator, fan convector, pressure vessel, double-entry radiator valve, microbore tubing and connectors of various sizes, manifold and pump. Tools are: hacksaws, hand pipe bender, external bending spring, pipe cutter, adjustable spanner and Stilsons, solder and blowlamp.

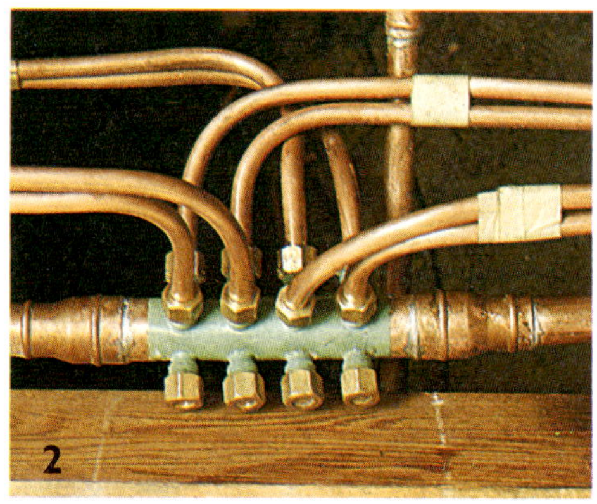

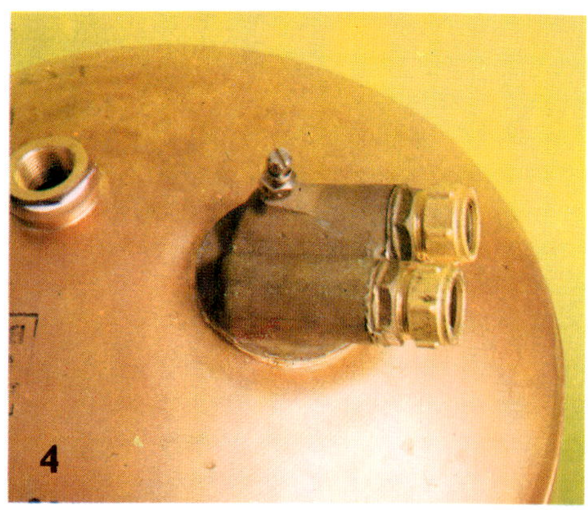

1. *Double-entry radiator valve with flow pipe nearer radiator.*
2. *Manifold is in two sections – one for flow, one for return pipes.*
3. *Installing immersion element in immersion heater boss on cylinder.*
4. *Connect flow and return to bosses and adjust flow with screw on top.*

ly positioned separator disc, which provides both flow and return chambers in one unit. Into this length of tube a number of stub bosses are soldered to form compression fittings which allow pipework to be connected easily.

Any boss not required can be capped and used at a later date for additional radiators. Any number of manifolds can be used in one system.

There are basically three types:

	no. of bosses for flow	no. of bosses for return	temp. drop 11°C	temp. drop 17°C
WM18 240mm	9	9	36kW	54kW
WM12 170mm	6	6	24kW	36kW
WM8 170mm	4	4	16kW	24kW

This is based on Wednesbury Micrafold range

Conversion units

A conversion unit is an immersion element used to convert an existing direct copper cylinder to an indirect cylinder. It can also be used in a new system but is not essential. Conversion units can be used on a pumped or gravity primary system. Various outputs are available:

output pumped	size
11.1kW	760mm × 4 blade
8.8kW	680mm × 4 blade
3.5kW	400mm × 4 blade

Pumped primaries and heating

The layout for a pumped primary heating system is exactly as the pumped smallbore system and there is no variation in the position of pump, valves, controls and boiler.

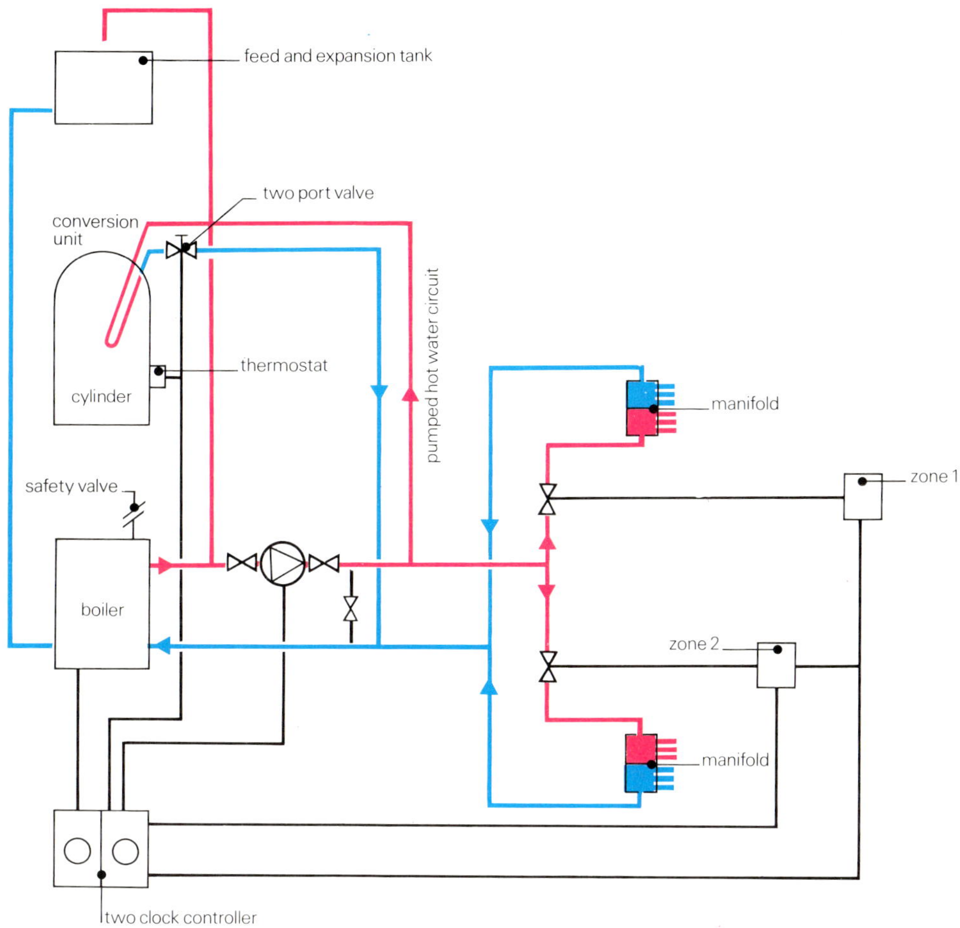

Above *Two-zone microbore system with pumped primaries and separate control of time and temperature for each zone.*

Installation

Installing a central heating system will cause considerable domestic upheaval. To reduce this to a minimum, plan as much of the work as possible in advance.

Work systematically, have everything to hand, and complete each stage before starting on the next. This cannot be stressed too much. Try to install everything possible before you cut into the domestic water system.

Tools

1. pipe cutters, hacksaw and files
2. Allen keys (to fit radiator blanking plug and air vent)
3. bending springs 15mm and 22mm
4. spanners or Stilson wrench
5. hammer and cold chisel (for holes through walls)
6. butane blowlamp (can be hired)
7. floorboard bolster and claw hammer (for lifting floorboards)
8. hand brace and bits and a saw
9. spirit level, screws No 12 and wall plugs
10. lead light

Materials

1. lead-free solder and flux
2. PTFE tape and non-toxic sealing compound
3. wire wool
4. heat-resistant mat to prevent burning
5. copper fittings

The different kinds of copper fittings fall under two headings:

Compression fittings have olives (rings) and nuts. If you have very little experience of copper installation this is the best type of fitting to use as only a small amount of sealing compound and a spanner to tighten the nut are needed, but these fittings are more expensive.

Capillary fittings come in two types. Some have a ring of solder included inside, which are known as integral ring fittings. The others are called end feed fittings to which the solder is added afterwards.

Capillary fittings are neater and cheaper, but need more skill to make good joints.

If a leak does occur with capillary fittings, part or all of the system may have to be drained down because of the presence of water.

All pipework and fittings must conform with British standards.

Buying equipment

Try to work out from your plan and room layout the amount of pipework, bends, and tees that are necessary to connect the equipment, as well as the equipment you will need.

Make a list, go to your supplier and ask for advice on what type of fittings are required. Also ask if you can return any that are not needed, because fittings are expensive.

When buying pipework allow extra, because without doubt you will make some mistakes and there will be offcuts that cannot be used.

Do not try to carry all the equipment in your car; it is heavy and awkward and it is well worth having it delivered.

Specialist tools needed to install central heating:
1. *Pipe bender and attachments.*
2. *Internal bending springs.*
3. *Butane blowtorch (if using capillary fittings).*
4. *Electric saw (useful for cutting floorboards).*
5. *Stilson.*
6. *Basin spanner (for fitting taps).*
7. *Adjustable spanner.*
8. *Pipe cutter.*
9. *Case opener.*
10. *Rat's tail files.*
11. *Half-round file.*
12. *Solder (for end-feed capillary fittings).*
13. *Flux and* **14.** *Wire wool (for capillary fittings).*
15. *Spirit level (to set radiator and pipe levels).*

Points to note when installing
When lifting floorboards try not to splinter them.

Never put banks of, pipework in the centre of a room as this is the weakest point of the joist. Try to run pipework with or under joists. Make notches cleanly and if making holes through joists make them through the centre.

Never fit pipework side by side. Make enough room in the joist for a gap to allow for expansion. Many installers place pieces of felt between pipes.

Modern thinking is that all pipework under floors should be insulated to save heat.

Radiators
Decide where the valves are to be fitted. Usually they are at the bottom, at opposite ends, which leaves the two top ends: one of these is blanked off with a plug and the other is fitted with a brass air vent valve. These are threaded and must be wrapped with PTFE tape and screwed in with a spanner. When fitting the air vent make sure that a key can be fitted in the end when the radiator is installed, so that it can be vented to release trapped air.

Steel panel radiators are hung on brackets (supplied) and fixed securely to the wall. You must take care to align the brackets horizontally because radiators that are not level get air locks in them.

Radiators are fixed about 150mm from the floor level to facilitate cleaning beneath them. If the radiators are fixed elsewhere than under a window, a shelf can be fitted about 75mm above to protect the wall from staining.

Painting radiators is no problem, but metallic paints such as aluminium can reduce overall output by up to 10%.

Skirting heating and fan convectors
The same principles apply except that it is not necessary to have valves at every point on the skirting heating beyond a balancing valve for the circuit.

Pipework and fittings
When installing copper or steel pipework it is vital that the pipework is cut squarely and then cleaned thoroughly with wire wool inside and out at the ends. The same cleaning is necessary for fittings otherwise the joint, especially soldered joints, will not be leak-free.

Use as few fittings as possible and try to install long lengths of pipework. This will reduce the chance of leaks and friction losses. All bends should, where practical, be formed using the bending springs. Never kink pipework when bending as this reduces the flow of water and causes noise.

Always lay out pipework either level or at a gradient to the point of venting. Do not be afraid to put in as many automatic air vents as you feel are necessary. About 90% of the faults on heating systems are due to air locks. Make sure that each compression fitting is tightened, but *not* over-tightened which will strip the thread or burr the olive ring inside.

If you are using capillary connections try to make them before placing them under the floors, to reduce the fire risk and possibility of leaking.

Pipes should be clipped to walls and joists at short intervals:

Pipe size	Horizontal installation	Vertical installation
10mm	750mm	1.50m
15mm	900mm	1.80m
22mm	1.05m	2.10m
28mm	1.05m	2.10m

CPVC pipe
An alternative to copper pipe is the CPVC (Chlorinated Polyvinyl Chloride) hot water pipe system which is now available on the UK market. This plastic material has many advantages, for instance it is corrosion resistant, lightweight, reduces heat loss from hot water, and is impact resistant. CPVC is available in 15mm and 22mm sizes. Joints are solvent-welded.

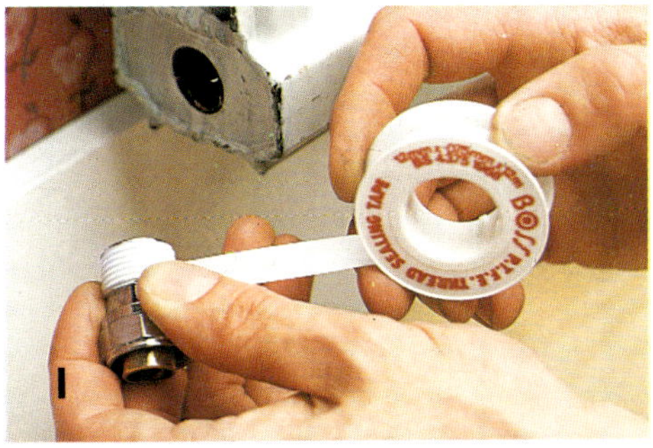

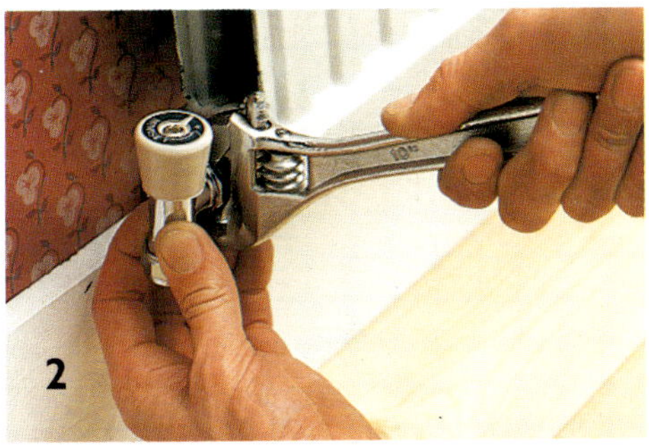

1. *Wrap PTFE tape anti-clockwise (as seen from position shown) round thread of valve connector to ensure watertight joint with radiator.*
2. *Hold valve at desired angle against connector and screw on coupling nut with adjustable spanner. Do not overtighten.*
3. *Measure centre-to-centre distance of fixing lugs on back of radiator and screw brackets vertically to wall at this spacing.*

Pumps

The pump can be fitted in the flow or return, next to or in the boiler or next to the hot water cylinder. However, it *must* be installed in an accessible position and in the correct plane according to the manufacturer's recommendations.

Boiler and flue or chimney

Boilers should always be placed on a level base which is made of non-combustible material. When installing a wall-hung boiler be sure that you use the template provided. Never install a boiler adjacent to or touching any kitchen units or furniture unless it is specifically designed to be installed in this way. Leave a gap of 75mm around the boiler. Remember that it is a machine and has to be serviced.

Working systematically

You must work systematically, firstly because putting in central heating is a reasonably dirty job, and secondly because in most households it is a problem to find enough storage space, unless a garage is available.

It is practical to make as many joints and connections as possible before the actual installation.

This is one system of working when installing a new system:

1. Put on overalls. Assemble all fittings, tools and materials.
2. Flush out the radiators, preferably with a hose to remove any sediment.
3. Fit lockshield, wheel valves, plugs and air vents.
4. Prepare and fit boiler connections to receive pipework, and pump if fitted inside.
5. Prepare and fit expansion tank connections.
6. Prepare and fit cylinder connections. Take great care when screwing up the joints to a copper cylinder because the cylinder walls are easily distorted. Fit immersion heater to the cylinder. This will allow you to have hot water until the boiler is working.
7. Install radiators or convectors.
8. Prepare wall or base and install boiler.
9. Install cylinder in position on two 100mm × 50mm wooden battens to allow air to circulate below the cylinder. This also allows a drain cock to be fitted at the lowest point.
10. Now you can lift all necessary floorboards since all the equipment is in place ready to receive the pipework.

So far the household has not lost its gas, or hot or cold water supplies, due to basic planning, and you have not had to enter the loft area. The next steps will help reduce the time that these services will be disturbed.

11. Connect up all the equipment with pipework as necessary.

The gas board must:

12. Fit the gas supply to the boiler. This can usually be taken from a branch fitting, made on the outlet side of the meter. Be sure that the pipework size is that required. It is usually shown on the inside of the boiler casing. Check with your gas authority

Layout of small-bore heating and water systems

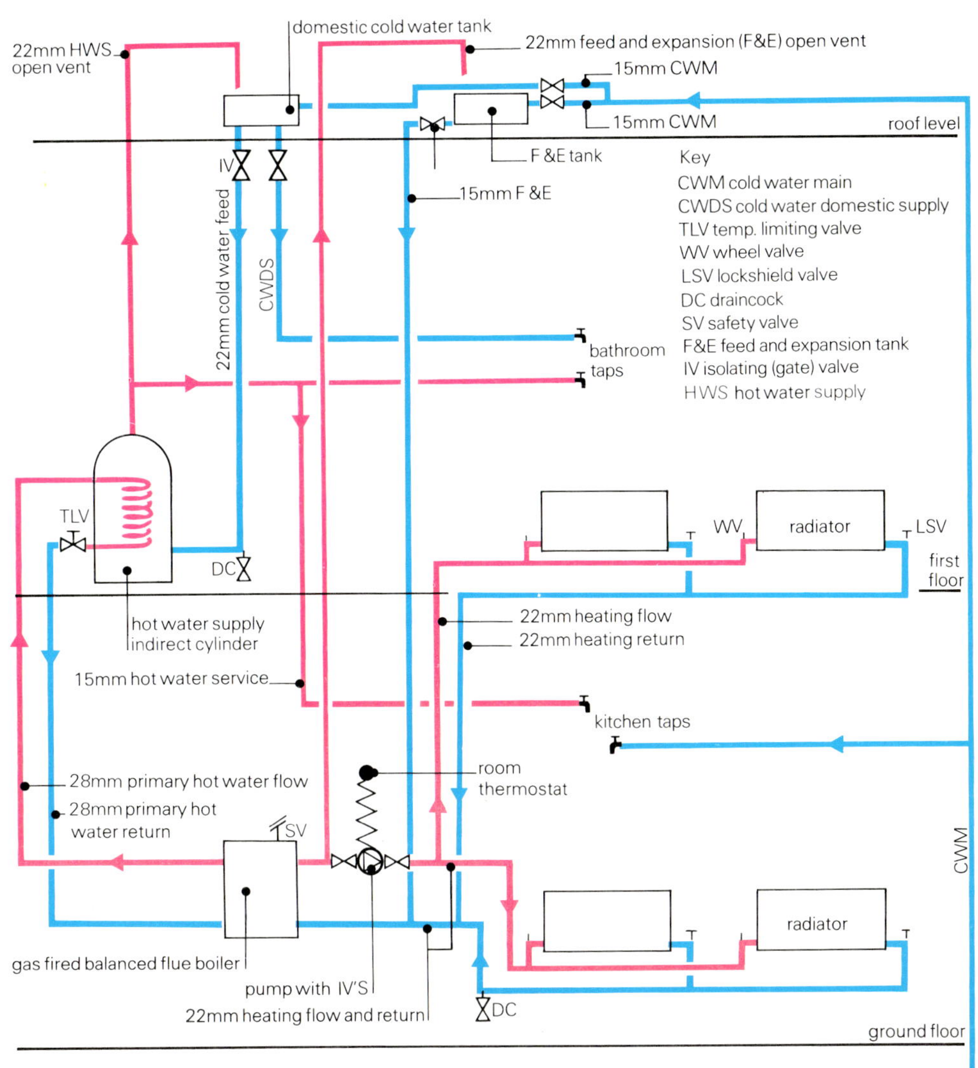

that the supply pressure is adequate to meet heating need, and, most important, never light a match until the supply is shut off at the meter.

Secondly, meet all the requirements for air supply to the boiler. These can also be obtained from your gas board.

13. Position the F & E tank in the loft, level with the cold water tank. You may need to make wood supports. Connect up all the pipework, but leave the cold water main connection to last.

14. Shut off the cold water main at the stop-cock internally or externally. Make the final connection to the F & E tank and from the cold water domestic supply make the connection to the cylinder.

15. Fill the system, check for leaks. If there are none flush out the system two or three times, pour corrosion-inhibitor into F & E tank and finally fill system.

16. Vent the system through the radiators when the valves are fully open and leave them open.

17. Wire in all thermostats and electrics.

18. Switch on the heating and balance the system through the lockshield valves. Balancing means to regulate the flow of water through each radiator so that the temperature drop (inlet to outlet) is equal on all radiators and gives the correct temperature in the rooms.

19. Check that all the controls are working satisfactorily and the heating and hot water is reaching temperature.

20. Make a final check for leaks and loss of pressure, particularly with a sealed system which operates at higher temperatures and pressures. As air is expelled from the system water levels have to be topped up. This is done automatically from the F & E tank.

Keep your system moving

Once the heating system has been installed, and all the checks made for leaks and air locks, it can be left for a couple of months. Then once again check for leaks and airlocks. If there are any, which is quite possible, they must be put right straight away.

If a radiator does not become hot at the top after venting then the level of the radiator is out. Close down the valves. The lockshield valve is closed by unscrewing the cap and then with a spanner turning the spindle clockwise.

The radiator can now be taken off the brackets when the compression joints have been loosened and the water drained off into a bucket. The radiator is then re-aligned, reconnected, filled up and vented. This usually cures any problem.

It is usual to clean the boiler once a year. This job has to be done exactly as the manufacturer recommends and it is best tackled during the summer months. It is not necessary to drain the system.

Saving heat

You wouldn't deliberately throw money away, so why do it unintentionally? This is just what you could be doing if your home is not properly insulated. In fact, for every £1 you spend on heating, 75 pence could be going straight outside. That is a waste of both money and heat.

Of course, many people fall into a sense of false security by thinking that their home is insulated because there is some glass fibre matting in the loft. If this was put down some years ago, it is unlikely to be up to modern standards, so check your insulation now!

If there is not any insulation in your loft, then enquire at your local council offices for up-to-date information on insulation grants to which you are probably entitled. But do this before the material is bought or the work started.

Heat losses can be reduced by insulation, but never eliminated. The drawing shows the proportions of heat lost by the various parts of a typical semi-detached house without any insulation, and how effective insulation can reduce this heat loss by more than half.

Insulating materials

Glass fibre matting Light, cotton-wool-like glass fibre material supplied in rolls. Thickness is 100mm. May irritate sensitive skins so you should wear gloves. Cut to length with scissors or a sharp knife.

Mineral wool matting Similar to glass fibre matting, but made from spun mineral wool.

Vermiculite granules Made from heated mica which expands to form spongy, lightweight granules. A loose-fill material which is supplied in sacks and simply tipped out and spread as desired. Chest ailment sufferers should wear a dust mask when handling this material.

1. *Foil-backed glass fibre.*
2. *Hot-water cylinder jacket.*
3. *Expanded polystyrene.*
4. *Staple gun.*
5. *Scissors.*
6. *Trimming knife.*
7. *Loose-fill material.*
8. *Gloves.*
9. *Expanded polystyrene.*
10. *Pipe insulation.*
11. *Glass-fibre matting.*

Depending on the construction and style of building, heat losses will vary from house to house, but here are the averages for a typical suburban 'semi'. In a bungalow, for example, more heat will be lost through the roof than through the walls, and in a house with large panoramic windows the heat losses here can be considerable. Of course, a proportion of the heat produced in a house is usefully used warming the building and the occupants. Of the heat lost to the outside, this illustration shows the typical heat losses in the various areas and how these losses can be reduced by improving the home with insulation.

Expanded polystyrene beads Granules of expanded polystyrene sold as a loose-fill material.

Expanded polystyrene slabs Expanded polystyrene moulded into large lightweight slabs that vary between 13mm and 75mm thick. Cut to fit with a sharp knife or breadsaw. Decorative expanded polystyrene tiles can be used for ceiling insulation.

Building paper Stiffish waterproof paper which can be used as a lining in lofts and sheds to reduce draughts. Also available with a foil surface that will reflect radiant heat.

Aluminium foil A thicker and stronger version of the familiar kitchen foil. Reduces radiant rather than conducted heat losses. Special coated foil to prevent tarnishing is available for fixing behind radiators on outer walls. The foil may be self-adhesive or fixed by double-sided sticky tape. Some types have an additional layer of foam.

Moulded foam pipe insulation Split foam plastic or rubber sleeve which clips around water pipes. Available to suit all sizes of

pipes. Paper-backed insulating bandage is an alternative material for insulating pipes.
Double-sided adhesive tape Transparent tape with adhesive on both sides which can be used for fixing thin, clear plastic sheet to windows.
Plastic sheet double glazing Self-adhesive magnetic strips attach to window frame (timber or metal) and perimeter of 2mm thick acrylic sheet.
Double glazing channel Clear or white soft vinyl channel which is used to edge glass to form a simple frame. Turnbuckle clips hold the frame in place. A cheap form of double glazing for timber windows.
Double glazing kits May have plastic or aluminium frames to give fixed, hinged or sliding secondary sashes. Vary in sophistication and quality of finish.
Hot water cylinder jackets Must conform with British Standard 5615:1978. Available in several sizes, so measure height and diameter of cylinder before buying.

Draught excluders
Mastics Non-setting mastics will prevent draughts getting through cracks around window and door frames. Available in white, brown, grey, black and other colours. Usually supplied in an injector pack with screw-down applicator, or for use with a mastic gun.
Silicone rubber sealant Special packs (some containing release tape) are available for sealing irregular gaps in window frames. When cured, the sealant adheres to the frame, but the release tape prevents it from sticking to the window.

1. *Fitted carpet taken a short distance up the skirtings will eliminate under-skirting draughts. L-shape hardwood moulding glued and tacked to the skirting finishes the exposed edge.*
2. *Any type of non-setting mastic will also seal under-skirting draughts. Various colours are available so choose one that will match the eventual decor colour. A trigger-operated mastic gun makes application easy.*
3. *Quadrant moulding as shown, or scotia moulding which has a concave face, can both be used to seal a skirting-to-floor gap.*

A selection of draught excluders and other insulating materials. Moving from left to right along the bottom are: bristle strip excluder, rise-and-fall excluder; threshold draught excluder; interlocking door bottom strip excluder. On the top are: all-purpose double-sided tape for fixings; rubber-backed draught strip and synthetic strip for doors and windows.

Door threshold excluders Rigid PVC or aluminium carrier incorporates a row of bristles or soft vinyl flap. The carrier is screwed to door to prevent under-door draughts. The brush type can be used on hinged and sliding doors. Some threshold excluders fix to the floor directly under the door. These are usually aluminium with a soft vinyl or rubber arch which seals by pressing against the bottom of the door.
Threshold excluders and weatherbars Used where draughts and rainwater come under a door. Consist of two parts – usually a combined aluminium weatherbar and vinyl seal draught excluder which screws to the threshold, and an aluminium weatherboard which screws to the base of the door.
Letterbox excluders Long bristles in a plastic frame prevent draughts, even when newspapers are left in the opening.
Vinyl foam self-adhesive tape Plastic foam draught excluder with self-adhesive backing – the surface to which it is fixed must be clean, firm and dry. Foam is available in various thicknesses and with ordinary or wipe-clean surface. Colour usually white. Cheap, but not very long-lasting.
Rubber foam tape Also self-adhesive, but harder wearing than vinyl foam tape. Wipe clean surface. Coloured grey or black.
Nylon pile tape Another self-adhesive draught excluder, but with a nylon pile, carpet-like surface. Suitable for surfaces that slide together.
Rigid brushstrip Draught excluder with rigid PVC or aluminium holder in which a row of bristles is inserted, or incorporating a soft plastic or rubber buffer. The strip is tacked to the outside of a door or window frame with the brushstrip or soft buffer forming the seal.

Sprung draughtstrip Flat flap of stiff plastic or phosphor bronze with nail fixings at one side for fixing to the inside edge of door and window frames. The unfixed flap edge forms a seal against the door or window.

Draughtproofing

Ill-fitting doors and windows are the main sources of draughts, but other points of entry are via chimney flues and floors.
Warning Beware of total draughtproofing if the room contains a fuel-burning appliance, unless it is a balanced flue type in which case it automatically draws its air from outside. For other appliances, particularly paraffin and bottled gas heaters, an air supply is needed. Either ignore the

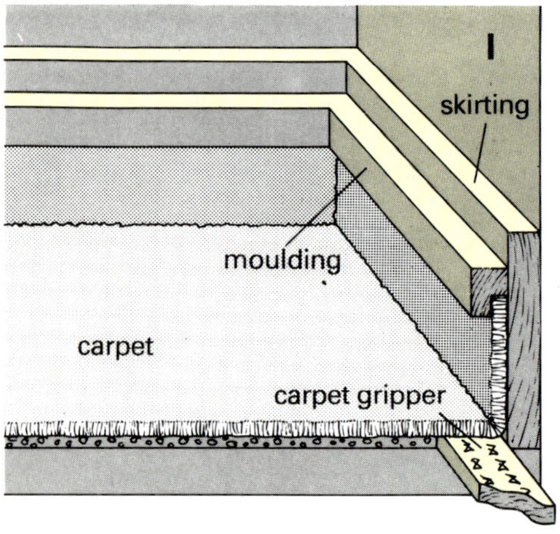

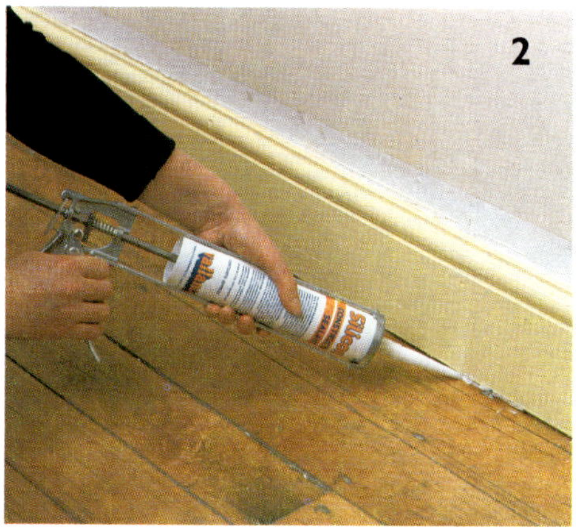

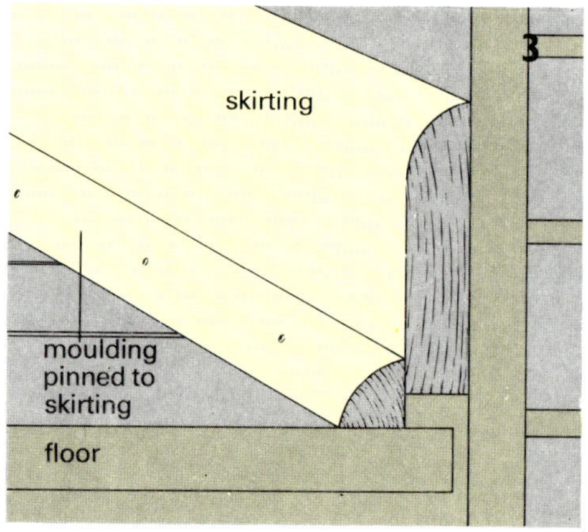

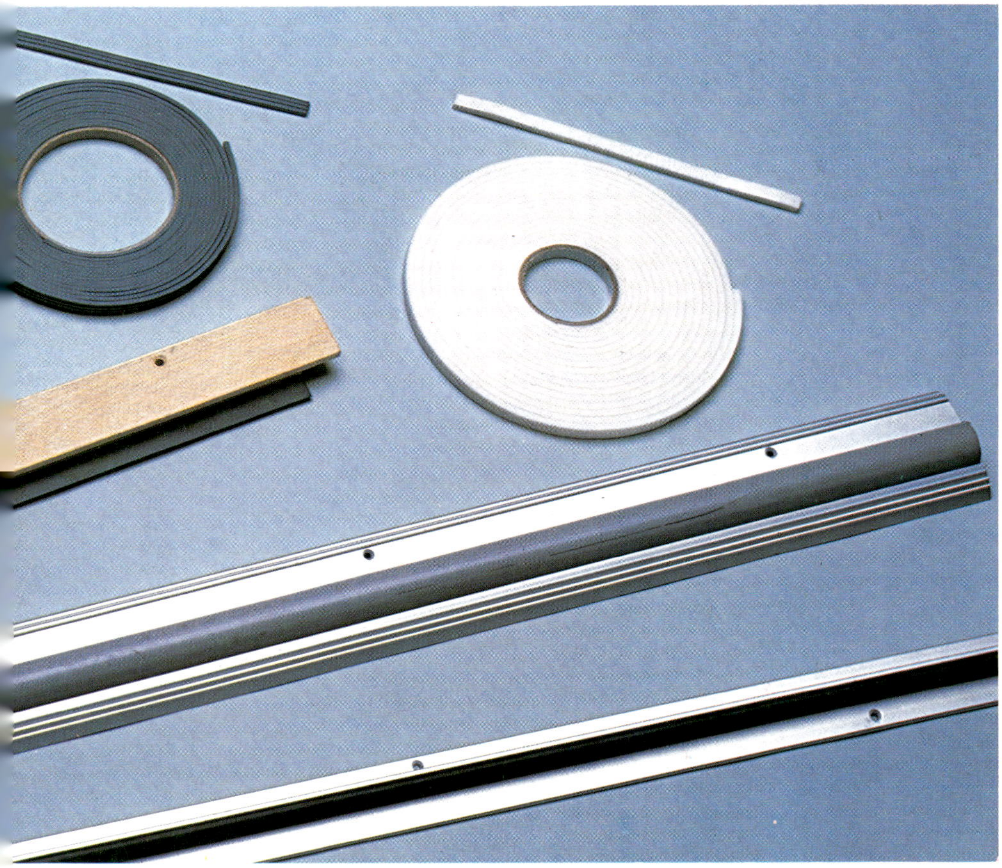

draughts or, ideally, fit ventilator plates or air ducts close to the appliance so it can draw its air from outside, either straight through an outside wall, or indirectly from under the floor via the airbricks and an opening cut in the floorcovering.

Floor draughts

With timber floors in ground floor rooms it is common to get draughts coming up between the boards and through the gaps between the floorboards and the skirtings. Do not be tempted to cure the problem by blocking air bricks – an underfloor air supply is vital to keep floor timbers in good condition.

First decide whether you want to insulate the floor – see page 100 – otherwise proceed as follows.

Obviously, fitted carpets are ideal for eliminating floor draughts, and if the carpet is taken a short distance up the skirting it will also effectively seal skirting draughts, as well as minimising accidental paint chips on the skirtings. Use an L-shape hardwood moulding to seal the exposed carpet edge.

Alternatively, seal floor-to-skirting cracks with a bead of non-setting mastic, which is available in white and brown. The mastic is sold in injector packs for application using a screw-down plunger or trigger-operated applicator gun.

If preferred, the gaps can be sealed by tacking scotia or quadrant timber moulding around the perimeter of the room. It is usually best to press the moulding against the floor and then glue and tack it to the skirting so that any movement between the floor and the skirting will not open up the easily seen moulding to skirting joint.

Where the floorboards will not be covered by a floorcovering, use papier mâché to seal the gaps between the boards, or use timber laths if the gaps are more than about 4mm thick.

Flue draughts

To prevent draughts coming down disused chimneys, make a cover for the fireplace opening. This can be a plywood, hardboard or composition board sheet tacked to a timber framework wedged in the fireplace opening. Cut a hole at least 100 × 50mm in the panel and fit a neat ventilator plate to provide gentle ventilation, which is essential to keep the flue dry.

Door draughts

Because doors are opened and closed frequently, hard-wearing draught excluders are required. For the sides and top of the door frame there are a variety of suitable types.

Sprung hard-plastic or metal strip is widely used. The strip is cut to length and nailed to the door frame with the raised edge facing towards the rebate (step) in the frame. As the door is closed it slides past the sprung strip which then rests against

Sealing gaps between floorboards

1. *To seal gaps between floorboards with timber laths the first step is to clamp the lath on its side and plane it to the approximate thickness of the gap at its widest point. Apply PVA adhesive and tap into place.*

2. *The batten should be slightly proud of the surface and it can then be planed down to produce a perfect fit. Finally, you can stain the timber laths so that they match the colour of the boards.*

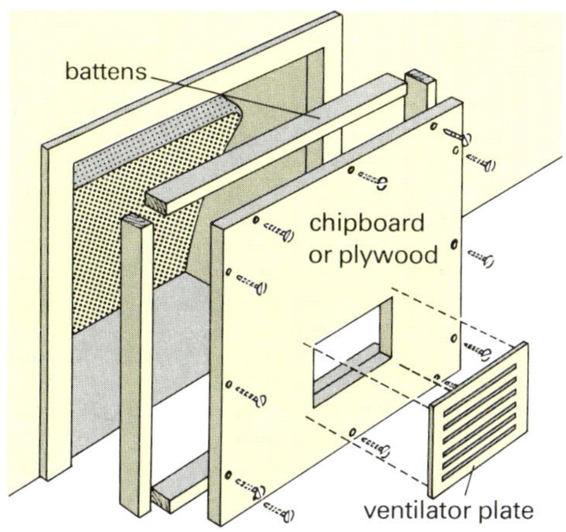

A method of blocking an unused fireplace. A frame of 25 × 38mm timber can be wedged in the opening to which the blanking plate is fixed.

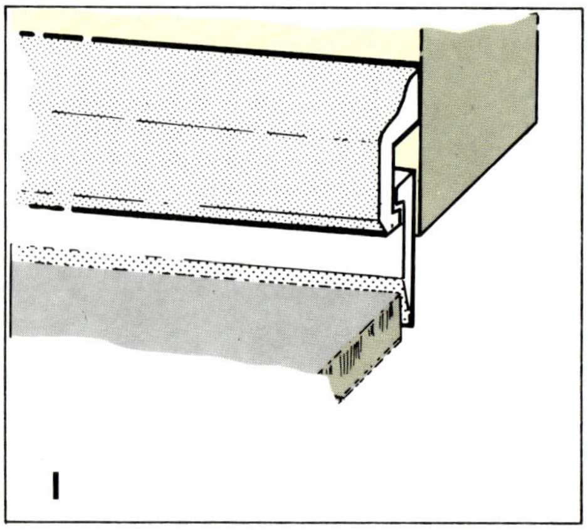

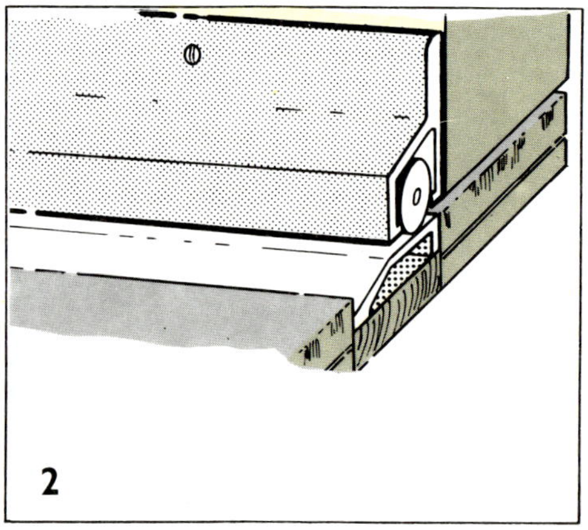

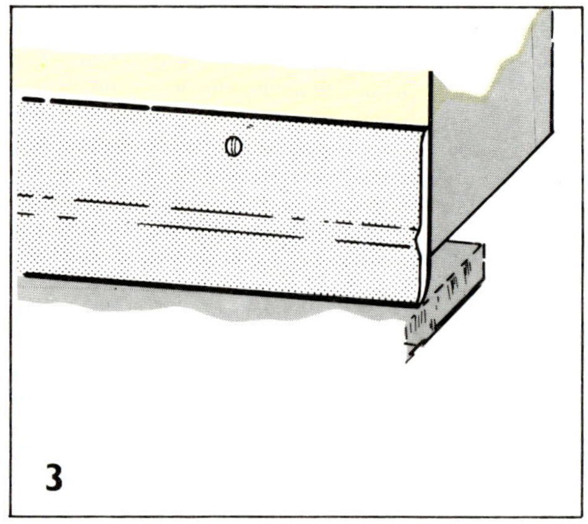

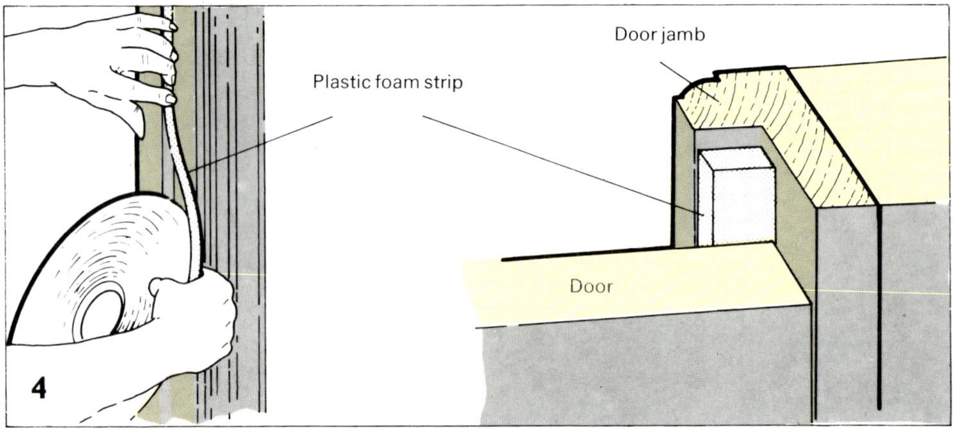

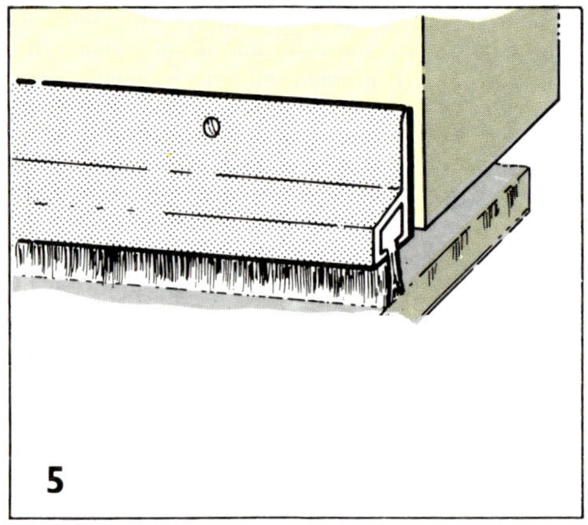

1. *Bottom of door draught excluder with a lifting flap which allows the draught excluder to move easily.*
2. *This type of door-bottom draught excluder has a rubber buffer which seals against a threshold strip fixed under the door.*
3. *A cheap, flexible plastic strip excluder for under-door draughts.*
4. *Rigid stripbrush draught excluder may have PVC or aluminium holder.*
5. *Fixing self-adhesive draught excluder on the frame's closing face.*
6. *On the hinge side the excluder is fixed to the side face.*

the edge of the door forming a good seal. Remember to leave the lock plate clear.

Where there is room, an easier draught excluder to fit is self-adhesive soft rubber tape which simply presses into the rebate along the top and lock side of the frame, and on to the inside edge of the frame on the hinge side. To ensure good results, make sure the frame is thoroughly clean before fixing the tape.

For difficult-to-seal door frame gaps, a long-lasting solution is to use the slightly more costly rigid plastic or aluminium strips fitted with brush strips, or soft plastic or rubber beads of various designs. The strips are cut to length and simply nailed around the sides of the door frame with the sealing edge lightly pressed against the face of the door so that draughts are stopped, but the operation of the door is not impaired.

A commonly used draught excluder for under-door draughts is the stripbrush with a plastic or aluminium holder that screws along the bottom edge of the door. Others may have a flexible plastic or rubber blade, and some are sprung so that the flap lifts automatically when the door is opened to clear carpets and mats.

Where there is a tendency for rainwater as well as draughts to get under an external door, fit a two-part threshold draught excluder kit which fixes both to the sill and the bottom of the door for a perfect seal.

Brush type seals can be screwed behind letterbox openings to cure draughts here when newspapers are pushed through.

Windows

Hinged and pivoted windows are easy to draughtproof using self-adhesive foam tape to seal the surfaces that close together. Many draught excluders are suitable for doors and hinged windows.

The action of sliding sash windows tends to push off ordinary draught excluders, so use nylon pile self-adhesive tape, or ideally nylon stripbrush in a PVC or aluminium holder. Tack it around the frame with the stripbrush pressing against the sash.

The irregular gaps often found on metal casement windows can be sealed with silicone rubber sealant which is injected into the gaps after the window face has been protected with release tape which can be clear sticky tape. The sealant sets, but sticks only to the frame.

Loft insulation

You can save up to 17 pence in every £1 spent on home heating by having effective insulation in the loft, which means having 100mm thick insulation. Usually the insulation will be placed directly between the joists over the bedroom ceilings. Where the loft space is used, as a workroom or darkroom, say, it will be necessary to fix the insulation to the underside of the roof rafters.

Fitting insulating matting

Glass fibre or mineral wool matting are the best materials to use in unlined lofts because they are not blown about by draughts

Laying insulating matting

1. *Cleaning out the loft space with an industrial-type vacuum cleaner.*
2. *Starting at the eaves, unroll the insulating matting and tuck it between the ceiling joists. Protect your hands with gloves.*
3. *Insulation matting is easy to cut with a large pair of scissors.*
4. *Remember to insulate the loft hatch. Tie the matting to the hatch so that it does not move around when you open it.*

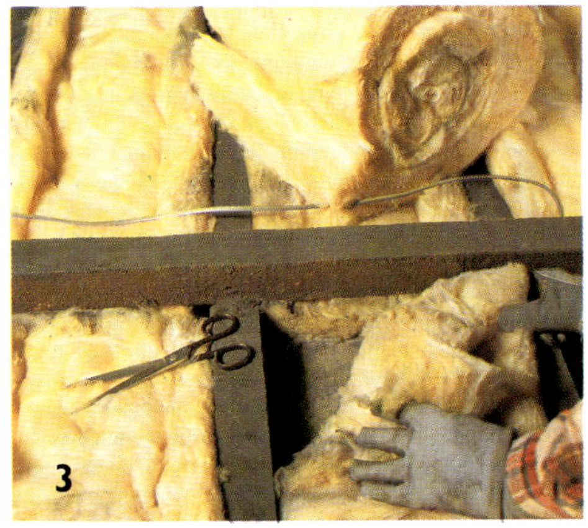

in the same way that loose granules can be.

Start by cleaning the loft, at the same time checking the roof timbers for dampness and woodworm damage which should be remedied before the insulation material is laid. Where the house has plasterboard ceilings it is a simple, if somewhat dirty, job to sweep between the joists with a dust pan and brush. It is better to use a powerful industrial vacuum cleaner for this job, and this is the only way to clean a loft where the ceilings are the old lath and plaster type. However, great care must be taken here not to knock off the plaster nibs which hook over the laths and hold up the ceiling.

To keep the loft reasonably clean, and to prevent snow from being blown in and settling on the insulation, it is a good idea to pin building paper to the rafters.

Avoid putting a foot through the ceiling by working from boards laid on the joists.

The insulating matting is simply unrolled between the joists, starting at the eaves and finishing in the middle of the loft area. The end of each strip of matting should rest over the outer walls of the house. With an unlined roof (where you can see the undersides of the tiles or slates) the matting can be tucked into the eaves as far as you can reach in order to block up some of the draughts, but where the roof is lined with felt or boards, it is best to pull back the matting to leave the soffit boards in the eaves uncovered. Then from the outside, a series of 18mm holes can be drilled through the soffits to ensure adequate ventilation in the loft space.

The matting can lie flat between the joists or, where it is a little wider than the joist spacings, tucked in between them. The matting is easily cut with a trimming knife, sharp breadsaw, or scissors. The ends between one strip and another are simply closely butted together.

Remember to fix insulation above the loft hatch, but do not take any under the cold water storage cistern as it will stop warm air from following under the cistern and preventing freezing.

Installing loose-fill materials

Loose-fill materials are quick and easy to lay, especially in awkward corners, around obstructions, and where the joist spacings are uneven. However, they can be blown about if the roof is very draughty, so it can be a good idea to line the loft with building paper when loose-fill insulation is used, paying particular attention to seal the eaves.

A big advantage of loose-fill insulation lies in the fact that it can be poured, making it ideal for insulating attic rooms where the sloping ceilings are fixed direct to the rafters. As long as there is access to the roof space above the attic room, the granules can

1. *In modern houses where the roof is lined under the tiles and the rafters are set at a low pitch, the insulation should be kept clear of the eaves and the soffit boards should have holes drilled for ventilation.*
2. *In an old house with an unlined roof the insulation should be tucked into the eaves.*

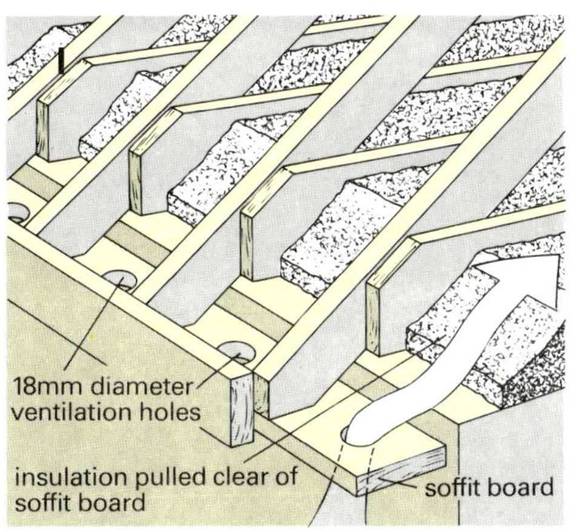

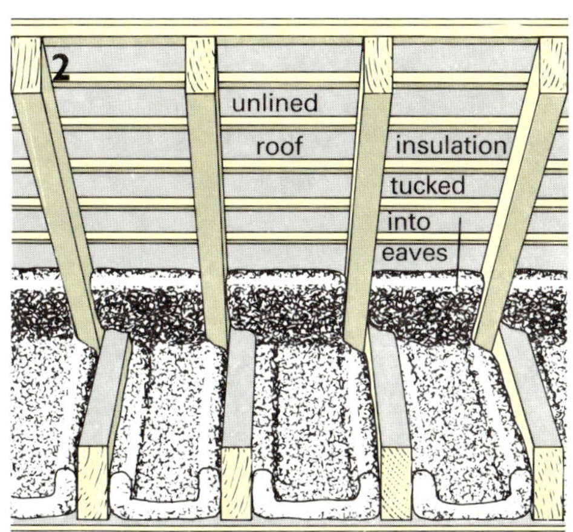

simply be poured into the voids between the rafters. But first the lower outlets from the voids should be sealed with wads of insulating matting.

In a loft, measure the depth of the ceiling joists before installing loose-fill. The joists should be at least 100mm deep so they are not completely buried by the insulation. If they are covered it will be virtually impossible to walk about in the loft in the future. In the case of shallow joists, either use insulating matting, or nail timber blocks to the joist tops to which permanent timber walkways can be fixed.

Loose-fill materials are difficult to clear away to give access to pipes and cables, so make a careful check of these before installing the insulation, and if necessary carry out any plumbing or electrical work beforehand. Also check over the roof timbers and clean the loft area as described for insulating matting.

Before installing loose-fill, drape building paper over any water pipes which run between the joists so that the loose-fill insulation does not run under them and insulate them from heat rising from below. Then simply pour out the loose-fill between the joists and rake it level. The ideal tool for this is a 500mm length of wood, notched at each end to rest over a pair of joists so that when the wood is drawn along the insulation is levelled to the required depth. Gaps at the eaves of an unlined loft should be sealed with lengths of building paper.

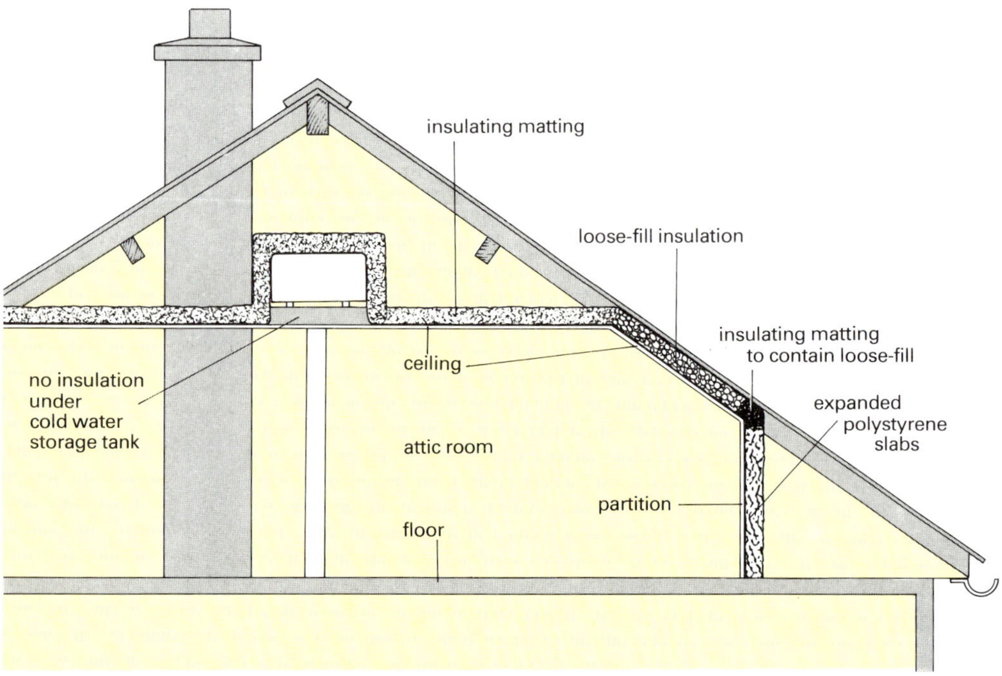

Insulating a loft or attic room. Normally the only way to insulate the area of sloping ceiling close to the roof is to pour loose-fill granules into the void after sealing up the lower ends of the voids with insulating matting. It will probably be necessary to cut a hatchway through the partition wall to give access to the eaves space.

Installing loose-fill insulation

1. *Water pipes that run close to the ceiling should be covered with waterproof building paper which will prevent the loose-fill from trickling under the pipes and insulating them from heat rising from below.*
2. *Push waterproof building paper into the eaves to stop draughts blowing the loose-fill about.*
3. *Loose-fill material is simply tipped between the joists.*
4. *Then it is raked out using a specially shaped board which will leave it at the correct thickness. Remember that walkways must be fitted if the joists are shallow and the loose-fill covers them. Otherwise there will be a danger of stepping through the ceiling.*

Insulate a loft hatch with glass fibre matting, or use loose-fill by nailing a 10cm deep box-like frame to the top of the hatch, pour in the loose-fill granules, and then keep them in place with a lid, such as a piece of hardboard. Another method of insulating the hatch is to put the loose-fill material in a polythene bag and attach this to the top of the hatch. It is always easier, though, to use insulating matting for this job.

Lining under rafters

There are basically two types of underrafter linings. The most common is a simple lining used as an adjunct to loft floor insulation to keep the loft-space clean, draught-free and weatherproof. The second type of lining involves fixing effective insulation under the rafters so that the entire loft space becomes a useful heated area, and water pipes and tanks within the

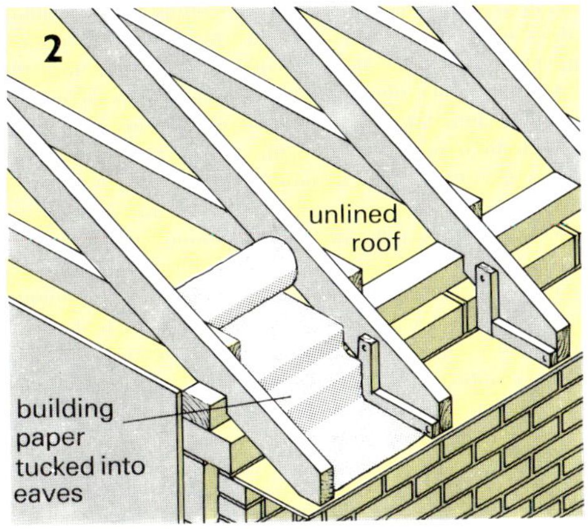

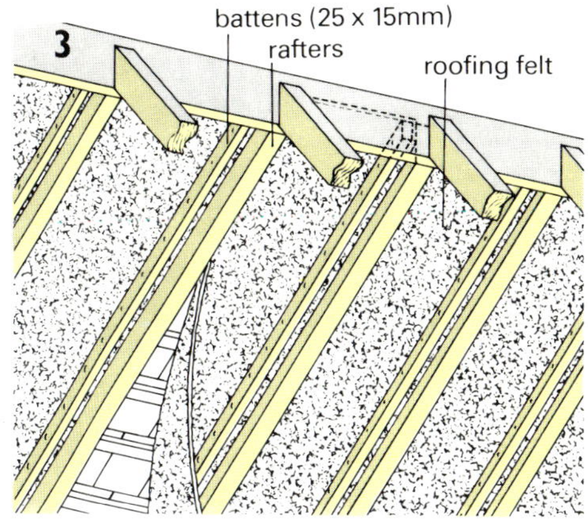

1. *Lining under rafters with waterproof building paper. This is fixed in horizontal strips starting at the apex of the roof and working down to the eaves. Fix with wire staples driven through squares of cardboard.*
2. *If the roof is unlined under the tiles, tuck building paper well into the eaves before fixing the last strip of horizontal lining paper as this will channel in-blown snow and rain into the eaves.*
3. *When lining a roof with roofing felt it is a good idea to run the strips from ridge to eaves; fixing them with battens tacked to the sides of the rafters.*

area do not need to be individually protected from frost. However, this is a more costly and time-consuming way to insulate than laying insulation directly on the loft floor.

Lining with building paper

Use ordinary building paper, or foil-backed building paper. Both will keep out draughts, but the foil-backed type gives additional insulation of radiated heat which keeps the loft space warmer in winter and cooler in summer.

The paper should be fixed to the undersides of the rafters in horizontal strips, working from the apex of the roof and finishing at the eaves. A staple tacker is the ideal tool for fixing the paper, using a small square of scrap card to reinforce each fixing. Overlap each strip by about 50mm so that any in-blown rain or snow will be channelled down to the eaves. Fix foil-backed paper facing inwards.

Lining with roofing felt

Roofing felt is a more durable material for lining a loft to keep it draught-free. Fix it in horizontal strips as building paper, or cut the felt into strips about 200mm wider than the rafter spacing and fix the strips between the rafters running from the apex of the roof down to the eaves. Use thin timber battens and 25mm galvanised nails to fix the felt to the sides of the rafters.

Insulating lining

For entire loft insulation it is necessary to fit insulation between the rafters and then cover this with boards to give a smooth finish and perhaps add a further degree of insulation.

For insulating between the rafters, insulating matting is ideal and this can be pushed into place and temporarily held with lengths of springy bamboo canes wedged between the rafters until the surfacing boards are fitted. Alternatively, use slabs of thick expanded polystyrene cut to fit between the rafters. These can be temporarily held with tacks until the surface covering is fixed.

Wallboards

For surfacing there is a wide choice of wallboards. Thermal board and fibre insulating boards are insulating in their own right, or you can rely solely on the inter-rafter insulation and use ordinary lining boards, such as vapour-check plasterboard, tempered hardboard, plywood, and so on.

Ceiling and wall insulation

In loft rooms, in flats and maisonettes, and in houses with flat roofs, it may not be possible to go into the loft to lay insulation between the ceiling joists. The solution is to fix insulation to the ceiling.

The simplest method is to stick expanded polystyrene or insulating board tiles directly to the ceiling. These tiles should be at least 13mm thick – the thicker the better. Wash the ceiling with sugar soap and scrape off any flaking paint. Ensure good adhesion by painting the ceiling with stabilising solution.

Mark out the ceiling carefully so that if the tiles need to be trimmed this can be done evenly around the perimeter. Fix whole tiles first, working adjacent to the longest wall. Spread adhesive over the back of each tile and then press it into place

1. *Before fitting insulating matting between rafters first tack strips of waterproof building paper between the rafters running from the ridge down to the eaves. This will prevent any moisture that penetrates the roof from soaking the insulation material. As insulating matting is unrolled, it is tucked between the rafters and held in place with springy bamboo canes.*
2. *If preferred the inter-rafter spaces can be lined with slabs of expanded polystyrene.*
3. *In this case the loft area is being lined with fibre insulating boards.*

firmly against the ceiling. With polystyrene tiles, a square of wood makes a useful presser that avoids finger identations being made in the surface of the tiles.

Using thermal board – plasterboard and a vapour-check membrane bonded to an expanded polystyrene backing – it is possible to make a new insulated ceiling directly beneath the old one. Use a bradawl or narrow screwdriver to probe the old ceiling to discover the joist positions, then pencil them in. Simply nail up the thermal board using long plasterboard nails into the joists. Use jointing tape and filler to hide the cracks between adjacent boards.

Another method, which lowers the ceiling further but gives more effective insulation, is to fix timber battens beneath the ceiling, fixing through the battens into the ceiling joists. Battens should be the thickness of the desired insulation and they can be fixed to coincide with the joists, or to run at right-angles to them. A good size for the battens is 50 × 50mm. Screw the battens to

1

2

1. *Tongued and grooved fibre insulating board tiles which are available pre-painted and with a variety of decorative finishes.*

2. *If thermal plasterboard is to be fixed under an existing ceiling it is simply a matter of nailing it up after the joist positions have been marked on the existing ceiling as a guide to nailing. Use galvanised nails which will penetrate the joists by at least 25mm.*

1

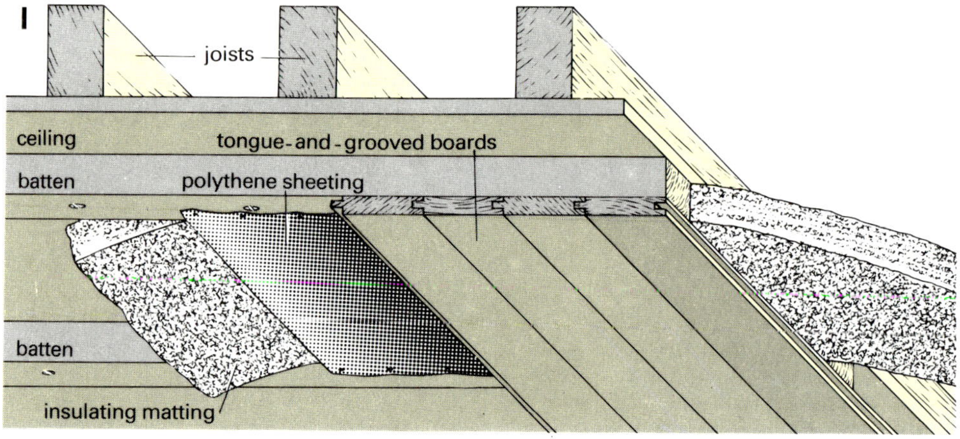

2

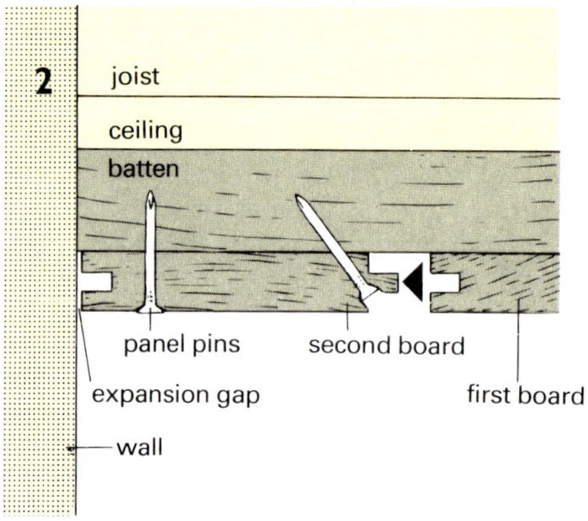

3

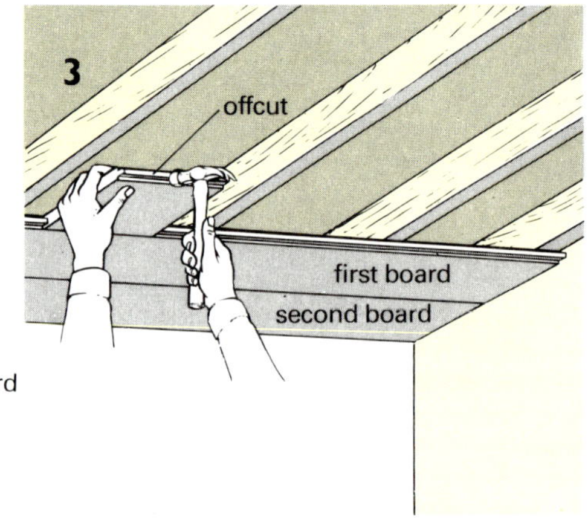

1. *For even more effective under-ceiling insulation this is how insulating matting can be fixed above a timber board or other surface lining which can itself be an insulating material. The joist positions are located by probing, and battens of the thickness of the desired insulation, and running at right-angles to the joists, are screwed through to the existing ceiling. The result is attractive and practical.*

2. *Tongued and grooved boards are fixed with pins. The first must go through the face and it will be hidden by a moulding fixed last around the perimeter of the room. Subsequent pins are driven at an angle as shown.*

3. *An offcut allows boards to be butted tightly before being fixed. This protects the delicate edges of the tongue and groove from the hammer blows.*

the ceiling to avoid dislodging the plaster. When fixing the battens, use a spirit level and straight board to check that the surface of each one is level, and if necessary pack them out with scraps of hardboard.

Insulating material is fixed between the timber battens and can be expanded polystyrene slabs to make up the 50mm thickness, or insulating matting. The matting can be temporarily supported by tacking polythene sheet to the battens. The polythene forms a useful vapour barrier.

Finally, finish off the ceiling by nailing up sheets of thermal board, or use ordinary plasterboard, insulating fibreboard, or tongued and grooved timber boards.

Another method is to fix a suspended ceiling but for maximum insulation the infill panels should be of the insulating type rather than the usual translucent ones.

Heat loss from walls

One third of the heat lost from a house can go through the walls and effective insulation can reduce this figure by two-thirds.

First it is necessary to ascertain the type of outside walls used in the house. Older houses (those built before about 1920) probably have *solid walls*, distinguishable because they are likely to have half-bricks showing in the pattern of bricklaying. Newer houses are built with *cavity walls* – a double skin of bricks with a 50mm wide cavity between them. This type will have only full bricks showing in the outer wall. They are better at saving heat than solid walls, but heat is lost due to convection within the cavity; this space can be filled.

Cavity wall insulation

This is not a DIY job, but it can be well worth having the job done in terms of improved comfort and lower fuel bills. The savings in heat will take from five to ten years to pay for the cost of installation.

There are basically three types of cavity infill – urea formaldehyde foam, mineral wool fibre, and expanded polystyrene

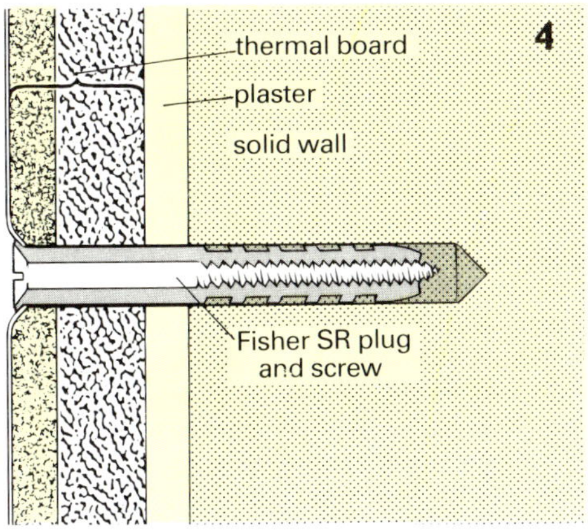

Putting up thermal board

1. *Thermal board can be cut with a hand saw. Less dust is created if both surfaces are cut through with a trimming knife and then the board is snapped over a straight edge.*
2. *Bands of fixing adhesive are applied using a notched spreader.*
3. *The thermal board is pressed on to the wall in the desired position.*
4. *Boards must be held additionally with wallplugs and screws.*
5. *After fixing, the joints between boards are reinforced with jointing tape.*
6. *More paste is applied and joints are feathered smooth.*

beads. In each case the job involves drilling holes in the outer wall and injecting or blowing the insulating material into the cavity.

Get quotations from reputable contractors who will either carry out the work to British Standards 5617 or 5618, or can show a current Agrément Board Certificate for their work.

Lining with thermal boards

There are ways of insulating solid walls on the outside (insulation under cladding, for example), but generally it is best to do the work on the inside as this is cheapest and does not alter the external appearance of the house. Remember that only the external wall in a room needs to be treated.

One of the best lining materials is thermal board which consists of plasterboard backed with expanded polystyrene, and with a polythene vapour-check membrane between the two. After fixing, the joints have only to be filled to give a flat wall surface equal to that of plastering.

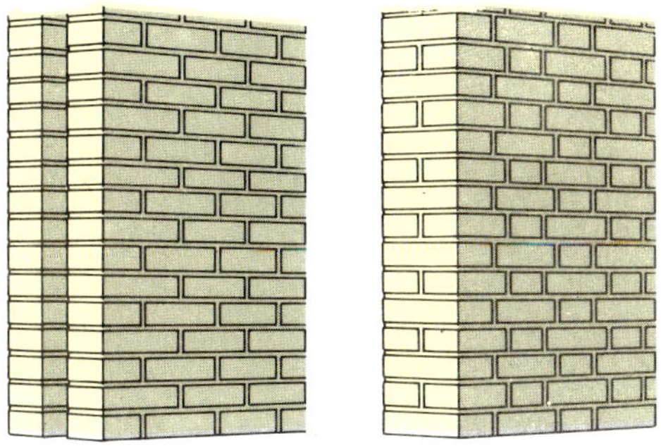

Above *on the left is a cavity wall – no half bricks show on its surface, except at the ends. On the right is a solid wall – there are half bricks in its surface.*

The thermal board can be nailed to timber battens previously fixed to the wall but where the wall surface is flat and firm it is better to bond the thermal board directly to the wall using special thermal board adhesive.

The wall should be clean and dry, skirting boards, door architraves and other decorations removed, and electrical outlet boxes repositioned to take account of the thickness of the boards (22 to 65mm).

The adhesive is applied to the walls in bands, the board is pressed into place and then fixed additionally with nine spaced out wallplugs and zinc-plated screws to assist in maintaining the lining in the event of a fire.

It is well worth using this technique on out-buildings, particularly ones used as workshops, or even on a garage.

Lining with insulating boards

By using a gap-filling adhesive or contact adhesive other materials, like plain and painted insulating fibreboards, may also be fixed direct to sound, solid walls using an adhesive.

Gap-filling adhesives are applied in the form of a narrow bead around the perimeter of each board and at regular intervals across it. The board is pressed into place and held for a few minutes until the adhesive hardens. Contact adhesive is suitable for flat walls, and is applied in wide bands on the wall and on the back of the boards. The adhesive is allowed to dry and then the board is pressed on to the wall. The boards can, of course, be cut to shape or around any features.

Lining on battens

A good method of lining an uneven solid wall is to use various wallboards or timber cladding fixed to a framework of timber battens screwed to the wall and lined with insulating material. The method is more costly and time-consuming than using thermal board, but it allows greater flexibility in the choice of wall finish.

Clear the wall of skirting boards, door architraves and other decorations, and also

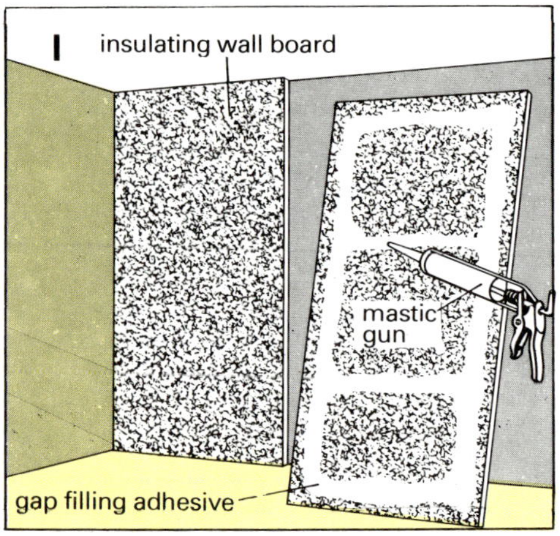

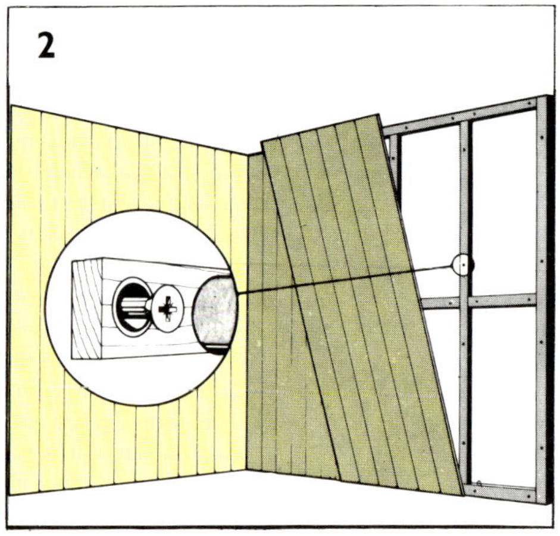

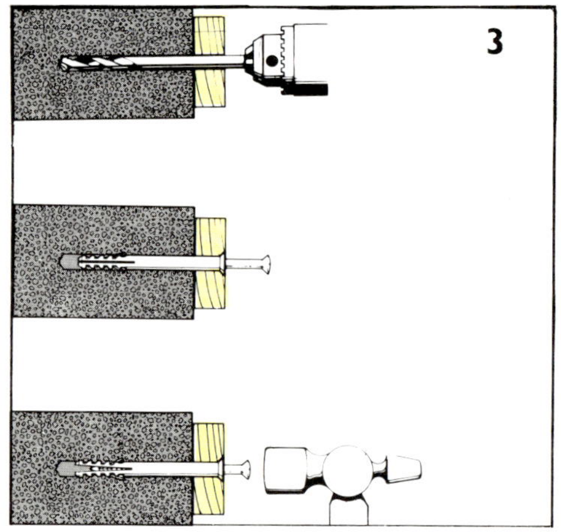

1. *Work fast if you are lining a wall direct using a gap-filling adhesive. The adhesive is sold in a cartridge and is applied like toothpaste, using a mastic gun.*
2. *Fixing batten framework to wall before applying wallboards.*
3. *Methods of plugging battens to wall.*

remove electrical fittings *after isolating them at the main switch.* Using wallplugs and screws, fix up a framework of 50 × 25mm battens to the wall with the 50mm wide face against the wall. The framework should go around the perimeter of the wall, door and window openings, and the vertical battens should be positioned to support the edges of the wallboards when fixed. To ensure the centres of the boards are well supported, also fix a number of 38 × 25mm intermediate battens between the main framework. Improve insulation by covering the wall in aluminium foil or foil-backed building paper held under the battens as they are fixed. If the wall is not flat, pack under the battens with pieces of hardboard. Use a straight edge to check that the face of the batten framework is flat. Fill the spaces between the battens with slabs of 25mm thick expanded polystyrene, or use insulating matting. Now fix in place the chosen wallboards or timber cladding to finish the job.

Lining behind radiators

With both solid walls and cavity walls, a good way of reducing the amount of direct heat lost from radiators on external walls is to line the wall behind each radiator with reflective foil. Ordinary aluminium cooking foil tends to tarnish after a short time, but special coated radiator foil is available for this purpose. The foil may be self-adhesive, or fixed with double-sided sticky pads, and it is simply smoothed on to the wall behind the radiator using a T-shaped applicator which is usually supplied.

A radiator shelf fixed above a radiator also helps to deflect heat into the room. However, do not overload the shelf with magazines and books.

Floor insulation

A lot can be done in the way of insulation to reduce the amount of heat lost through a floor. A very simple way to insulate all types of floors is to lay aluminium foil or foil-backed building paper under a heavy rubber foam-backed carpet.

Solid floors

A solid floor that feels cold is quite likely to be damp, so put in a damp-proof membrane at the time of installing floor insulation. Take off the skirting boards so the d.p. membrane can be linked with the damp-proof course in the wall. The membrane can be brushed on to the floor as a thick bituminous solution which dries to form a rubbery layer. Alternatively, a sheet of thick polythene can be used. This is laid on floor surface and turned up the wall behind the skirting.

Lay 13 to 50mm thick slabs of expanded polystyrene over the d.p. membrane and then slot together panels of tongued and grooved flooring-grade chipboard on top of the polystyrene to form a floating floor. Lay the panels in brickwork fashion so the joints in the chipboard and polystyrene do not align. The method will take up slight

1. *Wall battened over aluminium foil.*
2. *Detail of lining for window reveal.*
3. *Insulation is cut to fit the spaces between the battens before the plasterboard is fixed.*
4. *Battens must frame a window opening.*

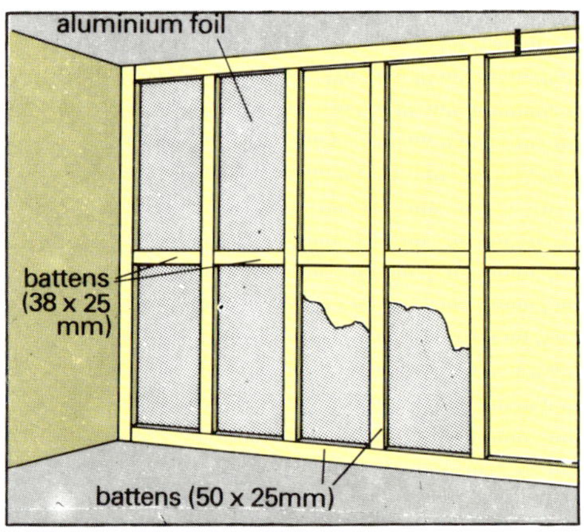

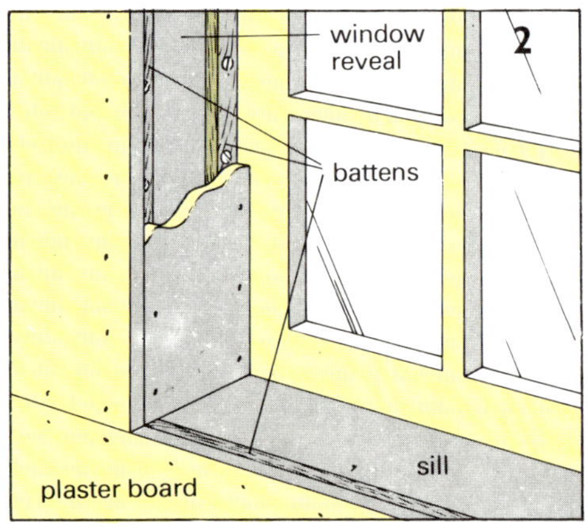

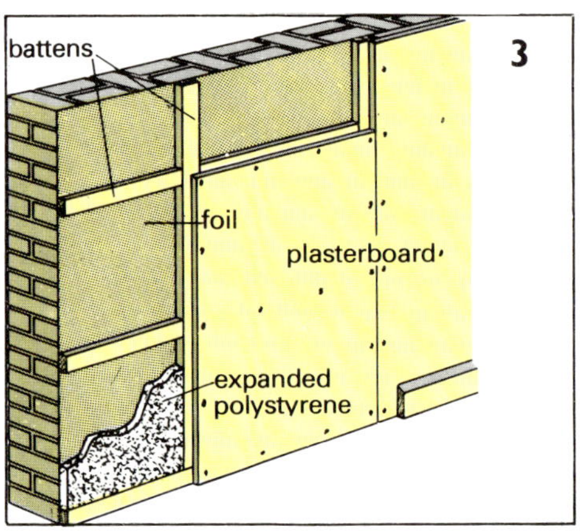

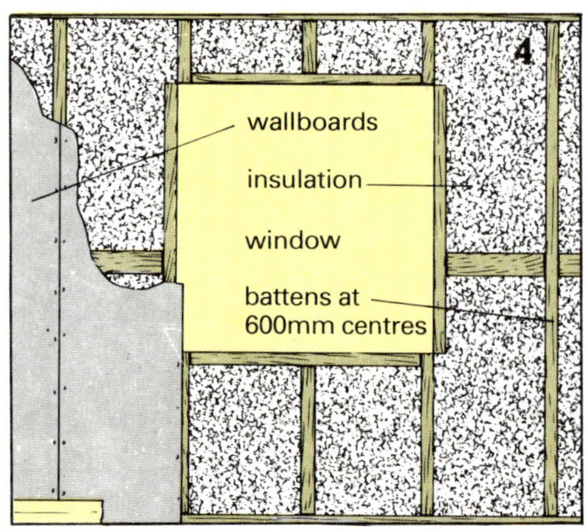

irregularities in the surface so it is useful on old quarry-tiled floors.

Another method is to fix sheets of insulation fibreboard to the floor using bituminous flooring adhesive and then surface the fibreboard by gluing down sheets of hardboard. The method is similar to that described below for timber floors.

Of course, both methods raise the floor level, and if this is not desired, the only alternative is to dig out the old floor, lay a new polythene d.p.m., cover this with slabs of expanded polystyrene, and then lay at least 75mm of concrete on top.

Timber floors

Methods of dealing with draughts through timber floors were dealt with on page 34.

The methods described here will also draughtproof the floor while insulating it at the same time.

An effective method is to cover the floor with sheets of insulation fibreboard covered with sheets of hardboard. Both the insulation board and the hardboard should be conditioned by standing them on edge for 48 hours in the room where they will be laid, using spacers between the boards so the air can circulate around them.

The insulation board should be cut into sheets measuring about 1200 × 600mm and fixed to the floor using nails or bituminous adhesive. Lay the sheets so the joints are staggered. The hardboard should also be cut into small sheets and laid at 90 degrees to the insulation boards so that none of the joints align. Again, the hardboard should be fixed by nailing or gluing with bituminous flooring adhesive.

This method raises the floor level, and where this is not desired the insulation must be fixed under the floor. If there is sufficient headroom it may be possible to lift a few boards and crawl under the floor joists to lay the insulation. Otherwise, the floor must be lifted so that expanded polystyrene slabs can be laid on battens between the floor joists, or polythene-backed glass fibre matting can be stapled between the joists.

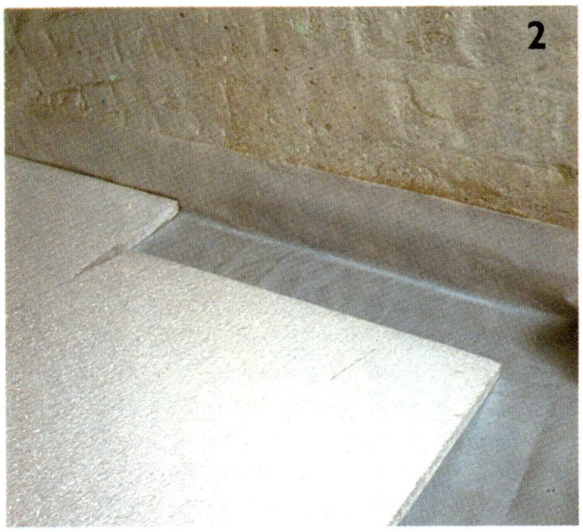

Insulating a solid floor

1. *A solid floor can be insulated with a floating wood floor. Start by laying a damp-proof membrane which can be liquid bitumen, or heavy gauge polythene sheeting, as shown.*
2. *Now lay the slabs of expanded polystyrene on the damp-proof membrane.*
3. *Complete the job by laying sheets of tongued and grooved flooring grade chipboard on top of the polystyrene. The first few sheets should be trimmed to ensure that the joints between the flooring do not coincide with the polystyrene.*

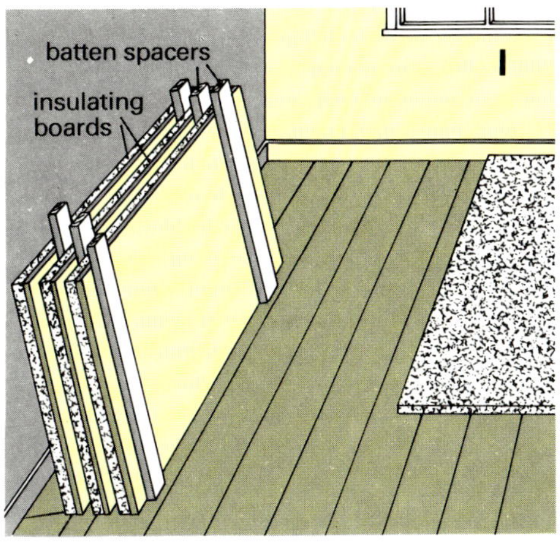

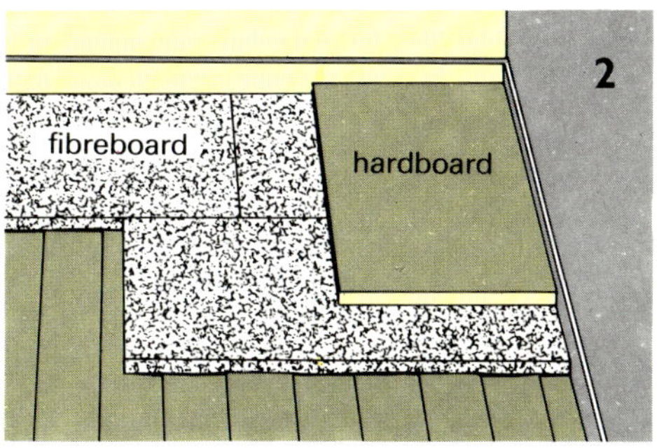

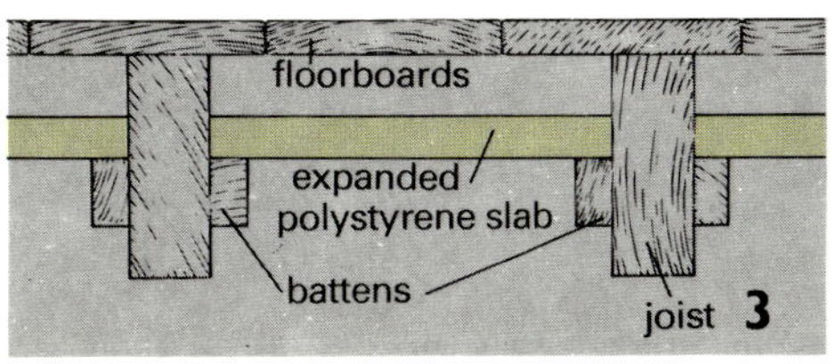

1. *Levelling and insulating a timber floor using fibre insulating boards surfaced with hardboard. First the boards must be conditioned by standing them on edge with battens to separate them so that air can circulate around them. After 24 hours lay the fibre-board sheets by nailing or gluing.*
2. *Lay the sheets brickwork fashion so the joints do not align, then lay the hardboard sheets at 90 degrees to the fibreboard so that the joints are staggered.*
3. *For underfloor insulation expanded polystyrene can be rested on battens.*

Window insulation

Up to 15% of the heat loss from a house can be through the windows. Double glazing can halve this loss, although the cost can be considerable, especially if you choose commercially installed sealed-unit replacement windows. However, with a low-price DIY system you may be able to get your money back in five to 15 years, depending on the fuel used and the size of the windows. You should also take into account the additional comfort provided by double glazing, the extra noise insulation, better security and the greenhouse effect which helps to heat the rooms on any sunny day, even in winter.

Fire safety

When installing double glazing, pay special attention to the following points so that your windows can be used in an emergency if the usual means of escape is cut off.

1. Do not install a fixed, sealed double glazing unit unless there is an adjacent opening window (not a fanlight). Secondary sash units should have at least one sliding or hinged pane.
2. Always glaze opening sashes or casements separately.
3. To give sufficient warning for a safe exit to be made by the usual means, fit a smoke detector on every level of the dwelling and

interconnect them to ensure an effective alarm, even if you are asleep.

4. If you are in any doubt about fire precautions, contact your local fire prevention officer and ask his advice. The telephone number is under the name of your local county council, fire brigade department, in your local directory.

Remember, the benefits of heavy lined curtains for window insulation. These are effective at reducing heat loss in the evenings and at night, and they may be preferable to double glazing if the room is not heated by day and only in the evenings. The benefits of curtains are enhanced further if they are backed by aluminium foil reflective loose linings (known as Milium).

Plastic film

This is the very simplest form for double glazing and is ideal where a low-cost temporary system is required. For windows with small panes, such as the Georgian style, self-cling kitchen film can be applied directly to the frames. If these have been recently painted, the film will cling perfectly. Larger frames can be treated in the same way if a light timber framework is made up to divide the frame into areas in the Georgian style.

Another method is to double glaze the window with clear plastic film, or even clear polythene sheet as a low-cost alternative. The plastic sheet can be held to the frame using double-sided adhesive tape. Opening windows should be double glazed separately from the fixed frames so that the windows can be used without removing the film. Make sure the windows are draughtproofed or the film will move noisily in the wind.

Plastic sheet

Thick, clear, rigid plastic sheet is cheaper than glass and much quicker to fix, but care must be taken in cleaning to avoid scratching the surface. The cheapest type is clear polystyrene, but the more expensive acrylic (Perspex) sheet will not yellow in normal use.

Plastic sheet can be fixed with double sided adhesive tape, although the sheets are very difficult to remove for cleaning. Another system uses self-adhesive plastic channel on the window frame into which the sheets are clipped. The best system uses two-part self-adhesive magnetic strip around the perimeter of the sheets to hold them to the window, yet allow them to be removed easily for cleaning. All these self-adhesive systems are ideal on metal frames.

Insulating glass

These hermetically sealed units consisting of two panes of glass are normally fitted in replacement window frames, but they are available for replacing a single pane win-

1. *Clear plastic sheet can be cut to size using a sharp trimming knife with a steel rule to ensure a clean, straight cut.*
2. *Sliding acrylic sheet into a hinged carrier previously fixed to the frame.*
3. *Polycell UPVC horizontal sliding secondary sash double glazing. This type of double glazing forms one of the best systems. It is easy to fit, opens easily, and blends well with white-framed windows.*

Installing UPVC double glazing

1. *Cutting the track to length.*
2. *Using a spirit level to check that the side frames are vertical.*
3. *Fitting the carriers to the glass.*
4. *Lifting the sash into the track.*

1. *Section through three types of hermetically sealed double glazing panes. The fused double pane and the factory sealed unit must be fitted in frames with deep glass rebates suitable for this type of double glazing, but the stepped units are useful for improvement work because they can be fitted in place of conventional glass in a standard window. Make sure the frames are in good condition.*
2. *A detail of the finger-operated catch on the Polycell UPVC vertical sliding sash secondary double glazing system.*

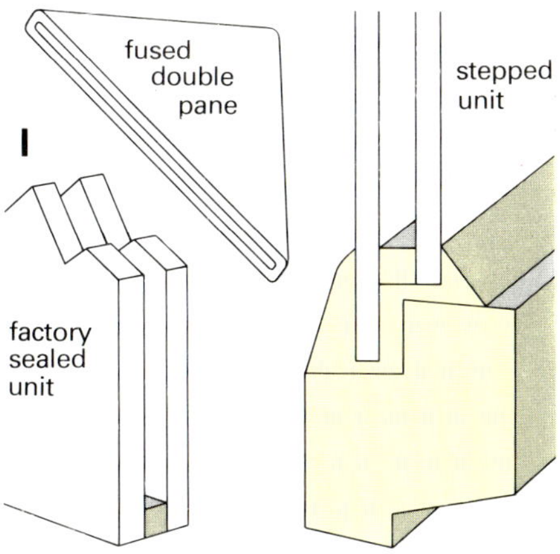

dow in a conventional frame. It is a very efficient system.

There are two types of insulating glass units – standard and stepped. The stepped units can be fitted in a conventional frame without alteration to the depth of the glass rebate (step). The frames must be in good condition to make the expense and effort of replacing the glass worthwhile. The benefit of this double-glazing system is that the appearance of the window is unaltered. But the insulating properties are greatly enhanced.

Plastic channel and glass

This very simple secondary glazing system uses flexible U-shape plastic channel which is simply cut to length and fitted over the edge of a sheet of glass to provide a neat edge and a tight seal when the glass is pressed against the window frame. The channel can be cut with scissors and V-shape cuts are made in the corners to form neat mitres. Plastic clips hold the glass and channel assembly to the window frame. Treat frames individually so that opening windows can be used, and large sheets are avoided which otherwise may crack when the panels are unclipped for cleaning.

Secondary sash double glazing kits

These are the best forms of d-i-y double glazing in which standard 4mm glass is held in rigid plastic or aluminium frames which are attached to the existing window frame, or to the inside of the window recesses and sills. The units may be fixed (for non-opening windows), hinged, or sliding (for horizontal or vertical sliding sash windows). Of course, hinged units can be used on fixed windows to make cleaning easier.

The secondary sashes are usually fitted on the insides of the window, but some systems can be fitted to the outside of the frame where this is preferred.

Before buying a double glazing kit, measure up the windows very carefully to ensure that the kit is the right size and of the right type for the particular window. Also be very careful to use glass of the correct thickness, and cut to the right size (the manufacturer's fitting instructions tell you how to measure). Check after fitting that the sashes butt tightly against the frames to reduce the risk of condensation forming between the frames.

Although secondary sashes reduce draughts caused by poorly fitting windows, for the maximum effect, the windows should be properly draught-proofed at the time the double glazing is fitted.

With metal windows, the secondary sashes are best fitted to the main timber frame.

Installing aluminium double glazing

1. *The tracks for this aluminium sliding, secondary sash, double glazing system are screwed to the face of the timber window frame surround.*
2. *The glass carriers are joined at the corners with screw-fixed corner pieces for extra rigidity and strength.*
3. *The same carrier channel is used for both sliding and hinged double-glazing. The hinge pivots slide into a groove on the outer edge of the carrier, and fit into sockets screwed to the window-frame surround.*
4. *Hinged units should be supported in the open position with a stay to prevent them from being blown back against the window reveal, and broken or damaged.*
Note *Measure very carefully before buying double glazing kits. You should also check that there is enough space to open both the original window and the new double glazing when the units are fitted. If in doubt, consult the manufacturer.*

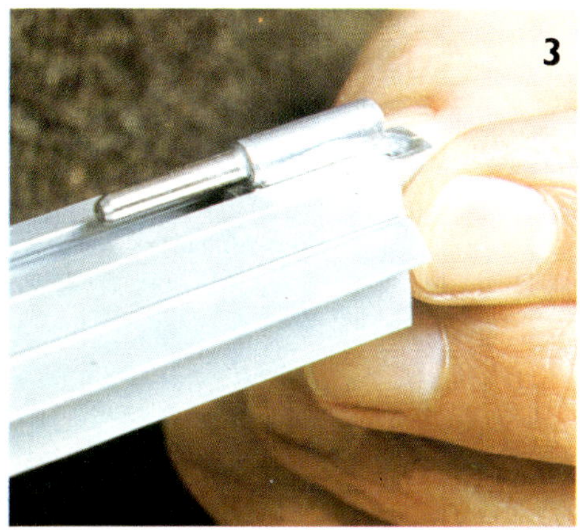

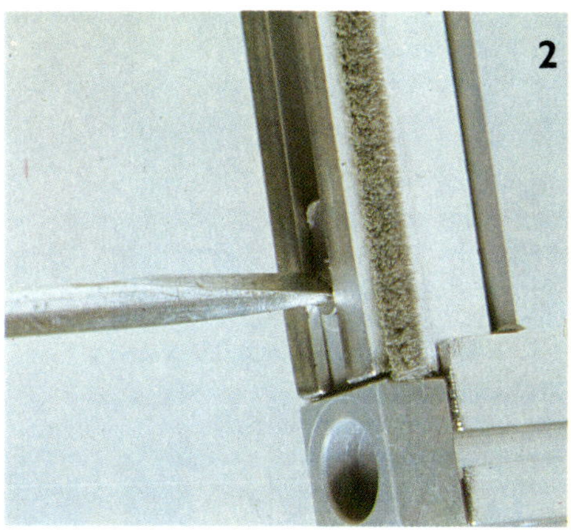

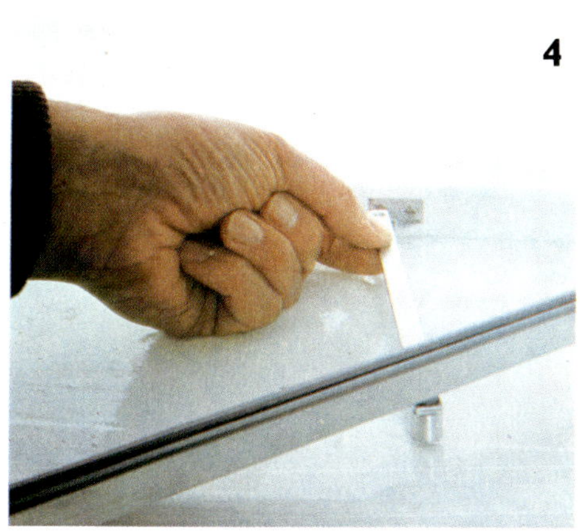

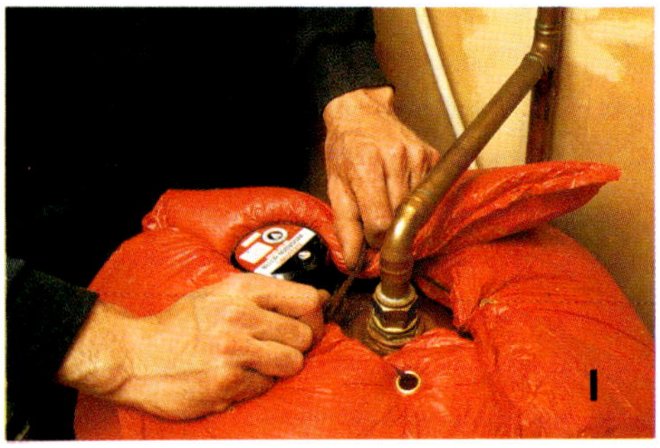

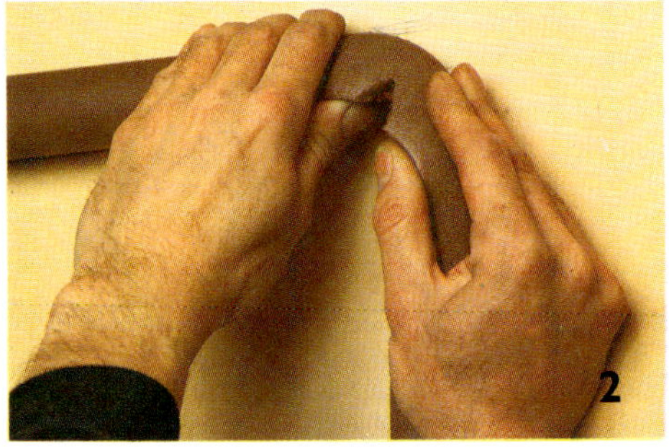

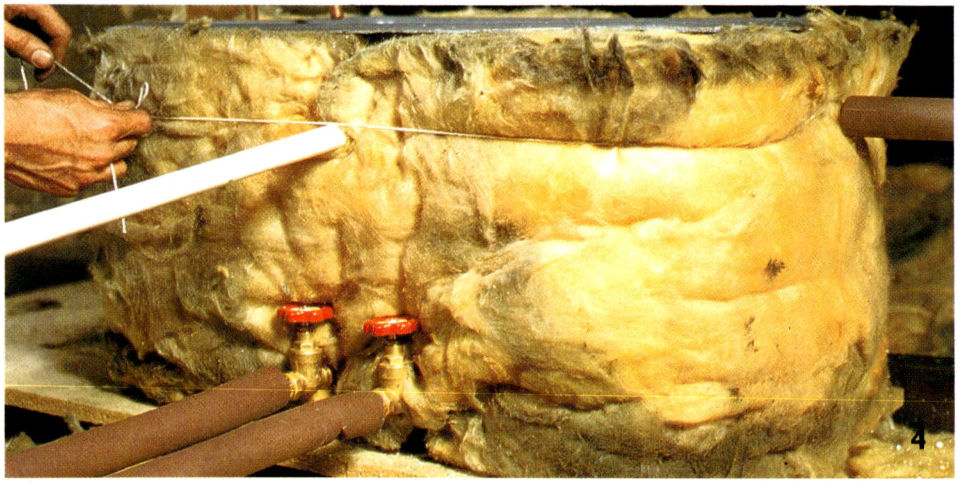

1. *To insulate a hot water cylinder the segments of the lagging jacket should be tied to a loop around the draw-off pipe at the top of the cylinder.*
2. *When taking split foam pipe insulation around a bend in a pipe a 45° mitre cut should be made halfway through the insulation at the mid-point of the bend.*
3. *To insulate a T-joint, shape the foam insulation as shown.*
4. *A cold water storage cistern wrapped with glass fibre matting which is secured with loops of string.*
5. *A cistern being insulated with slabs of polystyrene. In both cases the valves remain to be insulated.*

Plumbing insulation

When a loft is insulated it becomes vital properly to insulate exposed water pipes and storage cisterns, as these will be more liable to freezing. At the same time it is wise to check the thickness of insulation around the hot water cylinder where a lot of heat can be wasted. A new jacket can pay for itself in a matter of weeks.

Hot water cylinder

Pre-lagged hot water cylinders offer a substantial fuel saving over the conventionally lagged type, so if you are fitting a new or replacement cylinder, buy the former. To lag a conventional cylinder, the jacket should be at least 80mm thick to conform with British Standard 5615:1978. Measure the height and diameter of the cylinder to make sure the correct size jacket is bought. Simply clip the jacket around the draw-off pipe at the top of the cylinder letting the segments drape around the sides. Lightly hold the jacket in place by fastening two tapes around the cylinder.

Pipe insulation

All exposed water pipes in a loft should be insulated, including overflow pipes and the expansion pipes of heating systems.

Pipes close to the loft floor should be covered by the loft insulation. Other pipes should be individually lagged, particularly bends where freezing often occurs first.

The best material is moulded foam pipe insulation. This is split down one side so it can be slipped over the pipe and secured with adhesive tape or string.

The older type paper-backed insulating pipe wrap is wound around the pipe spirally like a bandage and held in place with string.

Keep draughts out of overflow pipes by taping a flap of polythene tubing over the end of the pipe.

Cold water storage cistern insulation

Make sure that loft insulation is not taken under the cistern so that a little warmed air can rise from below.

The cistern must be fitted with a lid to support the insulation and to keep out dirt. The lid will be subject to a lot of condensation, so use an impervious material, such as a slab of expanded polystyrene or plastic tray if a purpose-made lid is not available. Wood is not usually suitable unless it is wrapped in a double thickness of heavy gauge polythene held in place with adhesive tape.

The simplest form of cistern insulation is insulating matting, draped over the cistern and held in place with loops of string around the sides.

Another method is to use slabs of expanded polystyrene at least 25mm thick, cut to fit around the sides and top of the cistern and held in place with meat skewers or cocktail sticks.

Loose fill insulation can be used for cistern insulation by making a simple box around the cistern, and a little larger than it. The loose fill can then be tipped into the cavity. The lid can be a slab of expanded polystyrene, or a tray filled with loose fill with a hardboard lid.

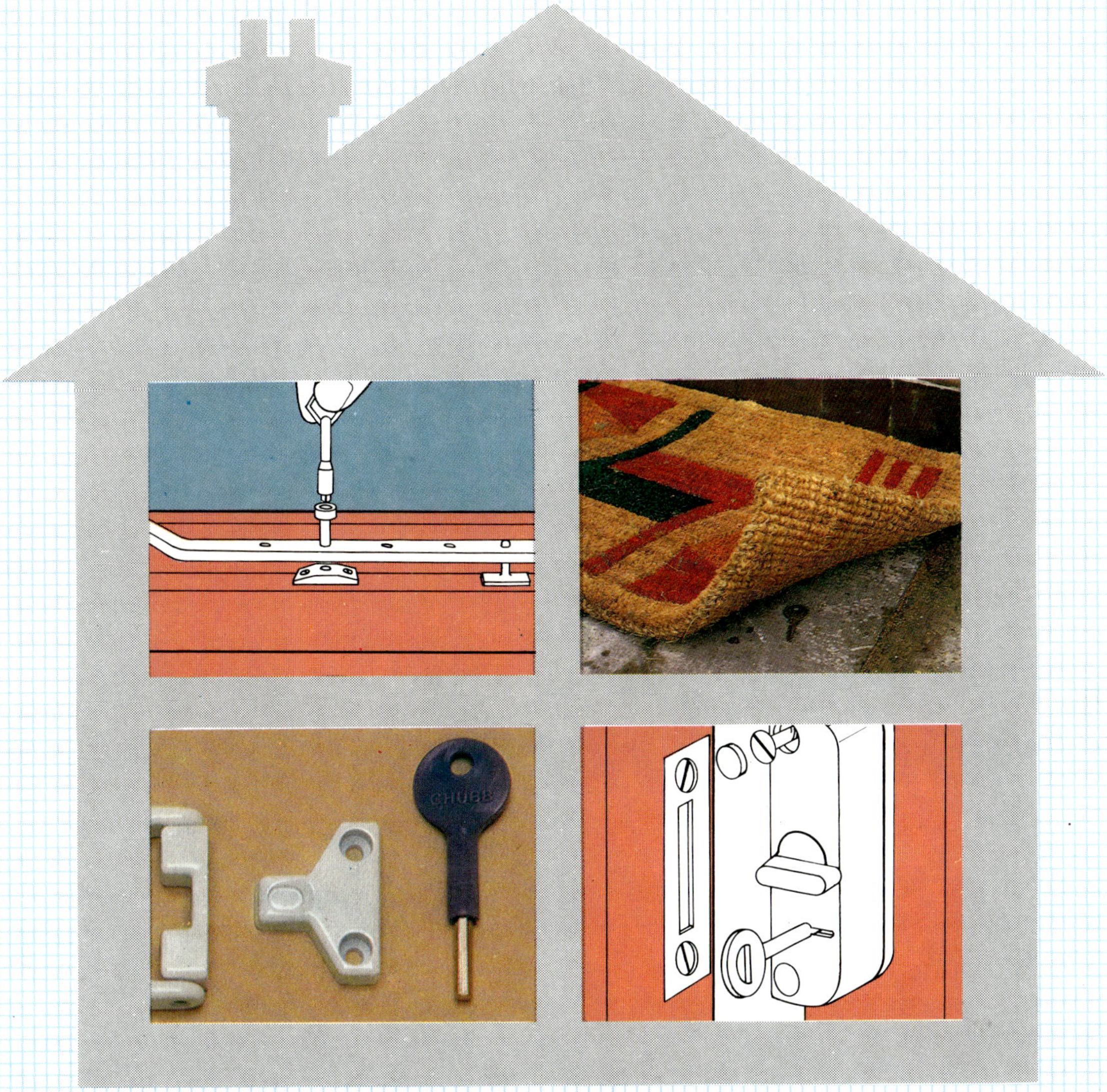

SECURITY

One of the most important aspects of looking after your home today is to make sure that all entrances and exits are firmly secured. This section gives you a thorough understanding of what you can use and buy to ensure a competent level of security and safety. It deals systematically with the exterior and the interior of the home and covers most types and styles of windows and doors. Advice is given on types of mortise locks, rim locks, door bolts, window locks and burglar alarm systems. It also discusses security lighting, personal security and fire precautions, including detectors and extinguishers.

Taking precautions

'As safe as houses' is a saying which no longer rings true and it is necessary to pay increasing attention to security – both the security of the home and our possessions, and personal security. A break-in is a traumatic experience, with loss of personal belongings, desecration of the home, which is always associated with a break-in, and possibly even personal physical injury by the intruder. Such facts must be faced and action taken to guard against them.

This section deals with all these aspects of security, and also includes precautions against fire which is another potential hazard to a house and its occupants.

Before going into details, there are some general observations on home security which are worth bearing in mind. Obviously, there is tremendous value in locking all external doors and windows (and removing the keys from the locks) as this in itself often deters the casual, opportunist thief. With regard to locking internal doors, this must be a personal decision. Modern internal flush doors are so flimsy that it is probably best not to lock them, because once indoors the thief will not hesitate to smash them, causing even more damage. However, in an older house where the doors are a lot more substantial, it can be a good idea to lock those which lead into the hall from rooms which are vulnerable to entry, such as those with French windows or those leading to an attached garage, for example. In this case, security rack bolts at top and bottom of the door are called for.

When choosing locks, examine them carefully to satisfy yourself that they are strong enough for the required purpose; quality can vary considerably from one make to another. If you are uncertain as to what type to buy, remember that for excellent free advice on this subject, and indeed on all aspects of home security, you can consult the crime prevention officer at your local police station.

When you fit security devices to doors and windows bear in mind that they will be useless if a burglar can unscrew them. So where this seems likely to be possible, fix the device with cross-slot, Supadriv-type screws and, after fitting, drill out the screw heads to the depth of the recess so that it is impossible to remove the screws.

Remember, too, that windows are a very popular means of entry for an intruder, so anything you can do to improve the security of the glass will be worthwhile. Fitting safety glass, which is very difficult to break, is a good precaution, and so is fitting double glazing, especially factory-sealed units. Ordinary glass can be made more secure by fixing clear, self-adhesive safety film over the inside surface. Do, however,

1

2

3

4

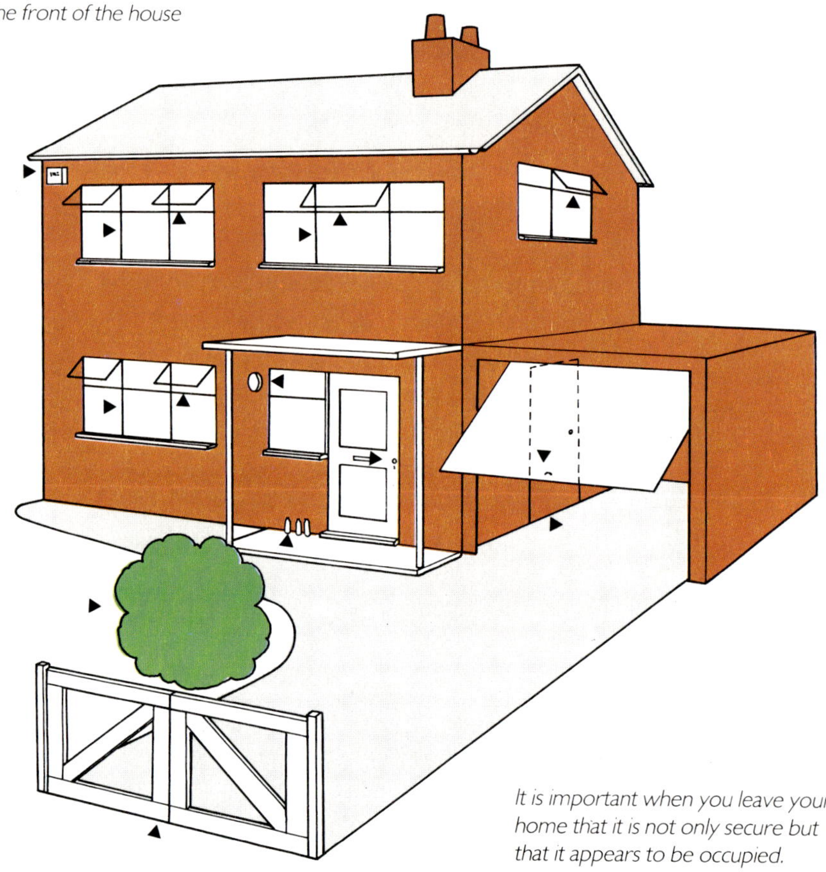

The front of the house

It is important when you leave your home that it is not only secure but that it appears to be occupied.

5

6

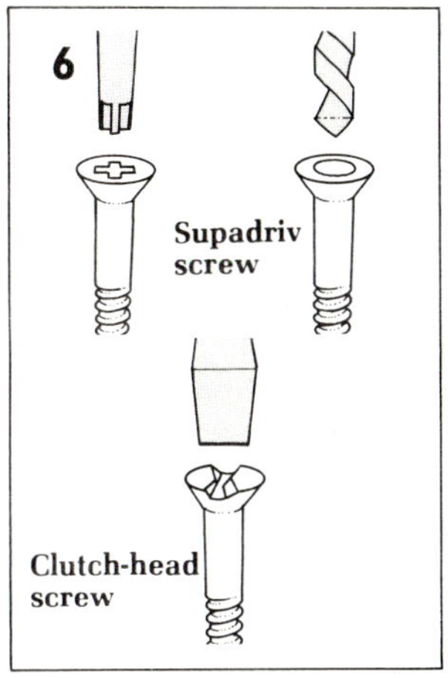

1. *Open invitation to a cat burglar.*
2. *Fit a cat flap – don't leave a window open.*
3. *Don't hang keys through the letterbox.*
4. *The door mat, too, is no hiding place.*
5. *Cancel all deliveries before holidays.*
6. *Drill out heads or use clutch-head screws.*

The rear of the house

The back of the house is just as important, as a burglar can work more easily when unobserved.

make certain that the opening windows can be unlocked easily, by key, from the inside in case of fire.

Danger points

Some parts of the house are far more liable to break-ins than others, so it pays to learn where these danger points are and to take extra-special care here. If nothing else, extra locks in these areas can delay a thief's entry and this may even be enough to deter him in favour of other easier pickings.

Good visibility

Ground-floor doors and windows are obviously the most vulnerable, so try to make the thief's task as hard as possible by ensuring that all doors and windows are visible to neighbouring properties. This means keeping trees and bushes around the house clipped well back. Also try to ensure that anyone approaching the house is in clear view by keeping the front-garden path and driveway clear of bushes and making sure that the area is well-lit at night.

External doors

The front door should be fitted with both a deadlocking rim latch which cannot be opened using flexible plastic pushed between the edge of the door and the frame, and a five-lever mortise deadlock which is much better than a rim latch in resisting drilling, forcing and picking. Also fit a door viewer and security chain to foil the barge-in thief.

Garage doors should be firmly secured with a strong lock and bolts, or a padlock and locking bar. A communicating door between an attached garage and a house should be fitted with a mortise deadlock, plus lockable bolts top and bottom on the house side. Back- and side-entrance doors need similar protection.

Glass doors should be fitted with toughened glass or sealed double-glazing units. French doors and patio doors are usually very vulnerable, so fitting additional locks and security devices to these is essential.

Windows

With windows, double-glazing units are a good deterrent. Some louvre windows are danger points because the glass slats are very easy to remove, while top-hung casements are a risk because, once open, they allow the thief to reach and operate the side window-handles. Therefore, fit window locks to all opening windows.

Upstairs windows above the roof of a porch or attached garage are particularly at risk, and so are those accessible from a drain-pipe, such as the bathroom window. Even skylight windows, particularly those with external hinges and fasteners, are vulnerable, especially if near a flat roof.

Finally, be sure to lock away ladders and DIY tools which may be easily taken from an unsecured shed or garage.

External doors

External doors should be secure enough not only to prevent break-ins, but also to act as a barrier to stop intruders who may have got into the house via a window from leaving with your bulkier belongings.

It is no good relying on locks and bolts alone as these will be useless if the door is weak and easily smashed. So make sure that doors are in good condition and are an exterior-quality type, at least 44mm thick and, ideally, are made from hardwood. Weak door-frames can be reinforced by screwing a length of angle-iron to the inside of the frame and to the adjacent wall. If the door has glass panels these should be either laminated or toughened safety-glass. Apart from being safer in an accident, safety glass is much more difficult for an intruder to break.

Because the front door is the one by which you leave and enter the house it tends to be the most vulnerable from the security aspect because it cannot be bolted when you are out. In addition to security deadlocks (see below), fit good bolts at the top and bottom for use at night and if you are out of earshot in the back garden. Side and back doors also need bolts at the top and bottom to prevent them from being kicked in.

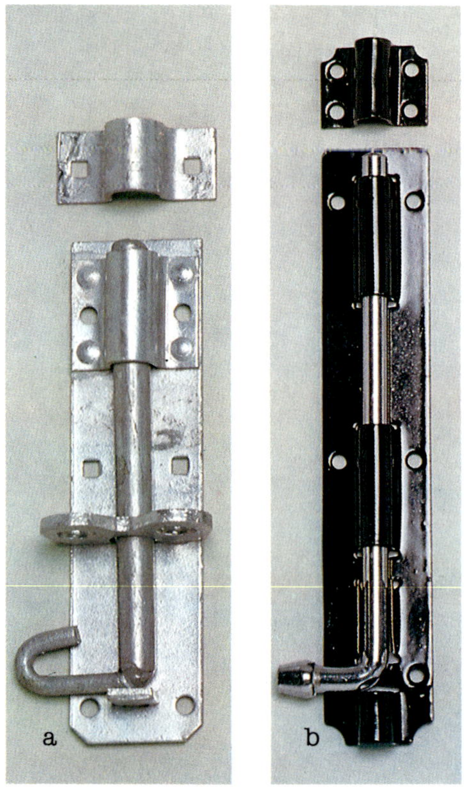

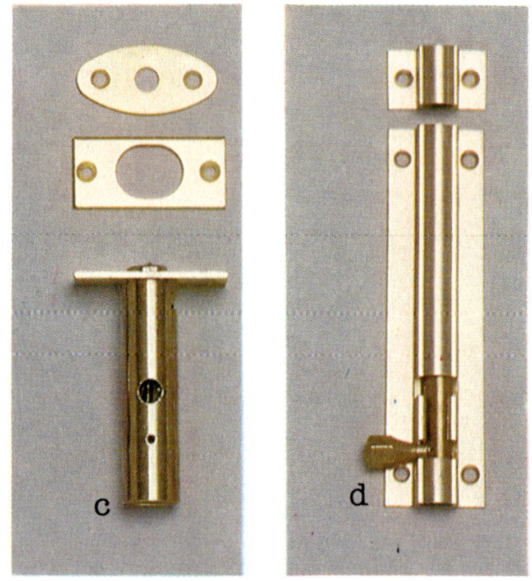

a. *Padbolt, for use with a padlock.*
b. *Tower bolt.*
c. *Mortise security rack bolt.*
d. *Barrel bolt.*

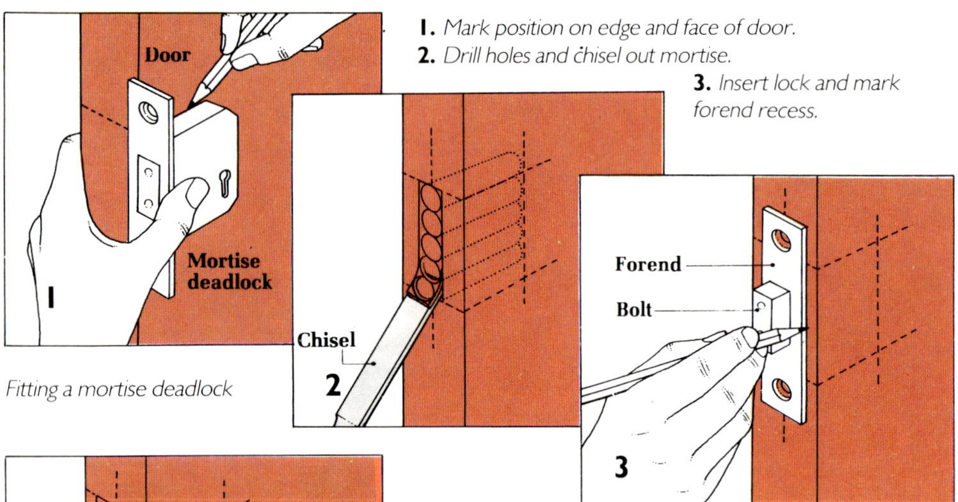

1. *Mark position on edge and face of door.*
2. *Drill holes and chisel out mortise.*
3. *Insert lock and mark forend recess.*

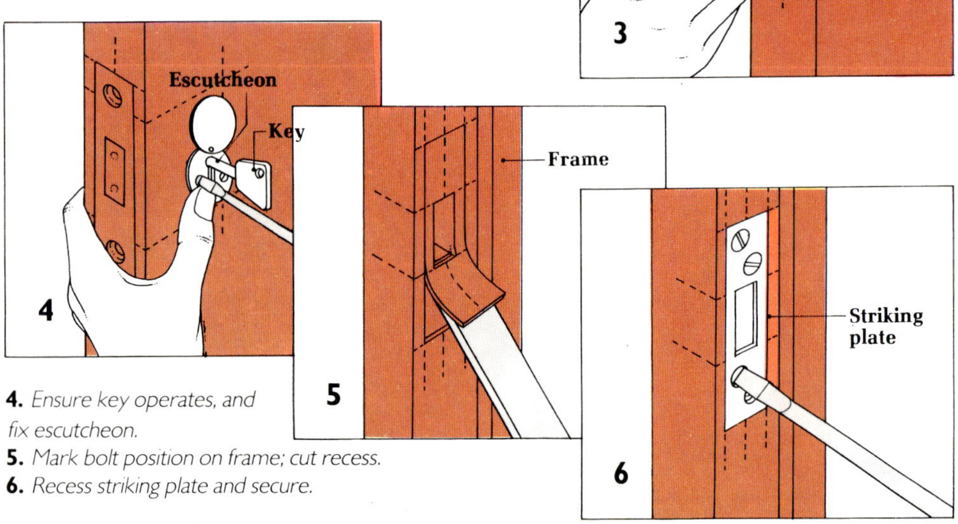

4. *Ensure key operates, and fix escutcheon.*
5. *Mark bolt position on frame; cut recess.*
6. *Recess striking plate and secure.*

Fitting a mortise deadlock

Surface-mounting bolts

The most common bolts are the traditional, surface-mounting sliding bolts. These are available in various sizes and patterns in steel and brass. The steel bolts are the stronger and a minimum bolt length of 200mm is required for external doors. Because the staple for bolts of this type tends to be made from thin steel and be held to the frame by only two screws, these bolts are fairly easy to force. Also, if a bolt is quite near to a window pane, it can often be a simple matter to reach it and slide it back. Apart from using long round-head screws to hold the staple, the strength can be considerably improved by mounting the bolt vertically so that it slides into a hole in the floor and in the head of the frame.

Mortise bolts

The best type of bolt is the mortise rack bolt, or security mortise bolt. These are fitted at the top and bottom of the door in holes drilled in its edge, which makes them difficult to tamper with. Also, since the bolt, which is wound out by a special key, shoots securely some distance into the door-frame, it is virtually impossible to break it out.

Mortise locks

The most secure lock for an external door is a mortise deadlock which is fitted into a slot cut in the edge of a door. In the case of a side or back door this may be the only type of lock on the door, but with a front door it is a good idea to fit this type of lock even if there is already a rim latch fitted. With mortise locks, turning the key shoots a bolt into a hole cut in the adjacent door-frame, and when the key is removed the bolt is deadlocked, which means that it cannot be

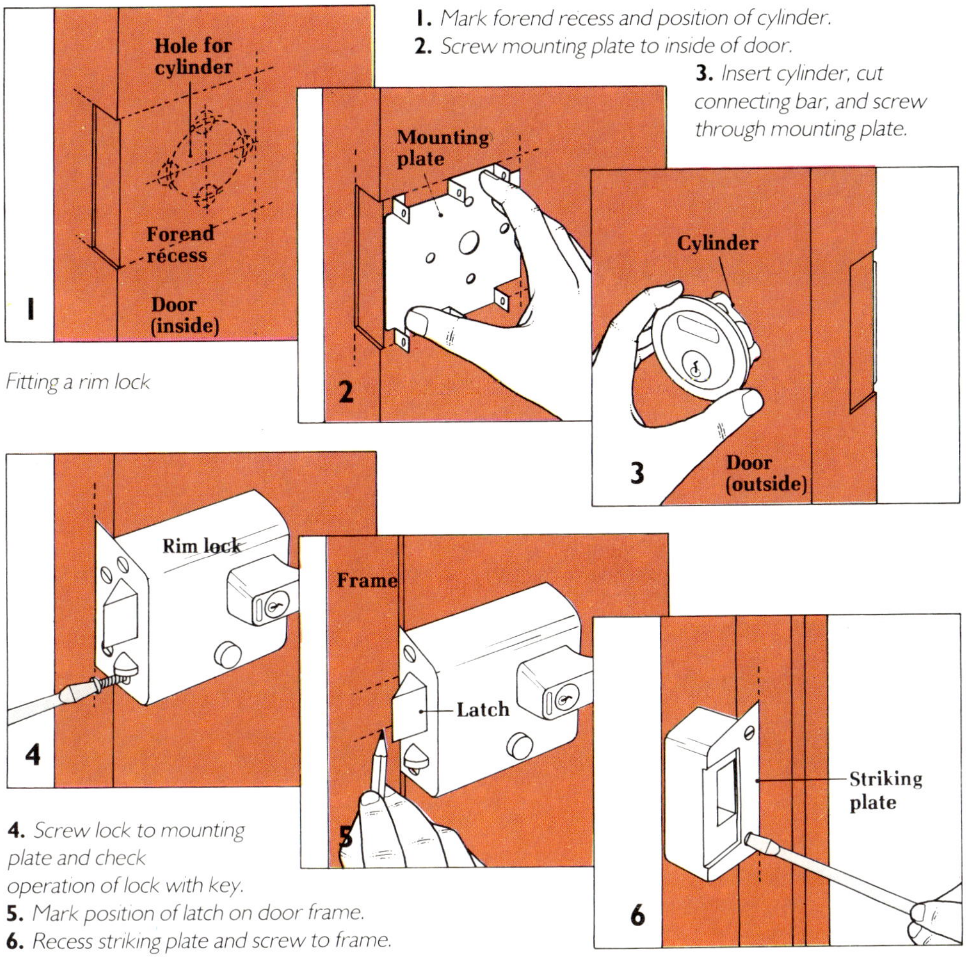

Fitting a rim lock

1. *Mark forend recess and position of cylinder.*
2. *Screw mounting plate to inside of door.*
3. *Insert cylinder, cut connecting bar, and screw through mounting plate.*
4. *Screw lock to mounting plate and check operation of lock with key.*
5. *Mark position of latch on door frame.*
6. *Recess striking plate and screw to frame.*

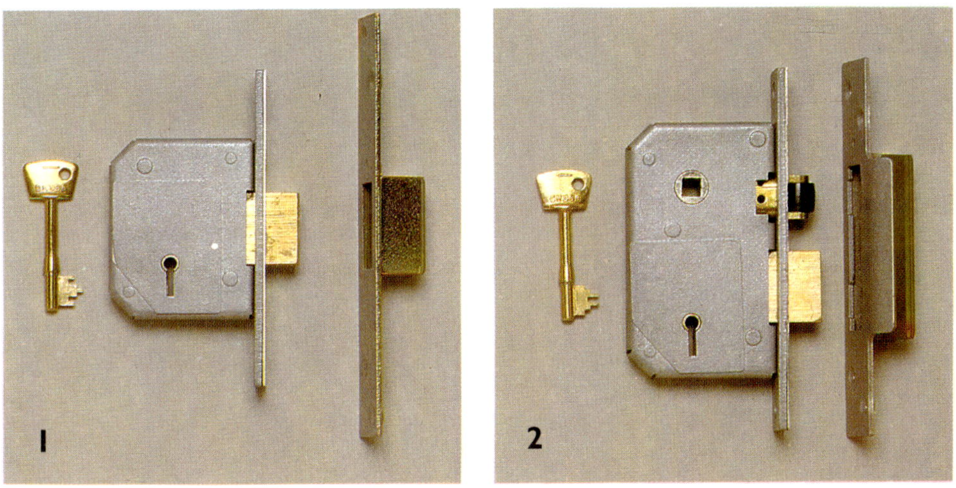

1. *Standard mortise deadlock.*
2. *Two-bolt, for back and side doors.*

retracted without using the key.

As long as the lock meets British Standard BS 3621 it will give a high degree of security. However, fitting this type of lock can weaken a door, and for glass-panel doors with narrow stiles there are special slim versions which reduce the problem. If the door will be severely weakened by fitting a mortise lock (that is when the stile is less than 44mm thick or 63mm wide) then fit a deadlocking rim latch instead.

Types of mortise lock

For a front door, most mortise locks will just have a key-operated deadbolt because the door will be held closed automatically by the rim latch, but for side and back doors it is usual to fit a two-bolt mortise lock. This type has a conventional key-operated deadbolt, and in addition a springbolt which is operated by a handle or a door knob. This type of lock allows the door to be used from either side without a key, yet by using the key the door can be locked from inside or outside. Again, these locks must be to BS 3621 (or be five lever and of equivalent security) – two- or three-lever locks are inadequate.

Keys to pass

When ordering front- and back- or side-door mortise locks at the same time, you can ask for a key to be made 'to pass'. This will operate both locks saves bulk on your key-ring and means less keys to be lost.

Rim locks

Rim locks are simply mounted on the inside face of a door. They are useful in addition to a good mortise lock on a front door, or they can be used as an alternative where the door is too thin or the stile of the door too narrow to allow a mortise lock to be fitted.

Types of rim lock

There are various types of rim lock. The simplest is the cylinder rim-nightlatch which is totally insecure as it can be opened easily in several ways, such as by breaking an adjacent pane of glass, by pushing back the latch with a sheet of plastic, or by exerting the minimum of force on the door.

For security, either an automatically deadlocking rim latch, or a deadlockable latch is required, both of which should be made to BS 3621. The automatically deadlocking rim latch has a springbolt with a mechanism to prevent the bolt being forced when the door is shut. This lock should be key-operated from both sides of the door to deadlock the internal handle, knob or lever. With a deadlockable latch the springbolt is not automatically deadlocking, but it can be deadlocked, together with the internal handle, by turning the key. Apart from being essential with glass-panelled doors, deadlocking latches are useful in any case because they prevent intruders from leaving the property easily.

Patio doors

There is little that can be done to improve locks fitted to sliding patio doors, so make sure that a secure type is fitted from the outset. The best type is a cylinder-operated hook-bolt lock. One problem with aluminium doors is that the metal, being soft, is very easily drilled and prised open. To overcome this, some manufacturers fit a locking mechanism with bolts which shoot out of the top and bottom of the door to prevent it from sliding and from being lifted out of its track.

With an existing patio door there is little to do except fit sliding-door locks to the top and bottom of the fixed frame. A steel bolt, which is locked by means of a key, can be pushed into a hole drilled in the sliding frame. A second hole can be drilled a short distance from the first to allow the door to be opened fractionally for ventilation.

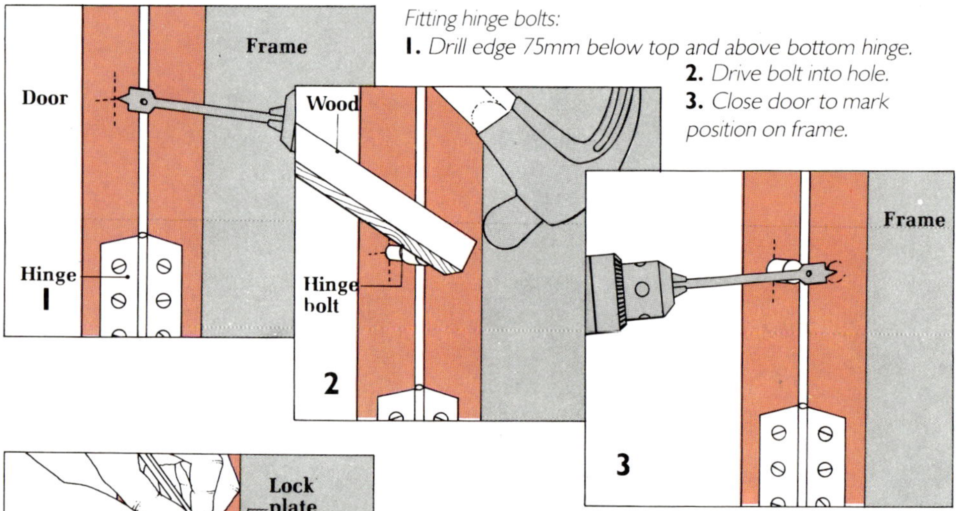

Fitting hinge bolts:
1. *Drill edge 75mm below top and above bottom hinge.*
2. *Drive bolt into hole.*
3. *Close door to mark position on frame.*

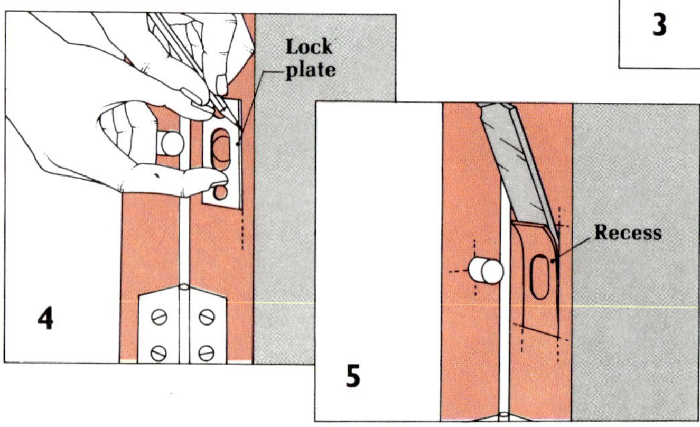

4. *Mark round lock plate.*
5. *Recess and secure flush with frame.*
Locks for French and sliding patio doors:
6. *Hinge bolts.*
7. *Espagnolette bolt.*

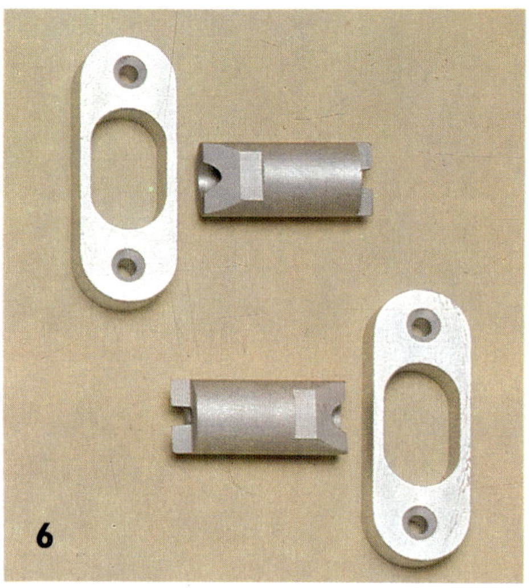

7

Timber French doors
Being glazed and situated facing a garden where they may not be overlooked, these doors are always vulnerable and should be protected in several ways. Normally fitted with both doors opening outwards, the first closing door should be fastened with either flush bolts at top and bottom, recessed into the edge of the door and hidden by the second leaf, or with mortise rack bolts installed to shoot into the sill and head of the frame. The second closing door should lock to the first leaf with either a mortise deadlock or a hook-bolt mortise lock and also be secured at top and bottom with mortise rack bolts which shoot into the sill and head of the frame.

An alternative lock which can be fitted to French doors is an espagnolette bolt which extends the full length of the door and consists of two sliding bolts which by means of a central handle extend into recesses at the head and sill of the frame. Ideally, the handle should be lockable. If it is not then an additional mortise lock will be required.

Hinge bolts
A problem with doors which open outwards is that the hinges are exposed. It is possible that these can be tampered with, allowing the door to be opened on the hinge side. To prevent this from happening, hinge bolts should be fitted. These consist of a fixed bolt fitted into the edge of the door close to the hinge position and a matching locking plate recessed in the fixed part of the door jamb. When the door is closed, the bolts engage in the locking plate preventing the door from being removed from its hinges.

Windows

The majority of break-ins, over 60% in fact, occur through windows, so you must take window security very seriously indeed. A wide variety of window locks have been produced to help you make your windows more secure. Most of these are effective and simple to fit. The type you choose depends on how your windows are designed.

Most at risk are small-paned windows because the glass in these is usually fairly easy to break without making a great deal of noise which would attract attention. Once

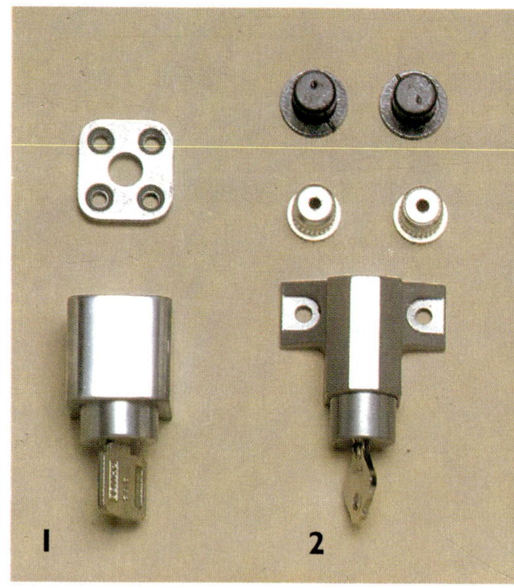

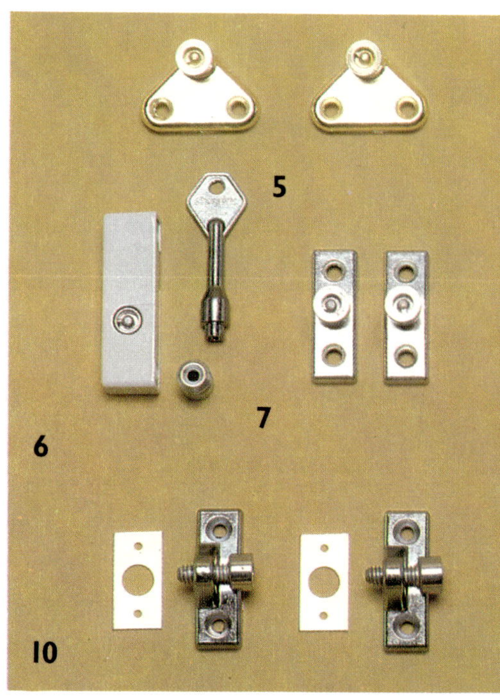

the pane is broken the intruder can reach in to open the window and make his entrance.

With timber windows in particular, before fitting any type of lock, first make sure that the window frame is sound and that the putty holding the glass is in good condition. Secondly, do not take the easy way out and simply screw down opening windows so they cannot be opened. Even if the windows are not opened very often it is important to retain the option of opening them for ventilation when required. More important still, you should be able to open the window quickly in the event of a fire. In this respect some of the more expensive window security devices which operate by key are better than the cheaper devices which screw together and are therefore slower to unlock. The latter, if they are detachable, are also easily mislaid when they have been removed.

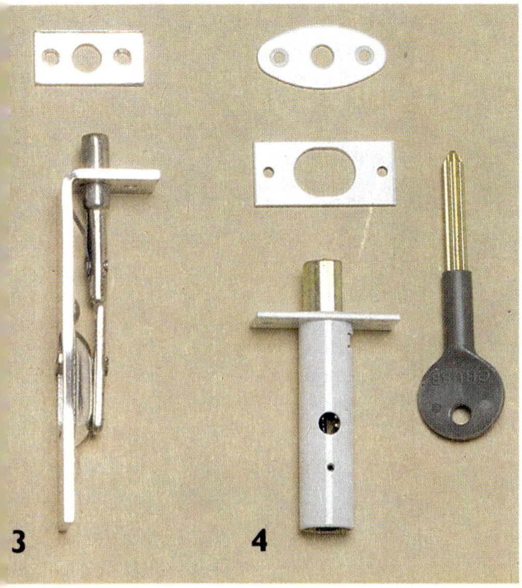

Casement-window locks

With casement (hinged) windows the best way to improve security is to change the fasteners for key-operated locking types. A cheaper alternative is to fit supplementary locking devices.

One of the best devices is the locking cockspur handle which is fitted in place of the standard type. Alternatively, the cockspur handle can be retained and security supplemented by key-operated casement-window locks. For maximum security you should fit two of these close to the top and bottom of each casement. These locks can also be used to secure top-hung fanlight windows. Another device is the automatic self-lock for hinged windows. This type locks automatically when the window is closed and is released with a key.

Mortise rack bolts

An excellent supplementary device for securing hinged-windows closed is the mortise rack bolt which is fitted in exactly the same way as it is to doors (see page 108). The bolt is slightly shorter than the door version. Surface-mounted dual screws work in a similar way, but they are not so neat in appearance.

Locks for windows and sliding doors
1. & 2. *Key-operated patio door locks.*
3. *Flush bolt.*
4. *Mortise rack bolt.*
Locks for timber casement windows
5. *Screw stops for stay without holes.*
6. *Self-locking window lock. Stud fits on window, lock body fits on frame.*
7. *Screw stops for stay with holes.*
8. *Mortise security rack bolt.*
9. *Catch- and key-operated lock.*
10. *Screw-down casement locks.*
11. *Pivoting lock.*
12. *Automatic lock with wedge for fitting to tapered frames.*
13. *Locking cockspur handle.*
14. *Catch- and key-operated lock on window.*
15. *Screw stop on stay with holes.*
16. *Screw stop on stay without holes.*

Stops

A cheap and quick way to secure hinged windows is to fit casement stay-screws and stops. Although these are not as strong as the previously mentioned devices, they do have the advantage that they can hold a window in a partially open position.

Timber sash windows

Although horizontal sliding timber-framed windows are occasionally found, the vast majority are vertical sashes. Many of the locks for this latter type can be used on horizontal sliders, but if you are in doubt take the advice of your crime prevention officer.

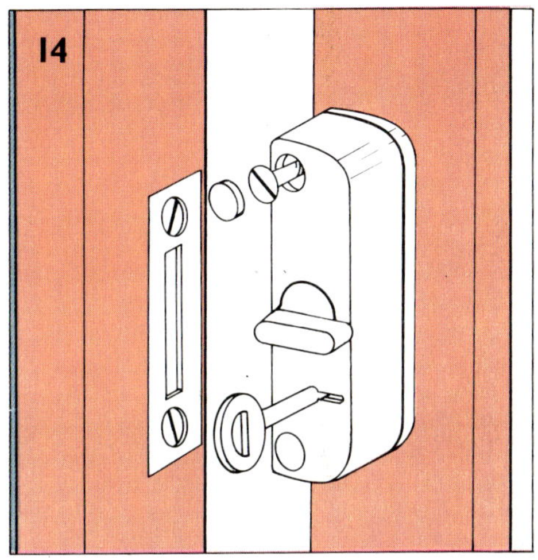

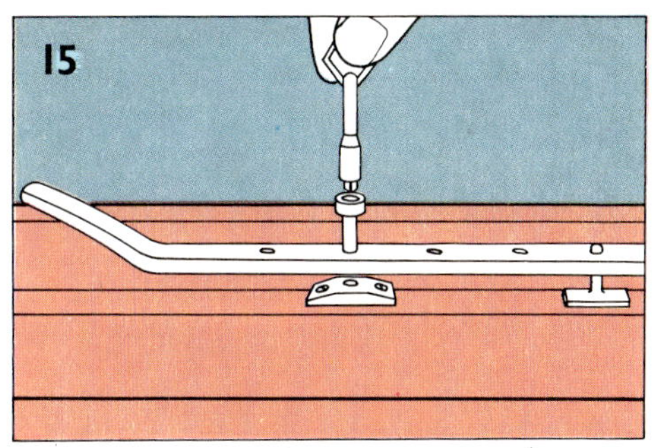

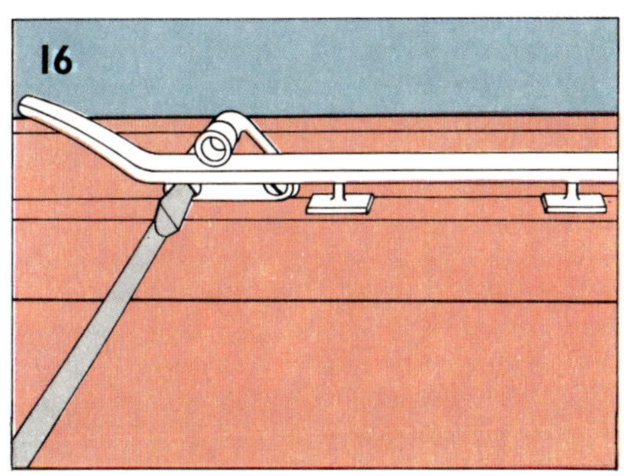

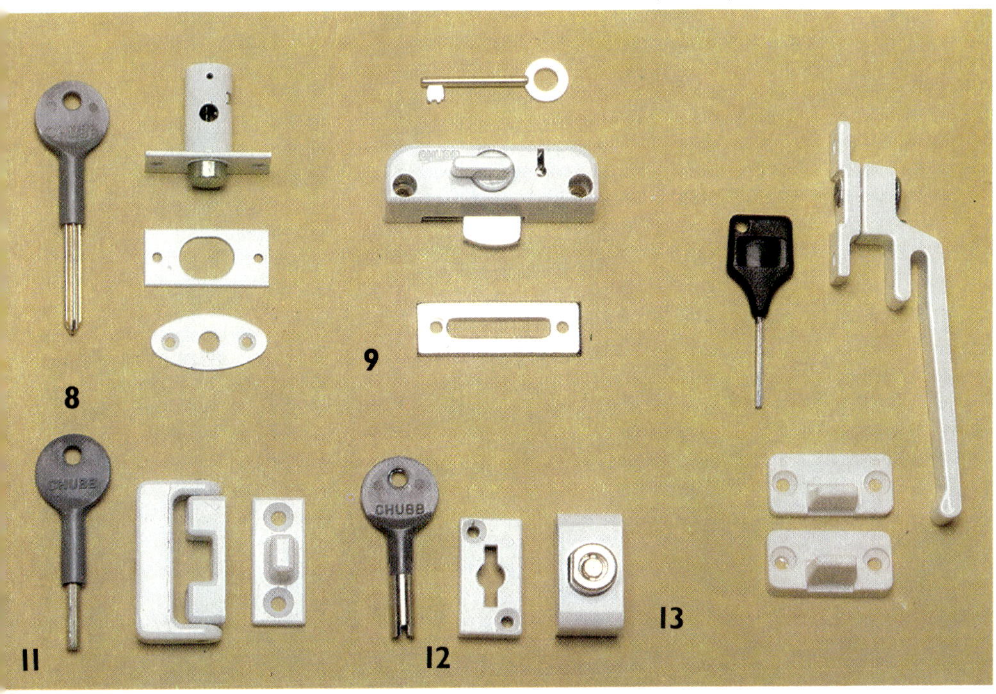

Fasteners
The first stage in securing sliding sash windows is to fit a secure type of fastener. The old type of pivoting sash-fastener, which can be opened with a knife blade from outside, should be discarded and in its place either a cam-type fitch fastener or a screw-type Brighton fastener should be fitted. The action of closing these fasteners draws the sashes together which not only aids security but also considerably reduces draughts which can blow between the meeting bars.

Sash locks
In addition to improved fasteners you still need to fit security locks which cannot be undone simply by breaking the glass. However, there is an easy way out with windows you never open for ventilation and that is to screw the meeting rails together, although you must never screw all the windows in a room together in this manner because there must always be an escape route in the case of fire.

The quickest-acting sash window security device is the key-operated sash lock. Fit one of these on each side to the top edge of the lower (inner) sash. By operating the key the body of the lock can be slid forwards so that a bolt enters a hole in the outer (top) sash. By drilling two holes the top sash can be lowered a little for ventilation. Because this type of lock is key-operated it offers better security than the other devices mentioned below.

Stops
The first of these is the locking stop. In this case a metal plate is screwed to the outer sash, and into the plate a small stop can be screwed using a special key. At the top of the lower sash a protective metal plate is fitted and when the stop is in place the movement of the top sash is restricted. Although the stop cannot be removed by hand it is easy to remove it with a key of the right make. Again, two locking stops should be fitted per window.

Dual screws
A neater type of sash window lock is the dual screw which consists of a screwed bolt within an outer barrel. The barrel is fixed in a hole drilled in the rail of the lower sash and when the key is turned this screws in the bolt which engages in a hole drilled in the meeting rail of the top sash preventing the window from being opened, but not allowing ventilation.

Metal casement windows
Many of the locks described under timber windows may also be used on metal ones but check on the pack before buying.

Steel windows
The majority of metal casement windows are made from steel or, more recently, galvanised steel. In the same manner as hinged timber windows, they are secured with cockspur handles and metal stays. There are a number of security locking devices for this type of window.

Cockspur-handle locks
Unlike those on timber windows, the cock-

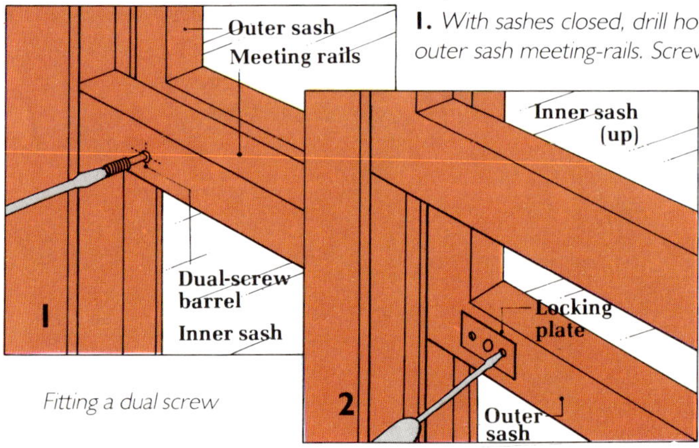

Fitting a dual screw

1. *With sashes closed, drill hole through inner and 15mm into outer sash meeting-rails. Screw or hammer in barrel.*
2. *Lift inner sash and screw locking plate (or hammer in locking barrel) to meeting-rail of outer sash.*

Sash-window locks and fasteners:
a. *and* **b.** *Spring- and sliding-bolts.*
c. *Brighton fastener.*
d. *Screw stop.*
e. *Easy-fit dual screws.*
f. *Fitch fastener.*
g. *Standard dual screws.*

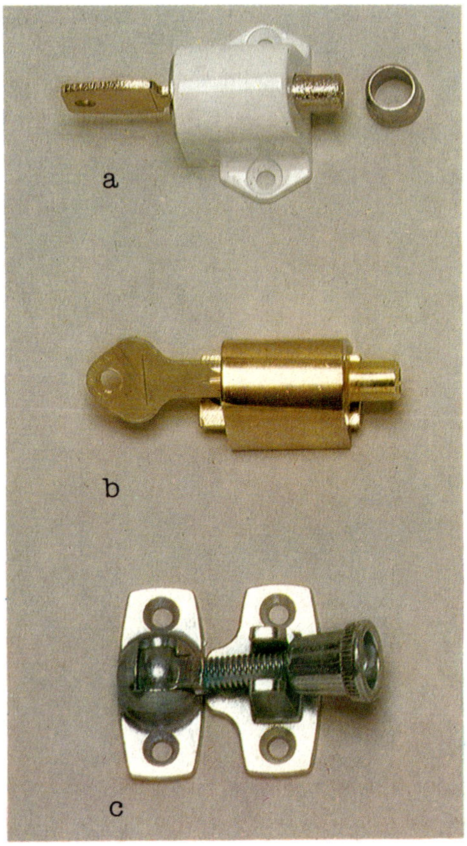

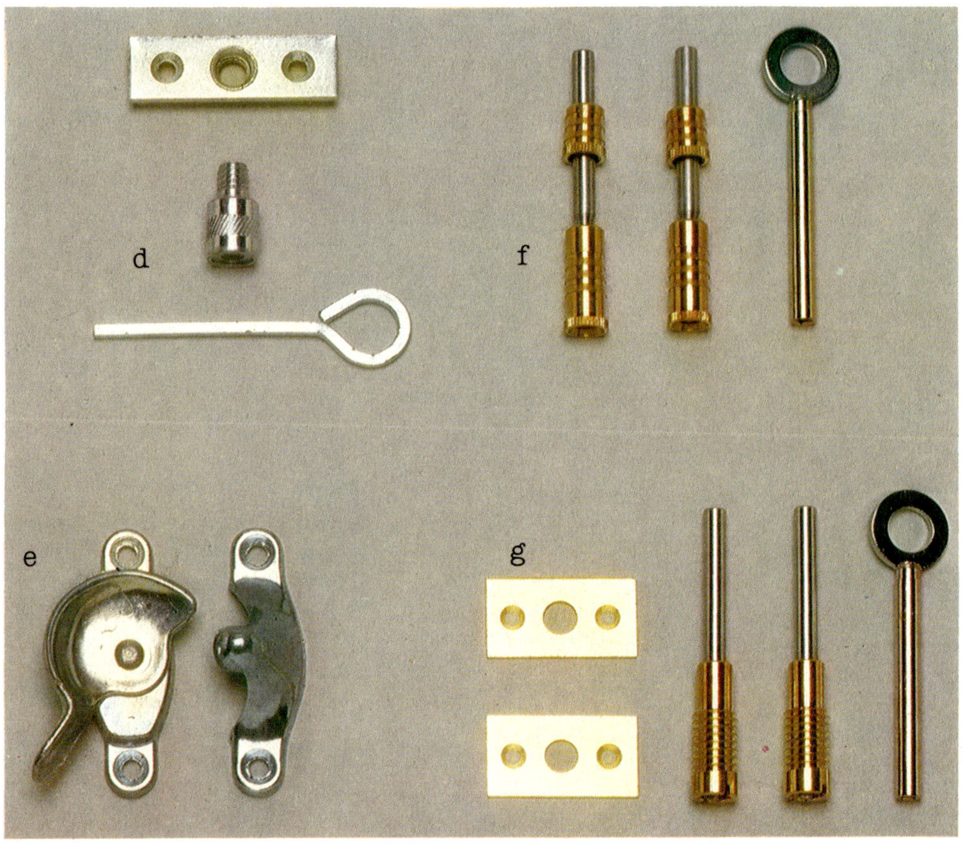

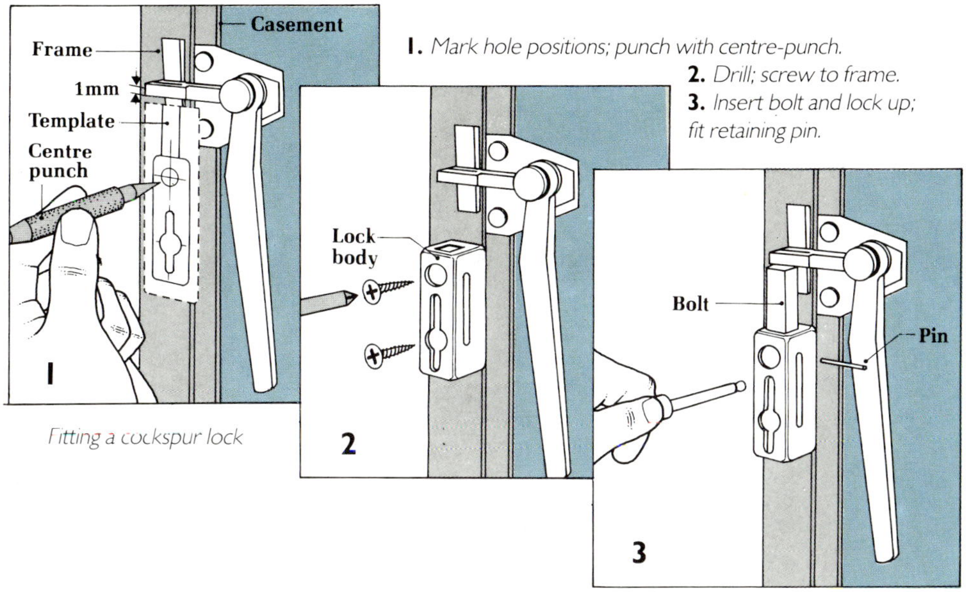

1. *Mark hole positions; punch with centre-punch.*
2. *Drill; screw to frame.*
3. *Insert bolt and lock up; fit retaining pin.*

Fitting a cockspur lock

spur handle on steel windows is very difficult to change for a key-operated locking version, but there is a good alternative and that is to fit a cockspur-handle lock. There are various types of this lock which screw to the fixed frame below the handle fixing position and which have a sliding or pivoting bolt which can be locked into position with a special key to prevent the handle from being operated. As long as the handle has a secondary ventilation slot these devices will allow a degree of ventilation and it is fairly easy to release the bolt to allow the window to be fully opened.

However, where metal casement windows are rarely opened there are cheaper window-latch locks available which by means of a key provided, lock directly on to the cockspur handle to prevent it from being opened. The advantage of this type is that it can be fitted without needing to drill the window for screw fixing.

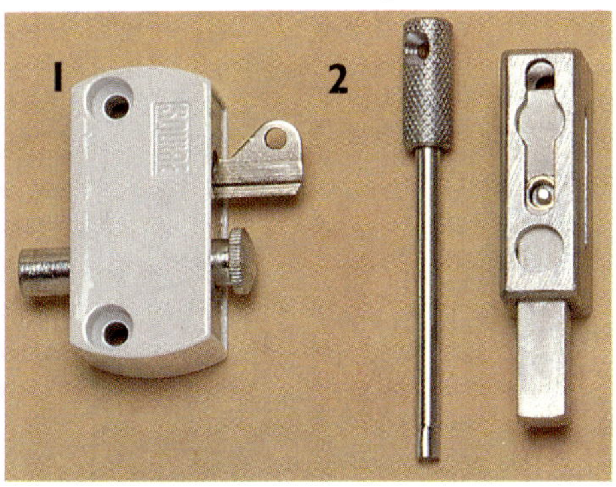

Locks for metal casement windows:
1. *Cockspur-handle lock, attached with spring clip.*
2. *Sliding body cockspur-handle lock, screw fitting.*
3. *Clamp-on cockspur stop.*
4. *Pivoting lock.*
5. *Clamp-on cockspur stops.*
6. *Catch- and key-operated lock.*
7. *Protruding bolt lock.*
8. *Sliding-bolt cockspur-handle lock, screw fitting.*

Key-operated casement-window locks

Those key-operated locks which can be fitted to timber hinged windows can also be fitted to metal windows. In this case the lock is positioned on the opening frame so that there is maximum engagement of the bolt on the fixed frame. The frame has to be drilled carefully so that the window glass is not damaged and the lock is fixed using the self-tapping screws supplied.

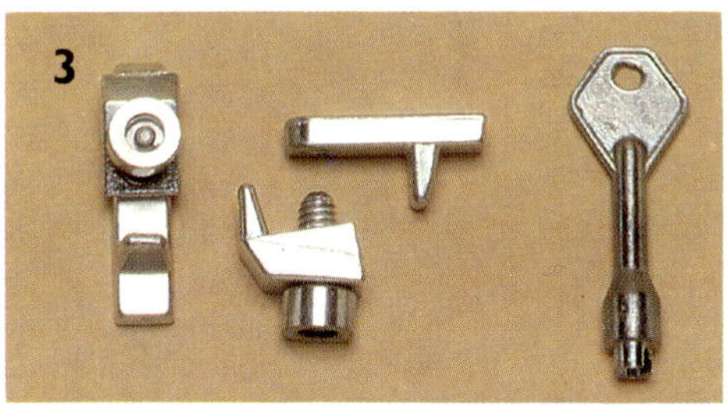

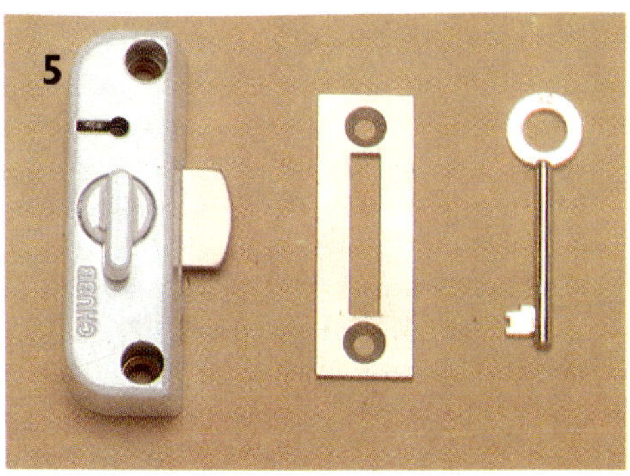

Sliding-wedge lock

A problem with surface-fitting locks is that they are obtrusive and can be tampered with. An excellent securing device for metal casements is, therefore, the sliding-wedge lock, which is fitted inside the channel within the metal frame and is thus not only unobtrusive but also cannot be tampered with. The device should be fitted about 100mm below the window catch and requires only one hole to be drilled in the fixed part of the frame through which the lock is secured. When the key is turned in the lock the sliding wedge expands, preventing the window from being opened. The only snag with this lock is that it fits only medium section frames, so take careful measurements of the frame dimensions before purchasing.

Stay locks

There are also various devices for locking the window stay in position and this type is particularly useful with metal fanlights which are particularly vulnerable to break-ins. One screw-operated type of stay lock works like a clamp which very simply holds the stay on to its rest. Another type uses a key-operated locking screw through one of the holes in the stay to hold a bar under the stay retainer. There is also a type with a pivoting locking-bar, operated by

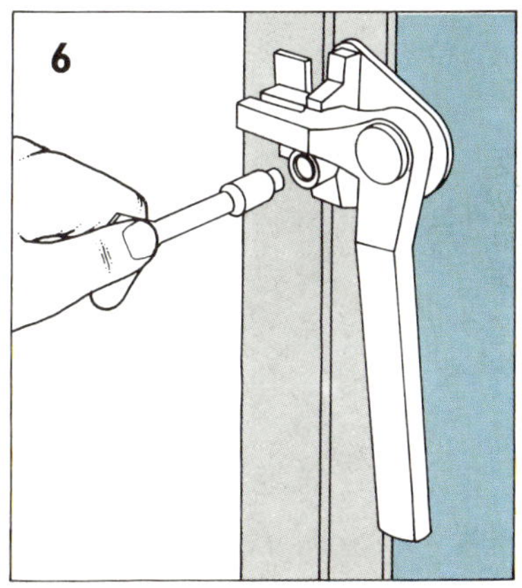

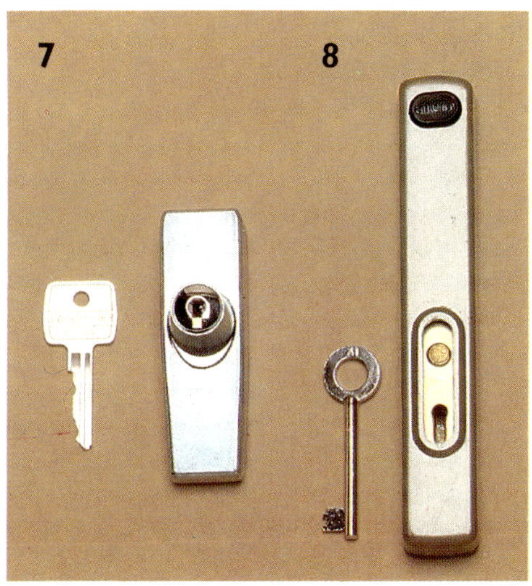

key, which is permanently attached to the window stay. The bar can be locked in place under the retainer to prevent the stay from being lifted.

Aluminium windows

Because the metal is so soft there is not a great deal that can be done to improve the security of aluminium replacement windows. Therefore, great reliance has to be placed on the locks originally fitted by the manufacturer. Some of the devices which are described for steel windows can be fitted to aluminium types, but in the latter case it is best to take the advice of your crime prevention officer. When buying new aluminium windows make sure that the security locks conform to BS4873 which will ensure as far as possible that the windows are secure.

Sliding windows

The best way to improve the security of horizontal or vertical sliding metal windows is to fit a key-operated lock, as recommended for patio doors, which screws on to the edge of the inside window and allows it to be locked to the outer pane.

If the window is not sufficiently wide to allow one of these locks to be fitted, fit instead a clamp-on type of lock which is attached to the sliding track to prevent the window from being opened.

Pivoting windows

Centre-pivot windows, both metal and timber types, can be secured with most of the devices intended for casement windows.

Louvre windows

By their nature these windows are very insecure. With the cheaper louvre mechanisms in particular, it is very easy to remove whole panes of glass from the metal clips. Make sure that the glass is well fitted in a good quality mechanism. It may pay to glue the glass in place with epoxy resin. Consider changing the window for a more secure type, or improve security by fixing an expanding metal-grille over the window.

Summary

If you have timber casement windows, the best protection is provided by mortise rack bolts, although key-operated cockspur handle locks are also good and are easier to fit. With timber sash windows, use the type of bolt that locks the two parts of the window together – these afford much better security than the basic catches found on most sash windows. Of the latter, Brighton

Fitting sliding-wedge lock to metal casement window:

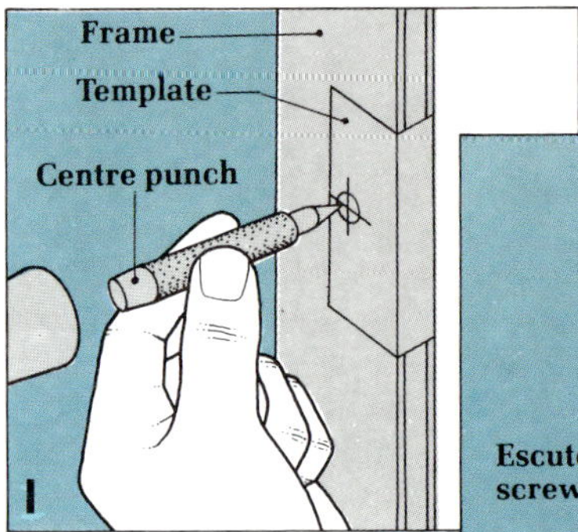

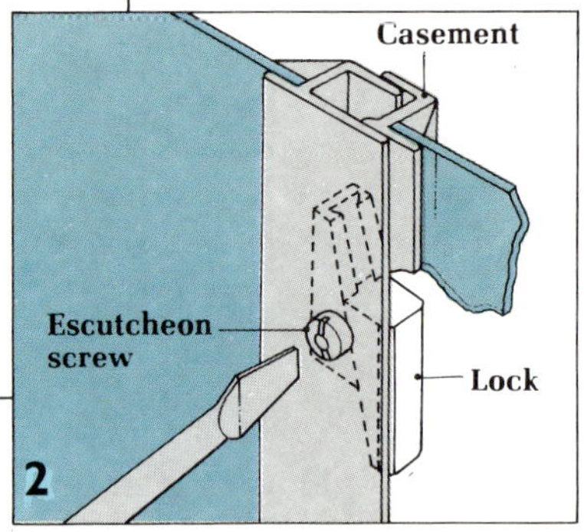

1. *Fold paper template round frame, 100mm below catch. Centre-punch hole position and drill.*
2. *Position lock in frame channel and fix by screwing escutcheon screw through frame*

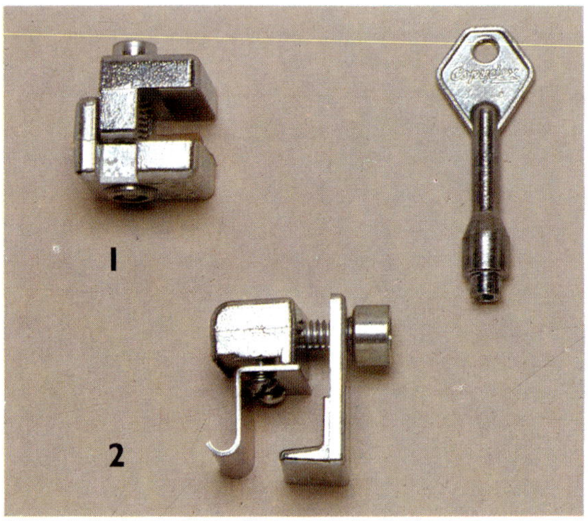

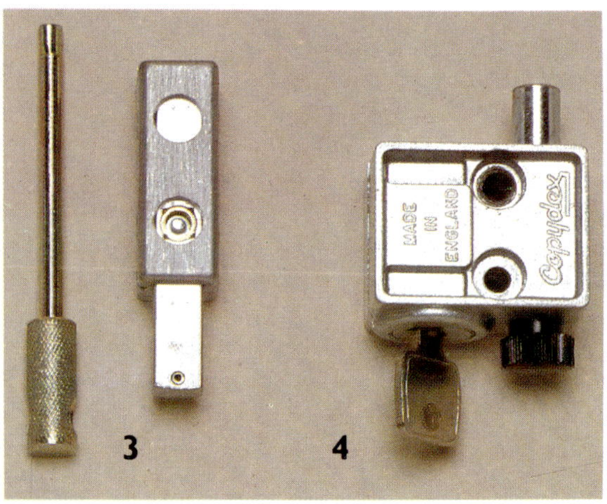

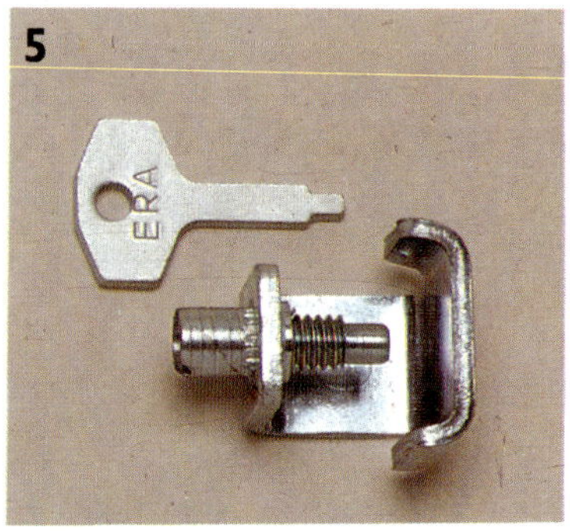

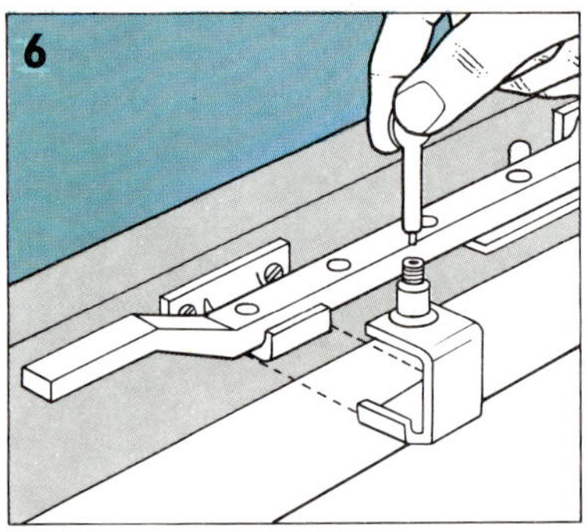

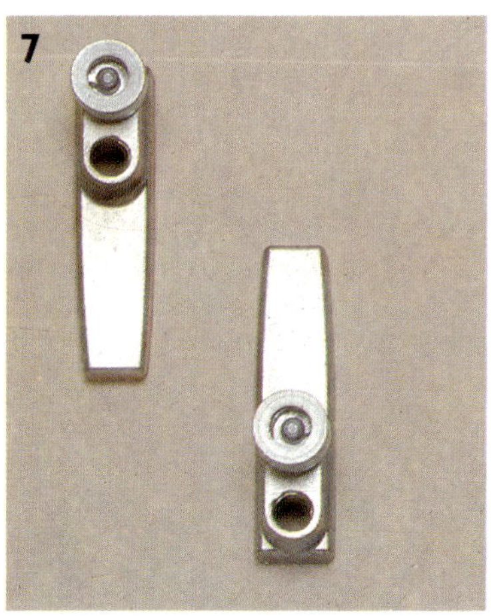

1. *Clamp-on lock for sliding windows.*
2. *Clip-on metal-casement lock.*
3. *Sliding-bolt stay or fanlight lock.*
4. *Protruding-bolt sliding-window lock.*
5 *and* **6.** *Clamp-on stay or fanlight lock.*
7. *Metal casement stay screw.*

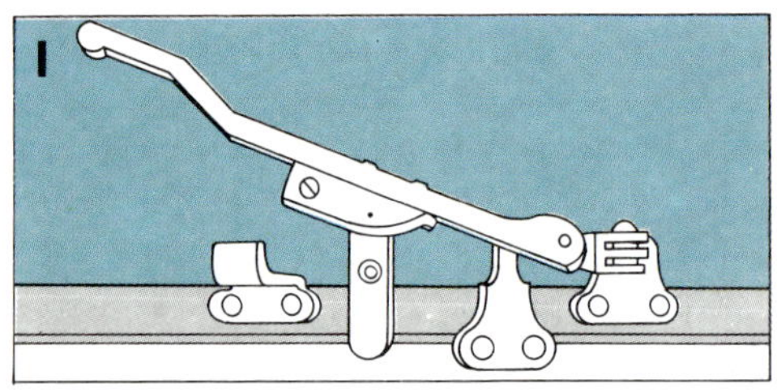

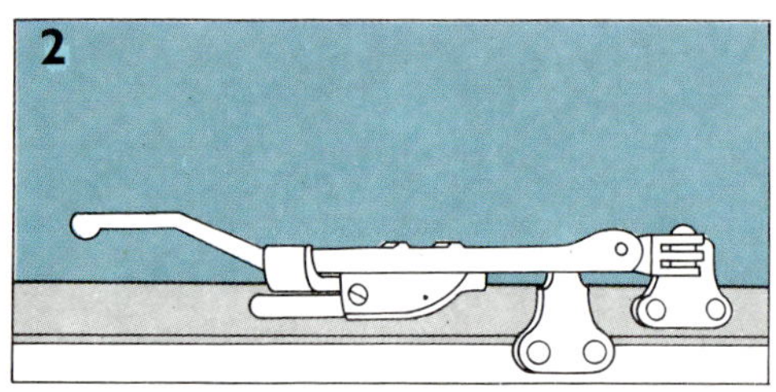

Above *Pivoting-bolt lock for casement stay, shown in both the closed position – when the stay cannot be raised – and open.*

Components of typical burglar alarm kit:
a. *Pressure mats.*
b. *Control unit.*
c. *Magnetic sensors.*
d. *Cable.*
e. *Panic switch.*
f. *Alarm bell.*

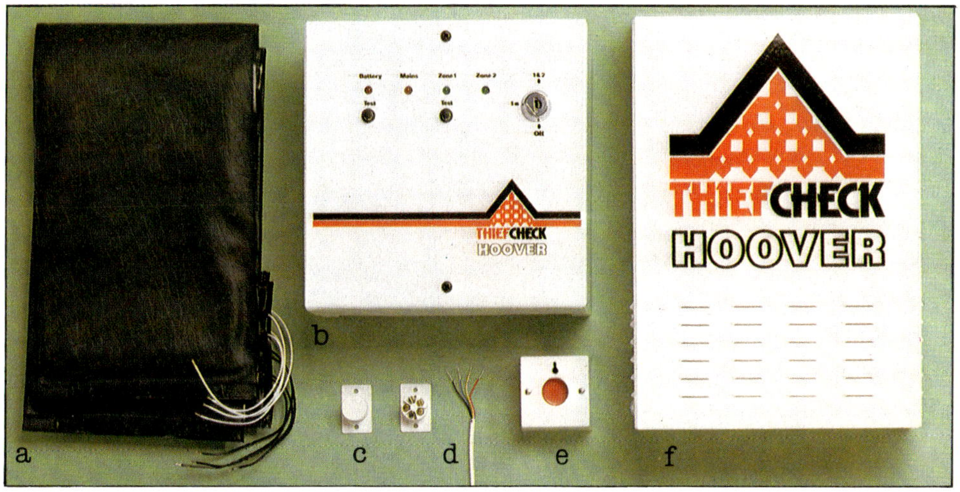

fasteners give more protection than the simple fitch types. If you have metal casement windows, fit sliding wedge locks if possible – these are ideal because they are hidden and cannot be tampered with by an intruder. With metal sliding windows, try one of the screw-on or clamp-on locks. If you are having new windows fitted, pay particular attention to security, especially if you have chosen aluminium double-glazed windows. It can be difficult to fit security devices to these.

Other precautions

Alarm systems

A burglar alarm is not a substitute for good security locks on doors and windows, but it is excellent in conjunction with them – the exterior bell box acting as a visual deterrent and the alarm system itself detecting an intruder before he has time to steal property or create havoc inside the home. It is important that you arm the system at night and whenever the dwelling is empty, and that it is reliable. A number of false alarms will prevent police and neighbours taking notice of a genuine alarm call, and may even dissuade you, the householder, from using the alarm regularly.

The usual DIY burglar-alarm kits are wired-circuit alarm systems consisting of a control unit, an external self-actuating alarm bell or siren, specialised detectors and sensors, which in most kits comprise magnetic contacts for doors and windows and pressure mats, and one or more panic switches together with the necessary cable, clips and connectors to form an electrical circuit. A good kit will contain both closed circuit devices, such as magnetic contacts, in which the alarm sounds if a continuous current is broken, and open circuit devices, such as pressure mats, in which the alarm sounds if a circuit is completed. Open circuit devices should not be used alone because if the connecting wires are cut the alarm will not be triggered off.

Another type of alarm is the ultrasonic unit which detects an intruder within a defined area. These self-contained units can resemble hi-fi speakers and simply plug into the mains supply and have back-up batteries. They vary in sophistication and may have a walk-test facility, which lets you set the pattern of the area to be guarded, remote alarm, and other features.

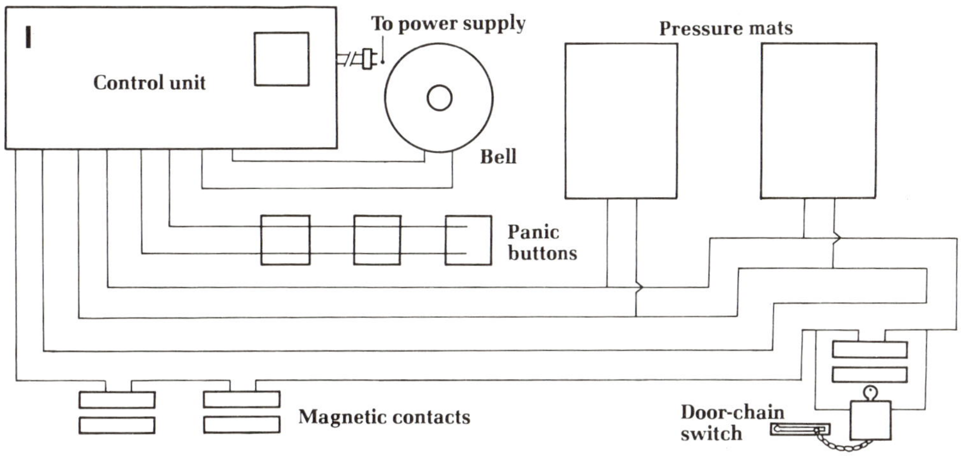

1. *Typical wiring of open and closed circuits.*
2. *Positions of magnetic sensors. Magnet fits on door or window, switch on frame.*
3. *Location of alarm components.*

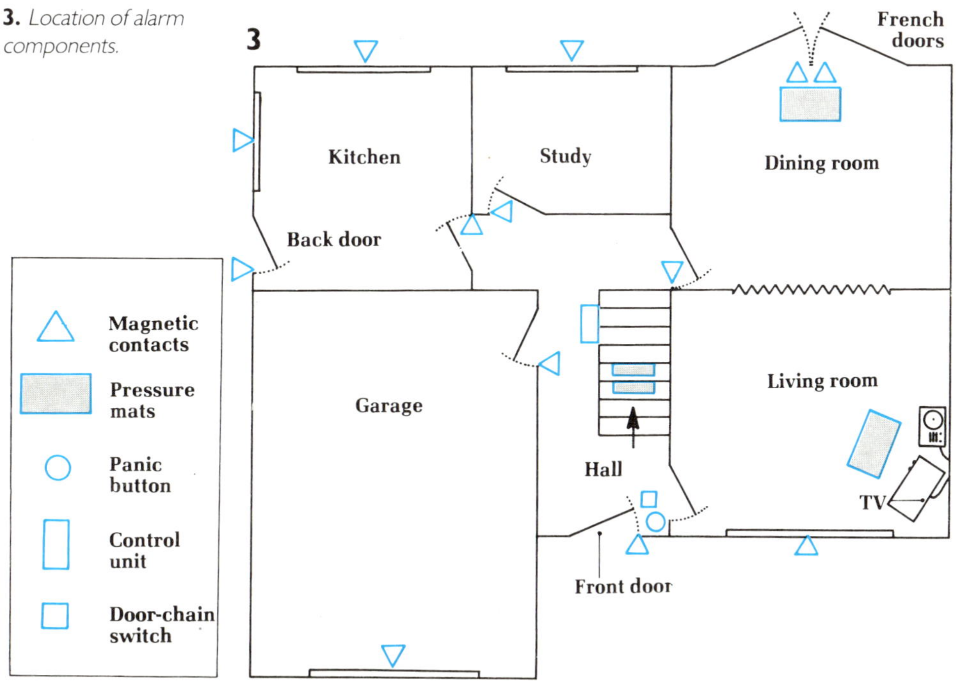

A passive infrared detector triggers the alarm if any change in the heat of the room occurs, such as the heat from the body of an intruder. Careful positioning of the detector is necessary to prevent false alarms.

Both ultrasonic and infrared units may be incorporated into a conventional alarm system and used to protect high-risk areas.

Installing a system

Start by familiarising yourself with the various items in the kit. With short lengths of wire, connect up the control unit and exterior bell or siren to ensure that all the pieces are working correctly before they are finally installed when fault-finding is more difficult. Smother the alarm with a cushion during these tests.

The next stage is to decide where the various devices will be installed. A typical domestic layout is shown in the diagram. This illustrates how the likely entry points can be protected and how carefully placed pressure mats will quickly detect the movement of an intruder inside the house. It is not a good idea to have pressure mats between the control unit and front door as this would deny the keyholder free entry and exit, unless the control box incorporated a time-delay facility or there was a key-switch outside the door.

The actual installation of the various devices is quite easy if you follow the manufacturer's instructions. Usually, it is just a simple wiring job using 2-core cable supplied in the kit.

Security lighting

Lighting can help security in two ways – it can make the house seem to be occupied when it is not, and it can illuminate dark areas outside the house to make it harder for an intruder to lurk unseen.

Indoor lighting

In the evenings, a dark house is almost certainly unoccupied so it usually pays to leave a light on somewhere, although not solely in a hallway, and not in a ground-floor room with the curtains drawn back so that anyone looking through the window can see that the room is unoccupied.

If you are going away for a long period you should not leave lights burning by day (another sign that a house is unoccupied) and by night. It is best to fit some sort of time-switch so that the lights come on automatically in the evening and go off again at bedtime.

Time-switches

The simplest time-switch is the plug-in type which fits into an ordinary socket outlet (power point). Time-switches can usually be set to allow up to two on/off switchings in a 24-hour period, although there are more expensive models allowing a

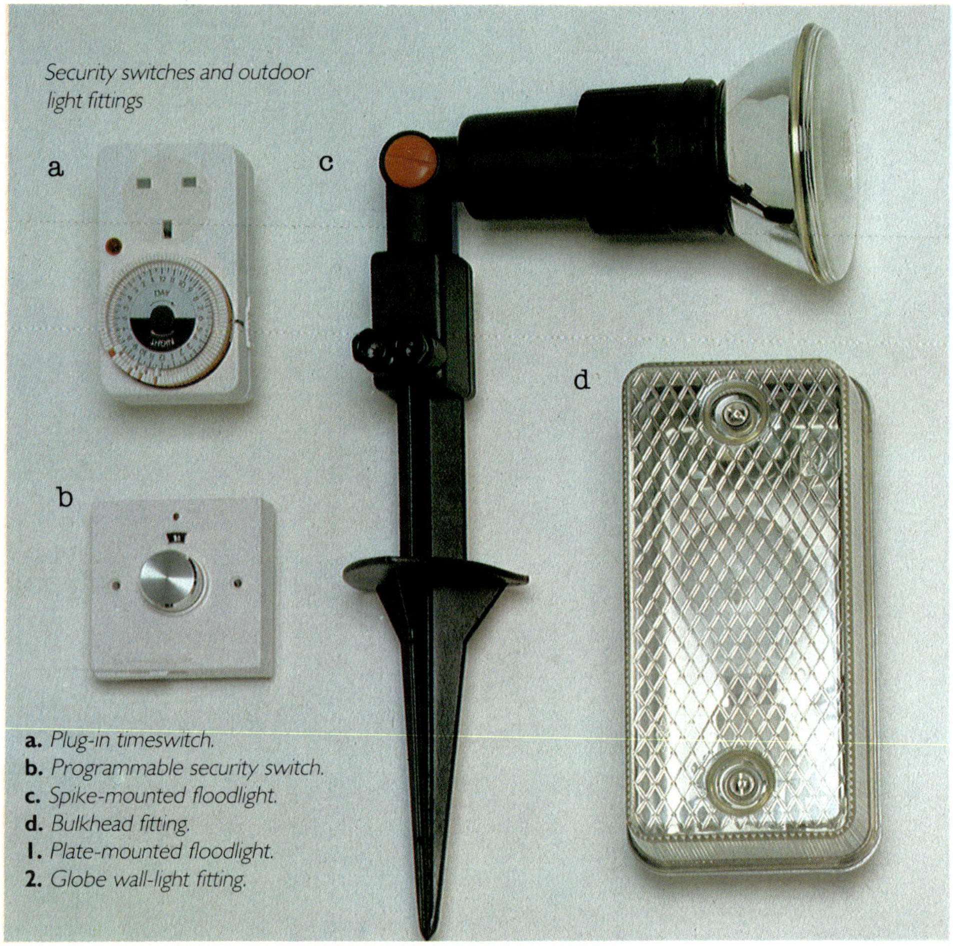

Security switches and outdoor light fittings

a. *Plug-in timeswitch.*
b. *Programmable security switch.*
c. *Spike-mounted floodlight.*
d. *Bulkhead fitting.*
1. *Plate-mounted floodlight.*
2. *Globe wall-light fitting.*

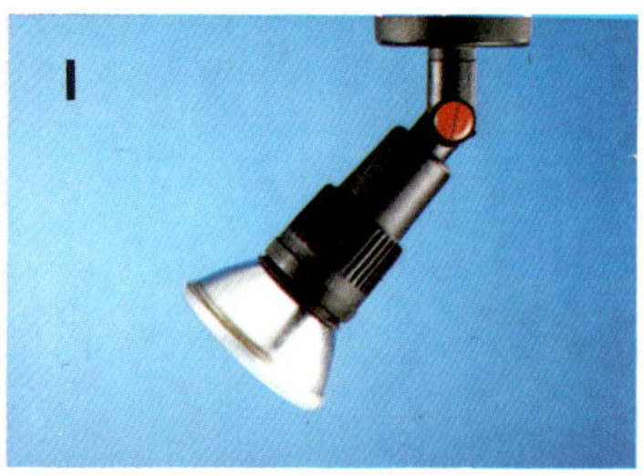

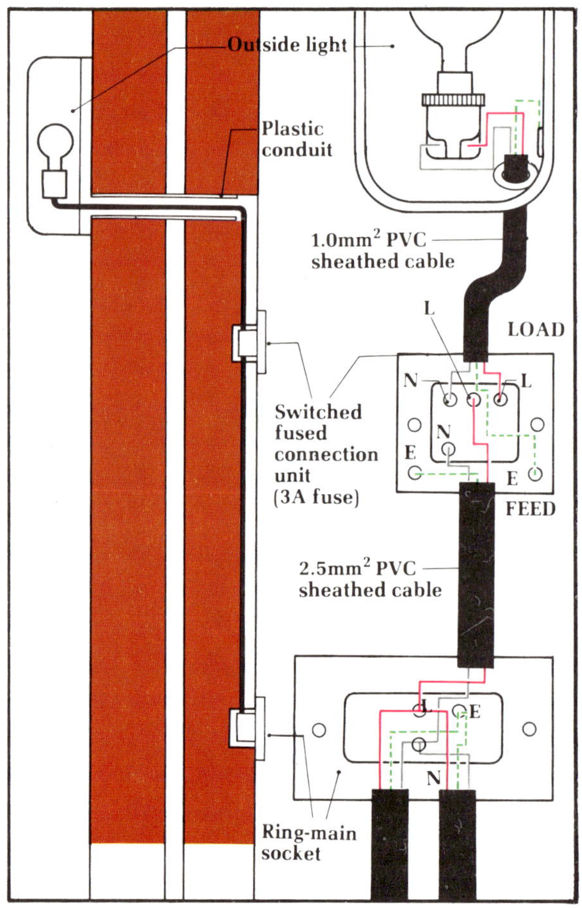

Right *Connect feed terminals of switched fused connection-unit to ring-main socket and load terminals to light fitting.*

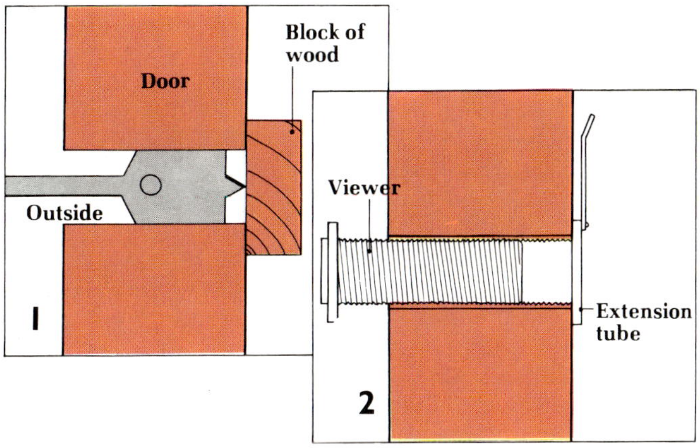

Measure door thickness before buying door viewer. To fit:
1. *Drill specified hole through door with block of wood against other face to stop splintering.*
2. *Insert viewer and washer from outside, extension tube (with cover) from inside, and screw together.*

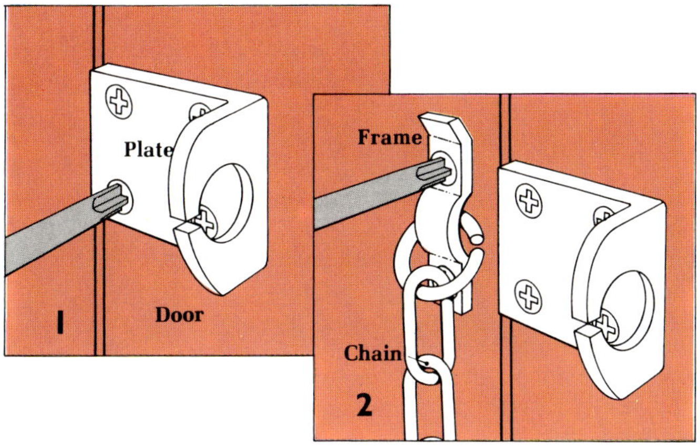

Fitting door chain:
1. *Screw plate to door, close to opening edge.*
2. *Fix staple with chain to door frame.*

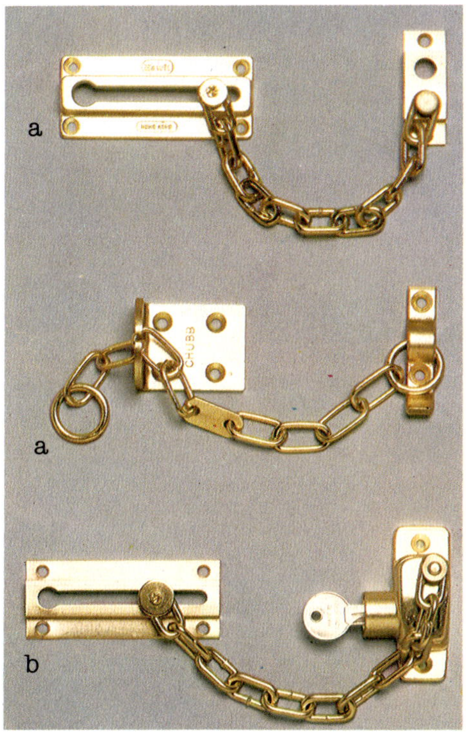

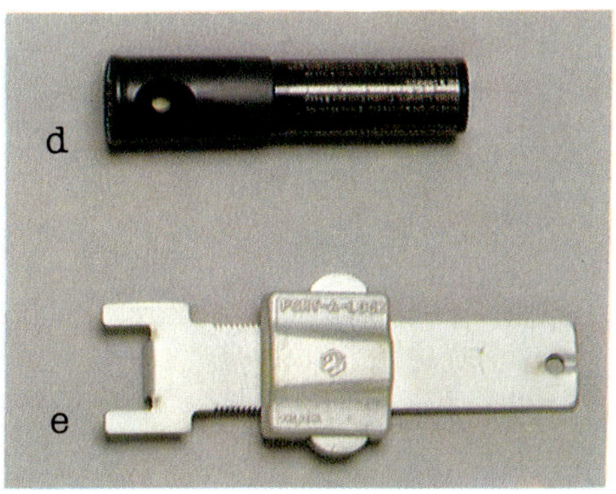

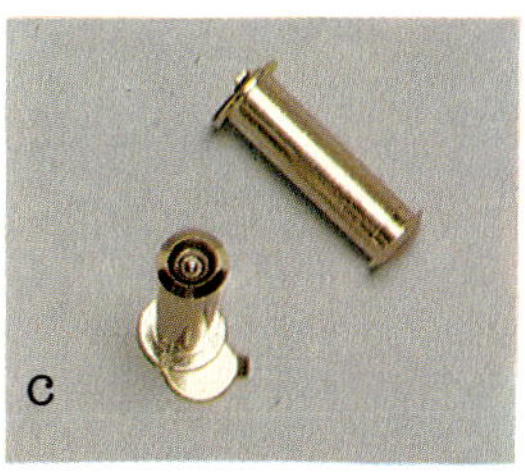

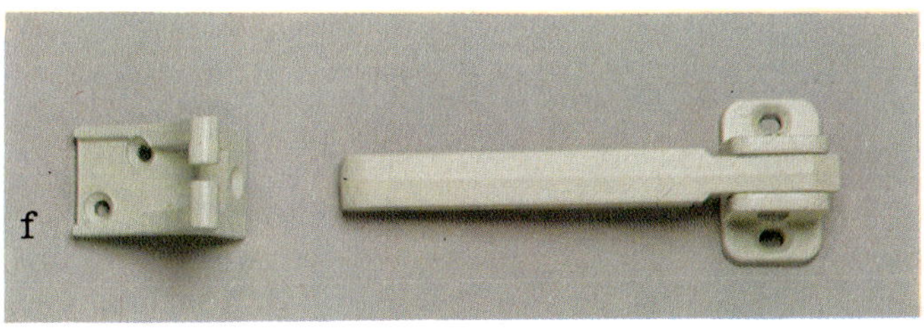

a. *Door chains.*
b. *Lockable door chain; can be resecured when leaving the house if it is still occupied.*
c. *Anti-personnel whistle; operates from compressed air.*
d. *Portable door lock; clamps against door and is held in place by latch striker-plate.*
e. *Door viewers.*
f. *Door limiter; a solid alternative to the door chain.*

greater number of switchings. They can only be used for plugged-in lights, such as table lamps or standard lamps, and not to switch the central room-light on and off. However, used in a bedroom or living-room, they can give the effect that the house is occupied, although anyone studying the house over a period of days may notice that the lights go on and off at identical times each day.

Security switches

To avoid this there are random switching devices available and one of the best of these is a unit which replaces the wall switch in a room and can therefore control the main light. The switch can be used as a conventional light switch, but it is also programmable and will either 'learn' and repeat automatically the way the light is normally used over a period of time, or it can be programmed to switch the light on and off a number of times in any 24-hour period. These times are varied up to half an hour each day to give random switching.

Outdoor lighting

It is a good idea to fit a wall-mounted lamp above both the front and back doors. Small, powerful wall-mounted floodlights are available for illuminating patios, driveways and other parts of the garden. If lights are installed in the garden these should be either 12 volt garden lights working from a transformer which is kept indoors, or if mains-operated, a professionally installed system connected by means of armoured outdoor cable. Low voltage cable should be buried in a trench and covered with tiles to prevent accidental damage.

Personal security

All the measures described so far have been aimed, in the first instance, at protecting property. Unfortunately, however, there is an ever-increasing need to take account of personal security. It is a sad fact of life that even at home you cannot be certain that you will not be subjected to a personal attack from an intruder, and the barge-in type of theft is on the increase, particularly in flats.

Two very easy ways to increase your security at home are to fit a door viewer and a door security chain.

Door viewers

A door viewer contains a special lens which gives a very wide angle of view when mounted at eye height in a front door, allowing you to identify callers before opening the door. It is supplied in two parts and fitting is simply a matter of drilling a hole through the door and screwing the two parts of the viewer together after inserting one part from the front of the door and the other section from the back.

Door chains

These should be strong, and fixed with large, long screws to minimise the risk of the chain fittings being wrenched from the door. The chain anchor should be screwed to the door-frame and the metal channel in which the other end of the chain can slide is fixed to the door. Some door chains have the chain attached to a key-operated plunger which allows the chain to be secured when you leave the property as well as in the conventional manner but it should never be used in place of a security lock. Get into the habit of always securing the door chain when you are at home.

Electronic devices

A further aid to personal security is provided by many burglar alarms which incorporate panic buttons or personal-attack switches into the system. The panic buttons are usually mounted near the front door and beside the bed, and pressing one of these buttons in an emergency sounds the alarm regardless of whether the main system is switched on or off.

Another electronic aid to security is the doorphone. This can simply be a two-way intercom system which will enable you to identify a caller, as an alternative to a door viewer, or it can be a sophisticated system, which may include a television door-viewer, and incorporate an electric door-release mechanism which can be especially useful in flats to minimise trips up and down stairs.

Portable devices

As a deterrent to attacks outdoors there are several, small anti-personnel whistles and sirens working off a canister of compressed air or batteries which emit a painful noise to drive-off attackers and attract the attention of passers-by.

Fire precautions

While some fires are caused by faulty electrical wiring, the vast majority are a direct result of carelessness, and the victims of these incidents tend to be children and the elderly who are least able to fend for themselves. Yet by taking simple precautions many incidents need not happen, or, if they do, at least you can be prepared for them.

Guarding against fires

Almost half of all domestic fires start in the kitchen so be especially vigilant here. Particularly with electric cookers there is a risk of leaving the cooker on and unattended. The position of the cooker is important too – it should be well clear of the door.

Never leave a chip-pan unattended on a cooker which is turned on. If the fat gets too hot it can ignite spontaneously. Be careful when adding wet chips to hot fat as the fat can splash and ignite. Do not leave tea-towels and clothes to dry over a cooker. Avoid curtains in a kitchen; if the window is left open there is a danger that the curtain will blow into a gas burner. Window blinds are safer in this respect. Make sure that electrical appliances are frequently checked for frayed flexes, broken plugs and loose connections. Never overload socket outlets by using multiple adapters.

In other areas of the house, make sure that portable electric and gas fires are not left where they could ignite furniture and curtains, or where someone could trip over them. Make sure that open fires are guarded. Chimneys for open fires should be swept at least once a year. Never move or fill oil-heaters when they are alight. Make sure that the heater is kept out of draughts and if possible fix it to the floor. Never use electric blankets when creased or folded and never leave them on all night unless they are the overblanket type. Unplug television sets before going to bed, check that fires are on their night-time setting; check ashtrays for smouldering cigarette ends, and close internal doors to inhibit the spread of fire.

Smoke detectors and extinguishers

It is an excellent idea to fit a smoke detector to give warning of a fire at an early stage. Most domestic smoke-detectors are battery-operated ionisation units which detect invisible products of combustion at an early stage and then sound an alarm. A good unit should sound a warning when the battery needs to be replaced and there should be a test button to check that the unit is working properly.

A range of fire extinguishers is available. Dry powder and vaporising liquid types are the most versatile and can be used on any type of fire.

Finally, and very important, ensure that everyone who needs to know – members of the family, guests and baby-sitters, for example – is aware of the position of essential keys and how to use them, in the event of an emergency.

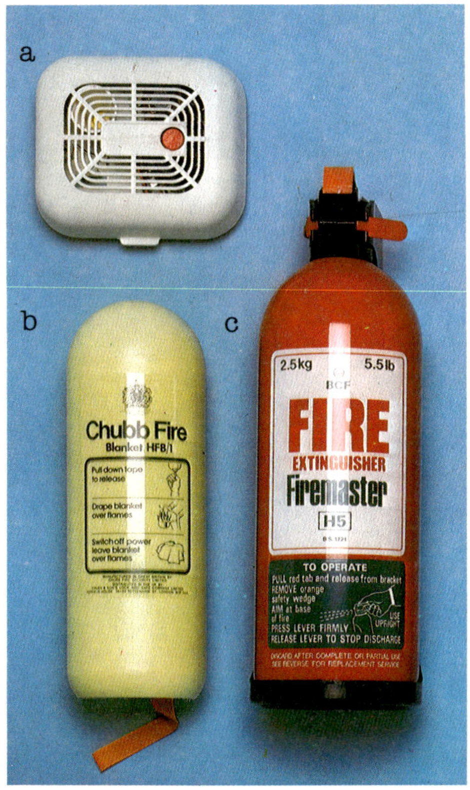

a. *Smoke detector.*
b. *Fire blanket.*
c. *Halon extinguisher.*
d. *Dry-powder extinguishers for electrical, flammable liquid and other types of fire.*

WOODWORKING

This section covers the basic requirements needed to master working with timber and chipboard, and the tools needed. To start with, it guides you through the process of buying timber; how to gauge its strength, age and suitability for the job you have in mind. It also introduces the main types of manufactured boards – hardboard, chipboard, plywood and laminated board which includes block board and pine-board. From the point of view of tools, those for measuring, cutting, cramping, jointing and fixing are covered. Fixings include types of nails, varieties of screws, and adhesives. Finally a general introduction to construction is given, including putting up shelves and box construction.

Timber

Ignorance of the nature of the materials you are using can cause a project to fail. Timber is a natural material and it is necessary to know something about the way it grows in order to understand how it can best be used and how it will behave in use.

Briefly, trees grow by adding new layers round the outside of the trunk, just underneath the bark. This makes the well-known annual rings. The sap which feeds these new layers also passes through to the centre or heartwood along the medullary rays which we call the figuring when the wood has been cut into planks. This means that the first few centimetres of the tree immediately under the bark are not fully grown cells and the mature timber is found towards the middle of the tree. The actual centre is known as the pith. These distinct areas behave differently in use.

Sapwood, that is the outer, immature wood, shrinks more than the inner heartwood. It is therefore more liable to twist. Shrinkage takes place round the direction of the annual rings from the outer part of the tree towards the central heart. If the tree is simply cut straight through into wide planks they will contain more sapwood on one side than the other and will warp away from the heart side, as the sapwood dries out and shrinks more than the heartwood. The pith should be avoided for all but the least important jobs because it is the most likely to twist as it dries or seasons.

When buying timber, as well as looking for the obvious defects such as large knots, shakes and cracks, and at general appearance, look also at the end grain, as it will tell you a lot about the future movement of the wood. The best pieces have the annual-ring marks fairly vertical across the narrowest width. Square timbers should not have the rings running diagonally as this will distort the shape.

Points to watch when choosing timber

- Choose timber which is both straight in its length and free from twist.
- Avoid large knots or dry dead knots which are likely to fall out.
- Choose vertical end grain.
- The closer the growth rings, the denser and more durable the timber.
- As well as obvious splits, or shakes as they are called, look for cup shakes which follow the curve of the growth rings.
- Avoid waney edge; this is the outer part of the tree and may still have the bark attached. It would need preservative.
- Sapwood of some of the softwoods is prone to blue staining. This is a type of mould and not serious, but because it indicates immature wood, a preservative should be applied for protection.

Other diseases to look for (which mainly apply to secondhand timber) are:

- Wet rot; dies when water is removed.
- Dry rot, in which the wood is dry, brown, crumbly and cracked into squares.
- Woodworm (3mm holes).

a. *Wider and closely spaced dark rings, higher strength.*
b. *Waney edge with bark removed.*
c. *Drying shakes reduce strength.*
d. *Rupture from sharply sloping grain.*

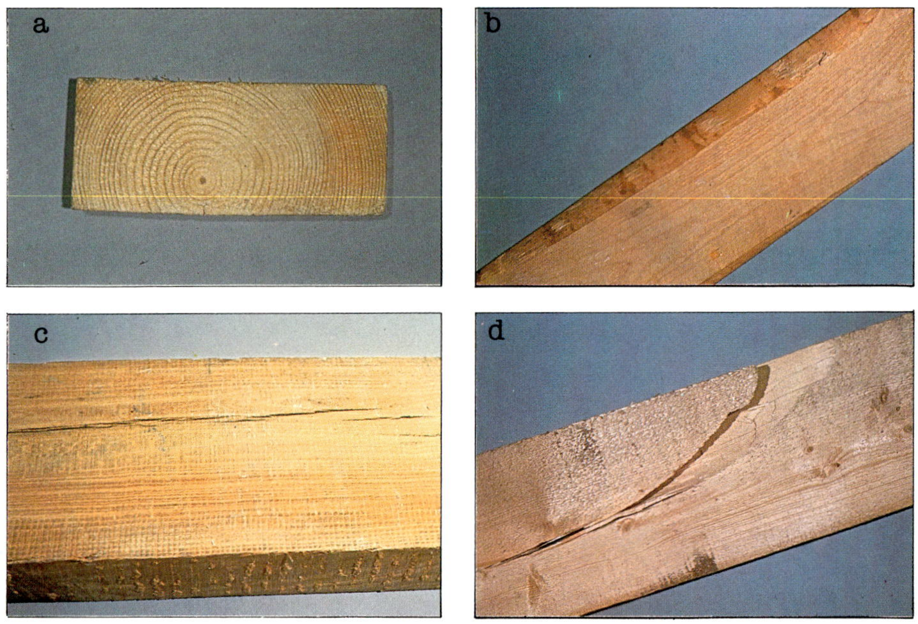

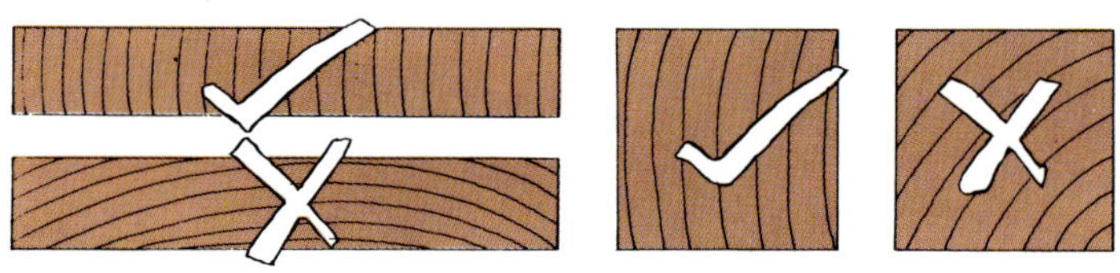

Left *Good and bad end-grain patterns for rectangular and square sections of timber.*

Usage of timber

Timber not only dries and shrinks but also takes up moisture and swells. Its tendency to change shape affects the choice of wood and the way it is used. For example, you should always put the timber heart side up for table tops and the tops of wooden stools, and table tops should not be fixed firmly, only buttoned or attached with slotted plates to allow for this movement.

Further, if wide boards are to be made up using a number of narrow boards edge-jointed together, it is best to arrange the boards so that they are alternately heart side up and heart side down. This will cause them to pull against each other and in this way help to hold them flat. The battens underneath, which are used to hold the boards, must be screwed through slots not through tight screw holes. In this way the whole top can adjust itself to the atmospheric conditions.

These comments apply to both hardwoods and softwoods, although the movement of softwoods is greater than that of hardwoods. However, the movement of the latter can often have a more damaging effect because these timbers are used for furniture show woods.

Hardwoods and softwoods

The terms hardwood and softwood are based on the structure of the wood and the characteristics of the trees. In general, soft-

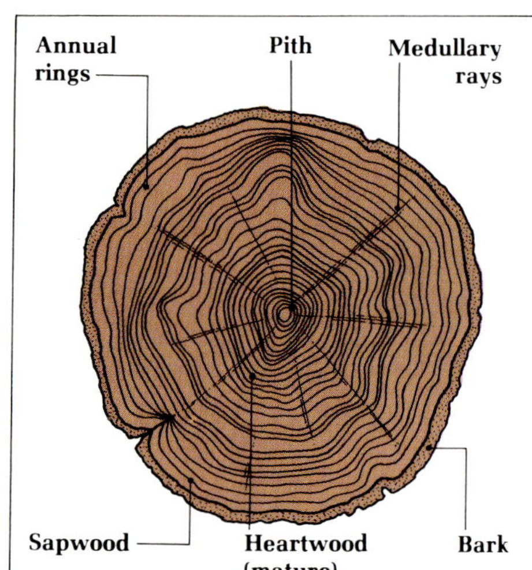

Cross-section through a tree showing important features.

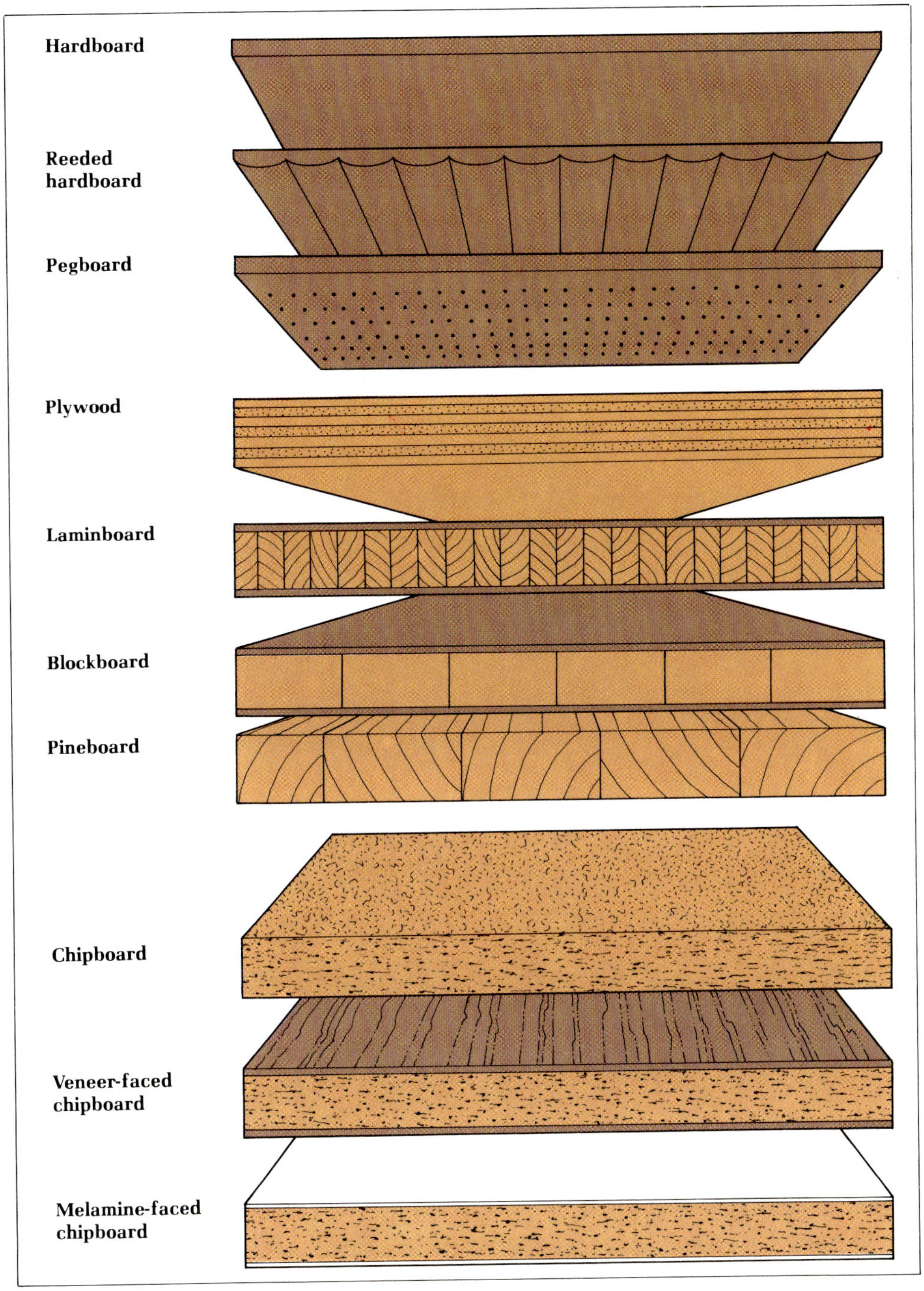

Timber sizes

Thickness (mm) / Width (mm)

Softwood	25	38	50	75	100	125	150	225
12	•	•	•					
16	•	•	•	•	•			
19						•		
22		•	•	•	•	•		
25	•						•	•
38		•	•					
50			•	•	•			

	6	9	12	15	18	21	22	33	35	45	47	145	220
Ramin													
6	•		•		•		•		•				
9				•			•		•		•		
12			•				•		•		•		
22							•		•		•		
Lauan													
9		•		•				•		•			
15				•									
21						•				•		•	•
45										•			
Japanese Oak													
9		•											
15												•	•
Iroko													
21						•				•		•	•

Table of commonly available sections of softwoods and hardwoods.

woods are from the cone-bearing and evergreen trees; while hardwoods are from trees which shed their leaves in autumn. For practical purposes, softwoods are used for general joinery and structural work while hardwoods are generally used for furniture and show woods.

Buying boards

There are three main types of manufactured wooden boards – hardboard, chipboard and plywood (including blockboard). They are sold by the square metre, hardboard and plain, standard chipboard being cheaper than veneered chipboards, plywoods and blockboards of the same thickness.

Hardboard is shredded timber which has been pulped and remade as large sheets. It can be plain or patterned and there is an oil-tempered type which is for use externally. Hardboard is used for the base of boards finished with a woodgrain pattern or tiled finish. Fretted pattern boards are also made and form good decorative grilles.

Chipboard is made from timber chipped into flakes and then pressed, with a resin binder, to make a large sheet of material. It is available in stock sizes of length and width, and with a range of timber-veneer or plastic facings. Special grades are available for flooring. Chipboard is also available faced with different decorative surfaces. Most popular are wood-veneered chipboard and Melamine-faced chipboard which is ideal for use in kitchens and bathrooms.

Plywood is made in a very wide range of sizes and thicknesses. The number of plies varies according to the thickness required which can be from about 4mm to 25mm. All kinds of facing veneers are available from plain birch to mahogany and teak. For panelling there is a planked-pattern finish as well as plain wood.

Laminated boards consist of a core of wood strips glued or laminated into one solid piece, faced with veneer. They are obtainable in similar finishes to plywood. Pineboard also comes under the general heading of laminated boards. It is made from strips of pine edge-glued together and is available in a range of widths and lengths.

Usage of boards

Hardboards and softwood-faced plywoods can be used for similar purposes. When buying them take care that the sheets are completely flat, because once they have taken up a curved or distorted shape they are difficult to straighten.

Chipboards and blockboards also have similar uses and for the same reasons care must be taken that they are flat. Both boards are stable, but as shelving, blockboards will hold greater weights over larger spans. Blockboard has a surface which will accept a finish without further work, but chipboard needs to have a decorative surface applied to it.

Tools

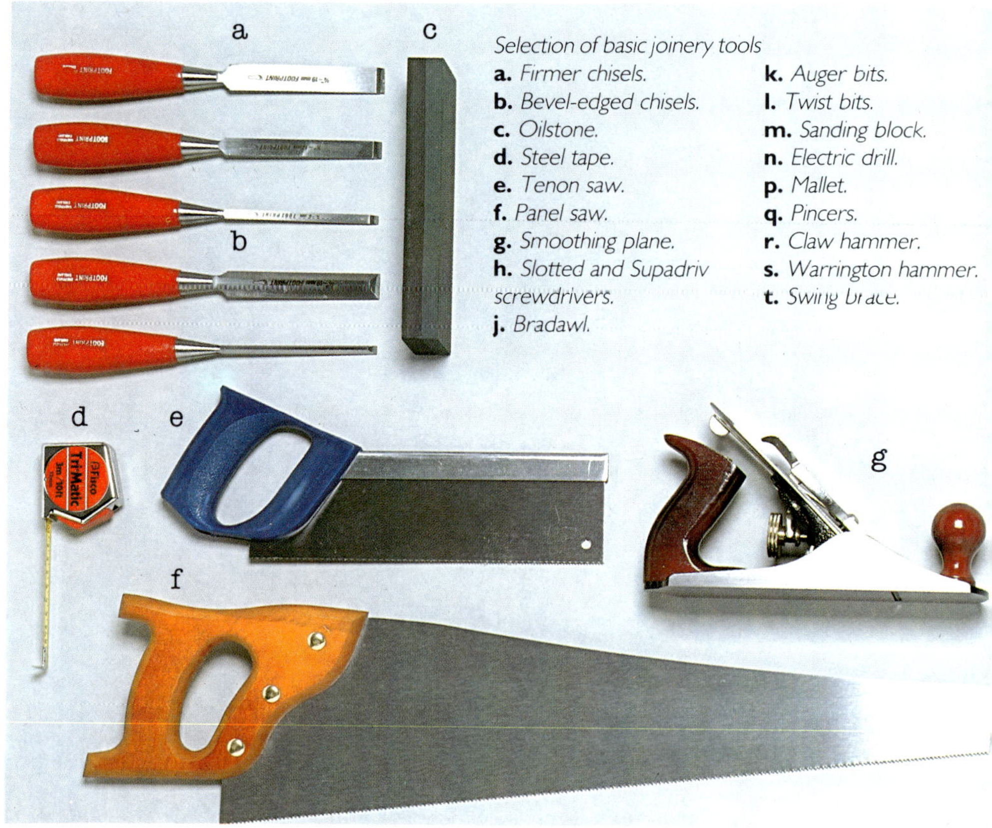

Selection of basic joinery tools
a. *Firmer chisels.*
b. *Bevel-edged chisels.*
c. *Oilstone.*
d. *Steel tape.*
e. *Tenon saw.*
f. *Panel saw.*
g. *Smoothing plane.*
h. *Slotted and Supadriv screwdrivers.*
j. *Bradawl.*
k. *Auger bits.*
l. *Twist bits.*
m. *Sanding block.*
n. *Electric drill.*
p. *Mallet.*
q. *Pincers.*
r. *Claw hammer.*
s. *Warrington hammer.*
t. *Swing brace.*

Exactly what constitutes a basic tool kit will depend to some extent on what kind of work you intend to do.

Measuring and setting out

In furniture construction and general workshop joinery there is always measuring to be done, whatever the job. For setting out on the bench the best measuring tool is a good quality folding rule. For measuring around the house use a steel tape. A two or three metre long model will meet most requirements. Get one which has both metric and imperial markings but be sure you only work in one or other system.

A square is needed to mark wood for cutting and although a try-square with a blade 200 or 230mm long is used for benchwork, a 300mm adjustable combination square and mitre square with a sliding blade is more useful for other work. For marking out the cutting lines you will need a setting-out, or marking, knife and a pencil sharpened to a chisel point (this is more accurate than a pointed one).

Cutting

To cut the timber you will need a panel saw 500 or 550mm long with 10 teeth per 25mm. This is a suitable size for general work. For bench work you need a tenon saw. This should have 12 or 14 teeth per 25mm. When sawing, the saw should not be forced to cut but pushed evenly so that it can cut at its own speed.

Shaping

Bevel-edged chisels are the best choice for bench work, but for general purposes use a firmer chisel which has square sides and is stronger. Widths of 19 and 6mm would enable you to make a start.

There is a wide range of planes available, from small block-planes up to the long trying-planes used for obtaining straight edges. The latter is not often needed now as most timber can be bought planed straight.

Planing

A block plane comes in very handy for rough shaping; buy one which has screw adjustment for the blade. It can be held in one hand, with the forefinger resting on the front knob of the plane, and the top of the wedge and the cutting blade in the palm of your hand. The larger, 250mm smoothing plane requires two hands to operate it successfully: one holds the handle at the back and the other holds the front knob. The hand on the knob holds the plane level at the start of the cut and raises it slightly at the end of the cut. Failure to lift the plane in this way will cause the end of the timber to be made slightly rounded as the plane drops at the end of the cut.

With both these types of plane, adjustment of the blade is made by turning a knob under the blade. This is just in front of the rear handle of the smoothing plane. Side adjustment is made by a lever.

For right-handed people, hold the blade or handle firmly in the right hand, with the left hand resting on the flat blade steadying it and providing an even pressure. This is particularly important with wide plane blades as the edge must be kept square. However, the corners of the plane blades have to be rubbed off a little to prevent them digging into the wood and making marks on the surface.

Use the full width of the stone when sharpening chisels as it will otherwise wear hollow in the middle and be unable to sharpen wide blades properly.

Drilling

Drilling holes, whether for fixing or for assembling projects, is another essential part of woodwork. An electric drill is a boon for holes up to 9mm, although a simple hand-drill (or wheel brace) will do the job. For holes above this size you have a choice of using flat-bits in an electric drill or buying a carpenter's swing brace which will take a wide variety of auger bits for making deep holes of almost any size. Adjustable bits are available, and for work in confined spaces, a ratchet brace is useful. For additional information on choosing and using electric drills, see pages 127-9.

Assembling

When it comes to assembling furniture and fittings you will need a hammer for driving nails, and a screwdriver or two. Suitable screwdriver lengths would be 150mm and 230mm. You will need tips suitable for cross-head (Supadriv) as well as the traditional slotted-head screws. A ratchet screwdriver will be very useful if you have a lot of screws to insert. A bradawl is essential for making a small hole for starting the screws.

A Warrington-pattern hammer is best for bench use and it should be about 12oz in weight. This is the type with the cross pein at the opposite side of the head to the striking face. This chisel-shaped pein is used for starting small panel-pins held between the finger and thumb. The claw hammer, much favoured by carpenters, is ideal for heavier fixings around the house and is of greater weight, about 20oz. If you have only a Warrington-pattern hammer you will need pincers to pull out nails.

Assembling furniture made with conventional woodworking joints calls for a mallet. This tool used to be essential for use with chisels, but the modern plastic handle is able to withstand the use of a hammer. The wider head of the mallet and its softer nature makes it less likely to mark the timber when projects are being assembled. The main difference in using these tools is that the hammer is swung with a wrist action whereas the mallet is swung from the elbow.

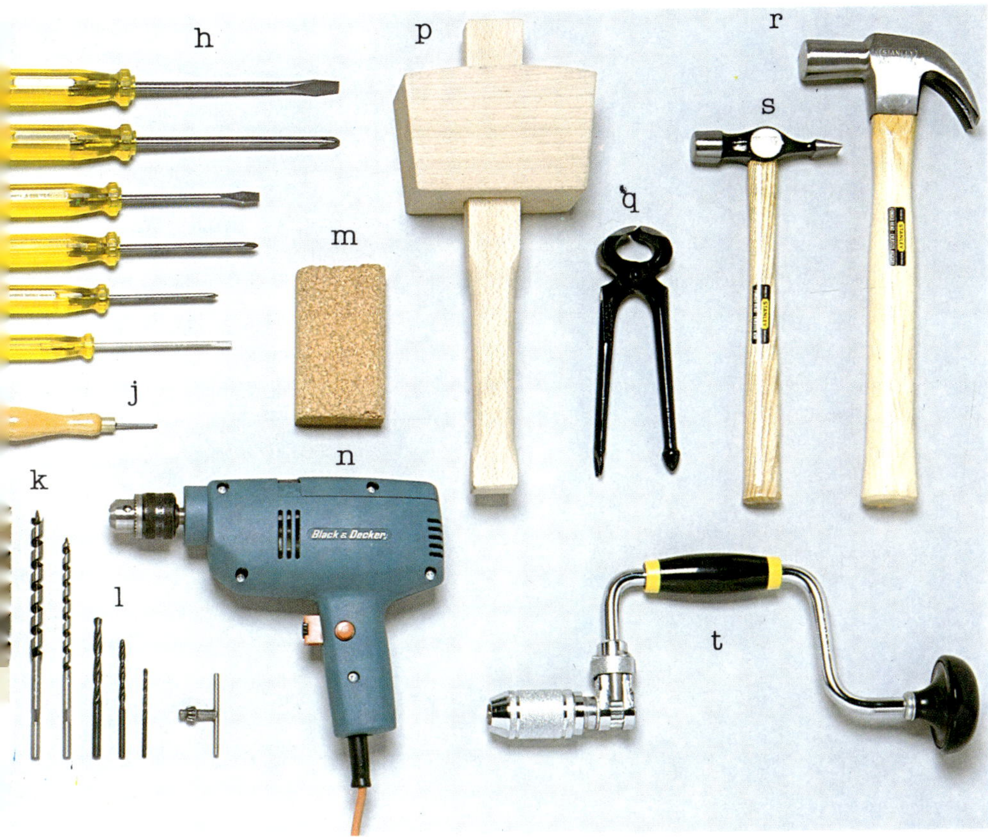

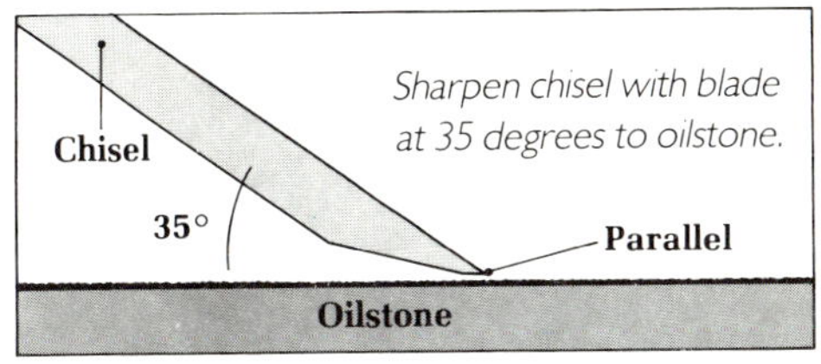

painting. A comfortable sanding block either cork or cork-faced is ideal for holding these papers on flat surfaces.

Sharpening

An oilstone is required for sharpening these tools and a medium grade provides a suitable edge for a beginner, but later you may want a finer stone in order to hone a keen edge on tools used for benchwork. The cutting edges of chisels and planes have two bevels, one at about 25 degrees made by the grindstone, and the other at about 35 degrees which is the sharpening bevel. Do not raise the handle of chisels and other blades too high when sharpening them or the cutting bevel will become too steep, reducing the ability to cut cleanly.

Holding devices

If you have a workbench you will be able to fix a vice to it so that you can hold timber firmly while working on it. When it comes to assembling the parts you will need other holding devices.

Bench hook

The simplest of holding devices is the bench hook. This can be made out of a piece of 75×50mm timber about 225mm long. It is cut out at each side so that a 50×25mm block is left at each end, on opposite sides of the wood. In use, it is placed on the bench so that one of the blocks is downward and hooks against the bench top, and the other faces upward so that the timber to be cut can be held firmly against it.

An alternative form of this hook is made from a broad piece of wood approximately 150mm wide, with a block screwed to opposite sides at opposite ends. Make these blocks about 25mm shorter than the width of the board and you can cross-cut timber held against the stops and when the saw comes through the wood it will not damage the bench top.

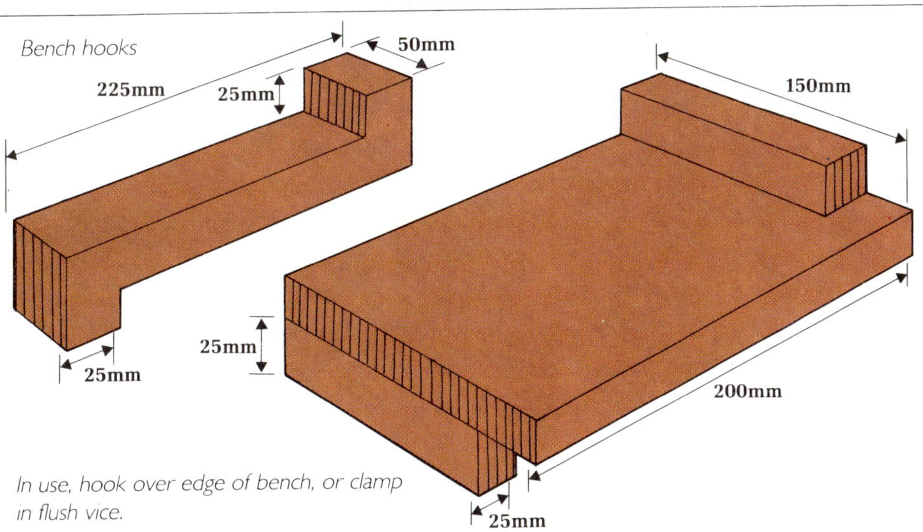

In use, hook over edge of bench, or clamp in flush vice.

Finishing

When projects have been completed there remains the finishing. Whether this is to be paint, varnish or polish a certain amount of preparation is necessary. Hardwoods are the most difficult to prepare because the grain may be twisted, figured or reversed and though this provides a pleasant appearance, it does take some effort to produce a good finish. When this kind of grain is to be polished or varnished it has to be scraped first.

An ordinary scraper is simply a rectangle of metal and it is sharpened with a hard steel rod by first drawing it along the edge of the scraper, square to the sides, and then tilting the rod at a slight angle and drawing it along the edge of the scraper again. This has the effect of first creating a burr on the metal then bending the burr over slightly.

The scraper is held upright with the thumbs at the back: it is pushed forward over the surface of the wood where the burr will take off very fine shavings. It takes a considerable amount of practice to sharpen and use this tool.

The alternative is abrasive paper. There are many grades of abrasive papers and many different types of grit. Very fine ones are used for preparing wood for polish and varnish, but the coarser grades of glasspaper are all that are needed to prepare timber for

Cramps

Whether you use patent, traditional or home-made cramps using folding wedges, the important part of the operation is holding the members of the structure tightly until the glue has set or screws, nails or other permanent fixings have been employed.

Sash cramps

One of the most useful devices is the sash cramp of which there are patent types as well as the simple, traditional cramp. This consists of a long metal bar with a screw-adjustable jaw at one end and a movable jaw which slides along the bar. The latter is fixed at the required point by a pin which passes through holes in the bar. Two of these cramps are needed for pulling up the joints of frames, but four or even more would be ideal for furniture making if you are using traditional cabinet-making methods of construction.

Frame cramps

For cramping chairs, frames or other similar constructions there are frame and web cramps. The frame cramp consists of a length of strong nylon cord with four corner blocks and a cleat. The corner blocks are put in position and the cord is passed round the frame over the blocks and tightened on the cleat. This puts an even pressure on all four corners.

Web cramps

The web cramp consists of nylon webbing passed through a ratchet lever device which is used to tighten it. Web cramps are useful for holding together objects with irregular shapes.

G-cramps

Another useful tool is the G-cramp. This, as its name suggests, is in the shape of a letter G. It has a long, threaded jaw with a swivel head to grip at most angles. These cramps are made in a wide range of sizes from about 75mm to 300mm or more. Again, two would be useful, but four or more of various sizes would be the ideal.

Mitre cramps

One specialised type of cramp which is useful if you are making picture frames, or similar constructions, is the mitre cramp. This metal corner device has two screw-operated jaws which hold both pieces of wood firmly together. It has the advantage over the frame cramp that it may have a saw guide incorporated so that the mitres can be cut accurately while they are held in the cramp. The disadvantage is that only one corner is held at a time.

In addition to these traditional cramping devices there are other patent cramps which are designed to perform two or three different cramping actions. There are also portable workbenches which incorporate a cramping mechanism.

You can make a cramp by screwing a block to each end of a length of wood and fitting the framework to be cramped between the blocks. Then drive folding wedges between the framework and the blocks at one end.

Using cramps

Whenever cramps are used there is the danger that the edges of the timber will be marked by the pressure of the jaw, so a piece of waste wood should be placed between the jaw and the workpiece.

To overcome the tendency for frames to bend or twist under pressure, you should fit a cramp both on the top and underneath the workpiece so that they pull against each other. Frames can also be squared up by cramps. When one diagonal of the frame is longer than the other, the cramps are moved so that they are angled the same way as the frame is leaning. When the cramps are tightened it will have the effect of pulling the frame into the square position.

Setting out

The start of any project, after the initial measuring up, is the setting out of the various parts. This must be done accurately if the completed work is to be satisfactory.

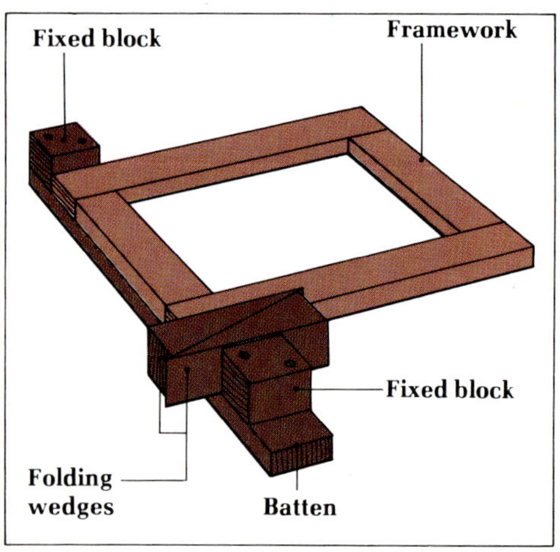

Simple cramp consisting of two blocks nailed to a batten, and folding wedges to apply the pressure.

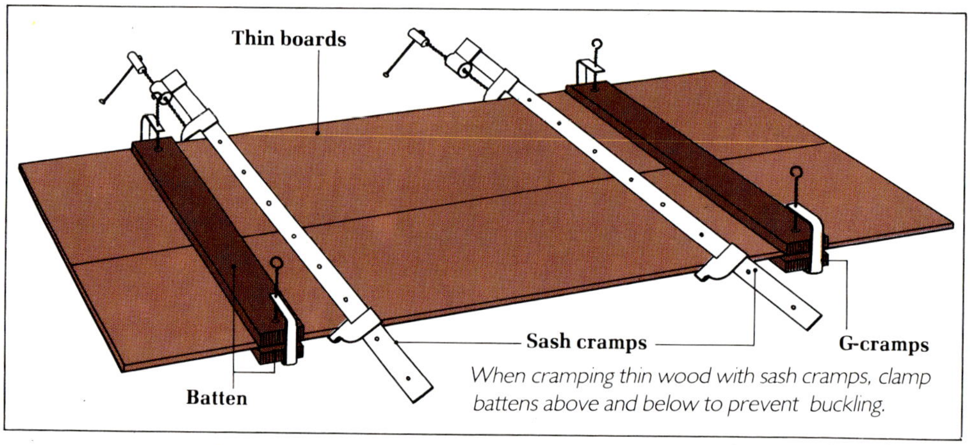

When cramping thin wood with sash cramps, clamp battens above and below to prevent buckling.

Selection of cramps for general purpose and specialist uses.

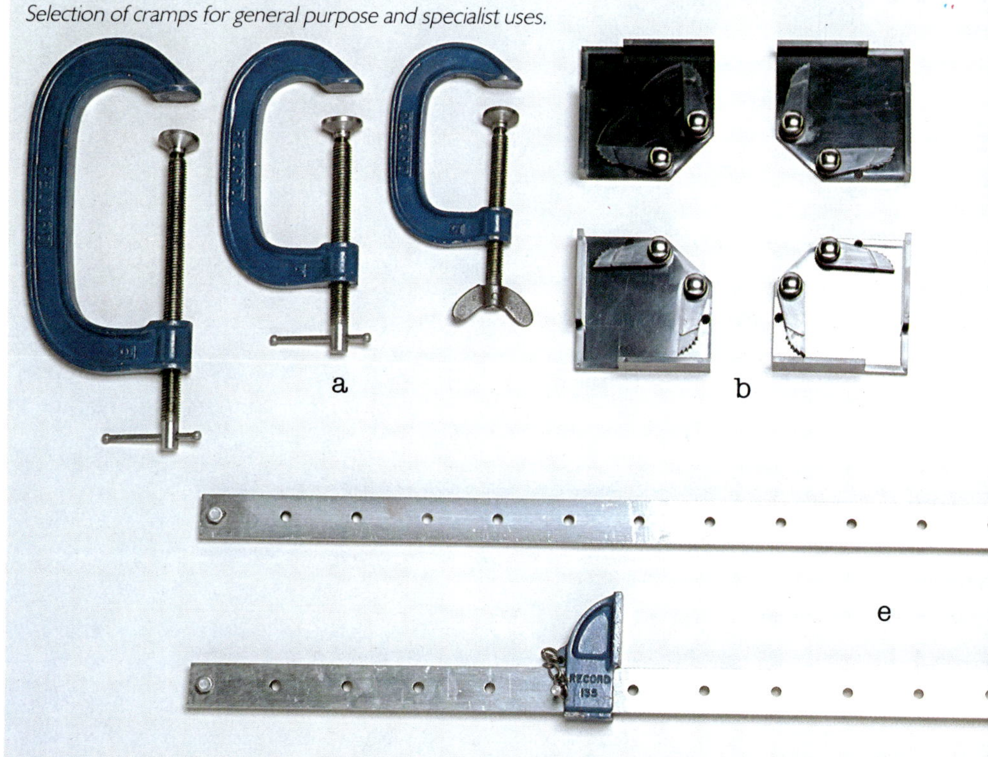

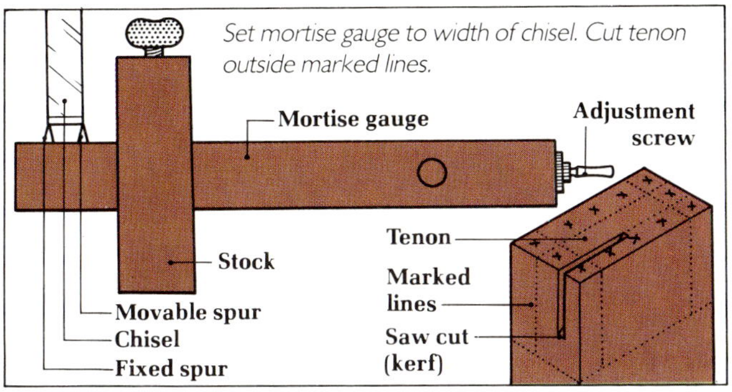

Right *Setting out dowel joints using template (top) and marking pins.*

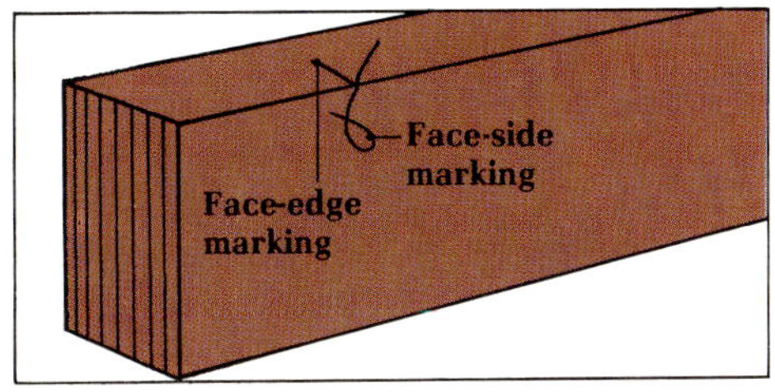

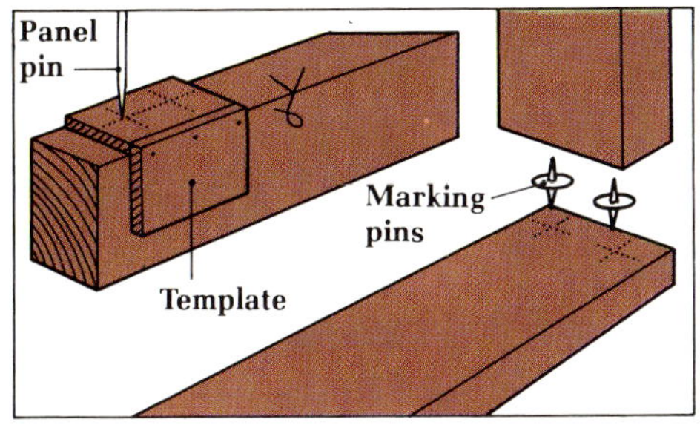

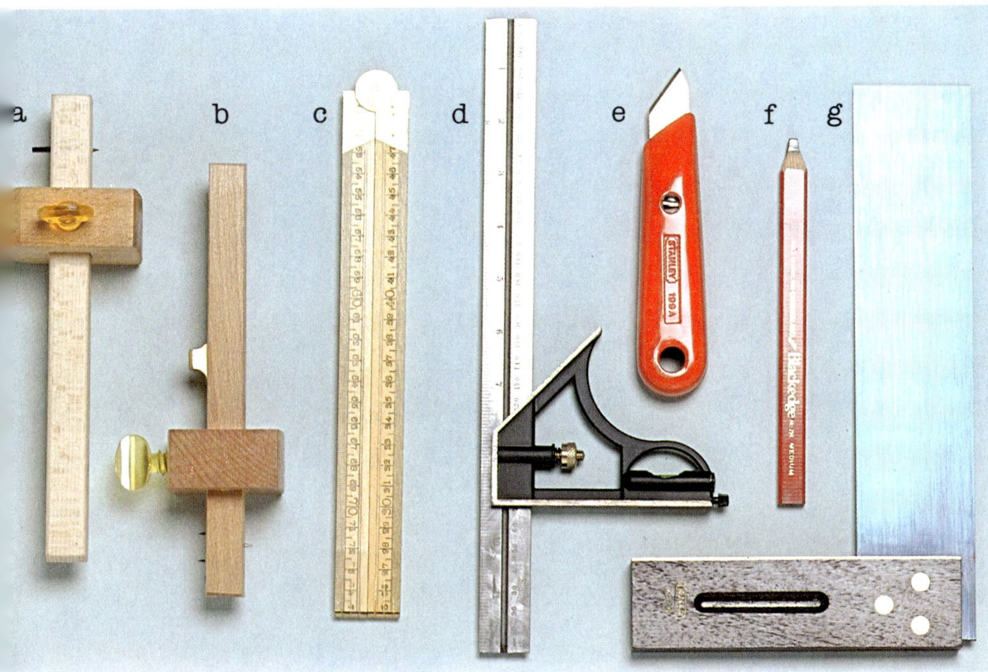

Setting-out tools:
a. *Marking gauge.*
b. *Mortise gauge.*
c. *Folding rule.*
d. *Combination square.*
e. *Marking knife.*
f. *Carpenter's pencil.*
g. *Try-square.*

a. *Three sizes of G-cramp.*
b. *Set of mitre (picture-frame) cramps.*
c. *Mitre-cutting cramp.*
d. *Web cramp.*
e. *Pair of sash cramps.*

A wooden rule, either folding or straight, a chisel-pointed pencil, a setting-out (or marking) knife and a square are the essential tools, but others will be needed for special joints in timber.

Use the rule on its edge for greater accuracy and use the knife in place of the pencil where possible. There are in fact only five places where the pencil must be used: all rough measuring; where a cut line would be seen on the surface of the wood; for most curves; for lines which are at an angle to the grain of the wood, because a knife would tend to follow the grain; when marking out chamfers, because the cut would show as a damaged edge.

The first task on setting out is to determine which is the best side of the wood for use as the face and this should be marked so that it is easily recognisable. One edge must also be chosen as the face edge and all setting out is done from these surfaces.

Setting out dowel joints

Dowel joints, which are used a great deal when working on chipboards and blockboards, are simply marked in pencil for position. The dowel holes can be drilled by means of a jig, of which there are two or three types, providing that they are at the ends of the boards. When dowel holes are needed in the middle of the board a different approach is necessary.

Accurate measurement will provide the position of one set of holes, but to get the other set in exactly the right position to match them it is necessary to use dowel marking pins. These are simply two short, sharp metal points separated by a ridge, like a washer. One point is pressed into each marked position, then the second piece of board is placed on the points in the exact position that it is required. The points mark this piece so that when they are removed the holes can be drilled, using a vertical drill-stand, and will match perfectly.

Marking gauges

For accurate setting out of joints a gauge should be used where possible. A marking gauge with one spur will do for most setting out when depths of cut are being marked for halved joints and for housings and similar joints. This gauge can also be used for marking mortise and tenon joints, but because it has only one spur, when all the joints have been marked with one groove, the gauge has to be reset to mark the other side of the mortise and tenon.

Marking out these joints for furniture where there are a lot of tenons is much easier and far more accurate if a mortise gauge, which has two spurs, is used. With this gauge the two spurs are set at the mortise width first, usually by placing the chisel to be used between the two points and adjusting them using the screw at the end of the stem. When they are correctly positioned, the stock is set on the stem so that the mortise will be marked in the required position which is usually in the centre of the wood. Whichever gauge is used, it is important that the marking is done with the stock against one face surface of the wood.

Setting out batches

Where a number of pieces of timber, for the legs of a table, for example, are to be set out the same, they should be cramped together to hold them while the edges are marked. These marks are later squared round the sides of the wood when they have been separated again. When pieces have to be set out as pairs they are placed with their face sides together and their face edges upwards and set out as before.

Where a large number of pieces of timber are required to be set out in the same way, it is often best to set out a pattern piece and cramp it to a small number of pieces. Then set them out in batches rather than try to set them all out at once. If there are complicated joints to make, they can be drawn out full size on a length of timber or plywood so that the piece for the pattern can be laid on the drawing and the joint positions marked directly on to it.

Whatever you are making, the setting out is the most important part of the job; if you don't set out accurately you cannot expect a well-fitting final product.

Nails and screws

The range of fixing devices for timber is immense. Here is a selection of some of the most popular nails and screws, together with their uses.

Nails

Round-head wire-nails are suitable for general and outdoor work where appearance is of little importance.

Round or oval lost-head nails are often used for fixing floorboards in place of the old-fashioned cut-nail. Lost-heads do, in fact, have a slight head.

Oval wire-nails are used for the same purposes as the round-head wire-nails, but because of their oval heads they can be punched below the surface so that the small hole they make can be filled with putty or other material. They can then be painted over so that they do not show.

Panel-pins are simply small slim versions of lost-head nails and are used for fixing thin material such as panels or mouldings where, being thin, they are easily covered and hidden.

Hardboard nails are also made specially for panel fixing. They have a slightly pointed head which is supposed to allow you to drive them into hardboard without having to punch them below the surface. These nails often have square shanks and are copper finished.

Clout nails are usually short, galvanised and have large heads. They are used for fixing felt to roofs.

Nails come in all lengths from 12mm pins to 150mm constructional nails. They are made in a variety of thicknesses too, so be sure to get a type which is suitable for the job. Thick nails easily split thin wood.

Nails are also made from aluminium and copper, but there is not the same range of types and sizes. There is also a limited range of galvanised or sherardised nails.

Screws

Screws are equally prolific, although they are most freely available in a more limited range of preferred sizes. You can still get the non-preferred sizes, but you may have difficulty finding them, and they may be more expensive.

The main types of head are countersunk for all general applications, raised countersunk which are usually plated and used for fixing metal fittings, and round head which are often used for fixing flat metal and may be used in conjunction with washers. There are also pan heads which are similar to round heads but have a flatter section. Other heads are made and are often used for heavyweight coach-screw fixings.

Screws are made in steel, brass, aluminium, stainless steel or silicon bronze. There are also a number of finishes including sherardised, nickel plate, chromium plate, brass plate, bronze metal antique, dark Florentine bronze and black japanned.

The plated finishes are only suitable for interior work. For external applications the solid brass, stainless steel and sherardised screws should be used. Aluminium screws are ideal for fixing cedar as they will not stain the surface. They are also, as are solid brass screws, suitable for fixings in kitchens, bathrooms and other damp areas.

There are two types of threads on screws. The first and most often used is the tapered thread which has a single spiral running down the shank. The other type is the chipboard screw. This has two spirals running round a parallel shank. The shorter lengths of these screws are threaded up to

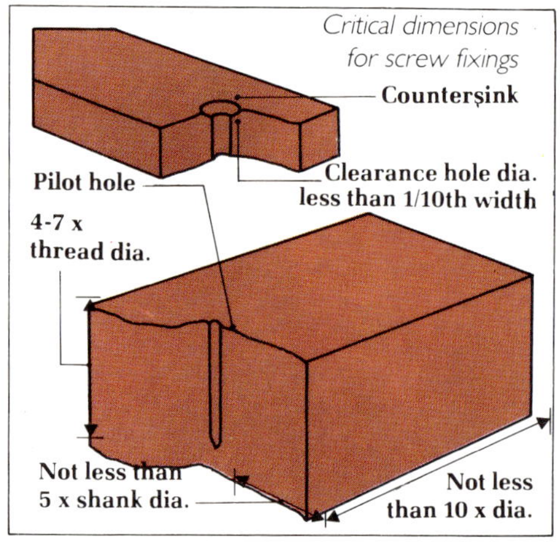

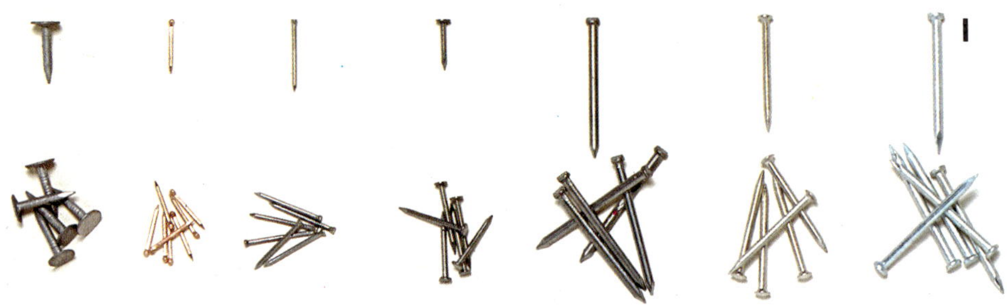

1

2

1. Clout nail; Hardboard nail; Panel pin; Round-head wire-nail; Oval wire-nail; Batten-head nail; Masonry nail.

2. Chrome-plated brass round-head woodscrew; Zinc-plated chipboard screw; Chrome-plated brass raised-head woodscrew; Four sizes of steel countersunk woodscrew.

the head. The parallel shank reduces the tendency to split the chipboard.

Using screws
Whichever screws are being used it is always best to drill pilot holes. If these holes are the same diameter as the shank of the screw below the thread, then a full grip will be obtained without danger of the wood splitting.

The size of wood screw required for a particular application depends upon the width and thickness of the timber. The diameter of the screw should not exceed one tenth the width of the wood into which it will be inserted. You should also ensure that at least four diameters of thread, and if possible up to seven, are engaged in the wood. If the screw is fixing a piece of wood, its length should be not less than three times the thickness of the wood it passes through. If pilot holes are drilled the screws can be positioned up to ten times the diameter from the end of the wood or five times the diameter from the edge. If pilot holes are not drilled then the screws must be kept 20 times the diameter from the end of the wood.

Woodworking adhesives
For small woodworking projects you can use most household adhesives. The most universal is the PVA type of adhesive which will bond many materials to wood as well as fixing wood to wood. It has the advantage that surplus glue can be wiped off the surface with a wet rag before it sets.

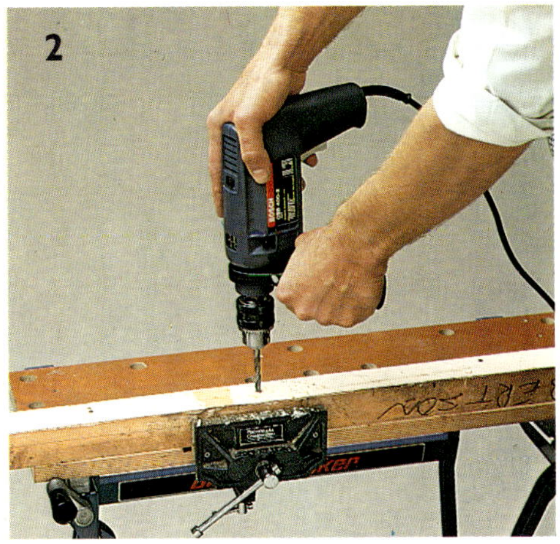

1. *The modern power tool will give years of trouble-free operation. As a constant work companion it is important that the tool you buy should feel comfortable and easy to handle. Try a selection of different makes to find which suits you.*
2. & 3. *The typical DIY power drill can be held in either the conventional pistol grip or the palm grip as shown here. The palm grip is said to be more effective because it puts pressures directly in line behind the drill bit. Buy a drill with an auxiliary side handle which can be fitted for those drilling jobs where maximum control is required.*

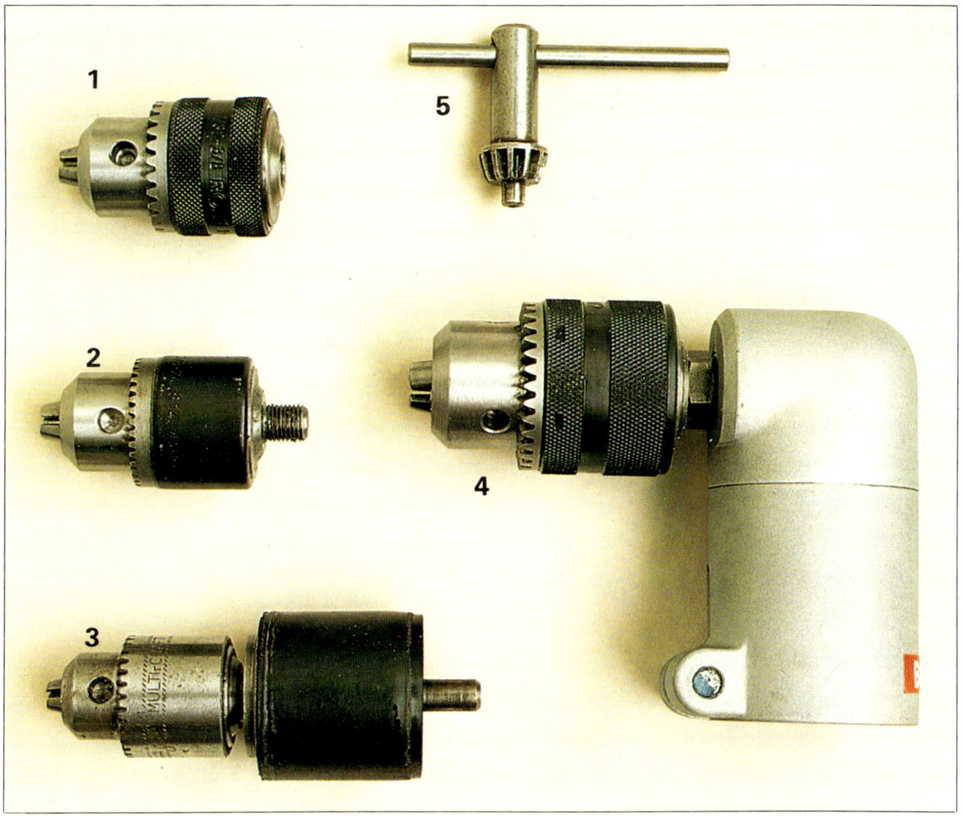

Chuck sizes on DIY drills generally range from 6mm (¼in) to 13mm (½in). The motors of such drills have a power range of just under 300 watts to around 500 watts. Generally twice the size of the chuck indicates the maximum drilling capacity in wood, one and a half times the capacity for masonry and the same capacity for steel.
1. & 2. *Chucks screw either on to or into the drill.*
3. *Percussion adapter is gripped in drill chuck and bit held in adapter chuck. Hold body of adapter for hammer action.*
4. *Right-angle attachment.*
5. *Chuck key.*

When veneering in wood you can still use Scotch glue or PVA, but when fixing plastic laminates to timber you have to use one of the contact adhesives. The type which gives instant grip is suitable if there is scope for finishing operations which would hide any slight error in positioning the laminate. The alternative is to use one of the contact adhesives which allow a slight movement before the final pressure is applied.

For extra strength there are the epoxy resins which are two-part adhesives requiring the application of a catalyst or hardener to create the required bond.

Power tools

Today's wide range of power tools helps you make light work of jobs around the home that were once difficult, tedious or plain impossible. With practice in using them any handyman can now work faster and to a higher standard than ever before.

Variable-speed drills

One of the most significant developments in DIY power tools has been the introduction of the electronically controlled variable-speed drill. This is the most suitable model for the home handyman because it can drill holes at the ideal speeds required for different materials.

Developments in micro-electronic technology have made possible variable-speed drills where the speed is automatically maintained regardless of the resistance encountered in a particular material.

Two-speed drills

You should not be misled into thinking that a single-speed drill with a high speed rating will effectively cover all drilling requirements. Considering the variety of jobs you may undertake the single-speed drill is positively unsuitable and should not be seriously considered.

Every material has its own ideal drilling speed. Also the size of the hole to be drilled is important. As a general rule the larger the hole the slower the speed that is required.

A two-speed drill is normally adequate for most drilling jobs around the home. The slower speed is used for drilling masonry and larger size holes in most materials, and the higher speed is used to drill most small holes and to drive attachments.

Hammer drills

Percussion or hammer drills make easy work of drilling in masonry and concrete. They form an increasing proportion of the DIY drills sold.

Rotary drills can be used to drill masonry and ordinary house brick but regardless of how powerful they are this tends to be extremely hard work and causes excessive wear on the drill bits.

The percussion device delivers rapid blows to the drill bit at a rate of up to 35,000 blows per minute. This hammering, combined with the normal rotary action, breaks up any small stones or flint at the drill point and considerably speeds up the drilling of holes in masonry.

__1.__ There are two basic types of two-speed drills. The first and more recently developed type has a speed change operated through an electrical diode and the change from high to low speed is controlled by a two-position trigger switch.
__2.__ The second and more expensive type of two-speed drill has a mechanically operated gear box with an extra train of gear wheels. The speeds are changed by either turning a knob or a simple lever on the gear box. The mechanical gear box is the more effective of the two types.

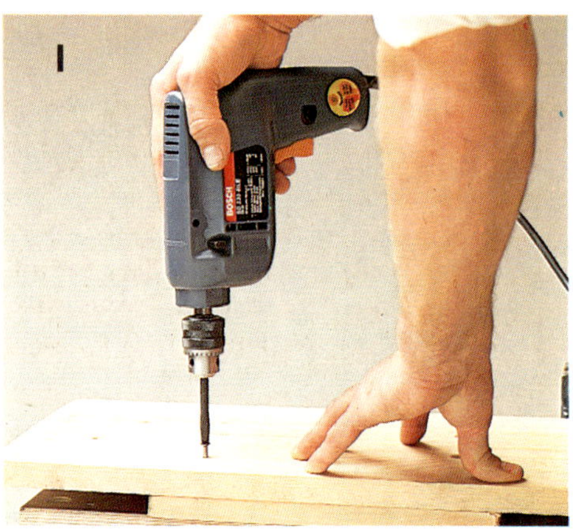

__1.__ If you are undertaking a lot of fixing work there are variable-speed drills with reversing facilities. This means that fitted with the appropriate bit the tool can be used to drive in screws and take them out.
__2.__ A variable-speed drill is particularly useful for some of the more tricky drilling jobs around the home or outside. For example, fitting a curtain or shower rail in a bathroom may mean drilling through ceramic tiles into masonry. Using a slow starting speed eliminates the risk of the tile cracking. The speed can then be increased to drill into the wall behind.

__3.__ Advances have been made in the development of cordless drills which are powered by rechargeable batteries. These are ideal for use where there is no main power supply available. For light drilling work such as small holes in soft materials the cordless drill is perfectly satisfactory. When heavier drilling of large holes is carried out it is likely that the battery will drain much more quickly and frequent recharging will be required.

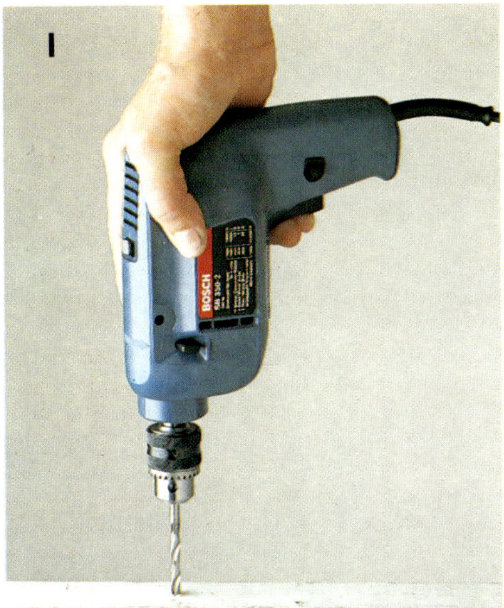

1. *The work that you can tackle depends on the features of your drill. If for example you buy a cheap 6 or 8mm single-speed rotary drill with a small motor it will be hard work drilling materials such as masonry and it would be impracticable to drill 13mm holes without overloading the motor so use a good dual purpose drill as shown here.*

2. *It is very difficult to drill through glass, ceramics or brick with a lower powered single-speed drill and probably this type will be underpowered to drive attachments effectively. Always use a drill that has plenty of power in reserve.*

3. *Look beyond your immediate needs: be prepared to spend a little more on a drill which is versatile enough to tackle the variety of tasks you will no doubt wish to put it to at some point in the future.*

Ideally you should be thinking about a rotary/percussion drill with a variable speed facility and a chuck size of at least 10mm. This will be versatile enough for both wood and masonry drilling, and for a wide range of hole sizes.

2

1. & 2. *You should ensure when buying a percussion drill that it is the dual purpose type with a switch or selector ring. This allows the hammer action to be switched on and off when simple rotary drilling is required.*

3. *The rotary percussion drill is invaluable for fixing jobs in brickwork or concrete such as wall plugging for putting up shelves and curtain rails.*

The final choice

When you have seen the range of power drills available, consider carefully before making a final choice. Prices can vary enormously between different makes and types, but do not attach too much importance to price. There is no point in buying a drill because it is cheap only to discover later that its use is too limited.

It is important that you buy a drill which will cope adequately with the envisaged workload. However, it is likely that you will soon discover how the electric drill can open up new horizons, making possible many previously impossible jobs.

Circular saws

The circular saw has one basic function, to cut fast and accurately in a straight line. Circular saws are classified in size by the blade diameter. They can be divided into three general types. The smaller 150mm (6in) has a maximum depth of cut of around 36mm (1½in). This is reduced to 18mm (¾in) when a bevel cut of around 45° is made. This type is sufficient for most light cutting work.

However, if rebuilding or renovation work is being done it will involve for example cutting planks of 4×2in timber. For this type of work a larger saw around 190mm (7¼in) is necessary. This type has a depth of cut of just over 60mm (2 7/16in) and should cope adequately with most jobs around the home. The larger 225mm (9in) industrial circular saw should be considered for heavy work.

Using the correct blade the circular saw can cut a wide variety of materials. Consult the manufacturer's specification for recommended types of blade.

Blade types

For general purpose fast cutting in timber use a crosscut blade. For a fine finish in timber use a flooring blade. This is designed specially for cutting old floors and suchlike where nails may be encountered. Note that only the specially hardened flooring blade is recommended for sawing where there may be nails. Nails will destroy the teeth of other blades. Aluminium oxide abrasive discs are used for iron and steel. Silicone carbide abrasive discs are used for stone, brick, slate and marble. The tungsten carbide tipped blade is one of the hardest known materials and one of these blades will keep a sharp cutting edge up to 40 times longer than a normal blade. While costing between two and five times as much they represent excellent value for money, saving the resharpening and replacement costs of a normal blade.

Check the set of the teeth frequently to keep drag to a minimum.

Be very careful when using a circular saw. The blades are sharp and travel very quickly. It is essential that both upper and lower blade guards are fitted.

Jig saws

The jig saw is more versatile than the circular saw. It can be used for intricate, curved work as well as straight cutting. The compact design of the jig saw means it is also more suited to cutting in places where space is limited.

The selection of blades available for the jig saw is of a similar variety to those for the circular saw. As a general rule a blade with widely spaced teeth is used for rough, fast cutting of timber. For fine or cross cutting of timber a blade with teeth set well together is used. A blade similar to the hard hacksaw type is used for metal and plastics and a knife edge blade cuts leather, rubbers and plastics.

When cutting thin metal sheet clamp it on to a backing sheet of softwood or plywood. This minimises vibration and the risk of tearing the metal. Make sure that the backing wood is soft enough to be cut with the metal blade.

Spread some lubricant along the cutting line. This stops the blade clogging and keeps it cool. Use oil for steel and paraffin or turpentine for non-ferrous metals such as copper, aluminium and brass.

It may well be that you will do enough cutting work to utilise both a circular and a jig saw.

Where only occasional cutting is envisaged the jig saw is certainly the more desirable model because of its versatility.

Joints

There are many cases where joints such as the mortise and tenon, used for table and chair legs, are still necessary in spite of modern resin adhesives. However, the strength of traditional woodworking joints is enhanced by a resin bond.

1. *To ensure that the maximum number of teeth are cutting at any one time, set the depth of cut so that the blade only just protrudes beneath the underside of the workpiece. This gets the job done with less drag on the blade, preventing overload.*

2. & 3. *Always cut material with the good side down. The circular saw blade cuts upwards so any splinters and chips will be on the topside of the workpiece. With the good side down the blade can make a clean bite into the material.*

4. *Allow the blade to reach its full speed before starting to cut. The blade guard will retract automatically as the saw is fed into the work. With the saw fixed the guard covers the blade. If the machine is forced the blade will slow, dropping below the ideal cutting speed and risking damage to the motor.*

A selection of blades.

1. Most modern jig saws have a soleplate or baseplate which is adjustable to allow cutting close up to return surfaces such as skirting boards. A valuable facility on some jig saws is the jet of air exhausted from the front of the machine to keep the cutting line clear. This enables the user to follow the most intricate of lines easily.

2. A two-speed jig saw is the best buy with the high speed used for straight cutting while the slow speed gives extra control on awkward work. Most DIY jig saws will give a maximum depth of cut of around 50mm (2in), making them adequate for most cutting jobs around the home. The depth of cut on a jig saw cannot be set because of the up and down cutting action.

1

2

1

2

3

1. & 2. A common use for the jig saw is to cut a shape out of a piece of wood. Drill a hole first of all somewhere within the cutting line. Naturally the hole should be large enough for the blade. Note that if the required shape has 90° or pointed corners it will be necessary to round these off coming back later to trim each corner.

3. As with the circular saw the jig saw can be used with a rip fence for fast, accurate, straight cutting. This is particularly handy as the single thin blade can easily wander off the straight line unless care is taken. Very often the rip fence can also be used as a circle guide for cutting perfect circles out of sheet material.

Mortise and tenon joint

This is used for framed-up constructions including door and cupboard frames, chairs and tables. It gives the strongest connection and the best-looking finish.

The setting out and the tools required have been described. You also need to know the correct size for the joint. A tenon should be one third the thickness of the wood and for a rigid joint it should have a shoulder all round it. If a mortise and tenon is needed at the end of a piece of wood, such as when joining the top rails of a table to the legs, then to avoid the mortise being an open-ended slot the tenon is made only two thirds the width of the rail and a stub called a haunch is made for one third of the width. An extra 25mm of timber can be allowed on the leg length to avoid it splitting. This is cut off later when the glue sets.

Dowel joint

Splitting is a problem with the dowel joint, which is used as an alternative to the tenon. The dowel joint can never be as strong as the mortise and tenon joint because the size of the dowels is limited. There is no point in increasing the diameter of a dowel as this will seriously weaken the rail. A rail 25mm thick would support a dowel or tenon about 8mm thick and leave about 8mm each side to support the dowel or to form a shoulder to the tenon. If the strength of the joint needed to be increased for any reason, the tenon could be nearly doubled in thickness to 15mm, still leaving a shoulder of 5mm at each side which would provide stability to the joint. If a dowel was increased to this size there would only be 5mm at each side of the hole to support the dowel and this could prove insufficient. This is one of the reasons for failure of the dowel joints between chair legs and rails.

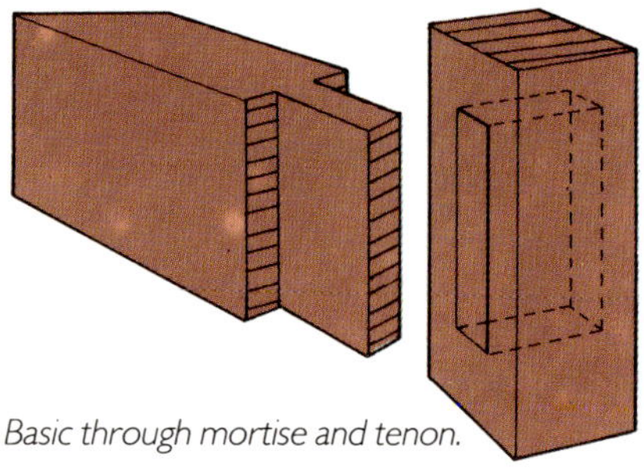

Basic through mortise and tenon.

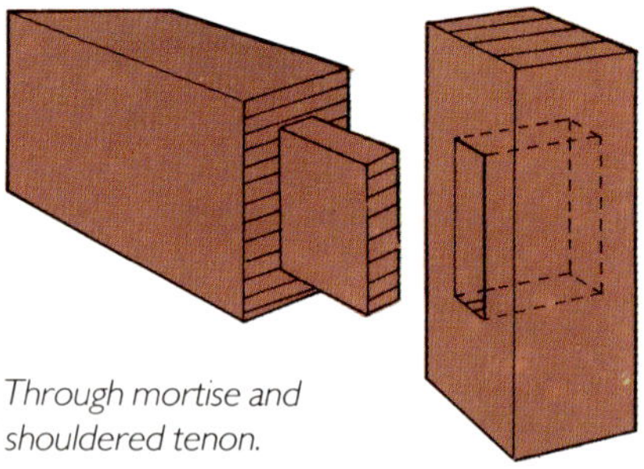

Through mortise and shouldered tenon.

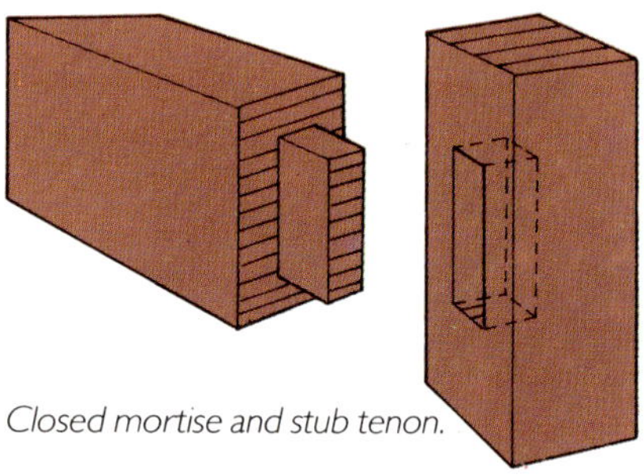

Closed mortise and stub tenon.

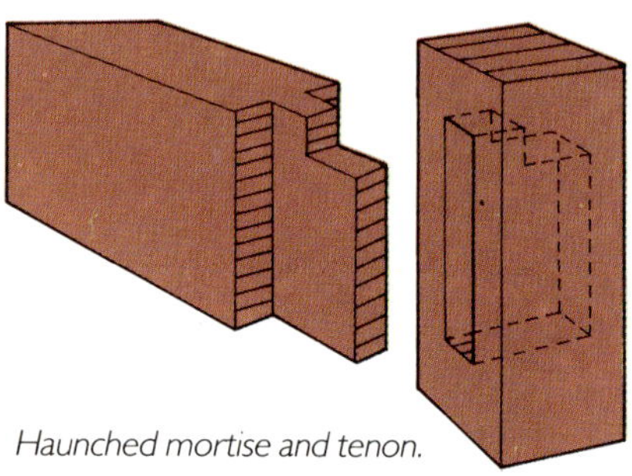

Haunched mortise and tenon.

Halved and lapped joint

Another strong alternative to the mortise and tenon joint is the halved and lapped joint. Usually just called a halving joint, it needs no special jig to set it out. It can be marked out using a marking gauge and cut with a fine-toothed saw, preferably a tenon saw. As its name suggests it is made by simply cutting away half the timber of each piece of wood so that the two pieces will fit together flush with each other. The joint is made in the same way even if the two pieces of wood are of different thickness. In this case the gauge is set to half the thickness of the thinner piece and both timbers are marked from the face side. The

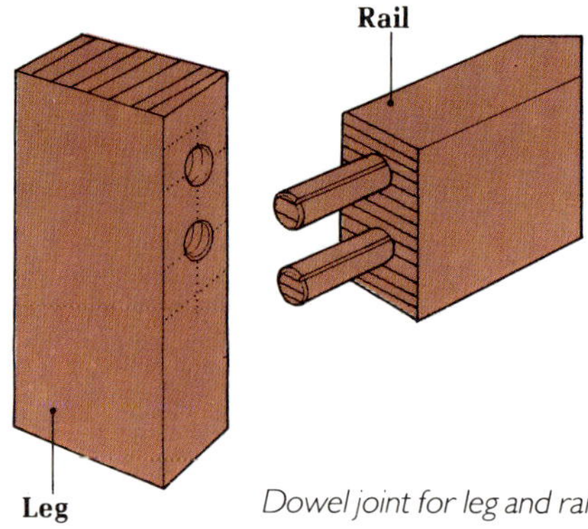

Dowel joint for leg and rail.

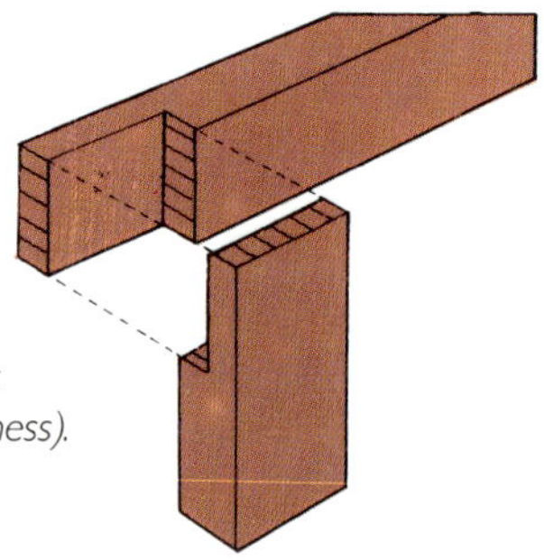

Halving joint (same thickness).

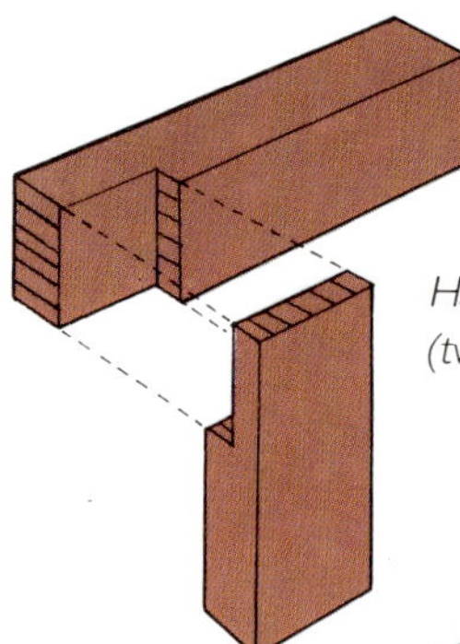

Halving joint (two thicknesses).

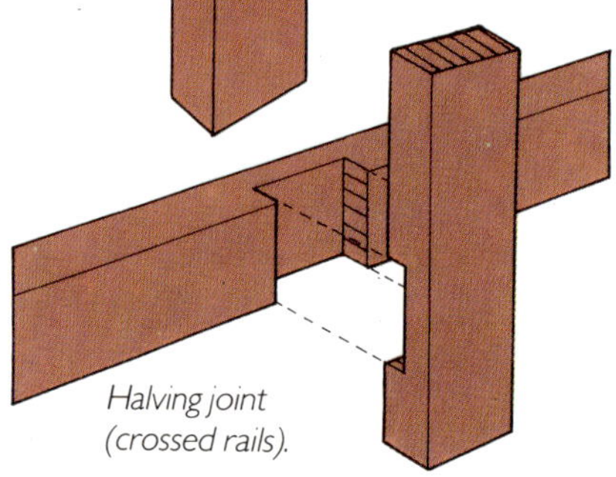

Halving joint (crossed rails).

face side is left intact on the thinner piece and the back is removed. The opposite is done to the thicker piece where the joint is cut on the face side to a depth of half the thinner piece. The joint can then be assembled with the two face sides being flush with each other.

The joint is both glued and screwed. Where possible the screws are inserted from the back of the joint so that they do not show when the project is completed.

Apart from corners being halved, the joint can also be used where timbers cross each other. Such places are the diagonal cross-rails at the bottom of table legs and any form of diagonal bracing.

Housing joint

The traditional joint for shelves which are fitted into cupboards and bookcases is the housing joint. This is a groove cut into the side member and it must not be deeper than one third the thickness of the side. In solid timber the depth need only be a quarter of the thickness. In order to prevent the joint showing, the housing can be stopped about 25mm from the front edge.

Housing joints are not really suitable for chipboard because the boards are not very thick and the edges of the groove are prone to breaking away. A chipboard shelf, even though it is not suitable for heavy weights, needs better support, and this can be provided by a thin strip, or batten, of timber glued and pinned inside the cupboard.

Butt joint

Simple butt-jointed constructions, which are made by cutting the ends of boards exactly square both in width and thickness, are suitable for solid timber which can be glued and nailed or screwed at the joint. Chipboard would have to be fixed by means of a corner block.

Butt-jointing of narrow boards to make up a wide board such as a table top is done by planing the edges perfectly straight and square in thickness and then gluing the edges before cramping the boards together. They may later be given additional support by screwing battens to the underside. Again, this type of jointing process is not suitable for chipboard construction.

Reinforcing butt joints

Although they are used as a substitute for a mortise and tenon, dowels should really only be used to strengthen ordinary butt-joints. A minimum of two dowels must be used in each joint to avoid any tendency to twist. A groove or saw cut should be made along the side of the dowel to allow the air trapped at the bottom of the hole to escape; excess glue will also be released this way. The holes in each piece of timber should be slightly countersunk to make it easier to remove excess glue cleanly. Chamfering the ends of the dowels will enable them to enter the holes more easily.

Mitred joint

This is usually made in mouldings and is secured by small nails or pins. Where extra strength is needed the joint can be reinforced by veneer keys, glued and driven into saw cuts across the point of the mitre. This is sometimes used for picture-frames.

Notching

Another simple carpentry joint is notching, which is cutting a small recess or housing in one piece of timber so that another piece can be secured in it. This is a method often used for securing the shelf-bearers where racks or shelving are being made.

Bird's-mouth joint

Where an angled timber meets a horizontal timber, a bird's-mouth joint is used. In this joint, a cut is made to fit the vertical face of the horizontal piece and another cut made to match the top horizontal face. The result is a right-angled v-shaped joint of a type much used in roofing work.

Bridle joint

Another carpentry joint, used in rough woodwork instead of the mortise and tenon, is the bridle joint. In this construction, which is set out like a mortise and tenon, instead of cutting a hole for the tenon, the sides of the mortise are cut away leaving the centre solid. The end of the mating piece of timber then has what would have been the tenon cut out leaving the two sides as a forked joint which will fit over the centre web.

At a corner the bridle joint looks like a mortise and tenon which has been cut too near the end of the wood leaving one end of the mortise open to make a slot. The joint is as strong as a mortise and tenon when it is made in the middle of the rail, but when used as a corner joint it lacks stability. The recess in the middle of a rail holds it firm.

Box and framework construction

There are two main types of construction in woodwork. One is box construction in which the project is mainly composed of sheet materials which are fastened together without being attached to a framework (see page 135). The other is frame construction in which lighter panels are supported on a framework. As this framework is made rigid by the various joints which are used in its construction it is better able to support doors and is less likely to sway with the movement of the doors.

Mortise and tenon joints

The basic joint for framed construction is the mortise and tenon. This is used because the shoulders of the tenon make the frame rigid and the tenon itself enables the members to be joined without seriously weakening the timber at that point. For cupboard frames the ends of the top and bottom rails are tenoned to fit into mortises in the sides or stiles, while for door frames and window frames the joint is made the opposite way round: the sides or jambs are tenoned to fit into mortises in the head and sill. The mortise and tenon is one of the most useful joints and has several forms (see opposite page).

Halved and lapped joints

These joints can be used as a substitute for the mortise and tenon, but when this is done the appearance should be preserved by allowing the stiles of the cupboard frame to run up the face of the top and bottom rails. They cannot be used for window and door frames, but a housing joint can be made in the head and sill so that the jamb can fit into it. This joint would have to be well nailed. Doors which are to be clad with hardboard or plywood can also be made with halving joints. It is best to fix the hardboard panel to the frame using an adhesive because the nails always seem to show through the paint however careful you are in punching them down and filling the hole.

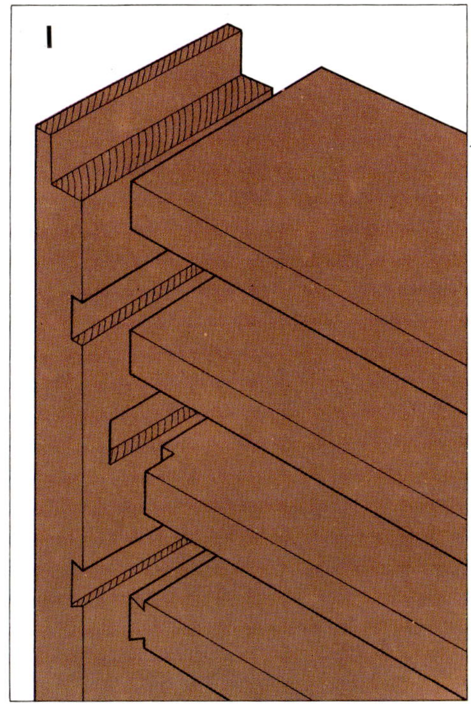

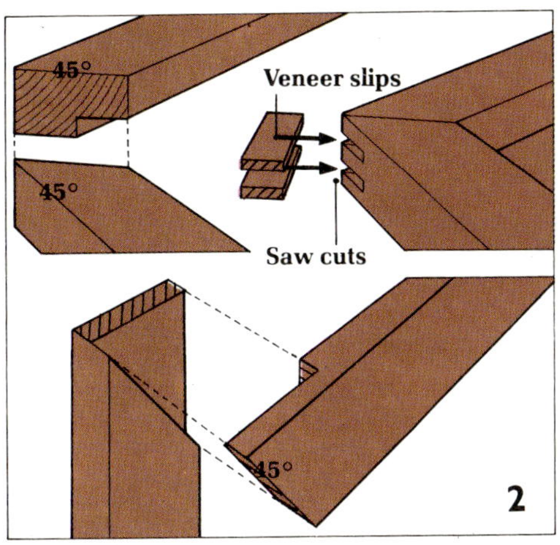

1. Rebate; Through housing; Stopped housing; Dovetailed housing.
2. Mitred joint and reinforcement and mitred halving joint.
3. Simple horizontal, bevelled horizontal and bevelled angled notches.
4. Simple bird's-mouth and recessed bird's-mouth joints.
5. Corner and through bridle joints and box joint.

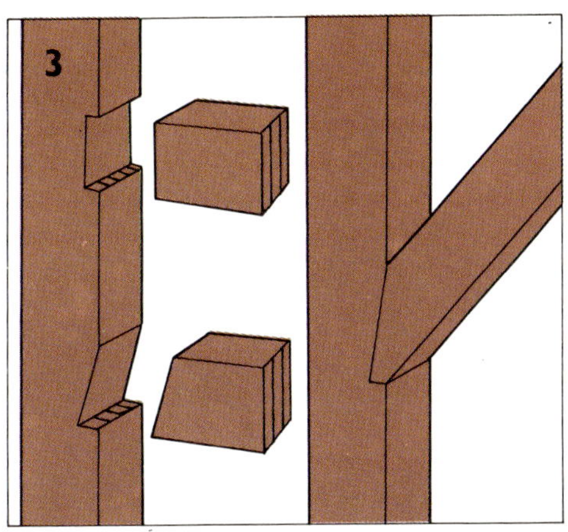

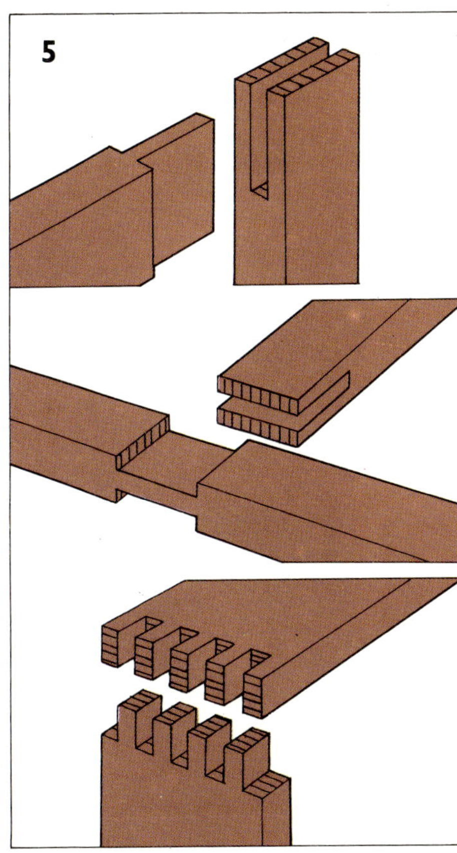

Dovetail joints

Traditional box construction uses dovetail joints as these give a pleasing appearance at the corners of the furniture. This joint is not used much today because of the amount of veneered chipboard which is used for furniture, and dovetails cannot be made successfully in chipboard. Some machine-made dovetails are used in quality furniture but they lack the decorative appearance of hand-made joints because the dovetails and the pins which separate them are all the same size.

However, dovetails provide a joint which will resist a lateral pulling force better than most other joints, so they are especially useful when making wooden brackets. Here the dovetail is cut in the top member, and the top end of the upright member has the cut-out for the tail to fit into. If the angled member of the bracket is let into the top and upright member, then the bracket will have considerable strength.

The correct angle for the sides of the dovetail is one in eight (7 degrees) for hardwoods and one in six (9½ degrees) for softwoods. If the sides are made too steeply angled the pointed corners of the tail will break and if the angle is too shallow it will have little resistance and pull apart easily.

Four-legged constructions

Where constructions such as chairs and tables are being made, the mortises for the rails, which are at right angles to each other, meet inside the leg. This means that the tenons must be mitred at their ends to give the maximum length to each.

Tops of solid-wood tables must be fixed by means of slotted metal plates or by wooden buttons which engage in grooves in the inside face of the top rail. This is to enable the wide wooden top to move with changes in atmospheric conditions. Solid tops which are battened on the underside must also be allowed to move. This is done by not gluing the battens, and making slots for the screws instead of tightly fitting holes. Failure to provide for the movement of natural timber tops could cause serious splitting in a warm atmosphere.

Side panels fitted into grooves in the framework must also be allowed to move and therefore they are not made a tight fit and they are not glued or pinned. Chipboard and laminated boards do not suffer this and can be securely fixed.

The legs and rails of chairs and tables, for example, must be cramped up carefully to avoid the whole article becoming twisted. Sight across the construction, viewing one rail against the same one on the opposite side, and you will be able to see whether they are in line or whether they are sloping in opposite directions. If they are not all in line, the piece of furniture will rock or wobble on its feet.

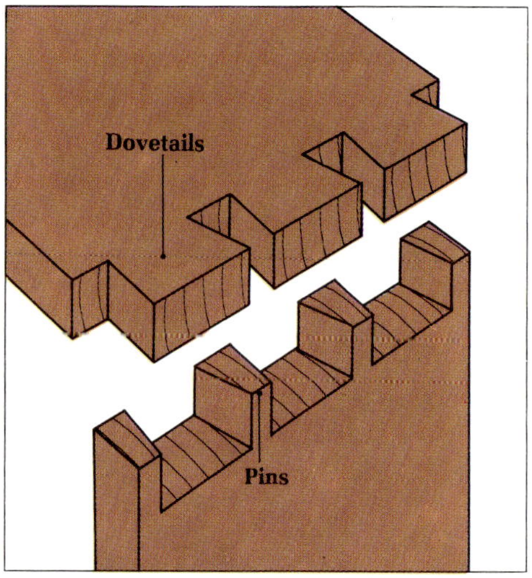

To make dovetailed bracket, cut angled notches in vertical and horizontal pieces to house bracing piece.

To make a wobbly chair or table stand firmly, wedge it level on a flat, level surface. Take a strip of wood about 3mm thicker than the amount the leg is short and mark a cutting line against the top of it on each leg. Never cut one leg to suit the others.

Box construction

Working with man-made boards requires different techniques to conventional joinery and involves very few cut joints.

Chipboard

Much modern furniture is basically boxes made from veneered chipboard. Construction is often of the knock-down type so that the units can be taken apart and fitted into a cardboard box which will go in a car boot or on a roof-rack. Any permanently constructed units are generally joined by means of dowel joints. There are two main requirements for making furniture like this and they are the ability to cut a straight, square line and to drill neat, perpendicular holes. This latter requirement is easily met with a dowelling jig or a vertical drill-stand.

Various proprietary connectors are available, including a plastic chipboard plug, and a barbed bolt which is tightened with an Allen key. This type of furniture is ideal for the beginner to make, as the boards can be bought cut to length and plastic blocks can be used for the joints and for supporting shelves. The blocks are simply screwed into place using double-threaded chipboard screws, enabling you to produce the furniture quickly. Doors can be of the lay-on type so that there will be no need to plane them to fit into an opening. Hinges can be of the concealed lay-on type which need no cut-outs and are just screwed into place.

Laminated boards

Working in blockboard and pine-board follows a more traditional method, as some woodworking joints can be employed. This kind of board will accept a mortise and tenon joint as well as a notch or a rebate in the edge. The boards will also accept screws in the edge which is not a good practice when using chipboard. To some extent you can make housings into the board so that shelves can be fitted.

Hardboard

This can be used for making doors and for cladding other types of framing, but it must be conditioned first by damping the back of the board, using about 1 litre of water to a 2440×1220mm sheet. The wet sheets should be placed back to back for 48 hours before use. This process enables the board to stretch so that when it is fixed and dries

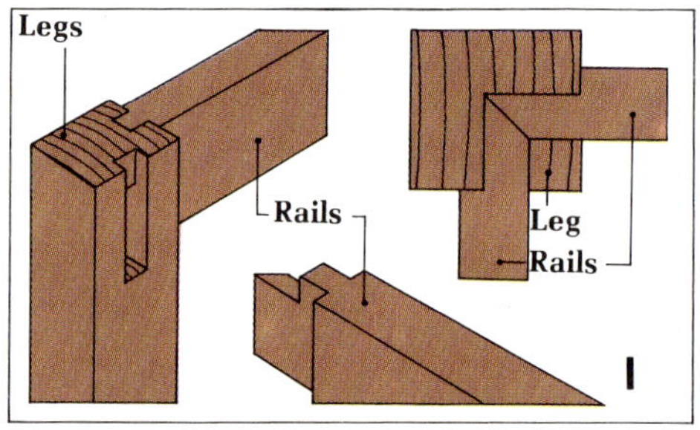

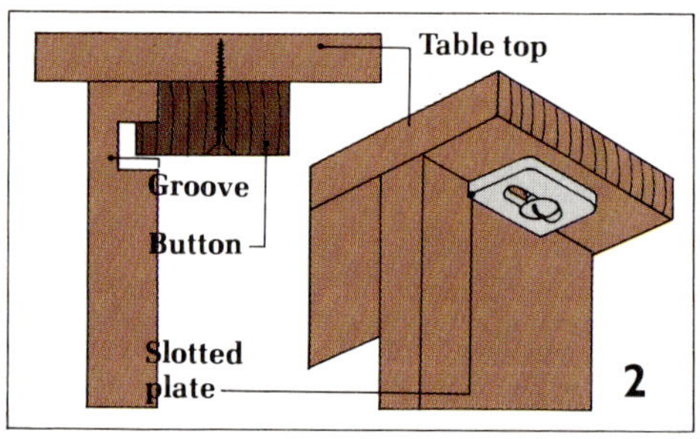

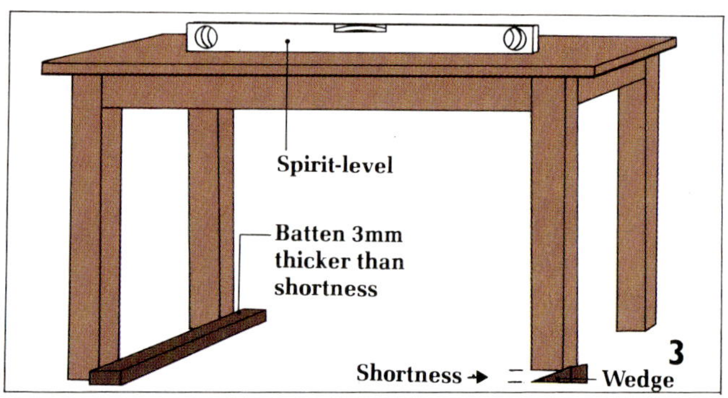

1. *Mitred haunched tenon joining rails to top of table or chair leg.*

2. *Join wooden table-top to base with wooden button (left) or slotted metal plate to allow for movement of timber.*

3. *Trim all four legs to level a wobbly table.*

to the moisture content dictated by the conditions in which it is being kept, it will tighten up and will not buckle. It would do so if it were perfectly dry when it was fixed to the framework and was then taken into a more moist atmosphere. The treatment is not necessary for free-moving panels.

Cutting boards

Sheet materials, especially thin boards like hardboard and plywood, are cut most easily if they are supported along the whole length of the cutting line on both sides of the cut. Lack of support allows the sheet to sag or bend and jam the saw.

Rigidity

Because there is no basic framework to hold the whole construction rigid, stability depends on the hardboard back of the unit being fixed securely to the sides and rails or shelves. In addition, any plinth or top rail will help to prevent the front of the unit swaying. This can prevent sliding doors from meeting the sides properly and it will make hinged doors swing open or closed.

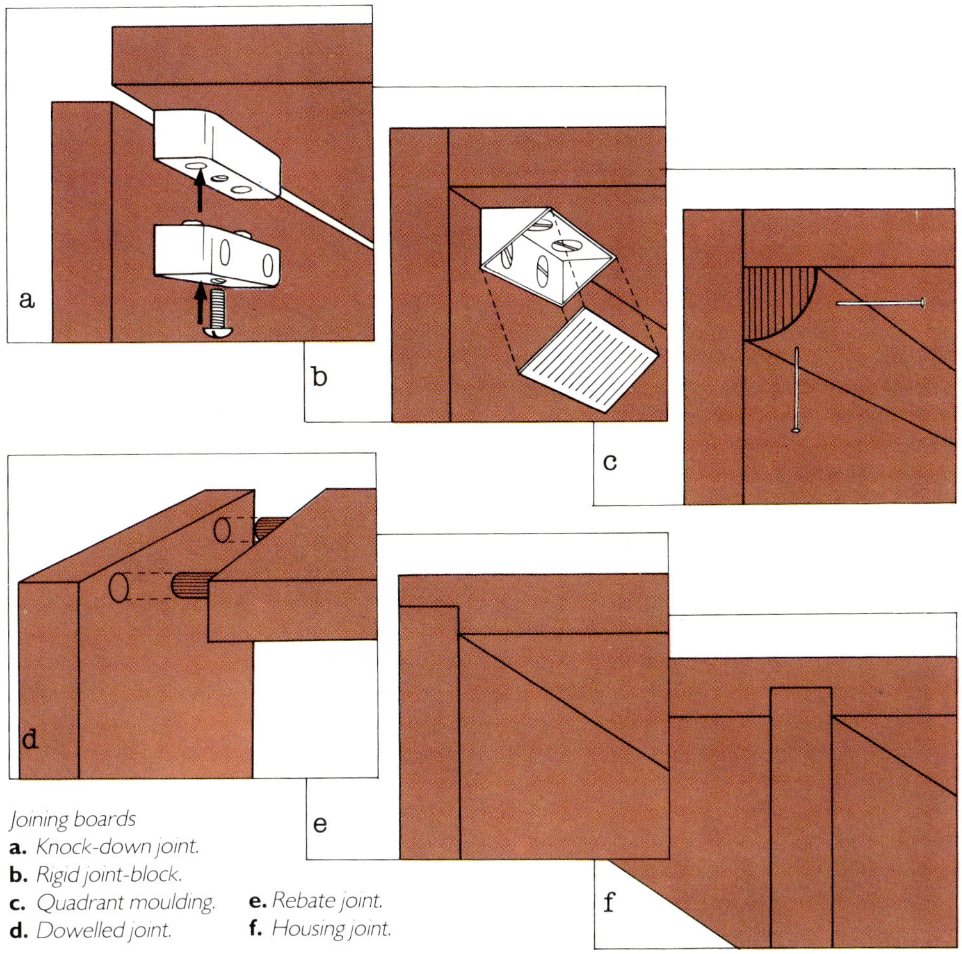

Joining boards
a. *Knock-down joint.*
b. *Rigid joint-block.*
c. *Quadrant moulding.*
d. *Dowelled joint.*
e. *Rebate joint.*
f. *Housing joint.*

Wood finishing

When using stains and varnishes, the technique depends on the type of material.

Board finishing

The plywood facing of blockboard and the surface of pine-board can be stained, polished or varnished without preparation other than sanding. This also applies, of course, to veneered chipboard and plywood, but plain chipboard needs some degree of filling, or preferably veneering, before a suitable finish can be applied.

Cut edges of chipboard can be a problem, but they can be trimmed using iron-on veneer strips which are obtainable in finishes to suit the finish of the boards you are using. Careful planning will enable you to use standard sizes and therefore reduce the number of cut edges. You can also arrange for the cut edges to be at the back, where they will be covered by the hardboard back of the unit, or in a position where they will be covered by other boards.

When plain chipboard is being used and is to have a decorative laminate applied to it, it is important that a similar laminate, which will be cheaper because it is not decorative, is applied to the back as well. Without this balancing veneer, the chipboard will tend to bend. However, the balancer is not essential when the board is being used for worktops or table tops because these can be screwed securely to the frame which will restrain it. Unlike natural timber, chipboard does not need to have the freedom to move with the changes in the atmosphere's relative humidity.

Timber finishing

All articles made of wood need treating with a preservative or finish, not only to preserve and protect the surface, but also to bring out the inherent beauty of the grain and the texture of the timber. The quality of finish is extremely important, as it is by this that the work is usually judged. Although painting will hide any slight surface defects any blemish in wood becomes even more noticeable when a clear finish, or a stain and clear finish are applied. It is important also that all woodwork except that which is being treated with a preservative such as creosote, is perfectly clean and smooth.

The main processes in finishing are filling, stopping, staining and applying the finish. When a clear finish is to be applied, it is essential when an orbital electric sanding machine has been used that the surface is still finished afterwards by sanding with the grain, by hand. If this is not done, small circular scratches resembling fish scales will be seen in the final coat.

Preservatives

Fences and sheds can be treated with creosote to BS 3051. If the brown colour is not acceptable, preservative of another colour can be used. Where the timber will be in contact with plants, such as on the inside of greenhouses and forcing frames, a green horticultural preservative should be used. Colourless preservatives are also available, for use on interior and exterior woodwork; these can be painted when dry.

Painting

Emulsion paint can be applied direct to sanded wood and no knotting, primer or undercoat is required. Before applying solvent-based paints, any knots in the wood should be sealed with pure shellac knotting and allowed to dry. Any cracks or dents should then be filled with wood-stopping, which should be applied slightly proud of the surface to allow for shrinkage and, when dry, papered smooth. Next, a pink or white primer, followed by an undercoat of a similar colour to the top coat, should be applied. If a first-class finish is required, lightly rub this smooth with fine glasspaper when it is dry, and apply a second coat. This too can be rubbed down before applying the finishing coat.

Because paint is pigmented it does not usually have as good a flow as varnish and, to make sure that no brush marks are left on the surface, it should be 'laid-off' to a greater extent than a varnish. The paint should be applied in one direction, then with a slightly lighter pressure at right angles, then with lighter pressure still diagonally, finishing off with the minimum pressure, drawing the brush lightly across the surface in the original direction of application.

The best results are always obtained by using good quality brushes of the correct size. For example, it is no good using a 1″ brush for painting a door – a 2½″ brush would be more suitable. Immediately after use, brushes should be cleaned with white spirit or a proprietary solvent.

Exterior wood-stains can be used on timber instead of paint. These are not to be confused with the transparent wood-stains or dyes used for staining wood prior to the application of clear finishes. They contain a

French polishing:

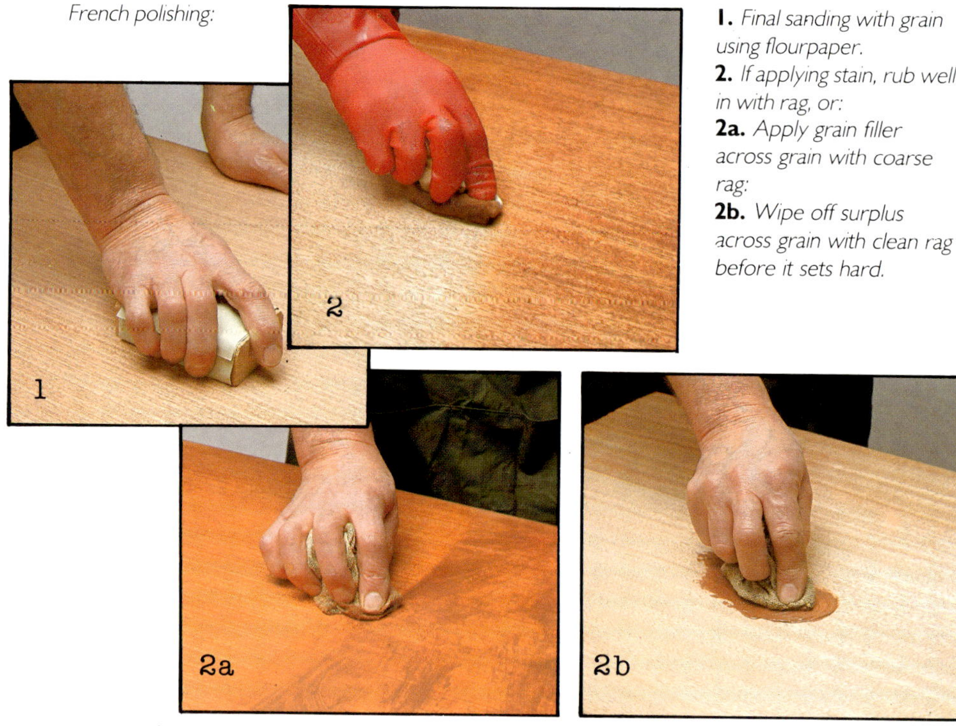

1. *Final sanding with grain using flourpaper.*
2. *If applying stain, rub well in with rag, or:*
2a. *Apply grain filler across grain with coarse rag:*
2b. *Wipe off surplus across grain with clean rag before it sets hard.*

pigment and tend to obliterate the grain, but they are easy to apply and maintain.

Non-pigmented finishes

All finishes alter the colour of wood to some extent and some woods, for example, mahogany and walnut, turn much darker even when a completely clear finish is applied. An approximate idea of the colour the wood will become when finished with a clear solution can be seen by damping a small area with water. If this colour is too light, then the wood can be stained before finishing. It is only possible to stain wood to a darker colour; for a lighter shade it must be bleached.

When staining wood, it is advisable to test the stain on a square piece of wood, or on an area which would not normally be seen as it is difficult to remove stain which has been recently applied. If the wood has an open grain, and a smooth finish is required, then a grain-filler should be used for filling the pores, or extra coats of the finish would have to be applied and then rubbed down with an abrasive paper. Any cracks or holes in the wood should be filled with wood-stopping before staining.

The final finish may be of a type which leaves a surface film, such as French polish, varnish or polyurethane. The last two are available in gloss, satin and matt finishes. Varnish stains are also available which will colour and finish the wood in one operation. It is important to note, however, that each extra coat of varnish stain will darken the colour and, unless brushed out very evenly, the colour will vary as the thickness of the film varies. When wood is stained with a penetrating dye, the colour will not vary however many coats of clear finish are then applied. When varnishing an external door, it is important that at least one coat is applied to the top, bottom and side edges to prevent water being absorbed at these

1. *Different finishes and veneers.*
Top to bottom: *Gloss polyurethane on rosewood; Matt polyurethane on sen; Yacht varnish on padauk; Plastic coating on burr walnut; Teak oil on teak; Danish oil on Baltic pine; Satin polyurethane on coromandel.*

2. *Selection of dyes on sycamore.*
Top to bottom: *Light oak; Dark Burmese teak; Light Scandinavian teak; Dark oak; Walnut; Medium oak; Brown mahogany; Ebony; Red mahogany; Pine.*

points, which would eventually cause the varnish to fail.

Alternatively, oiled finishes may be used, such as teak oil and Danish oil. These finishes are far easier to apply than the previous types as they are merely wiped over the surface with a cloth. Teak oil leaves the wood with a soft, lustrous finish. When a high gloss finish is required on exterior woodwork, a yacht varnish should be used. These usually contain tung oil which has outstanding exterior durability.

Waxing

This type of finish is popular on wood such as pine and oak. Before applying wax the wood should be sealed with French polish if a golden colour is required, or with transparent French polish, which will not alter the colour of the wood. Two coats of French polish should be applied with a brush or rag and, when dry, lightly rubbed down with fine glasspaper. The surface can also be rubbed down with fine steel wool and wax polish. This treatment will give an acceptable satin finish. If, however, a higher gloss is required, then the wax polish should be applied with a soft cloth or a shoe polishing brush and allowed to harden. The surface should then be buffed with a soft yellow duster or soft shoebrush.

French polishing

For further information on this process send a stamped addressed envelope to the manufacturer of the product.

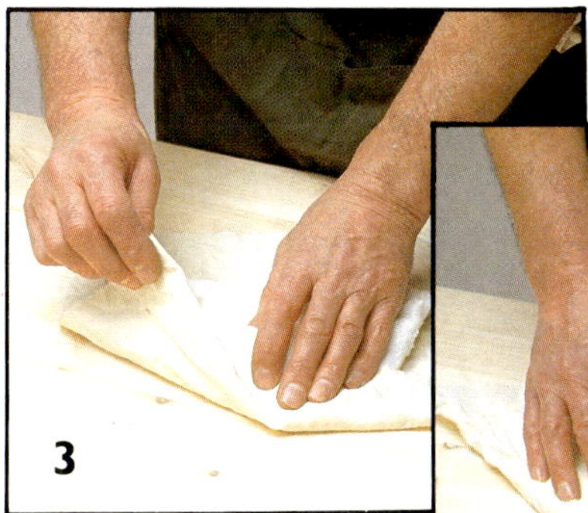
3

4

5

3. to 5. *Preparing rubber from cotton wool and linen rag.*

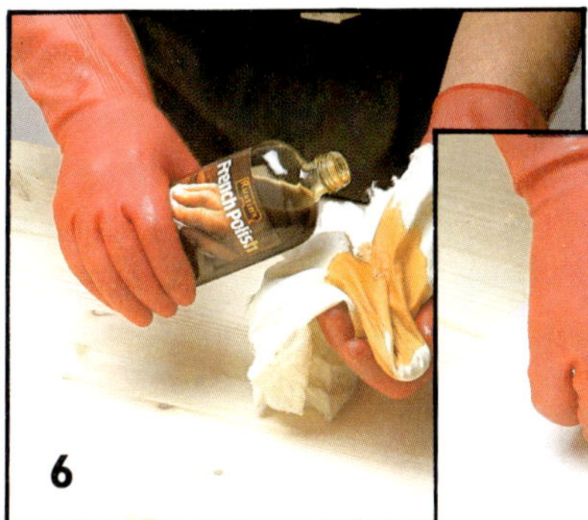

6
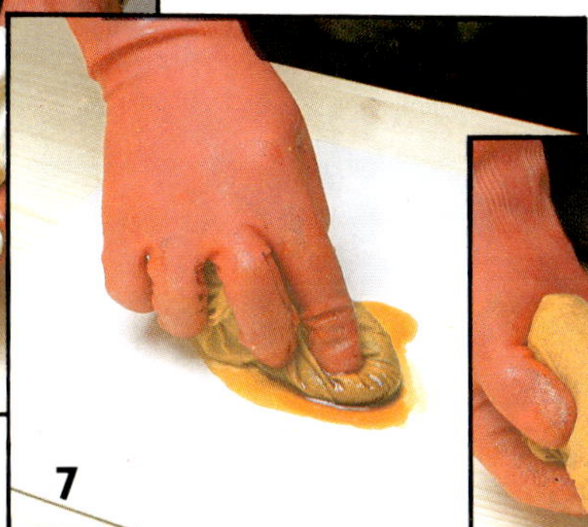
7

8
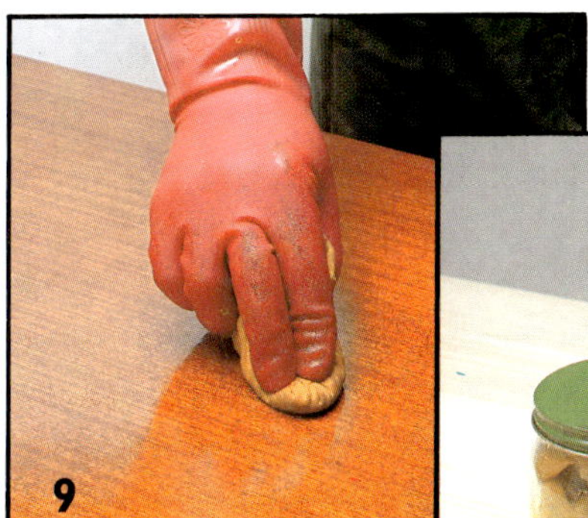
9

10

6. *Saturate cotton wool with French polish.*
7. *Squeeze out excess polish on piece of card.*
8. *Dab a drop of linseed oil on to base of rubber.*
9. *Rub in overlapping circles, gliding rubber on and off surface. Finish by rubbing evenly with grain using a nearly-dry rubber.*
10. *Put rubber in airtight jar between applications.*

Fixings

One of the commonest jobs around the house is making fixings, usually to walls, to carry such things as cupboards, shelves and so on. The type of wall dictates the fixing method used. There is a wide range of fixing devices to choose from.

Fixings into solid walls

The old fashioned fibre wallplug has now been largely superseded by the plastic variety. These have expanding ridges and teeth to grip the sides of the hole into which they are inserted when a screw is driven into them. Some are preformed, and have a lip which keeps the plug at the mouth of over-deep holes; others are cut to length from longer pieces, and should fill the entire depth of the hole. There are several sizes, and it is important for a firm fixing that a hole of the recommended size for the plug is drilled in the wall, and that a screw of the recommended gauge and length is used.

Wallplugs are suitable for fixings into all types of solid wall, and will carry quite heavy loads, provided they are set into solid brick or blockwork and not into the mortar joints between. The colour of the drill dust will indicate whether you have hit solid masonry or not. It is also important to ensure that a wallplug is long enough to reach through thick plaster into the masonry beneath.

Where you have to make a fixing into an existing hole that has become enlarged, plastic fillers can be used instead. These are formed into a plug and rammed well into the hole, which should be undercut if possible to prevent the plug from pulling out. The screw to be used for the fixing is then turned into the moist filler to cut its own thread; it is tightened fully when the filler has hardened.

For heavy-duty fixings, expanding anchors with metal wings should be used instead of wallplugs. These come complete with a machine screw, bolt, or threaded hook or eye, and when this is tightened the anchor expands to grip the sides of the hole.

Fixings into partitions

Where you are faced with making a fixing into a plasterboard wall or a modern hollow-core door, you have to adopt a different method. There are many proprietary fixings designed for use in these situations; all work on the principle of spreading the load over the inner face of the board.

Gravity toggles have swivel toggles which drop to the vertical position when inserted through a hole in the panel. Spring toggles each have two spring-loaded wings which open after the toggle is inserted. With both of these types, the toggle is lost in the cavity

Nylon plug.

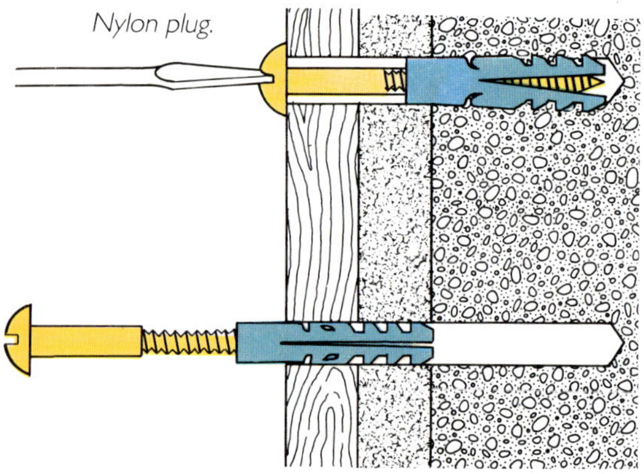

Nylon plug.

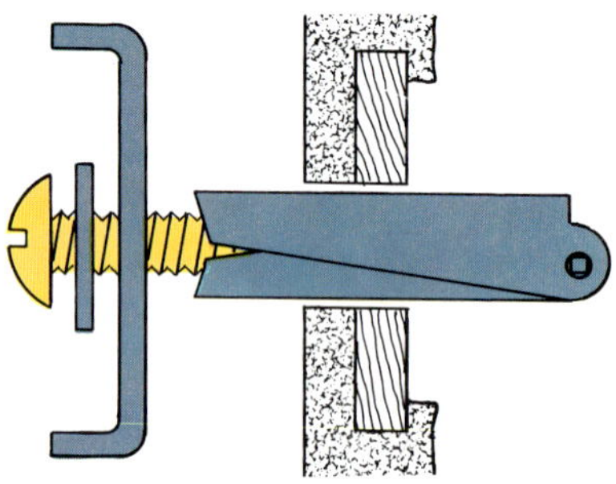

Spring toggle.

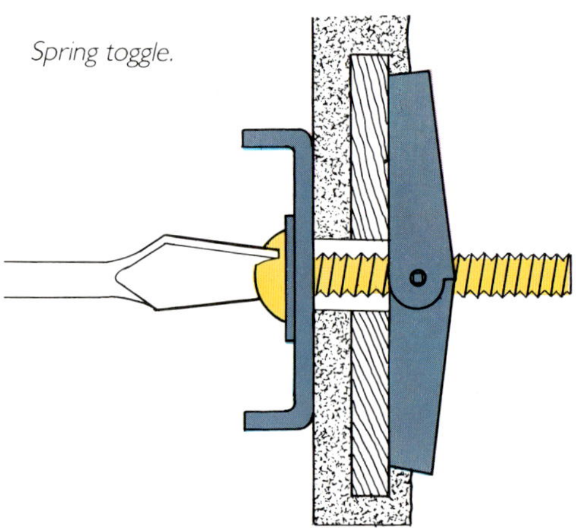

if the machine screw is withdrawn. Nylon types with a captive toggle are available; these neatly avoid this problem. With all three types, you must have sufficient clearance in the cavity to allow the toggle to operate.

An alternative is the collapsible anchor, made of metal, plastic or rubber. In this case tightening the screw collapses the anchor back against the inner face of the panel, so providing a firm fixing. In this type the anchor stays in place if the screw is removed.

On a partition wall, none of these devices will support a heavy load such as a wall cupboard or a bookshelf. These should be screwed direct to the timber uprights, which can be located by making trial borings into the wall. Where the fixing cannot be made into the uprights, a batten should be screwed across adjacent uprights to form a firm ground for the final fixing.

Masonry nails

These are specially hardened nails used for such jobs as fixing battens, picture rails, skirting boards and the like. They can be driven direct into masonry with a heavy hammer, and grip by compacting finely crushed material round their shanks as they penetrate. They come in a range of thicknesses and lengths, and are very difficult to remove once in place. Wear goggles when using these nails.

Drilling holes in walls

Beware of hidden pipes or cables when drilling holes in walls. Never drill vertically above or below an electrical fitting as this is where the cable is most likely to be. A cheap electronic detector is available which will indicate the presence of hidden metal objects such as pipes and wiring conduits. It also detects live wires.

You need special masonry drills for making holes in walls. For most drilling, 8mm to 12mm drills are ideal, although you may need larger sizes to fix expanding anchors. They should be used at slow speeds in a two-speed electric drill. For drilling very hard masonry and concrete, a rotary percussion drill can make life easier by hammering and breaking up the masonry.

Make sure that holes are drilled at right angles to the wall surface, and that the drill does not wander and produce a conical hole; an attachment for electric drill can help to prevent these problems. Allow the drill to cool occasionally, and keep it turning as you withdraw it to prevent it jamming.

Fixed brackets

When there are no end walls on which to fix the shelf bearers, the shelves have to be supported on brackets. For simple storage the brackets need be only plain and strong, but where shelves are to be used in a living area for display purposes there are better looking types available.

The plain brackets are usually pressed steel with a central fold to form a strengthening rib. These brackets are usually either black or grey finish, but some may be found that are enamelled in white or colours. Wrought iron brackets are decorative and are made in various patterns finished in white or black. Simple flat steel angle brackets which are unpainted and have no strengthening rib can be used for light shelves, although they are really intended for use in strengthening the corners of boxes and other frameworks.

Brackets may be fixed directly to the wall or they can be fixed to wooden uprights secured to the wall. If it is a partition wall of timber and plasterboard you will be able to screw the brackets directly into the wooden uprights. They will be about 400mm centre

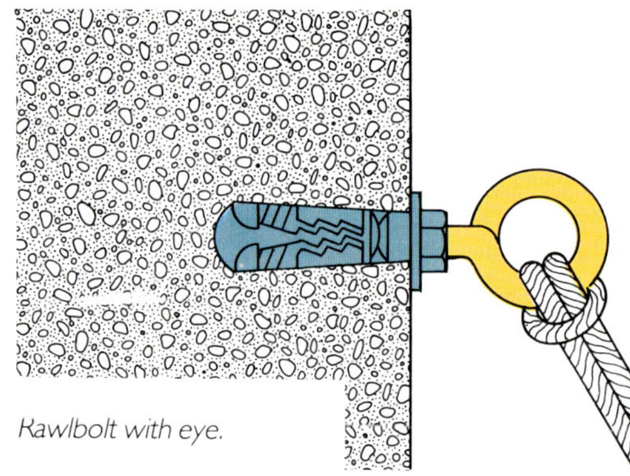

Rawlbolt with eye.

Rawlbolt.

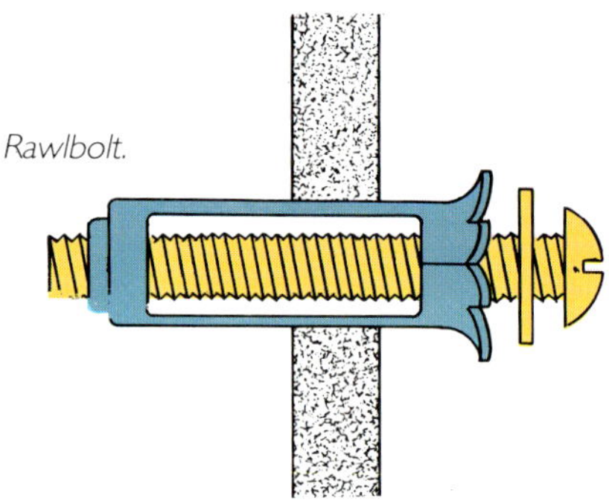

Collapsible anchor.

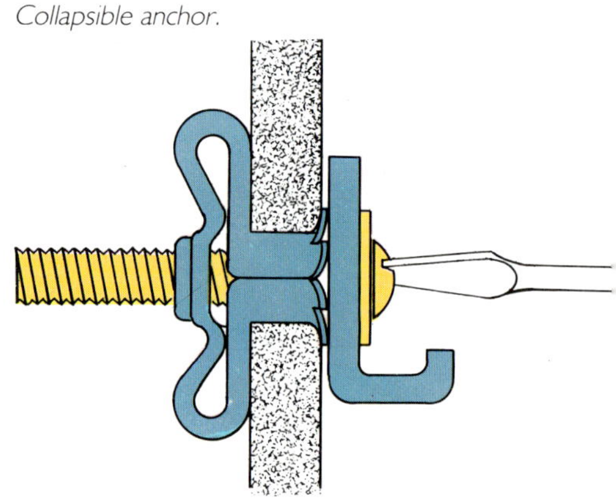

to centre. Screwing directly to walls which have to be drilled and plugged is not so easy as the drill may move from the place where it was started. To help overcome this, drill one hole and fit a plug in it. Then screw the bracket in place and drill the other holes through the bracket screw holes.

With masonry walls it is easier to fix wooden uprights than to try to fix the brackets directly to the wall. The top of the upright can butt up to the top shelf and with careful planning the fixing screws can be hidden by the brackets. If the wall can be drilled without the bit wandering, you can make the holes in the timber first and use them to mark the positions on the wall.

The alternative is to plumb the timber upright in the required position and then mark each side. Drill and plug the wall, then hold the upright against the plugs so that their positions can be marked on the wood. Square the line across the face of the upright and then measure the position of each plug from the pencil line on the wall. Measure this distance from the edge of the upright to make a mark for the centre of the screw hole.

Screw all the uprights in place and then fix the brackets on each end upright. A string-line can then be used to bring all the intermediate brackets into line. If the span is too great for levelling from one end to the other, level an intermediate bracket first and then carry on to the end. The string-line is then used in the same way. The shelves should be ready for immediate use and serve to enhance the room and create more space.

Various methods of supporting shelves

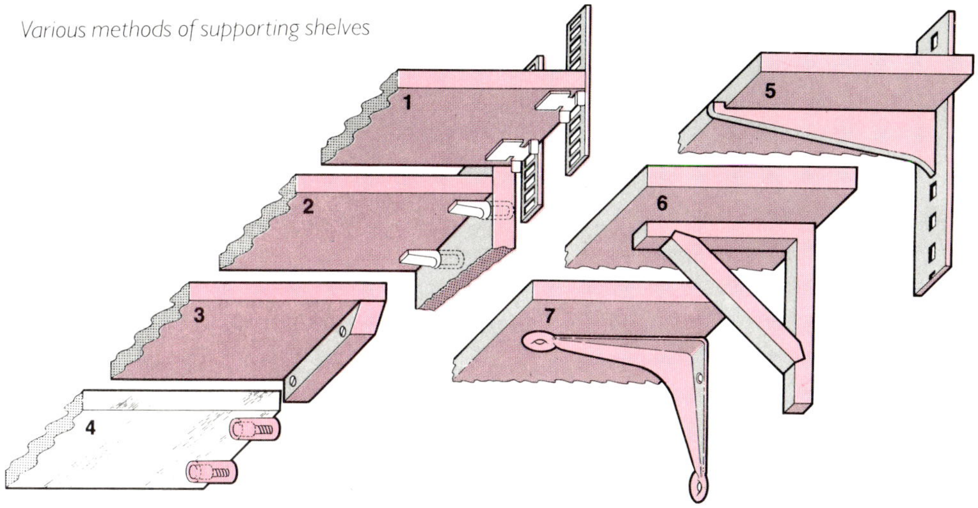

Shelving systems

If your shelving requirements vary and you need the flexibility of being able to move the shelves up or down, or if you need to be able to add cabinets or cupboards, but you are not sure where or at what level, then you need an adjustable shelving system. Basically, most systems consist of metal uprights with slots into which the shelf brackets are hooked. An alternative is channel-shape uprights into which brackets will lock where needed.

Fixing these systems follows very similar procedures whichever product you chose. The distance between the uprights depends on the type of shelf and on the weight which is to be supported. For general use the spacing is about 750mm.

First, position an upright against the wall and mark the top hole. Drill the wall using a 5mm drill to a depth of at least 40mm dependent on the thickness of plaster. You must get a firm grip of at least 25mm in solid brick or block and you may have to drill as deep as 50mm to achieve this. You can, of course, make a fixing to plasterboard or lath and plaster using toggles, but the weakness of the plaster will limit the weight the shelves will hold.

A plastic or fibre plug is inserted into the hole, ensuring that it really is flush with the plaster so that it does not foul the upright. Screw the first upright in place, but do not drive the screw tightly. Plumb the metal upright using a spirit level, although if the upright hangs free it should plumb itself. Mark the rest of the screw holes, drill them, fit the plugs and screw the upright tightly into place.

Measure the position of the next upright to ensure that it will be parallel with the first one. Level the tops of the two uprights using a straight-edge and spirit level and mark the top screw-hole. Drill the wall, plug and screw the upright into place as for the first upright. If a long length of shelving is to be installed, carefully position the two

1. *Metal strips and studs suitable for fitting inside bookcases. These are fully adjustable to suit different book sizes.*
2. *Metal or plastic studs drilled into the sides of bookcases. The degree of adjustability depends on the number of holes that are drilled in the side of the bookcase.*
3. *Wooden wall-bearers.*
4. *Studs used for glass shelves.*
5. *Adjustable bracket systems. Many different types are produced, most conforming to this basic design.*
6. *Hand-made wooden gallows brackets.*
7. *Pressed steel brackets.*
8. *A strong bracket for carrying heavy loads.*

8

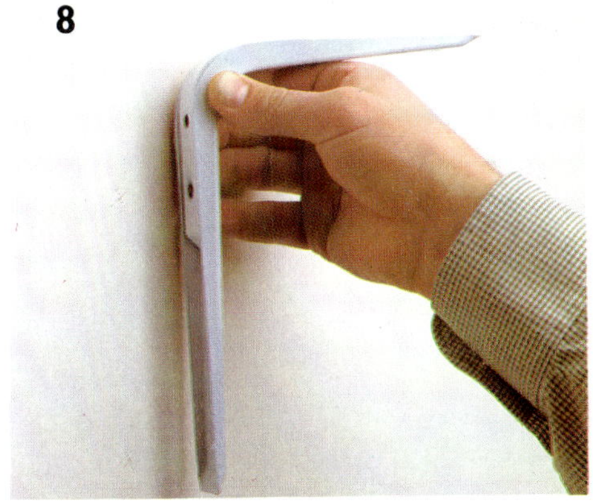

1

2

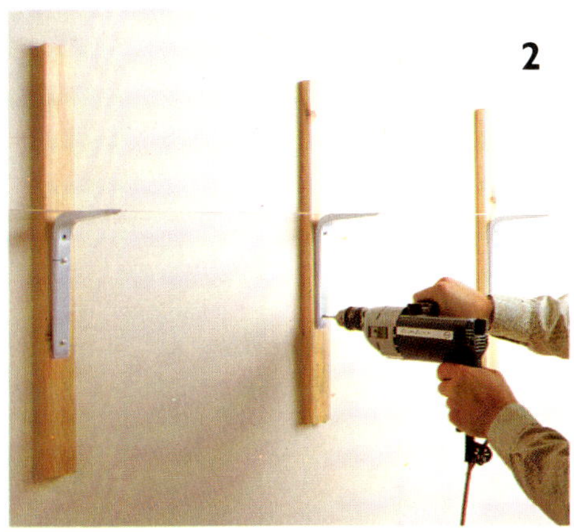

3

1. *For heavy loads a wooden upright is plugged and screwed to the wall and a stout bracket screwed to it.*
2. *The outer brackets are fixed first and the centre ones are positioned using a string-line. A pilot hole will avoid splitting the timber.*
3. *For a neat fit, the shelves are notched to fit around the wooden uprights before being screwed into place.*

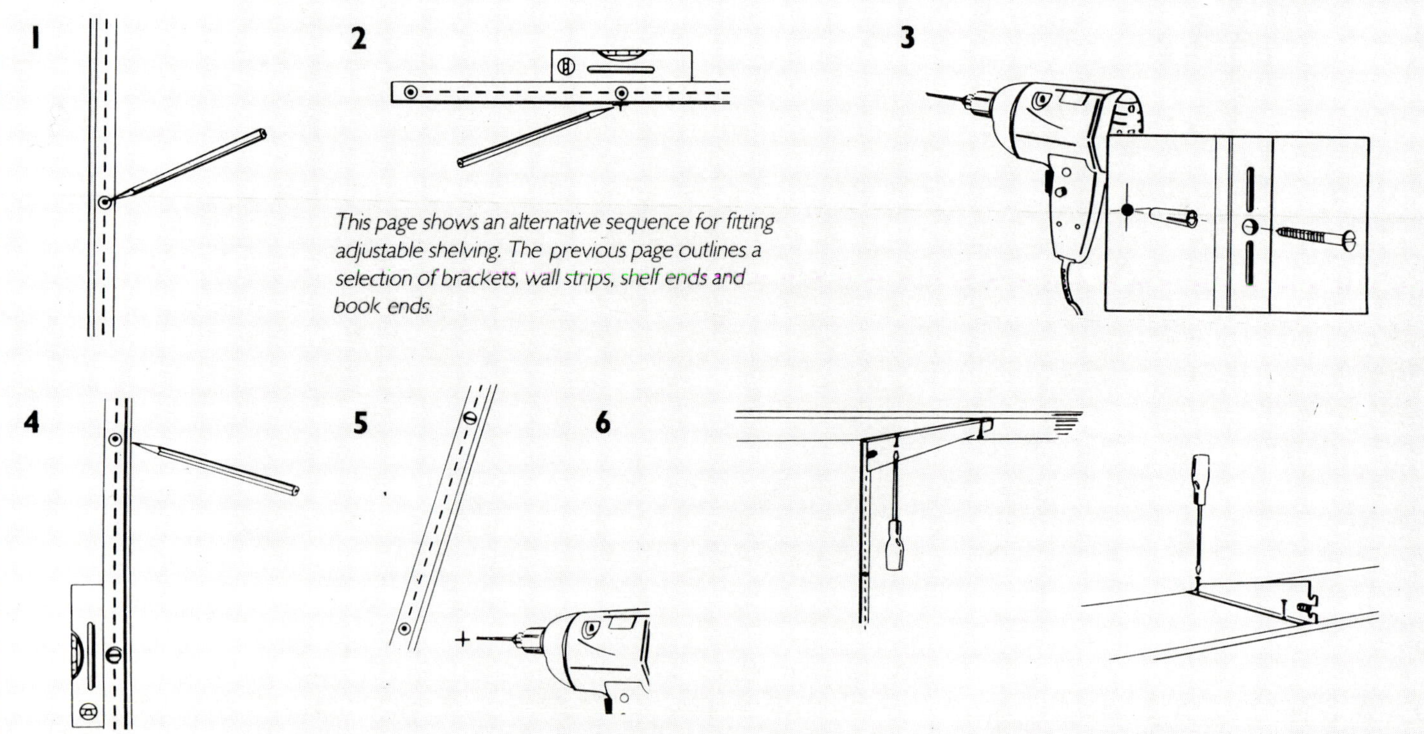

This page shows an alternative sequence for fitting adjustable shelving. The previous page outlines a selection of brackets, wall strips, shelf ends and book ends.

1. *Refer to your plan. Hold wallbar to wall in chosen position. At about waist height mark through fixing hole.*
2. *Using a spirit level and straight-edge, mark position of identical hole in adjacent wallbars.* ***ENSURE*** *marked hole positions are level and correctly spaced.*
3. *Drill hole at each marked position. Insert fixing and screw wallbar in position.*
4. ***ENSURE*** *wallbar is vertical. Mark through for other fixing holes.*
5. *Untighten securing screw and swing bar sideways. Drill other marked positions, insert fixings and screw up.*
6. ***EITHER*** *slot bracket into wallstrip, position shelf and screw to bracket, uppermost shelf first.* ***OR*** *position shelf, mark through bracket, remove shelf and bracket and screw together. Slot into wallbar in one piece.*

end uprights and use a string-line to line-up the intermediate ones.

This is all the fixing required and the brackets and shelves can be fitted. If the uprights have been levelled properly, the hook-in brackets will line up and the shelves will be level. If you use the locking type system, the brackets will have to be levelled by placing a spirit level on the shelf and adjusting the brackets to suit.

Shelves on bearers

Fixed shelving in alcoves is generally supported on wooden bearers which are fixed to the walls. One bearer at each end of the shelf is usually sufficient, but for books and other heavy objects, a long supporting rail along the back wall will help prevent the shelf sagging. Brackets can be used instead in the middle of the span.

Plugging the wall follows the same procedure as for adjustable shelves. Use a masonry drill or a hammer and jumper. If you use the latter, remember that quick blows that are rhythmic and not too heavy will drill the hole neater and quicker than wrist aching heavy blows with a heavy hammer. Also, keep turning the jumper bit as you hammer it.

Square-cut end bearers look clumsy, so make them in pairs with the ends cut at about 45deg. from about 10mm from the top. Smooth the end grain and chamfer the exposed corner. Screw holes can be bored at this stage. You will not need more than two, unless the shelf is very wide.

The alternative is to drill and plug the wall first and mark the bearers by holding them in place and squaring a line across to the face of the bearer.

Level the bearer in its finished position and mark the wall. Then, measure from the mark to the centre of each plug (they may vary in position) and measure this distance from the top of the bearer down the squared line. Drill the holes and countersink them for the screw heads. This method is useful when the drill tends to wander in the wall preventing you getting the holes in exact positions.

Having fixed the bearers at one side of the alcove, level across to mark the positions at the other side. If a rail or bearer is needed across the back of the alcove it is fixed in the same way and it is best if it is fixed first, then the joints in the corners will be better concealed.

A variation on this method of supporting shelves is one that is suitable for shelves which are for light display work. The wall is plugged and screws are driven into them until only the plain shank is showing. Then the heads are cut off. A slot is sawn in the end of the shelf just wide enough to take the screws. A power saw will give just about the right cut and can be stopped before the cut shows on the front edge.

The shelf can then be slid on to the screw shanks. This is not suitable for chipboard, unless the weight to be carried is only very light. It is best used with solid timber shelves which can be chamfered on the underside of the front edge to reduce the apparent thickness.

Heavy duty shelving

There are occasions when the storage of heavy goods calls for extra strong shelves and supports. As this usually occurs in garages and workshops the actual appearance is not so important as strength.

The shelving is erected using the same methods as those used for the more ornamental indoor shelves, but the fixings are slightly different. For instance, instead of ordinary wallplugs, wall anchors are used. You may have to use a star drill to make the holes for these. This is like a large jumper tool used with a hammer and it needs heavier blows than the jumper tool.

Heavy duty metal brackets can be screwed to the wooden uprights or you can make the uprights into wooden brackets. To

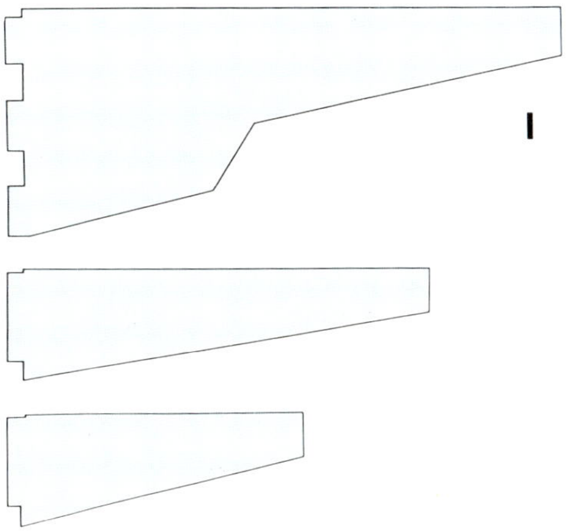

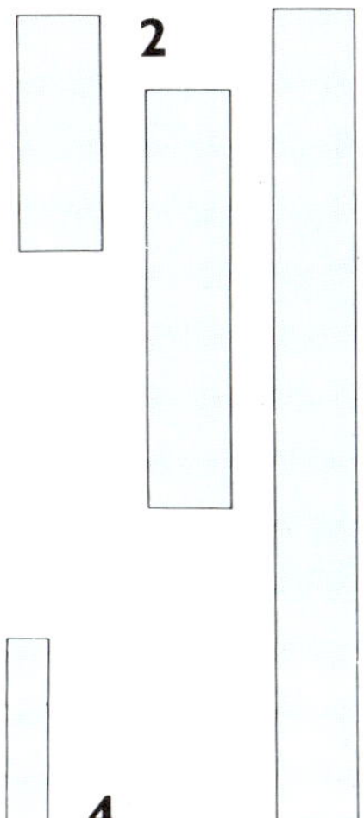

1. *Heavyweight and extra heavy-duty shelf brackets.*
2. *Wall strips in a range of sizes.*
3. *Shelf ends and bookends to keep shelf contents neat and tidy.*

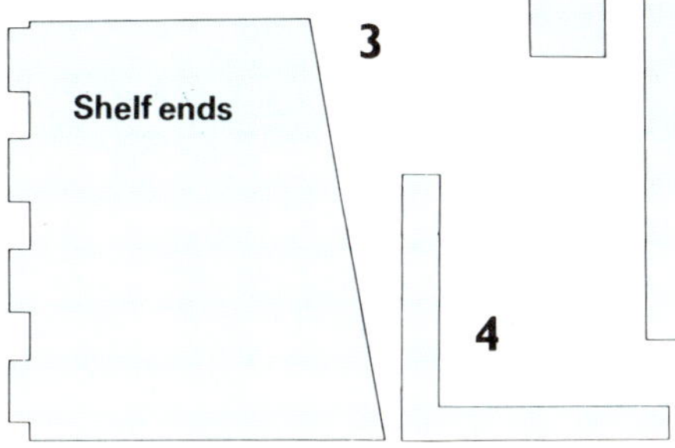

do this lay all the uprights together and mark the positions of the shelves. Notches 10mm deep are marked and cut out to take the bearers. A timber brace is then marked with a 45deg. angle halving joint and one end of the bearer is also marked with a 45deg. halving joint. These are then cut and screwed together. The bearer and brace are then placed in position on the upright and the angled notch for the brace is marked and cut. The two are then screwed to the upright and when all are complete the set of brackets is bolted to the wall.

With this kind of shelving it is not always necessary to use full-width shelving. Open slats are often sufficient and are cheaper than solid wooden shelves. The thickness of the slats depends, of course, on the type of materials to be stored but they should not be less than 25mm.

If you prefer metalwork to woodwork, you can make the shelving out of angle iron in a similar manner to that used for making free-standing shelves. If the structure is bolted to the wall it will not need to have braces across the corners.

Shelves can be of solid wood, or chipboard can be used if the spans are short and the shelves supported on the long edges. Plywood can also be used, but again, it needs support along the front and back.

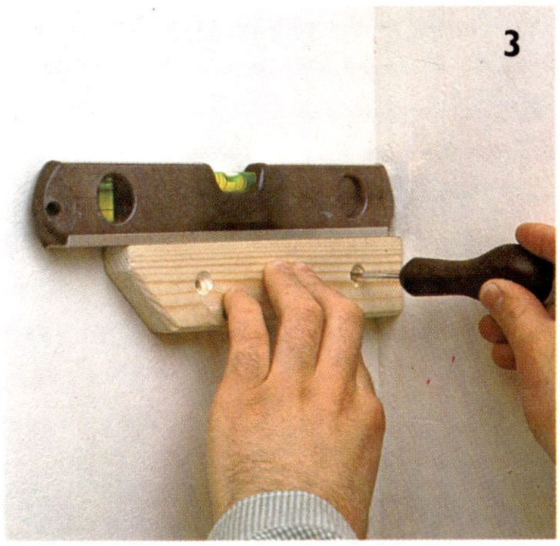

Putting up shelves on wooden bearers

1. *Bevelling the end of a wooden bearer.*
2. *Drilling and countersinking the bearer.*
3. *The bearer is levelled against the wall and the positions of the holes are marked.*
4. *When the first bearer has been fixed a straight-edge is used to level the position of the bearer at the other side of the alcove. The second bearer can then be fitted in the same way as the first.*

Note *If you are using a material such as plywood for the shelf, or if you plan to put heavy loads such as books on it, fit a supporting rail along the back wall.*

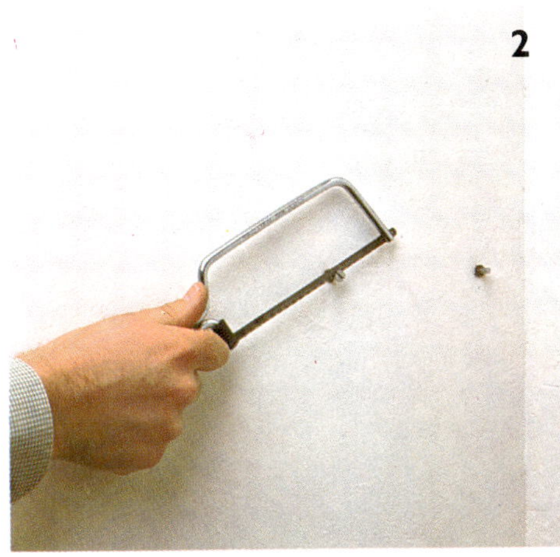

Putting up shelves with hidden supports

1. *For hidden fixings, screws are driven into plugs in the wall until only the plain shank shows. The heads are then cut off.*
2. *A saw cut is made in the end of the shelf which can then be slid on to the projecting screws. This secret fixing can only be used for shelves which are to carry light loads such as glasses or small ornaments.*

When metal supporting structures are being made it is best to use galvanised angle iron, but if plain metal is used it should be cleaned and primed with a rust-resistant paint, such as calcium plumbate, and then given its finishing coats as soon as possible; otherwise it will quickly get rusty and become very unsightly.

Folding shelves

The main difference between the fixings for a normal shelf and the fixings required for a folding or drop-down shelf is that the latter needs a horizontal board on which to hinge the shelf.

When fitting a simple flap support stay, the horizontal board need be wide enough to take only the wall section of the stay. This timber, which is as long as the shelf, must be securely plugged and screwed to the wall close to the point where the stay will be attached. One screw at the top of the board and one at the bottom will be sufficient for general purposes, but for heavy weights double the screws.

The shelf is hinged to a narrow timber of the same thickness as the shelf, which is screwed firmly to the top edge of the horizontal board attached to the wall. The width of this board depends on the projection of the flap stay when in the closed or down position as obviously the shelf must fall freely in front of it.

You can hinge the shelf using ordinary butt hinges set into its edges and its support in the usual manner. To avoid having to make recesses, you can use piano hinges. These are obtainable in lengths of up to about 2m.

Folding table tops and worktops can be supported on wooden brackets. Timber 50×25mm will make a strong bracket. The right-angle halving joint at the top is made first and is screwed together, then checked with a square to ensure its accuracy. The bracing piece is then laid across the two legs of the bracket at an angle of 45deg. Both timbers are then marked where they cross and the depth of the joint is marked on the edge of the timber. If possible, this is best done with a marking gauge, but if you have not got one you can make a gauge by driving a countersunk-head screw into a small piece of scrap wood until the head projects just the right amount for the depth required. Slide this gauge along the face of the wood so that the head of the screw cuts a line into the side. Then square the joint lines down to this depth line to guide you when cutting the joint.

Saw down to the depth line at each side of the joint and into the waste to make chiselling easier. Cut the waste from the face of one half of the joint and from the back of the other. Screw all the joints together and fix the bracket, with hinges, to an upright plugged and screwed to the wall.

1. *Serviceable general-purpose wooden shelving can be made from lengths of timber. Brackets are made with one horizontal piece and a diagonal strut, attached to each other and the upright with halving joints as shown.*

2. *Uprights are screwed to the wall at regular intervals and the battens that make up the shelves are screwed to the brackets.*

3. *Use wall anchors for a really firm fixing.*

4. *For heavy-duty workshop shelving, metal Dexion is ideal. It is both strong and versatile. More attractive versions are also available for use in the home.*

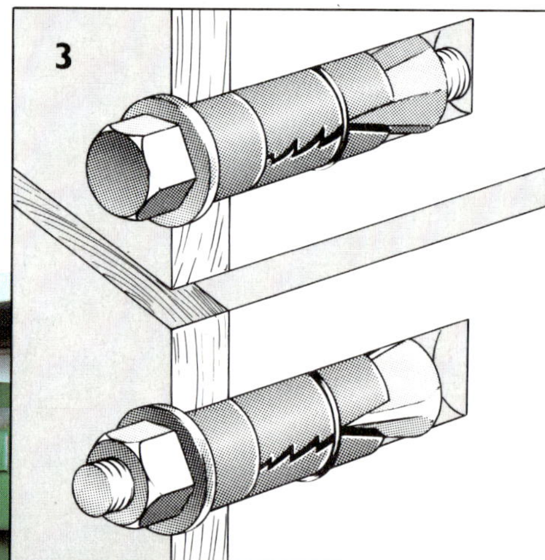

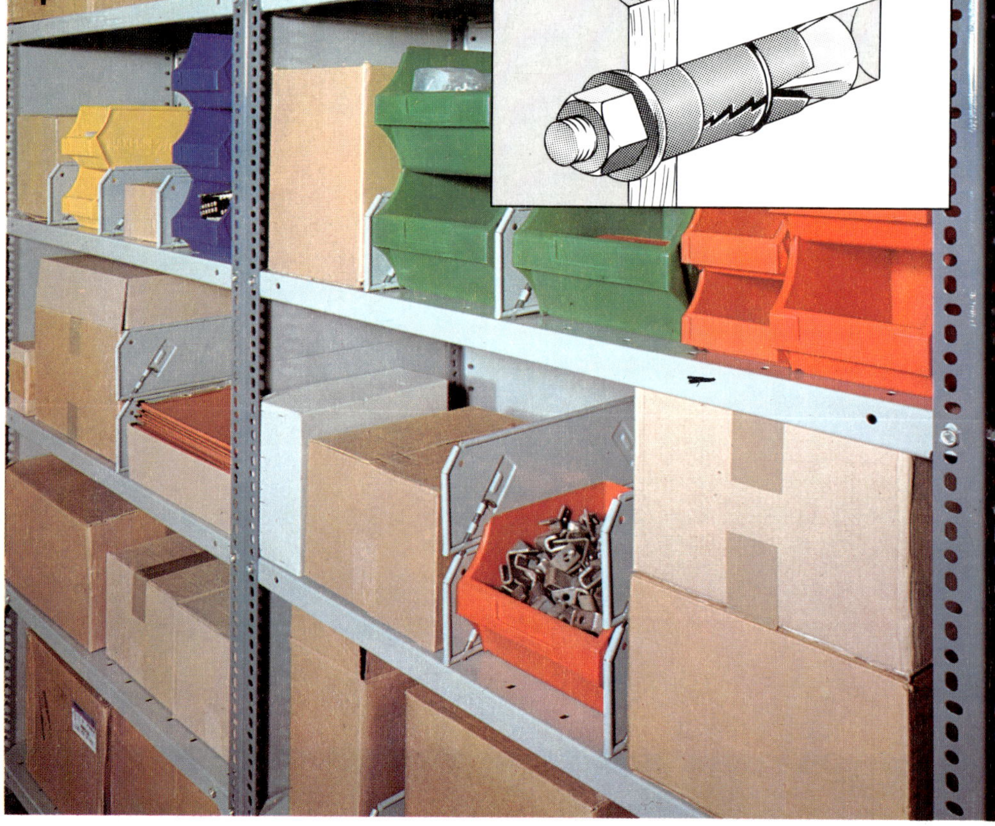

Cabinet fittings

The two main problems you will encounter with storage cupboards are putting on doors and dealing with fittings such as catches and handles.

Doors

Hanging doors calls for care and neatness if the finished job is to look acceptable. The framework must be rigid if the door is to be hung within it. You can use a piano hinge screwed directly to the edge of the door or you can use butt hinges which have to be let into the edge of the door and the cabinet side. In either case, the door must be carefully fitted into the framework so that it will show about 1.5mm joint all around when it is hung. With a piano hinge you will need to make the door equal to the width of the opening less 1.5mm and the thickness of the hinge. Butt hinges need an even joint all around as they are let into the wood.

It is obvious that to make a good job takes a little extra care and if the framework is not rigid it will move slightly when the door is hung and cause it to bind at some point.

These problems can be overcome by having the door laid on the face of the framework. It will then be cut to the same size as the outer dimensions of the cabinet with no need to plane it to an accurate joint. There are two types of lay-on hinge, one that is partly let into the door and one that simply screws into place.

The lay-on hinge is screwed to the door allowing for the thickness of the cabinet side. The door is then hung with the hinge screwed flush with the front of the cabinet. This hinge can also be used for inset doors if the hinge is screwed to the side of the cabinet set back the thickness of the door and also set back from the edge of the door the thickness of one leaf of the hinge.

The other type of hinge for lay-on doors has a round boss on one leaf that has to be let into the door. A special end mill bit is necessary for boring the blind hole. An ordinary bit has the centre point too long and it will pierce the front of the door before the hole is deep enough. The best end mills, which are 26 or 35mm diameter, have built-in depth stops to ensure that the holes are milled to exactly 12.5mm deep.

Holes are 3mm from the edge of the door

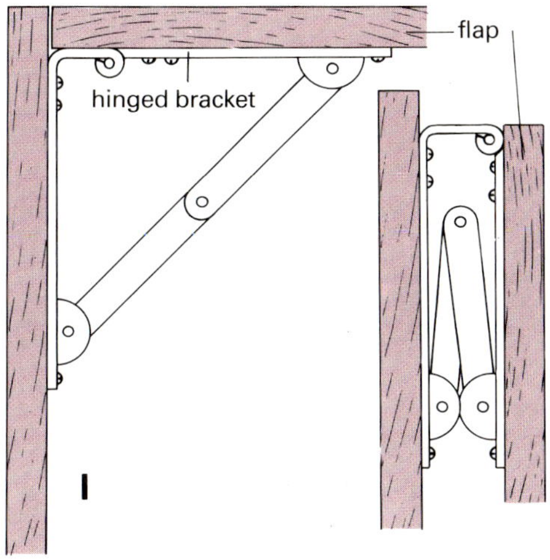

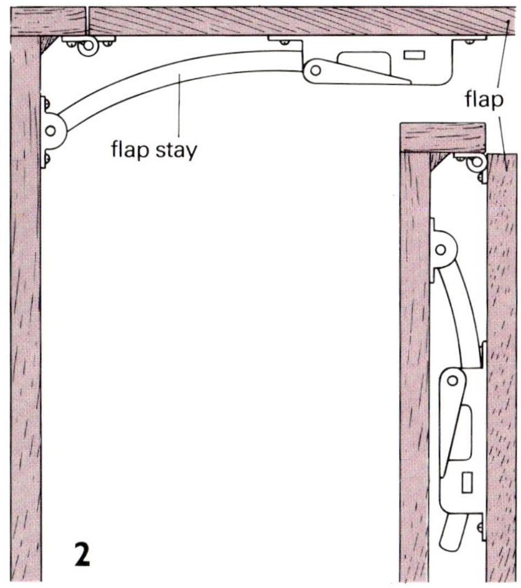

1. & 2. Two methods of making folding shelves using flap stays or hinged brackets as supports.

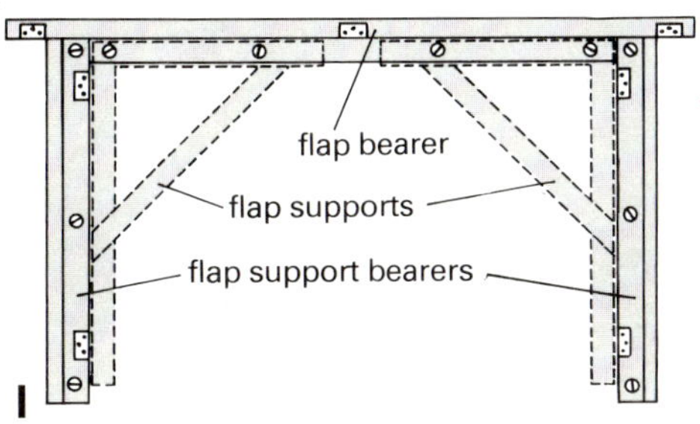

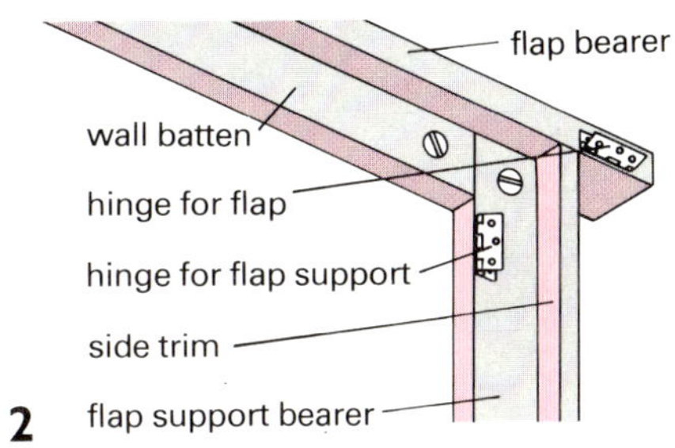

Making a folding table

1. and 2. *Folding shelves or tables can be supported on large hinged gallows brackets.*
3. *Butt hinges are used and they do not need to be let into the wood.*
4. *The flap hinge looks better if it is let into the wood.*
5. *The brackets can be made using halved and lapped joints which are glued and screwed together.*

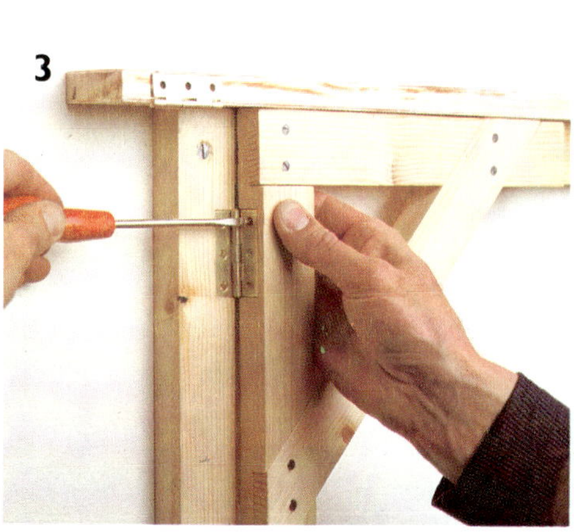

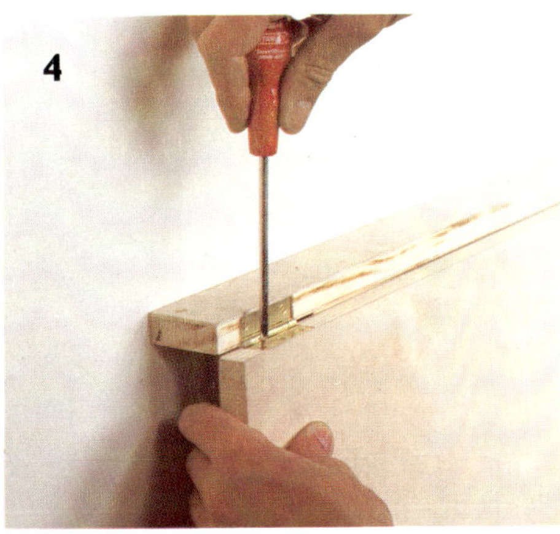

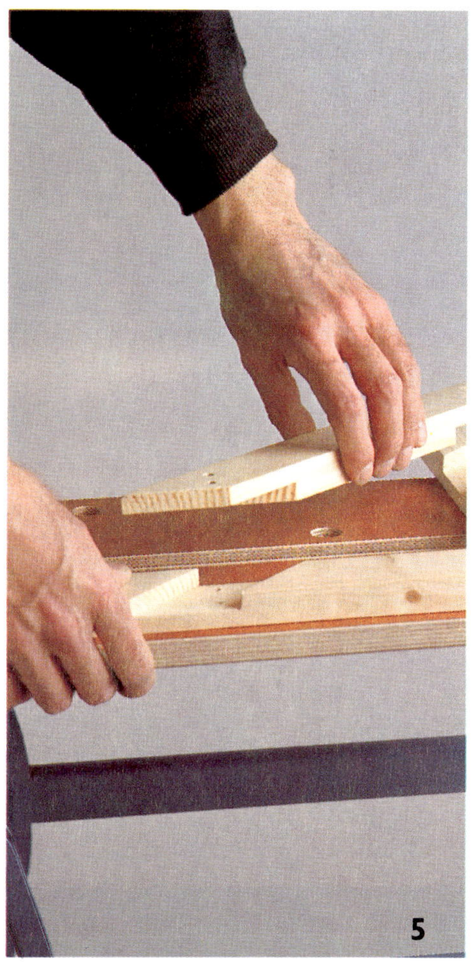

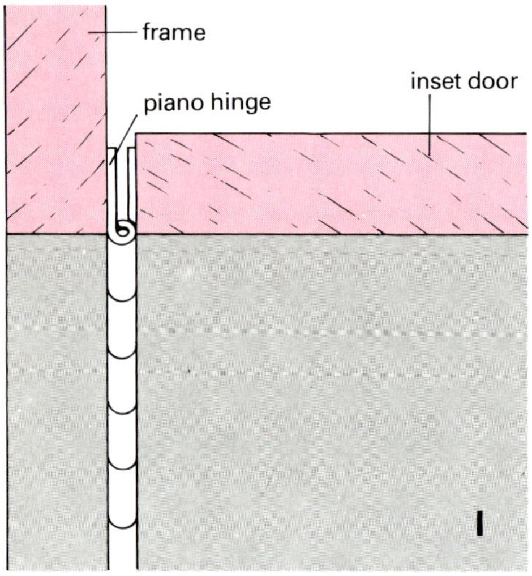

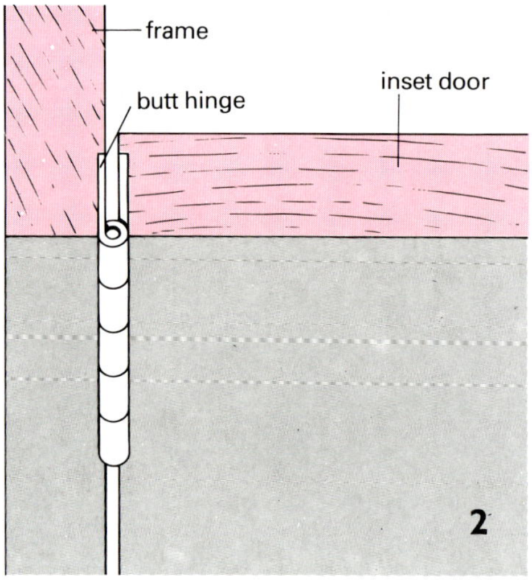

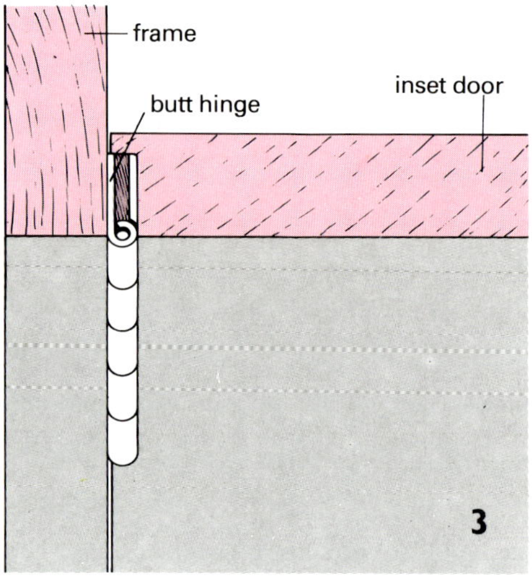

which makes 20.5mm to the centre of the hole for 35mm diameter and 16mm from the edge for the 26mm diameter holes. The boss is set into the hole and screwed into place. Then the door is offered up and the cabinet marked so the base plates can be screwed into position. Next, the door is hung by screwing the leaf of the hinge on to the plate where the correct closure of the door can be adjusted by two screws.

Handles, catches and hinges

Hinges are available in patterns to suit any cabinet. The most popular for kitchen cabinets is the concealed type that gives the door a pivoting action so that the cabinet can be fixed close into a corner. Some of these hinges incorporate a spring so that the door locks itself into the open or closed position, doing away with the need for a separate catch.

The simplest hinge for a glass door has a pivot action. A hole is drilled about 10mm deep in the top and the bottom of the cabinet and a plastic bush is inserted. Into this bush fits the pivot of the hinge, then the glass is slid into its channel where it is held in place by grub screws.

Handles must be chosen to suit the cabinet and its location. For kitchens, robust metal channels are generally used as they will stand up to heavy use. The more decorative handles used for lounge or bedroom furniture can be in wood or metal and may screw into the face of the door or drawer or, in the case of the ringpull types in brass, they need to be carefully let into the surface to produce a flush finish.

Magnetic catches are the easiest to fix and are neat in appearance. Some catches are of the touch-latch type which open partly at a light touch allowing the door to be fully opened. Spring operated touch latches are also available. In all cases fitting involves screwing the catch to the framework; recessing or drilling is not often required.

Bolts for the insides of double doors such as wardrobes and bookcases are usually in brass and are flat, not round. They may screw directly to the door or they may be let into the surface.

Adjustable shelves can be provided in bookcases by means of slotted strips screwed to the sides of the cabinet. A small clip fits into the horizontal slots to support the shelves. Four strips are required for each cabinet.

More difficult to position accurately, but less obtrusive, are shelf studs. These need carefully set out and drilled holes into which the studs are pushed. Two columns are required at each side of the cabinet.

Sliding door gear is obtainable in all sizes from simple channels to heavy overhead rollers. It is necessary to choose from the range made for the weight and type of door which you wish to hang.

Whatever type of cabinet you are preparing to build, always ensure that the fittings of the type you need are obtainable in the sizes you require before starting work. It is best to have all the fittings to hand at the outset, otherwise you could get into problems if you look for fittings only after the

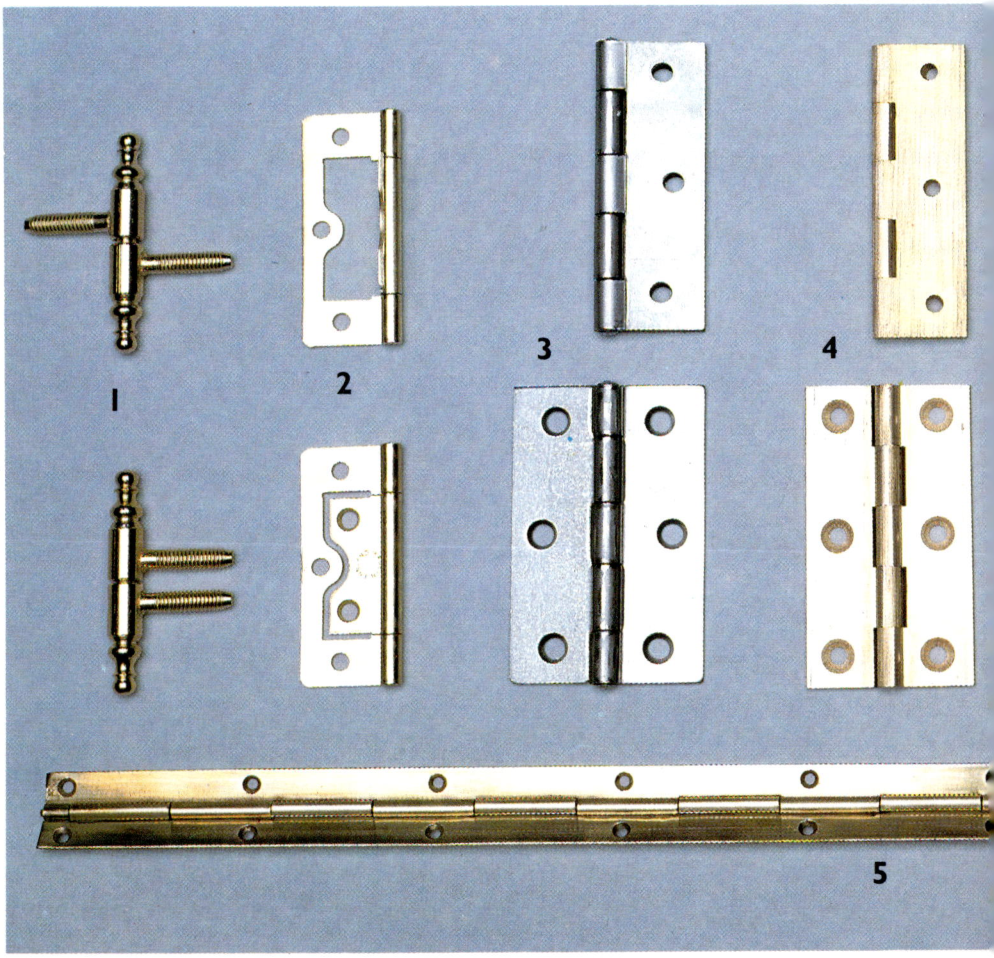

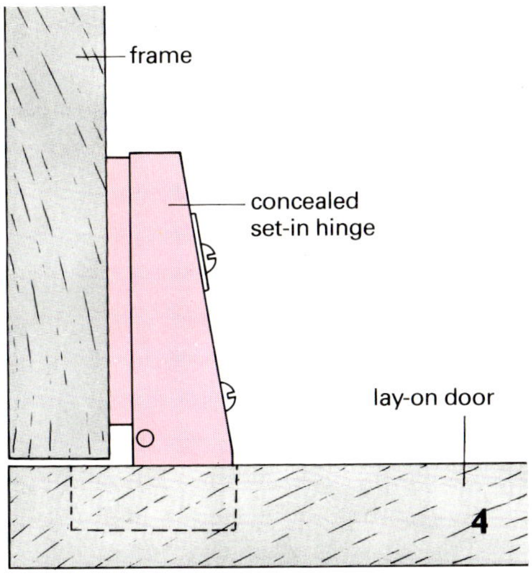

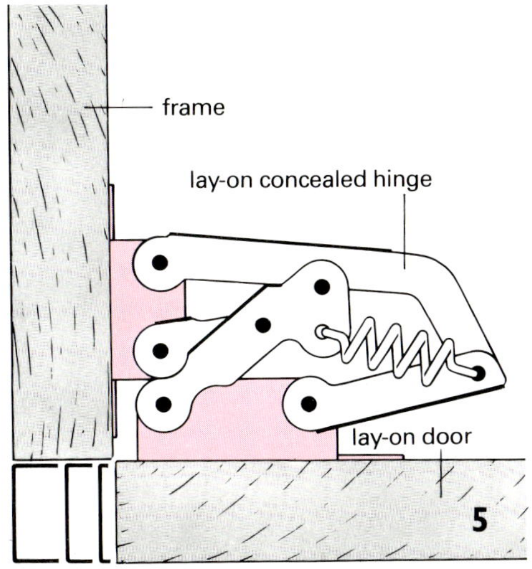

Two of the main types of hinge are illustrated here: piano and butt hinges which are suitable for the doors of furnishing cabinets and concealed hinges which are more suitable for the doors of kitchen cabinets.

1. *Piano hinges are useful for chipboard doors because they cover the raw edge and offer a large number of screw positions.*
2. *Butt hinges can be let into the frame and the door.*
3. *Both leaves of the butt hinge can also be let into the door.*
4. *The concealed hinge needs a circular recess in the door.*
5. *The lay-on hinge needs no recesses.*

work is well advanced – well thought out planning is essential.

Cupboards

One useful way of using the woodworking skills outlined in this chapter is to build simple cupboards and display cabinets. These are basically wooden boxes, and you can make good use of dowel joints, knock-down fittings and similar labour-saving devices.

Display cabinet

This need be only a light wooden case with glass or wooden shelves and either with or without glass doors. As the cabinet is intended to be looked at, it is best to make it using some form of concealed joint rather than the plastic blocks which make storage cupboards easy to construct.

One of the simplest concealed jointing systems is the dowel joint. It does require some form of jig to get the holes in exactly the right places. If only a few dowels are to be used, twin-point locaters are all that you need. These are metal discs with a centre point at each side. The board edge is pierced by the locater at the required position. A dowel or small tube can be used to press it home. The board to be mated is then positioned accurately and pressed on to the exposed point of the locater. Both board and locater are then separated and the pin marks are used to centre the drill. For accuracy, the holes should be bored using a purpose made dowel bit which is similar to a metal twist drill except that it has a centre point and side spurs for clean cutting and accurate centring.

When a lot of dowel joints are to be made, it is better to buy a dowelling jig. There are two or three different types but the basic principle is the same. A metal block contains holes of various sizes and set at right angles to each other. These holes are used to guide the drill for face and edge boring. Usually they take bits of 6, 8 and 10mm diameter.

Methods of adjustment for the positioning of the holes for the dowels and the sizes of timber that can be accommodated vary according to the make of the jig.

Glass shelves for ornamental displays can be supported by studs let into the side of the cabinet. Decide on the number of shelves and the adjustment needed, then drill a plywood strip with holes at the required spacings and use this as a template

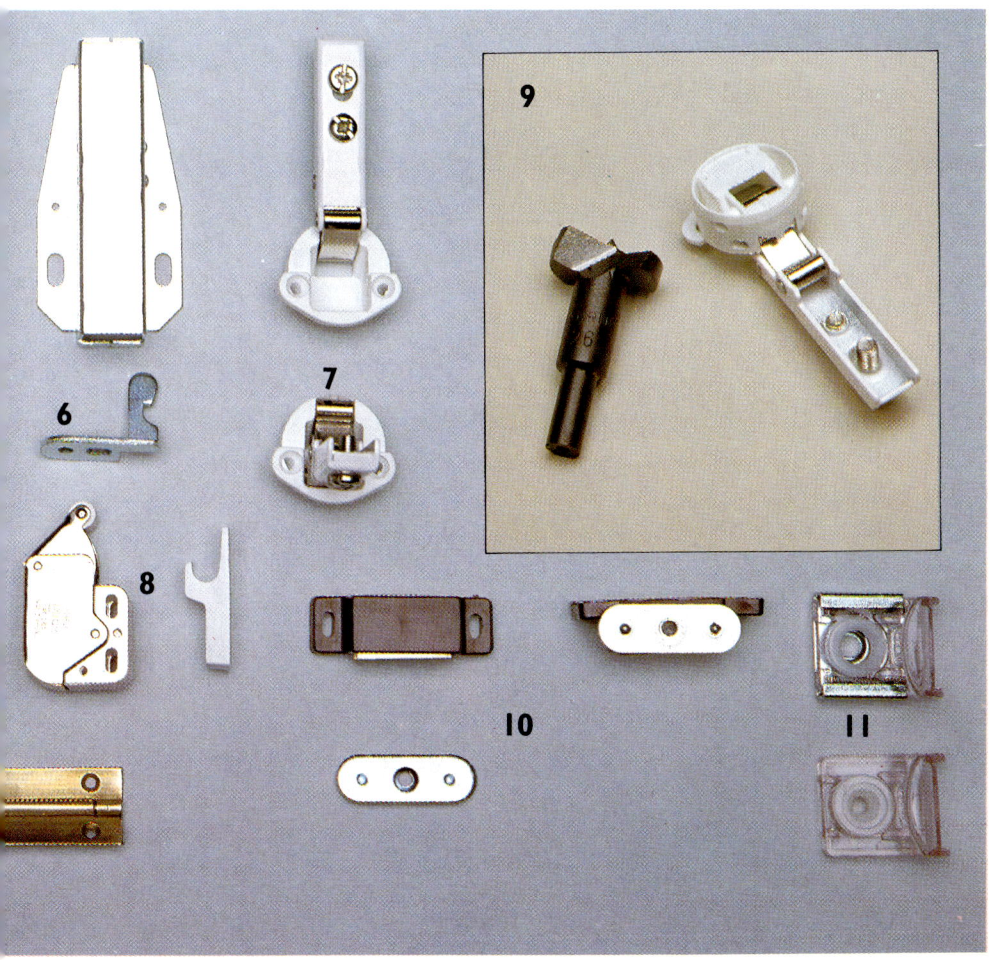

These small hinges and catches are easy to fit and are suitable for all kinds of cabinets.

1. *Pivot hinges.*
2. *Flush hinges which require no recess.*
3. *Pressed-steel hinges.*
4. *Narrow-leaf brass hinges.*
5. *Piano hinge.*
6. *Touch latch.*
7. *Concealed hinge.*
8. *Automatic latch.*
9. *Concealed hinge with drill bit.*
10. *Magnetic catches, open and closed.*
11. *Mirror clips.*

1

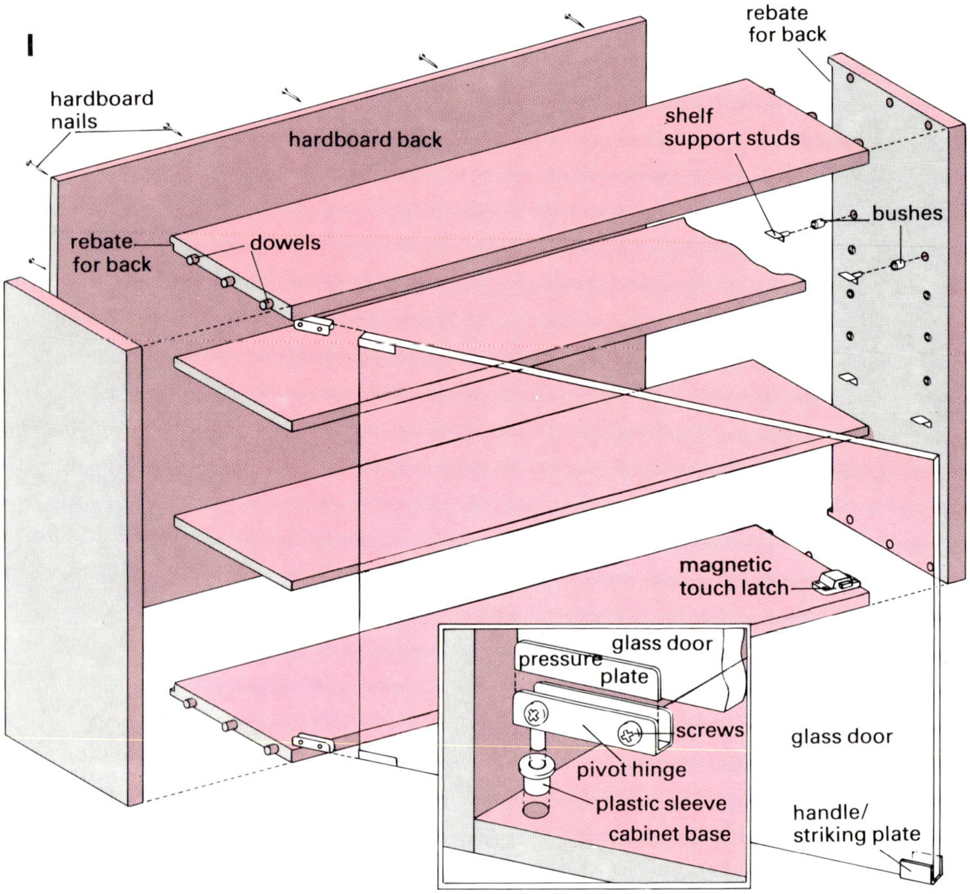

2

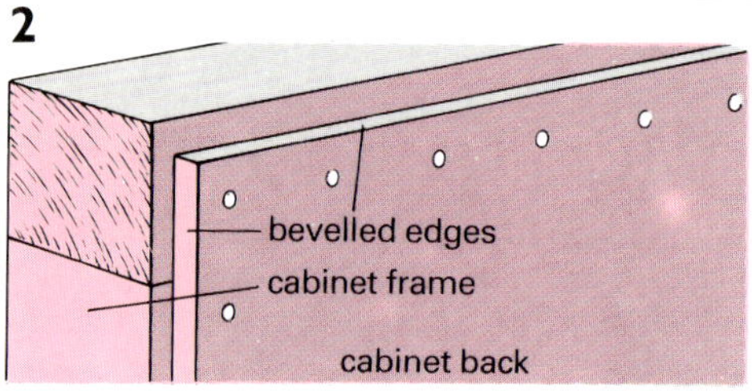

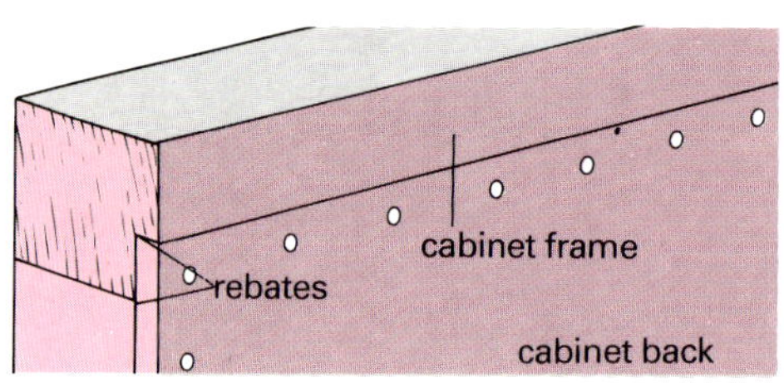

Making a glass-fronted cabinet

1. *An exploded view of a simple display cabinet showing shelf supports and dowel joints with, inset, a detail of the pivot hinge for the glass door which needs no holes or special cut-outs.*

2. *Two methods of fitting the back of a cabinet.*
3. *Making dowel joints using a dowelling jig.*
4. *Making a template as a guide when drilling holes for shelf supports.*

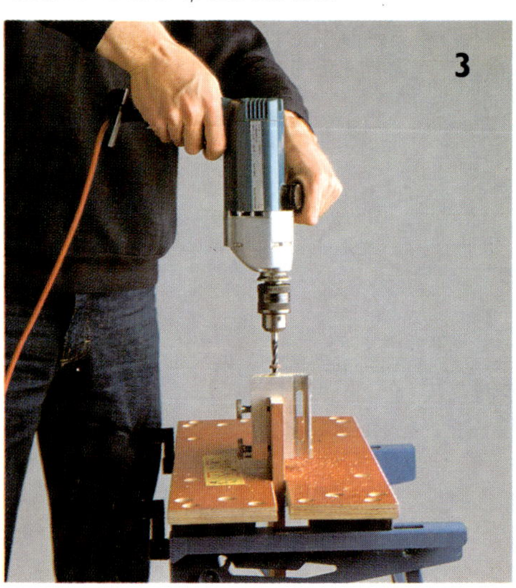
3

4

when drilling the holes in the cabinet sides.

If possible, drill these holes before assembling the unit. A bush is then pressed into the hole and into this is pushed the stud on which the shelf rests. Always use a depth stop of some kind when drilling these holes, to prevent you boring too deep and damaging the face side of the boards.

A well made dowel joint will make a fairly rigid cabinet, but rigidity and appearance are improved if a back is fitted. This can be hardboard painted to match the woodwork or for better finishes use veneered plywood. If you have the facilities a rebate can be made to take the back, otherwise bevelling the edge of the board will make it less obtrusive when viewed from the side. The fit must be close.

Storage cabinets

There are two main types of storage cabinet. One is of the quality suitable for use in living rooms and the other is the more sturdy store room type.

Cabinets for use as furniture are made using veneered boards and for these the dowel joints described in making display cabinets are most suitable. Plastic block connectors are quite suitable for general storage cabinets and for kitchen cabinets.

As these units have a fair weight of materials to support, it is more usual to house the shelves into the side of the cabinet, unless plastic blocks are being used. For the best appearance, the housing should be stopped and not cut right through

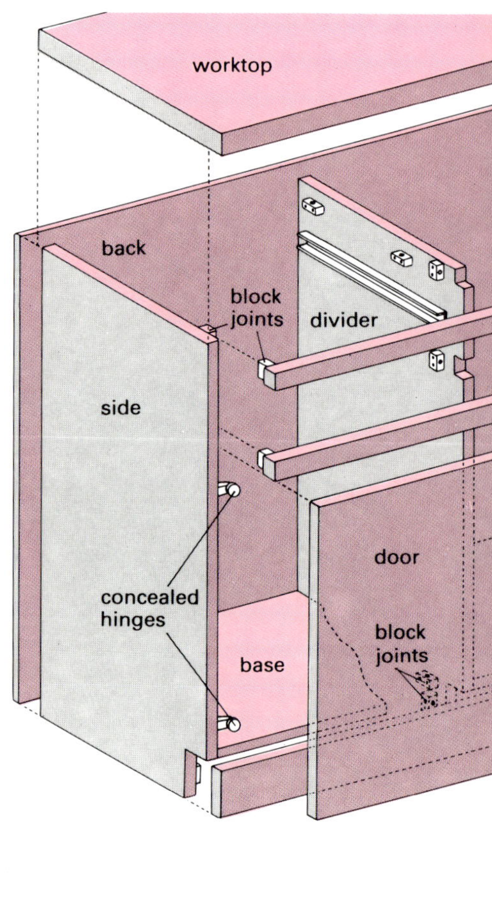

to the front of the side pieces. Mark the position and thickness of the shelves, then square the lines across the boards. Mark the depth of the housing and bore two or three shallow holes at the stopped end of the housing. Clean out these holes to make a small recess and you will find this a help when sawing each side of the housing. The waste is best cut away with a chisel and finished off with a hand router. If a router is not available, you will have to take great care in getting the housing level and even.

The front edge of the shelf is cut back to clear the end of the stopped housing and the shelves are glued into place. These shelves are slid into the cabinet from the back after the top and bottom have been dowelled and fixed.

When the shelves are installed the back can be fitted. This is either set in a rebate, or if that cannot be made the cabinet must be squared by measuring the diagonals, which must be the same length, and the back nailed to the sides and bottom edges. Extra nails into the shelves will make an even more rigid job.

Rigidity is very important if a door is to be inset, any movement of the cabinet would cause the door to bind and jam. Face fitted doors hung on adjustable concealed hinges are the best for this type of unit as any slight discrepancies can be overcome by the adjustment of the hinge.

Wall-hung cabinets must be firmly fixed and this means making provision for fixing when making the cabinet as well as providing a secure fixing in the wall. One method for use where heavy weights are expected, is to fit a supporting batten underneath the top and the shelves. The shelves and the top can be screwed down into these battens and the battens then plugged and screwed to the wall.

Brass mirror plates, which are screwed to the edges of the top or sides and then fixed to the wall, are really satisfactory only when solid timber is being used. Chipboard soon gives way at the edges.

Measurements have not been included in the illustrations as they are intended to show the methods used when constructing the complete unit.

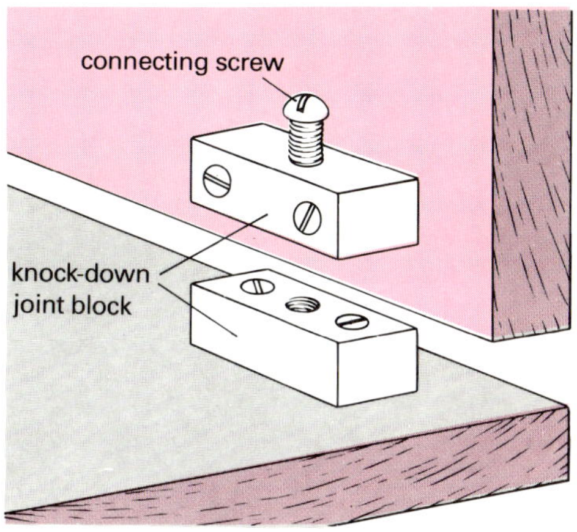

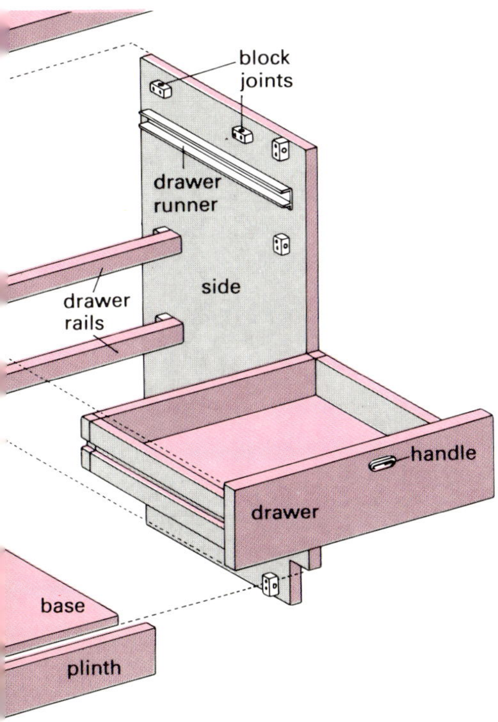

A typical storage cabinet with details of the joints used. Although the entire unit can be constructed using plastic blocks, secret fixings such as dowel joints and housings look more professional for living room furniture. The cabinet top can either overhang the sides or be inset between them. Dowel joints can be used in either case. The back will hold the frame rigid so the shelves can be fixed in housings or they can be made adjustable by using one of the support systems suitable for bookcases.

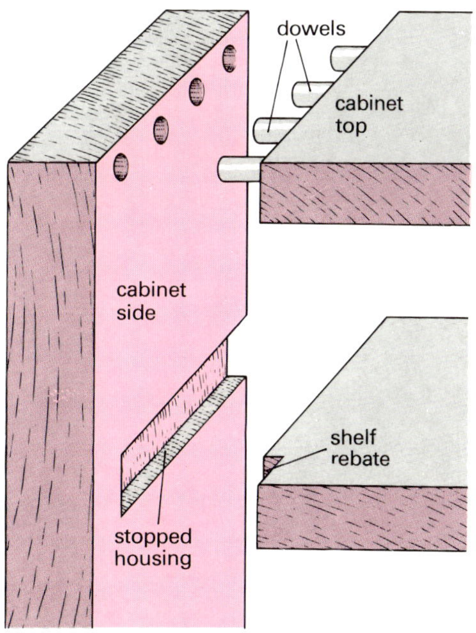

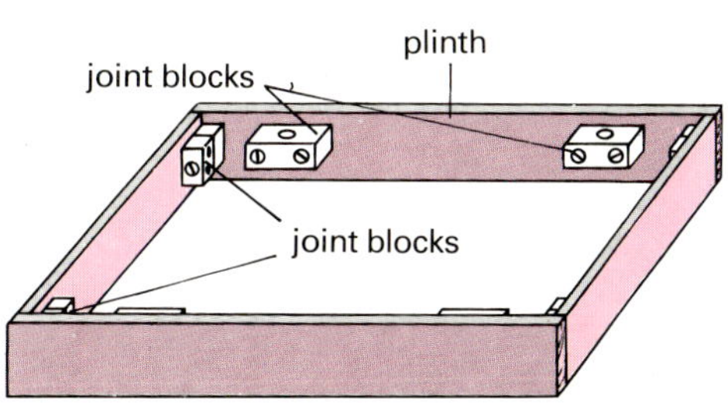

Box unit.

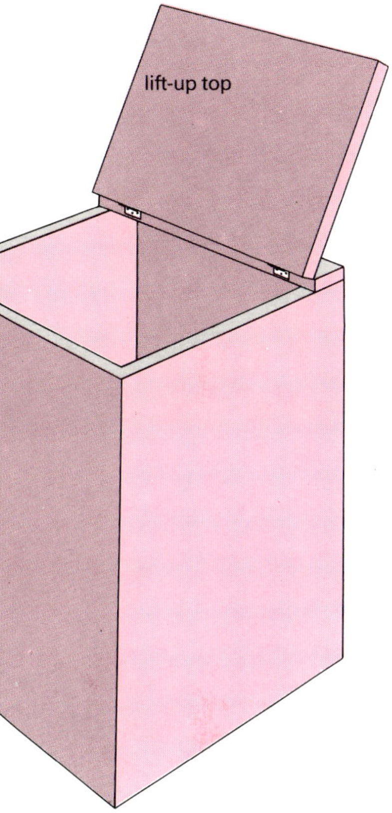

Corner unit.

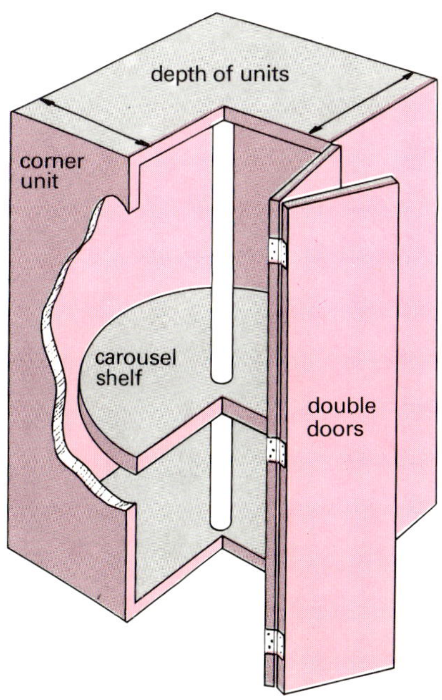

Drawers

Making drawers can be a tedious and time-consuming job and it is unlikely that you would want to go to all the trouble of making dovetail joints for the fronts. Housed joints will do the job just as well and, if you prefer it, you can use plastic extrusions instead of wood.

There are one or two different plastic drawer systems, but most include a corner joint which enables the drawers to be assembled using only square cut materials. Using these drawer systems does limit the depth of the drawers to that of the extrusions. If you want to have a more varied choice you will have to use wood and chipboard.

The easiest type of drawer is the one with the front wider than the sides so that it fits over the face of the cabinet. The drawer itself is then made as a square box with the ends housed or rebated into the sides. These joints are glued and pinned.

Ideally, the bottom of the drawer is fitted into a groove in the sides and front, and the back of the drawer is made shallower than the sides, finishing level with the top edge of the groove so that the bottom can be slid into place and pinned to the bottom edge of the drawer back.

A rebate can be made for the drawer bottom, but it is not very good as it does not leave much for the drawer to run on. The drawer will not run freely if the bottom is simply fixed directly to the bottom edges of the sides.

Side runners are therefore the best solution. A strip of hardwood, glued and screwed to the outside of each side of the drawer, slides on a similar strip of hardwood fixed to the inside of the cabinet. This means that the drawer tray is made 20mm narrower than the opening to make a space for the two 10mm runners. The false front, which overlaps the sides of the cabinet, is screwed into place.

Using side runners means that there need be no cabinet rail showing between the drawers which will then present a flush finish. If rails are needed to strengthen the cabinet, they can be fixed by letting them into the sides or screwing them through the sides, dependent on the quality of finish required. In this case the width of the drawer front will have to be adjusted to cover the rails.

Drawers can be run on bottom rails if the drawer bottom is fixed to battens glued and pinned to the inside of the drawer about 10mm above the bottom of the sides, but this reduces the storage depth of the drawer.

Always remember to make your drawers as strong as possible so that the weight they bear will be well supported.

1

2

3

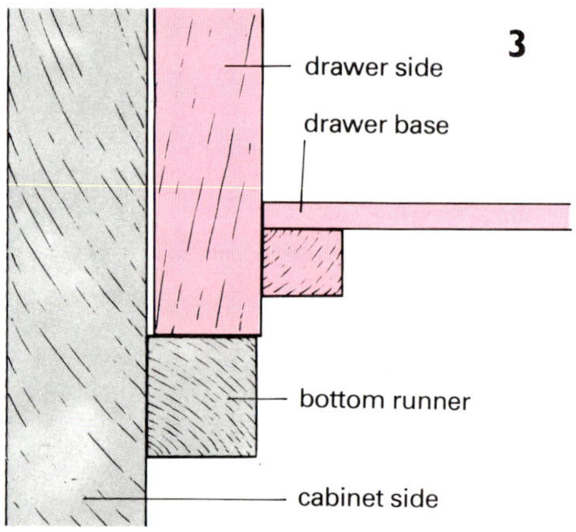

4

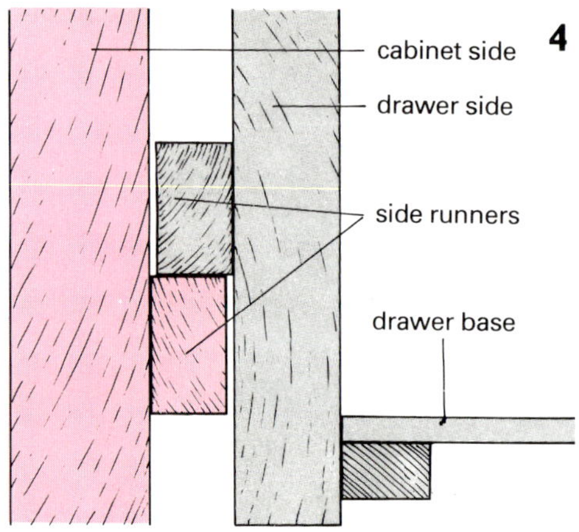

5

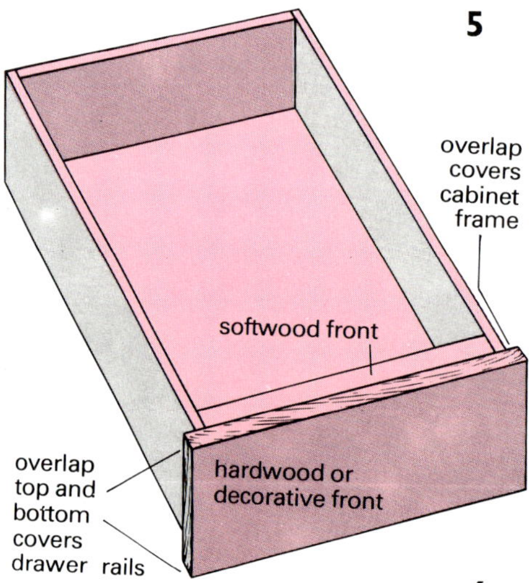

6

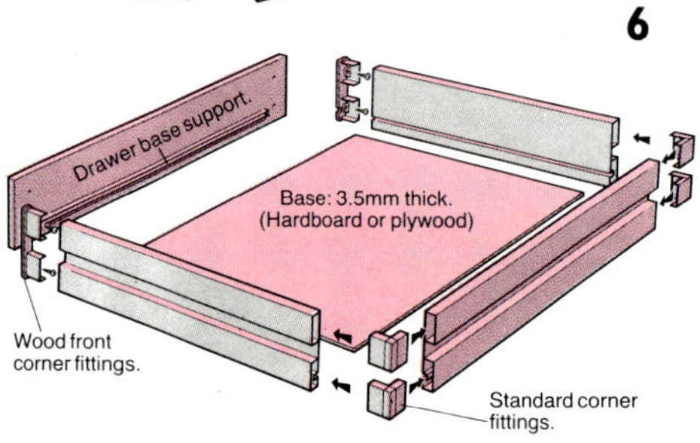

1. *The bottom of a drawer slides into grooves in the sides and the back is fitted and fixed into place.*
2. *The back also has a groove into which the base fits. The bottom holds the drawer square, so it must fit neatly into the back.*
3. *The drawer slides on a hardwood runner screwed to the side of the unit.*
4. *Hardwood runners are screwed to both the sides of the unit and to the sides of the drawer. The former method is often used where front rails form a feature of the unit. In the latter method the two hardwood runners wear better and the drawer fronts are not separated by the front rails of the cabinet.*
5. *The drawer can have a decorative front screwed to a softwood backing.*
6. *This illustrates how drawers are made-up using one of the plastic drawer making systems which are generally obtainable as complete kits.*

EXTERIOR REPAIRS

A modern house is warm, comfortable and convenient, built with mass-production materials that will last for many years. But the seasons are always trying to reduce our efforts to nil, with winds, rain, snow and – sometimes – sunshine. So we have to be on our guard, ready to repair the ravages of the weather.

Knowing how a home is constructed and what materials and tools are available to make necessary repairs is essential for the home owner and this guide is intended to help you understand house construction, recognise the signs when something is going wrong and know how to put it right.

Before you begin

The outside shell of a house is a complex assortment of features, built with a variety of materials and techniques, with but one practical purpose: to protect its occupants from the weather. However picturesque the building may appear, it has to keep wind and rain at bay, and if it is not given its fair share of maintenance and repair it will soon deteriorate.

Anatomy of exterior repairs

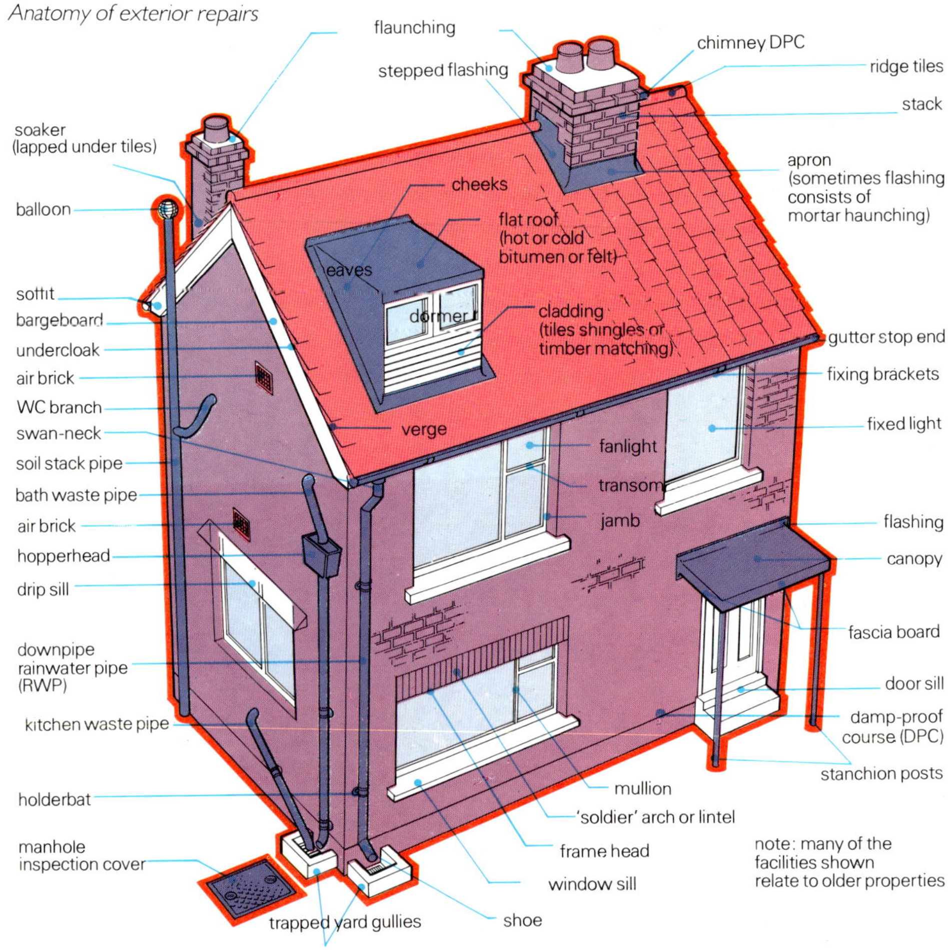

The guided tour

To get an idea of what is involved in keeping your house shipshape, go on a guided tour, with notebook in hand to make a brief record of the various features and their condition. You will then be able to plan a maintenance checklist, and to establish a routine of regular inspection and repair that will stop minor problems growing into major ones through neglect.

Start at the top with the roof and any chimney stacks you may have. Chimney stack faults are a common cause of damp penetration; the pots themselves may crack or shift in the mortar bed on top of the stack, while the masonry of the stack may crack because water has penetrated defective pointing between the bricks. Where the stack meets the roof slope, the apron flashing of lead or zinc sheet that is supposed to seal the junction may have become porous, or may have split, allowing water to penetrate. The same problem can occur where flues and soil pipes pass through the roof.

If you have a pitched roof, it will most likely be covered with tiles or slates. If these are displaced, missing or cracked, water can penetrate, especially at the roof ridge and on the sloping hips. Valleys – internal angles where roof slopes meet – are lined with lead or felt, which may be torn or porous. Flashings are waterproof junctions where the roof slope meets a vertical such as a dormer or a parapet wall; problems can also occur in this area.

With flat roofs covered in felt and chippings, problems are difficult to spot. The roof covering may have become porous, or may be damaged at one or more points, allowing water to find its way in. Where such roofs meet the house wall, a felt, metal or mortar flashing is used to seal the join; this too is a common point of failure. Flat roofs should in fact have a slight slope to allow water to run off to gutters at one edge, and the overhang must direct water into the gutters, not over them or between them and the fascia board.

Gutter and downpipe problems are usually easy to spot. The gutters may sag, pouring water down the house walls, or may actually be broken; blockages cause overflows. Bad connections between the gutter and the downpipe also allow water to run down the house walls, causing damp to penetrate, while the joints between successive downpipe sections may have opened up. Box gutters, found behind parapet walls and where two roof slopes meet, are usually felt or metal-lined, and may have become porous with age causing leaks.

Exterior woodwork is particularly prone to rot and decay. The fascias to which gutters are fixed, the soffits behind them and the bargeboards at gable ends may be rotten, while windows, doors and their frames may also need attention if they have not been properly protected against the weather. Exterior paintwork usually needs re-doing every five years.

Some paints and varnishes are more suitable than others for exterior use, especially in south-facing positions. A recent 'flexible' paint will not crack when exposed in this way, and some hardwood finishes contain ultra-violet light stabilisers which give high resistance to fading of the timber and breakdown of the finish.

Check that putty is sound and properly painted, and that gaps have not opened up between the frames and the masonry.

The next area to check is the surface of exterior walls. The surface of brick and stone may be damaged because water has penetrated defective pointing, allowing frost to crack the surface. Water running down the wall may have caused discoloration and mould growth. Rendering and pebbledash may have cracked or flaked away, looking unsightly and allowing water to penetrate, causing dampness in the masonry behind and further damage to the rendering itself.

The damp course, which extends right round the house wall and is intended to stop moisture rising up the wall from the ground, may be bridged (by soil, incorrectly laid paths and patios or adjoining garden walls) and rising damp in the wall will result. Airbricks below the damp course must be clear, allowing air to circulate under suspended floors; if they are blocked, rot can attack under-floor timbers.

The drains need checking while you are on your tour of the house. Gullies taking waste water from the house and rainwater from the roof may be blocked, causing overflows and damp penetration. The brickwork of drain manholes may need repair, and manhole covers may be broken.

Check the condition of paths, drives and steps; the surface of concrete, stone or brick may be cracked and crumbling, allowing further deterioration of the subsurface and preventing proper drainage. Lastly, inspect garden walls, fences and gates; walls, especially earth-retaining ones, can soon be-

1. *Extend ladder, ensuring at least a three-rung overlap, and position the foot of the ladder in the wall-ground angle.*
2. *Raise the ladder hand-over-hand to the upright position then lift out the foot and stand it on firm ground or a board.*

Erecting a tower platform; the angled traces are essential for rigidity.

come unstable and dangerous, while fences and gates are at risk from rot and poor fixings which can cause complete collapse.

Access to the job

Perhaps the biggest problem with all exterior maintenance work is getting to the job. For any work above ground-floor window level, you will need some form of access equipment – either ladders or, for large-scale jobs, a scaffold platform. With a two-part extension ladder about 4m (13ft) long, extending to about 6m (20ft), you should be able to reach safely up to eaves level on a two-storey house. Where you need a more comfortable and more permanent working platform, a slot-together scaffold tower with a 1.2m (4ft) square base can be hired by the weekend or week, and can be built up to heights of around 8m (26ft), making them particularly useful for work on gable ends and side chimney stacks. For repairs to centre chimney stacks, and pitched roofs, you will need a special roof ladder that hooks over the roof ridge and provides a safe foothold while spreading your weight over the roof surface so that you do not damage the slates or tiles.

Using ladders safely

The first golden rule with ladders is not to climb if you do not like heights; you will only feel thoroughly unsafe, and so will risk a fall. The second is to check any ladder before you climb it, to make sure it is in good condition. All the rungs should be securely locked into the stiles (the long side pieces), and, if wooden, should show no signs of splitting. The stiles themselves, if wooden, should be free from splits, and should be dead straight – a warped ladder will be severely strained when you climb it. Aluminium ladders are, of course, far more durable than wooden ones and unless seriously misused will last a lifetime.

Always carry a ladder in the upright position to where it is needed. Then set the foot against the angle between wall and ground, with the ladder horizontal, and lift the top end, working it up towards the vertical by walking your hands down the rungs. With the ladder upright, lift the foot out from the wall to a distance equal to one-quarter the height of the ladder top. If it is set on hard, level ground, tie it to stakes set in the ground at either side, or weight the foot of the ladder with a sack full of earth. At the top, tie the ladder to a conveniently sited window frame, or to a stout hook driven into a fascia board or window sill. Never trust gutter fixings or downpipes to be secure enough for this. On soft ground, set the foot of the ladder on a plank to which a wooden batten has been screwed, to prevent the ladder from sinking in. On slight slopes, use the same board with a wedge under one end; never put wedges under just one stile.

When you climb a ladder, do not be alarmed when it flexes under your weight. Hold both stiles as you climb, and look straight ahead as you do so. Carry tools in pockets or in an apron, or haul them up in a bucket once you have climbed the ladder, securing the bucket with a ladder hook over one of the upper rungs.

Once you are up the ladder and ready to start work, do not lean out too far to each side. Keep your body within the line of the stiles, and always hold on with one hand.

If you are using an extension ladder, always maintain a three-rung overlap when the ladder is extended. On any ladder, do not climb higher than about four rungs from the top. Do not rest ladders on guttering; if you need the ladder that high, fit a ladder stay at the top to hold the ladder clear of the wall. If you need access to the awkward-to-reach area immediately above a window, lash a length of wood across the ladder wide enough to bridge the window and rest on the masonry at either side.

If you are using your ladder to gain access to the roof, make sure it protrudes at least 1m (3ft 3in) above the eaves, and that it is securely tied. Then get a helper to pass up the roof ladder, hooked end first, and push it up the roof slope on its small wheels until the hook reaches the ridge. Then turn the roof ladder over, with the hook over the ridge, and check that it is securely held. Tie the lower end to the top of your extension ladder before climbing on to it.

Using slot-together platforms

These tower platforms are very easy to build; parts of H-shaped frames are simply slotted together to build the tower up to the desired height, and then planks and handrails are added at the top to form the working platform. They must be erected on firm ground, unless stout planks are placed under the feet; slight slopes can be accommodated by means of adjustable feet fitted below the bottom frames. On level, paved areas castors can be fitted to allow the tower to be moved along; these must be locked when the tower is in position.

If the tower is more than about 2.5m (8ft) high, it should be secured to the house near its top, by tying it to a window frame or stout fascia hook. Toe boards – platform planks placed vertically round the edges of the working platform – should be used to stop tools and equipment falling off.

When climbing a tower of this sort, always climb up the inside, never the outside, or you may tip the tower over.

Chimney repairs

Chimney repairs should be undertaken only by competent and confident people, using the correct access equipment (see page 151). Depending on the scale of the repairs, it may be necessary to haul up mortar, bricks and even new chimney pots, and a variety of bricklaying tools may be needed. The job will be a comparatively lengthy onc, including putting up and taking down the access equipment. Stout rubber-soled shoes, thick trousers and gloves are recommended.

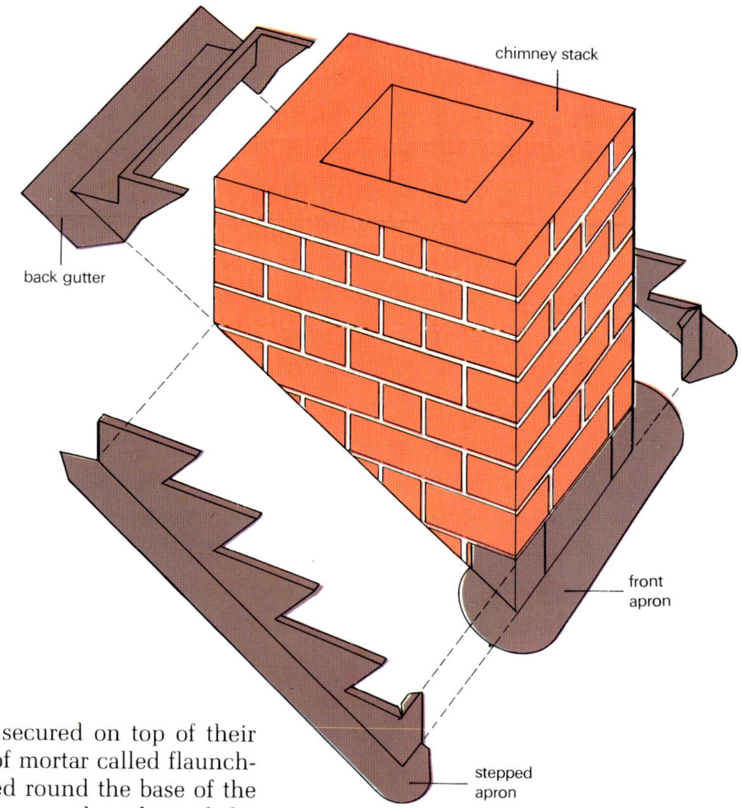

Chimney flashing

Chimney pots

Chimney pots are secured on top of their stacks with a bed of mortar called flaunching which is shaped round the base of the pot and sloped away to the edges of the stack. If this has cracked or crumbled away, it must be hacked off and replaced with fresh mortar. If the pot is cracked or broken, it should be replaced at the same time or removed if the flue is no longer in use.

With the old flaunching removed, the pot should be lifted off – it may be very heavy – and either secured to the ladder or lowered to the ground by rope if no longer needed. Then a bed of new mortar, 1 part cement to 3 parts sharp sand, should be laid on the top of the stack, and the pot replaced. If the stack brickwork and the pot are wetted first, the adhesion of the mortar will be improved. Then the mortar can be built up around the pot to a thickness there of about 75mm (3in), and trowelled to a smooth slope towards the edges so that water will run off. Ideally, when dry it should be given a coat of silicone water-repellent to stop water penetrating it in future.

Stack repairs

If the stack is of brick or stone, you may find that the pointing is crumbling. Rake the old mortar out to a depth of at least 18mm (¾in) and damp the brickwork before repointing with a mixture of 1 part cement to 4 parts soft sand. Press the mortar firmly into the joints, and finish off neatly with your trowel.

Where the stack has been finished off with rendering or pebbledash, you may find that this has cracked or fallen off altogether. In this case it should be hacked off completely, and the stack re-rendered (see page 158 for details).

Sealing the flue

If a flue is no longer used, the pot should be removed and the flue capped with a piece of slate over the flue opening, or with a small ventilating cowl. If slate is used, it should be set in mortar and covered over with sloped flaunching; to maintain some ventilation in the flue, an airbrick should be let into the side of the flue in the roof.

Waterproofing flashings

The junction between the chimney stack and the roof slope is waterproofed with an apron flashing, usually of lead or zinc. These are mortared into the brickwork of the stack, are tucked under the tiles above the stack, and laid over them below it. Repoint if necessary where the flashings meet the stack, and press the flashing down over the tiles if it has been lifted by the wind. Then brush bitumen emulsion over the surface of the flashing to seal any pinholes and make the apron completely waterproof. If the sheet has deteriorated badly, you will have to remove it completely and use it as a pattern to cut a new apron from sheets of lead, zinc, aluminium alloy or semi-rigid bitumen-based felt.

Making new flashings

Flashings are formed either from sheet material – lead, zinc, bituminised felt – or from mortar. The former may be torn or porous, while the latter simply cracks and breaks away. It is comparatively straightforward to repair or replace flashings, as long as they can be reached safely.

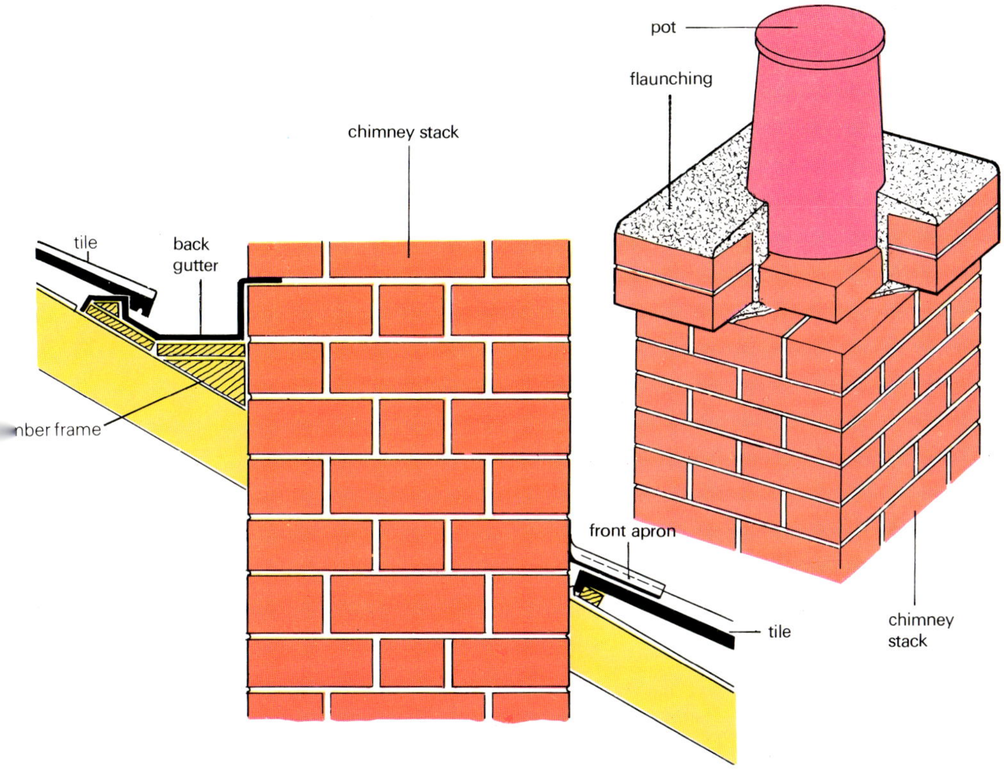

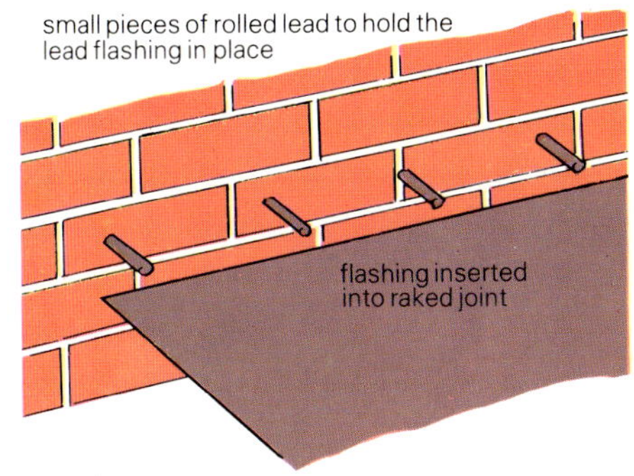

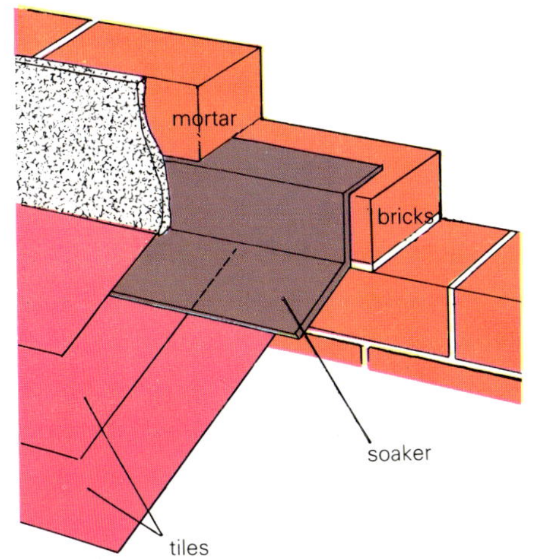

Waterproofing flashings

If a sheet flashing is letting in water, there are three possible reasons. The upper edge of the flashing, which should be let into a mortar course in the wall, may no longer be secure because the pointing is defective. In this case the old pointing should be raked out, the flashing wedged securely in place and the pointing replaced, using a mortar of 1 part cement to 4 parts soft sand.

The lower edge of the flashing should either be pressed down firmly over the surface below, or should be tucked under the upper layer of a multi-layer felted roof. In the first case wind pressure may have lifted the flashing, which should be gently pressed back into place. Bitumen mastic can be used to bed the flashing in place and prevent it lifting in future. In the second case, an imperfect seal may be allowing water to penetrate, and the join should be sealed with one or two applications of bitumen emulsion.

If the flashing is too badly damaged for this sort of repair to be effective, you will have to remove the entire flashing and use it as a pattern for a new flashing. While you can use traditional metal sheet materials for this, you will find it easier to use a proprietary flashing strip which can be cut to length and shape with old scissors and is bedded into a coat of bituminous emulsion. Provided adhesion to the wall above the flashing is good, there is no need to turn the top edge into the mortar course. The strip can be formed around corners and over minor obstructions that may be present.

Mortar flashings that have cracked and crumbled should be hacked away completely and replaced. Use a mortar of 1 part cement to 4 parts soft sand, mixed with a PVA additive to improve adhesion, and apply it in two layers to lessen the tendency for it to crack as it dries out. Cross-hatch the surface of the first layer, and when it has dried apply the second layer, trowelling the surface smooth. Try to avoid feathering out the edge of the mortar too thinly; it will only crack all the more easily. To prevent (or at least discourage) water penetration, brush a couple of coats of silicone water-repellent over the new flashing when it has dried.

Using flashing strip

1. *Coat the area to be sealed with bituminous emulsion primer.*

2. *Bed the flashing strip into the emulsion, pressing down firmly to ensure a good seal.*

Roofing repairs

As with repairs to chimney stacks, only the competent and confident handyman should attempt roof repairs. Safety is even more important in this case, since you will be working on the roof slope without even a friendly chimney stack to hold on to. Roof ladders are essential unless the repair needed is within easy reach of the eaves, and all access equipment should be secured. Tools needed are fairly limited – a hammer, a number of timber wedges and a tool called a slater's ripper if you are working on a slate roof.

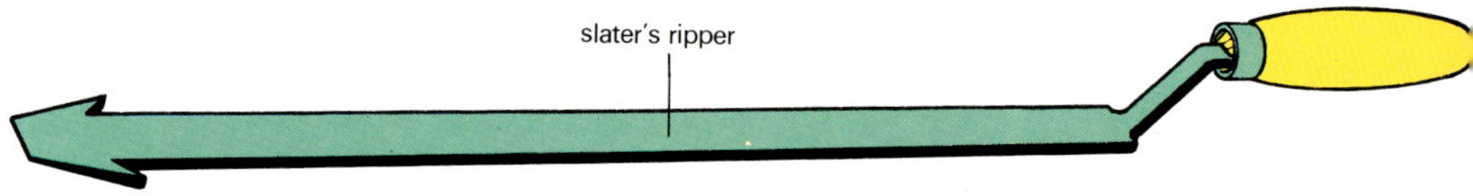

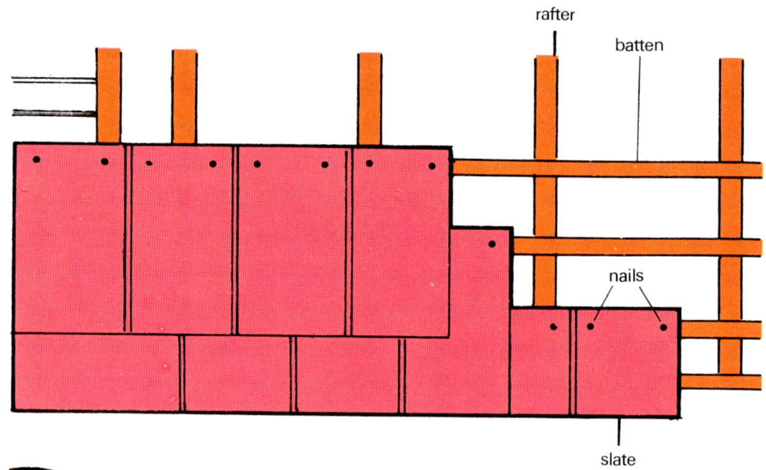

Slate roof, showing how the nails are fixed to battens

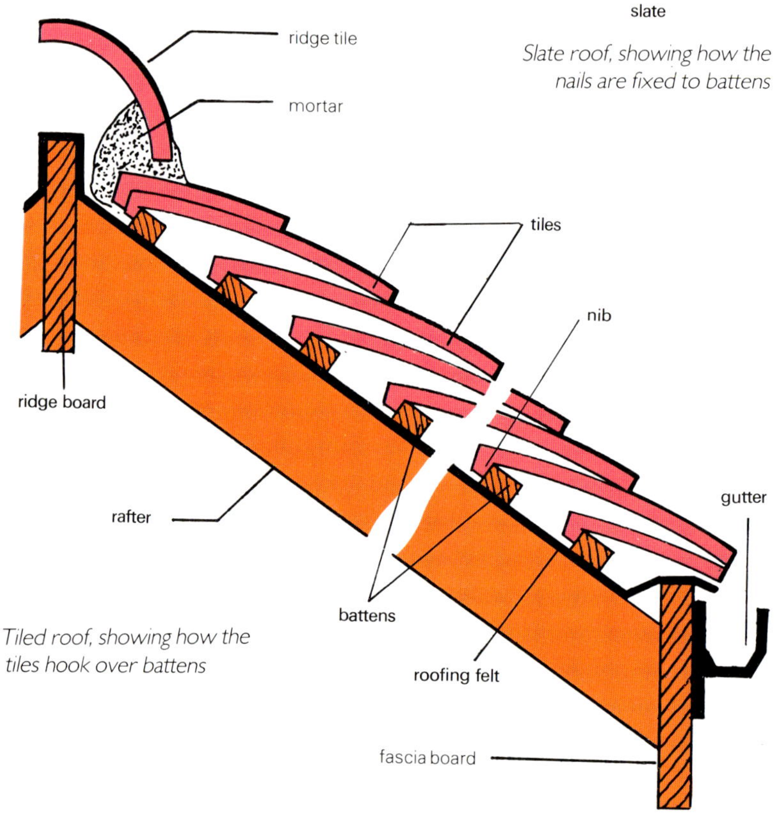

Tiled roof, showing how the tiles hook over battens

Refixing loose slates

Slates are held in place on the roof slope by nails driven through their centres or their top edges into battens. They usually slip because these nails have rusted away, or because the slate has split near the nail hole. It is usually possible to slide a slipped slate back into position, and to secure it with a strip of lead or other metal called a tingle. First you must slide the old slate out completely, allowing you to nail the tingle to a batten through the gap between the two slates underlying the one you removed. Then the old slate can be eased back into place, with those above it wedged up very slightly to give enough clearance. When the slate's lower edge is aligned with others in that course, the end of the tingle is bent up and folded over the lower edge of the slate to hold it in place.

Replacing slates

If slates are cracked or badly split, the only remedy is to remove the damaged slate and replace it with a new one. To do this you need a tool called a slater's ripper, which has a hooked end designed to be slipped up under the offending slate and around the nails holding it. By jerking the ripper downwards, the hooked blade is made to cut through the nail, so freeing the slate. Then the new slate is carefully pushed up into position and secured with a tingle, as already described.

Replacing loose and damaged tiles

Most types of tiles are held in place by nibs behind their top edges which hook over battens nailed across the roof slope, and by the weight of the tiles in the next course up resting on them. If the nibs are damaged, the tile will have to be fixed back in position like a slate, or replaced completely. But if it has simply been dislodged by high winds, you should be able to slide it back into place with the nibs hooked over their batten. In either case, you will probably have to wedge up surrounding tiles slightly to allow the offending tile to be replaced. Do this gently, or you may crack other tiles, which will then have to be replaced too.

Replacing ridge tiles and slates

Ridge tiles and slates are bedded in mortar, and may have to be reset if movement in the roof has cracked the mortar. The loose tile or slate should be lifted off, and all the old mortar chipped away. It should then be re-bedded in a mortar of 1 part cement to 3 parts sand, laid along the ridge. Place the tile on this, tamp it down carefully, level with its neighbours, and finish off by pointing up the gaps between it and them and along the ridge tiles' lower edges.

Waterproofing pitched roofs

If a tiled or slated roof is in poor condition, with a lot of loose and missing tiles or slates that have become porous with age, the only satisfactory long-term remedy is to have the roof stripped and re-covered. But you can make a short-term repair by covering the entire roof surface with bitumen emulsion, bedding a coarse scrim material in the emulsion and applying further coats to form a waterproof skin. There are a number of proprietary systems available for this purpose.

Exterior woodwork

At eaves level, the ends of the various roof timbers are protected by planks of wood. Fascia boards are nailed to the cut ends of the rafters at the eaves, while bargeboards protect the ends of the roof purlins and tiling battens at the gable end of a roof. The barge and fascia boards will have their inside faces flush with the house wall if the timbers are cut off flush with the masonry; where the timbers protrude to give overhanging eaves, there will be soffit boards fixed at right angles to the fascia and bargeboards to fill the gap between the board edge and the wall. All this wood is prone to attacks of rot.

Replacing fascias and soffits
Since the house gutters are fixed to the fascia boards, these must be taken down first (see page 156). You can then prise away the old timbers with a crowbar or bolster, and extract any nails left in the rafter ends.

If you are replacing both fascia and soffit, the new soffit is cut and fixed first. It must be a perfect fit against the house wall, so timber slightly wider than necessary is nailed temporarily in place. A block and pencil is then used to scribe the wall's contours on to the soffit board, which is then cut and nailed into place. Next, the fascia boards are cut and nailed into place so that their lower edges protrude beneath the soffit. Joins between adjacent boards are made over a rafter end, and should be tightly butted together to prevent water penetration. The guttering can then be re-fixed.

Replacing bargeboards
You follow much the same procedure to replace bargeboards, fitting new soffits first if needed. At this point, a shaped tailpiece must be cut and nailed to the lower end of the bargeboard to fill the gap between it and the horizontal soffit behind the fascia.

Preserving the new wood
Because fascias, soffits and bargeboards are so exposed to the weather, it makes sense to try to prevent rot from getting a foothold in your newly installed wood. Use timber that has been preservative-treated by your timber merchant.

Flat roofs
Flat roofs are usually constructed of several layers of roofing felt bedded in bitumen mastic or hot bitumen and covered with a layer of chippings rolled into a further bitumen layer. Joins between adjacent sheets of felt are overlapped rather than butted, and are arranged so that joins in successive layers do not coincide causing a weakness.

If a flat roof starts to leak, pinpointing the trouble can be extremely difficult. Begin by scraping off as many of the chippings as possible, and inspect the roof for signs of splits or other damage caused, for example, by ladders standing on the roof. You may find blistering where water has penetrated beneath one or more of the felt layers; these should be slit with a sharp knife so that bitumen emulsion can be brushed underneath the edges and the felt re-stuck. The damaged patches can be cut out and a patch of new roofing felt let in, bedded in bitumen emulsion. Then in all these cases the entire roof surface should be coated with a further layer of bitumen emulsion and the chippings replaced.

Tiled roof construction

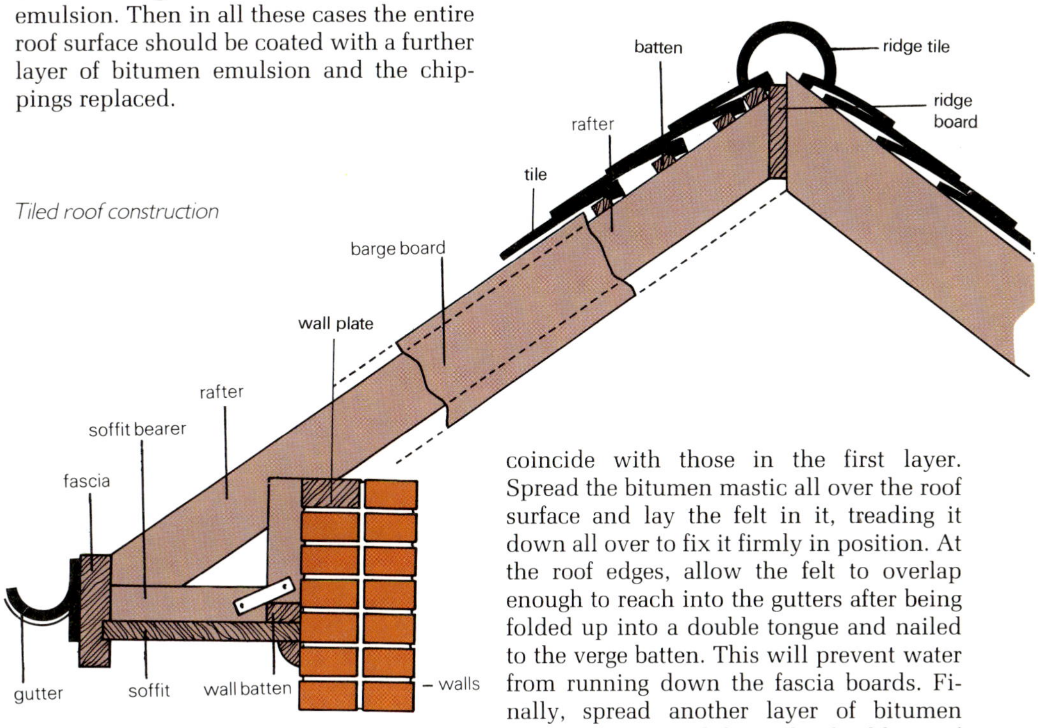

Re-covering a flat roof
If repairs and all-over waterproofing do not work, you will have to re-cover the roof. Begin by folding up flashings where the roof meets a wall, and then cut and strip all the old felt. Inspect the roof timbers beneath, replacing any that are showing signs of rot. Then lay the first strip of felt so that it just overlaps the edge of the roof above the gutters, and nail it at 150mm (6in) intervals all over. Lay succeeding strips so that they overlap by at least 50mm (2in) to complete the first layer.

Start laying the second layer at a slightly different point, so that the joins do not coincide with those in the first layer. Spread the bitumen mastic all over the roof surface and lay the felt in it, treading it down all over to fix it firmly in position. At the roof edges, allow the felt to overlap enough to reach into the gutters after being folded up into a double tongue and nailed to the verge batten. This will prevent water from running down the fascia boards. Finally, spread another layer of bitumen emulsion and tread down the third layer of felt, again avoiding coinciding seams. Finish off by folding down existing flashings or fitting new ones (see pages 152-3) and spread another layer of bitumen to hold the final layer of stone chippings.

1. *Repair a flat roof by brushing on bitumen emulsion.*

2. *Seal glazing bars of roof-lights with waterproof flashing tape.*

Guttering repairs

One of the most useful improvements in house construction in recent years has been the widespread use of plastic gutters and downpipes, which need virtually no maintenance or decoration and which are easy to install and remove. Their predecessors, mainly cast iron, can corrode away, and once cracked or broken can be difficult to repair. An inspection of your rainwater system will tell you what state of repair it is in.

Clearing blockages

At least once a year, climb up to eaves level with a trowel and bucket, and remove debris where it has collected; then take your garden hose up on the next trip and swill the whole system out thoroughly. Hose downpipes through to clear any debris that you may have allowed to fall down them while cleaning the gutters.

Repairing rainwater systems

You may find that sections of gutter have sagged because the fixings are inadequate, or because joints between lengths or components have come adrift. Sagging sections will accumulate debris, and will usually have water standing in them. With a plastic system, it will be comparatively simple to unclip the offending section, reposition the fixing brackets to restore the correct slope and clip the gutter back into place. But if you have a cast iron system you may have bigger problems. You can repair leaking joints with bituminous mastic or flashing tape, and you may be able to patch cracks or missing pieces in gutter sections in this way too. Leaks in downpipes are more difficult to repair, and you may have to dismantle the entire run to patch them. Broken and sagging gutter brackets must be replaced, and unless you want to take down the entire run you will have to use brackets that screw to the fascia board rather than the rafter ends. To position them you will have to wedge up the gutter somewhat by carefully driving strong nails into the fascia.

If you are taking down cast iron guttering, be warned: it is extremely heavy, and you should not attempt the job on your own.

Downpipes are secured by nails driven through lugs at the top of each length into the masonry, or into wooden plugs. Refix them if necessary using masonry nails fitted with retaining washers. At the bottom end of each downpipe, make sure that the shoe is undamaged and is discharging water into the gully; if it is not, you may get damp.

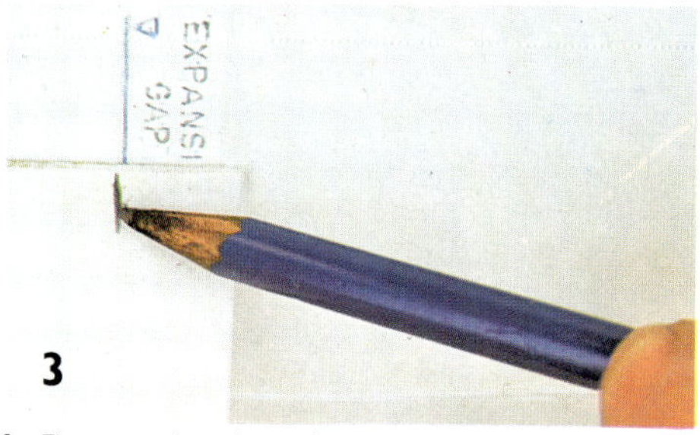

1. *Fix gutter brackets along a string line to ensure an even fall.*
2. *Check the fall with a spirit level.*
3. *Allow an expansion gap between the lengths of guttering when cutting to size.*
4. *Use a plumbline to ensure that downpipes are vertical.*

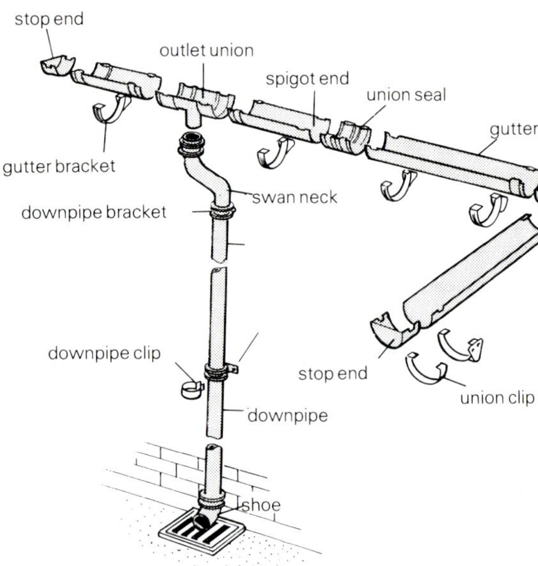

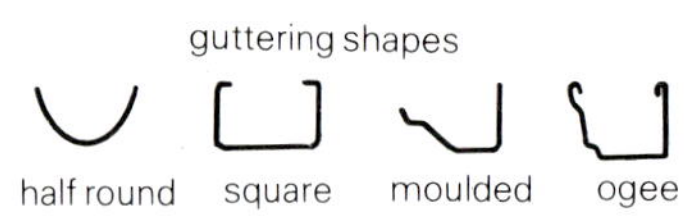

Guttering shapes and components

Putting up a new rainwater system

Modern plastic guttering systems offer a range of components that allow you to cope with every eventuality. Joints are usually made by clipping the cut ends of the gutter sections into unions containing neoprene gaskets for a waterproof join. Simple brackets support the gutters, and these must be set along the fascia to give the guttering run a slight fall towards each downpipe – a drop of about 25mm (1in) on a 3m (10ft) run. A length of string is used to align the brackets along the run, and these are then screwed into place at 1m (3ft) intervals.

Where the gutter parts join, you must allow an expansion gap of about 12mm (½in) at the union. With the guttering run completed you can put up the downpipes, fixing them at roughly 2m (6ft) intervals with clips and checking with a spirit level or plumb line that the run is vertical. A swan neck allows the pipe to reach the gutter outlet where the eaves overhang, while a shoe at the lower end discharges water into an open gully. If you are having to dig a soakaway to take water from new downpipes, take the opportunity to install a better closed back-inlet gully.

Brickwork

Although you will probably want to leave major wall repairs to a professional, there are some jobs you can do yourself.

Brickwork repairs

Even if your outside brickwork is sound, it will benefit from an occasional scrub down with a stiff broom and clean water. Mould or algae can be removed by scrubbing the surface with a mixture of household bleach and water, but a fungicide is better. Efflorescence, a surface deposit of powdery white crystals caused by water penetrating the brickwork and then evaporating and bringing dissolved salts to the surface, should be brushed off from time to time; washing it off only causes the salts to redissolve and reappear at a later date.

1

2

3

1. *You can drill out defective pointing easily with a special chasing bit.*
2. *Keyed pointing is formed with a rounded piece of metal.*
3. *Weathered pointing is formed with a trowel.*

Replacing damaged bricks
Brick is porous, absorbing moisture when the weather is wet and allowing it to evaporate when the weather is dry. On very porous bricks, water may accumulate in the brick and freeze in cold weather, causing the surface of the brick to break away or spall. Such damaged bricks need replacing.

Use a club hammer and brick bolster, cutting back until you reach the solid brick behind, in a solid brick wall. Cut a new brick in half along its length, and bed it into the hole with a thick mortar backing, so that its surface is flush with that of its neighbours. On a cavity wall one brick thick, you will have to loosen the pointing around the damaged brick, and then use a narrow cold chisel to lever it out. Where necessary, you will have to break up surrounding bricks. Then line the opening with mortar after chipping away all the old mortar, and tamp the new brick into place. In either type of wall, finish off by pointing around the new brick for a weatherproof joint.

Repointing
Even if the bricks themselves are sound, you may find that the mortar pointing between them has begun to crumble and fall out. If this is the case, use a club hammer and cold chisel or mortar rake to chop out the old pointing to a depth of about 18mm (¾in) and then brush out all the dust and debris. Soak the brickwork to stop it absorbing all the water from the new mortar. Mix up enough mortar (1 part cement to 4 parts soft sand) for about two hours' work, and start at the top of the affected area, taking mortar from a hawk to fill the crevices between the bricks. Press the mortar firmly into place, and trim off the excess roughly as you work. When you have completed a reasonable-size area go back and finish off to match the rest of the wall.

Flush pointing is left until the mortar is almost dry, and then the excess mortar is rubbed off with dry sacking. Weathered pointing is formed by drawing the edge of the trowel along the top edge of each horizontal join, and either the right-hand or left-hand edge of each vertical one – it does not matter which you choose as long as you are consistent – to leave a sloping surface to the pointing. A raked or recessed joint is scraped out with a pointed rod, while keyed pointing is given its rounded shape by drawing a dowel rod or a shaped piece of metal along the pointing. The final touch is to brush off the last traces of mortar with a stiff brush.

Rendering repairs
Rendering is a layer of mortar applied to exterior brickwork or blockwork as decoration or weatherproofing, and may be given a smooth or textured finish, or may have pebbles or fine shingle bedded in it. Once the surface begins to show cracks, moisture can penetrate and cause more widespread damage, eventually causing large areas to crumble and fall away from the masonry surface. It is therefore essential that any rendered surface is kept in good condition.

Undecorated rendering or pebbledash, however sound, soon begins to accumulate dirt and to discolour, and will benefit from an annual wash and scrub down with water and a stiff brush. Decorating with masonry paint or exterior-quality emulsion paint will enhance the looks of the surface, and will also help to protect it by sealing the surface, so preventing dirt from adhering to it so readily and also cutting down on the rate of water absorption. Small hairline cracks should be filled with exterior-quality filler before they have a chance to enlarge and allow further deteriorating.

Patching rendering

Where areas of rendering have crumbled away, you must chop out all loose material back to a sound edge before attempting a repair. Loose material should be brushed off and the wall surface damped ready for the first mortar coat, which should be applied with a float so that its surface finishes about 12mm (½in) below the level of the existing rendering. It should be scored when almost set to provide a key for the second coat. Leave the first coat to set for 24 hours, and then apply the second layer slightly proud of the surrounding surface. Draw a batten over the surface of the existing rendering and the patch to remove excess mortar, using a sawing to-and-fro motion. The surface can then be polished with a steel float if a smooth finish is required, textured to match the wall or covered with pebbles pressed into the final coat.

New rendering

If you have to re-render an entire wall the technique is broadly similar to that for patching. It is best to divide up the wall surface into bays by pinning battens the same thickness as the final rendering – usually about 20mm – to the wall surface. Make the bays a maximum of 1.5m (about 5ft) wide. Then apply the mortar in two or three layers, cross-hatching the surface between layers to provide a key for the next layer – see picture sequence.

Damp

Rising damp is moisture rising up the house walls from the ground as a result of failure in, or absence of, the damp-proof course of impervious material just above ground level. The result is a band of staining on inner walls, rising well above skirting board level in some cases, causing wallpaper to peel and adjacent timber – floors, skirting boards and so on – to rot. It can be cured only by inserting a new damp course, which can be done by one of several methods, most of which are usually professionally installed.

The first is the insertion of a new damp course of felt or slate. This is done by using a power saw rather like a chain saw to cut through the wall – usually along a mortar course. The damp course is inserted as the slot is cut, and is mortared into place. Both leaves of cavity walls must be treated.

The second method involves drilling holes in the wall at regular intervals, and injecting special chemicals which are

Applying rendering to a wall

1. *Begin by pinning battens to the wall surface to divide it up into bays and check that they are vertical.*
2. *Damp the wall and float on the first layer of rendering.*
3. *Cross-hatch the surface.*
4. *Apply the second coat of rendering.*
5. *Flick pebbles on to the wet rendering for a pebbledashed finish.*
6. *Use the float to bed the pebbles firmly in place.*
7. *At corners, work to a batten pinned to the wall for a neat finish.*

1

2

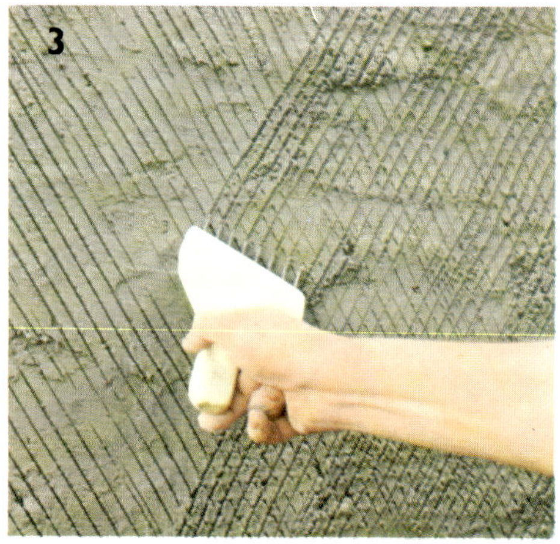
3

4

5

6

7

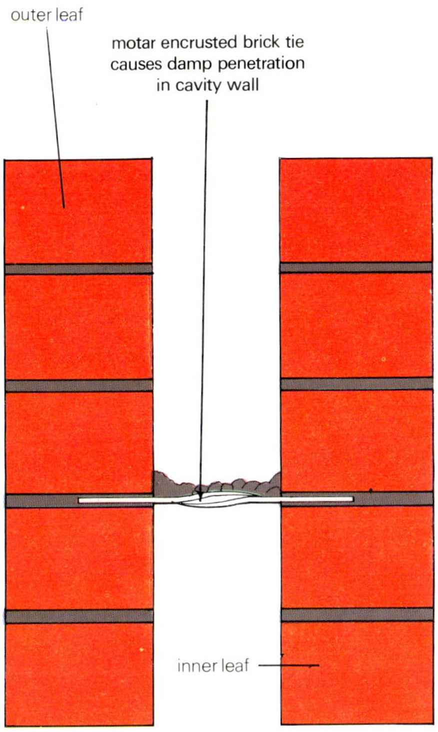

absorbed into the masonry and dry to form a damp-proof barrier. Again, both leaves of cavity walls must be treated. The fluid can either be injected under pressure, or else allowed to flow in under gravity.

The third method is called the electro-osmotic method, and involves inserting a ribbon of copper wire into the wall at the required level. This is then connected to a copper earth electrode driven into the ground. This method works because a small electrical charge is associated with the rise of water droplets up the wall, and the copper strip discharges these to earth, so preventing the droplets from rising. It is installed by damp-proofing contractors.

It is worth remembering that rising damp can also be caused by the damp course being bridged, allowing moisture to bypass it. The commonest cause of this is earth from flower beds being banked up against the house wall, but adjoining paths with their surfaces next to or even above the damp course can have the same effect, as can garden walls abutting the house wall without a vertical damp course between the two.

Solid floors should incorporate a damp-proof membrane too. If this is defective or absent, the floor surface can be sealed with a damp-resistant pitch-epoxy chemical, but this must be linked to the damp course in the walls. If this is not possible, the floor will have to be lifted and a new floor laid over a damp-proof membrane of heavy-duty, 500-gauge, polythene.

Coping with rot

Rot attacks wood in which the moisture content has risen to around 20 or 25 per cent, either because the house structure is defective and water has penetrated structural timbers or, in the case of exposed woodwork, where surface protection has broken down and the wood has become saturated. Structural timbers are particularly prone to dry rot, which can seriously weaken them, while exterior timber is usually attacked by wet rot. In the former case a professional inspection is advised to gauge the extent of the trouble, since the fungus can affect masonry as well; treatment involves cutting out and replacing all infected timber, and spraying nearby timber and masonry with special chemicals to prevent reinfection.

In the case of wet rot, minor attacks can be cured by allowing the wood to dry out, and if necessary cutting out and patching affected areas with wood filler or new wood. The use of wood preservatives on all new work will help to prevent the incidence of wet rot, but the best protection of all is to ensure that exterior woodwork is painted or varnished on all surfaces and that joints are tight and sealed with filler, so that water cannot penetrate and start an attack.

Concreting

Concrete is made by mixing together aggregates (sand, and gravel or stones) and cement with water. For most DIY jobs you can use all-in aggregates, or ballast.

There are different types of cement available but for most DIY jobs ordinary Portland cement will do. This is light grey in colour and is normally supplied in 50kg bags. It is possible to buy smaller bags when only a little is needed for small projects or repairs. Portland cement is a type, not a brand name, so provided that it is manufactured to British Standard BS12, it matters little which brand you use.

For all general purpose jobs a mix of 1 part cement to 4 parts ballast (by volume) is suitable. For footings, foundations and bases for pre-cast paving, use 1 part cement to 5 parts ballast.

Self-mix or ready-mix

The simplest way to order your materials is to tell your supplier the exact dimensions of the area to be concreted, the thickness of the slab, and the concrete mix you will be using

Putting in a new damp-proof course

1. *A powerful saw can be used to cut through the masonry so that a felt damp course can be inserted.*
2. & 3. *Damp-proofing chemicals can be injected after drilling a series of regularly spaced holes into the wall, in this case at 45° to the vertical.*
4. & 5. *An electro-osmotic damp-proof course is installed in a chipped-out mortar joint, and the copper strip is connected to an earth electrode.*

and let him calculate the number of bags of cement and the number of cubic metres of ballast required. As a rule of thumb, a cubic metre is about 25 wheelbarrow loads.

Although the ballast can be stored on a clean, firm area for any length of time, provided that it is protected from the attentions of animals and children, the bags of cement should not be kept more than a week or two in case moisture in the air penetrates the paper bags and causes hardening. Store the bags flat, under cover, on a dry surface. If they have to be kept in the open then place them on strong boards supported on bricks and covered with plastic sheeting.

The alternative to buying separate materials and mixing your own concrete is to use ready-mix. There are several specialist firms who will supply concrete in this form and their addresses can be found under 'Concrete' in Yellow Pages, and in the local press. Specify the amount of concrete required and for what it is to be used, and the supplier will agree a time for delivery.

Ready-mix has certain advantages and disadvantages. The biggest factor in its favour is that it saves a lot of time and effort in mixing the concrete. If the area you want to concrete is readily accessible to a large lorry then you could have the whole load poured straight between the formwork for spreading and levelling.

This 100 litre electric mixing machine operates from a 13 amp socket.

The main disadvantage is that, with certain firms, you will be expected to deal with the load in a restricted amount of time which means having to line up plenty of friends with wheelbarrows – especially if the concrete has to be transported a fair distance from the road. Some firms help here by agreeing to work at your pace but you must remember that a large load can be pretty exhausting to cope with.

The other way to buy concrete ready-mixed is in dry-mixed bags. This method is handy for small jobs or repair work but it is not economical for big jobs. Don't keep dry ready-mix in store for more than a couple of weeks and always store in the same way as bags of cement.

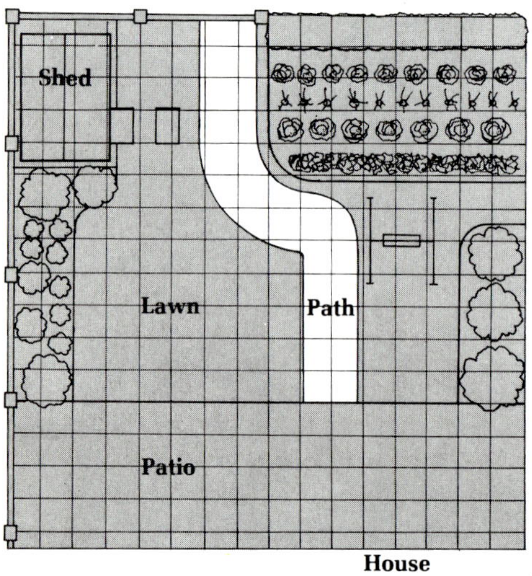

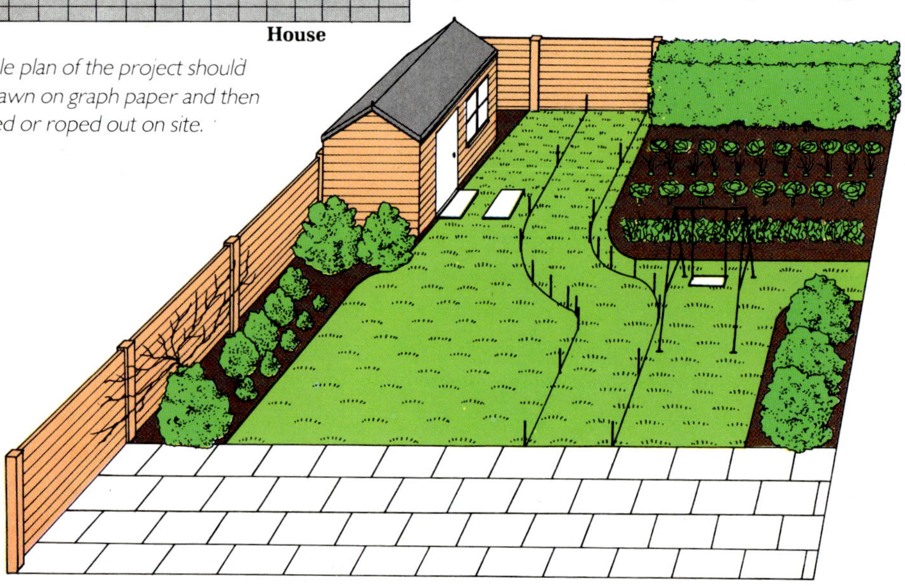

A scale plan of the project should be drawn on graph paper and then pegged or roped out on site.

Equipment

For transporting materials and laying the concrete, you will need:

Spade and fork for generally clearing the site and digging foundations.

Garden roller or punner for firming subsoil and hardcore in foundations. A punner is a home-made alternative for a garden roller. Make a square timber mould about 150×150×100mm in size and fill it with concrete. Insert a broom handle or length of pipe vertically in the mould and keep it supported until the concrete has hardened fully. Remove the timber mould and you have a heavyweight compacting tool.

Hammer, saw, straight-edge, spirit-level, tape-measure, string line and wooden pegs for setting out a level site and formwork to retain the concrete.

Builder's square for accurate marking out of right-angled corners in formwork when making a rectangular concrete base. Make one from three pieces of wood in the proportions 3:4:5; a useful size would be 450×600×750mm. Join the pieces with L-shaped metal brackets and screws. If you work accurately, the angle between the shorter sides will be 90 degrees.

Use a mixing machine for any sizeable job. For mixing small amounts of concrete by hand you will need:

Two shovels and two same-size buckets, one of each for measuring out the cement, the other for adding ballast and water to the mix and for the actual mixing.

Mixing platform or solid area available for mixing. Make a platform about 1200mm square from timber boards on battens, or from 18 or 25mm thick plywood. Add small side-pieces to keep the mix on the platform.

Sturdy wheelbarrow to transfer the materials from the storage or delivery site on to the work area. Also arrange for some strong boards if the barrow has to be pushed over soft ground or steps.

Shovel for transferring the wet, mixed concrete into the formwork (the mixing shovel can be used for this).

Rake for roughly levelling the concrete.

Tamping beam for final levelling of the concrete in the formwork. A narrow path can be levelled using a piece of 100×50mm timber on edge. A wider path or patio needs a stouter timber of 150×50mm to which strong handles have been fixed. In both cases the timber should be about 300mm longer than the width of the formwork.

Steel or wood float, or soft or coarse broom for achieving the preferred surface finish.

Polythene sheet, straw or sacking to protect fresh concrete from the harmful effects of frost or hot sun while the concrete sets.

Preparation

A job such as a base for a shed does not involve a great deal of planning. You will have found out its required dimensions and know roughly where you want it to be. However, a path, patio or drive needs more thought. It is best to make a scale plan of the project first to see how it fits with its

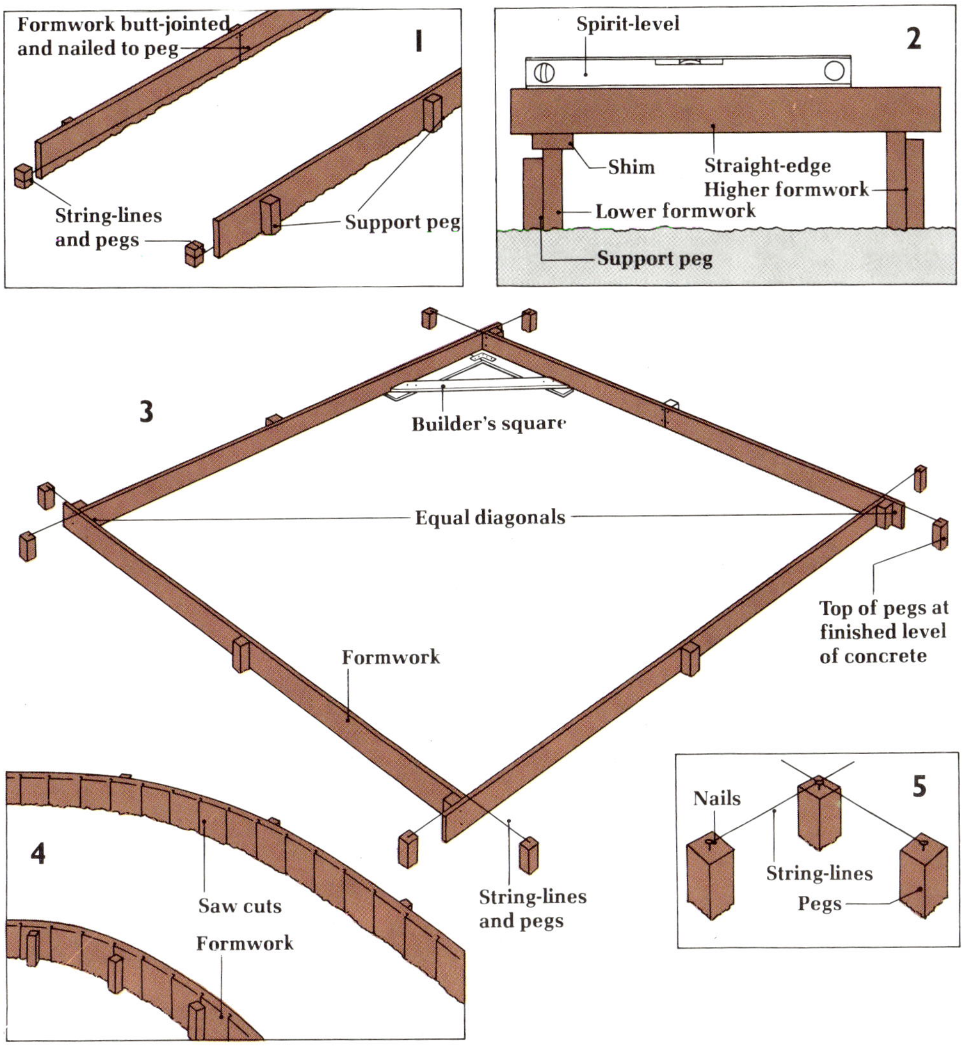

1. *Build formwork against string lines.*
2. *Shim used to set crossfall.*
3. *Cut through half thickness to curve formwork.*
4. *Setting out a rectangular area.*
Check corners with builder's square.
5. *Nail string lines to tops of pegs.*

surroundings. A curved path or an ornately shaped patio can be 'drawn' out on site using a length of string or rope or a sprinkled layer of sand.

Clear the site of all weeds and roots which are likely to cause problems later on. For most jobs the concrete can be laid directly on well-compacted ground with stones being used to reinforce any soft patches. However, on weak ground, clay or peaty soils you will need to lay a 100mm thick base of hardcore – broken bricks and stones – and compact it well with a roller or punner. Dig out the ground bearing in mind where you want the surface of the concrete to be, and take into account the thickness of any hardcore base plus the thickness of the concrete layer.

All concrete has to be laid within a formwork of strong boards which act as a mould to retain the wet concrete until it is set. The boards are left in place for about a week after concreting. Any reasonable straight-edged boards will do provided that they are at least 12 to 18mm thick. If a path needs to curve, bend formwork timbers by sawing through them at several close spacings to about half their thickness.

Setting out

A long path will first have to be defined by stretching two string lines and fixing them to pegs at each end of the site. The formwork boards can then be laid on edge, and supported by stout pegs driven into the ground so that their tops lie below the top edge of the formwork. Butt-join lengths of formwork half-way across a peg and nail through into the peg, ensuring that the nail heads are flush. All paths need a slight crossfall in order to shed rainwater so allow for this by building in a slope of about 12mm in 1m from one side to the other. To set this slope in the case of a 1m wide path, therefore, you would place a 12mm thick shim of wood on the lower formwork and use a spirit-level on a straight-edge across the shim and the other formwork. Adjust the height of the formwork to give a level reading.

A rectangular slab which is to be a base for a shed or garage, for example, has to be level. Here you would first need to set up string lines fixed to pegs, then check with a builder's square that the corners are true right-angles and with a steel tape that the diagonals are equal. When all is correct, set in the formwork timbers and check that they are level all round.

Hand mixing

Mixing concrete by hand is arduous so only do so if you are well used to tough work, and then only for small batches.

First measure out the required quantity of ballast in a bucket and pour it on to the ground or mixing platform; make a hole in the top of the heap and add the necessary amount of cement. Now turn the heap over and over with the shovel until the ballast and cement become thoroughly mixed and the heap takes on a uniform grey colour. There must be no streaks of ballast in it.

Make a crater in the middle of the heap with solid 'walls' round it. Pour some of the water into the crater – don't overdo it or the water may run out of the sides. Gradually shovel dry material from the edges of the crater on to the water and start turning the mix over and over with the shovel. Use the shovel in a chopping motion occasionally to help the mixing process. Again form a crater in the middle of the partly mixed heap, add more water and continue to mix in dry material. Keep repeating this process until the materials are well mixed together. The concrete should be easily workable but not too crumbly or sloppy. Test this by trowelling the surface with the back of the shovel – it should remain solid but moist.

If you are using a bag of dry-mixed materials then pour all the contents out of the bag before adding water to mix them together. If you want to use only part of the bag still pour the whole lot out and mix it up dry. Then shovel the unwanted material back into the bag before adding water to the remainder which is to be used. This is done because the cement in a dry-mixed bag tends to settle at the bottom so you would not get a true mixture by pouring out part of a bag.

Machine mixing

A mixing machine can be hired locally. For most jobs around the garden a mixer of 100 litres capacity is ideal. Petrol- and electrically-operated types are available. Place the mixer on site and ensure that it is level and that the wheels are chocked to keep it still. If it can be positioned alongside the formwork then the mixed concrete can be tipped directly into the formwork. The alternative is to discharge it into a wheelbarrow for taking to the formwork.

Put half the ballast and half the water into the revolving drum, let it turn over for a while then add the cement and the remainder of the ballast. This will make the mix crumbly and dryish. Next, slowly add the remainder of the water and allow it to turn over until correctly mixed. A total mixing time of about two minutes is about right. At this point the mix should fall cleanly off the blades of the mixer but shouldn't be sloppy. At first it is worth testing the consistency of each batch as described for hand-mixing.

You should never leave the mixer for a long time without cleaning it out. If you take a break, pour half the ballast and water for the next batch into the drum and leave it revolving.

Laying concrete

One problem when shovelling and levelling concrete in the formwork is that 'air pockets' may be left, especially around the edges. These cavities will eventually cause broken edges or hollows to form. So when each batch of concrete has been tipped or shovelled into the site it should be well tamped down – the heel of your boot is often the best method of ensuring that edges are well filled.

When enough concrete has been poured to fill about a metre of the formwork right across its width, use the back of a rake to leave the surface slightly proud of the top edge of the formwork – allow about 10mm for every 100mm of finished thickness. Now use the tamping timber to level off the mix with the top of the formwork; rest the tamper on the formwork and work it backwards and forwards in a sawing movement, then mix and shovel more concrete on to the site and level off this batch.

Mixing concrete by hand

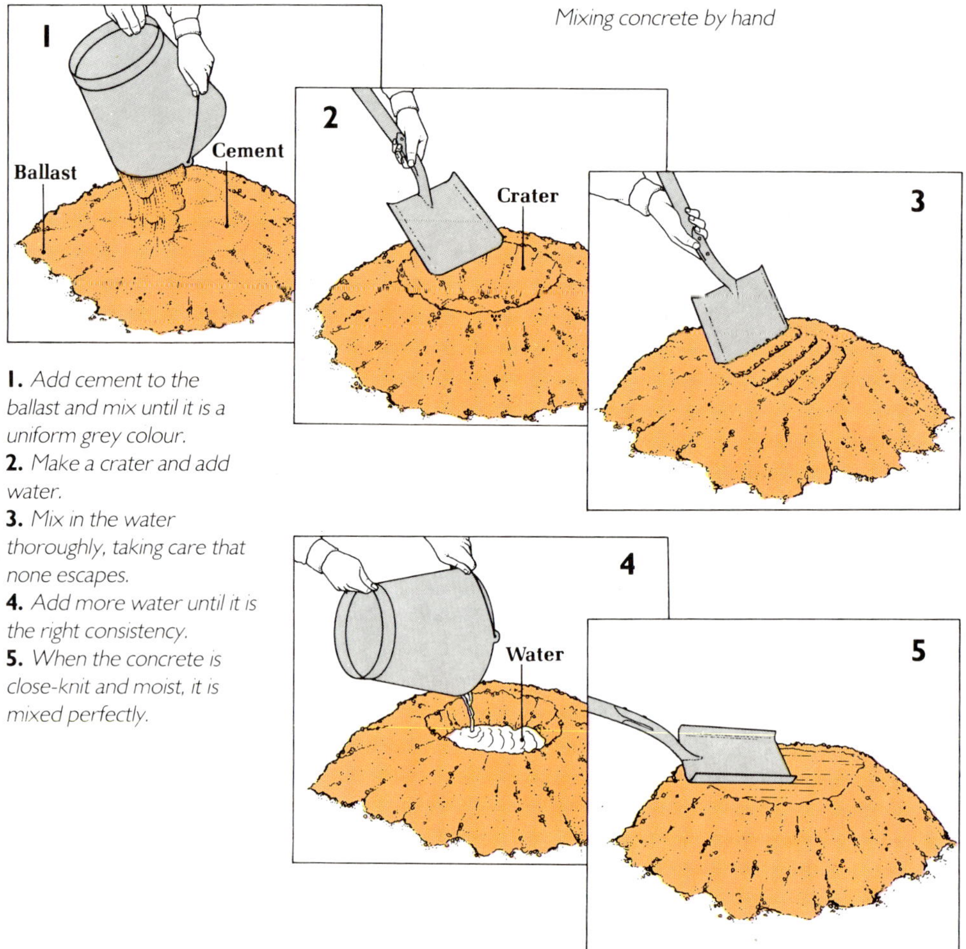

1. *Add cement to the ballast and mix until it is a uniform grey colour.*
2. *Make a crater and add water.*
3. *Mix in the water thoroughly, taking care that none escapes.*
4. *Add more water until it is the right consistency.*
5. *When the concrete is close-knit and moist, it is mixed perfectly.*

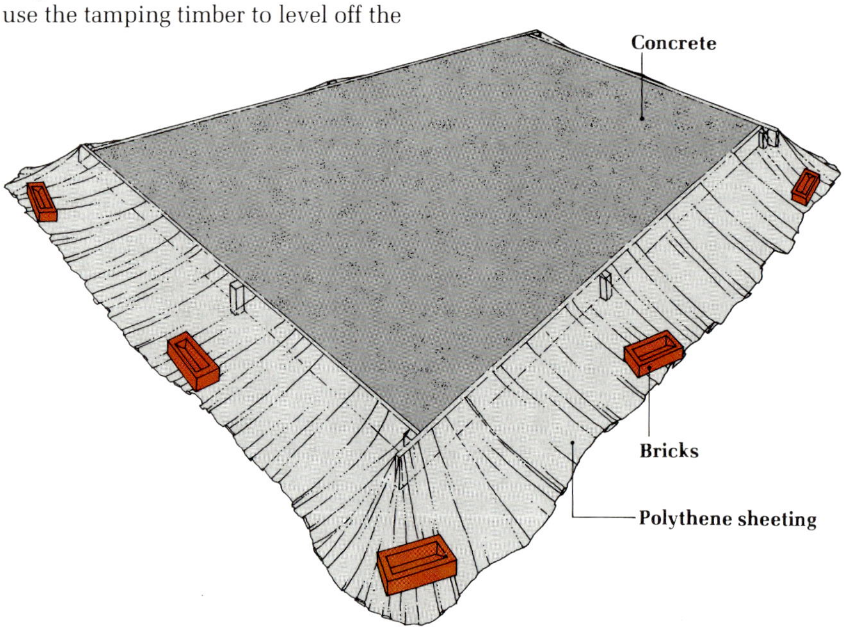

Volume (m^3)	0.5	1	2	3	4	5
1:4 mix:						
cement (50kg bags)	3½	7	14	21	28	35
Ballast (m^3)	0.5	1	2	3	4	5
1:5 mix:						
cement (50kg bags)	3	6	12	18	24	30
Ballast (m^3)	0.5	1	2	3	4	5

Finishes

Different surface finishes, smooth or wrinkled, can be achieved. After tamping, the surface will take on a sort of rippled washboard appearance.

There is a variety of brushed finishes which can be used for various effects. The results depend on the type of brush bristles used and at what stage in the setting of the concrete the work is carried out. It is a good idea to practise on a small unimportant area to get the technique right before tackling the whole job. With a narrow path it should be possible to stand on the ground alongside while working. For a wide drive, however, you will have to use a strong plank supported clear of the concrete.

For a smooth finish use a soft broom to gently brush the concrete immediately after it has been compacted. Always use the broom in the same direction. A more pronounced ripple will be formed by a nylon or stiff bass broom used immediately after compacting the concrete. The correct technique is to drag the bristles across the surface, holding the brush at a shallow

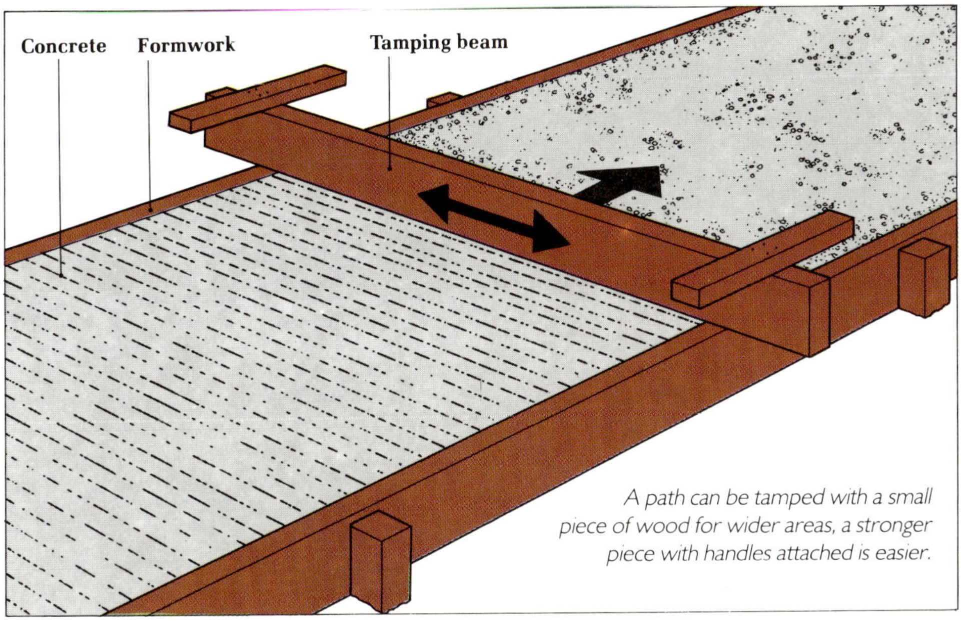

A path can be tamped with a small piece of wood for wider areas, a stronger piece with handles attached is easier.

The alternate bay method, used against walls. When these bays have set, the neighbouring bays can be concreted.

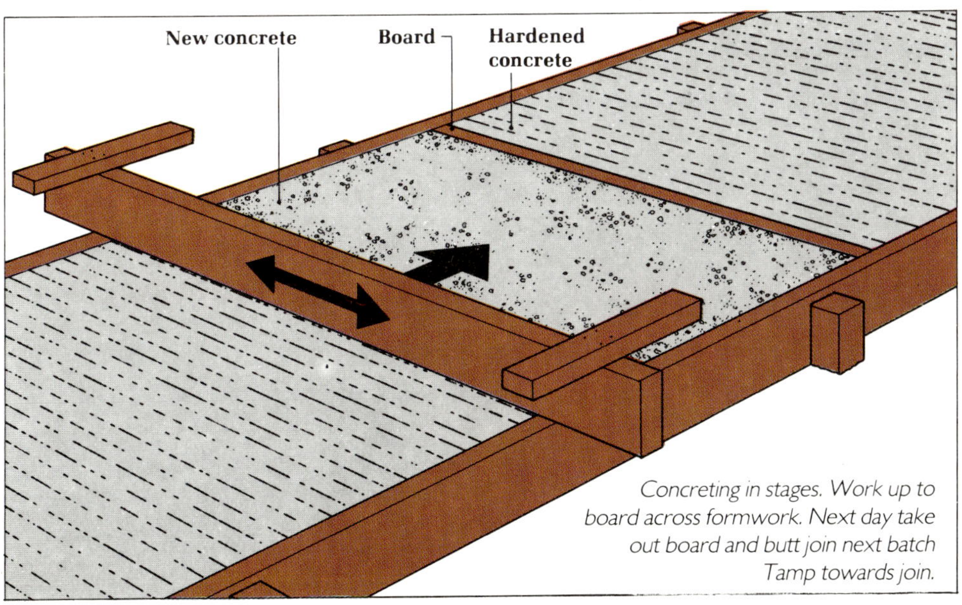

Concreting in stages. Work up to board across formwork. Next day take out board and butt join next batch Tamp towards join.

angle so that the surface is indented but not torn up.

For a textured aggregate effect, spread a thin layer of ballast on the surface after compacting and then firm it into the surface with a float. Allow the concrete to harden further until the aggregate is well gripped and then lightly spray with water and brush the surface to remove any loose material and leave the stones slightly proud of the surface. Use a stiff broom a couple of days later to finish off.

Other finishes are attainable with a float. A wood float used on fresh concrete will give a sandpaper texture. If the mix is allowed to build up on the face of the float a coarser texture will result. If the float is used in overlapping circles then an attractive 'fish-scale' appearance will develop. A steel float gives a smooth, fresh finish. As its name implies the tool should literally be skimmed or floated over the surface to avoid leaving marks. Also avoid over-vigorous trowelling of fresh, new concrete, as this will draw water on to the surface, producing a weak layer which will be prone later to dusting or surface damage. If the surface has been allowed to stiffen before steel trowelling, a very tight, hard-wearing finish will be achieved.

An unusual circular combed-finish can be made with a scrubbing brush after the back of the shovel has been 'floated' on the surface. It is also possible to create random or fixed patterns in a smooth steel-float finish which has been allowed to harden for a while. Using a pointed implement, a crazy-paving design can be drawn or a regular brick-bonding formation can be set out. The latter entails the use of a taut string-line stretched across the concrete so that an accurate line can be 'drawn' at uniform spacings.

The edge of a concrete slab will be sharp when the formwork is removed. Not only will this tend to break off easily but it could also be painful for an ankle to knock against. It is best, therefore, to round it off after the finish has been completed. Make a suitable implement for the job using a piece of sheet metal bent round a piece of rod or dowel. Run the tool along between the concrete and formwork to make the edge neat and uniformly rounded.

Protection

Unless concrete is allowed to dry out in its own time it will be weak and prone to damage. Hot sun will cause rapid drying, leading to shrinkage cracks; frosty conditions can freeze concrete, causing cracks.

As soon as the surface of the concrete is hard enough not to be marked it should be protected from extreme elements. In hot weather cover it with a blanket of polythene sheeting or hessian sacking. Weight down the material at the edges to stop wind

Paving in a variety of colours, shapes, finishes and sizes. Half-hexagons are of two shapes, shown with edging stones.

blowing underneath it. Tape joints between plastic sheets and sprinkle the sheets with sand to prevent them ballooning in gusty weather. Hessian sacking must be kept damp by sprinkling it with water. Whichever method is used, leave it in place for about three days.

You should only concrete when there is no danger of frost. If it is unavoidable, however, cover the surface with a layer of straw, retained by polythene sheeting or a sprinkling of earth or sand.

Paving slabs

Choose your paving according to type of construction, colour, surface finish, shape, and size. Hydraulically pressed slabs are about 37mm thick and are strong enough to support the weight of a car provided that they are laid properly. Cast concrete slabs are about 50mm thick and are heavier but their method of construction makes them weaker and suitable for paths and patios subject only to foot traffic.

Sizes and finishes

Paving slabs are available in a good range of colours so there should be something to suit all tastes. There are four common surface finishes. Smooth slabs have a non-slip finish; textured slabs have a relief surface and the aggregate in the surface is exposed; patterned slabs have a surface giving decorative brick, tile or cobblestone effect; riven looks like naturally split stone.

Most slabs are square or rectangular but there are circular, hexagonal and other geometric shapes available. Sizes of slabs vary. A popular size is 450×450mm because this can be easily handled, but sizes from 675×450mm down to 225mm square are also available. It is best to stick to one manufacturer's range when choosing your slabs – mixing ranges can cause problems as some are made to metric dimensions and others to imperial sizes. Most ranges, however, will be made to a standard module size, normally 225mm, so that slabs of different sizes can be combined to make patterns.

The slabs may have squared or slanting edges. The latter type automatically provide uniform joint lines after laying which are intended to be filled with mortar. Square-edged slabs are intended to butt up closely so obviating the need to fill joints. They can be laid with a gap of about 8 to 10mm which is later filled with mortar.

Planning on paper

Especially where an ornate-shaped patio or

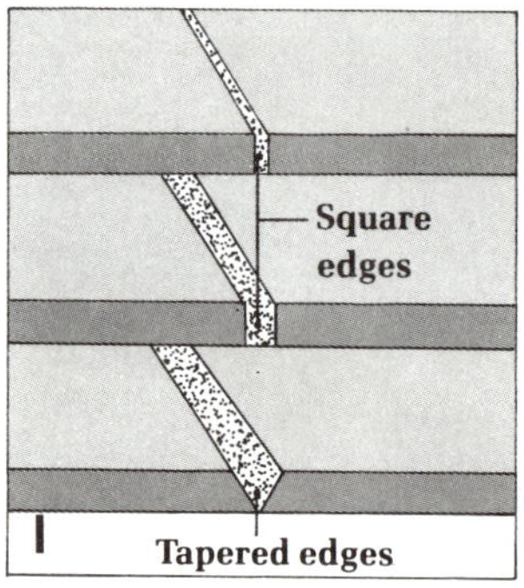

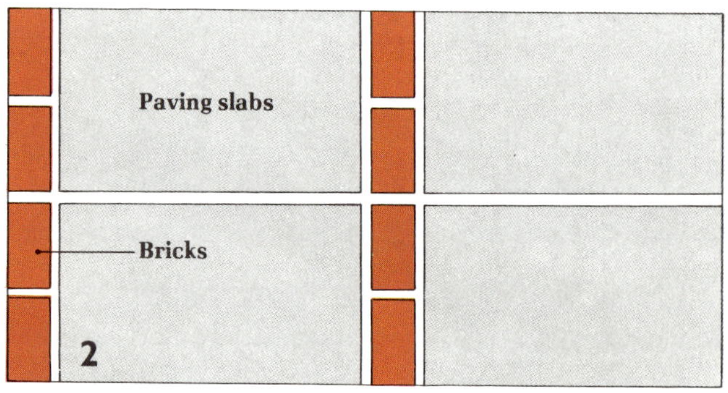

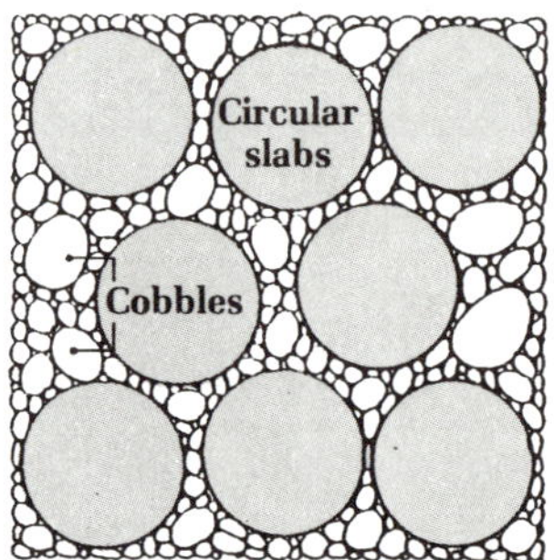

3

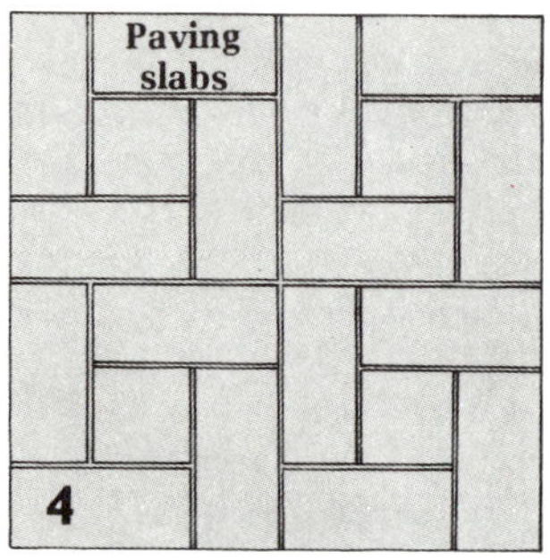

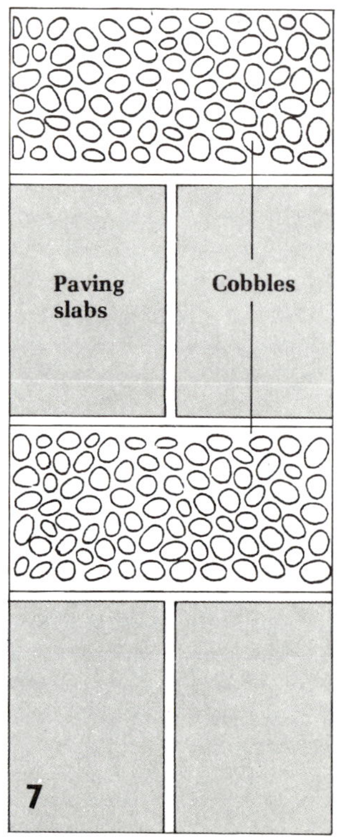

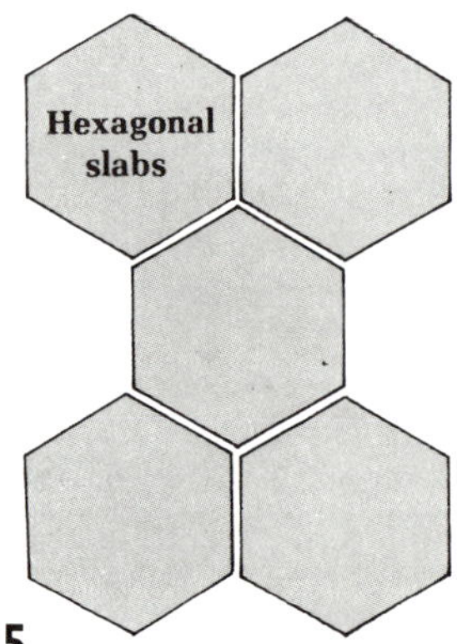

5

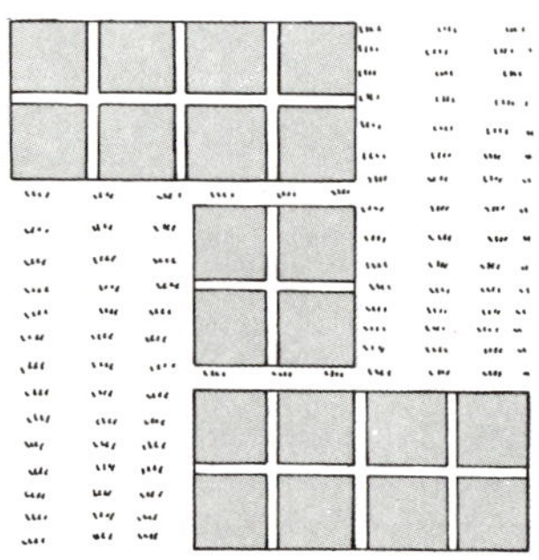

1. *Different edge patterns.*
2. *Alternating paving slabs and bricks.*
3. *Using circular slabs with cobbles.*
4. *Combining square and rectangular slabs.*
5. *Hexagonal slabs.*
6. *Making a pattern across a lawn.*
7. *Alternating slabs and cobbles.*

drive is being laid, it is best to plan the project carefully on graph paper. Having selected a range of slabs and noted the sizes available it is then easy to create an accurate plan showing the exact number of slabs and sizes needed. Where a multi-coloured design is required, make use of coloured pencils to reproduce the final effect and so avoid the design becoming gaudy and overbearing. Try to design the project to full size slabs to avoid having to make lots of cuts. If you do have to include a lot of part-sized slabs then the job is going to be more time-consuming. You should order a few extra slabs to allow for breakages while cutting. Most manufacturers offer suggestions for patterns in their brochures and one of these might appeal.

When the slabs are delivered you will have to carry them to the storage area yourself. Be careful when handling them since even individually they are awkward and heavy. Stack them on edge in a row on a hard surface and leaning against a solid wall. Ensure that the row is stable.

Preparing foundations

It is important to provide firm and level foundations. Strip away any vegetation and topsoil and replace it with well-rolled hardcore topped with a layer of ballast. When laying a driveway, dig down to a depth of 100 to 150mm; the shallower depth is suitable for firm, gravel soil and the deeper one for soft clay. For a path or patio you need only dig down to a depth of 75 to 100mm.

Roll or ram the site soil until it is firm before adding hardcore. Place larger pieces of hardcore at the bottom of the layer and spread smaller pieces on top. Finally, spread a layer of ballast over the surface and roll or tamp it down to compact the foundation work thoroughly.

You must always take into account the house damp-proof course (DPC) when laying a path, drive or patio which butts up to the wall. The surface layer should be at least 150mm below the DPC. This might mean having to dig down a little further when excavating for foundations. It is also important to ensure that the paving is laid to a slight fall away from the house so that rainwater drains readily away. A fall of about 25mm in 3m is sufficient.

Laying slabs

First set out taut string-lines tied to pegs as a guide to laying the edge slabs in straight lines and to the correct fall away from the house. Lay each slab on a 'box' of mortar; with larger (over 450mm square) slabs lay an extra band in the middle. If the paving has to support the weight of a car then spread an overall layer of mortar about 25mm thick under each slab. Use a mortar mix of 1 part cement to 5 parts sharp sand. Position each slab carefully on the mortar and, where it is intended to use definite joints, leave a gap of about 8 to 10mm. Uniform joints can be maintained by using pieces of wood as spacers.

Tap down each slab using the shaft of a club hammer or similar implement until it is level, at the same height as neighbouring slabs and shows no tendency to rock about. When all the paving has been laid, the joints should be filled with a dryish, crumbly mortar. Press this well into the joints, keeping it clear from the surface of the slabs. Only do this job when the slabs are dry and do make sure any surplus mortar is brushed away before it rains.

Cutting to fit

When you need to cut a slab, first mark the cutting line by scratching the slab with an old sharp tool held against a straight-edge. Lay the slab on a bed of moist sand and cut a shallow groove using a bolster chisel and club hammer. An alternative is a masonry-cutting disc fitted to a circular power-saw. Whichever method is used, ensure that the score line goes all round the slabs, including the edges.

Lay the slab face downwards on a timber batten and tap along the score line with the club hammer to make the break. Alternatively, work continuously with the bolster chisel and club hammer.

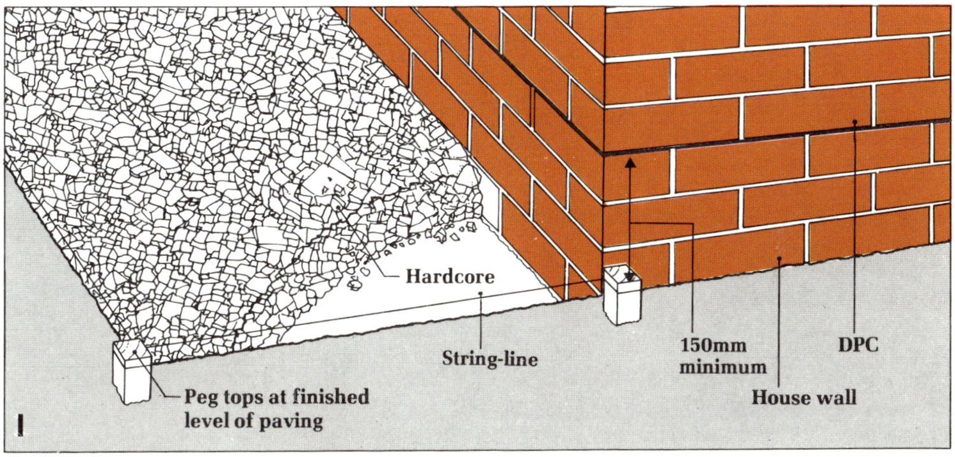

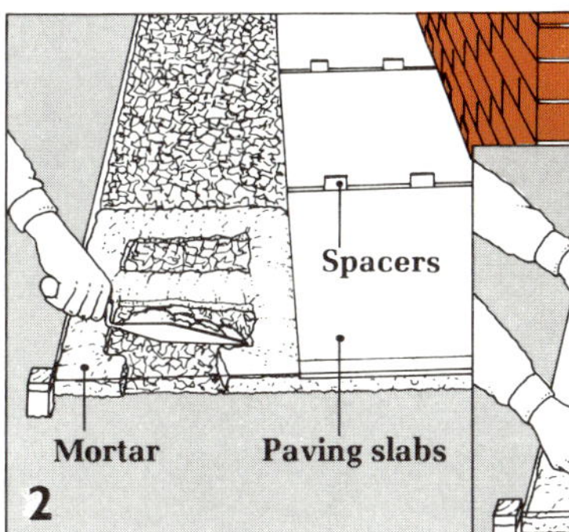

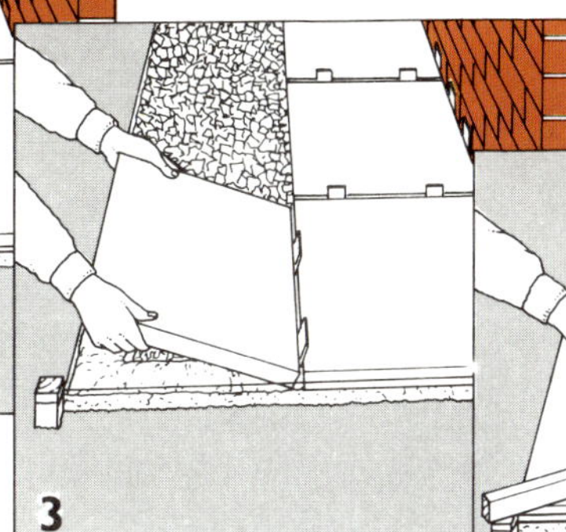

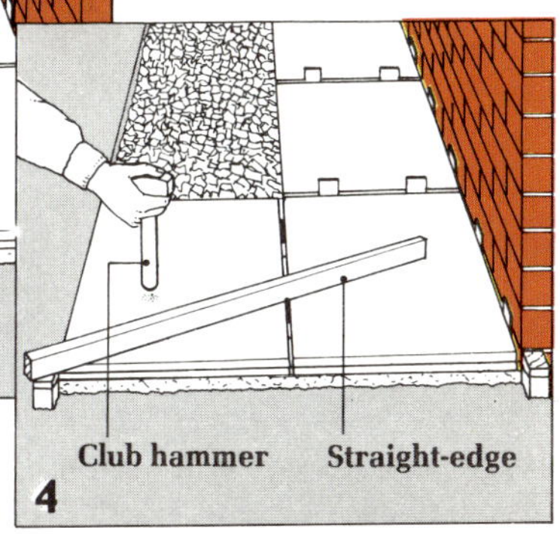

1. *Hardcore foundation.*
2. *Spreading mortar.*
3. *Positioning slab.*
4. *Tamping down.*
5. *Scoring cutting-line.*
6. *Cutting with bolster.*

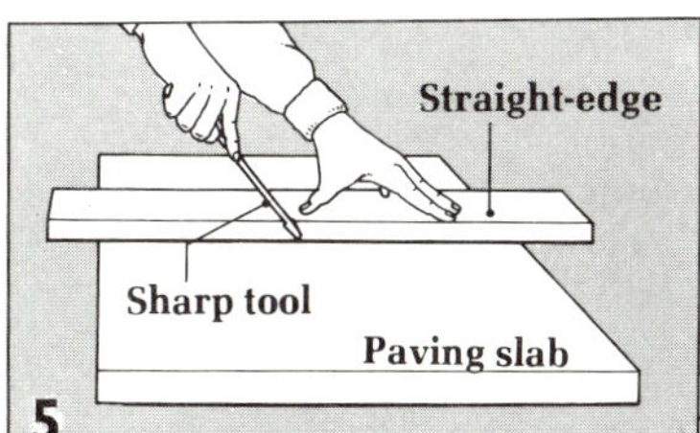

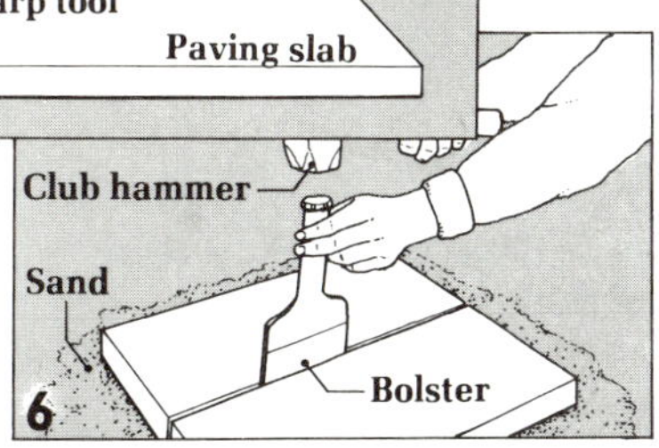

Stacking slabs.

Brickwork

When you look around you will see that there are many different types and colours of bricks available. A visit to a large stockist or a browse through a catalogue will enable you to choose something suitable. For garden walls you will probably want to choose a 'facing' brick which has an attractive decorative face and colour. The alternative here is to use second hand bricks.

All bricks are sold in one size – 225×112.5×75mm. This is a nominal size since a brick is in fact 10mm shorter on each dimension. The 10mm is a 'built-in' allowance for mortar joints. It is therefore easy to calculate the exact number of bricks needed for a project.

The V-shaped indentation present in many bricks is called the frog. Generally speaking, bricks are laid with the frog uppermost since this allows for the mortar to lie in the brick and so produce a stronger bond, although, in fact, the frog exists only as a result of the manufacturing process.

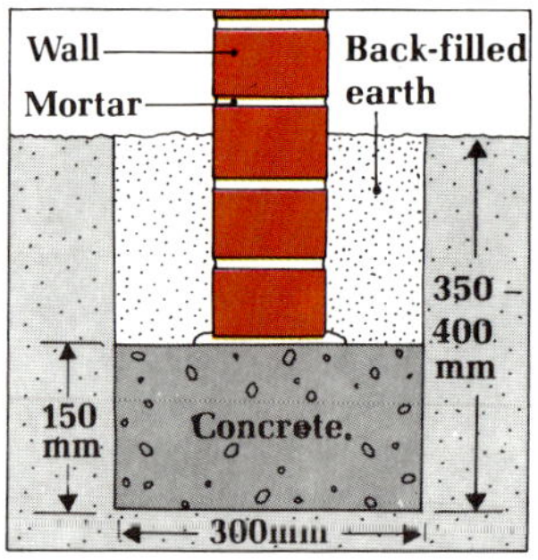

1

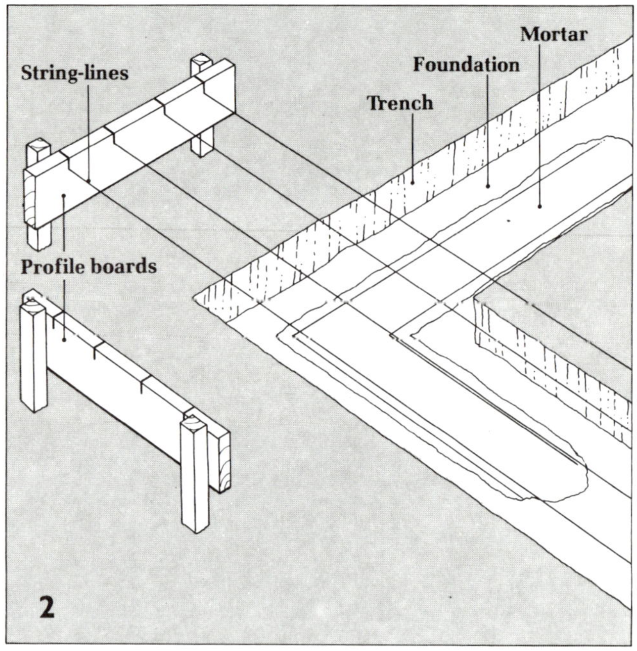

2

1. Foundation for a half-brick wall. Backfill the trench on both sides of the wall when the mortar has set hard.
2. Profile boards and string lines mark the line of the trench (outer strings) and wall (inner strings).

Mortar

For general bricklaying the mortar is made from 1 part Portland cement to 1 part hydrated lime to 6 parts clean sand. Where a wall needs to be stronger to withstand the elements, a mix of 1 part Portland cement to 3 parts sand is used. This mix should also be used for brickwork below ground level. A small amount of liquid plasticiser added to the mix will make it more workable. Also available are dry mortar-mixes in handy-sized bags, and these are especially useful for smaller jobs. The materials are in exact quantities ready for mixing with water. A 50kg bag is enough for 60-70 bricks.

However you make mortar, aim for a stiffish consistency – sloppy mortar will not support the weight of a brick. Mortar goes off in about an hour – less in hot weather – so only mix up small amounts at a time.

Every wall, whatever its height, must be built on firm, level foundations. Hard and fast rules about foundation depths are difficult to make since soil conditions vary; clay in particular is likely to cause seasonal movement so here a minimum foundation depth should be 900mm. If you find it difficult to analyse whether your soil is firm or weak then err on the cautious side and go deeper.

As a general guide for a small wall up to 1m high the following can be applied:
For a 215mm thick wall (two skins of brick) lay 230 mm of concrete in a 500mm wide trench at least 500mm below ground level. For a half-brick wall (single skin of brick) lay 150mm of concrete in a 300mm wide trench, 350 to 400mm below ground level. The concrete for foundations should be a mix of 1 part cement to 5 parts ballast.

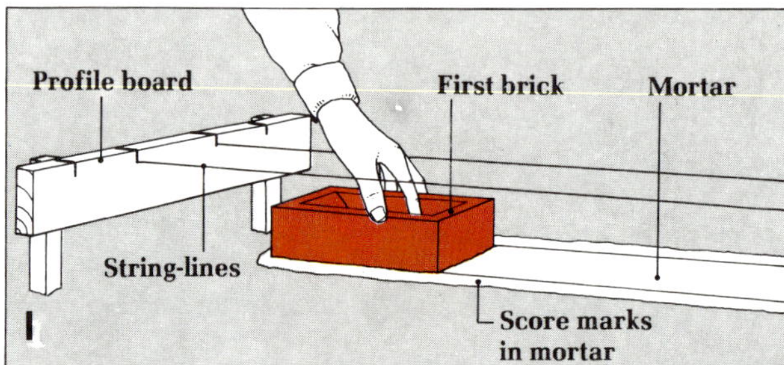

1

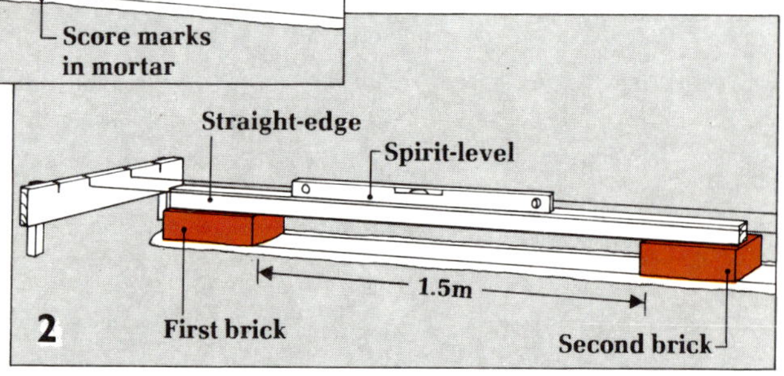

2

Laying first course:
1. Mark position of inner string lines in mortar and position first brick.
2. Position second brick 1.5m away and check it is level with first one.

Preparing the site

Set out the site by putting up profile boards at each end of it and well back from the trench. Cut notches in the top edge of each board and stretch string lines between them to represent the thickness of the wall and the width of the trench. It makes life a lot easier if the length of the wall is built to exact brick dimensions – this minimises cutting.

Dig the trench and drive timber pegs into the bottom. The tops of the pegs must be at the proposed surface-level of the concrete and should therefore be made level with a timber straight-edge and a spirit-level. Lay the concrete, compact it thoroughly and allow it to harden for at least four days before starting to build the wall.

Bonds

A wall relies on the way the bricks are bonded for its strength. The vertical joints between bricks in adjacent courses must not coincide either on the face of the wall or across its thickness. There is a variety of possible bonds. A half-brick wall up to 1m high can be built in stretcher or open bond. You should bond in piers (328×215mm) at the ends of the wall and at a maximum of 1.8m centres. A 215mm wall can be built using either English or Flemish bond. Careful cutting is needed at junctions and corners to avoid continuous vertical joints through two or more courses of brick.

Laying bricks

Having mixed up some mortar on a clean board close to where you intend laying the bricks, transfer some to the mortar board. Start at one end of the foundation trench and spread a 15mm thick layer of mortar on the concrete. The mortar should lie between the inner profile lines. The first course of bricks is the most critical as it governs the line and level of the whole wall.

Place the first brick on the mortar and check it is horizontal using the spirit-level. Next lay a second brick 1.5m or so away from the first and check that the two are level by laying the spirit-level on the straight-edge across them. If necessary, use the handle of the trowel to tap down 'high' points of the second brick until the bubble in the spirit-level shows horizontal. Complete the bottom row of bricks, buttering some mortar about 10mm thick on the end of each brick before laying it. Ensure that it is straight and level with the first two bricks. When you come to the second brick laid, you may have to reposition it but by this time you will have a length of horizontal brickwork to use as a datum.

Next build up the ends or corners of the brickwork to about six courses so that a stepped formation is reached. Use the gauge rod as a guide to the uniformity of vertical courses and also use the spirit-level as a check that the end of the wall and its outer or inner face is vertical. If the gauge rod increments coincide with the top of each brick all is well.

With the ends of the wall complete, the centre can be bricked in. Attach the string line and pins into the joints at each end of the second course and use this as the guide to placing the bricks. Transfer the line to the course above as work proceeds. On a long wall the line may tend to sag in the centre. If so, a small metal device called a tingle can be used to support the line in the centre.

Spread the mortar along three or four bricks in the previous course at a time and more on to one end of each brick before it is laid. On a hot day in particular it pays to dip each brick in water before it is laid to make the mortar stick. As each brick is laid and tapped down, surplus mortar will squelch from beneath it. Remove this straight away by drawing the edge of the trowel along the bottom edge. When a course of bricks is complete, shape the joints using a pointing trowel or draw a small rounded piece of metal through the mortar to give it a concave appearance. An old bucket handle is handy for this or you can buy an inexpensive tool designed for the job.

Where a corner is reached the return wall can be treated as an entirely separate construction. Just check that the corners are truly horizontal and vertical.

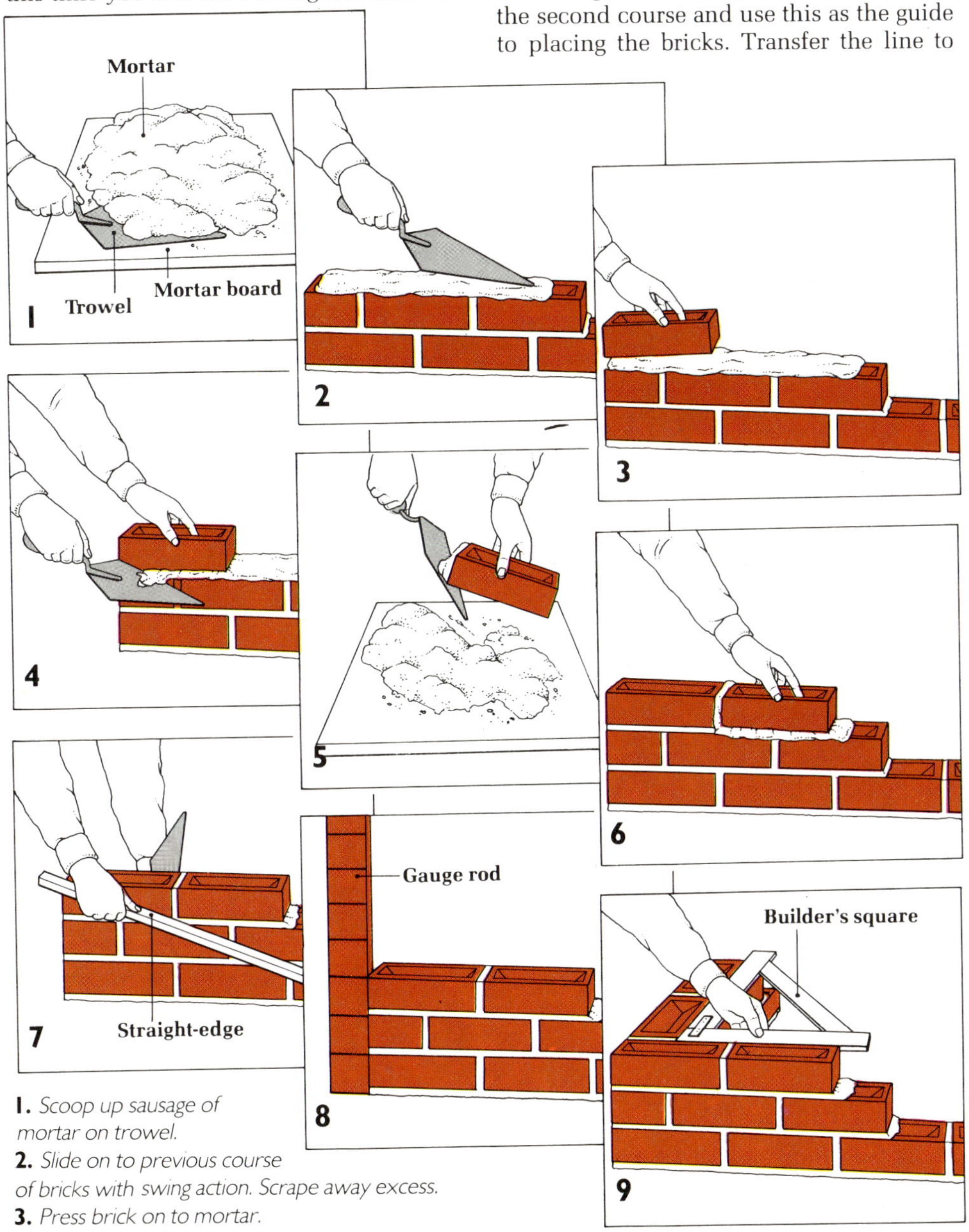

1. Scoop up sausage of mortar on trowel.
2. Slide on to previous course of bricks with swing action. Scrape away excess.
3. Press brick on to mortar.
4. Scrape away further excess mortar.
5. Butter mortar on to end of next brick.
6. Place brick, ensuring uniform joints.
7. Check horizontal and vertical level and face alignment of each brick laid.
8. Use gauge rod to check vertical courses.
9. Check corners with builder's square.
10. Mark cutting line on brick with chalk.
11. Cut groove on all faces with bolster chisel.
12. Place on bed of sand and break with sharp blow.

Cutting bricks

If you have chosen a bond that necessitates cutting a brick then do so as follows. First mark the line of the cut with chalk. Use a sharp brick-bolster and club hammer to cut a groove on all faces of the brick. Place the brick on a smooth bed of sand and place the edge of the bolster in the groove. A single sharp tap from the hammer on the bolster handle should result in a clean cut.

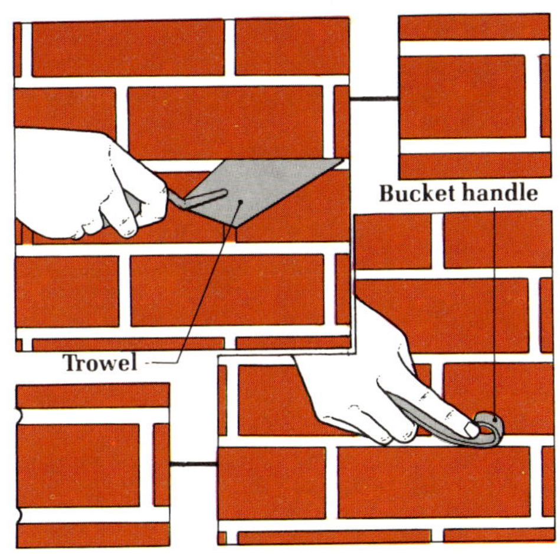

Flush joint formed with trowel. Bucket handle forms recessed joint.

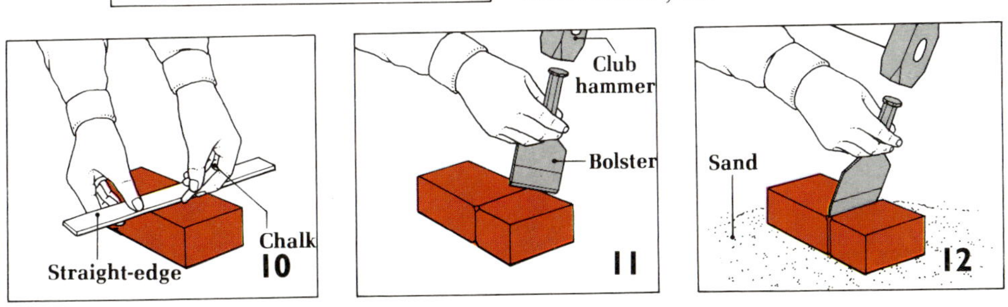

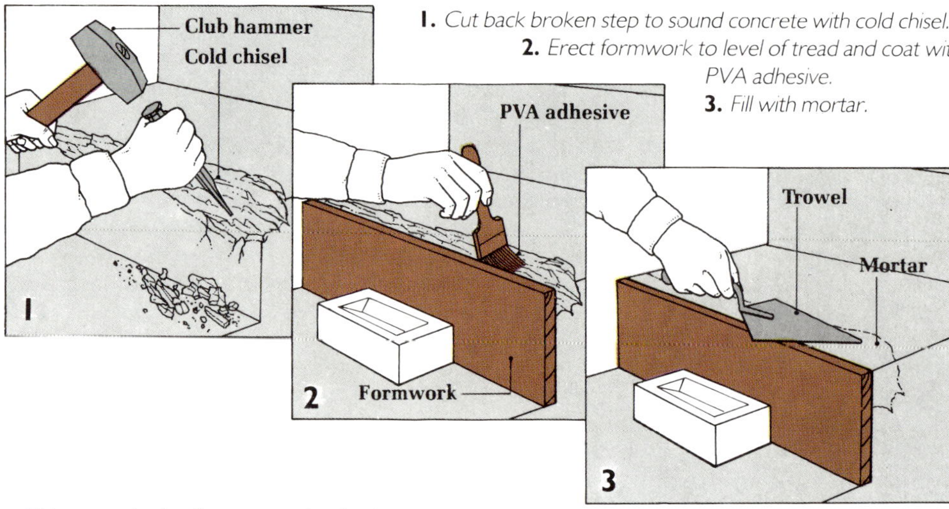

1. *Cut back broken step to sound concrete with cold chisel.*
2. *Erect formwork to level of tread and coat with PVA adhesive.*
3. *Fill with mortar.*

Concrete repairs

Repairs to concrete are easy to conceal, provided that you take care to match the finish to the existing surface texture.

Cracks

The occasional crack in a concrete path can occur for various reasons and it is simple to fill in the damage. However, where there are numerous cracks and depressions the cause is likely to be poor foundations in which case there is little alternative but to break up the concrete and start again from scratch.

For an occasional crack use a mix of 1 part cement to 3 parts sand or buy a suitable bag of dry-mixed cement mortar. In either case it is well worthwhile adding a little PVA adhesive to the mix; this acts as a bonding agent to ensure a firm grip between the old and the new concrete. Check the manufacturer's instructions for exact details for using the adhesive.

Use a cold chisel and club hammer to undercut the crack – this forms it into an inverted 'V' shape with the point of the 'V' at the surface. The filling material will then be well anchored. Clean all dust from the crack and then brush a coat of diluted PVA adhesive on to the crack to serve as a primer. Provided that the repair mix is on the dry side it will be easy to pack it down well into the crack and to level it off with the surface. Sometimes a steel float makes it easier to leave a level finish.

Holes

Holes in the surface are mostly found near cracks. They can be caused by weak foundations too (if there are several the concrete mix may have been too weak). Repair them as for cracks.

Crumbling edges

These are often caused by removing the formwork before the concrete was fully hardened. Another possibility is that the concrete mix was not pushed well down into the edges, leaving an air pocket below the surface.

Break up the crumbling edge with a cold chisel and club hammer, going back to firm material. Remove loose material and tamp down the foundations, adding new hardcore if needed. Set up a formwork alongside the repair (see page 161) and brush PVA adhesive on to the exposed edge. Mix up a batch of 1 part cement to 5 parts ballast (or use a bag of dry-mix) and add a little PVA adhesive. Press the mix well down into the edge of the formwork. Allow four weeks before removing the formwork.

Depressions

Hollows where puddles form can be filled successfully only if they are more than about 12mm deep. If less than this, the area will have to be broken up and relaid. Repair the hollow using the mix and techniques specified for cracks. Formwork is needed if the edge of the concrete is affected.

Brickwork repairs

If a zig-zag crack runs through the mortar between a couple of bricks in the top courses of a low wall then it is simple to tap away the affected bricks, clean off the old mortar and rebuild the wall using the same mortar and techniques described on page 167. A loose brick or two can be treated similarly. However, problems such as extensive vertical cracking through courses of bricks, a leaning wall or detachable movement mean totally rebuilding the wall.

Steps

To resurface a step it is first necessary to provide a key for the new mortar by scoring the surface using a bolster chisel and club hammer. Next erect formwork to a slight fall and 12mm above the old surface. Coat the step with diluted PVA adhesive and fill with a mortar mix of 1 part cement to 3 parts sand. Finish with a wood float for a non-slip surface.

Crumbling edges are filled by chipping away the broken concrete with a cold chisel, erecting formwork to the level of the surface, coating with PVA adhesive and filling with mortar as above.

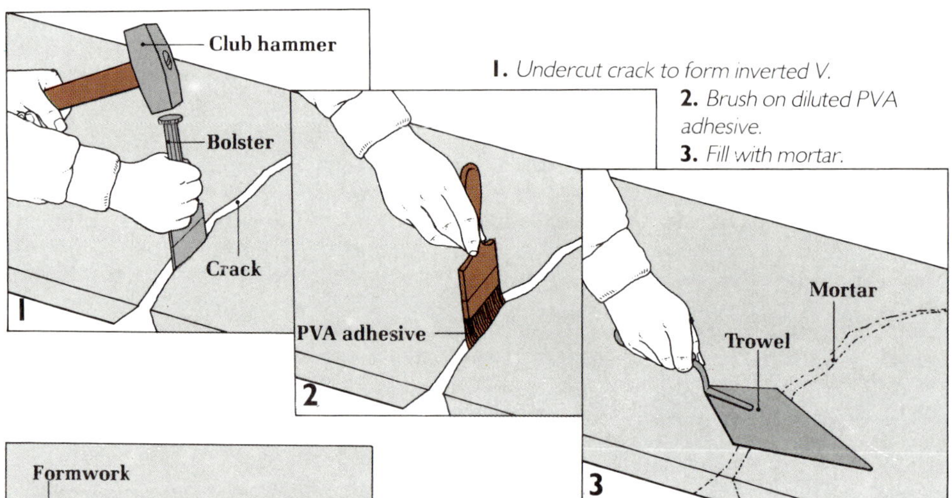

1. *Undercut crack to form inverted V.*
2. *Brush on diluted PVA adhesive.*
3. *Fill with mortar.*

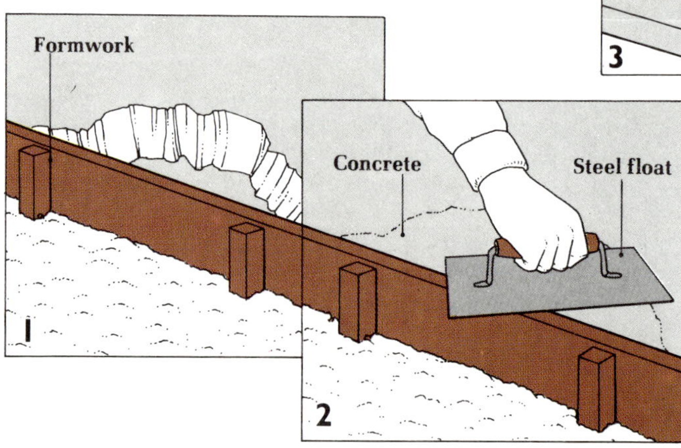

1. *Break up crumbling edge back to firm concrete, remove debris and erect formwork.*
2. *Fill with concrete and texture surface as existing finish.*

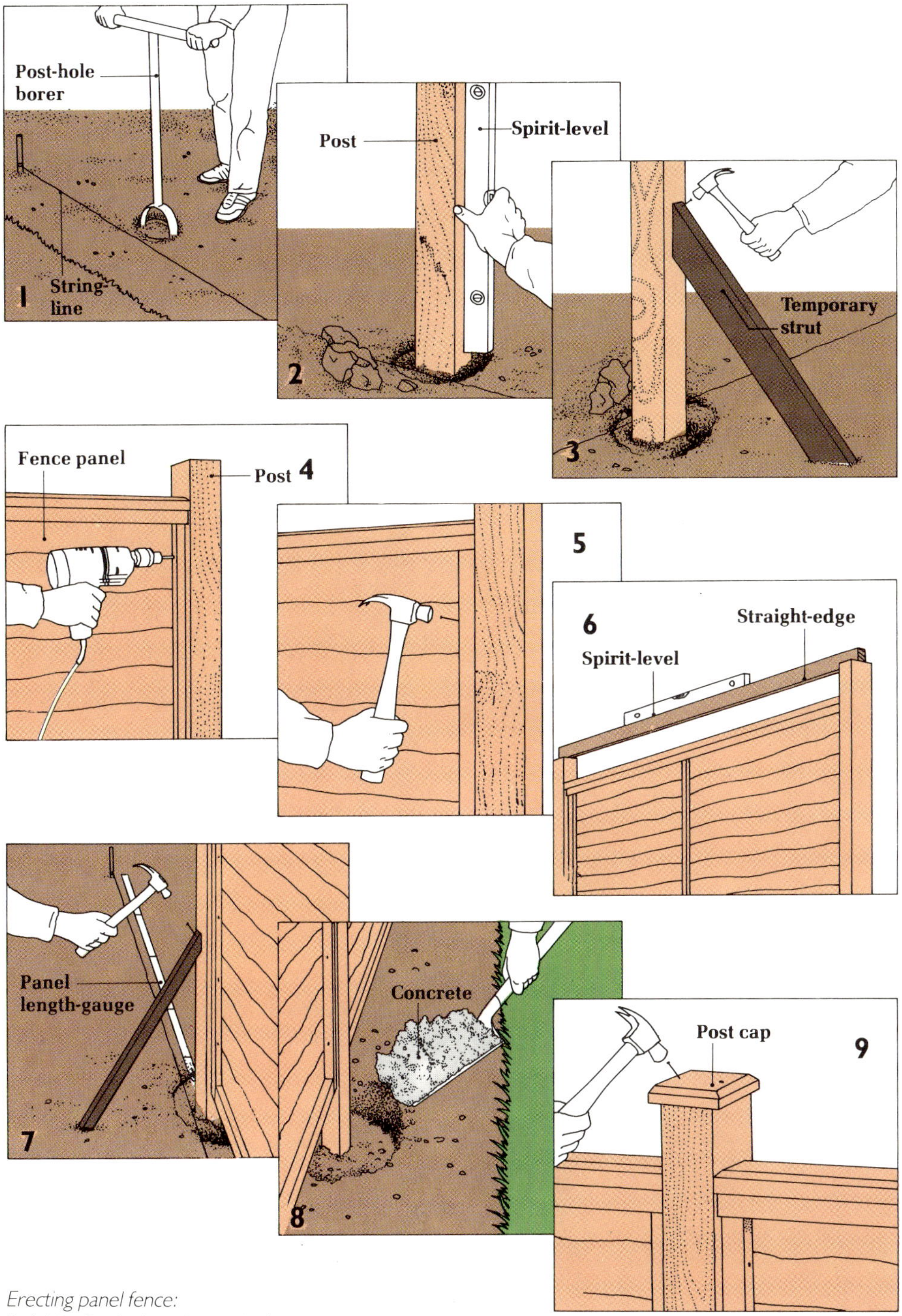

Erecting panel fence:
1. *Make first hole with post-hole borer adjacent to string-line.*
2. *Insert post and wedge in vertical position with rubble.*
3. *Support post with temporary angled strut nailed to it.*
4. *Hold panel in position and drill holes in end-rail for fixing nails.*
5. *Nail to post with galvanised nails.*
6. *Erect next post and check post tops are level using spirit-level.*
7. *Support post with strut and mark out next hole position with gauge.*
8. *Nearly fill holes with rubble and top off with dryish concrete mix.*
9. *When concrete has set, protect posts with timber caps.*

Start by stretching a string line where you want to erect the fence. Sturdy timber pegs at each end will keep the line in place. If, for example against a wall, there would be no room for one of the pegs when the first post was erected, remove the peg and tie the string line to the post instead.

Fences

Posts in holes

The traditional way to put up fence posts is to dig the holes for them. The best way is to use a post-hole borer which makes a smaller and neater hole than digging with a spade. Post-hole borers can be hired and in this case it is a good idea to make all the holes before setting in any posts, in order to keep the hire period as short as possible. Use a piece of wood the length of a panel as a gauge to ensure that the holes are the correct distance apart.

Make the holes slightly deeper than actually necessary so that each post can be stood on a brick as this will help to reduce rotting. Hold each post so that it is square to the line of the fence and vertical in both directions. Put a straight batten across the post tops to ensure that all posts are set into the ground an equal amount. Put additional packing pieces under those which are too low. Hold each post in place by ramming bricks and rubble into the hole. While the rubble is being added, the posts can be temporarily strutted with lengths of timber at an angle.

Post supports

To save making post holes metal post supports can be used. Some types have a tilt-and-turn adjustment which is useful for getting the posts exactly vertical after the post support has been driven into the ground. With the non-adjustable type great care has to be taken to ensure that the support is driven accurately into the ground. There is a driving tool with a tommy-bar handle which makes this task much easier. When the metal post support is in the ground the post is dropped into the socket and the clamp bolts are tightened.

Erecting panels

Once the first post is positioned, the panel is lifted into place and is wedged up on bricks so that its top is perfectly level. With a helper supporting the free end, the panel is fixed to the post using 75mm galvanised nails. Drill holes in the panel end-rails to prevent the nails from splitting the wood. Drill three holes on each side of the panel, and at each end. Alternatively, the panels can be fixed with panel clips which are simply screwed to the posts and panels.

The next post is then placed in its hole and held against the fixed panel. It is wedged vertically and then the panel is nailed to it before another panel is positioned. The process is continued to the end of the fencing run.

Grooved concrete posts

More permanent, but perhaps not so attractive in a garden setting, are grooved concrete posts. The panels simply slot into the grooves on top of gravel boards. The posts should be spaced at centres equal to the length of the fence panel plus the thickness of the post between the bottoms of the grooves, and should be set in concrete. One disadvantage is that the posts are very heavy to handle.

Maintaining fences

Prevent attack and prolong the life of a fence by treating it at least every other year with a good quality, branded wood-preservative which will be more effective than the cheaper creosote. Treat the fence when it is dry. Cover the ground beside it with plastic sheets and also cover any nearby plants to protect them from the preservative which is harmful to them. There is a new, water-based preservative stain which is harmless to plants, but this is only suitable for treating wood which has been previously treated with preservative. Apply the preservative with a brush in a good, flowing coat, taking special care to treat end grain, or use a garden pressure-sprayer with a coarse spray. Work on a calm day to avoid spray drift and cover the soil with polythene sheeting.

Loose posts

Posts which have come loose have probably rotted at soil level. They can be repaired without dismantling the fence by using concrete spurs. The loose posts are bolted to the spurs with two coach-bolts long enough to pass through the post and the spur. First dig a hole alongside the broken post so that the bottom part of the spur can be dropped into place. Then hold the spur against the post and use the bolts to mark where the bolt holes are required in the post. Remove the spur and drill the post for the bolts. Pass the bolts through from the other side of the post and bolt the post and spur together. Use struts to hold the post upright and then pack rubble round the spur, topping off with concrete. When the concrete has set, remove the struts.

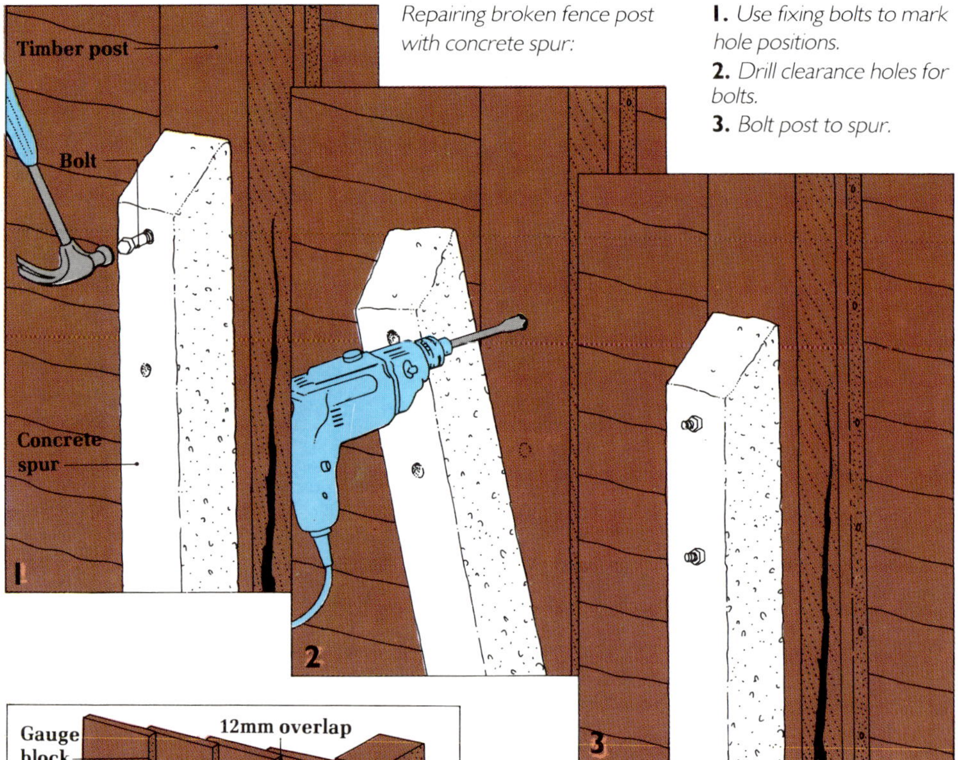

Repairing broken fence post with concrete spur:

1. Use fixing bolts to mark hole positions.
2. Drill clearance holes for bolts.
3. Bolt post to spur.

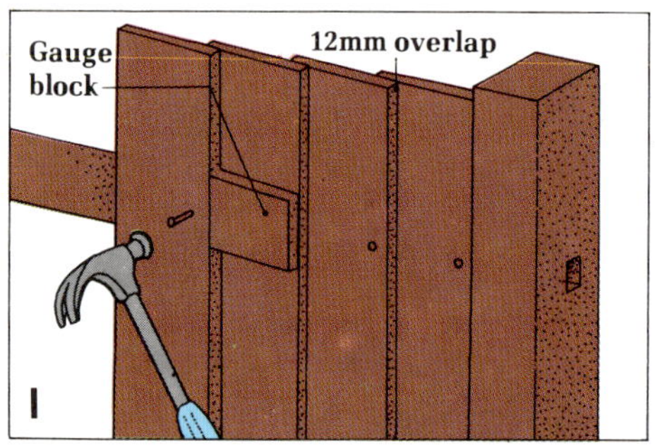

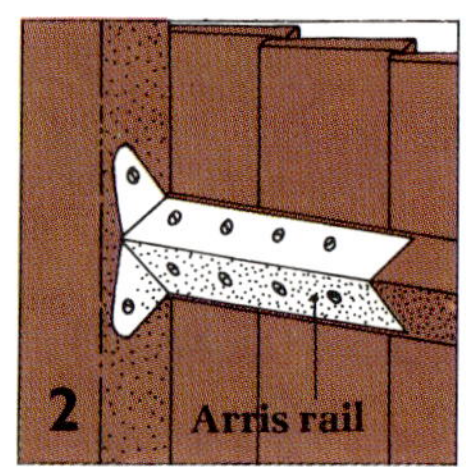

1. Mend a broken arris rail with a galvanised bracket screwed to post and rail.
2. Use a timber gauge block for spacing feather-edge boards.

Spraying a fence with wood-preservative using a garden pressure sprayer.

Broken arris rails

Arris rails are the triangular rails fixed between posts to which feather-edge boards are nailed. They occasionally snap where they slot into the posts. Again there is no need to dismantle the fence; you can repair it with a galvanised-steel arris-rail repair-bracket. There are various types of these and some are 'handed' so make a note of which end of the rail has broken before buying the bracket. Fix the bracket to the rail and the post, using zinc-plated screws for the strongest repair, or galvanised nails.

Loose or broken boards

If feather-edge boards have come loose or need replacing, the new boards are simply nailed in place with the thick edge covering the thin edge of the adjacent board. The galvanised fixing nail should pass through the thick edge into the thin edge of the board it overlaps, and into the arris rail.

Screen-block walls

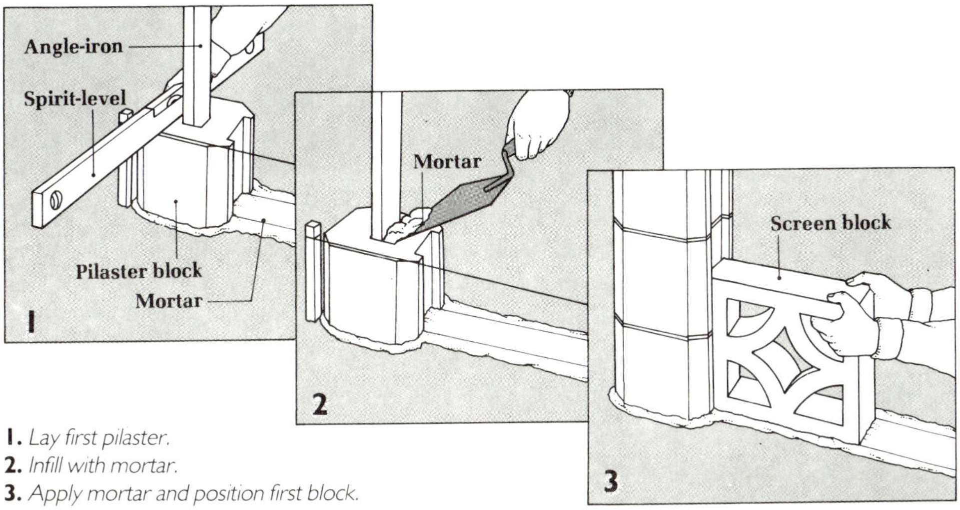

1. *Lay first pilaster.*
2. *Infill with mortar.*
3. *Apply mortar and position first block.*

Diamond, square and Maltese cross screen-block patterns, coping, end and intermediate pilasters, and pier cap.

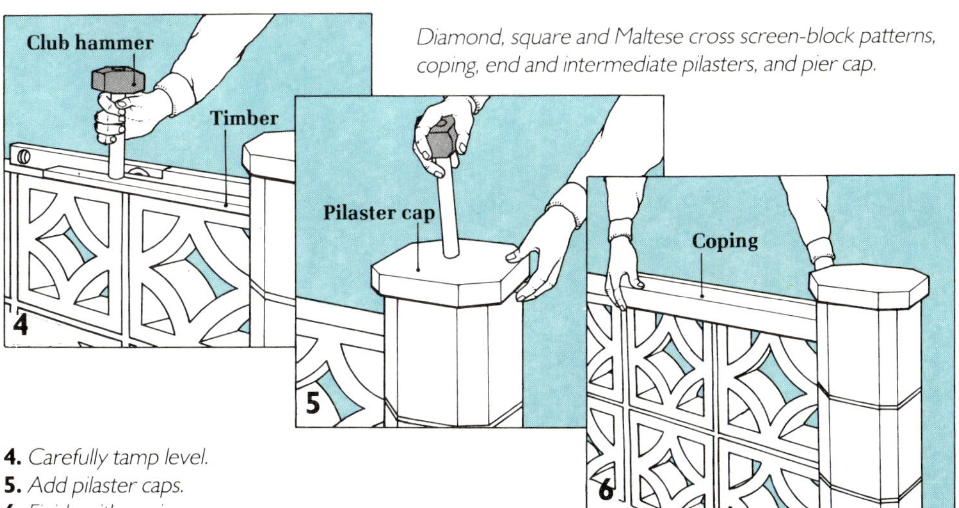

4. *Carefully tamp level.*
5. *Add pilaster caps.*
6. *Finish with copings.*

A screen-block wall should not span more than 3m without intermediate pillar supports. You cannot cut screen blocks nor the pilasters, so check the exact dimensions when planning. Blocks normally measure 300 × 300 × 90mm thick, and pilasters 195 × 195 × 200mm high including joints.

Foundations

For a low wall, foundations should consist of 100mm of hardcore topped by 100mm of concrete and be 300mm wide. Use a mix of 1 part cement to 5 parts ballast. Check with manufacturers for high walls. If using screen blocks on a sloping site it is necessary to lay a 'plinth' of bricks.

Stretch string lines through the site (see page 166) then dig the trench and lay the foundations. Although not strictly necessary on low walls of up to three courses, it is nevertheless well worthwhile reinforcing the pilaster blocks by setting an iron rod or angle-iron into the foundations. The pilaster blocks are lowered on to the reinforcement as the wall is built, so obviously the positioning of the angle-iron is vital. It must also be truly vertical and protrude from the ground to within a few centimetres of the top of the pilaster column. The mortar mix should be 1 part cement to 5 parts builder's sand and must be pliable. If you want the mortar joints to blend in colour with the blocks use white cement and light-coloured sand. For a contrasting colour use ordinary grey cement. To fill the pilaster blocks use a fluid mix of 1 part cement to 3 parts sand.

Laying blocks

First lay a row of blocks and pilasters along the foundations to check positioning. The first pilaster can then be laid on mortar and checked both horizontally and vertically for level. It must also align with the string guide-line. Repeat the procedure with the other end pilaster and intermediate pilasters. If there will be more than three pilaster blocks in each column, pour in reinforcing mix after each is laid.

Spread mortar on the base and inside the pilaster groove, then position the first screen block in the groove. Check it for level and, if necessary, tap it down with the shaft of the club hammer. Screen blocks are quite fragile so, when tapping down to level, lay a piece of timber on the block to spread force of the light taps. Build up the wall checking as you go for both horizontal and vertical alignment. In addition to the horizontal layer of mortar on which a block is laid, trowel some on to one side before it is positioned, to serve as a vertical joint. Make this a little more sloppy to aid sticking.

When the required height is reached, add caps and coping, and point the joints.

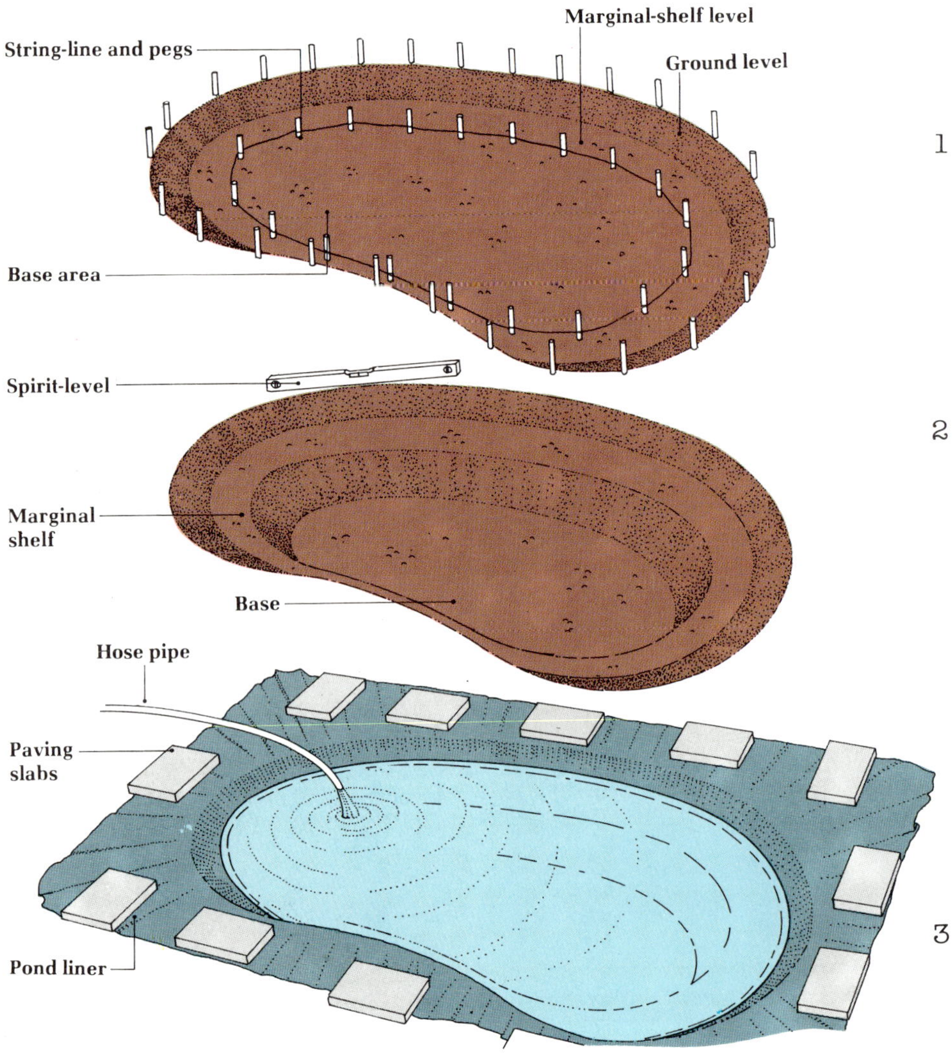

Garden ponds

Stages in making a liner pond
1. *Mark outer shape of pond with string-line, excavate to level of marginal shelf, then mark out base.*
2. *Excavate centre portion and check base, shelf and surround are level.*
3. *Lay liner over hole, weighting edges. Fill pond gradually, easing off weights to allow liner to be carried into hole. When full, trim surplus liner and cover edge with paving-slabs or upturned turves.*

There is nothing like a pond to add sparkle and movement to a garden, and it need not occupy a great deal of space – the minimum satisfactory surface area is 3.5sq m (m^2). The optimum depth to aim for is 600mm. Even the largest garden-pond need be no more than 750mm deep while 400mm should be considered the minimum depth. Avoid making a saucer-shaped pond – the sides should slope outwards at about 20 degrees to the vertical and round the edge you should form a shelf about 250mm deep and 250mm wide on which marginal water plants can be grown in plastic baskets.

There are basically two modern materials from which to make a pond – flexible plastic and moulded, rigid plastic. Flexible plastic is used for pond-liners which give you complete control over the shape of the pond, while the rigid plastic the size and shape of the pond are controlled by the manufacturer.

Moulded plastics

These are installed simply by digging a hole and putting the moulding into it. The best (and most expensive), rigid glass-reinforced plastic types are almost self-supporting and there is no need to be too careful over their installation. However, the thinner moulded-plastic ponds can crack if they are not installed in a hole carefully packed round with sharp sand. To install this type, stand the moulding on a base of damp sand and pack round the sides with damp sand as it is filled with water. Take particular care to pack the sand under the shelves to ensure that these are well supported.

Liners

The best liners are made from butyl rubber sheeting, which is the material often used to form reservoirs. Second to butyl rubber are nylon-reinforced PVC liners, and there is a third, cheaper sort, which is just laminated PVC.

Planting

Planting should take place between late April and early September, and you can begin a few days after the pond has been filled, although you should wait for two to three weeks before introducing fish. Apart from floating plants, all the other types – marginals and oxygenators – are planted in heavy garden soil in plastic planting-crates which are surfaced with a layer of pea gravel. The crates of the shallow marginal plants, such as water irises, are stood on the planting shelf while plants which need deeper water, such as the oxygenators and water lilies, are placed on the pond base.

Fountains, lights and waterfalls

Low-voltage submersible pumps are available to form fountains or waterfalls. The pump is simply placed in the pond and the low-voltage cable is taken back to the house, through a hole drilled in a window frame, to connect with an indoor transformer which is plugged into the mains supply. Low-voltage lighting sets are connected in a similar way.

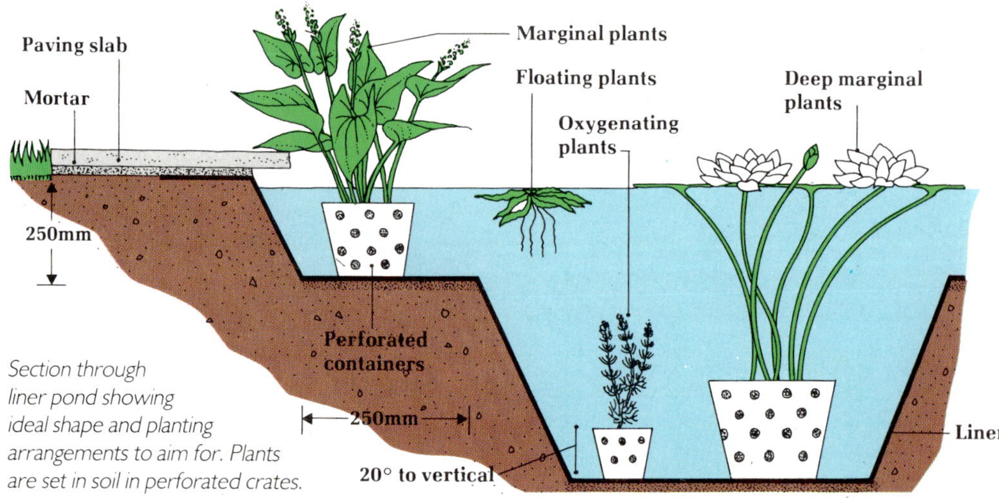

Section through liner pond showing ideal shape and planting arrangements to aim for. Plants are set in soil in perforated crates.

INDEX

A

B

C

D

E

SAFETY TIPS

Think safety. Remember that the safety warnings and manufacturer's instructions on any piece of equipment are designed for your safety and health. Always use the proper equipment and wear the correct clothing. Never wear a tie or anything else that could get caught in machinery. Take particular care with electrical work and whenever you are working with chemicals. Always protect your eyes with goggles when the situation demands it. Never interfere with, or remove, safety guards on power equipment. Concentrate on safety at all times – and do not rush work – it is never worth it.

- Familiarize yourself with the positions of all the main gas taps, stopcocks and electricity supply switches, so that you can turn them off in emergencies.
- Do not hang clothes over heaters, or put them where they could fall on to a heater and cause a fire.
- Keep radiant heaters well away from curtains.
- Make sure heater air grilles are always kept clear.
- Keep chimneys and flues clear.
- Take care with paraffin heaters – never allow them to be knocked over; turn them off before refilling.

ELECTRICITY

- Always work with great care and never attempt electrical work if you don't understand what you are doing.
- Turn off the main switch before beginning work on the household installation.
- Take out the appropriate fuse and put it in your pocket so that it is impossible for someone else to put it back.
- Unplug any appliance before you start any repairs or adjustments.
- Switch off the light before replacing a bulb.
- Don't patch broken or damaged flex – replace it with a complete length of new flex of the right size and type.
- If an appliance has provision for an earth wire it must always be used. Bad earth connections can cause serious electrical shocks.
- Never overload sockets or run appliances from lampholders.

GAS

- Act quickly if you smell gas. Put out all flames, open doors and windows, turn out every gas tap in the house, and do not use any electrical switches. Call the gas board.
- Have gas repairs carried out by a qualified gas fitter.

FIRE

- Evacuate the building.
- Close doors behind you to stop the spread of smoke and flames.
- Call the fire brigade.
- Remember that in a smoke-filled room a narrow band of air immediately above the floor will be smoke-free.